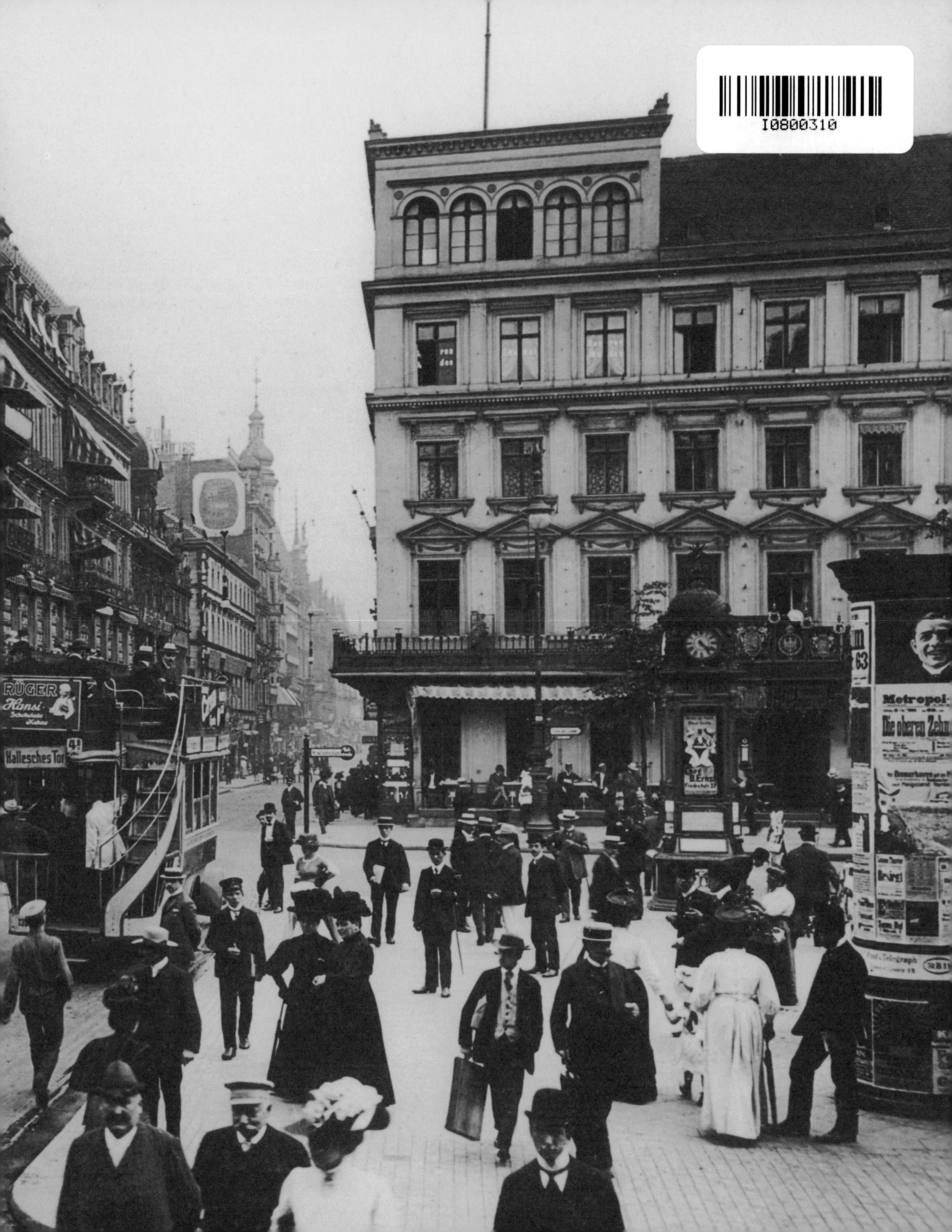
Hallesches Tor
Metropol-
Die oberen Zehn

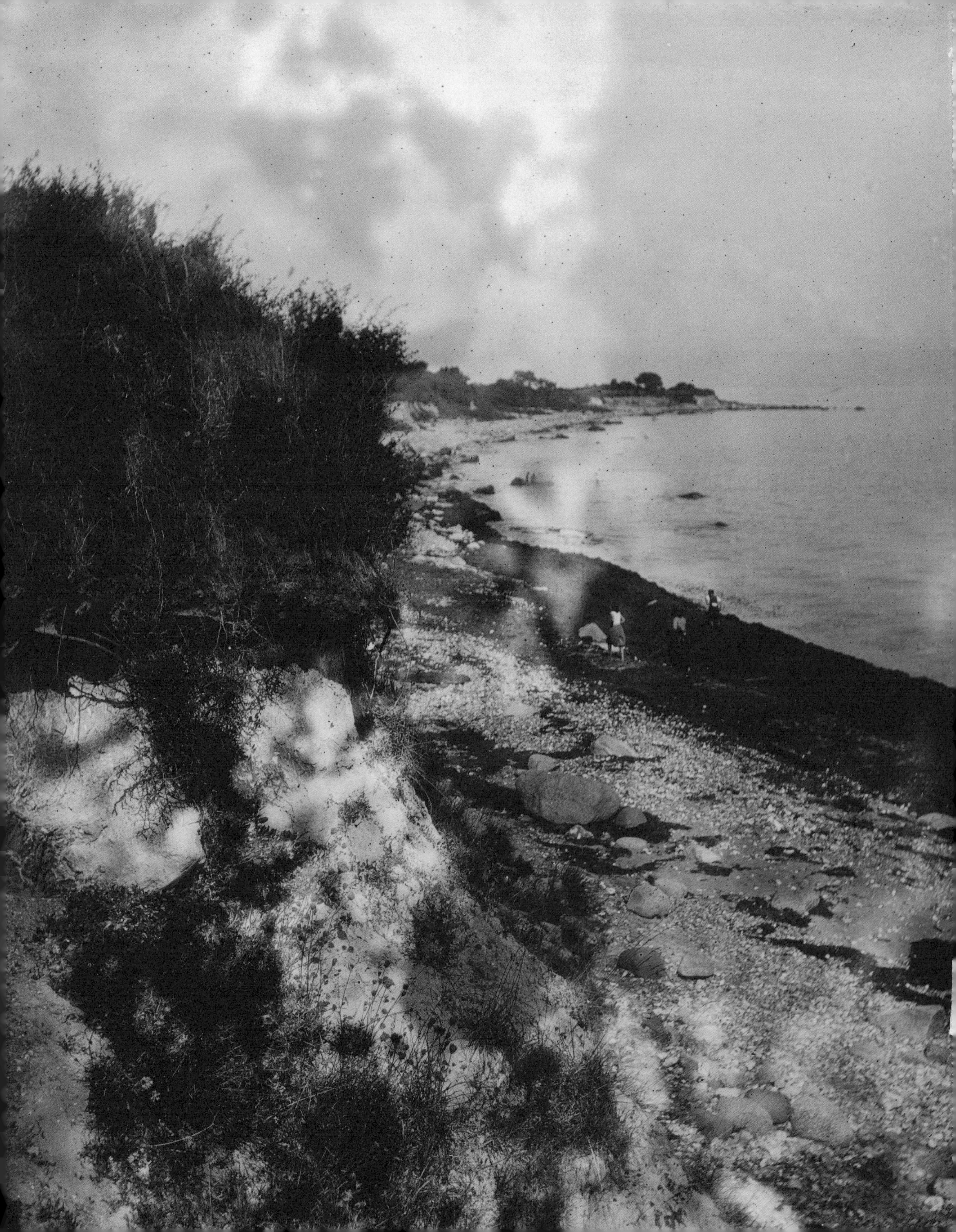

Vibrant Metropolis
Idyllic Nature

Kirchner — The Berlin Years

Vibrant Metropolis
Idyllic Nature

Kirchner — The Berlin Years

Kunsthaus Zürich | HIRMER

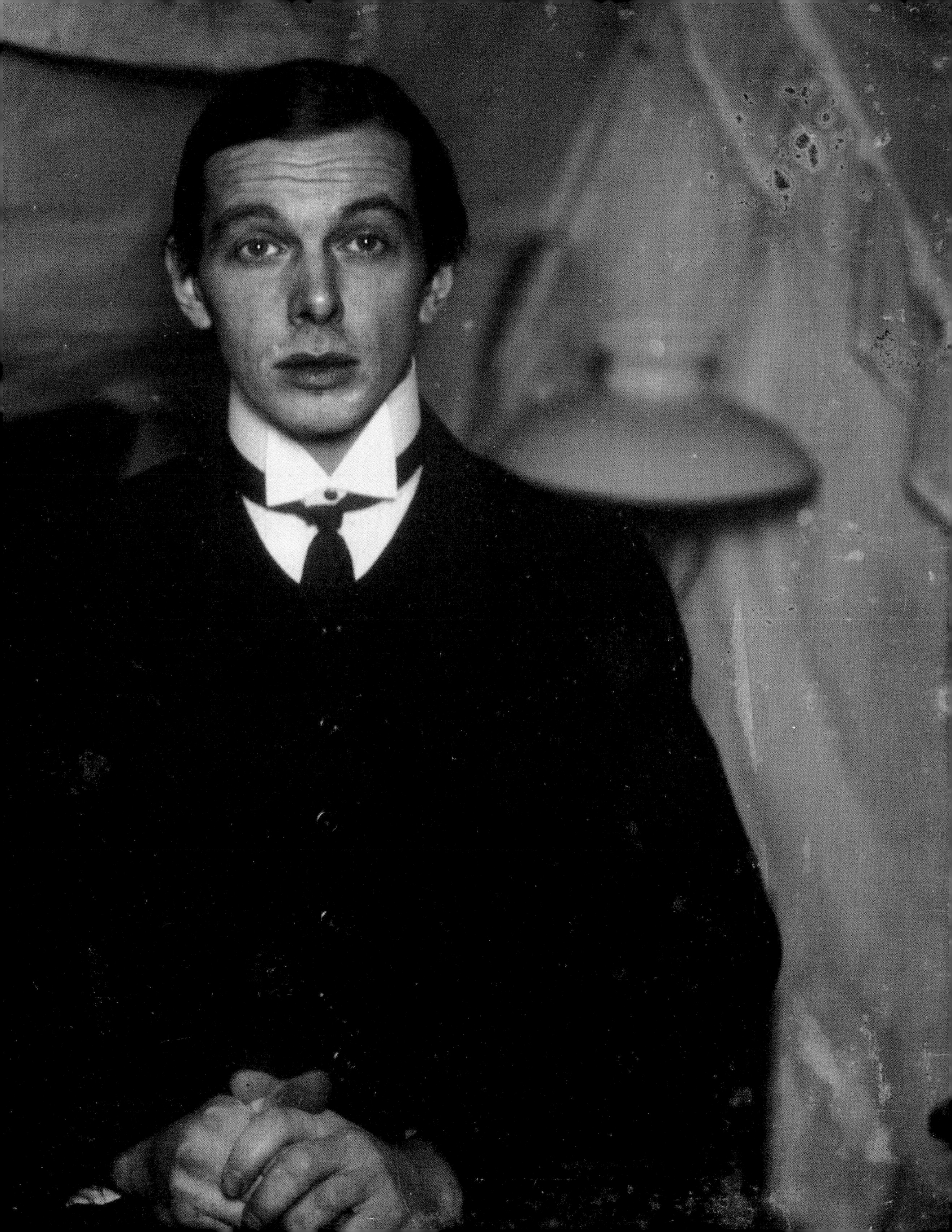

In grateful remembrance of our generous friend and benefactor

Dr Hans Vontobel
4 December 1916–3 January 2016

Essays

Catalogue

Appendix

Acknowledgements

We thank all the following lenders for their generous support:

Aargauer Kunsthaus, Aarau, Madeleine Schuppli, Thomas Schmutz

Stedelijk Museum, Amsterdam, Beatrix Ruf, Bart Rutten

Museum Frieder Burda, Baden-Baden, Frieder Burda, Helmut Friedel, Judith Irrgang

Kunstmuseum Basel, Bernhard Mendes Bürgi/Josef Helfenstein, Anita Haldemann

Karl and Emy Schmidt-Rottluff Foundation, Berlin

Stadtmuseum Berlin Foundation, Paul Spies, Martina Weinland

Kunstmuseum Bern, Nina Zimmer, Matthias Frehner

E.W.K. Collection, Bern/Davos

Kunstsammlungen Chemnitz, Ingrid Mössinger, Beate Ritter

Kunstsammlungen Chemnitz, Museum Gunzenhauser, Ingrid Mössinger, Anja Richter

Bündner Kunstmuseum, Chur, Stephan Kunz, Lynn Kost

Columbus Museum of Art, Ohio, Nannette V. Maciejunes, David Stark

Hessisches Landesmuseum Darmstadt, Theo Jülich, Klaus-D. Pohl

Kirchner Museum Davos, Thorsten Sadowsky

Rosemarie Ketterer Foundation, Davos

Museum Ostwall im Dortmunder U, Dortmund, Kurt Wettengl, Regina Selter, Nicole Grothe

Lehmbruck Museum, Duisburg, Söke Dinkla, Marion Bornscheuer

Leopold-Hoesch-Museum & Papiermuseum Düren, Renate Goldmann, Markus Mascher

Kunstsammlung Nordrhein-Westfalen, Düsseldorf, Marion Ackermann, Anette Kruszynski

Museum Kunstpalast, Düsseldorf, Beat Wismer, Kay Heymer, Gunda Luyken

Museum Folkwang, Essen, Tobia Bezzola, Mario-Andreas von Lüttichau, Tobias Burg

Olbricht Collection, Essen, Thomas Olbricht, Julia Rust, Sarah Sonderkamp

Deutsche Bank Collection, Frankfurt am Main, Paul Achleitner, Friedhelm Hütte, Claudia Schicktanz

Städel Museum, Frankfurt am Main, Max Hollein/Philipp Demandt, Felix Krämer, Jutta Schütt (†)

Stiftung Dome und Schlösser in Saxony-Anhalt, Kunstmuseum Moritzburg Halle (Saale) and Hermann Gerlinger Collection in the Kunstmuseum Moritzburg Halle (Saale), Thomas Bauer-Friedrich, Wolfgang Büche

Hamburger Kunsthalle, Hamburg, Hubertus Gaßner/Christoph Martin Vogtherr, Karin Schick

Estate of Erich Heckel, Hemmenhofen, Hans Geissler, Renate Ebner

Staatliche Kunsthalle Karlsruhe, Pia Müller-Tamm, Alexander Eiling

Museumslandschaft Hessen Kassel, Bernd Küster, Christiane Lukatis

Franz Marc Museum, Kochel am See, Cathrin Klingsöhr-Leroy

Museum Ludwig, Cologne, Yilmaz Dziewior, Stephan Diederich

Würth Collection, Kunzelsau, C. Sylvia Weber, Sonja Klee

The Getty Research Institute, Los Angeles, Thomas Gaehtgens, Marcia Reed

Die Lübecker Museen, Museum Behnhaus Drägerhaus, Lübeck, Alexander Bastek

Museo Thyssen-Bornemisza, Madrid, Guillermo Solana, Paloma Alarcó

Kunsthalle Mannheim, Ulrike Lorenz, Inge Herold

Merzbacher Art Foundation, Werner Merzbacher and Gabrielle Merzbacher-Mayer

Milwaukee Art Museum, Daniel T. Keegan/Marcelle Polednik, Brady Roberts

Bayerische Staatsgemäldesammlungen, Pinakothek der Moderne, Munich, Bernhard Maaz, Oliver Kase

The Museum of Modern Art, New York, Glenn D. Lowry, Ann Temkin, Leah Dickerman

Solomon R. Guggenheim Museum, New York, Richard Armstrong, Susan Davidson

Carnegie Museum of Art, Pittsburgh, Lynn Zelevansky, Louise Lippincott

Hilti Art Foundation, Schaan, Michael Hilti, Uwe Wieczorek

Staatsgalerie Stuttgart, Christiane Lange, Ina Conzen

Art Gallery of New South Wales, Sydney, Michael Brand, Maud Page

Kunstmuseum Liechtenstein, Vaduz, Friedemann Malsch, Christiane Meyer-Stoll

Albertina, Batliner Collection, Vienna, Rita and Herbert Batliner, Klaus Albrecht Schröder, Gisela Fischer

Leopold Museum, Vienna, Hans-Peter Wipplinger, Franz Smola

Colby College Museum of Art, Waterville, Sharon Corwin

Estate of Ernst Ludwig Kirchner, Courtesy Galerie Henze & Ketterer Wichtrach/Bern, Ingeborg Henze-Ketterer, Günther Ketterer, Wolfgang Henze

Kunstmuseum Winterthur, Dieter Schwarz, Simona Ciuccio

Von der Heydt-Museum, Wuppertal, Gerhard Finckh, Antje Birthälmer

Werner Coninx Foundation, Zurich

We are particularly indebted to Magdalena M. Moeller, director of the Brücke-Museum, Berlin, without whose generous loans this exhibition would not have been possible.

We would also like to thank those who prefer to remain anonymous.

For stimulating discussions we are sincerely grateful to Günther Gercken, Hermann Gerlinger, Lucius Grisebach, Eberhard W. Kornfeld, Felix Krämer, Mario-Andreas von Lüttichau, Thorsten Sadowsky, Karin Schick and Wolfgang Wittrock.

We have had invaluable support from Wolfgang Henze, the Ernst Ludwig Kirchner Archive, Wichtrach/Bern; we are also grateful to Ingeborg Henze-Ketterer, Carola Ertle-Ketterer and Günther Ketterer.

For their dedicated assistance and support in the research and preparation for this exhibition we would also like to express our gratitude to Sarah Ackermann, Angelika Affentranger, Timothy Benson, Bernadette Broeskamp, Christian Bührle, Tania Maria Camenzind, Birgit Dalbajewa, Hans Delfs, Isabelle Durrer, Anja Foerschner, Annick Haldemann, Daniela Hardmeier, Christian Häussler, Andrea Hodel, Jürgen Hoffmann, Yvonne E. Kaehr, Olivia Levental, Claudine Metzger, Bertold Müller, Ergün Özdemir-Karsch, Emilia Philippot, Stefan Puttaert, Werner Raeune, Thomas Rosemann, Birgit Sander, Daniel J. Schreiber, Christine E. Stauffer, Toni Stooss, Jeanne Sudor, Annegret Thoma, Esther Tisa Francini and Kyllikki Zacharias.

Foreword

Ernst Ludwig Kirchner is the most important representative of German Expressionism. Why is that? Not only was he one of the motivating forces behind the world-renowned Brücke artists' group, which he helped found in 1905, but it was in large part his works from the decisive Berlin phase of his career that led to that period being designated the "Expressionist era".

In Berlin, Kirchner and his small circle of artist friends and models were definitely outsiders, a group of anarchic bohemians in search of instant good fortune and innovation in art. At the same time their lives played out, as it were, in the penumbra of a cosmopolitan city. Their Berlin had none of the metropolis's glamour, wealth and glitter; instead, it was a city of dimly lit streets, wet pavements, crowded bars, questionable figures and empty absinthe glasses. The juxtaposition of Kirchner's Berlin pictures with those from his anti-urban retreats on the island of Fehmarn underlines the raw force with which Expressionism arrived on the scene in the twentieth century. The Wilhelmine establishment paid scant attention to these young savages; it knew them only from hearsay—enough for it to dismiss them lock, stock and barrel. Soon enough these outsiders and their distinctly non-conformist art would be condemned as "degenerate", confiscated from its collectors and, what is more disturbing, either sold or destroyed out of sheer opportunism by any number of museum directors.

Expressionism so completely disappeared from public view that it would be a full decade after the Second World War before its works gradually began to come to light and be displayed again. Critics and art historians came to see Expressionism as a uniquely German contribution to the art of the twentieth century. A kind of reparations campaign began, and trade in Expressionist paintings and graphics flourished. It was only between the 1950s and 1970s that this somewhat disparate art movement came to be fully appreciated.

The broader public came to value German Expressionism only long after the Second World War. The Brücke-Museum, opened in Berlin in 1967, contributed greatly to its acceptance. With its sixteen paintings and roughly five hundred works on paper it houses one of the most extensive Kirchner collections in the world, one that includes excellent early graphic works donated by his artist colleague Erich Heckel in the years 1964 to 1967 as well as paintings and any number of key drawings, especially from his Berlin years and the four summers he spent on the Baltic Sea island of Fehmarn.

In the relatively short time between 1911, when he moved from Dresden to the German capital, and 1917 Kirchner produced an extraordinary number of artistically highly important works that showed him to be an outstanding protagonist of figurative art in the early modern period. It is because of them that we have made this period the focus of our exhibition—the first to present such an abundance of this work in Switzerland. It was here, under very different conditions, that the second half of Kirchner's eventful career unfolded. In his Davos years beginning in 1917 his work took a new direction, one that for once is not featured in the show but represented by a few select works.

For a long time it has been our wish that our two institutions might work together, for with its various activities the Brücke-Museum has contributed greatly to the recognition and understanding of Kirchner's art. Thanks to the work of numerous colleagues in both museums that wish has now been fulfilled. We are indebted to our private and institutional lenders for giving our exhibition additional distinction with truly outstanding works from this period. The authors of this catalogue are all long-time Kirchner scholars and in their contributions they have managed to present a vivid picture of his turbulent Berlin years. We have been encouraged in this ambitious project by generous support. We are especially grateful to the Vontobel Foundation for its long, dependable support of the Kunsthaus Zürich; it is with deep respect and gratitude that we remember the late Dr Hans Vontobel, a good friend and patron of the Kunsthaus for many decades.

An imposing number of noted foundations have helped us to mount the exhibition: the Ars Rhenia Foundation for the Trans-regional Promotion of Art and Culture, the A-Charity Foundation, the Truus and Gerrit van Riemsdijk Foundation, the Dr Georg and Josi Guggenheim Foundation, and other donors who wish to remain anonymous. We are grateful to all the foundations' board members for their enthusiastic interest and confidence in our work. And we are especially indebted to the Federal Office of Culture for its gracious assistance in securing insurance coverage for the many highly valuable works of art.

We sincerely thank Sandra Gianfreda, who shortly after joining our curatorial staff took up a suggestion by our colleague Cathérine Hug and developed it further. We are also grateful to Martina Pfister and Franziska Lentzsch for their considerable research and organisational work; to the Kunsthaus's entire technical team and restoration department for managing the work of making the exhibition a reality so smoothly; to Lena Huber for the design of the catalogue; to our thoughtful editor at Hirmer Verlag, Markus Kersting; and to Ulrich Zickler for his architectural staging of around 160 works of art in the more than 1,000 square metres of the Bührlesaal in the Kunsthaus. Our exhibition is unprecedented in its richness and quality and is intended to foster a new recognition of this major artist both in Switzerland and far beyond its borders. We are delighted to be able to share with you the result of years of collaborative effort.

Christoph Becker
Director, Kunsthaus Zürich

Magdalena M. Moeller
Director, Brücke-Museum, Berlin

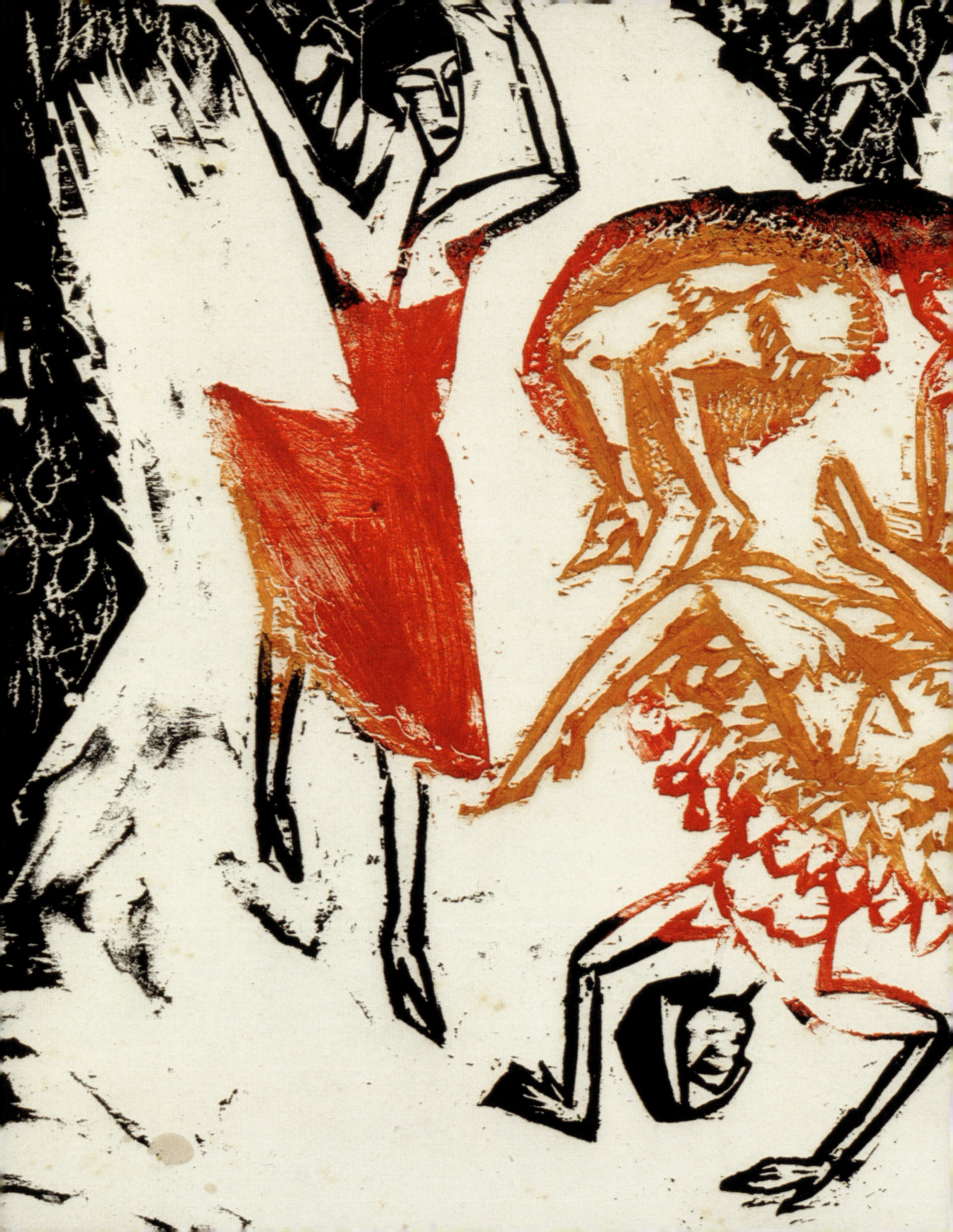

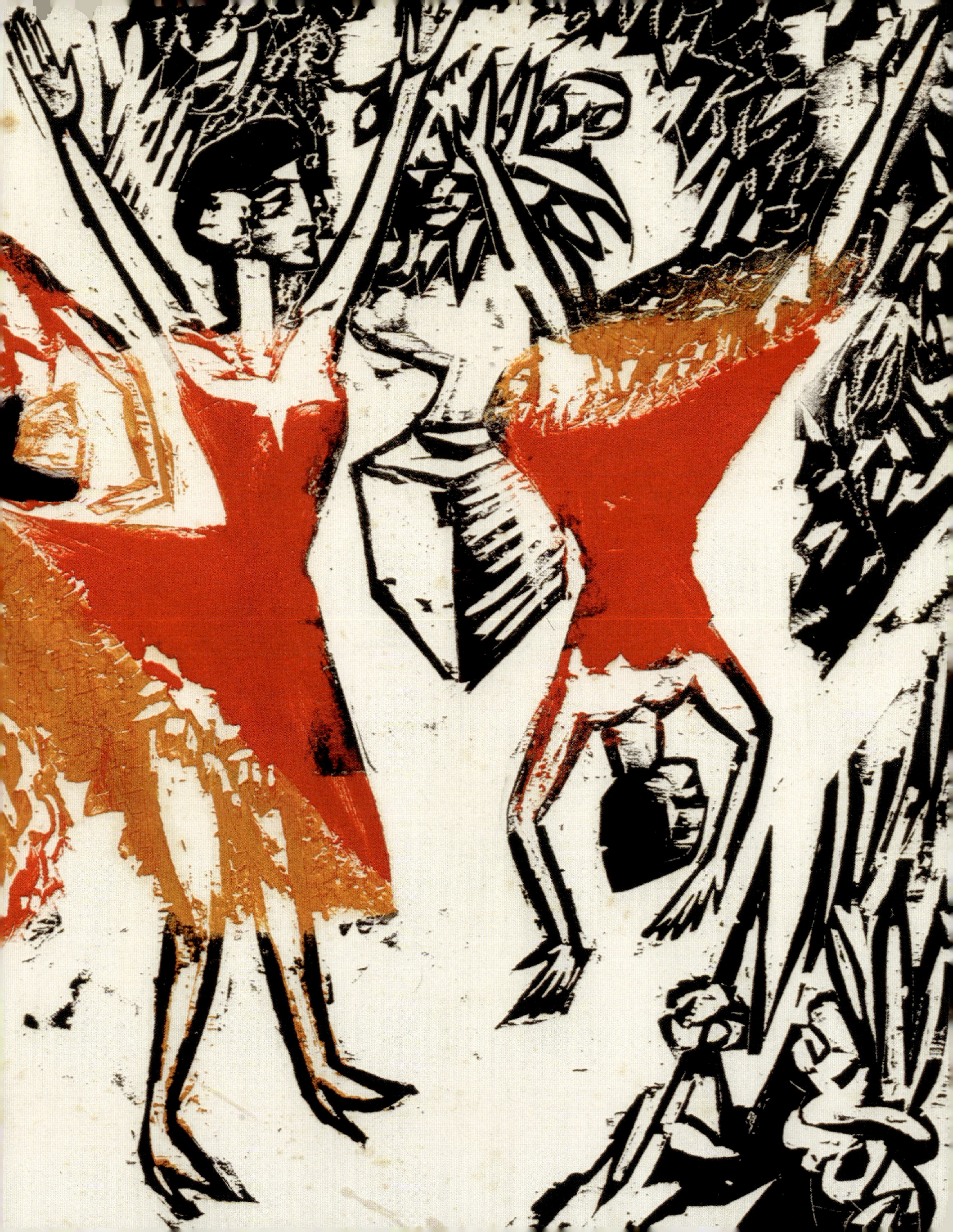

Introduction to the Exhibition

In late October 1911 Ernst Ludwig Kirchner moved from Dresden to Berlin. The thirty-one-year-old artist would rather have moved to Paris,[1] but since the Brücke colleagues with whom he had set out to revolutionise art in 1905 had chosen the Prussian imperial capital as a new centre for their lives, he followed their example. Within a century Berlin had expanded from a sleepy royal residence of some 170,000 souls in around 1800 to become one of Europe's most modern metropolises. At the beginning of the twentieth century it was home to two million people. Rapid economic and industrial development had drawn hundreds of thousands of workers to Berlin, where they were housed in multistorey tenement blocks. The majority of the populace lived in the most miserable conditions. Despite such bitter poverty, the well-situated bourgeoisie and nobility found ample entertainment in the vibrant big city. Splendid shopping streets illuminated at night with electric lights and lined with swanky cafés, large department stores, luxurious hotels, opera houses and theatres drew the public in vast hordes, and the most up-to-date public transport made it easy to get around in the metropolis. Among the busiest spots in Berlin at the time were Potsdamer Platz and Friedrichstrasse. There countless elegantly dressed women caught the eye, and it was difficult to distinguish between upstanding bourgeois ladies and cocottes. In contrast to other cities in the German Empire, prostitution was prohibited in Berlin and the street women had to be discreet in their search for customers.[2] So it is hardly surprising then that a city like this, presenting as many opportunities as risks, would have also attracted artists hungry for success. As a centre for avant-garde artistic movements Berlin was at the time quite young. It was only in 1898 that the Berlin group of artists headed by Max Liebermann split off into the Berlin Secession in order to give artists with Impressionist leanings an opportunity to be seen by the public. Then in 1910 a new generation of artists again broke away and exhibited its works under the name *Neue Secession* (New Secession). Its president was Max Pechstein, who had been a Brücke member since 1906 and had lived in Berlin since 1908.

Shortly after his arrival in Berlin, Kirchner, together with Pechstein, founded the MUIM Institute (Moderner Unterricht in Malerei / Modern Instruction in Painting), a school of modern painting and other techniques. They hoped to pass along to other artists their revolutionary concept of art and at the same time assure themselves of a regular income. But the whole point of their move to Berlin was the greater possibility they had there of establishing themselves as artists. Yet making a living in the metropolis was not easy, as Kirchner was also to experience. On 28 February 1912 he wrote to Luise Schiefler, the wife of the regional court director in Hamburg, and art patron Gustav Schiefler: "I believe I haven't yet answered your last card. This is because of the unsettled nature of life in Berlin for anyone struggling to get by. Things are dreadfully boorish here. I see that under these conditions it is impossible to cultivate a genteel way of life in a free cultural environment and I would like to leave as soon as I have overcome this deep depression."[3] He was clearly disappointed with Berlin, and in June/July 1912 and in January 1913 he once again considered moving away and settling in Cologne or at least in the Rhineland.[4] Yet at the same time he found the metropolis "interesting and rich".[5]

In his first Berlin years he suffered two setbacks in his struggle to make a living. Due to a lack of interest — it had attracted only two pupils — Kirchner and Pechstein were forced to officially close the MUIM Institute in December 1912. Less than six months later the artists' association Brücke, established so successfully in Dresden in 1905, broke apart — Kirchner himself being in large part responsible for its dissolution — so that henceforth each of its members had to make his own way. What is more, in Kirchner's private life the move from Dresden to Berlin had brought to an end his long-time relationship with the Dresden modiste Doris Grosse, one of his most important models since 1906. Consequently, Kirchner's new beginning in Berlin was a difficult period. In his art, however, he gradually began to make the city his own. He would ramble about for hours, whiling away the time on the streets and squares, in cafés, music halls, the circus and presumably in the company of cocottes, just as he had in Dresden.[6] In fact, the majority of his picture motifs in Berlin were already prefigured in his Dresden works. There he not only painted his first street scenes but also a number of dance and music-hall subjects.[7] Outdoors, and especially in such places of amusement, he could study people "moving freely",[8] while remaining wholly unobserved. Equally, the bathing scenes he produced between 1909 and 1911 at the Moritzburg Ponds anticipated his pictures from Fehmarn.

In Berlin, Kirchner soon surrounded himself with a new circle of acquaintances. In addition to the two MUIM pupils Hans Gewecke and Werner Gothein and the dancers Gerda and Erna Schilling, who became his two most important models, these were above all writers and intellectuals who frequented Der Neue Club and the Neopathetisches Cabaret—the series of events the club hosted—as well as the gallery Der Sturm. Through Pechstein he had met Herwarth Walden, the director of the gallery and publisher of the journal of the same name, in which, between April 1911 and March 1912, Kirchner was able to publish woodcuts. In this circle Kirchner came into close contact with the poet Simon Guttmann and the practising psychiatrist and writer Alfred Döblin and produced portraits of both men in drawings, prints and paintings. A Döblin essay on prostitution that appeared in the journal *Der Sturm* in 1912[9] and his one-act *Countess Mizzi,* a play set in a bordello that Kirchner illustrated with woodcuts,[10] left a lasting impression on him. In addition, Kirchner could have drawn analogies between his efforts to create works wholly "unconsciously" and the demands Döblin published in the essay "To Novel Writers and Their Critics", which appeared in *Der Sturm* in 1913 under the title "Berlin Programme". There Döblin called for the novel writer to practise "elimination of the self", "self-renunciation" and "depersonalisation", stipulating that "the hegemony of the writer must be broken; the fanaticism of self-denial cannot be taken too far. Or the fanaticism for self-renunciation; I am not I, but rather the street, the street lights, this or that occurrence, nothing more".[11] Kirchner appears to have first come closest to such self-dissolution on Fehmarn. In a letter to Schiefler from 28 December 1914 he wrote, "It was very difficult for me to leave [Fehmarn] so suddenly, for this year I almost completely merged with the landscape and life up there and could work almost unconsciously."[12] And in "Das Werk", written about himself in the third person in 1925, he explained: "The first [actually second (author's note)] stay on Fehmarn brought Kirchner's abilities in this direction to their full potential. The observation of his fellow men produced a rebound effect and allowed his observation of himself to become more intense. The island's isolation produced mystical sensations in relation to his wife. He developed an ability to see and depict himself as if he were a third person."[13] He had already written in a similar vein about his figural pictures in general, and his portraits and street scenes in particular, in a letter to Eberhard Grisebach in December 1917: "The possibility of self-elimination to the point that one can enter into this union with the other";[14] and a few days later to Karl Ernst Osthaus: "It seems to me the old goal of my work is to be able to completely dissolve myself in my perception of the surroundings, so as to be able to present this in a cohesive painterly form."[15]

Along with his contacts with the literary avant-garde, in Berlin Kirchner also had an opportunity to get to know the works of foreign artists searching, like him, for new forms of expression appropriate to the time. In the spring of 1912 Kirchner saw in the Sturm gallery works by the Italian Futurists, who introduced time as a fourth dimension into their pictures and devoted themselves to the simultaneous depiction of sequences of movement. Kirchner, who spoke at various times about the importance of movement in his work, could not have been unmoved by these works, especially since Döblin had positive things to say about the Futurists.[16] Movement, dynamism and changing points of view characterise Kirchner's works from the Berlin years and led him in retrospect to style his painting "a painting of movement".[17]

The move from Dresden to Berlin had also brought with it a change in Kirchner's style. The artist completely abandoned the soft, rounded forms and planes of colour of his last Dresden years in favour of pointed, angular forms and swift, hatching-like brush strokes. At the same time, he freed himself from strong colour contrasts and increasingly came to employ muted tones or tertiary colours. This change of style is generally associated with the hustle and bustle of the metropolis and the tough struggle to survive there. To be sure, Kirchner's development of a new kind of imagery can already be seen in works produced on the scenic Baltic Sea island of Fehmarn in 1912, i.e. before he painted his now-famous street scenes. This stylistic development was therefore presumably far less a response to the place where it occurred than the result of Kirchner's effort to find a way to express his experience of space and movement appropriate to the time. He would first capture his observations with swift pencil and brush strokes in his sketchbooks on countless rambles through the city and out in nature and would then solidify them in prints and paintings.

Berlin and Fehmarn—the big city and the nature idyll: At the latest since the publication of Donald E. Gordon's monograph with catalogue raisonné in 1968, Kirchner's two sources of inspiration from the years 1912 to 1914 have been seen as opposing poles. Here frenetic, nervous metropolitan life, there repose in rural isolation; here the misery and alienation of the city dweller, there a harmonious life in union with nature. The two places could not have been more dissimilar. For the most part they have also been treated separately in exhibitions and publications, with the street scenes given greater importance. Through the decades these scenes have also come to be interpreted in ways the artist may not have intended. As a rule they are seen as negative criticism of the metropolis. It may well be that a retrospective comment in the draft of a letter from 1919, first mentioned in a publication from 1979, is largely responsible for this. Writing to an art historian (probably Carl Georg Heise), he expressed himself as follows: "My street scenes. They were produced in 11–14, one of the loneliest periods of my life, when an agonising restlessness drove me again and again day and night into the long streets filled with people and automobiles." At the same time, Kirchner called them "perhaps the most valuable part of my work".[18] To many art historians his loneliness and restlessness in Berlin and his obviously conflicted relationship with the city—described later, at a time when Kirchner was quite unwell—were reason enough to read his street scenes as a rejection of modern civilisation and the opposite of Kirchner's Fehmarn pictures. Among the few exceptions are Charles W. Haxthausen, who more than twenty-five years ago argued against this "interpretative dichotomy", and Magdalena M. Moeller in her 1993 book on Kirchner's street scenes.[19] I agree with their affirmative reading of the street scenes. Both writers consider the contemporary context as well as Kirchner's larger oeuvre. Neither the artist himself nor his early reviewers saw the big-city subjects as indications of the demise of civilisation. Instead, the street scenes should most likely be viewed as "an aestheticization of urban life" and are "primarily about motion",[20] for which the artist sought and found an appropriate style. In his above-mentioned text "Das Werk" the artist expressed his search for form as follows: "Kirchner found that a city's pervasive feeling can be depicted in the manner of lines of force. In the way people behave in crowds, yes even in trains, in the way they ran, he found the means to capture whatever he was experiencing. There are pictures and graphics of his in which a mere scaffolding of lines with almost schematic figures captures the most vibrant street life."[21] In this way Kirchner recorded Berlin's metropolitan bustle, just as it was described in a contemporary guide book.[22]

The study of bodies in motion occupied Kirchner on Fehmarn as well. At the same time, while there he could explore a different sort of experience of space than he could have in the big city. In her essay in the present volume Karin Schick has sought to illuminate the Fehmarn pictures in this light and for once not link them to contemporary reform notions and the "escape from civilisation", although of course these also played a part in them.

Both sources of inspiration—metropolitan Berlin and the island of Fehmarn—document Kirchner's search for a life outside bourgeois conventions. In Berlin this was expressed not only by his conduct—his nocturnal jaunts around the city, his visits to places of amusement like music halls, the circus and cafés where people from the margins of society performed — but also by his unconventionally furnished live-in studio. The artist decorated his first Berlin studio at Durlacher Strasse 14 as well as his second one at Körnerstrasse 45 with textiles, furniture and objects he had made himself, inspired by non-European artefacts. When furnishing his rooms, Kirchner focused on nudes, generally in nature, and undisguised sexuality. In this ambience he then created numerous scenes of nude models in natural movements as well as portraits, interiors and still lifes. For three summers on the island in the Baltic he and his new Berlin girlfriend Erna Schilling lived an untroubled life under the open sky, visited by his companions at the time Erich Heckel and his girlfriend Sidi Riha, Otto and Maschka Mueller and the MUIM pupils Gewecke and Gothein referred to above. There they spent their days bathing nude, playing on the beach and amusing themselves while Kirchner captured their doings in numerous sketches and drawings that would later be reworked in prints, paintings and sculptures. Despite the budding nudist culture around 1900, their lifestyle there was extremely unconventional.

Just how greatly Fehmarn influenced Kirchner and his artistic development is expressed in his own reminiscences and in the large number of works with motifs from the island produced between 1912 and 1914. The artist already knew the spot from his visit there in 1908 in the company of the siblings Hans and Emy Frisch. In 1912 he doubtless chose to return to the island, readily reached by train and ferry from Berlin, because there was no tourism, in contrast to other coastal escapes, and the landscape was filled with lush vegetation.[23] In December 1912 Kirchner wrote to Schiefler, "As you probably know, after a pause of five years [actually four (author's note)] I was again on Fehmarn this summer. I want to go back next year as well; the very powerful impression from my first visit there only intensified, and I painted pictures there, as far as I can judge, of absolute maturity. Ochre, blue and green are Fehmarn's colours, wonderful coastline, in spots with the wealth of the South Seas, gorgeous flowers with fleshy stems."[24] His most fruitful stay would be his longest in the summer of 1913, which must have lasted from fifteen to twenty weeks. In that year Fehmarn motifs account for more than half of his painterly output. After his last stay, cut short by the outbreak of the First World War on 1 August 1914, he designed fabrics that decorated one of the two mansard niches in his live-in studio at Körnerstrasse 45. For them he devised a personal iconography based on his island impressions, and in that way managed to bring Fehmarn to Berlin. In our exhibition the surviving textiles are displayed in a space, reconstructed for the first time in Switzerland, that reproduces the setting of the studio in Berlin-Friedenau.[25] Significantly, Kirchner also drew on the iconography of their carefree life on the beach in 1916 for his wall painting of the well tower at the Kohnstamm Sanatorium in the Taunus, where he stayed on several occasions in search of recovery.

Our chief goal was to bring together these two poles in Kirchner's work — metropolis and nature idyll — in a single exhibition and its accompanying catalogue, and to have them experienced as two related aspects of Kirchner's life. Their interconnectedness is even visible on some of his canvases. The artist painted a full 13 per cent of them on both sides, whether for want of materials, for financial reasons, out of concern for storage space or for other reasons — opinions vary. There is also disagreement about whether one can speak of front and back in such cases or whether both sides are of equal merit, and which one — or both — should be exhibited. Six of these double-sided canvases present a Berlin street scene on one side and a Fehmarn motif on the other, not necessarily with the same orientation.[27] Since discussion of these issues has only recently flared up again,[26] in our exhibition and its catalogue we have decided to present and illustrate both sides of two of these works pp. 172–173, 196–197. In addition there is a third canvas that pairs a studio situation in Berlin with two nudes and nude bathers on the Baltic Sea island pp. 203, 205. This practice is by no means unique to Kirchner; other artists, like his Brücke colleagues Erich Heckel and Max Pechstein resorted to the same expedient, as did Vincent van Gogh and Pablo Picasso.

At the height of his Expressionist career Kirchner was first thrown off track by the outbreak of the First World War in August 1914, then by his mental and physical breakdown in September 1915. Despite his worsening condition — he suffered from severe anxiety attacks and extended bouts of paralysis in his hands—or indeed because of it, he continued to produce works of the highest poignancy. He was not the only artist to suffer in the difficult conditions of the time. Otto Dix and Max Beckmann created equally remarkable works in response to the crisis. In his enlightening essay in this publication Uwe M. Schneede undertakes a critical comparison of their output during this period. It is highly significant that in times of hopelessness both Kirchner and Beckmann turned to imagery from the Apocalypse, Kirchner at the beginning of his stay at the Bellevue Sanatorium in Kreuzlingen in the autumn of 1917, Beckmann on commission from his close acquaintance Georg Hartmann, the director of the Bauer type foundry in Frankfurt, during his exile in Amsterdam during the Second World War in 1941/42. Kirchner's designs for a woodcut cycle on the Apocalypse, drawn on the backs of cigarette packets for want of better materials, are here exhibited for the first time in the context of a Kirchner museum exhibition pp. 79–91. The twelve watercoloured drawings have been in the archive of the Getty Research Institute in Los Angeles since 1985 but were only rediscovered in 2014.[28] Günther Gercken provides a close analysis of the sketches in his essay in the present volume.

After repeated sanatorium stays in Königstein im Taunus and in Berlin, at the urging of his Jena friend Eberhard Grisebach, Kirchner first went to Davos in early 1917. And after interruptions to his treatment in Berlin and Kreuzlingen, in 1918 he settled in Davos Frauenkirch, together with Erna, where he stayed for the rest of his life. Here, after a prolonged recovery, he experienced a new urge to create. It is with this new turning point in his life that our exhibition ends. Within the space of a few short years, from 1911 to 1917, Kirchner produced his finest Expressionist work in Berlin and then fell—triggered by his experience of military training—all the more precipitously into an existential crisis that threatened his artistic identity. The drawings, graphics and paintings he produced during these brief six years are among the most striking works of art created in Europe at the beginning of the twentieth century.

1 Ernst Ludwig Kirchner to Gustav Schiefler, postcard stamped 27 September 1911; also to Luise Schiefler, letter from 17 October 1911, in Wolfgang Henze et al. (eds.), *Ernst Ludwig Kirchner/Gustav Schiefler: Briefwechsel 1910–1935/1938* (Stuttgart/Zurich, 1990), pp. 45, 46.

2 Robert Hessen, *Die Prostitution in Deutschland* (Munich, 1910); Hans Ostwald, *Im Sittenspiegel der Großstadt*, vol. 1, *Das erotische Berlin* (Berlin/Leipzig, 1910); Abraham Flexner, *Prostitution in Europe* (New York, 1914); Hans Ostwald, *Die Berlinerin: Kultur- und Sittengeschichte Berlins* (Berlin, 1921), especially pp. 365–397; Richard J. Evans, "Prostitution, State and Society in Imperial Germany", *Past & Present* 70 (1976), pp. 106–129.

3 Ernst Ludwig Kirchner to Luise Schiefler, letter from 28 February 1912, in Henze et al., *Kirchner/Schiefler* (see n. 1), p. 57; see also p. 48, as well as Kirchner to Sidi Riha, postcard from 7 February 1912, in Annemarie Dube-Heynig, *Ernst Ludwig Kirchner: Postkarten und Briefe an Erich Heckel im Altonaer Museum in Hamburg*, ed. Roman Norbert Ketterer with the collaboration of Wolfgang Henze (Cologne, 1984), pp. 196, 207.

4 Ernst Ludwig Kirchner to Gustav Schiefler, undated letter from June/July 1912, in Henze et al., *Kirchner/Schiefler* (see n. 1), p. 59; Ernst Ludwig Kirchner to Gertrud Osthaus, letter from 4 January 1913, in Hans Delfs (ed.), *Ernst Ludwig Kirchner: Der gesamte Briefwechsel*, vol. 1, *Briefe von 1901 bis 1923* (Zurich, 2010), pp. 77–78.

5 Ernst Ludwig Kirchner to an as yet unidentified female correspondent (presumably Luise Schiefler), undated letter (c.1912/13), in *Ernst Ludwig Kirchner: Großstadt, Eros und Natur; Aus den verborgenen Sammlungen der Region*, ed. Barbara Alms, exh. cat. Städtische Galerie Delmenhorst (Bremen, 2005), pp. 118–119, facsimile with a drawing of cocottes and gentlemen.

6 For Kirchner's experience with a prostitute in Dresden, see his letter to Erich Heckel, probably from 12/13 May 1910, in Dube-Heynig, *Postkarten* (see n. 3), pp. 94–100, 242–243.

7 See not only the works presented in Gordon and Gercken and the artist's countless drawings but also the drawings in letters and on postcards from Ernst Ludwig Kirchner to Erich Heckel, in Dube-Heynig, *Postkarten* (see n. 3).

8 Lothar Grisebach (ed.), *Ernst Ludwig Kirchners Davoser Tagebuch: Eine Darstellung des Malers und eine Sammlung seiner Schriften*, new edn., rev. Lucius Grisebach (Ostfildern-Ruit, 1997), p. 74.

9 Alfred Döblin, "Jungfräulichkeit und Prostitution", *Der Sturm* 3, nos. 125/126 (1912), pp. 141–142, and nos. 127/128, p. 7.

10 Gercken 637–639.

11 Alfred Doblin, "An Romanautoren und ihre Kritiker", *Der Sturm* 4, nos. 158/159 (1913), pp. 17–18; see also Döblin, *Aufsätze zur Literatur*, vol. 8 of *Ausgewählte Werke in Einzelbänden* (Olten/Freiburg im Breisgau, 1963), p. 18.

12 Ernst Ludwig Kirchner to Gustav Schiefler, letter from 28 December 1914, in Henze et al., *Kirchner/Schiefler* (see n. 1), pp. 68–70.

13 Grisebach, *Davoser Tagebuch* (see n. 8), p. 78.

14 Ernst Ludwig Kirchner to Eberhard Grisebach, letter from 1 December 1917, in Delfs, *Briefwechsel* (see n. 4), p. 215; see also Ernst Ludwig Kirchner to Botho Graef, letter from 21 September 1916, in ibid., pp. 144–145.

15 Ernst Ludwig Kirchner to Karl Ernst Osthaus, letter from 23 December 1917, in ibid., pp. 220–221.

16 Alfred Döblin, "Die Bilder der Futuristen", *Der Sturm* 3, no. 110 (1912), pp. 41–42.

17 Ernst Ludwig Kirchner, "Die Arbeit E. L. Kirchners" [1925/26], in Eberhard W. Kornfeld, *Ernst Ludwig Kirchner: Nachzeichnung seines Lebens* (Bern, 1979), pp. 339, 341, 344; entry in Sketchbook no. 156, c.1929/30, quoted in Gerd Presler, *Ernst Ludwig Kirchner: Die Skizzenbücher; "Ekstase des ersten Sehens"; Monographie und Werkverzeichnis* (Karlsruhe/Davos, 1996), p. 415; Ernst Ludwig Kirchner, "Bemerkungen über Leben und Arbeit", *Das Werk* 17, no. 1 (1930), p. 3.

18 Roman Norbert Ketterer, with Wolfgang Henze (eds.), *Ernst Ludwig Kirchner: Zeichnungen und Pastelle* (Stuttgart/Zurich, 1979), p. 250 (no. 4); the previous quote is taken from *Ernst Ludwig Kirchner: Werke, Dokumente, Bücher*, auction cat. Galerie Kornfeld, Bern, Auction 189, 21 June 1985, p. 174, Lot 143. It appears that the notebook in question has not been fully published in transcription. At the time of publication of this catalogue we have been unable to determine its present whereabouts. For the possible addressee of Kirchner's letter, see the entry from 21 July 1919 in Kirchner's Davos diary, in Grisebach, *Davoser Tagebuch* (see n. 8), p. 36.

19 Charles W. Haxthausen, "'A New Beauty': Ernst Ludwig Kirchner's Images of Berlin", in Charles W. Haxthausen and Heidrun Suhr (eds.), *Berlin: Culture and Metropolis* (Minneapolis, 1990), pp. 58–94. http://www.academia.edu/20327726/_A_New_Beauty_Ernst_Ludwig_Kirchners_Images_of_Berlin (accessed 10 October 2016); Magdalena M. Moeller, *Ernst Ludwig Kirchner: Die Straßenszenen; 1913–1915* (Munich, 1993).

20 See the essay by Charles W. Haxthausen in the present volume, pp. 20–31.

21 Grisebach, *Davoser Tagebuch* (see n. 8), p. 78.

22 Moeller, *Straßenszenen* (see n. 19), p. 26.

23 Ernst Ludwig Kirchner to Gustav Schiefler, postcard stamped 31 July 1912, in Henze et al., *Kirchner/Schiefler* (see n. 1), p. 60.

24 Ernst Ludwig Kirchner to Gustav Schiefler, letter from 31 December 1912, in ibid., p. 61.

25 There have already been reconstructions of this living-room corner at the Neue Nationalgalerie Berlin (2005), at the Mathildenhöhe Darmstadt (2010) and at the Staatsgalerie Stuttgart (2012).

26 Gordon 275, 363, 367, 369, 379, 427.

27 See most recently *Der doppelte Kirchner: Die zwei Seiten der Leinwand*, ed. Inge Herold, Ulrike Lorenz and Thorsten Sadowsky, exh. cat. Kunsthalle Mannheim and Kirchner Museum Davos (Cologne, 2015).

28 Thomas W. Gaehtgens and Anja Foerschner, "Ernst Ludwig Kirchner's Drawings of the Apocalypse", *Getty Research Journal* 6 (2014), pp. 83–102; *Nothing but the Clouds Unchanged: Artists in World War I*, ed. Gordon Hughes and Philipp Blom, accompanying volume for the exhibition *World War I: War of Images, Images of War*, The Getty Research Institute, Los Angeles, and Mildred Lane Kemper Art Museum at Washington University, St. Louis (Los Angeles, 2014), p. 124.

Vibrant Metropolis / Idyllic Nature
Kirchner — The Berlin Years

Essays

Fig. 1 Ernst Ludwig Kirchner
Potsdamer Platz, Berlin, 1914
Oil on canvas, 200 × 150 cm
(Gordon 370)

Staatliche Museen zu Berlin, Nationalgalerie

Motion Pictures: On Kirchner's Berlin Street Scenes

On the recto of the canvas, two fierce-looking whores cruise a Berlin street. On the verso two nude young women splash in the surf *(Two Women on the Street* and *Two Bathers in Surf)* pp. 196–197. The two sides of this single canvas exemplify the two sides of Ernst Ludwig Kirchner's art during these years: on the one, the edgy, intense maelstrom of the metropolis; on the other, a seemingly prelapsarian paradise on a remote, isolated corner of the Baltic Sea island of Fehmarn. There Kirchner, together with his companion Erna Schilling, spent part of each summer from 1912 to 1914. What to make of the acute contrast between these two image worlds? For some they have suggested an antagonistic relationship: modern urban anxiety and alienation contrasted with harmonious wholeness within a timeless nature; a critique of the one and a celebration of the other.[1] Donald E. Gordon, author of the first scholarly monograph on Kirchner and the catalogue raisonné of his paintings, believed Kirchner's images of Berlin revealed "better than the vision of any other twentieth-century artist [...] insight into a desperately diseased European society whose few remaining days are numbered."[2] For Wolf-Dieter Dube, co-editor of a catalogue raisonné of Kirchner's prints, the underlying theme of the artist's images of Berlin was "the hectic and unnatural condition of the modern metropolis", revealing the "desolation of the alienated man, which he was himself".[3] Although by no means universally shared, this dark, apocalyptic view of these pictures has persisted to this day.[4]

Nearly thirty years ago I argued against this interpretative dichotomy.[5] I proposed that "on the whole Kirchner's images of Berlin were born of an essentially affirmative attitude toward the metropolis", that he "saw his art not as an expression of urban alienation and anxiety, but as a contribution to an aestheticization of urban life".[6] In making this case I considered several factors. First there were Kirchner's own remarks about these works. In his Berlin street scenes, he wrote in retrospect, he had deployed "new means to give the relations among human beings a new poetic expression".[7] There are many such statements by him. With rare exceptions they were devoid of any suggestion of the negative world view art historians later read into his Berlin paintings.

A second factor influencing my assessment was the reception of Kirchner's Berlin pictures by his contemporaries, especially by leading German critics of the interwar period. These stood in sharp contrast to the dark interpretations in more recent commentary. These early writers praised Kirchner for capturing the dynamism and vibrancy of the city, hailing him as the greatest German painter of the modern metropolis. "No other artist experienced the metropolis Berlin, as it was in the last years before the war, with every fiber of his being as did Kirchner," wrote Curt Glaser, curator of the Berlin Kupferstichkabinett. "Kirchner gave artistic form to this world."[8] Karl Scheffler, noting that many contemporaries reproached Kirchner for owing too much to Manet, countered that precisely that was his virtue: "In terms of feeling he is still close to the Impressionists. There is something sensuously melodic in his works." One savoured this "artistic sensuousness in the figural paintings of fashionable persons on the street or in interior spaces, in which worldly elegance has, as it were, been spiritualized".[9] In Will Grohmann's monograph, which was stringently vetted by Kirchner, there is no suggestion of critical or apocalyptic sentiments in his urban subjects.[10]

Most of the works of Kirchner's Berlin years continue the themes of the Dresden years, the images of popular culture—circus, dance, music hall; nudes in the studio and in nature. In Berlin, as in Dresden, Kirchner also painted a number of *Stadtansichten,* works that took the Berlin cityscape as motifs, such as *Elisabethufer* p. 124 and *Street at Schöneberg City Park* p. 125. Yet the pictures that have come to define his Berlin period are

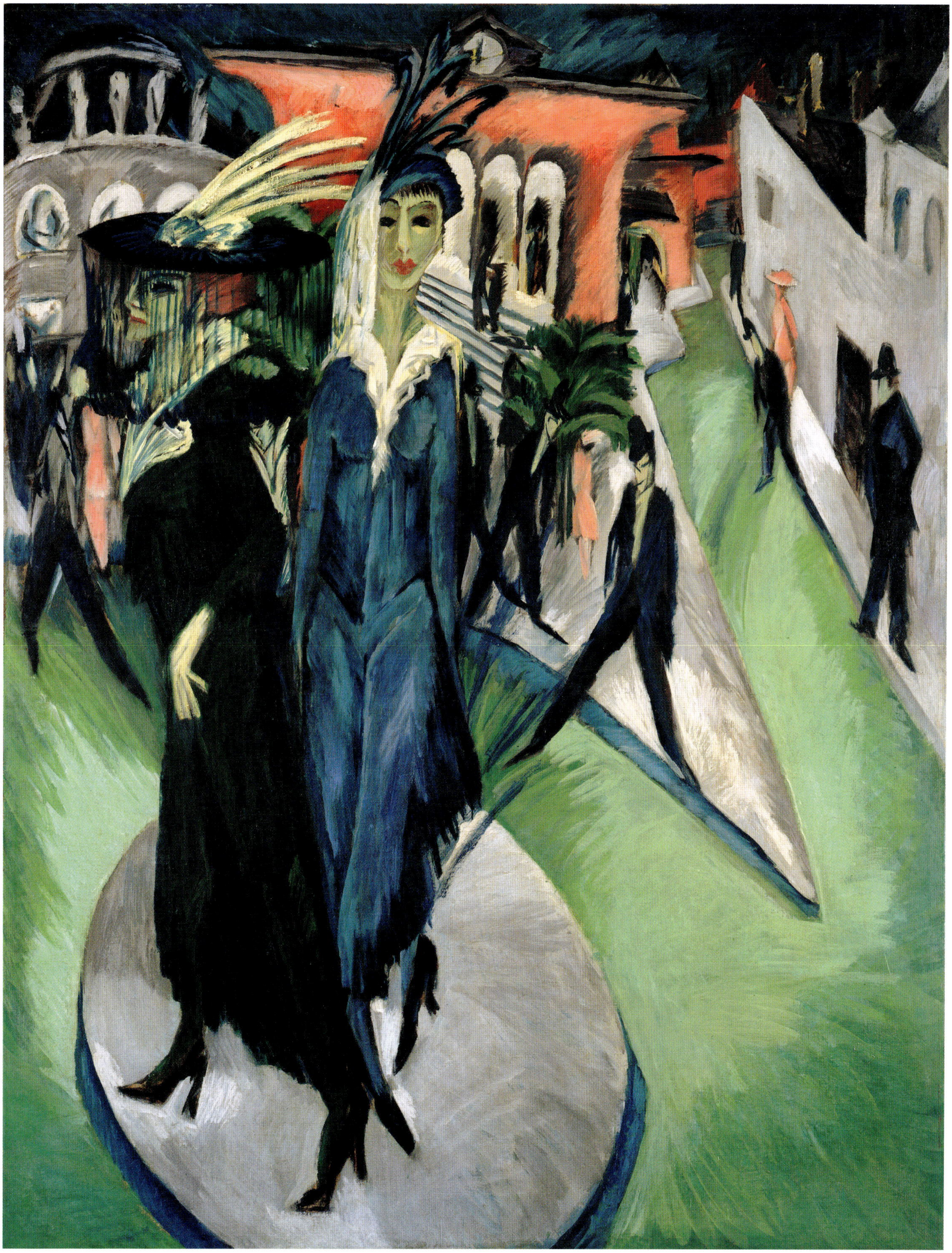

the *Strassenszenen,* the street scenes, and they constitute his most distinctive artistic achievement, the creation of a "new iconographic type":[11] these show people—among them are obviously prostitutes—strolling Berlin's streets. For Gordon they manifested Kirchner's "active distaste for the image of urban sin. [...] The Dresden champion of instinct in nature had become the Berlin critic of sex in the streets."[12] Rosalyn Deutsche, in a widely cited article, described the street scenes as "pictures of an unnatural, thoroughly dehumanized world". In these works, she argued, Kirchner "went beyond the mere depiction of alienation to observe its actual cause—the dominance of a money economy".[13] Yet nowhere in Kirchner's own remarks on the street scenes is there any evidence of a moralistic or critical stance toward prostitution. Gordon conceded his own puzzlement over this discrepancy, noting that Kirchner wrote about his street scenes "more in aesthetic than in ethical terms".[14]

For Deutsche, Kirchner's prostitutes exemplified "the objectification of human relations in economic exchange".[15] Yet at the time I was struck that none of these paintings (in contrast to certain prints) show women overtly engaged in solicitation. Attempting better to understand the context of the street scenes, I looked to sources of the period on the practice and regulation of prostitution in Berlin, material that had been previously ignored in the commentary on these works.[16] The most significant fact I discovered was that Berlin differed from cities like Hamburg, Paris and Vienna in its proscription of brothels. The "cocottes" therefore had to seek their clients on the streets, and consequently, as George Grosz later recalled in his first impressions of central Berlin in 1912 when he was nineteen, "the Friedrichstadt district was crawling with whores".[17] To be sure, prostitution was officially illegal, but it was tolerated under strict regulation.[18] The "women known to be for sale" could "under no circumstances glance behind them, or step up to a shop window, or stand still beside a man, or even speak to one. They should float by in a 'ladylike' manner"; otherwise they ran the risk of being arrested by the plain-clothes morality police.[19] Accordingly, most prostitutes had to be extremely circumspect as they strolled the streets seeking johns, resulting in an ambience vividly conveyed by one contemporary author:

"In the streets between the Zoo railway station and Wittenbergplatz and along the Kurfürstendamm there is, at every time of day, a crowd of *promeneurs* in which women predominate. Young women, schoolgirls, youthful-looking mothers with their grown daughters. [...] Sometimes with the serious face of a school teacher or student, sometimes with longing lips and eyes, mouth blood-red with lipstick or blackened eyelashes and eyebrows and a pallid powder-coated face. Or maternal, with defensive glances. And yet, countless sideward glances: "Make me yours!"—Intermingling with them are old and young men, mostly tradespeople, lawyers, engineers, a few with an artistic look. [...] And the glances of the women divided between the men and the gleaming shop windows. [...] That woman over there—she could perhaps be a famous film actress; that one—a cabaret dancer. But here one often doesn't know: perhaps she is the daughter or the wife of the man who walks beside her—for here the glittering colour of the demi-monde is also the style of dress. And that plain woman over there is perhaps soliciting."[20]

This pervasive erotic ambiguity was also characteristic of several of Kirchner's painted street scenes—they "approximated very closely the contemporary descriptions of the modus operandi of prostitution in Berlin". It was this very ambiguity, I suggested, not discretion or moral scruples, that had led most of Kirchner's early commentators to pass over the actual subject of these pictures in silence.[21] Instead of regarding the street scenes as the antithesis of his idyllic Fehmarn pictures, I speculated whether for Kirchner, this most flagrantly erotic German artist of his generation, these works might have been rather "a glorification of those same primordial energies within the modern metropolis".[22]

In the years since I published that essay there has been an exponential growth of scholarship on Kirchner, including several serious studies of the street scenes.[23] This has been aided by the substantial augmentation of documentation on Kirchner's life and art, including a monograph on his sketchbooks, accompanied by an annotated catalogue, and a four-volume edition of Kirchner's massive collected correspondence.[24] Moreover, in 2008

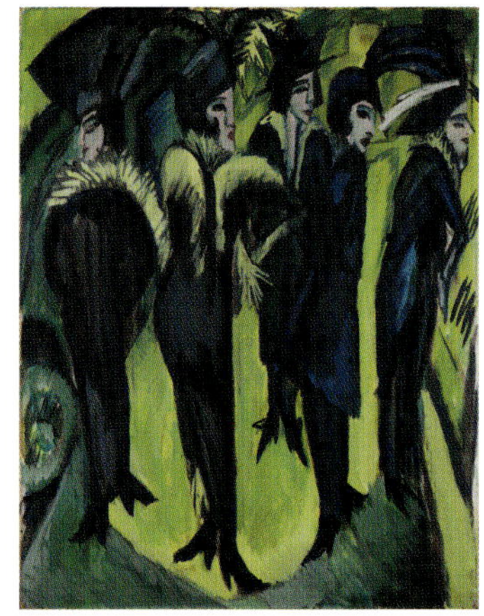

Fig. 2 Ernst Ludwig Kirchner
Five Women on the Street, 1913
Oil on canvas, 190 × 120 cm
(Gordon 362)

Museum Ludwig, Cologne

New York's Museum of Modern Art presented an exhibition on Kirchner's street scenes, where for the first and only time all seven of the paintings from the Berlin years could be seen and studied together.[25]

Given this expanded state of research I want to re-examine these endlessly fascinating works for the purpose of exploring a particular aspect of the street scenes that in my view has been insufficiently considered, that of *motion.* Kirchner had much more to say about the primacy of motion for his aesthetic vision than he did about cocottes. It was, he declared, "above all the observation of motion *[Bewegung]* that stimulates me to creation. From [motion] comes the intensified feeling for life which is the origin of the work of art."[26] He wrote quite eloquently about the importance of motion to his experience of the urban street. What I want to explore in the present essay is the relation between the theme of prostitution in the street scenes and the aesthetic sensation — that "intensified feeling for life" effected by the experience of motion — that inspired these pictures. How might these seemingly conflicting aspects of Kirchner's art be reconciled?

"A Painting of Motion"

In correspondence with Ludwig Justi, director of Berlin's Nationalgalerie, Kirchner referred to his street scenes as "the strongest and most mature of my works".[27] They are unique in his painted oeuvre in constituting a discrete series, one that coheres not only by subject matter but also by format. We are speaking of eight paintings in all: seven are of more or less equal dimensions, from 120 to 126 cm in height and 90 to 95 cm in width; the eighth, *Potsdamer Platz, Berlin,* fig. 1 is 200 by 150 cm, making it one of the largest paintings from Kirchner's Berlin period.[28] From the group of seven in the smaller format, one, *Street with Red Cocotte,*[29] was overpainted in the 1920s, so that six are considered to have come down to us in their original state.[30]

Kirchner exhibited the street scenes under various titles during the 1910s and into the 1920s, which often makes it difficult to determine precisely which pictures were being shown. With the exception of *Street with Red Cocotte,* which was evidently not exhibited until Kirchner had overpainted it around 1925, none of the works, then as now, had titles identifying the women as prostitutes.[31] Presumably this was in some cases out of deference to Wilhelmine censorship laws and the then virulent debates about combating public immorality.[32] Yet although the titles often changed from one exhibition to the next, so far as we know in no case did they refer directly to prostitution. By contrast, the titles of ten of his twenty-four prints on this theme, as catalogued in the 1920s by Gustav Schiefler, are explicit.[33] The woodcut version of the painting *Five Women on the Street* fig. 2 — with *Potsdamer Platz, Berlin* fig. 1 the only painting for which there is a corresponding print — bore the title *Fünf Kokotten* (Five Cocottes) p. 168.[34] In addition, there are seven prints with titles comprising the word "cocotte", as in the etching *Cocotte Offering Herself* p. 194 and the lithograph *Cocottes on Kurfürstendamm* p. 185.

What are we to make of this difference between the titles of the prints of street scenes and those of the paintings? In a letter to Justi, Kirchner claimed that he wanted to reserve his street scenes for acquisition by museums — might he have believed it prudent to conceal their sordid subject matter?[35] In this regard it's amusing to see how he titled two of the street scenes in his 1917 Jena exhibition: *Strassenbild mit zwei Damen in Orange und Blau* (Street Scene with Two Ladies in Orange and Blue) and *Strassenbild mit Zwei Damen in Blau und Schwarz mit folgenden Herren* (Street Scene with Two Ladies in Blue and Black with Gentlemen Following).[36] To judge from the particulars in the titles, these must have been two of his most blatantly "cocottish" images — respectively, *Two Women on the Street* p. 197 and *Friedrichstrasse, Berlin* p. 191. Yet the genteel designation *Damen* (ladies) — not *Frauen* (women), which Kirchner used for some of these works — seems to have been intended to obscure their obvious subject matter.

Even more striking — and more curious — is the title Kirchner chose for *Street, Berlin* prior to its acquisition by the Nationalgalerie. In a 1918 Zurich exhibition it was listed in the catalogue as *Rosa Strasse mit Auto* (Pink Street with Automobile).[37] Two years later, reproduced in the magazine *Kunst und Künstler,* it was *Rote Strasse mit Auto* (Red Street with Automobile).[38] After entering the collection of the Nationalgalerie that year it became, simply, *Strasse* (Street).[39] Why did Kirchner emphasise the automobile, an only partially visible object on the edge of his composition, in this way? It seems unlikely that he chose the title as a decoy—he could simply have called the picture *Strassenszene* or *Strassenbild,* generic titles under which he sometimes exhibited such works. Moreover, it wasn't the first time he had included the word *Auto* in a title—in his 1916 exhibition at the Schames gallery in Frankfurt there were two street scenes, both dated 1914, one of which was *Strassenbild mit Auto* (Street Picture with Automobile).[40] This might have been the same picture shown at Zurich in 1918, or perhaps *Five Women on the Street* fig.2, for both of these paintings feature an automobile. A third picture, *Friedrichstrasse, Berlin* p.191, includes a vehicle that has been variously read as a carriage or an automobile; a fourth, *Berlin Street Scene* fig.3, includes a horse-drawn omnibus; and a small figural street scene of this time, *Leipziger Strasse with Electric Tram,*[41] includes that conveyance.

Such motifs are not limited to the street scenes. In these years we find in Kirchner's art more vehicles of various kinds—trams, trains, automobiles, omnibuses, and droshkies—than in the art of any of his contemporaries, with the possible exception of the Italian Futurists.[42] To cite three examples: *Streetcar and Train* p.173; the intersecting trams in *Nollendorfplatz* p.112; a trio of cars in *Brandenburg Gate, Berlin* p.212—in his drawings, pastels, and prints there are also many instances. The frequent presence of such motifs is not coincidental. In a sketchbook from the end of the 1920s Kirchner wrote, "My painting is a painting of motion *[Bewegung].* Born at a railway station, early on I drew locomotives, gradually I came to line, the sign of motion, and from the line composition to planar painting. I enriched it with new forms, the form that one sees when one is in motion oneself and which derives from objects in motion." (emphasis in original).[43] And in a manuscript from circa 1926: "My starting point is motion. [...] I believe that human experiences of seeing and of feeling come much more from this condition of motion and that consequently a form that is derived from motion speaks much more to people."[44] It seems probable that Kirchner saw vehicles not merely as visual facts or as icons of modernity but as *signifiers of motion,* motifs with the suggestive power of evoking the fluctuant perceptual experience of the metropolis. And this may explain why he chose to direct attention to the automobile with his original title for *The Street* (Die Strasse).

As a discrete series the street scenes show a development in Kirchner's treatment of motion, from the deployment of vehicles as signifiers of motion to the *generation* of effects of motion within the picture through the pictorial means themselves. If in *Five Women on the Street* fig.2 and *Street, Berlin* p.169 the automobile functions as a signifier of motion, in *Friedrichstrasse, Berlin* p.191, cited by Kirchner as one of his most successful street scenes,[45] there is something new: the vehicle is no longer a marginal element of the composition; it is pushed into the foreground alongside the towering figures of the two women. Nor does it merely signify motion: its wheels, by means of their dynamic circular forms, *generate* motion, injecting a surge of energy into the composition. The force sweeps the phalanx of women and men into its current, intensifying the thrust of their forward movement. This motion is reinforced by the parallel curves of the men's legs in the background, which rhyme with the hatchings that are spun off the rotating wheels and with the sweeping arc of the curb. One need only compare the painting with *Street, Berlin* and *Five Women on the Street* to see the much greater dynamism of *Friedrichstrasse, Berlin.*

This shift to creating an effect of motion within the picture by plastic means is carried even further in the largest and most ambitious of Kirchner's Berlin street scenes, *Potsdamer Platz, Berlin* fig.1. This square "had become a synonym for the German metropolis".[46] It was considered the busiest traffic junction in Europe.[47] In a contemporary account Hans Ostwald vividly described the "splendid bustling activity" around the square, in which a flurry of "trams, omnibuses, cars, droshkies, commercial vehicles, men, women, young groomed girls, and children fill the square and through a perpetual motion produce a

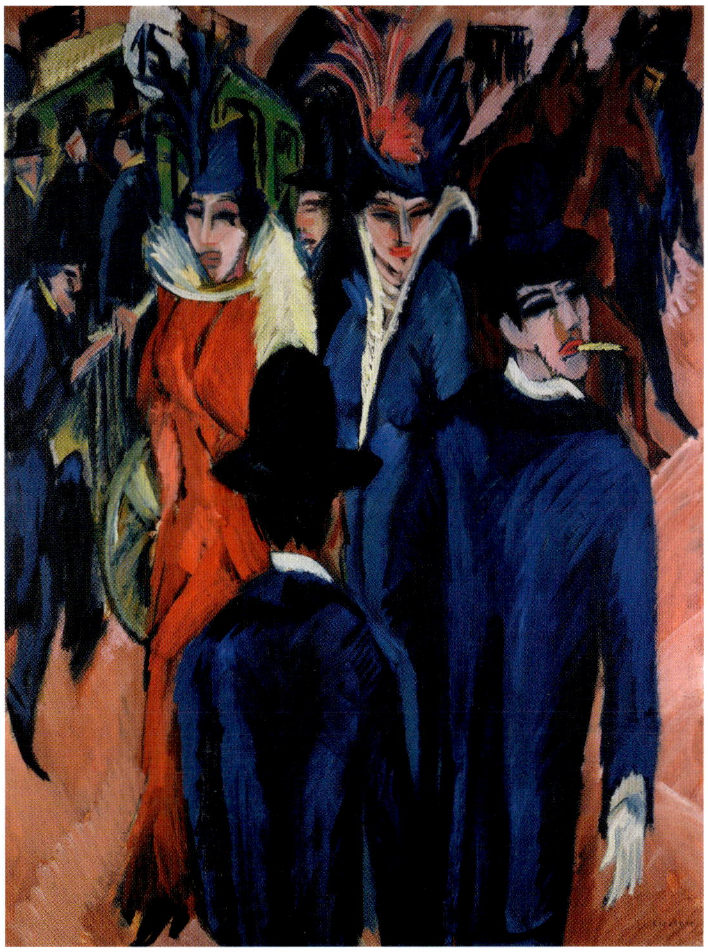

Fig. 3 Ernst Ludwig Kirchner
Berlin Street Scene, 1913
Oil on canvas, 121 × 95 cm
(Gordon 363)

Neue Galerie New York
and private collection

constantly changing scene".[48] Kirchner's painting offers a strong contrast to this image. We see no cars, trams, etc., hardly anything suggestive of "splendidly bustling activity". Might Kirchner have omitted vehicles in this painting because, building on *Friedrichstrasse, Berlin,* he discovered he no longer needed them as signifiers of motion? Because he had now found a purely *formal* means of generating effects of motion within the picture? The tipped-up circular form of the traffic island has become dynamic; "like a rotating disk [...] it seems to float above the luminous green street"—as Katharina Sykora quite aptly describes its effect.[49] This churning wheel seems propelled by the spiky shoes of the woman in black, radiating spiky hatchings onto the green surface. With their abnormally attenuated legs, the drastically diminished figures of the men approaching the traffic island seem sucked into this powerful vortex.[50]

Kirchner deployed another notable effect of motion in *Potsdamer Platz, Berlin.* In a long, undated autobiographical text from around 1926 he wrote, "One considers a picture to be what one can see from one point in space with a single view. That is a major limitation. This is how I do it: I move and collect the sequence of images within myself to an inner image. This I paint."[51] In other words, Kirchner explains here that he seeks not only to capture the motion of objects but also the motion of the perceiving subject in his continually changing spatial relationship to objects—"forms [...] that one sees when one is in motion oneself."[52] This effect he achieves through the introduction of contrasting angles of vision.

Kirchner used this multiple perspective to brilliant effect in *Potsdamer Platz, Berlin*—indeed, the painting seems like a montage of images seen from different viewpoints. We see this more clearly if we look at a photograph of the square more or less as it looked when Kirchner painted it fig. 4. He has reduced the tripartite station façade to its central section, in turn condensing its two stories into one. This he rendered in the reddish color that was present only in the flanking wings that he omitted. On the left, directly

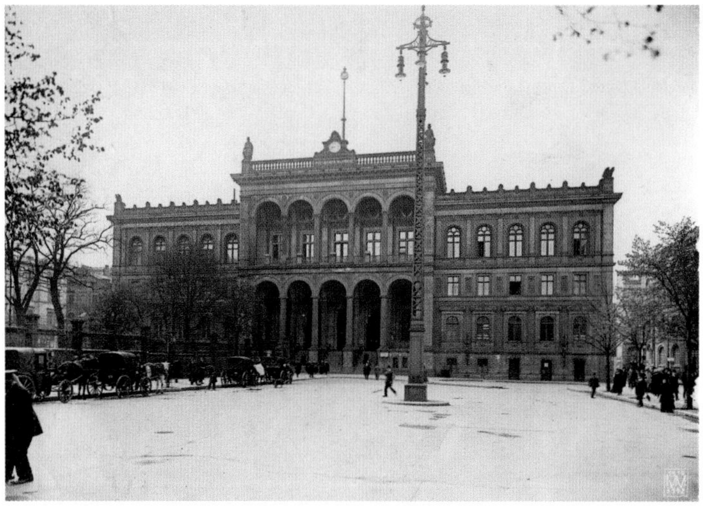

Fig. 4 Max Missmann
Potsdam Station,
Reception Hall, 1910
Original photograph,
16.5 × 22.8 cm

Stadtmuseum Berlin Foundation

juxtaposed with this façade was the newest architectural addition to the square, Haus Potsdam. Kirchner eliminated Köthener Strasse, the street separating the two structures, squeezing the new building tightly against the station façade. By contrast to this horizontal compression, in a vertical direction the pictorial space — and with it the visual field of the beholder — is dramatically expanded. We view the faces of the two women straight on, as though at their eye level, and when we look over to the cupola of Haus Potsdam on the upper left, as though from street level, the ground seems to tilt precipitously beneath us. Yet on the right we soar upward to gain an elevated view of the side street with its isolated pedestrians, drastically reduced in scale. In 1919 Kirchner shared with his friend Eberhard Grisebach his judgement that *Potsdamer Platz, Berlin* fig. 1 "is probably my best work and there will probably not be anything this good again".[53]

In a number of Kirchner's images of Berlin there is another distinctive aspect of his treatment of motion that I want to call *polydirectional.* This involves the incorporation of contrasting axes of motion in a single image. We can see this polydirectionality clearly in *Friedrichstrasse, Berlin* p. 191, in the juxtaposition of the forward movement of the figures advancing toward us with the sideways motion of the vehicle toward the right. We find it also in the differing orientations of the two women in *Potsdamer Platz, Berlin* one looking directly at us, the other sharply to the left. Polydirectionality can be found, too, in several Berlin streetscapes, such as *Nollendorfplatz* p. 112, *Railway Overpass* p. 175, and *Streetcar and Train* p. 173, all of them intersections incorporating contrasting axes of motion. As Grohmann noted, "intersections seem to exist only for the purpose of letting trolley car lines cross each other, metropolitan railway bridges only to indicate movement and speed above and beneath the earth".[54]

Basically polydirectionality is inevitably characteristic of the movements of people through the city. Anonymously — singly, in pairs or in smaller groups — they pass through the streets, without any necessary psychological connection to one another, without being united in any common action. They follow their respective paths through the city in various directions, generating contrasting patterns of motion. Of all the paintings, this is most evident in *Potsdamer Platz, Berlin,* made possible by its expansive deep space. For Kirchner this polyphony of motion was especially exciting. In his notes for the Grohmann monograph, he writes that he "found that that the feeling that pervades a city is represented by the character of lines of force *[Kraftlinien].* In the way people in crowds form into compositions, in the very trajectories of their walking, he found the means to capture what he experienced. There are pictures and prints by him where a purely linear scaffolding with virtually schematic figures nevertheless represents the life of the streets most vibrantly."[55]

This phenomenon finds perhaps its most vivid representation in Kirchner's prints, above all in the etchings and lithographs. A splendid example is the etching *Cocotte Offering Herself* p. 194. The dense, zigzagging hatchings take on a life of their own, producing

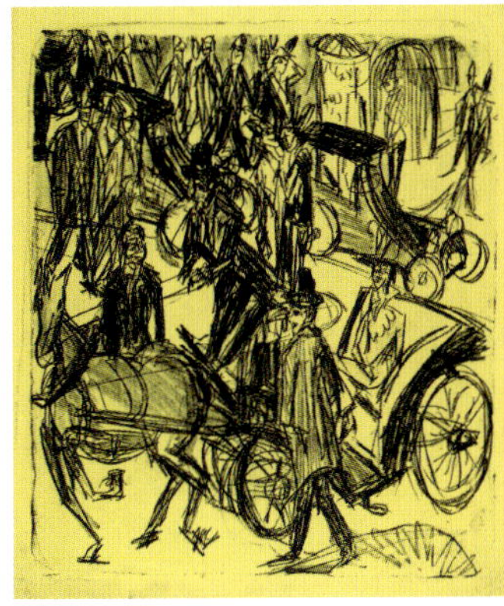

Fig. 5 Ernst Ludwig Kirchner
Leipziger Strasse, Intersection, 1914
Lithograph on yellow paper, image: 59.5 × 50.5 cm, sheet: 69 × 57.6 cm
(Gercken 669/I)

Private Collection

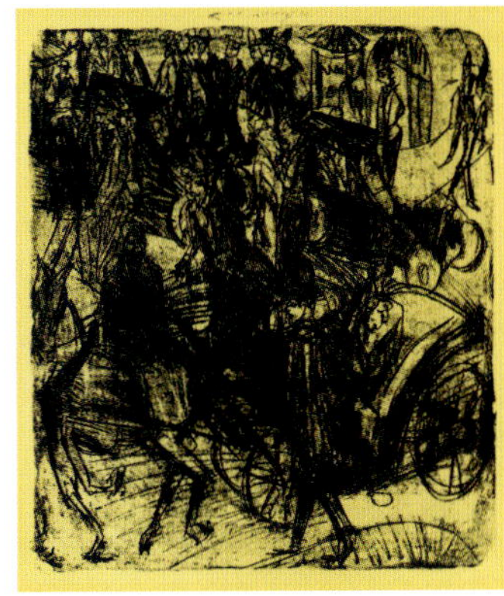

Fig. 6/Cat. 115
Ernst Ludwig Kirchner
Leipziger Strasse, Intersection, 1914
Lithograph on yellow paper, image: 59 × 50.6 cm, sheet: 70.5 × 55.9 cm
(Gercken 669/III)

Brücke-Museum, Berlin, Karl and Emy Schmidt-Rottluff Foundation

clusters of pure graphic energy, uncontained by objects. A consummate instance of such polydirectional "lines of force" is found in Kirchner's great lithograph *Leipziger Strasse, Intersection* figs. 5,6, the most complex of his images of street life, comparable to the painting of the nearby Potsdamer Platz in its richly figured commodious space. In the middle distance two cars roll forward in a rightward direction, in the foreground a droshky carrying a woman passenger moves toward the left. Individual men approach the carriage from opposite directions. Somewhat further in the background individuals and pairs move in their respective, seemingly random paths. In the first state of the print these motifs are clearly visible. Some of this clarity is sacrificed in the third state, in which Kirchner has added clusters of hatchings of parallel lines that function purely to emphasise the different axes of motion, giving the "lines of force" concrete form.

Among Kirchner's contemporaries none grasped and praised his aesthetics of motion better than Paul Westheim. What was at stake for the artist, he explained, was "to bring dynamism into the inertness of the painting surface. [...] Only in this way could one dare to take on the image of the metropolis, whose essence is motion, motion boundlessly and breathlessly intensified. This is what makes it possible to paint the rushing rows of houses, the Brandenburg Gate, Potsdamer Platz with its bustling tangled jumble of humanity, Friedrichstrasse with its streetwalkers, the Engelsufer, the cityscapes from Frankfurt, Halle, Dresden, representations that are not pictures, but a symphony of the big city" (original emphasis).[56]

For Kirchner, Westheim continues, this meant motion "not as motif", but as "a new life-rhythm, as the motoric energy of living things, motion as pictorial form, as play of line, as flow of colour masses, as unfolding of space".[57] Westheim was uniquely positioned to experience and appreciate this — he was the owner of *Two Women on the Street* p. 197.[58]

Kokotte = Zeitfrau?

In his paean to Kirchner's art Westheim mentioned "streetwalkers" only in passing, and they would remain marginal to the discourse on the street scenes until the 1980s. Since then it is generally assumed that all of the Berlin street scenes have prostitution as their subject. But can we be sure? In his short monograph on Kirchner's urban pictures Lucius Grisebach acknowledged his uncertainty about identifying the two women in *Street, Berlin* p. 169 as prostitutes — here they were characterised "not so obviously as cocottes, but as fashionably dressed women who are attracting the attention of the men. Probably they are intended as cocottes, but we lack any unequivocal way of judging their role."[59] Such ambiguity — remember, this was a picture Kirchner once titled "Pink Street with Automobile" — reproduces a distinctive feature of Berlin prostitution itself: for "here one often doesn't know".[60] This uncertainty could also be extended, I believe, to *Berlin Street Scene* fig. 3, as well as to some of the prints of street scenes that make no reference to prostitution in their titles, such as *Flâneurs in the Street* fig. 7, that are compositionally related to scenes explicitly identified as depicting prostitutes.

Given that streetwalkers are undoubtedly the subject of, at the very least, five paintings—*Five Women on the Street, Friedrichstrasse, Berlin, Potsdamer Platz, Berlin, Two Women on the Street* and the reworked *Street with Red Cocotte*—why do they dominate the pictures Kirchner called "perhaps the most precious of my works"?[61] Why were these the pictures that he singled out for giving "the relations among human beings a new poetic expression"? To return to our original question, what is the relationship between the subject matter of the street scenes and Kirchner's aesthetic agenda?

Two statements by Kirchner seem particularly relevant here. The first is from a long text, a self-representation in the third person, which he prepared for Grohmann's monograph. There he writes, "The danger of getting stuck on subject matter didn't exist for Kirchner. He thought too much like a painter for that. The best evidence are the prints and paintings and pastels of the street scenes, in which sensations are rendered purely plastically, one would like to say almost abstractly [*gegenstandslos*, or, literally, without subject matter]."[62] Yet two years later he seemingly contradicted this statement: "I must confess to you", he confided to Schiefler, "that I am heretical enough to attach a lot of value to content and subject matter. For me the decisive factor in taking up the profession of painter was that I could express something through pictures that I could not express otherwise. Consequently, from the very beginning I have always drawn and painted compositions that meant something."[63] Might both of these statements be true? What then might be the meaning of the street scenes? Could, paradoxically, the very subject of prostitution be integrally linked with Kirchner's transcendence of the subject in his aesthetic response to the metropolis?

A passage in an essay by Alfred Döblin provokes such a thought. Wolfgang Henze was the first to link the street scenes with Kirchner's friendship with the writer, for whose one-act play on a Viennese brothel, *Countess Mizzi,* the artist was making woodcut illustrations about the time he began the series of paintings.[64] But Henze also suggested a further, arguably more significant link connecting the street scenes with Döblin, namely an essay on prostitution he had in published in 1912 in *Der Sturm.*[65] We cannot know whether Kirchner read this, yet it certainly seems highly likely that while working on Döblin's brothel play he could have, at least in conversation, had the opportunity to become familiar with the ideas the author had expressed in his *Sturm* essay. Henze cites a passage in which Döblin describes the prostitute as a woman with "sex organs [but] without sexuality. Further, she exhibits a coldness below freezing point."[66] This observation Henze links with "the conspicuous coolness with which Kirchner sees womanhood offering itself and making itself available."[67] This "conspicuous coolness", I believe, certainly fits the affect of the cocottes in *Potsdamer Platz, Berlin* fig. 1 or *Two Women on the Street* p. 197. Yet in my opinion another passage from Döblin's essay may be of greater relevance for our question, and it is this: "The genitals are directed to another sex, but not to another person. The basis of prostitution is the lack of a compulsion towards a specific object, the absence of a fateful determination of a sexual counterpart, the aimlessness of the drive to connect."[68] This squares very well with contemporaneous accounts of Berlin prostitution: the cocotte as *flâneuse* within the anonymity of the city, impersonal, always on the move, seeking "another sex, but not [...] another person", no "specific object". This enforced perpetual movement—for she risked arrest if she paused or lingered—made the prostitute the very image of the anonymous, perpetual motion in the metropolis that so enchanted Kirchner and inspired the paintings he regarded as his greatest works.

Probably around 1914/15, as he was painting the street scenes, Kirchner scrawled a curious, isolated phrase on a page of a sketchbook: *Kokotte = Zeitfrau.*[69] The term *Zeitfrau* is anomalous—it was evidently Kirchner's invention. What did he mean by it? "Woman by the minute",[70] a woman for temporary hire as a sex object? Or might *Zeitfrau* be, rather, analogous to *Zeitgeist*—the omnipresent ambulatory Berlin cocotte as the ultimate representative of the age? In view of Kirchner's aesthetic vision, this latter meaning seems to me the more likely one.

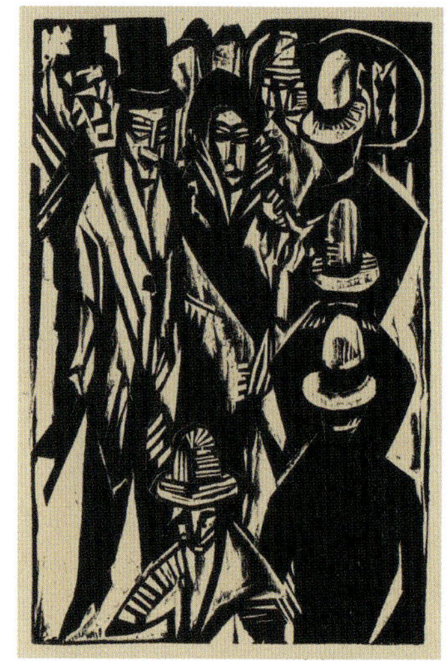

Fig. 7 Ernst Ludwig Kirchner
Flâneurs in the Street, 1914
Woodcut on brownish paper, image: 29.2 × 18.2 cm, sheet: 49.2 × 33.3 cm
(Gercken 647/II)

Saarlandmuseum Saarbrücken, Saarländischer Kulturbesitz Foundation

Ultimately, for Kirchner these pictures were probably primarily about motion: "The modern light of cities in combination with the motion of the streets continually gives me new stimuli. It spreads a new beauty over the world, one *that does not lie in the particulars of the subject matter"* (my emphasis).[71] For such an art Westheim's musical metaphor, "symphony of the big city", is absolutely fitting.

1 See, for example, Wolf-Dieter Dube, "Kirchners Bildmotive in Beziehung zur Umwelt", in *Ernst Ludwig Kirchner: 1880–1938*, ed. Lucius Grisebach and Annette Meyer zu Eissen, exh. cat. Nationalgalerie Berlin (Berlin, 1979), pp. 12–13. (This and all following translations from the German are by the author.)

2 Donald E. Gordon, *Ernst Ludwig Kirchner* (Cambridge, MA, 1968), p. 86.

3 Wolf-Dieter Dube, "The Artists' Group *Die Brücke*", in *Expressionism: A German Intuition 1905–1920*, ed. Susan B. Hirschfeld, exh. cat. Solomon R. Guggenheim Museum (New York, 1980), p. 101.

4 For a summary of the darker interpretations in the recent literature on the street scenes, see Eleanor Moseman, "At the Intersection: Kirchner, Kubišta, and 'Modern Morality', 1911–14", *Art Bulletin* 93, no. 1 (2011), pp. 98–99, n. 44.

5 Charles W. Haxthausen, "'A New Beauty': Ernst Ludwig Kirchner's Images of Berlin", in Charles W. Haxthausen and Heidrun Suhr (eds.), *Berlin: Culture and Metropolis* (Minneapolis, 1990), pp. 58–94, http://www.academia.edu/20327726/_A_New_Beauty_Ernst_Ludwig_Kirchners_Images_of_Berlin (accessed 10 October 2016). German translation: "'Eine neue Schönheit': Ernst Ludwig Kirchners Berlinbilder", in Thomas Steinfeld and Heidrun Suhr (eds.), *In der großen Stadt: Die Metropole als kulturtheoretische Kategorie* (Frankfurt am Main, 1990), pp. 71–96. A shorter version of the argument appeared in my article, "Images of Berlin in the Art of the Secession and Expressionism", in *Art in Berlin 1815–1989*, ed. Kelly Morris and Amanda Woods, exh. cat. High Art Museum (Atlanta, 1989), pp. 61–82.

6 Haxthausen, "A New Beauty" (see n. 5), p. 61.

7 Louis de Marsalle [Ernst Ludwig Kirchner], "[untitled]", in *Ernst Ludwig Kirchner*, ed. Max Huggler, exh. cat. Kunsthalle Bern (Bern, 1933), p. 15.

8 Curt Glaser, *Die Graphik der Neuzeit: Vom Anfang des XIX. Jahrhunderts bis zur Gegenwart* (Berlin, 1922), p. 540.

9 Karl Scheffler, "Ernst Ludwig Kirchner", *Kunst und Künstler* 18 (1920), p. 226.

10 Will Grohmann, *Das Werk Ernst Ludwig Kirchners* (Munich, 1926), pp. 31–32.

11 Lucius Grisebach, *Ernst Ludwig Kirchner: Großstadtbilder* (Munich, 1979), p. 14.

12 Donald E. Gordon, "Ernst Ludwig Kirchner: By Instinct Possessed", *Art in America* (November 1980), p. 89.

13 Roslyn Deutsche, "Alienation in Berlin: Kirchner's Street Scenes", *Art in America* (January 1983), pp. 69, 71.

14 Gordon, "By Instinct Possessed" (see n. 12), p. 95.

15 Deutsche, "Alienation in Berlin" (see n. 13), p. 71.

16 Haxthausen, "A New Beauty" (see n. 5), pp. 79–81. Two particularly informative sources were Robert Hessen, *Die Prostitution in Deutschland* (Munich, 1910), and Abraham Flexner, *Prostitution in Europe* (New York, 1914). Magdalena M. Moeller subsequently cited these sources in *Ernst Ludwig Kirchner: Die Straßenszenen 1913–1915* (Munich, 1993), pp. 26–27.

17 George Grosz, *An Autobiography*, trans. from the German by Nora Hodges (Berkeley and Los Angeles, 1998), p. 91 (translation altered by the author).

18 Flexner, whose book appeared in January 1914 and is thus exactly contemporary with Kirchner's street scenes, published these regulations in his *Prostitution in Europe* (see n. 16), pp. 415–419.

19 Hessen, *Prostitution in Deutschland* (see n. 16), pp. 116–117.

20 Hans Ostwald, *Kultur- und Sittengeschichte Berlins* (Berlin, 1924), pp. 640–641. See Kirchner's lithograph *Cocottes on Kurfürstendamm*, p. 185 in the present volume.

21 Haxthausen, "A New Beauty" (see n. 5), pp. 80–81.

22 Ibid., p. 95.

23 See especially Moeller, *Die Straßenszenen* (see n. 16); Katharina Sykora, *Weiblichkeit, Großstadt, Moderne: Ernst Ludwig Kirchners Berliner Straßenszenen 1913–1915* (Berlin, 1996); Rita E. Täuber, *Der häßliche Eros: Darstellungen zur Prostitution in der Malerei und Grafik 1855–1930* (Berlin, 1997), pp. 91–99; Sherwin Simmons, "Ernst Kirchner's Streetwalkers: Art, Luxury and Morality in Berlin, 1913–16", *Art Bulletin* 82, (2000), pp. 117–148; Pamela Kort, *Ernst Ludwig Kirchner: Berlin Street Scene* (New York, 2008); and Deborah Wye, *Kirchner and the Berlin Street*, exh. cat. Museum of Modern Art (New York, 2008).

24 Gerd Presler, *Ernst Ludwig Kirchner: Die Skizzenbücher; "Ekstase des ersten Sehens"; Monographie und Werkverzeichnis* (Karlsruhe/Davos, 1996); Hans Delfs (ed.), *Ernst Ludwig Kirchner: Der gesamte Briefwechsel* (Zurich, 2010). The latter includes summaries of letters published elsewhere, most importantly in Wolfgang Henze et al. (eds.), *Ernst Ludwig Kirchner/Gustav Schiefler: Briefwechsel 1910–1935/1938* (Stuttgart/Zurich, 1990); and Hans Delfs, Mario-Andreas von Lüttichau and Roland Scotti (eds.), *Kirchner, Schmidt-Rottluff, Nolde, Nay ... : Briefe an den Sammler und Mäzen Carl Hagemann, 1906–1940* (Ostfildern-Ruit, 2004).

25 Moeller, *Die Straßenszenen* (see n. 16); Wye, *Kirchner and the Berlin Street* (see n. 23).

26 E. L. Kirchner, "Bemerkungen über Leben und Arbeit", *Das Werk* 17, no. 1 (1930), p. 3.

27 Ernst Ludwig Kirchner to Ludwig Justi, letter from 24 July 1919, in Delfs, *Der gesamte Briefwechsel* (see n. 24), no. 767.

28 Gordon 362, 363, 364, 366, 367, 369, 370, 427.

29 Ernst Ludwig Kirchner, *Street with Red Cocotte*, 1914/1925, Oil on canvas, 125 × 90.5 cm, Museo Thyssen-Bornemisza, Madrid (Gordon 366).

30 It appears, however, that the faces in *Street, Berlin* (p. 169) were retouched by Kirchner, probably in 1929, when it was in the collection of Berlin's Nationalgalerie. See his letter to Ludwig Thormaehlen, curator at the Nationalgalerie, 30 October 1929, asking for permission to undertake repairs, in Delfs, *Der gesamte Briefwechsel* (see n. 24). A comparison of the painting in its current state with the reproduction published in Scheffler, "Ernst Ludwig Kirchner" (see n. 9), p. 229, reveals changes in the faces of the three main figures.

31 As late as 1927 *Straße mit roter Kokotte* was titled *Straße in Berlin (Rote Frau)* (Street in Berlin [Red Woman]) in the catalogue (no. 16) of the Kirchner exhibition at the Nassauischer Kunstverein, Wiesbaden, May 1927. Apparently only in the Munich Neue Secession exhibition of 1929 was it first exhibited under its ultimate title.

32 On this, see Simmons, "Ernst Kirchner's Streetwalkers" (see n. 23), pp. 120–125, 130.

33 They are conveniently illustrated in Moeller, *Die Straßenszenen* (see n. 16), illus. 76–99.

34 Gustav Schiefler, *Die Graphik E. L. Kirchners bis 1924*, vol. 1, *Bis 1916* (Berlin-Charlottenburg, 1926), p. 91, no. 222.

35 Ernst Ludwig Kirchner to Ludwig Justi, letter from 27 June 1919, in Delfs, *Der gesamte Briefwechsel* (see n. 24), no. 747. Yet, by 1921 three were evidently in private collections: in the first catalogue of the Nationalgalerie published after its acquisition of Kirchner's *Die Strasse,* the entry makes reference to "counterparts *[Gegenstücke]* with Mr. Westheim in Berlin, and Messrs Hess in Erfurt and Wallerstein in Berlin." *Verzeichnis der Gemälde und Bildwerke in der National-Galerie zu Berlin* (Berlin, 1921), p. 61.

36 "Texte und Dokumente", in *Ernst Ludwig Kirchner: Von Jena nach Davos,* ed. Anna-Maria Ehrmann and Volker Wahl, exh. cat. Stadtmuseum Göhre in Jena (Leipzig, 1993), p. 115.

37 *Ausstellung,* exh. cat. Kunsthaus Zürich (Zurich, 1918), p. 8, no. 140.

38 Scheffler, "Ernst Ludwig Kirchner" (see n. 9), p. 229.

39 *Verzeichnis der National-Galerie* (see n. 35), p. 61.

40 *Arbeiten von E. L. Kirchner,* exh. cat. Kunstsalon Ludwig Schames (Frankfurt am Main, 1916), nos. 18–19.

41 Ernst Ludwig Kirchner, *Leipziger Strasse with Electric Tram,* 1914, Oil on canvas, 71.5 × 87 cm, Museum Folkwang, Essen (Gordon 368).

42 Parts of the following were first presented in my article "Framing Movement: Kirchner in Berlin", in Joseph Masheck (ed.), *Mostly Modern: Essays in Art and Architecture* (Stockbridge, MA, 2014), pp. 104–117.

43 Presler, *Die Skizzenbücher* (see n. 24), p. 415 (Skb. 156).

44 E. L. Kirchner, "Die Arbeit E. L. Kirchners", in Eberhard W. Kornfeld, *Ernst Ludwig Kirchner: Nachzeichnung seines Lebens* (Bern/Fribourg, 1979), p. 341.

45 Lothar Grisebach (ed.), *Ernst Ludwig Kirchners Davoser Tagebuch: Eine Darstellung des Malers und eine Sammlung seiner Schriften,* new edn., rev. Lucius Grisebach (Ostfildern-Ruit, 1997), p. 72.

46 Sykora, *Weiblichkeit, Großstadt, Moderne* (see n. 23), p. 40.

47 Grisebach, *Kirchner: Großstadtbilder* (see n. 11), p. 49, after a 1910 Berlin Baedeker.

48 Hans Ostwald, *Berlin und die Berlinerin: Eine Kultur- und Sittengeschichte* (Berlin, 1911), p. 422.

49 Sykora, *Weiblichkeit, Großstadt, Moderne* (see n. 23), p. 40.

50 For an analysis of similar effects in another major work of 1914, *Circus Rider,* see Haxthausen, "Framing Movement" (see n. 42), pp. 110–112.

51 E. L. Kirchner, "Die Arbeit E. L. Kirchners" (see n. 44), p. 344.

52 See above, n. 43.

53 Ernst Ludwig Kirchner to Eberhard Grisebach, letter from 20 September 1919, in Delfs, *Der gesamte Briefwechsel* (see n. 24), no. 788.

54 Will Grohmann, *E. L. Kirchner,* trans. anonymously from the German (New York, 1961), p. 54 (translation altered by the author).

55 Grisebach, *Kirchners Davoser Tagebuch* (see n. 45), p. 78.

56 Westheim, *Helden und Abenteurer: Welt und Leben der Künstler* (Berlin, 1931), p. 212; the metaphor "symphony of the big city" is probably a conscious reference to the 1927 film *Berlin: Die Sinfonie der Großstadt* by Walther Ruttmann.

57 Ibid.

58 Kirchner to Justi, letter from 27 June 1919 (see n. 35).

59 Grisebach, *Kirchner Großstadtbilder* (see n. 11), p. 16.

60 Ostwald, *Kultur- und Sittengeschichte Berlins* (see n. 20), p. 641.

61 Kirchner, in a notebook entry titled "Meine Strassenbilder"; for the citation in German, see Roman Norbert Ketterer and Wolfgang Henze (eds.), *Ernst Ludwig Kirchner; Zeichnungen und Pastelle* (Stuttgart/Zurich, 1979), p. 250.

62 Entry from 1925, Grisebach, *Kirchners Davoser Tagebuch* (see n. 45), p. 78.

63 Ernst Ludwig Kirchner to Gustav Schiefler, letter from 11 January 1927, in Henze et al., *Kirchner/Schiefler* (see n. 24), p. 371.

64 Wolfgang Henze, "Die Kunst Ernst Ludwig Kirchners in den Krisenjahren 1913–1917", in Ehrmann and Wahl, *Von Jena nach Davos* (see n. 36), p. 52. For the woodcuts, see Gercken nos. 637–639.

65 Alfred Döblin, "Jungfräulichkeit und Prostitution", *Der Sturm* 3 (1912), pp. 141–142.

66 Ibid, p. 142.

67 Henze, "Kirchner in den Krisenjahren" (see n. 64).

68 Döblin, "Jungfräulichkeit und Prostitution" (see n. 65), p. 141.

69 Presler, *Die Skizzenbücher* (see n. 24), p. 97, transcription p. 409. My thanks to Professor Presler for his opinion regarding the dating of the sketchbook page.

70 Kort, *Berlin Street Scene* (see n. 23), p. 30.

71 Kirchner, "Über Leben und Arbeit" (see n. 26), p. 4.

"Happiness in a Quiet Corner": Kirchner on Fehmarn

In the foreground of the painting *Bathers on Fehmarn Island* fig. 1 the fully dressed painter crouches with a visored cap and pipe. Around him stretches the slightly elevated coastline, bordered by greenery and framed by large trees. In front of him lie the ochre beach and blue sea, and nude bathers are gambolling on the beach and in the water. In his picture Ernst Ludwig Kirchner presents himself as a participant and observer in a paradise that can be taken to be either real or imagined.[1] The sketchy brush strokes and the thin, wet application of colour create the impression not so much of firm reality as of a shimmering vision. At the same time, this world is clearly constructed: the coastline appears as a diagonal, the tree trunks and figures form verticals, the horizon describes a curve. The area's expansiveness, the vastness of the sea and sky crowd into a rectangular format that offers both stability and depth.

Whereas Kirchner spent years or decades in the cities of Dresden, Berlin and Davos, he stayed on the Baltic Sea island of Fehmarn for a total of only around six months in the four summers of 1908, 1912, 1913 and 1914. Which makes it all the more astonishing how many works he produced either while on the island or a short time later in his studio: Kirchner captured his impressions of the island in roughly 120 paintings; 550 watercolours, pastels, drawings and sketches; 60 etchings, woodcuts and lithographs as well as a few sculptures and photographs.[2] He pictured the island's landscapes and buildings, painted interiors and still lifes but devoted himself primarily to depictions of nudes in nature, as in *Bathers on Fehmarn Island,* painted during his last summer there. In this composition with a self-portrait Kirchner combined his central artistic themes from that time. What was it that he sought and found on the island, and why did he still feel such nostalgia for it many years later?

In the Kirchner literature Fehmarn is generally treated as the antithesis of the metropolis Berlin, as a place to recover from the stress of life in the big city, the hustle and bustle of the daily routine and the art world, the tense pre-war atmosphere. The island represents Kirchner's retreat into an existence remote from the constraints of civilisation, and the lyrical works inspired by it are seen as expressions of such a world. This is accurate, but it does not go far enough: for one thing, Kirchner frequently subordinated his living necessities to the advancement of his art and, for another, he always knew how to explore the characteristic features of his particular surroundings to give form and content to his work. One suspects that his lasting affection for Fehmarn has to do with his determination to push his art forward. Thus the works he created there are of interest not so much as a cohesive group of works but rather as stations on a journey. They build on the past and prepare the way for something new.

Entry

The summers on Fehmarn came during a fraught, eventful period. Between 1908 and 1914—first in Dresden, then in Berlin—Kirchner, as a member of the Brücke artists' group and in the safety of his studio, revolted against the expectations of his family and society and experimented with a simple, almost primitive lifestyle. As an artist he rejected the "anaemic" traditions of the academy and looked for images filled with real life that would properly reflect a modern world based on movement.[3]

For Kirchner, man and the human figure would always be the main focus of his art, meaning that complete abstraction was not an option. He therefore had to struggle with a fundamental problem in modern objective painting: if one chooses to reject illusionism, or

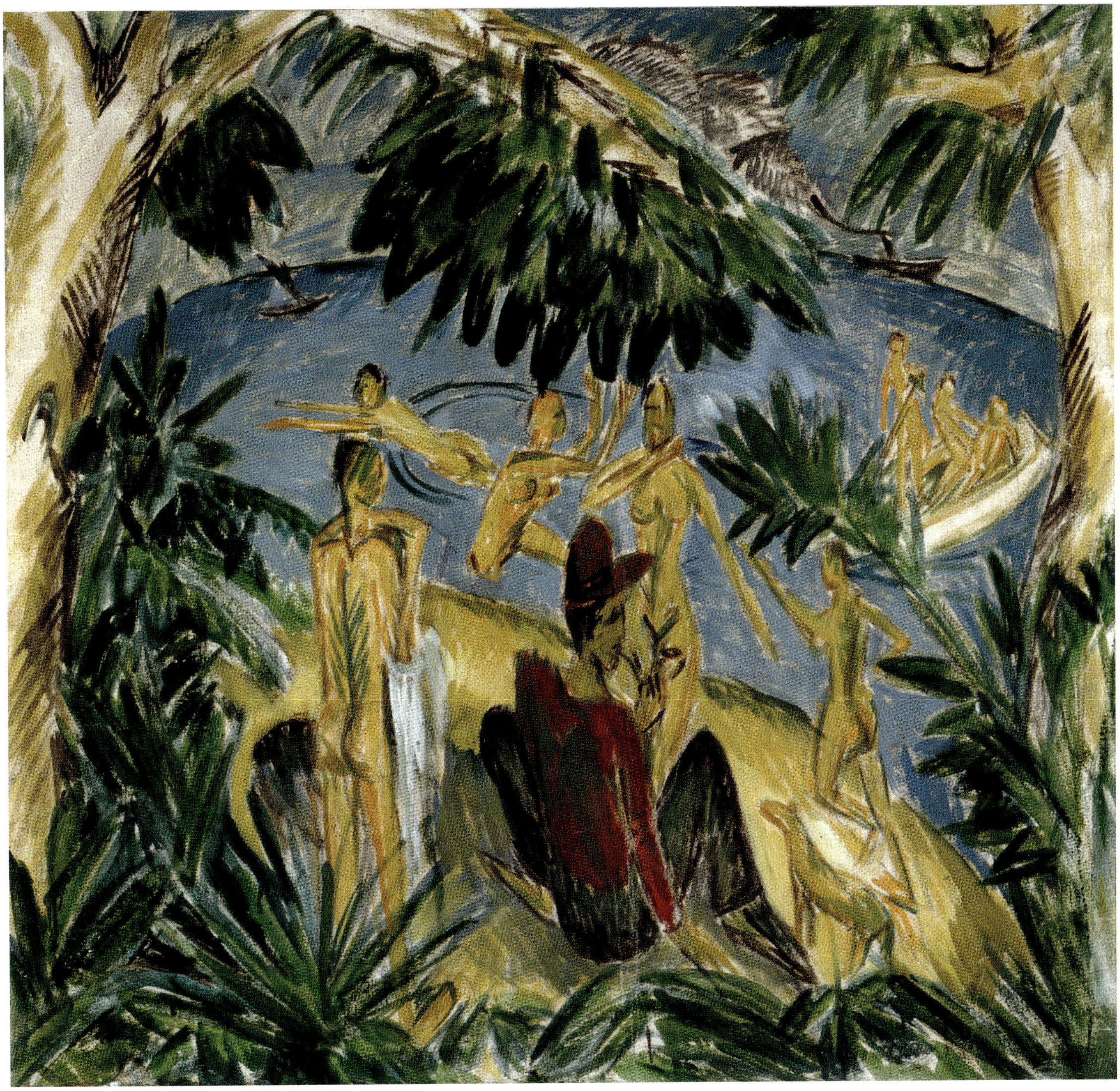

Fig. 1 Ernst Ludwig Kirchner
Bathers on Fehmarn Island,
1913/14
Oil on canvas, 114 × 117 cm
(Gordon 47v)

LWL-Museum für Kunst und Kultur, Münster

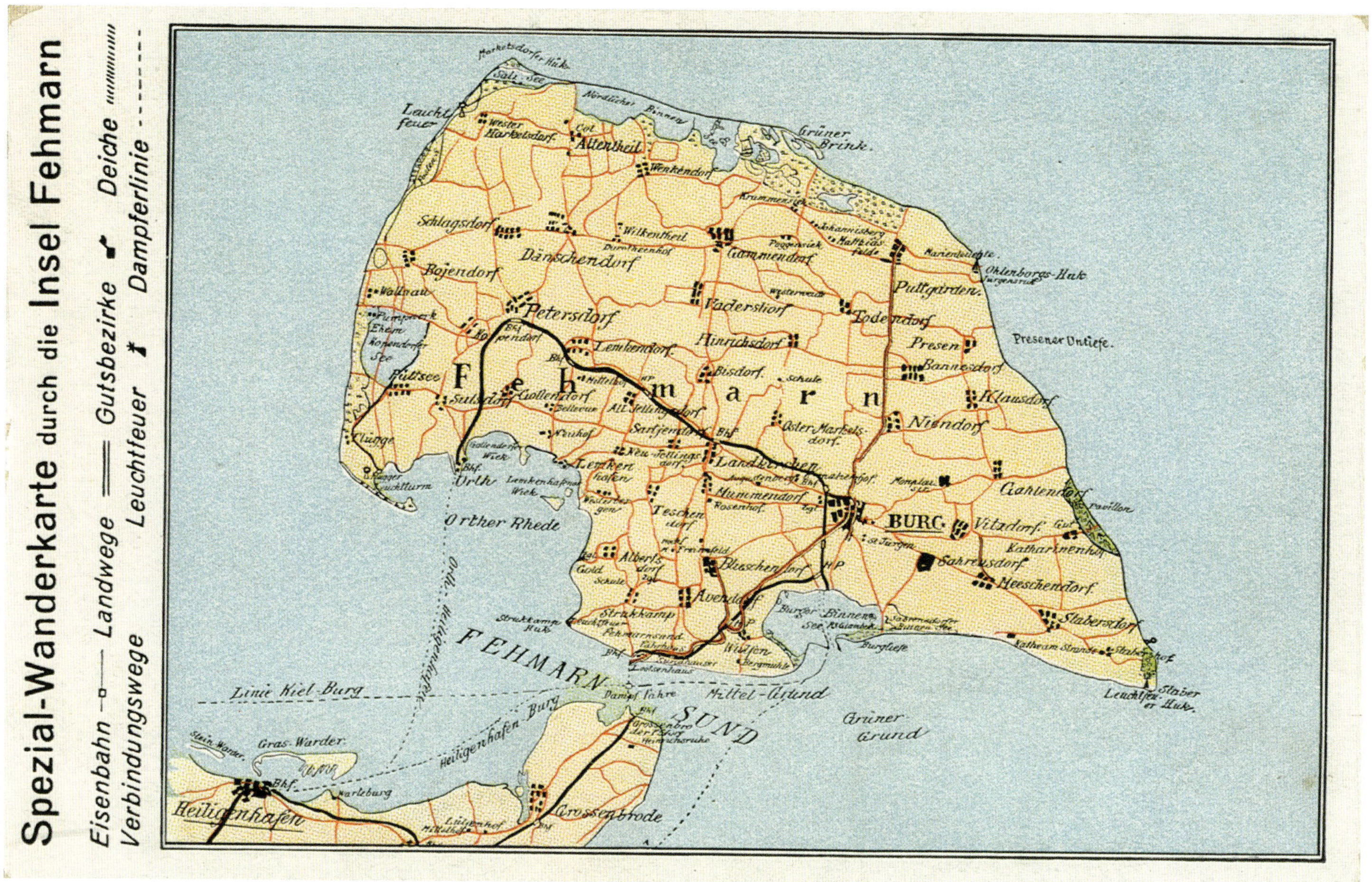

traditional realism, how is one to capture the three-dimensionality of figures and objects on the flat surface of the canvas? In his search for new representational methods, Kirchner, like many of his contemporaries, turned to the art of primitive peoples, whose works he was able to examine in anthropology museums in Dresden and Berlin.[4] If he studied the planar art of Africa, India and Oceania and integrated it into his work, it was because he was hoping for solutions for his own painting, though he was fully aware of the irrevocable disparities between this art and his own time. Looking back on his work in the spring of 1925, he noted the following in his diary: "In them [the primitive art works] he feels a parallel to his own striving, but also that his own form was something wholly different, and necessarily so, from that of these exotics [...] that the only path to a new modern art led through a purely naive study of nature without looking through the prism of a particular style."[5]

The conviction that precise nature observation was the only valid basis for the creation of art runs through all of Kirchner's statements. Yet his gaze was by no means naive: he was not only schooled by instruction in drawing and painting, but also by his four-year study of architecture in Dresden, from which he graduated in July 1905. It included freehand, ornamental, and figure drawing, but needless to say concentrated on surveying, building construction and geodetic drawing as well as analytical and descriptive geometry. Students were supposed to develop a spatial imagination, to appreciate the importance of movement for perspective and learn to transfer spaces and three-dimensional objects onto a flat surface.[6] Although Kirchner rarely discussed this training,[7] he was fully conscious of the knowledge he had gained and saw it as something that distinguished him from other modern artists.[8] It was also a skill set available to him when the Brücke members drifted apart after their move to Berlin and their unified approach to painting in Dresden based on contrasting colour fields gave way to different personal styles. The group announced its dissolution in May 1913, and shortly afterwards Kirchner withdrew to Fehmarn for a few months.

Fig. 2
Special walking map through the island of Fehmarn, c.1910
Postcard, 9.1 × 14 cm,
Julius Simonsen Kunstverlag, Oldenburg in Holstein

Author's archive

Places

In their search for unspoiled nature, the Brücke members had discovered isolated villages on the coasts of the North Sea and especially the Baltic;[9] Kirchner selected Fehmarn. Lying between the Kiel Fjord and the Bay of Mecklenburg, and only readily accessible by train and ferry since 1905, the island was not yet a tourist destination.[10] The "Sunny Island" and "Breadbasket of Schleswig-Holstein" was instead thought of as a productive agricultural area, characterised by fields, animal husbandry, farmhouses and windmills. It is not known just why Kirchner chose to go there in 1908; possibly it was at the suggestion of his companions, the siblings Emy and Hans Frisch, neighbours and friends of his since their early years in Chemnitz.[11] In any case, the three found lodging together in the town of Burg, and Kirchner found his motifs at the harbour, the city and its surroundings. In drawings, prints and a few oil paintings he captured the island's rural atmosphere, its openness to sun and wind. Although his painting *Fehmarn Houses* p. 101 with its pastose application of paint and broad palette represented an important experiment, its horizontal orientation, broad strip of sky and naturalistic colours were still indebted to tradition. By contrast, his *Fehmarn Windmill* p. 162, painted with swift brush strokes and few colours in the summer of 1913, seems revolutionary: in this dynamic composition the mill with its spinning blades is crowded into the picture's top right corner, and the yellow-green landscape with its blue road (or brook) in front of it responds to its spirited movement. Kirchner's new view of the island's buildings was visibly inspired by the cityscapes he produced at this same time: in Dresden in 1909 he had already discovered curving streets as motifs p. 99, and he frequently depicted roads or rivers leading into his Berlin compositions. We see this, for example, in his paintings *Elisabethufer* p. 124 and *Yellow Engelufer, Berlin* p. 135, in which the buildings have to make way for an extensive cityscape, just as the mill does for the surrounding landscape. In symmetrically ordered views like *Street at Schöneberg City Park* p. 125 or *Nollendorfplatz* p. 112 Kirchner pictured broad squares as empty or populated planes in the foreground.

He depicted a farm on Fehmarn, the Staberhof, in a similar manner. In various preliminary drawings he had first focused on the complex of buildings with the manor house, service buildings and barns from different angles before painting three oils.[12] For the largest work, *Staberhof Country Seat, Fehmarn I* p. 163, he selected the view between the service buildings, across the broad square onto the front of the barn with its baroque gable. With his rendering of a blue sky, windblown trees and birds flying up from a dovecote he captured a rural scene, yet at the same time he emphasised the imposing nature of the structure. He pictured it in stately symmetry and frontality from an elevated position and adorned the large open space with an elegantly dressed pair of flâneurs. Even in its nervous, feathery brush strokes and a palette dominated by yellow-green, the depiction of the estate matches metropolitan counterparts like *Nollendorfplatz* and like them it evokes the tense, foreboding atmosphere before the outbreak of the First World War.

From 1912 on Kirchner's more mature gaze was rarely directed inland at buildings, fields and dikes, let alone the everyday lives of the local people, but almost exclusively at the coast and the sea. It was probably at the side of the young Peter Wiepert, a local historian, that the painter had explored the island on his first visit[13] and discovered its extreme south-eastern tip fig. 2: from the Staberhof a long avenue of white poplars led past the Staberholz wood to the coast and to Staberhuk, with its tall lighthouse guiding ship traffic into Fehmarn Sound. And it is possible that, to Kirchner, Wiepert praised Staberhuk in the same terms he used decades later in a guide to the island: "Tall shoreline, heavy surf, lovely view of the Baltic as far as the Mecklenburg coast. Near the shore and far into the sea large stately boulders up to four metres long. When a storm rises, the sea rages here. Then one stands on the deserted beach and marvels at nature's glorious spectacle."[14] In any case, Kirchner chose this remote spot on the island as a place to live and work for three successive summers, with his life partner Erna Schilling renting rooms in the house of the lighthouse keeper, Lüthmann, and his family of ten and from time to time enjoying visits from artist friends.[15] So there was no shortage of models for his art.

The tower, placed in service in 1904, was the newest of the island's five lighthouses, and was an impressive sight: sturdily constructed of yellow bricks, it supported a red cast-iron lantern enclosed by a network of lozenges, with its apex at a height of over twenty metres. In numerous sketches and drawings Kirchner pictured the tower from all sides, and in two portrait-format paintings he placed it in the centre and had its yellow shaft loom up into the sky p. 121. In his perspective he again treated it like towers in the city, picturing the structure with its surroundings from an elevated position,[16] yet the unusual topography, the site right next to the sea, presented a challenge. In contrast with an urban setting, there was now a limitless view into the distance to deal with, the depiction of which had to be accomplished in new ways: he had the tower with its red lantern dramatically break through the double arch of two parallel curves. With their sharp curvature the lines of the coast and horizon form a dark globe that causes the site with its glowing shades of yellow and red to be strangely transfigured. With the Staberhuk as the tip of a pointed triangle of land at his back, he faced a stunning panoramic view of the open sea and an expansive sky. According to Nikolaus Lüthmann, a son of the lighthouse keeper, Kirchner would repeatedly stand on the beach with outstretched arms and cry: "Oh Staberhuk, how glorious you are, happiness in a quiet corner, a place of peaceful beauty!"[17] It was the first time he had experienced such a sense of space. His views in Dresden and Berlin were blocked by rows of large buildings; the Moritzburg Ponds with their reedy banks and small stands of trees lay in a landscape of gently rolling hills; and years later, in the Landwasser Valley around Davos, mountains rose steeply on either side. His experience of Fehmarn would remain unique.

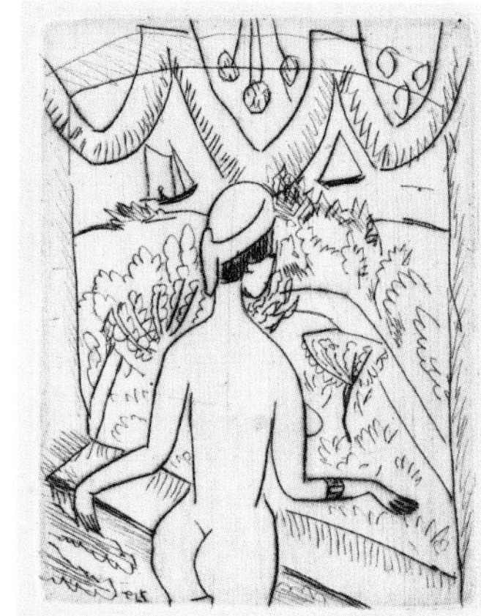

Fig. 3 Ernst Ludwig Kirchner
Nude Woman at the Window, Fehmarn, 1913
Dry point on copper, on copperplate printing paper, image: 15.9 × 11.8 cm
(Gercken 612)

Private collection, Hamburg

Spaces

Between Staberhuk and Katharinenhof to the north Kirchner found the island's most varied strip of coastline. He followed it on countless walks and photographed it from the coast p. 153. While the beach in the south of Fehmarn was flat and invited swimming, the east coast with its clay cliffs was steep and its beach rocky, dotted with large boulders and lined with trees, shrubs and grey hair-grass. In 1908 Kirchner had drawn the horizon line as an uninterrupted horizontal in the lithograph *The Sea at Staberhuk,*[18] but he now experimented with more exciting compositions. In endless new variants he sketched, drew and painted the coast as an elongated semicircle, bending northward to the left and away from the lighthouse p. 152 or southward to the right towards the tower p. 150. Whereas in the summer of 1912 he still conceived of the coast as a southern idyll, a "Mexico Bay" p. 122, and revelled in a rich repertoire of shapes of stones, plants, waves and clouds in intense shades ranging from green or blue to violet and pink, in the following year his compositions became increasingly spare: with a narrow spectrum of muted colours he presented the wide Fehmarn coast in landscape format, with a large boulder in the foreground and the lighthouse towering in the distance p. 150; in portrait format he pictured the ochre-coloured coast in strong curves edged by green and washed by blue water and yellow waves p. 152.

He could also see the coast from his gable room at the lighthouse keeper's house. In the etching *Nude Woman at the Window, Fehmarn* he pictured Erna Schilling, leaning on a windowsill and gazing into the distance past trees, roads, the beach and boats fig. 3. The motif of the nude in an interior appears to have interested Kirchner far less on Fehmarn than it had in Dresden or Berlin, so a self-portrait with Erna — in a sea-blue room — is one of the rare interiors painted on the island p. 151. He preferred placing figures in the landscape, at the same time blurring the boundaries between interior and exterior space. In one portrait he pictured Erna on the beach with one of the Japanese umbrellas that were part of the decor of the Berlin studio pp. 44, 148. On another occasion he posed her next to the sea in a long dress and red hat as though she were lounging on a sofa p. 146. Erna appears in the same costume in the painting *Lady with Red Hat on the Shore* fig. 4: filling the entire height of the tall format, she sits erect with her legs crossed on a rounded, pinkish rock as

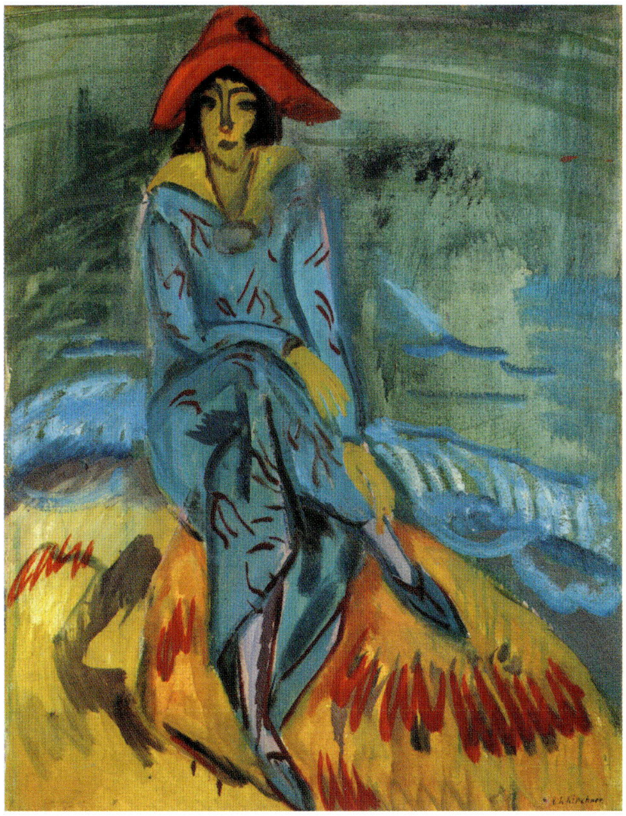

Fig.4 Ernst Ludwig Kirchner
Lady with Red Hat on the Shore, 1912
Oil on canvas, 100 × 75 cm
(Gordon 247)

Private collection

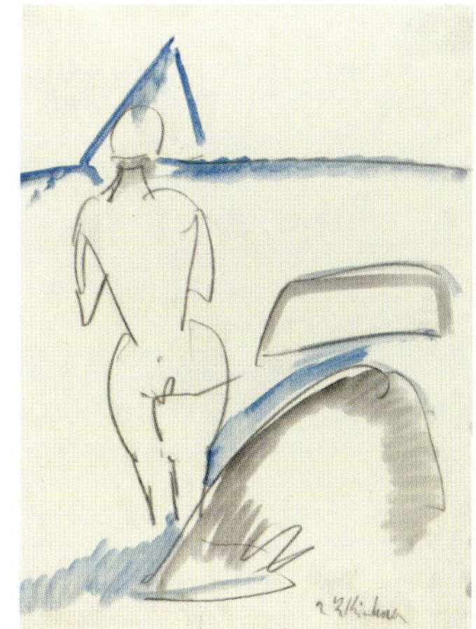

Fig.5 Ernst Ludwig Kirchner
Bather on the Beach, 1912/13
Black crayon with blue and grey wash on paper, 43.4 × 31.8 cm

National Gallery of Art, Washington, Gift of Mr and Mrs Jacob Kainen in honour of Charles Parkhurst

though seated inside on a chair. Her position in the picture echoes that of the lighthouse with its red lamp—a firm vertical against a curving coastline and an undefined seascape.

Erna, whose "angular, architectural body"[19] inspired Kirchner, also frequently appears as a nude in nature. Working from his own photograph, Kirchner depicted her with a group of boulders, straightening her seated figure, bringing it closer and reducing the coastal landscape to her human scale pp. 114, 119. *Seated Girl on the Beach,*[20] Kirchner's only female nude from 1908, shows Emy Frisch's cowering figure. At this point the subject is still seen up close and tightly framed but from 1912 on he gave the human figure increasing space, again and again exploring the relationship between the body and its surroundings: a seated bather bends into a diagonal p. 116, a woman in a hammock spreads out horizontally p. 147, a dancer on the beach stretches in every direction, with extended arms and one leg crossed far over the other p. 147. Even in his swift sketches Kirchner combined his immediate impression of scenes in nature with an analytical, organising gaze. In the reduced, almost constructivist watercolour *Bather on the Beach* fig. 5 he incorporated a female figure as a vertical in a portrait-format composition, let her head interrupt the blue horizon line, crowned it with a triangle—derived perhaps from a sail—and added to the figure rounded and angular stone blocks. With the same consistency, though with less focus on geometry, in the colour lithograph *Man Entering the Sea (Hans Gewecke)* p. 164 he placed a male nude extending from earth to sky and surrounded him with a semicircle of coastline. At the Moritzburg Ponds near Dresden, Kirchner and his Brücke colleagues had studied nudes in the landscape intensively, painting numerous scenes of bathers p. 100, and on Fehmarn he wished to get back to this. The conditions were ideal; unlike in Moritzburg, at Staberhuk it was possible swim naked undisturbed and experience "the ultimate unity of man and nature".[21] Moreover, the figures appeared to be absorbed in the expanse of land, water and sky, as Kirchner also captured in a photograph.[22] Whereas the bathers in his Dresden pictures ultimately remained models turned toward, and relating to, the painter and observer, on Fehmarn Kirchner conceived of them as elements in a complex context of content and form.

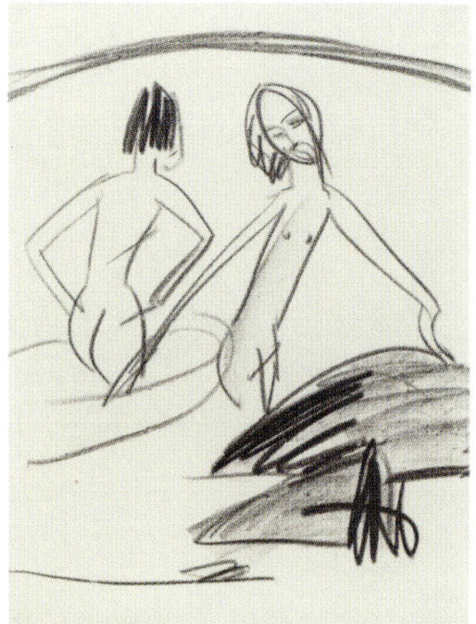

Fig. 6 Ernst Ludwig Kirchner
Two Bathers on the Fehmarn Shore, 1913
Charcoal on paper, 58 × 43 cm

Brücke-Museum, Berlin

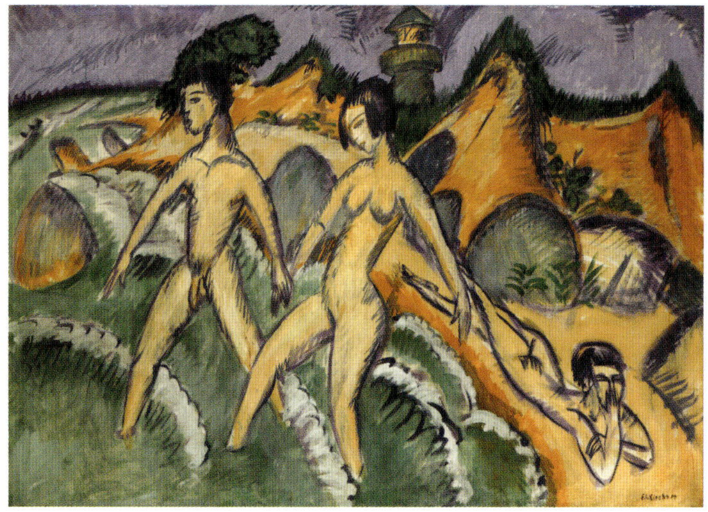

Fig. 7 Ernst Ludwig Kirchner
Striding into the Sea, 1912
Oil on canvas, 146 × 200 cm
(Gordon 262)

Staatsgalerie Stuttgart

Bodies

Constructing the pictorial space with just a single figure offered only limited possibilities. It was easier to explore and fill it with two, three or more figures. A fine example is the swiftly executed charcoal drawing reduced to mere outlines *Two Bathers on the Fehmarn Shore* fig. 6 : the figure in front is striding with outstretched arms toward a rock on the right, while the one at the back, her hands on her hips, is walking out into the open sea; a line at the bottom edge marks the solid shoreline and a curving line, the horizon circling the scene. Again and again Kirchner formulated such combinations of pairs and groups: two figures standing next to a tree p. 118 , leaning against boulders p. 200 , seeking shelter on the steep coast p. 159 or stepping into the sea p. 196 . In some depictions the figures tend to form a circle, as in the woodblock print *Women Bathing between White Rocks, Fehmarn* p. 117 , in others their movements are opposed. For example, the hand-holding couple taking great strides to the left in the painting *Striding into the Sea* fig. 7 is balanced by a recumbent figure stretched out in the other direction.

In quick sketches of multiple figures in only slightly altered poses, Kirchner produced almost filmic sequences p. 201 that give the impression that one is watching a single figure walking, twisting or bending over. He let the knowledge he had gained in nature flow into his paintings: in the picture *Four Bathers* p. 100 , from 1909, he had still placed single figures in various poses, but he now linked them into chains of movement fig. 8 .

During his extended stay on the island in 1913 Kirchner caused the figures to be absorbed more and more into the landscape or occupy different positions as a group. The elongated, light-coloured figures join in the waves p. 160 , press against slender tree trunks p. 158 or climb tall rock formations together fig. 9 . In some depictions, like *Five Bathers on a Rock,* women, men and children form a peaceful company; in the picture *Red Tree on the Shore* p. 149 five bathers in a small bay form a circle completed by dark stones. Three women with Japanese umbrellas appear to have created a natural room from the coastal clay formation p. 50: fig. 6 . Kirchner also repeatedly pictured the simple hut he had built that same summer p. 156 . In September 1913 he described it to his Berlin pupil Hans Gewecke not only as a dwelling, but as a piece of architecture responding to the forms of man and nature: "And just think, we have also built a hut on the beach with a feudal entrance. You would naturally say Gothic. It is delightful to sit in it. I built it in such a way that one can see the sea past a pink rock. Now when bathers come up the beach with their long verticals

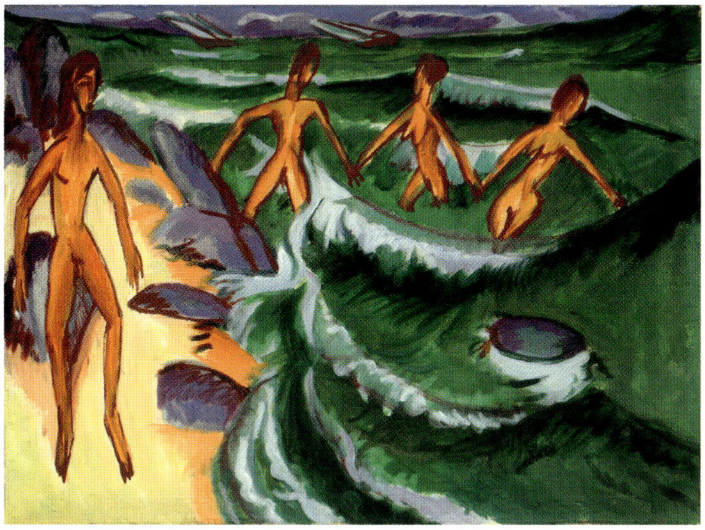

Fig. 8 Ernst Ludwig Kirchner
Bathers on the Shore, 1913
Oil on canvas, 76 × 100 cm
(Gordon 350)

Staatliche Museen zu Berlin, Nationalgalerie

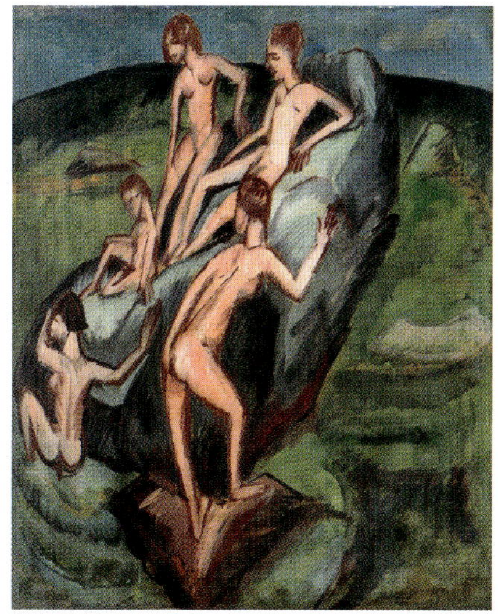

Fig. 9 Ernst Ludwig Kirchner
Five Bathers on a Rock, 1913
Oil on canvas, 111.5 × 88.5 cm
(Gordon 360v)

Wilhelm-Hack-Museum, Ludwigshafen

and appear in the pointed arch of the entrance and behind them the two black wedges of the rocks next to our swimming spot. How splendidly you would stand out among them."[23]

Kirchner again and again incorporated in his compositions sculptures he had created on Fehmarn, among them large nudes carved in wood like *Figure Looking Back* p. 154. When he included these ample, multi-perspectival figures in his pictures, he often made no distinction between real human beings and the re-created ones, as in a drawing from 1912 p. 115: two women appear to be talking to a gesticulating child that only on second glance proves to be a sculpture. The juxtaposition of actual and sculpted bodies in interiors had already interested Kirchner in his Dresden years, and he continued to produce such compositions up into his Davos period. In composed still lifes he would often replace people entirely with sculptures he had made himself, creating—on tabletops or in corners—controlled little worlds, protected places.[24] If one compares the paintings *Still Life with Sculptures and Flowers* fig. 10 and *Five Bathers on a Rock* fig. 9, the parallels are astonishing: male and female figures appear in an oval, earthly realm and gaze into an indefinite distance—surrounded by the elements and colours of nature.

Dimensions

The discoveries he had made on Fehmarn left their effects in Kirchner's work: for one thing, he increasingly consolidated compositional principles that he had tested before nature; for another, he combined different subjects into symbolic pictures. The painting *Three Bathers* p. 160 is the final stage in the development of a motif that began with a postcard to his artist friend Erich Heckel and a drawing in his sketchbook: both picture a couple in waves.[25] In the following year Kirchner reworked the motif in a number of prints, including *Three Bathers in the Surf* p. 165.[26] In all of these versions Kirchner now stacked several figures in the depth of the pictorial space. In a charcoal drawing he first added a seagull and a rock to the rhythmically intertwined bodies and waves p. 161, before further exploring this motif in the large-format painting and a lithograph.[27] In the drawing he had left the sex of the figure at the back indeterminate, but in the painting he definitely decided on three women: they appear to be rising out of the greenish-blue water in a uniform movement like creatures born from the sunlit sea foam, surrounded by a shell-like circle of

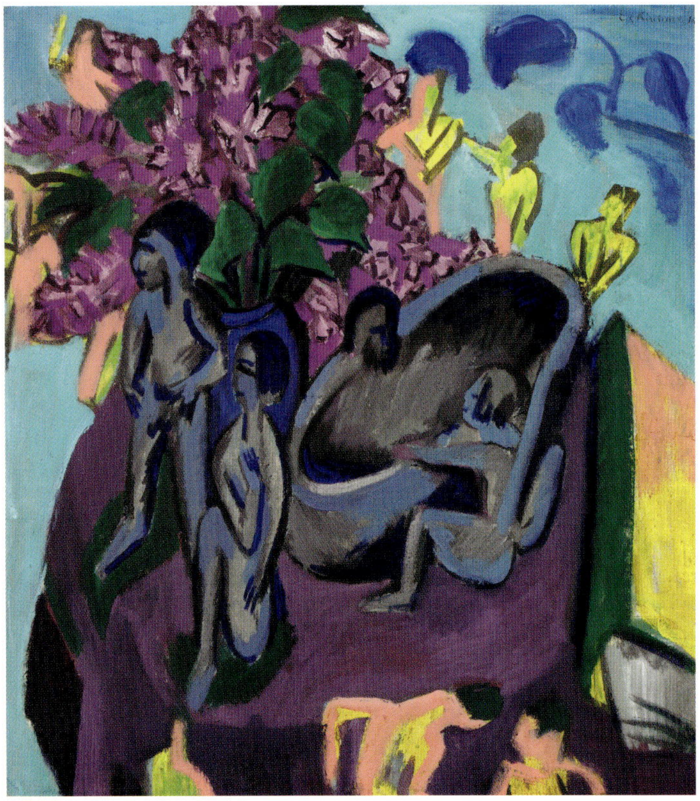

Fig. 10 Ernst Ludwig Kirchner
Still Life with Sculptures and Flowers, 1912
Oil on canvas, 90 × 80.5 cm
(Gordon 230)

Groninger Museum

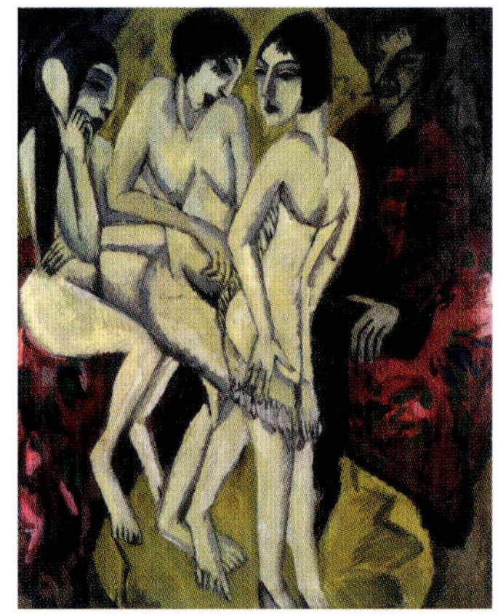

Fig. 11 Ernst Ludwig Kirchner
The Judgement of Paris, 1913
Oil on canvas, 111.5 × 88.5 cm
(Gordon 360)

Wilhelm-Hack-Museum, Ludwigshafen

spray. The light-coloured bird above them and the flower-like pink object behind them—a rock overgrown with algae?—seem like attributes of their natural beauty.

In that same year Kirchner produced a related composition: in the mythological painting *The Judgement of Paris* fig. 11 Aphrodite, Athene and Hera appear before the youth in the background—not as nudes, but in modern dress. Much like the bathers, the three goddesses are moving uniformly towards the bottom right, but now in an interior. When one turns *The Judgement of Paris* to its reverse side, *Five Bathers on a Rock* fig. 9, one's gaze follows the figural grouping back up and out into a coastal landscape with a curving horizon.

In his famous street scenes Kirchner continued to use the compositional principle of rhythmic alignment that he had explored with nudes in nature on Fehmarn: for example, in the painting *Women on the Street* from 1915 p. 213, and even more clearly in the 1914 painting *Friedrichstrasse, Berlin* p. 191 —on the backs of both canvases are single Fehmarn nudes filling the picture space.[28] In his compositions Kirchner paralleled the breadth of the sea and the expansiveness of the city, and aligned the element of movement both in the bodies caressed by wind and waves and in the figures surrounded by street traffic and crowds.

Kirchner's nocturnal scene *Fehmarn Moonrise* fig. 12 is a celebration above all of the landscape, rendered in intense green and muted violet. Surrounded by high grass, the man and woman in the foreground are difficult to make out. Behind them the horizon appears as an arc, and above them a bright moon glows between dramatic clouds. Nature appears equally portentous in the picture *Curving Bay (Laburnum Tree),* painted after 1914 p. 201. Below the weeping tree with its glowing yellow blossoms, three figures are dancing in front of three resting sailing boats. The blue-green sea behind them curves as though with the globe, and above it a flame-red sun floats between scalloped cloud formations. In retrospect Kirchner combined any number of impressions from Fehmarn—even the golden rain tree he had already pictured in a painting in 1912/13 p. 120 —yet this nature appears to be removed from reality. In its ornamental rhythm the composition is more reminiscent of the embroideries Erna Schilling created for the Berlin studio pp. 61–63 and in its mystical qualities, more like the five wall paintings created for the Kohnstamm Sanatorium in Königstein in 1916.[29] From there Kirchner, now physically and mentally ill, yearned for the island that

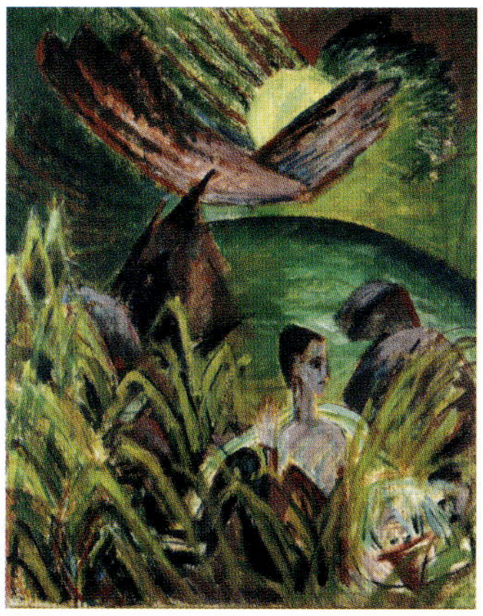

Fig. 12 Ernst Ludwig Kirchner
Fehmarn Moonrise, 1914
Oil on canvas, 150 × 120 cm
(Gordon 403)

Museum Kunstpalast, Düsseldorf, on permanent loan from the Friends of the Museum Kunstpalast e.V.

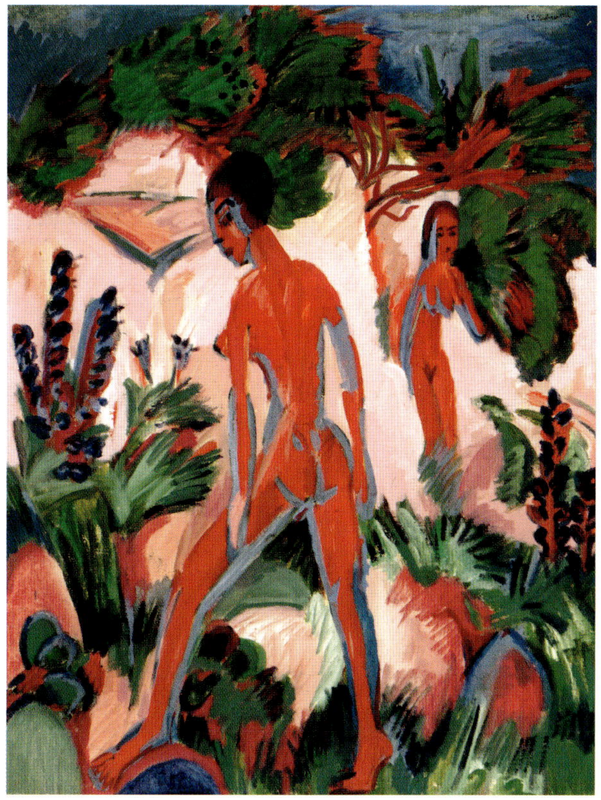

Fig. 13 Ernst Ludwig Kirchner
Red Nudes, 1913/1925
Oil on canvas, 120 × 90 cm
(Gordon 347)

Private collection

he had had to leave so abruptly in the summer of 1914 when it was declared a military zone, and he raved about the "sun, air and sea on Fehmarn".[30] Nudes in nature must have taken on for him a heightened importance in wartime as symbols of an ideal world at peace.

Exit

From 1918 on Kirchner transferred his nature visions onto his new surroundings, the Davos landscape and the Landwasser Valley. The spray-topped breakers became snow-covered peaks p. 242, and instead of a lighthouse it was now the Tinzenhorn mountain that towered into the sky. Instead of coming together on the beach, figures now appeared on the Stafelalp beneath a radiant full moon p. 241. In the high Alps with their long, hard winters there was little opportunity for depicting nudes in the landscape, yet in the mid 1920s Kirchner once again took up the theme and painted nude women in the forest or bathers in a mountain stream. In 1925 he also reworked the painting *Red Nudes* fig. 13 — created on Fehmarn in 1913 — in his new Davos style and contributed it to the volume *Das Werk Ernst Ludwig Kirchners* (The Work of Ernst Ludwig Kirchner), compiled by Will Grohmann, as one of only four colour plates.[31] The book was meant to acquaint the art public with the quality and range of his work and to have a special impact in Germany, for Kirchner was hoping to be given a professorship at an art academy there. In preparation for such a role, he worked up ideas in his diary, in particular sketching out "The Reform of Nude Drawing Instruction" and "Landscape Theory". At the outset he described the "Structural System of the Picture", using the terms "sky curve, earth horizontal, object verticals"[32] — he was doubtless drawing on his experiences from Fehmarn.

In the same text he clarified his ideas about the "knowing creation [...] that alone deserves to be called art", and argued for the free, intuitive application of learned rules by the mature artist: "Knowing is knowing one's means. Knowing how colour works. Experience in composition, knowing the rules of distribution, of harmony, of perspective, anatomy, the psychological effect of a specific form, etc./Feeling is the imagination, the invention of forms, of objectivity, the use of known rules to a specific end, everything, all that is left, that remains in the work of art that cannot be logically explained when we study it critically, and that yet amounts to the mysterious 'life' no work of art can do without."[33]

Back in December 1924 Kirchner had written from a chilly Davos to his fatherly friend Gustav Schiefler in Hamburg: "It is so frightfully lonely here [...] that I am planning to once more head out to Fehmarn for a summer by the sea. I would like to take along a few young people, then for a few months we could paint straight from life. Who knows how long one will live and be able to work, and I have still some things to do up there. Also, I'd like to see the old spots where we lived so happily and simply. [...] I look forward to seeing and painting real trees with leaves and branches again and the bay and the lovely old churches and windmills. If anything comes of it of course."[34]

Nothing came of Kirchner's plans — he was unable either to pass along his knowledge as a teacher or to ever return to the island. But Fehmarn lived on in his memory: as a realm of happiness and as a place that could teach an artist how to see and feel.

1 Kirchner pictured himself in his "Fehmarn Dress", which he also described on a drawing he did of himself. See *Ernst Ludwig Kirchner auf Fehmarn,* ed. Hermann Gerlinger and Heinz Spielmann, exh. cat. Schleswig-Holsteinisches Landesmuseum, Schloss Gottorf, Schleswig (Schleswig, 1997), p. 33, illus. 19.

2 For a complete introduction, see Gerlinger/Spielmann, *Kirchner auf Fehmarn* (see n. 1).

3 See the essay by Charles W. Haxthausen in the present volume, pp. 20–31.

4 For a full discussion of this, see Hanna Strzoda, *Die Ateliers Ernst Ludwig Kirchners: Eine Studie zur Rezeption "primitiver" europäischer und aussereuropäischer Kulturen* (Ph.D. diss., 2004; Petersberg, 2006).

5 Lothar Grisebach, *Ernst Ludwig Kirchners Davoser Tagebuch: Eine Darstellung des Malers und eine Sammlung seiner Schriften,* new edn., rev. Lucius Grisebach (Ostfildern-Ruit, 1997), p. 76: March/April 1925.

6 See *Ernst Ludwig Kirchner als Architekt,* ed. Ralf Beil and Katharina Siegmann, exh. cat. Mathildenhöhe Darmstadt (Munich, 2011); especially "Stunden- und Semesterplan 1901–1905", pp. 130–133.

7 For a listing of the autobiographical texts, see Karin Schick, "Color in Black and White: Kirchner's Compositions", in *"No One Else Has These Colors": Kirchner's Painting,* ed. Karin Schick and Heide Skowranek, exh. cat. Kirchner Museum Davos (Ostfildern-Ruit, 2012), p. 74.

8 See, for example, Ernst Ludwig Kirchner to Will Grohmann, letter from circa 2 June 1926, in Hans Delfs (ed.), *Ernst Ludwig Kirchner: Der gesamte Briefwechsel,* vol. 2, *Briefe von 1924 bis 1929* (Zurich, 2010), pp. 1056–1057: "[Gino] Severini has written a book about the application of mathematics in art but, alas, in it he exhibits the knowledge of a high-school pupil, nothing more. A person like me who studied descriptive geometry at college has to laugh at the ceremony and fervour with which the simplest things are expounded."

9 See, for example, *Erich Heckel an der Ostsee,* ed. Magdalena M. Moeller, exh. cat. Brücke-Museum, Berlin (Munich, 2006); also *Karl Schmidt-Rottluff: Ostseebilder,* ed. Magdalena M. Moeller, exh. cat. Museum Behnhaus Drägerhaus, Kunsthalle St. Annen, Lübeck, and Brücke-Museum, Berlin (Berlin/Munich, 2010).

10 In Karl Baedeker's *Handbuch für Reisende: Nordost-Deutschland (von der Elbe und der Westgrenze Sachsens an) nebst Dänemark* from the years 1908 and 1911, Fehmarn is mentioned in only half a sentence.

11 It was not until 1910 that Kirchner met his later Brücke colleague Otto Mueller, who also stayed on Fehmarn in 1908.

12 Donald E. Gordon, *Ernst Ludwig Kirchner* (Cambridge, MA, 1968), nos. 322, 323, 324; no. 925 verso was left unfinished.

13 See Karlheinz Gabler, *E. L. Kirchner: Dokumente; Fotos Schriften Briefe,* ed. Museum der Stadt Aschaffenburg (Aschaffenburg, 1980), p. 106 (there with the year 1910); also Hermann Gerlinger, "Die Fehmarn-Aufenthalte Ernst Ludwig Kirchners", in Gerlinger/Spielmann, *Kirchner auf Fehmarn* (see n. 1), p. 14 (with the year corrected to 1908).

14 Peter Wiepert, *Führer durch die Stadt Burg und die Dörfer der Insel Fehmarn: Ein heimatkundlicher Beitrag* (Berlin, 1941), p. 123; by this time Wiepert was an ardent National Socialist, and the book was published by the Verlag Ahnenerbe-Stiftung.

15 These included Erich Heckel and Sidi Riha as well as Otto and Maschka Mueller.

16 See, for example, the picture *The Red Tower in Halle,* 1915, oil on canvas, 120 × 90.5 cm, Museum Folkwang, Essen; Gordon, *Kirchner* (see n. 12), no. 436.

17 See Dietrich Reinhardt, "Zeitgenössische Zeugnisse von Kirchners Fehmarn-Aufenthalten", in Gerlinger/Spielmann, *Kirchner auf Fehmarn* (see n. 1), p. 39.

18 Günther Gercken, *Ernst Ludwig Kirchner: Kritisches Werkverzeichnis der Druckgraphik,* vol. 1 (1904–1908) (Bern, 2013), no. 254.

19 Ernst Ludwig Kirchner, "Die Arbeit E L Kirchners", in Eberhard W. Kornfeld, *Ernst Ludwig Kirchner: Nachzeichnung seines Lebens* (Bern, 1979), p. 336.

20 Gercken, *Druckgraphik* (see n. 18), no. 249.

21 Kirchner, *Arbeit* (see n. 19), p. 337.

22 Roland Scotti (ed.), *Ernst Ludwig Kirchner: The Photographic Work* (Göttingen, 2006), cat. 22.

23 Ernst Ludwig Kirchner to Hans Gewecke, letter from 24 September 1913, in Hans Delfs (ed.), *Ernst Ludwig Kirchner: Der gesamte Briefwechsel,* vol. 1, *Briefe von 1901 bis 1923* (Zurich, 2010), p. 84.

24 See Karin Schick, "Ruhelose Ordnung: Ernst Ludwig Kirchner und das Stillleben", in *Ernst Ludwig Kirchner: Die Stillleben,* ed. Karin Schick, exh. cat. Kirchner Museum Davos (Davos, 2006), pp. 7–79.

25 *Ernst Ludwig Kirchner: Postkarten und Briefe an Erich Heckel,* ed. Annemarie Dube-Heynig, exh. cat. Altonaer Museum (Hamburg/Cologne, 1984), illus. p. 205; also Gerd Presler, *Ernst Ludwig Kirchner: Die Skizzenbücher; "Ekstase des ersten Sehens"; Monographie und Werkverzeichnis* (Karlsruhe/Davos, 1996), p. 220, Skb. 26 with illus.

26 Also Günther Gercken, *Ernst Ludwig Kirchner: Kritisches Werkverzeichnis der Druckgraphik,* vol. 3 (1912–1916) (Bern, 2015), nos. 618, 624.

27 Ibid., no. 623.

28 Gordon, *Kirchner* (see n. 12), nos. 427v, 367v.

29 Ibid., no. 1027.

30 Ernst Ludwig Kirchner to Carl Hagemann, letter from 20 May 1916, in Hans Delfs, Mario-Andreas von Lüttichau and Roland Scotti (eds.), *Kirchner, Schmidt-Rottluff, Nolde, Nay ...: Briefe an den Sammler und Mäzen Carl Hagemann, 1906–1940* (Ostfildern-Ruit, 2004), p. 56.

31 Will Grohmann, *Das Werk Ernst Ludwig Kirchners* (Munich, 1926); see Schick, "Color in Black and White" (see n. 7).

32 Grisebach, *Tagebuch* (see n. 5), p. 155.

33 Ibid., p. 166.

34 Ernst Ludwig Kirchner to Gustav Schiefler, letter from 10 December 1924, in Wolfgang Henze et al. (eds.), *Ernst Ludwig Kirchner/Gustav Schiefler: Briefwechsel 1910–1935/1938* (Stuttgart/Zurich 1990), p. 316.

Cat. 137
Erna Schilling and Ernst Ludwig Kirchner in the live-in studio in Berlin-Wilmersdorf, c.1913
Glass negative

Kirchner Museum Davos,
Gift of the Ernst Ludwig
Kirchner Estate 1992

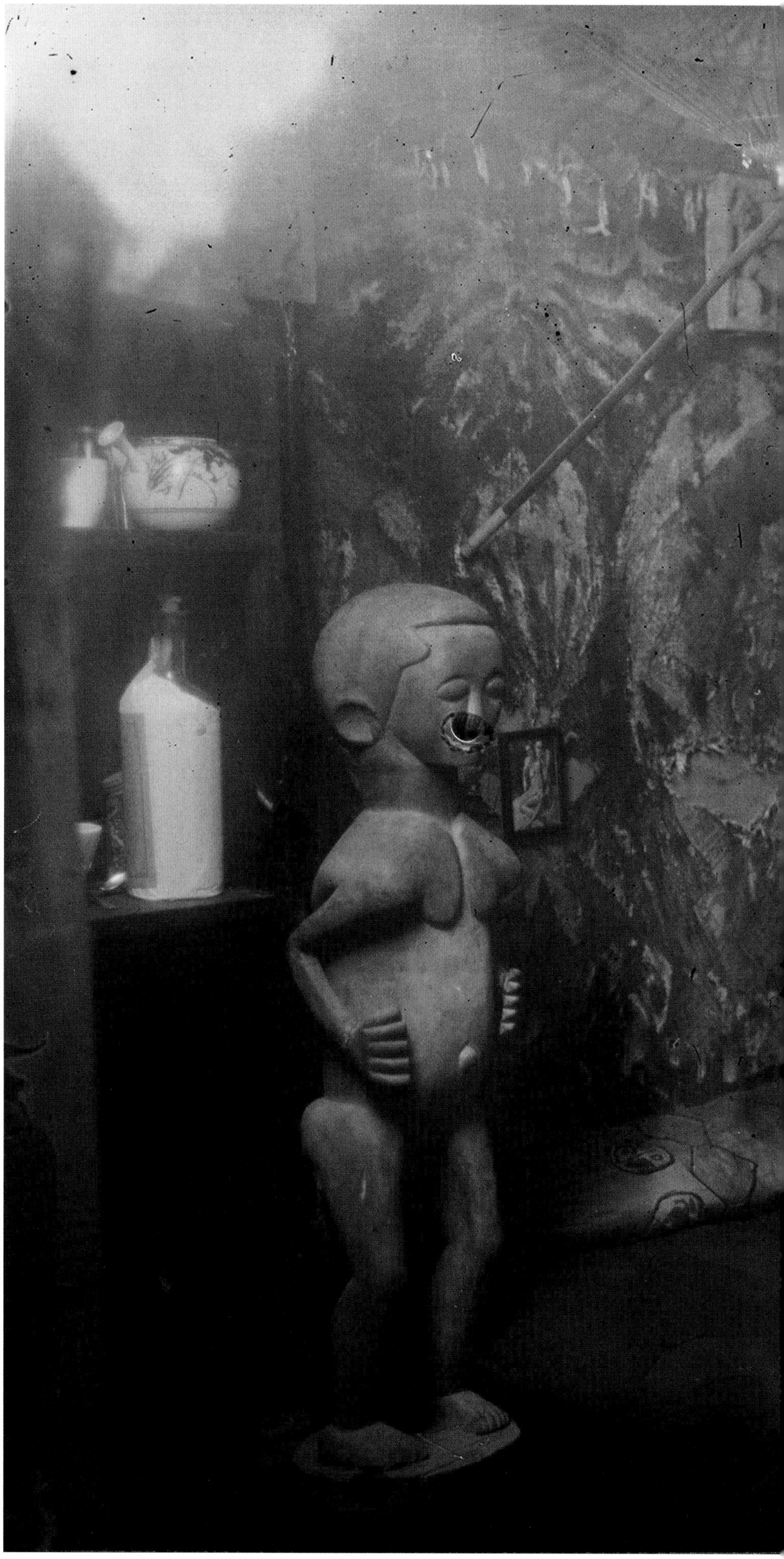

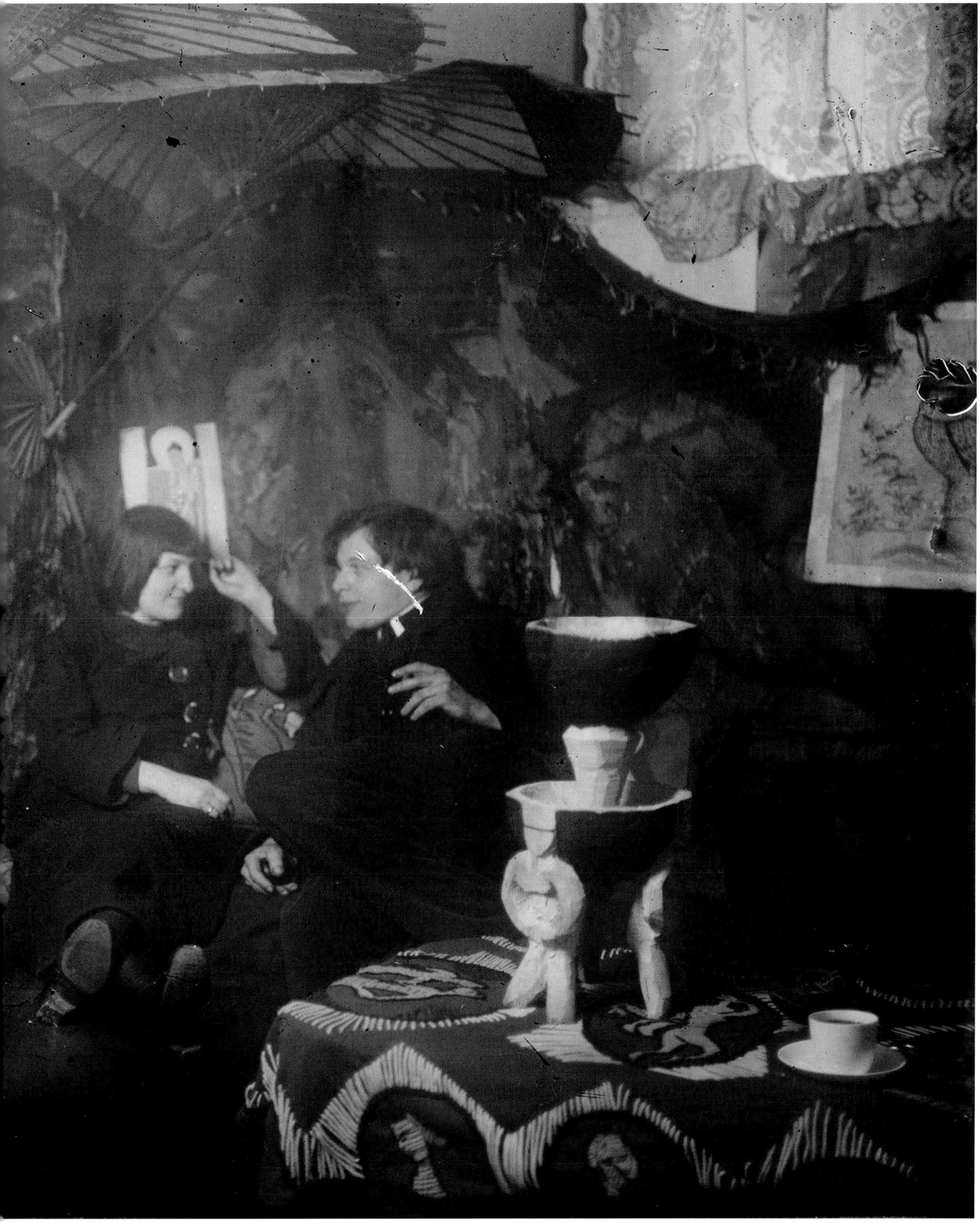

Self-Created Nature Idyll in the Metropolis: Kirchner's Live-In Studios in Berlin

There is scarcely any other studio whose furnishings have been so thoroughly studied as have those of Ernst Ludwig Kirchner's six live-in studios.[1] It is above all to Hanna Strzoda that we are indebted for our knowledge of each of these studios and, in particular, of the influence of various non-European cultures on the objects Kirchner created.[2] The artist furnished each of his studios in Dresden, Berlin and Davos with pieces of furniture, fabrics and objects he had designed or made himself. Inspired by the interior furnishings and artefacts from non-European cultures he was able to study in the originals in ethnographic museum collections in Dresden, Munich, Hamburg and Berlin or in relevant publications, he designed interior furnishings that were highly unusual for the time. His rooms left a lasting impression on the people he admitted into them, who were presumably relatively few in number.[3] For example, in 1927 the Hamburg art historian and Brücke patroness Rosa Schapire recalled in retrospect Kirchner's second studio in Dresden fig.1: "The walls were covered with Kirchner's own frescoes [actually wall hangings], a curtain he had batiked himself separated the narrow bedroom from the 'studio', carved wood posts in the manner of African sculpture flanked the doorway, furniture he had made himself out of crates served as seating and piles of drawings and prints covered the floor."[4] In similar vein, the writer and philosopher Karl Theodor Bluth, with whom Kirchner was friendly in 1915/16, described his experience of the studio in Berlin-Friedenau pp.58, 59 as follows: "Kirchner lived in a studio that he had put together out of an attic apartment. Every piece of furniture, every carpet he had made by hand. When you entered his room you felt you were on another planet or in some long-ago century."[5]

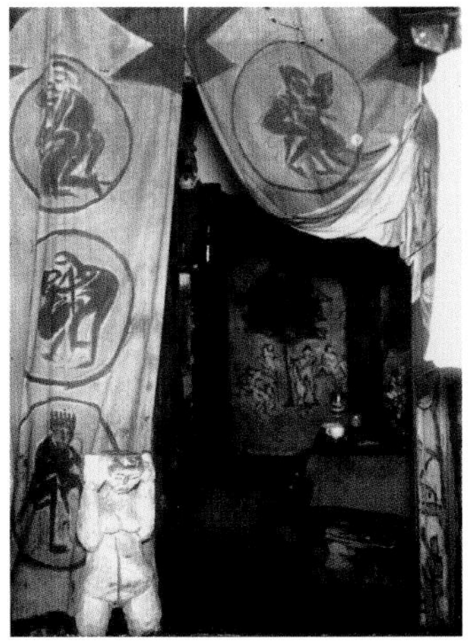

Fig. 1 Ernst Ludwig Kirchner
Kirchner's live-in studio, Berliner Strasse 80, Dresden, 1910
Glass negative, 13 × 18 cm
(Scotti 4)

Kirchner Museum Davos, Gift of the Ernst Ludwig Kirchner Estate 1922

At the beginning of the twentieth century artists' studios generally looked altogether different. The various familiar types from the time ranged from the minimally furnished work spaces of artists (either living minimal existences or bent on utmost convenience) to splendid salons—furnished with all kinds of objects, mostly from other cultural circles—that served as showplaces indicative of a distinguished artist's social standing.[6] The only studios that might be compared to Kirchner's were those of his colleagues of the Brücke—Erich Heckel, Karl Schmidt-Rottluff, Max Pechstein and Otto Mueller.[7] Whereas other artists were content to furnish their workrooms and living quarters with readily available pieces, the Brücke members preferred to design their furnishings themselves. At first this was doubtless largely owing to their limited finances,[8] but it was also partly their disdain for the aesthetics of industrially produced mass wares that led them to design their interiors themselves.[9] And quite soon it was their artistic stance that prevailed. Home-made furnishings—benches, beds, bedspreads, pillows, wall hangings, bowls and the like—came to express their concept of art and approach to life. As part of their innovative endeavours, their furnishings from the beginning of their careers reflect their abandonment of artistic and social conventions. They all—Kirchner especially—saw artefacts from non-European cultures as sources of inspiration in their desire to recapture the "immediacy" and "originality" in life and in art that had been lost in industrial and bourgeois society and thanks to the stringent rules of the art academies. In the lifestyles and artefacts of so-called "primitive" cultures Kirchner found forms of expression that provided alternatives to the dominant trends in art in Wilhelmine Germany—whether academic, realistic or Impressionist in style. In this he took inspiration in his art and way of living from Paul Gauguin and Henri Matisse. Through a "return" to "pristine" forms of expression not only art but also life could be freed from social constraints and thus from all self-alienation. Kirchner's attitude was essentially that of the *bohème.*[10]

His rejection of the bourgeois conventions that had characterised his upbringing was reflected in his outings into nature. Both at the Moritzburg Ponds near Dresden and on the

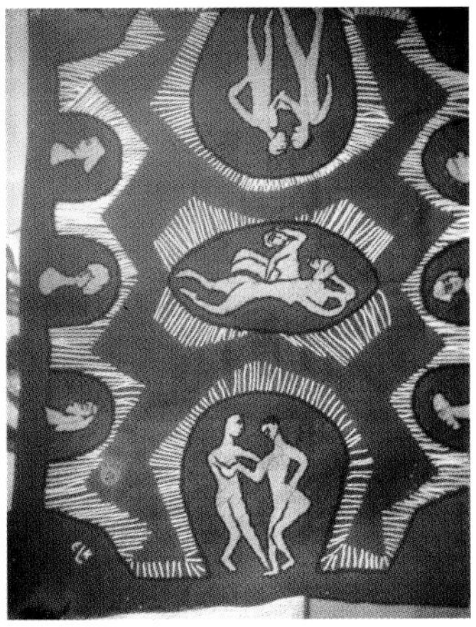

Fig. 2 Ernst Ludwig Kirchner
Tablecloth from Kirchner's live-in studio, Durlacher Strasse 14, Berlin, executed by Erna Schilling based on a design by Kirchner, c.1912
Glass negative, 24 × 18 cm

Kirchner Museum Davos, Gift of the Ernst Ludwig Kirchner Estate

island of Fehmarn off the Baltic coast Kirchner and his colleagues sought an unfettered existence in tune with nature. Being naked was, needless to say, essential to being able to study nudes out of doors; looking back at this period in 1925, Kirchner saw it as the first major culmination of his work up to that time.[11] Motifs of an unencumbered, carefree life in nature also found their way into the design of Kirchner's Dresden and Berlin studio furnishings. It is especially this aspect, with special focus on the Berlin studios, that is the subject of this essay.

The First Live-In Studio in Berlin

Since Kirchner was able to indulge in a way of living outside of bourgeois norms and thus find inspiration for his art primarily during his summer sojourns, it is unsurprising that he chose as the basic theme of his urban live-in studios the untroubled existence of nudes in nature. In October 1911 Kirchner moved from Dresden to Berlin, into a second-floor combined studio and living quarters at Durlacher Strasse 14 in Berlin-Wilmersdorf. It consisted of a living room, kitchen, toilet and an additional room. Pechstein lived at the same address and most likely on the same floor from November 1909 to April 1912. In late October 1911 they established the MUIM Institute there but had to close it in December of the following year owing to insufficient interest. The classroom was also on the second floor, presumably in the largest of the three studio rooms. It is altogether possible that at times instruction was given in either Kirchner's studio or Pechstein's, especially since the MUIM Institute officially had only two students. It is highly probable that Kirchner's new life partner Erna Schilling moved in with him just before the summer they spent together on Fehmarn in 1912.

Only a single photograph of the studio at Durlacher Strasse 14 survives p.44. But from sketches, drawings and paintings it is possible to describe Kirchner's first Berlin atelier in some detail. The space in the photograph was long thought to be that of the MUIM Institute. Yet based on its appearance as compared to the surviving floor plan and the sole presence of objects designed by Kirchner, Strzoda has convincingly argued that it must be Kirchner's "living room".[12] The photo shows Kirchner and Erna seated, facing each other, in a corner on a mattress, over which a spread with appliquéd geometrical forms had been thrown. The two have settled beneath two large, rectangular Japanese umbrellas mounted on one of the walls. Patterned pillows serve as cushions. On the basis of a Kirchner painting the cylindrical pillow on the left next to Erna can be identified as one with an orange-green fabric and a geometric pattern that Kirchner had previously designed for his Dresden studio at Berliner Strasse 80.[13] As in Dresden, Kirchner also covered the walls of at least one of his rooms with fabrics he had painted himself and, as before, they pictured stylised vegetation set off by ornamental framing arcades. In the Dresden studio the arcading were trapezoidal at the top fig.1, but for the room on Durlacher Strasse Kirchner gave them round arches. In the second arch on the left in the photo of the Berlin studio it is possible to make out the rudiments of a crouching figure with spread legs. Strzoda proposes that this figure could have been inspired by Palauan gable figures but it could also have been modelled after Cameroonian chieftains' stools, which she mentions elsewhere as important inspirations for Kirchner.[14] He was able to study sculptures from both cultures in museums in both Dresden and Berlin. The fabric is badly tattered at the level of the figure's thighs — probably from people leaning against it. At the same time, this wear is an indication that the photograph cannot have been made immediately after the room was furnished, but more likely in 1913. Another such figure occupied the second arch on the right, as is documented in a surviving drawing.[15] Whereas the Dresden design was characterised by the forthright sexuality of couples freely copulating in nature, in the first Berlin studio the eroticism, if no less graphic in spots, is somewhat muted. In addition to these large single figures flaunting their genitals, at the upper edge of the hanging on the left-hand wall one can see a couple making love. This is one of Kirchner's home-made tiles and had adorned one of the walls in his Dresden studio.[16] In addition, the fabric used as a tablecloth was embroidered with nudes. The three couples, like the busts along the edges, are ensconced in an arcade-like structure fig.2. For the stylised busts on the borders Kirchner borrowed from Coptic examples. The embroideries were done by Erna Schilling based on Kirchner's designs.

The nude is also the subject of Kirchner's large, African-inspired wood sculpture[17] as well as the small reproduction of a work by Pablo Picasso seen on the wall next to this figure. This was not *The Frugal Repast (Le Repas frugal)*—as has been indicated in the Kirchner literature since 1980[18]—but rather the gouache *Two Girlfriends (Les Deux Amies)* from Picasso's so-called Blue Period figs.3,4.[19] It features two seated nude female models gazing at the viewer. It is the only work by a European artist known to have made its way into Kirchner's "exotically" furnished interior. For an artist like Kirchner, who always stubbornly emphasised his independence and pioneering achievement, the inclusion of a work by Picasso in his studio is a revelatory detail. The unforced poses of Picasso's nude models could have been of particular interest to him. Since his Dresden period he had asked his models to move freely about the studio so that he could draw them in unaffected, natural poses. The reproduction of Picasso's *Two Girlfriends* reappears in Kirchner's second Berlin studio at Körnerstrasse 45, a further indication of how much he valued the work p.58.

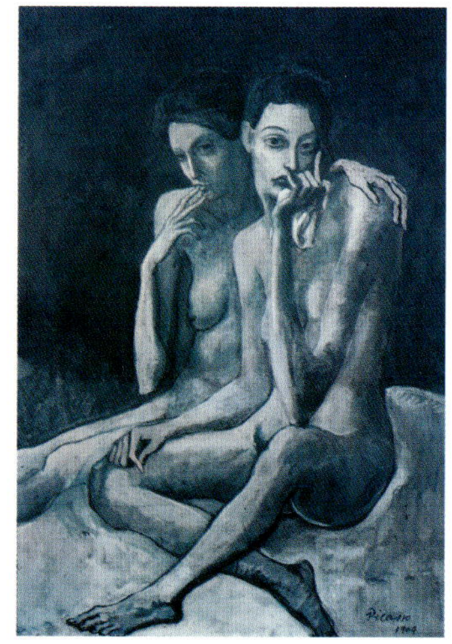

Fig.3 Pablo Picasso
Two Girlfriends, 1904
Gouache on paper,
55 × 38 cm

Whereabouts unknown

Mounted on the wall behind Erna's head is Kirchner's copy of an Indian Buddha figure that he had discovered in John Griffiths's work *The Paintings in the Buddhist Cave-Temples of Ajantá, Khandesh, India,* from 1896/97. His copy, like the above-mentioned tile, had hung in his second Dresden studio. The work on paper on the wall at the right edge of the photo has not as yet been identified. It could be a depiction of a bird in a landscape. Strzoda suspects that it is an East Asian print.[20] Kirchner also hung this print again in one of the rooms on Körnerstrasse p.251. Works of his own and by others important to the artist thus survived at least three moves, and thanks to their different configurations were placed in a new context at each new address.

The interior at Durlacher Strasse 14 (like Kirchner's Dresden studio at Berliner Strasse 80) proves to be a gathering of objects of varied materials, origins and inspiration. One is especially reminded of the studio furnishings of orientalist painters documented and published in the nineteenth century—for example, the "oriental studio" of the Munich-based painter Ferdinand Max Bredt in Ruhpolding[21] and the workroom of the French artist Georges Rochegrosse, which was photographed in the 1880s by Edmond Bénard for the series *Artistes chez eux* and widely circulated. In his interior, Rochegrosse, much like Kirchner, had employed as decor wall hangings, Japanese umbrellas and fans fig.5. It is highly probable that Kirchner knew similar interiors, possibly even having seen them first-hand during his stay in Munich from 1903 to 1904.[22] Kirchner's interiors differ from these earlier "exotic" settings in one essential point however: in contrast to them, non-European objects made up only a small percentage of his furnishings; the greater part, though inspired by foreign cultures, Kirchner had designed and made himself.

As for the colours of this room corner p.44, it is possible to consult a few of Kirchner's paintings, though, needless to say, the artist allowed himself a certain freedom in the chromatic scheme he chose. This is especially true of the Japanese umbrellas. *Couple under Japanese Umbrella* p.144 shows precisely the same situation as the photograph p.44. Here the two umbrellas mounted on the wall are rendered in a pinkish tone with green accents in the centre field and dark edges. In the *Portrait of the Poet Guttmann,*[23] however, which also pictures this corner, the umbrellas' basic colour is yellow and the edges are red, just as in the painting *Erna with Japanese Umbrella (Japanese Girl)* p.148—which was, however, painted on Fehmarn. In another picture painted there, *Fehmarn Dunes with Bathers under Japanese Umbrellas,* the umbrellas are a light blue with dark-blue borders and red accents in the centre panel fig.6. If one assumes that Kirchner did not own a number of umbrellas in colours differing from the two in the photograph, it is clear that he deliberately changed their colours. This could have been in the interest of colour harmony, as in his *Couple under Japanese Umbrella* or, conversely, a matter of placing contrasting accents, as in *Erna with Japanese Umbrella (Japanese Girl).* We see him treating the wall

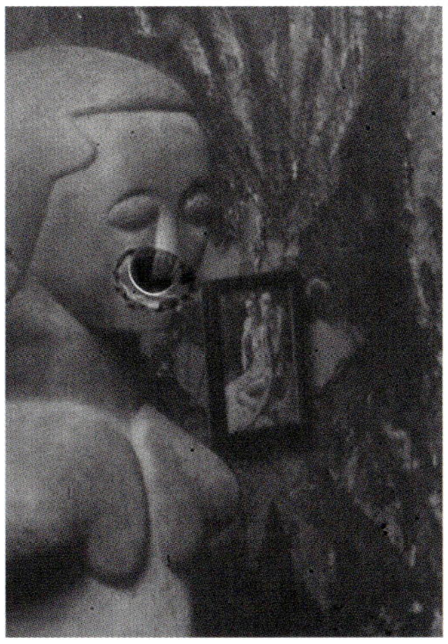

Fig. 4 Reproduction of Picasso's *Two Girlfriends,* 1904, on the wall in Kirchner's live-in studio, Durlacher Strasse 14, Berlin (detail of p. 44)

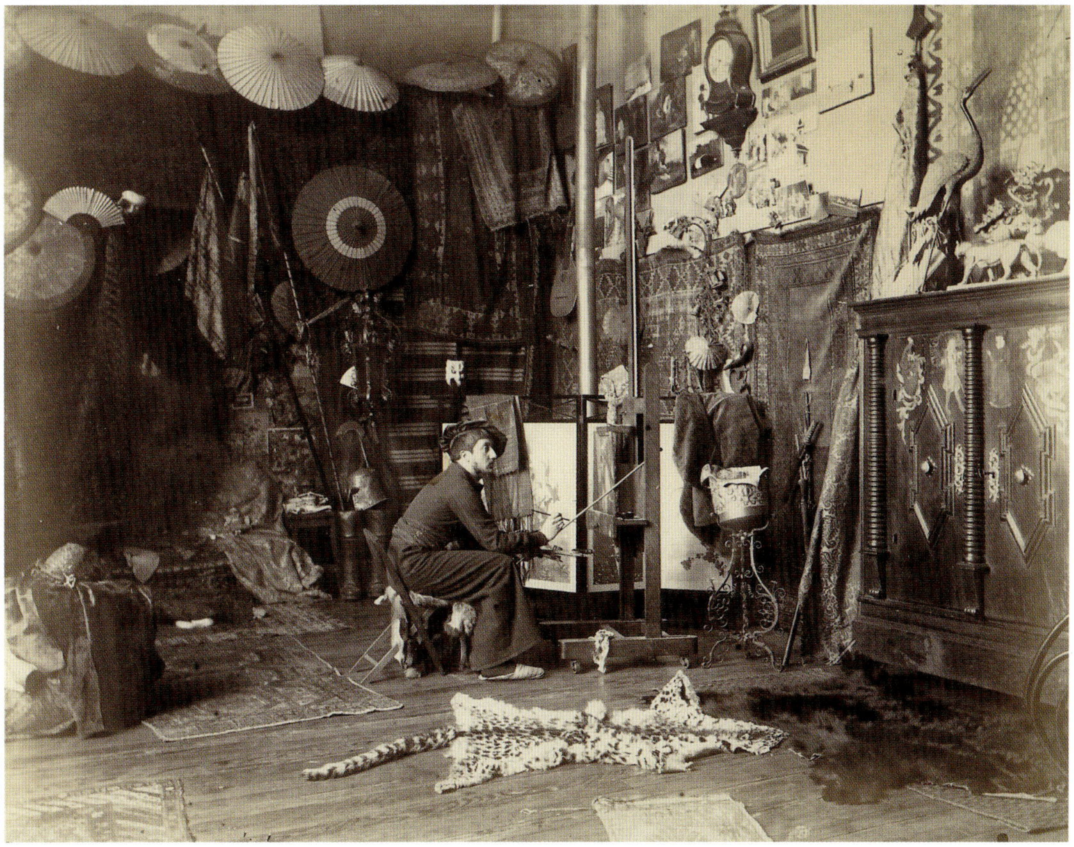

Fig. 5 Edmond Bénard
Georges Rochegrosse in his Paris Atelier, c.1885
Albumin print, 25 × 20 cm

Fratelli Alinari, Museum Collections, Florence

hanging in much the same way. In *Couple under Japanese Umbrella* it is rendered in grey, green and blue, with the figure in the arcading a pinkish beige. This colouring is repeated in other paintings, for example *Seated Woman with Wood Sculpture* fig. 7, with the exception of a single tone: the ornaments here rendered in yellow have a greenish tone in *Couple under Japanese Umbrella.* Apparently Kirchner here once again changed the colouring so as to achieve a chromatic harmony within the picture. However, in both paintings the dress is pink with green sleeves and collar. In *Seated Woman with Wood Sculpture* the collar is pinned together with one of Kirchner's brooches.[24] The fact that the dress is the same colour could indicate that it is not Maschka Mueller who is depicted in *Couple under Japanese Umbrella* but rather Erna. That it has hitherto been thought to be Maschka was based on the fact that the male figure was seen to be Otto Mueller thanks to the hat. Yet Mueller's second "attribute", his pipe, is lacking, so this figure could also be Kirchner himself. The male figure sits on a leopard stool p. 60 that Kirchner had probably acquired from Manfred Heckel, Erich Heckel's brother, in 1909.[25] By comparison with other pictures, the mattress cover proves to be a blue fabric with appliquéd shapes in red.[26] The tablecloth was most probably green with pink-and-yellow embroidery.[27]

The living-room corner in Kirchner's first Berlin studio captured in the photograph was accordingly very colourful, and distinctly different from the customary interior decor of the time. Plant-like forms and nude men and women are the dominant motifs — clearly an allusion to a nature idyll in which mankind is meant to feel free and unashamed.

Little is known about the other rooms at Durlacher Strasse 14. The picture *Nudes in the Studio* p. 127, also painted there, shows part of a room with a stove and a canopy bed looming in from the right that takes up almost the entire picture surface. On the left one can see a folding screen. The bed apparently consists of four heavy posts, carved in wood

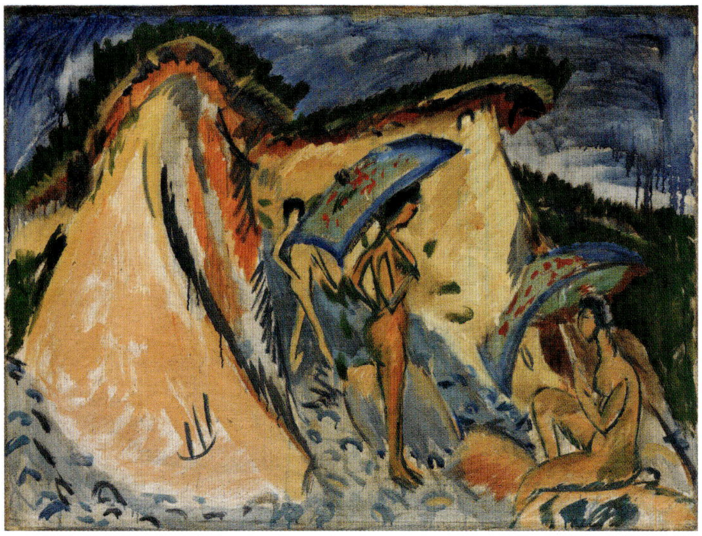

Fig. 6 Ernst Ludwig Kirchner
Fehmarn Dunes with Bathers under Japanese Umbrellas, 1913
Oil on canvas, 90 × 120 cm
(Gordon 709v)

Kirchner Museum Davos, Gift from a private collection, 2000

and adorned with figures, supporting a fabric canopy with extensive ornamentation. On the floor lies a patterned carpet in bright shades of ochre, red and blue. In front of the bed are three female models, either nude, stockinged or dressed in underwear. A fourth model can be seen on the bed. The women seem wholly relaxed, conversing with each other and oblivious to the artist watching them. As Strzoda doubtless correctly suspects, this room was the actual studio in which Kirchner was able to capture nudes in natural poses.[28] Leaning against the stove is what is presumably a painting of a nude. Since Kirchner did not truly separate his working space from his living space, the room depicted could also have been Kirchner and Erna's bedroom disguised as a studio; according to building regulations at the time, studio spaces could not be used as living quarters.[29] The ban presumably applied equally to Durlacher Strasse 14, the back wing of which had been built specifically as a studio tract. In one of the two rooms Kirchner had also put up the wall hanging he had painted for his Dresden studio at Berliner Strasse 80. In Dresden it had been mounted on the wall of the small room, in the doorway of which Kirchner had hung fabric he had batiked himself. The wall covering is documented for the Dresden studio in three photographs fig. 1.[30] In arcading filled with stylised figures stand trees of various shapes beneath which nude couples are copulating. The characteristic trapezoidal tops of the arcading are also seen in drawings and paintings he produced only after moving to Berlin.[31] One painting that can be dated to the early Berlin period based on its style and the models depicted—the sisters Erna and Gerda Schilling—shows this flat-angled arcading in the background above Erna's back p. 111. In addition, around the arcading one can see at least four nude figures in green against a blue ground that also point to the Dresden painting. The figures' unselfconsciousness (in the landscape) is thus transposed onto the models in Kirchner's studio. The interpenetration of life and work that Kirchner had begun to realise in Dresden—as well as his desire for a unity of man and nature—he made more explicit in his first Berlin studio and would take still further at his second address in the city.

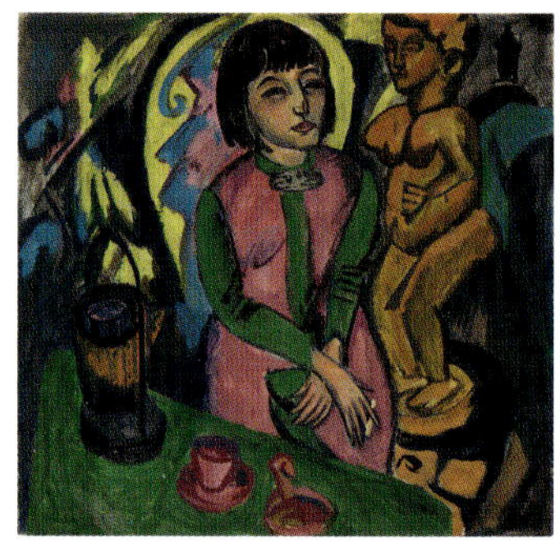

Fig. 7 Ernst Ludwig Kirchner
Seated Woman with Wood Sculpture, 1912
Oil on canvas, 97 × 97 cm
(Gordon 268)

Virginia Museum of Fine Arts, Richmond. Adolph D. and Wilkins C. Williams Fund

The Second Live-In Studio in Berlin

At the end of October 1913 Kirchner and Erna Schilling moved from Berlin-Wilmersdorf to Berlin-Friedenau. After a long search they had found the attic floor at Körnerstrasse 45.[32] It was probably a desire for more space that occasioned the move, not so much the failure of the MUIM Institute the previous December or Kirchner's falling out with his Brücke colleagues. Their association had been officially dissolved on 27 May 1913. Pechstein, with whom Kirchner clashed most violently, had already left Durlacher Strasse 14 in late April 1912. He too had moved to Berlin-Friedenau, to Offenbacher Strasse 1.

At the new address the couple probably had a total of five rooms: two conceived as a studio and three smaller ones. The two studio rooms were roughly four feet longer than

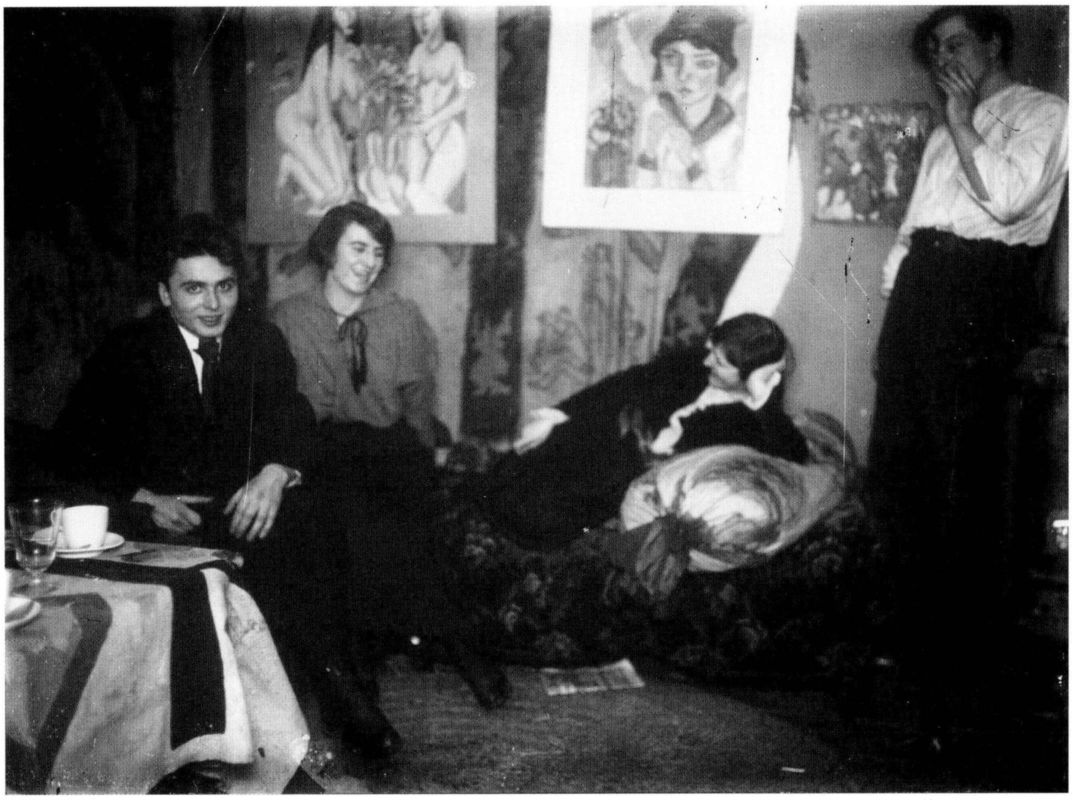

Fig. 8 Ernst Ludwig Kirchner
Werner Gothein, Gothein's girlfriend, Erna Schilling and Ernst Ludwig Kirchner in Kirchner's live-in studio, Körnerstrasse 45, Berlin, with wall hanging from his Dresden live-in studio, Berliner Strasse 80, c.1914
Glass negative, 18 × 24 cm
(Scotti 33)

Kirchner Museum Davos, Gift of the Ernst Ludwig Kirchner Estate 1992

the others, which was reflected by projections on the façade. A number of surviving photographs show how the spaces were furnished. But since the photos were made at different times and because Erna and Kirchner presumably changed the furnishings, it is not always clear which rooms are pictured.

The Dresden wall fabrics were once again installed in one of the spaces fig.8. At times Kirchner hung two of his paintings on top of them, one being his *Two Yellow Nudes with Bouquet of Flowers* p.204 from 1914. In it one can see behind the two nudes arcading with a stylised, palm-like tree from this painted fabric fig.9, the very spot now covered by the painting. Also dating from his time in Dresden are the brightly patterned batiked bedspread and the large pillow roll visible in the photograph. The wall fabrics from Durlacher Strasse 14 could also be reused at the new address. The pastel *Standing Nude in Front of the Tent* p.183 pictures them, not affixed to the wall but loosely installed in one of the corners of the room, causing the cloth to gather in thick folds. It is possible that this solution was reached because of their poor condition. The phrase "in front of the tent" in the pastel's title—which is certain to have been added later—is misleading. It suggests that the fabric itself functions as a "tent". But based on the pictured space, with two adjoining walls, it is a niche, most probably containing a door opening. Because the ceiling doesn't slant, Strzoda suspects that this must have been one of the doors in the centre of the building. Yet there is only one door in the entire floor plan, the door to the left-hand studio room, which was located in a niche. And in fact it was hung with a patterned fabric the artist had produced himself, as we can see from three photographs pp.66, 218.[33] The considerable folding does not allow us to definitively identify the curtain as the former wall covering from Durlacher Strasse. A slight indication that it could be is the round-arch pattern at the bottom edge, most clearly visible in the above-mentioned pastel. The fabric in the pastel also turns up in other paintings produced in the second Berlin studio, for example in *Female Nude Combing Her Hair* p.136. Here the curtain can be seen at the picture's right edge. Accordingly, this must be the same space pictured in the two photographs pp.66, 218. At least it contains the same round table with trapezoidal foot, a sisal rug and a stove.

For the more spacious studio new textiles were created as well. Kirchner applied to a wall in an unidentified room on Körnerstrasse a light-coloured fabric appliquéd with

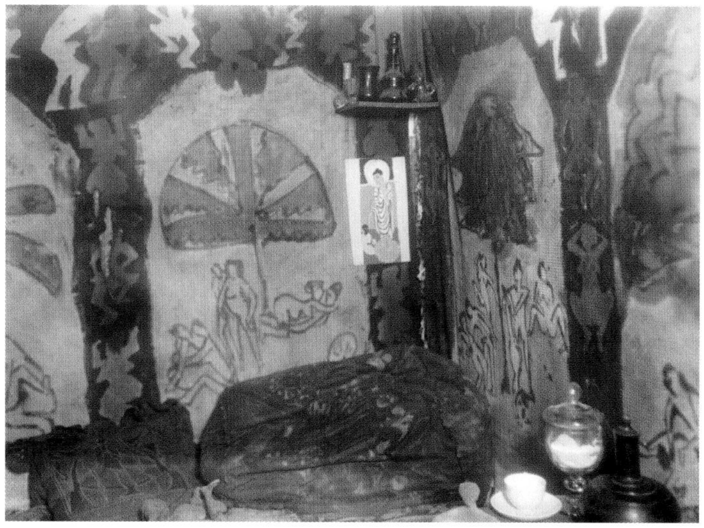

Fig. 9 Ernst Ludwig Kirchner
Kirchner's live-in studio, Berliner Strasse 80, Dresden, c.1910/11
Glass negative, 18 × 24 cm
(Scotti 17)

Kirchner Museum Davos, Gift of the Ernst Ludwig Kirchner Estate 2001

stylised figural and abstract forms in a dark colour p.58. In style they closely resemble the works on fabric Kirchner had produced for the tobacco merchant Josef Feinhals's booth at the Cologne Werkbund exhibition in 1914.[34] In this same room, in addition to the above-mentioned Picasso reproduction, there was also one of the rectangular Japanese umbrellas. For the new studio there was also presumably a divan throw fig.10 that no longer survives. On each of its long sides it depicted four nude women in nature, and the centre featured a recumbent or swimming nude. Kirchner's most successful interior design, meanwhile, featured a new, coordinated fabric ensemble for one of the two mansard niches.

Fehmarn in Berlin

After his last summer sojourn on Fehmarn, cut short by the outbreak of the First World War, Kirchner designed an entire textile ensemble for one of the two studio rooms at Körnerstrasse 45. He then documented this space in a photograph p.59, covering the window with a black cloth to do so. The ensemble consisted of a fabric covering for the trapezoidal window wall (often referred to in the literature as a *sopraporta,* two divan covers, two backrest covers, two cushions and a tablecloth. Fortunately, the majority of these fabrics — in contrast to the other textiles produced in Dresden and Berlin — are preserved pp.61–63. Whereas the ensembles in Kirchner's earlier interiors were made up of components created at different times and therefore heterogeneous, with the exception of the wooden furniture and sculptures the design of this sitting corner followed a single concept. It is quite rightly called the "design highlight" from Kirchner's studio apartments.[35] For these textiles, unlike the earlier ones, Kirchner created a personal iconography based on the couple's experiences on Fehmarn. The island's importance in Kirchner's life and art is apparent not only from the written sources but also from his artistic oeuvre. At the end of his longest stay on the island in the summer of 1913, which lasted from fifteen to twenty weeks, he wrote to his former MUIM pupil Hans Gewecke, who had visited the couple there that summer: "Sadly, sadly we soon have to return. You can't believe how hard this will be for us. I don't know whether the sea is most beautiful in summer or in autumn. I am painting as much as possible, so as to at least be able to take along something of the thousand things I would like to paint. In addition, the oak from the stranded ship is becoming more and more tempting for sculptures."[36] More than a year later, after his last, interrupted stay on Fehmarn, Kirchner wrote to Gustav Schiefler on 28 December 1914: "It was very difficult for me to leave so suddenly, for this year I was completely captivated by the landscape and the life up there and only needed to grasp hold of it, almost unconsciously. A few woodcuts and lithos date from this time. Here [in Berlin] I am working through the new finds. I have two large bathing pictures in mind and a number of smaller things."[37] And in 1924, ten years later, Kirchner was still homesick for Fehmarn. In a letter to Schiefler from 10 December he wrote from Davos: "It is so frightfully lonely here since Bosshart [the poet Jakob Bosshart] is dead that I am planning to once more head out to Fehmarn for a summer by the sea. I would like to take along a few young people, then for a few months I could paint straight from life. Who knows how long one will live and be able to work, and I have still some things to do up there. Also, I'd like to see the old spots where we lived so happily and simply. I am only slightly concerned about treading on German soil; since my name has become so well known and not the best things are being said of me, my life there is made more complicated."[38] He would never realise this plan, although by December 1925 he had overcome his anxiety and again travelled to Germany for a brief three months for the first time in nine years. For Kirchner, Fehmarn represented an Arcadian nature idyll in which he had doubtless spent the most carefree time of his life. The feeling of living in tune with nature that he had experienced there he transferred, by way of the fabric decoration, to one of his mansard niches in big-city Berlin.

The textiles differ in style from those he had previously designed. For them he selected an undyed linen, on which motifs from Fehmarn are embroidered with stylised black outlines and a sparing use of colours: various shades of green for the vegetation, a yellow-beige for the flesh tones of the nudes and the sand, blue for the water, pink for stones, the centres of flowers and sails, violet and dark red for hair, a boat and a ball. Male and female figures are captured in various situations. Some are lying or sitting on the sand, standing in the water, making "sand angels" or playing with a ball. Others are simply conversing or dancing on the beach. However, the surviving cover for the left-hand divan pictures a hunter lying on the ground with his rifle and accompanied by a woman. He is taking aim at one of the two seagulls in the water. The meadow in which the two figures are lying is dotted with various kinds of flowers. The scene recalls an experience of Kirchner's that he had captured in a sketchbook in July 1913: "I am lying in the grass by the sea next to my wife and gazing at the delicate shapes of the plants up close. Against the brownish-yellow ground of the soil the bright green of feathery leaves growing in a circle. Out of the centre the oval line ends with the blossoms. This same rounding in the elegant curve as in the leaves on the ground. Crossing the curve of the flower stalk is the slender, slightly bent zigzag line of grass. At the tip, pale yellow-green lancets. On them pale greyish-yellow blossoms with broad S-shaped bellies. The banal shape of clover leaves arranged in a triangle; on the long side of the flowers yellow in the shape of boomerangs. Quaking grass rises above all the rest, black, flattened egg shapes on bent strands. They are ornamented like South Seas oars. Above the grass violet heaps of seaweed. In a cove a white seagull is swimming in the blue water. I raise my shotgun and fire."[39] It is indeed documented that Kirchner went bird hunting with a small-calibre rifle.[40] Kirchner also captured the motif of the seagull hunter in paintings and graphics.[41] The cushion cover on the left-hand divan, probably no longer preserved, pictured a lighthouse — most likely the one at Staberhuk, where Kirchner and Erna stayed in the lighthouse keeper's home.

Personal experiences and impressions that Kirchner had captured in writing and in numerous sketches, drawings and paintings on Fehmarn served him as patterns for the coordinated fabric ensemble that Erna Schilling executed in satin-stitch embroidery in the autumn and winter of 1914/15. Whether he had long planned such a room decor or the idea was triggered by his premature departure from Fehmarn is difficult to say. It is certain that with this ensemble Kirchner brought "his" nature idyll back to his studio apartment in Berlin, and with it combined in a single spot the two most important sources of inspiration from those years — Fehmarn and Berlin.

Along with the textiles Kirchner arranged wooden objects from his Dresden period, for example the first Brücke piece of furniture, which he had carved himself in 1909. This consisted of a wooden bench, whose frieze and backrest are ornamented with figures based on Cameroonian and Palauan designs. Then there was the sculpture *Crouching Figure with Fruit Bowl* from 1911, patterned after African carvings.[42] Both of these are now lost, although the wooden leopard stool from Cameroon p.60 survives. Ever since Erika

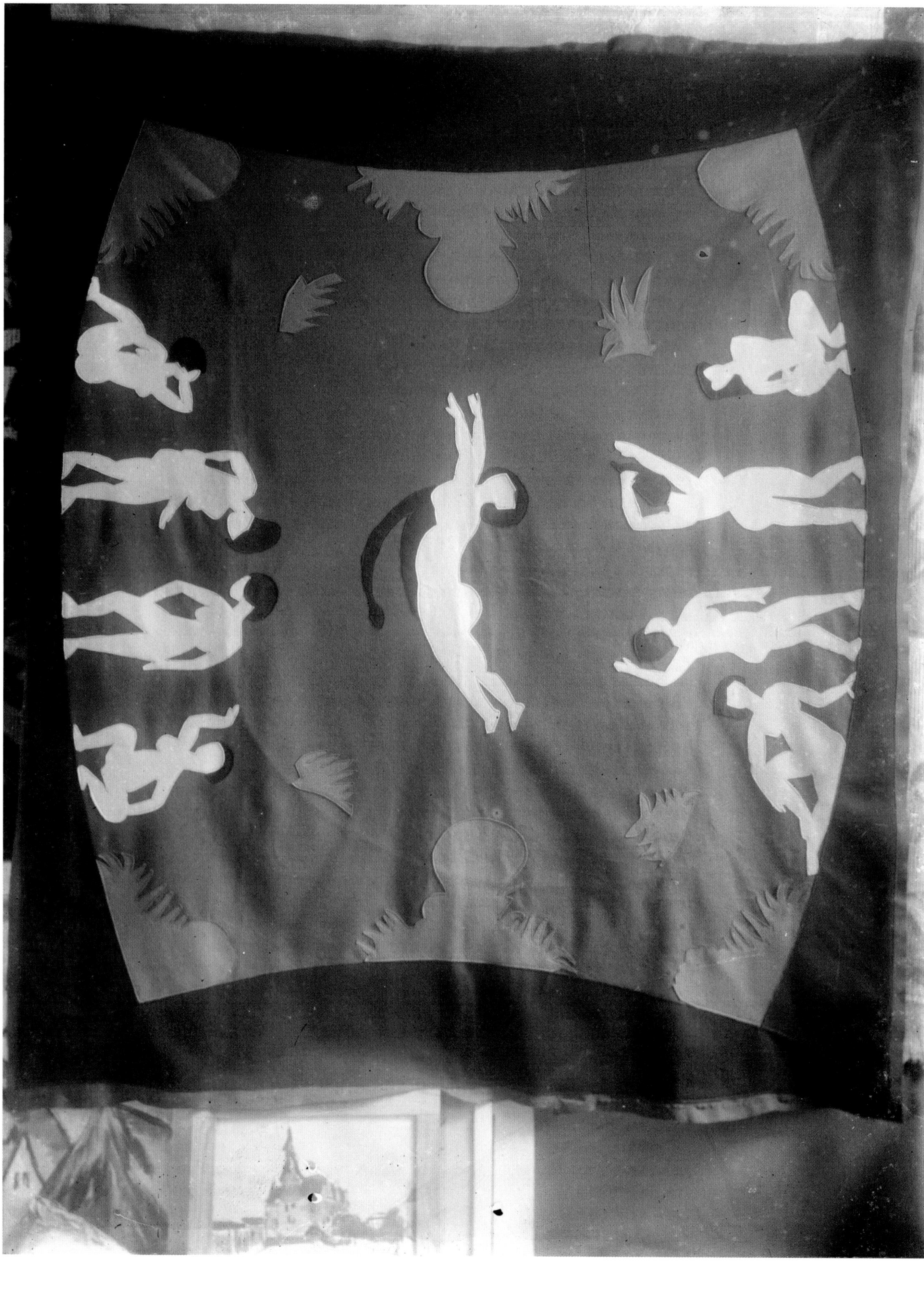

Fig. 10 Ernst Ludwig Kirchner
Divan cover with appliqué, executed by Erna Schilling based on a design by Kirchner, c.1913
Glass negative, 24 × 18 cm

Kirchner Museum Davos, Gift of the Ernst Ludwig Kirchner Estate

Billetter compared this "seating corner" to a Bedouin tent in 1979 and Roman Hollenstein described it as an "exotic-looking tent niche" in 1985, this mansard niche has regularly been referred to as a "tent".[43] And accordingly it has been variously interpreted: it has been associated with a nomadic, primitive way of life and oriental exoticism.[44] The term "tent", however, was never used by Kirchner himself.

The design of his rooms was not only an expression of his bohemian lifestyle, it also influenced and was influenced by his artistic development. Moreover, his surroundings flowed into many of his works, helping him find solutions for his artistic problems; or, as he put it in retrospect, "the course of development in these external things, from the first appliquéd coverlet in the first Dresden studio space to the fully harmonious space in the Berlin studio [...], is an uninterrupted logical progression, one that has gone hand in hand with my painterly development in pictures and graphics and sculpture. The first bowl that I carved [...] brought the three-dimensional form into the flat form of the picture, and thus the personal relic became fully incorporated in the various techniques down to the last detail." And in another passage: "This continuous effort finally resulted in the solution of the problem of how to depict nudes in nature in new ways. The bodies of people in the water or between trees glow in pure blues, reds, greens and yellows just as they do in the rooms that Kirchner tried to readjust by the simplest of means, with crates for furniture and painted fabrics, adapting them to the newly discovered forms and rules of his pictures. One generated the other. The newly created space was also painted, and accordingly brought with it new insights."[45]

1 These are the two studios in Dresden at Berliner Strasse 60 and 80, the two in Berlin at Durlacher Strasse 14 and Körnerstrasse 45, and the houses "In den Lärchen" and "Auf dem Wildboden" in Davos. In her dissertation on Kirchner's studios Hanna Strzoda also includes his attic in Dresden before the founding of Brücke as well as the hut he rented for four summers on the Stafelalp above Davos Frauenkirch. There is, however, no documentation relating to the decoration of these last two. See Hanna Strzoda, *Die Ateliers Ernst Ludwig Kirchners: Eine Studie zur Rezeption "primitiver" europäischer und außereuropäischer Kulturen* (Ph.D. diss., 2004; Petersberg, 2006).

2 Ibid.

3 Christian Saehrendt, *Ernst Ludwig Kirchner: Bohème-Identität und nationale Sendung* (Frankfurt am Main, 2003), p. 38.

4 Rosa Schapire, "Ernst Ludwig Kirchner", *Der Kreis: Zeitschrift für künstlerische Kultur* 4, no. 3 (1927), p. 144; also quoted in: Leonie Beiersdorf, "'Dass Leben und Arbeit eines sind': Gelebte Utopie bei Ernst Ludwig Kirchner und Rosa Schapire", in *Gesamtkunstwerk Expressionismus: Kunst, Film, Literatur, Theater, Tanz und Architektur 1905 bis 1925*, ed. Ralf Beil and Claudia Dillmann, exh. cat. Mathildenhöhe Darmstadt (Ostfildern-Ruit, 2010), p. 70.

5 Volker Wahl, "Von Jena nach Davos: Stationen eines Künstlerlebens", in *Ernst Ludwig Kirchner: Von Jena nach Davos*, exh. cat. Stadtmuseum Göhre, Jena (Leipzig, 1993), p. 28.

6 Strzoda, *Ateliers* (see n. 1), p. 10; see also Eva Mongi-Vollmer, *Das Atelier des Malers: Die Diskurse eines Raums in der zweiten Hälfte des 19. Jahrhunderts* (Ph.D. diss., 2002; Berlin, 2004).

7 Strzoda, *Ateliers* (see n. 1), pp. 262–273.

8 Ibid., pp. 18–20, 149.

9 As Kirchner wrote in retrospect in his diary entry from 6 March 1923, "the first bowl that I carved because you couldn't buy one that was pleasing brought the three-dimensional form into the flat form of the picture, and thus the personal relic became fully incorporated in the various techniques down to the last detail." For the citation in German, see Lothar Grisebach, *E. L. Kirchners Davoser Tagebuch: Eine Darstellung des Malers und eine Sammlung seiner Schriften*, new edn., rev. by Lucius Grisebach (Ostfildern-Ruit, 1997), p. 67.

10 Strzoda, *Ateliers* (see n. 1), pp. 274–281.

11 Grisebach, *Tagebuch* (see n. 9), p. 71.

12 Strzoda, *Ateliers* (see n. 1), p. 173.

13 Ibid., p. 176.

14 Ibid., pp. 142, 174 .

15 Ibid., pp. 173, 175.

16 Ibid., p. 122.

17 *Negro Sculpture (Experimental Figure)*, 1912, wood, height c.100 cm, whereabouts unknown (Henze 1912/05).

18 Karlheinz Gabler, *E. L. Kirchner: Dokumente; Fotos, Schriften, Briefe* (Aschaffenburg, 1980), p. 90.

19 Picasso had exhibited the gouache in February 1905 in the Galerie Serrurier in Paris. It was illustrated in Guillaume Apollinaire's review in *La Plume*; see Éliane Formentelli, "Écrire 'Picasso', d'Apollinaire", *Études françaises* 21, no. 1 (1985), pp. 11, 14, 19. It is unclear how Kirchner came to have a reproduction of it. See also Thorsten Sadowsky, "Kirchner, Picasso und die anderen", in *Picasso und Deutschland*, exh. cat. Museo Picasso Málaga and Kunsthalle Würth, Schwäbisch Hall (Künzelsau, 2016), pp. 296–311.

20 Strzoda, *Ateliers* (see n. 1), p. 178.

21 Ibid., p. 279.

22 Ibid., p. 242.

23 *Portrait of the Poet Guttmann*, 1911, oil on canvas, 80.5 × 65 cm, The Nelson-Atkins Museum of Art, Kansas City (Gordon 215).

24 This was most probably the brooch *Three Heads*, c.1910, embossed metal, width c.11 cm, whereabouts unknown (Henze 1910/22).

25 Strzoda, *Ateliers* (see n. 1), p. 137.

26 For example, *The Tent*, 1914, oil on canvas, 101.5 × 76 cm, Pinakothek der Moderne, Munich (Gordon 393).

27 See the painting *Still Life with Head*, 1911/12, oil on canvas, 70.5 × 76 cm, Brücke-Museum, Berlin (Gordon 374v).

28 Strzoda, *Ateliers* (see n. 1), p. 182.

29 Ibid., pp. 26, 273.

30 For the other two photos, see Roland Scotti (ed.), *Ernst Ludwig Kirchner: The Photographic Work* (Göttingen, 2006), cat. nos. 8, 17.

31 Strzoda, *Ateliers* (see n. 1), pp. 176–177.

32 See Ernst Ludwig Kirchner to Gustav Schiefler, letter from October 1913, in Wolfgang Henze et al. (eds.), *Ernst Ludwig Kirchner/Gustav Schiefler: Briefwechsel 1910–1935/1938* (Stuttgart/Zurich, 1990), p. 65, no. 39.

33 The third one is in Scotti, *The Photographic Work* (see n. 30), cat. no. 332.

34 Strzoda, *Ateliers* (see n. 1), p. 218.

35 Ibid., p. 208.

36 Letter from 24 September 1913, in Hans Delfs (ed.), *Ernst Ludwig Kirchner: Der gesamte Briefwechsel*, vol. 1, *Briefe von 1901 bis 1923* (Zurich, 2010), p. 84.

37 *Kirchner/Schiefler* (see n. 32), p. 70, no. 45.

38 Ibid., pp. 316–317, no. 260.

39 For the citation in German, see Gerd Presler, *Ernst Ludwig Kirchner: Die Skizzenbücher; "Ekstase des ersten Sehens"* (Karlsruhe/Davos, 1996), p. 401, Skb. 35. The texts in this sketchbook were most likely transcribed from Kirchner's notes by Erna Schilling.

40 Dieter Reinhardt, "Zeitgenössische Zeugnisse von Kirchners Fehmarn-Aufenthalten", in *Ernst Ludwig Kirchner auf Fehmarn*, ed. Hermann Gerlinger and Heinz Spielmann, exh. cat. Schleswig-Holsteinisches Landesmuseum, Schloss Gottorf (Schleswig, 1997), p. 38.

41 *Seagull Hunter in the Woods,* 1912, oil on canvas, Städel Museum, Frankfurt am Main (Gordon 272); *Seagull Hunter,* 1912, woodcut (Gercken 579); and the woodcut *Pigeon Hunter in the Woods,* 1914 (Gercken 709) with reference to two drawings.

42 *Studio Stool (Carved Stool),* 1909, wood, painted, height c.100 cm, whereabouts unknown (Henze 1919/10); *Crouching Figure with Fruit Bowl,* 1911, wood, painted, height c.56 cm, whereabouts unknown (Henze 1911/01).

43 Erika Billetter, "Ernst Ludwig Kirchner: Kunst als Lebensentwurf", in *Ernst Ludwig Kirchner 1880–1938,* ed. Lucius Grisebach and Annette Meyer zu Eissen, exh. cat. Nationalgalerie Berlin (Berlin, 1979), p. 16; Roman Hollenstein, "Die Atelierhäuser von Arnold Böcklin und Hermann Haller in Zürich und die Häuser von Ernst Ludwig Kirchner in Davos", in Eduard Hüttinger (ed.) *Künstlerhäuser von der Renaissance bis zur Gegenwart* (Zurich, 1985), p. 234; most thoroughly in Strzoda, *Ateliers* (see n. 1), pp. 219–256. Worth mentioning in this context is the painting *The Tent,* 1914, oil on canvas, 101.5 × 76 cm, Pinakothek der Moderne, Munich (Gordon 393). The white cloth in the background is, however, a curtain in front of the mansard window in one of the two studio rooms. According to Leopold Reidemeister, the title, which apparently pleased Kirchner, was evidently given to it by Edwin Redslob, the painting's first owner. See *Künstler der "Brücke" in Berlin (1904–1914): Ein Beitrag zur Geschichte der Künstlergruppe "Brücke",* exh. cat. Brücke-Museum, Berlin (Berlin, 1972), no. 105, unpaginated.

44 Strzoda, *Ateliers* (see n. 1), pp. 232–238.

45 Grisebach, *Tagebuch* (see n. 9), pp. 67, 76.

Cat. 143

Unknown young woman (Gerda Schilling?), Ernst Ludwig Kirchner, Erna Schilling and Hans Gewecke in Kirchner's live-in studio, Berlin-Friedenau, 1914/15
Glass negative

Kirchner Museum Davos,
Gift of the Ernst Ludwig
Kirchner Estate 1992

Cat. 142

Mansard niche in Kirchner's live-in studio, Berlin-Friedenau, 1914/15
Glass negative

Kirchner Museum Davos,
Gift of the Ernst Ludwig
Kirchner Estate 2001

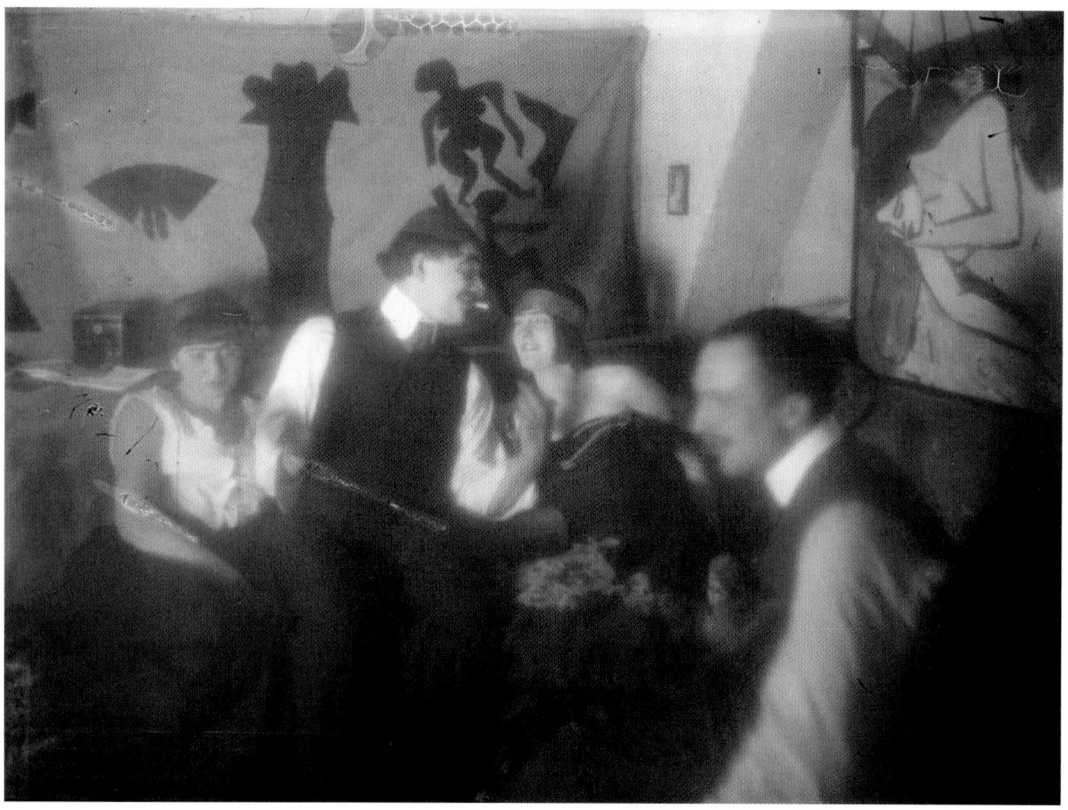

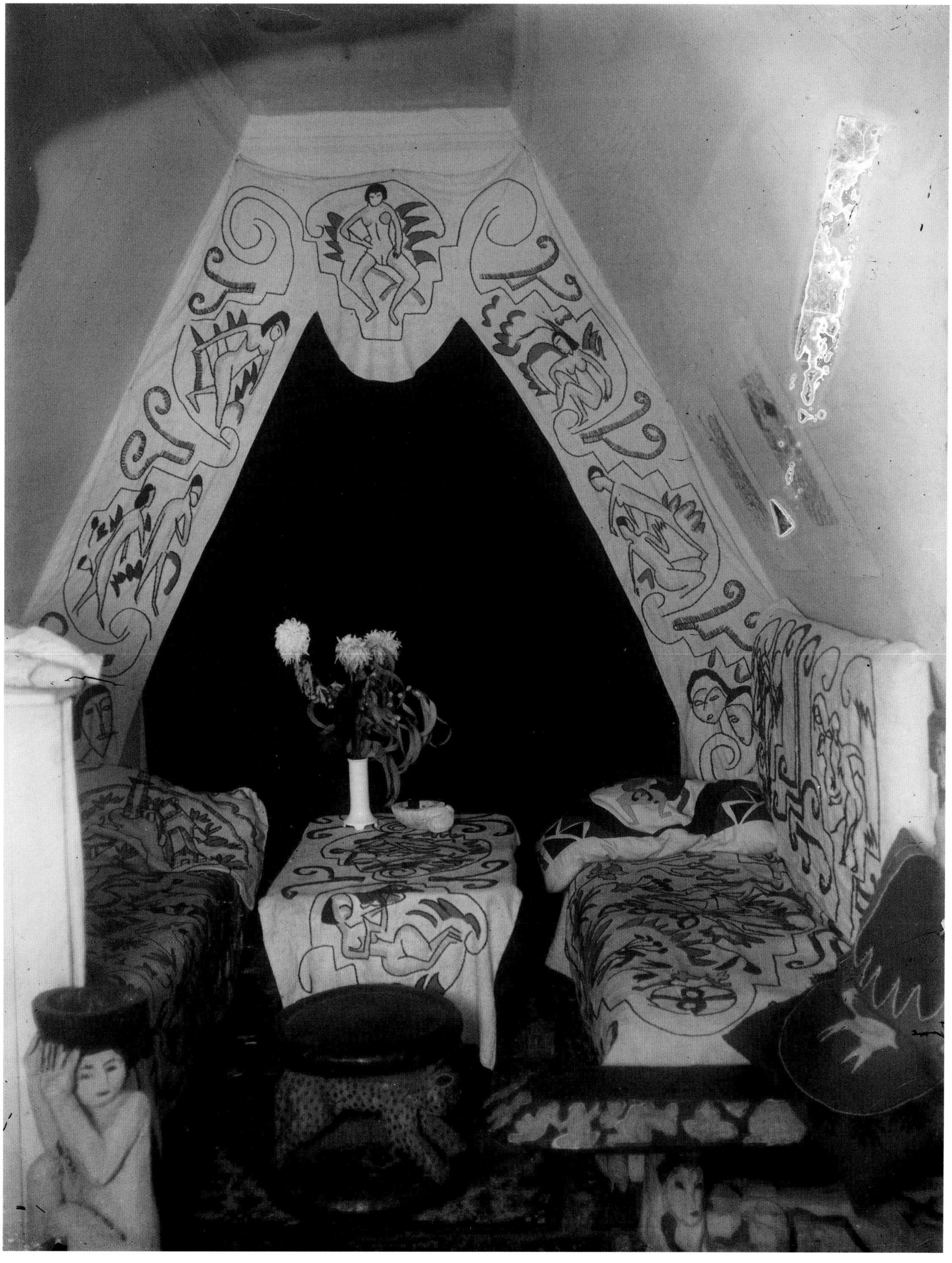

Cat. 149

Anonymous
Leopard stool (from the former collection of Ernst Ludwig Kirchner), 19th century
African obeche wood

Bündner Kunstmuseum Chur, Gift of Prof. Otto Tschumi, Bern (1954)

Cat. 150

Supraporte from Kirchner's live-in studio, Berlin-Friedenau, 1914/15
Wool embroidery on linen

E.W.K. Collection, Bern/Davos

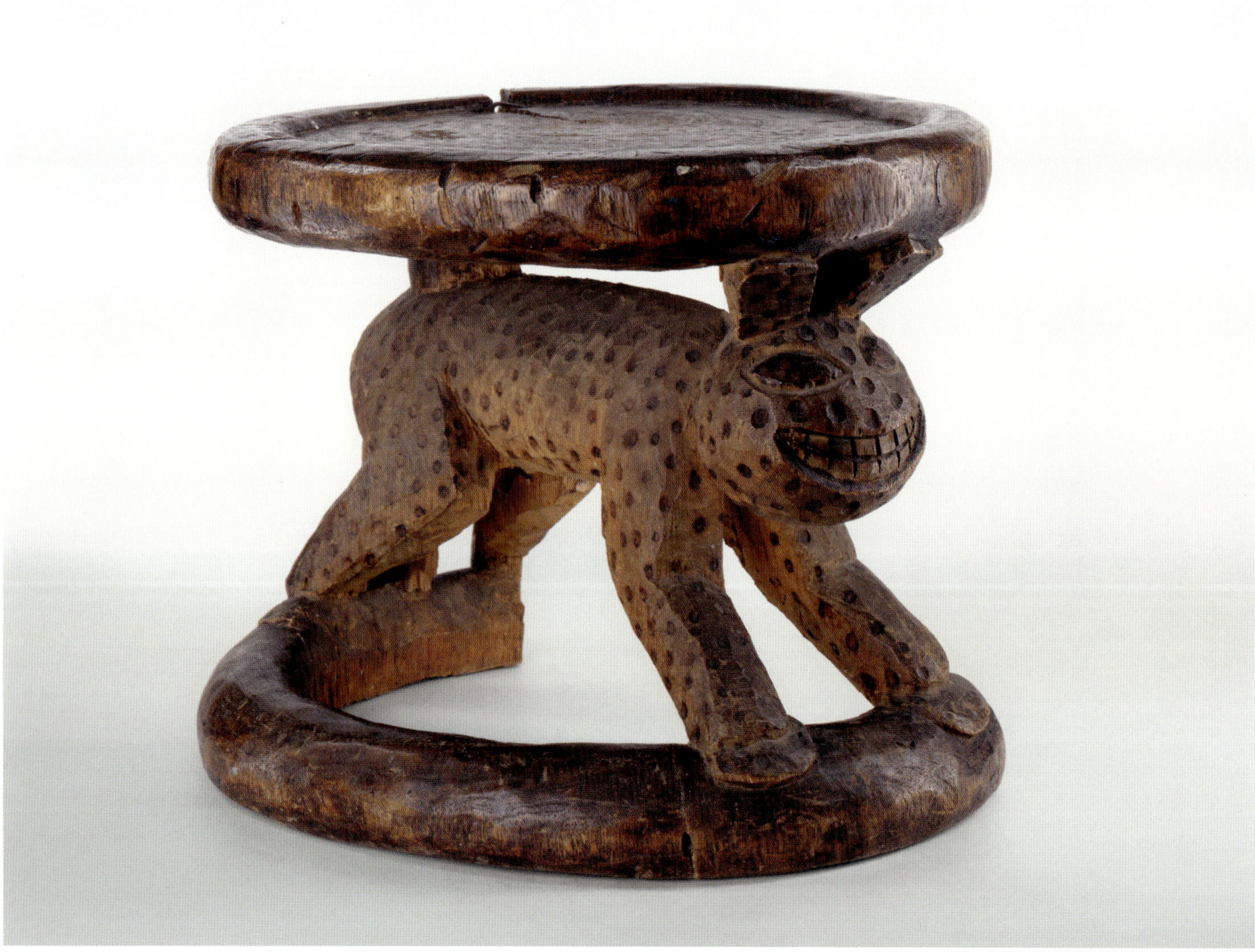

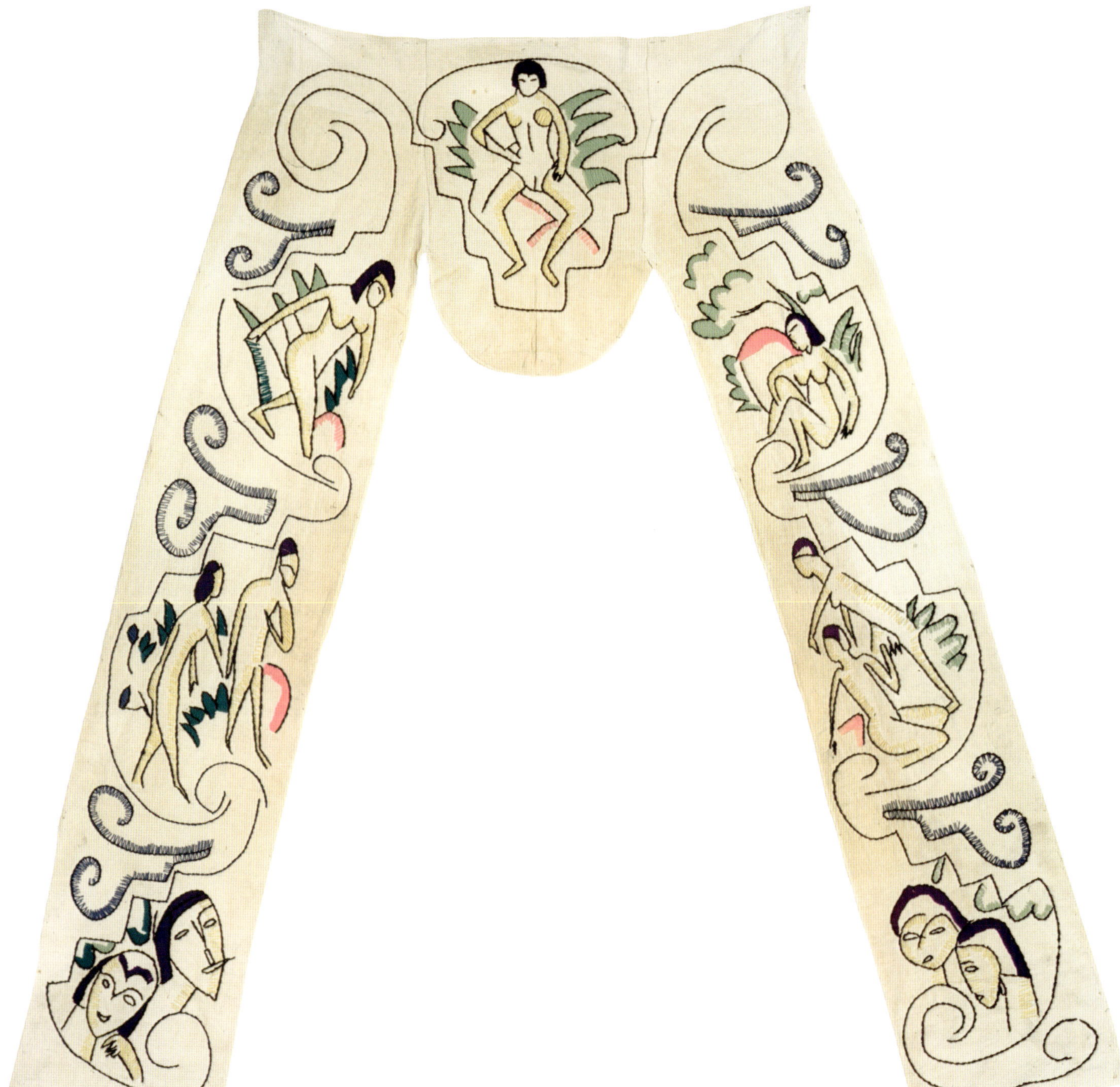

Cat. 153

Divan throw from Kirchner's live-in studio, Berlin-Friedenau, 1914/15
Wool embroidery on linen

Private collection

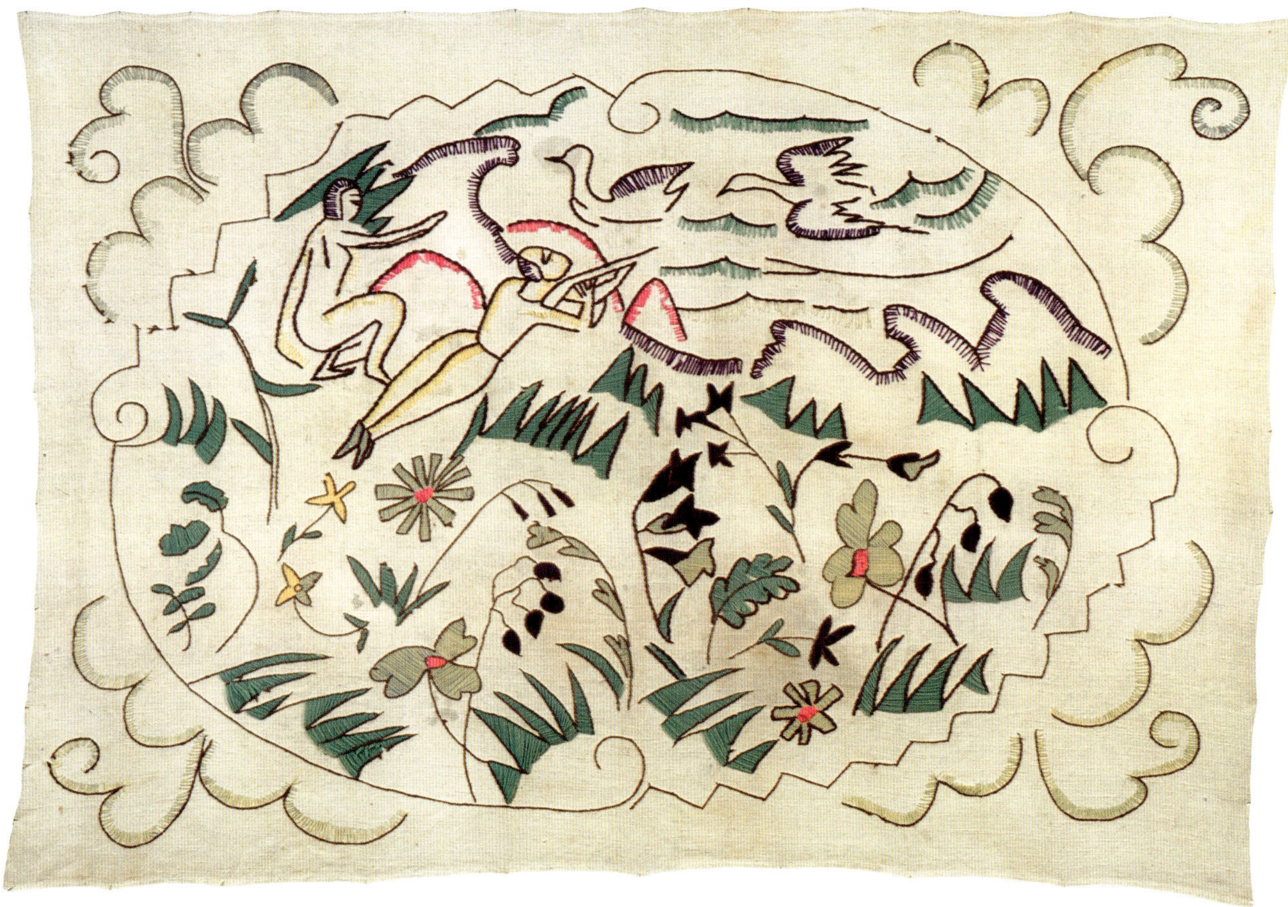

Cat. 151

Backrest cover from Kirchner's live-in studio, Berlin-Friedenau, 1914/15
Wool embroidery on linen

E.W.K. Collection, Bern/Davos

Cat. 152

Backrest cover from Kirchner's live-in studio, Berlin-Friedenau, 1914/15
Wool embroidery on linen

E.W.K. Collection, Bern/Davos

Cat. 154

Tablecloth from Kirchner's live-in studio, Berlin-Friedenau, 1914/15
Wool embroidery on linen

E.W.K. Collection, Bern/Davos

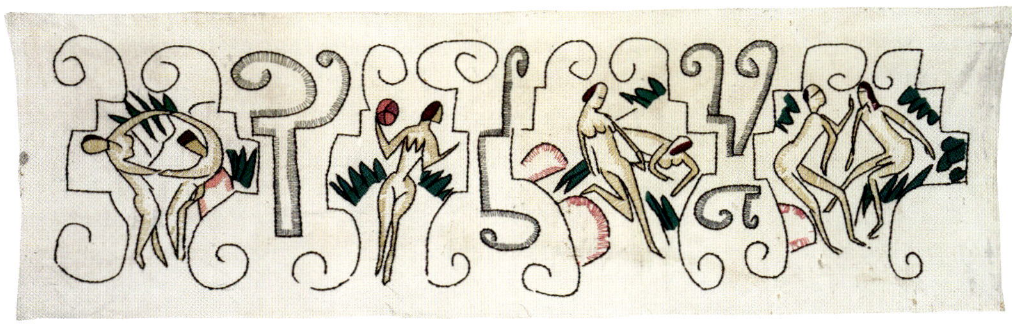

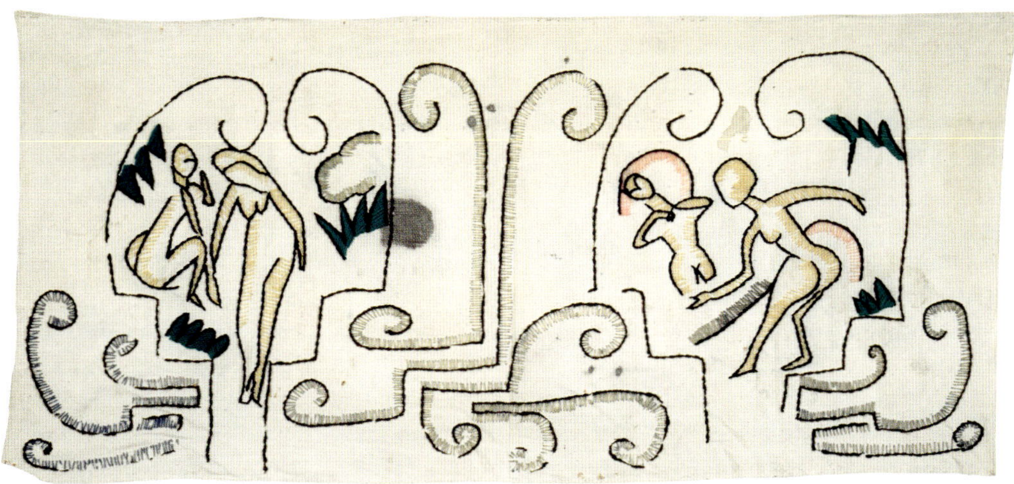

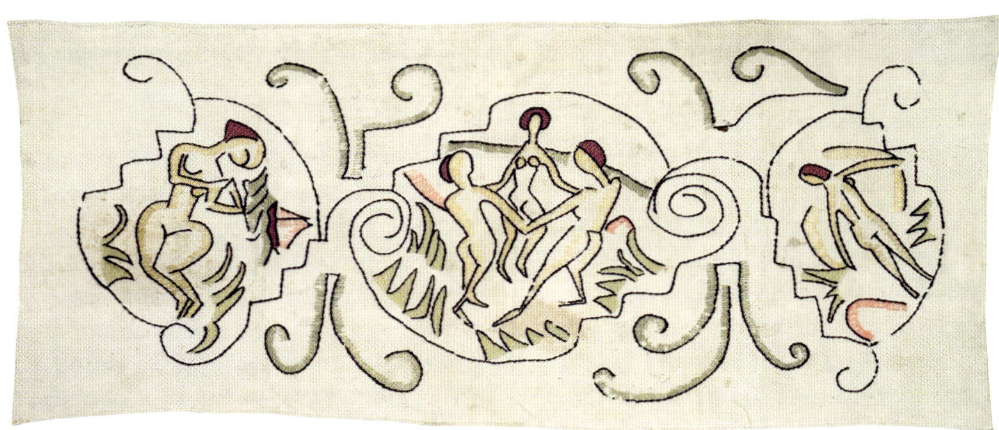

Cat. 130

Head of the Invalid — Self-Portrait as an Invalid, 1917
Woodcut on blotting paper

Brücke-Museum, Berlin

In the Crisis, In Spite of the Crisis: Ernst Ludwig Kirchner at the Time of the First World War

Whether German artists were forced to go to war in August 1914 or enlisted, either enthusiastically like Franz Marc or reluctantly like Max Ernst; whether they served as orderlies behind the lines or as artillerists at the front; whether they were quickly able to have themselves declared "unfit for service" like George Grosz or evaded it by fleeing abroad like Hans Arp or with a hunger strike like Rudolf Schlichter; whether they deliberately sought to experience the human depths like Otto Dix or were hoping for material from reality for their art like Max Beckmann — at that moment, with the start of the war, everything changed for them and for the art of the avant-garde. Their studios stood empty, artist friends on the other side of the border now had to be thought of as enemies, and their closest colleagues often became opponents: when Heinrich Campendonk went on a hunger strike in order to escape the draft, his friend and neighbour Franz Marc suddenly scorned him ("Thank God such types are the exception!"[1]), and when Marc proclaimed his enthusiasm for the war, his Blue Rider colleagues Wassily Kandinsky and Paul Klee turned away from him. By replacing their painting smocks with uniforms and, as Marc put it, "their brushes with cannons",[2] they became no longer creative individuals working on their own but members of a hierarchical organisation responsible for destruction and killing.

So art was set aside. Even though people kept making drawings where they could, continuous, wilful creativity — and thus the further development of pictorial style, which played a consistently decisive role in Modernism — was abandoned. The art business also came to a halt: avant-garde artists' groups were involuntarily dissolved; relations only recently established with art dealers and collectors by and large ceased; the art world fell apart. As Paul Klee attested for Munich: "The international circle is scattering in every direction."[3] One of the few artists to continue to work — in the crisis, in spite of the crisis — was Ernst Ludwig Kirchner.

At first, in November 1914, Kirchner thought he might be able to work "with particular intensity, as we are now living in the midst of these great matters",[4] and shortly afterwards he voiced the expectation that anyone who served in the war "came into contact with what it is to be human" and could therefore have a better appreciation for "the expression of emotions" in art — that is to say the new art.[5] Although he may have been thinking mainly of the recognition of his own art, he shared with many other artists the hope for a cultural new beginning through Modernism, leaving behind the torpor of the outdated empire.

Kirchner enlisted, apparently so as to be able to choose his branch of service and thereby avoid the infantry. In July 1915 he was assigned to the mounted Mansfeld Field Artillery Regiment 75 in Halle. But he immediately wrote that he was finding "the considerable physical exertions" very difficult and had therefore been "partially released from duty".[6] That it was terrible being able to do "less than the meanest recruit", while in one's studio one "could create something new"[7] — another lament about the interruption of continuity. In September 1915 Kirchner was placed on leave, with the proviso that he put himself in a doctor's care, but he continued to fear being called up again. He wrote to Karl Ernst Osthaus, "I feel half dead from the mental and physical torments,"[8] and to Gustav Schiefler, "I'm no longer fit for heavy military work and plan to enter a sanatorium in a few days to heal my nerves and my lungs. I have become half mad, and physical human feelings are still foreign to me even today." To this letter from December 1915 he added a brief passage that makes clear his altered stance with regard to the war: "War takes hold of me more and more. You now see almost nothing but masks, no faces any longer, it would be a good thing and necessary if an end were to come soon."[9]

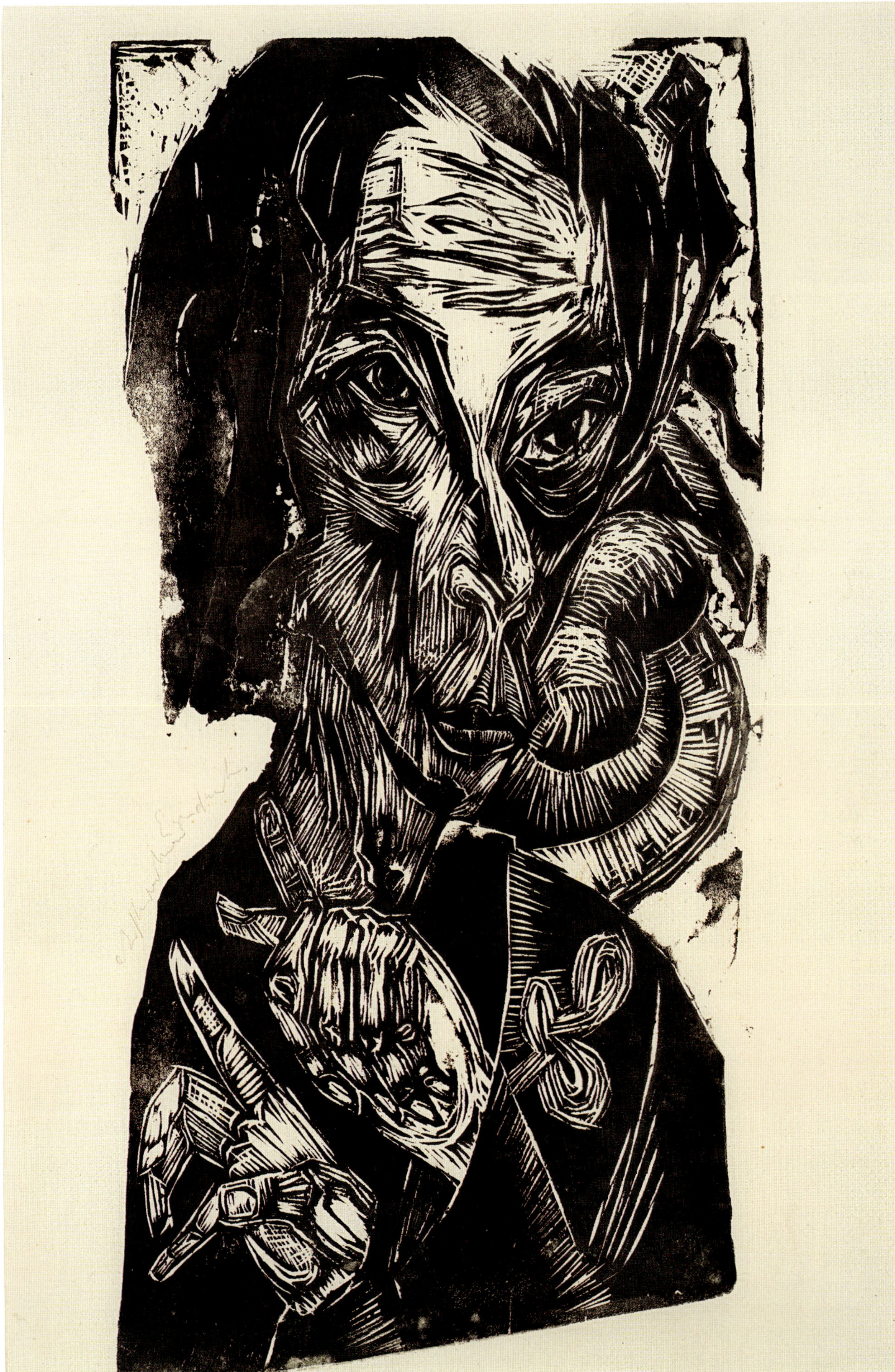

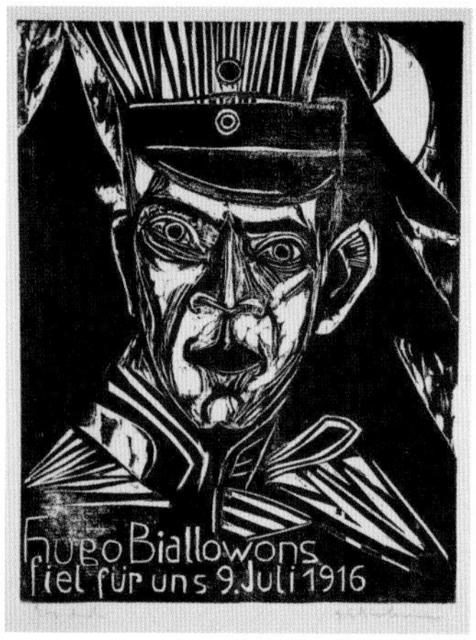

Fig. 1 Ernst Ludwig Kirchner
In Memory of Hugo Biallowons, 1916
Woodcut on blotting paper,
image: 46 × 34 cm,
sheet: 51 × 37.8 cm
(Gercken 823/II)

Städel Museum, Graphische Sammlung, Frankfurt am Main

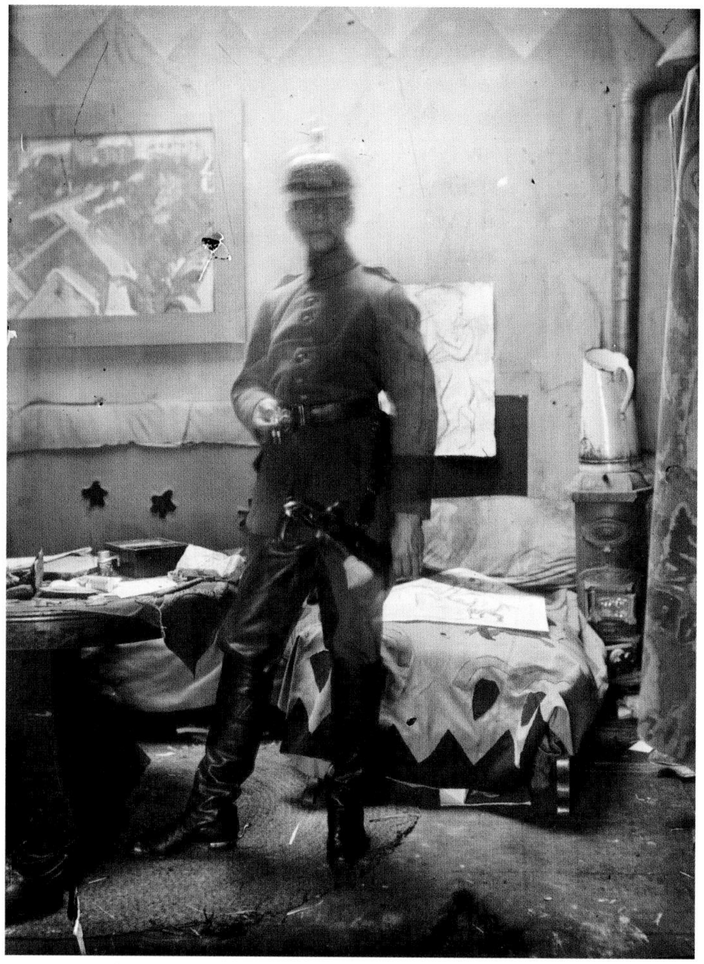

Fig. 2 / Cat. 145
Ernst Ludwig Kirchner
Self-portrait as a soldier in the live-in studio in Berlin-Friedenau, 1915
Glass negative, 18 × 13 cm

Kirchner Museum Davos, Gift of the Ernst Ludwig Kirchner Estate 1992

For Kirchner — as for almost all the other artists and intellectuals of his generation — his initial expectations of the war and first experiences of it were vastly different. Oskar Schlemmer announced the change as early as January 1915: "I'm no longer the fellow who enlisted in August. Neither physically nor, more especially, in my attitude."[10] Unlike many of his artist colleagues, Kirchner was spared an assignment at the front. But what seriously affected his constitution, never particularly strong, was apparently his experience of the hardship and coercion of military life — and then the prospect of being wounded and having to kill. To cap it all, the death of his friend Hugo Biallowons at Verdun in July 1916 was a heavy blow to him: "So everything is going hence, and the terrible war knows no end."[11] Kirchner immediately produced a commemorative woodcut for Biallowons fig. 1.

The change in attitude was general. Franz Marc, for example, originally enflamed with enthusiasm for the war, underwent a radical shift after the death of his friend August Macke on the Western Front. He began to sense the political dimensions of the war. It was no longer weapons that mattered, he now wrote, but rather economic interests: it was a mutual "shifting of the burdens of billions in taxes". It was high time to close this "most distressing chapter in European history" and put an end to the "age of armament".[12]

Kirchner now recognised the moral corruption, the "money-grubbing", the "speculation and greed" resulting from "this terrible war".[13] He constantly had "the impression of a bloody carnival" and was plagued by self-doubt and deep pessimism: "Now one is just like the cocottes I painted. Whisked away, no longer there the next time."[14] In this period his physical suffering increased. He first tried to recuperate with several visits to the Kohnstamm Sanatorium in Königstein im Taunus between December 1915 and July 1916. Then in late 1916/early 1917 he was forced to stay in Dr Edel's psychiatric clinic in Berlin, which obviously particularly upset him — he felt he had been "interned in a lunatic asylum".[15] This was followed by a stay in Davos in January 1917, and in May he moved there. From September

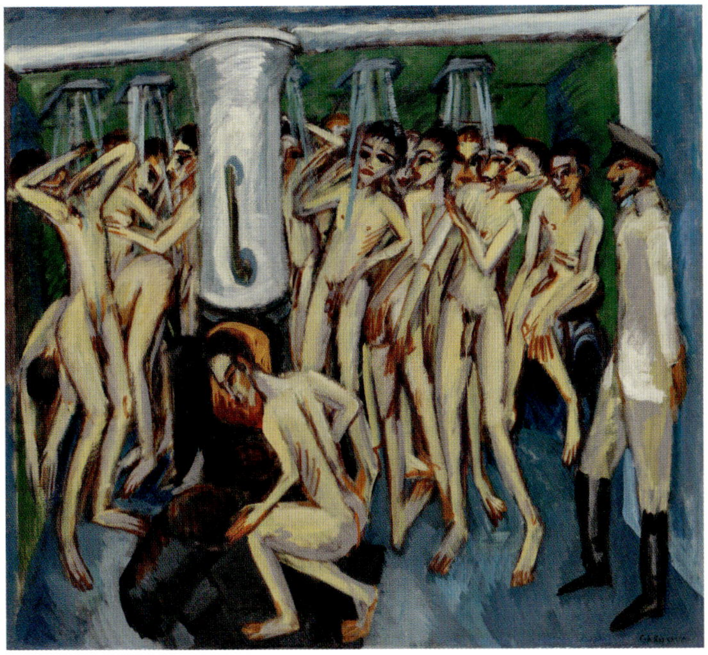

Fig. 3 Ernst Ludwig Kirchner
Artillerymen, 1915
Oil on canvas, 140 × 153 cm
(Gordon 434)

Solomon R. Guggenheim Museum, New York, by exchange, 1988

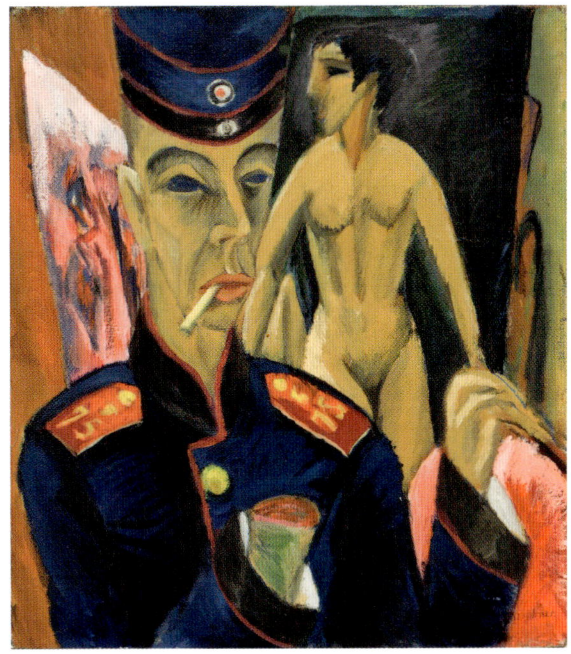

Fig. 4 Ernst Ludwig Kirchner
Self-Portrait as a Soldier, 1915
Oil on canvas, 69 × 61 cm
(Gordon 435)

Allen Memorial Art Museum, Oberlin College, Ohio, Charles F. Olnes Fund, 1950

1917 to July 1918 he took the cure at Dr Ludwig Binswanger's sanatorium in Kreuzlingen: alcohol, sleeping pills, morphine. He repeatedly complained of paralysis in his hands and legs, and wrote in October 1917, "I am utterly incapable of doing anything at all for myself because of the paralysis in my hands and feet. Yet I am seeing so much that is interesting and thousands of pictures that I could paint but cannot, and that makes me very miserable."[16]

Three Self-Portraits: A Protagonist, a Mould-Breaker, a Sufferer

One would think that in this desperately difficult situation, especially with his painting and woodcutting hand subject to paralysis, art would have had to be abandoned. But in this period Kirchner produced a great deal of work: twenty to thirty paintings a year in various genres, numerous woodcuts, including the highly important portraits, the *Schlemihl, Absalom* and *Triumph of Love* cycles and, in 1916/17, the unique series of reed-pen drawings. Only Paul Klee, serving at Bavarian military airfields and able to find drawing opportunities when not on duty, was similarly productive during this time.

There are no war motifs or even motifs evoking the war in Kirchner's work. But in 1915 he did produce a small group of paintings critical of the military, though it was not the potential for expressing his disapprobation that interested him so much as the organised group behaviour: *Hussars on Horseback; The Riders, Mounted Artillerymen, Artillerymen* fig. 3, — and *Self-Portrait as a Soldier* fig. 4. While *Artillerymen* resembles a snapshot, the *Hussars on Horseback; The Riders* p. 216 is like a scenic arrangement of colours: in the cool yellow in front of a violet mountain the hussars appear in green on black horses, and along the edge at the right, some of them elevated, slender black passers-by stop to observe them.

The *Self-Portrait as a Soldier,* however, is highly symbolic. It is necessary to see the work in its art-historical context. For in 1915 two other extraordinary and distinctive self-portraits were produced by German painters; their titles alone indicate their specific relationship to the war and in them, moreover, the prospects for art at that historic moment

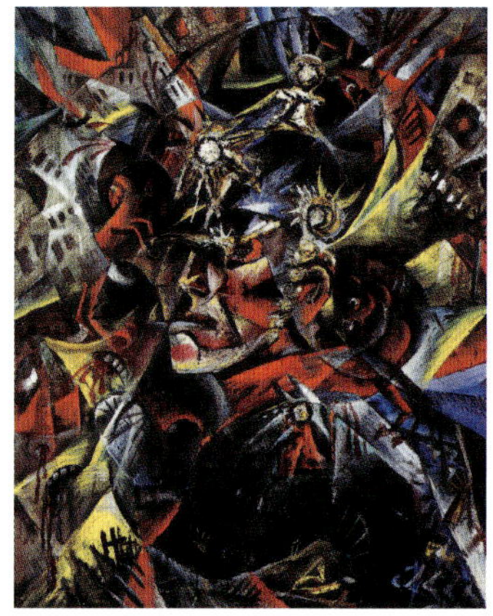

Fig. 5 Otto Dix
Self-Portrait as Mars, 1915
Oil on canvas, 81 × 66 cm

Städtische Sammlungen Freital

are articulated: Otto Dix's *Self-Portrait as Mars* fig. 5 and Max Beckmann's *Self-Portrait as a Medical Orderly* fig. 6 — to sit alongside Kirchner's *Self-Portrait as a Soldier.*

Dix produced a futuristic picture in the centre of which he poses as the god of war, dressed in uniform and wearing on his powerful head a helmet adorned with shiny cockades. Whether he was actually playing such a role or only trying it on — as the styles and poses of his very different self-portraits from this time attest — in this picture, painted at the time he was undergoing military training, he nevertheless presents himself as a man willing to go into battle. Interlocked in a futuristic vision are collapsing buildings, barricades, spotlights and, above all, red horses gushing blood. This emphatic, wholly unprecedented picture is expressive of fascination and horror. Dix had enlisted and first served with the field artillery in Dresden and Bautzen, before being shifted to the Western Front in September 1915. He fought for a time in Belarus as well and, until the end of the war, was deployed in northern France and Flanders as a machine-gun platoon leader.

Dix took part in the war willingly, not as a patriot or enemy of France but as an artist in search of liminality, terror and proximity to death, wishing to collect experiences outside the studio in a reality foreign to him, so as to then be able to create vivid art from life's extremes. He later professed that "the war was an abominable business, but nevertheless something tremendous. I wasn't about to miss it for anything! You have to have seen people in this unleashed state if you want to know something about them. Perhaps you have to have directly shared in it."[17] He had had to experience himself "all the pain and suffering", the "stifling filth", in order to be able to depict it.[18]

In this picture the artist appears as a warrior capable of attack in the midst of chaos and destruction, but here he is also an artist confronting the tension between inner battle readiness and external ruin by aggressively shattering the old way of making pictures. The external order is crumbling, but the artist is able to develop a new painterly order out of its debris; he is profiting artistically from destruction and disorientation.

In his *Self-Portrait as a Medical Orderly* fig. 6 Max Beckmann depicts himself against an indistinct background in his uniform but without any other attributes; everything external has been stripped away. He gazes sceptically and expectantly into the mirror, and thus directly at the viewer, holding a brush or crayon in his hand. When Beckmann painted the picture in Strasbourg, he had been relieved from the front following a collapse, but not released from military service. He had volunteered as an orderly and been sent to the Eastern Front, before being deployed in Flanders. In Strasbourg he began painting again, having abandoned it at the beginning of the war. The uniform in place of a painting smock assures us that the consequences of war are still prevalent. The painter is isolated, assuming a somewhat helpless pose, with a penetrating, searching, openly sceptical gaze, unennobled by any attitude — this is naked self-analysis. It is uncertain what he might be creating on his canvas or paper; everything remains uncertain for him at this moment. But it is possible to see the complete stylistic break within his oeuvre. Before the war Beckmann had chosen to show off with pictures of current events in the manner of the Secession; the extreme simplicity of this work signals a new beginning for him as a painter. In 1919 he admitted, "It's truly cheerless in its colours. I agonised over it a lot. There you see for the first time what I had, in the meantime, experienced in the war. From the line around the forehead and nose you can clearly see, I feel, how the later strict, solid form emerges."[19] With this he created a foundation for his development of an idiosyncratic pictorial imagery in the 1920s.

In his *Mars* picture Dix placed himself in the middle of a turbulent, deadly experience that he wished to expose himself to and yet defy. Beckmann had such experience behind him. His orderly's uniform shows that he was living with the consequences, yet he did not depict himself in his military function but rather as a painter, looking to the future despite all the uncertainty, and starting to be creative again.

Kirchner's setting in his *Self-Portrait as a Soldier* fig. 4 is his studio. He depicts himself wearing the uniform of his regiment, as indicated by the epaulettes with the number "75", and with a narrow, mask-like head. To the right stands one of his models, and on the left we see part of a canvas with wild streaks of colour. His left hand, strangely cramped and twisted, clutches the back of a chair and his right arm pokes out of his uniform sleeve as a red stump. The self-portrait could hardly be surpassed in its directness and vividness. Lucius Grisebach has written that the work is the "most gripping testament to the panicked existential angst at the time that led the artist to mental and physical collapse".[20] The arm stump is not real, only symbolic. His physical mutilation serves as a conspicuous indictment of the glaring limitations imposed by the military and the war. Since it is his right hand, the one he paints and carves his woodcuts with, the mutilation is simultaneously a plea for sympathy now that his creative powers are blocked. The picture is not simply a rendering of himself in wartime but an illustration of the destructive consequences of political events for Kirchner the artist.

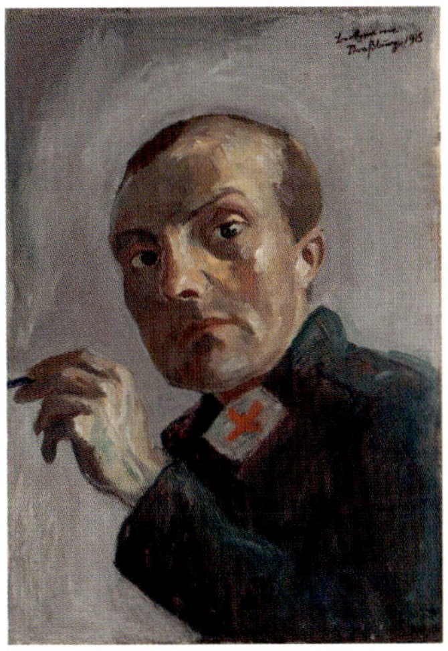

Fig. 6 Max Beckmann
Self-Portrait as a Medical Orderly, 1915
Oil on canvas, 55.5 × 38.5 cm

Kunst- und Museumsverein Wuppertal

The attitude of the head with cigarette and the pose of the right hand, as well as the pictorial quote at the left edge, recall a *Self-Portrait* p. 132 painted two years before. This was still before the outbreak of war and Kirchner was thirty-three years old — he had left Dresden and had been living in Berlin for two years. There he depicted himself as a painter, prominently brandishing in his right hand the paint brushes it is no longer possible for him to use in the self-portrait with the severed hand. Even here the dark-rimmed eyes, the greenish cheeks and the emaciated body cause the painter to appear as a sufferer with his own instruments of torture.

In the year he painted the soldier self-portrait Kirchner wrote, "I'm still haunted by a fear of uniforms to this day."[21] Even so, for the picture he once again donned the detested costume that here, unlike in Beckmann, functions as a working smock. The uniform makes it perfectly clear that the dominant impression produced by the self-portrait is one of suffering.

Three programmatic self-portraits with different approaches and contents, all from a single year during the war in the autumn of which Dix took part in the battle in the Champagne region near Reims and was promoted to sergeant, Beckmann collapsed and was transferred to peaceful Strasbourg, and Kirchner broke down and from then on increasingly tortured himself with physical and psychic ailments in sanatoriums. In his self-portrait Dix pictured himself amid explosive, seemingly inescapable turmoil; Beckmann, though internally burdened, with great concentration and the simplest of means began a radically new start; and Kirchner exhibited his own agony for all to see.

"I am struggling to express that in art as well" — Autobiographical Elements in the *Schlemihl* Cycle

Beginning in late 1915, there are passages in Kirchner's letters that are somewhat surprising, for in his difficult personal situation they suddenly open up an artistic perspective. In December 1915, for example, he wrote that he was happy to have been discharged, that he had "begun to depict what I have recently seen".[22] Then in November 1916 he explained that he was trying, despite all his despondency, to bring "order" to his thoughts and "to create out of the confusion a picture of the time" — adding the self-confident note, "which is my job, after all". Perhaps he would still manage to "gain mastery over things. Begin anew."[23] And again in March 1917: "I'm internally shattered and beset from all sides, but I am struggling to express that in art as well."[24]

It sounds as if he wanted not only to continue making art despite the internal and external crises but also, more importantly, to exploit them for his art and prevail in art and through art, and to do so with firm resolution, with the highest demands on himself: to begin anew, to express the disintegration in art, to create out of the confusion a picture of the time, which also meant capturing the confusion in an adequate likeness and form.

Once again expressing his fear of being called up, in early December 1915 Kirchner related that he was printing a *Schlemihl* cycle, and a few days later he wrote that it was finished.[25] This was a series of six colour woodcuts and a title page pp. 220–225 after Adelbert von Chamisso's *Peter Schlemihl's Wondrous Story,* written in 1813, the year of liberation

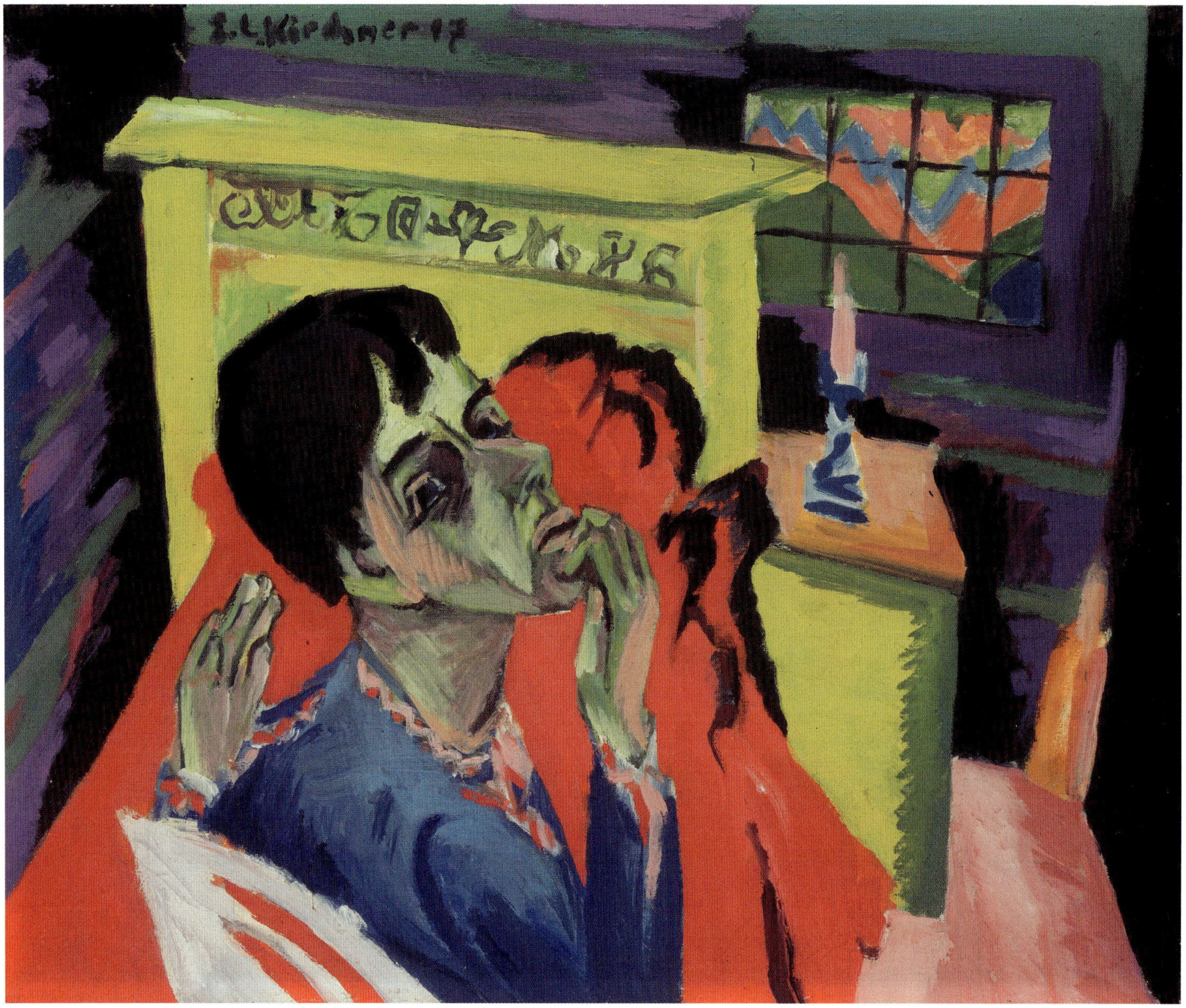

from French occupation. It was the story of a man who sold his shadow to the Devil for money. As Günther Gercken has written, "Kirchner recognised in Chamisso's literary reproach the ideal framework in which to depict his own fate as an artist. As an artist he is branded, and wears his curse the way Schlemihl wears his want of a shadow."[26]

In a highly illuminating commentary on the cycle in a letter to Gustav Schiefler from 1919, Kirchner himself emphasised the autobiographical references. The Schlemihl story was "actually the life story of a man with a persecution complex". By selling his shadow and with it his selfhood, Schlemihl lost his psychic balance. Of sheet 5, *Schlemihl's Encounter with the Little Grey Man on the Country Road* p.224, he wrote, "Schlemihl's military uniform derives from the fact that during this time I found myself in a similar psychic state." The sale of his shadow to the little grey man was his own "enlistment". And of sheet 6, *Schlemihl's Encounter with the Shadow* p.225, "He tries to place his feet in the shadow's footprints, under the illusion that he could thereby recover his selfhood. Analogous to the thought processes of a man discharged from the military."[27]

Reflecting on his voluntary enlistment in the army, his loss of identity there and subsequent inability to get back on his feet, Kirchner created in the *Schlemihl* pictures an ambiguous narrative in the fascinating form of experimental colour woodcuts. To achieve

Fig. 7 Ernst Ludwig Kirchner
Self-Portrait as an Invalid,
1918/1930
Oil on canvas, mounted on plywood, 59 × 69.5 cm (Gordon 496)

Bayerische Staatsgemäldesammlungen, Munich, Pinakothek der Moderne

this, he updated the romantic parable of Chamisso's fairy tale from the war-torn year of 1813 and directly referred to his own situation during the First World War. The cycle deals with the persecuted artist of Modernism as well as the personal fate of the artist Kirchner, who loses his orientation owing to the menacing proximity of war (in contrast to Dix, who feels himself to be in the thick of it). At the same time, as Günther Gercken has noted, the series marks a decisive stylistic turning point in Kirchner's work: "It is the summation and end point of ten years of ecstatic Expressionist work and looks ahead to the magnificent woodcut portraits and landscapes of his first Swiss years, the beginning of his second creative period."[28] Kirchner had hoped to begin anew, to express his inner conflict in art, to create out of the confusion a picture of the time. The *Schlemihl* cycle is one of the impressive results of this. It seems significant that he was unable to realise the planned seventh sheet: "It was meant to present the denouement, the reconciliation with his psychological shortcoming. [...] As yet I've not been able to find the composition of this sheet."[29] It was the disruption, his conflictedness, that actually led him to express it in art. The notion of salvation and an attendant positive resolution somehow failed to challenge him to the same degree. The reed-pen drawings that he began to create at this same time can also be seen as a bold new beginning, an attempt to render the chaos of the time in pictorial form in strong, uninhibited, radical networks of lines and at the same time present a frank picture of his own ruined health. *Self-Portrait in Morphine Rush* p. 237 from 1917 is a grandiose example.

"To create out of the confusion a picture of the time"

In 1917 Kirchner moved to Davos, and a year later he moved into the house "In den Lärchen" in Davos Frauenkirch. His *Self-Portrait as an Invalid* fig. 7,[30] painted in October and November 1918, documents his stay in this cottage. It illustrates the artist's personal troubles. He shows himself lying in bed, wearing a blue peasant's smock, with bright-red bedclothes in a greenish-yellow peasant's bed; the complementary colour contrasts heighten the work's expressiveness. He seems physically deteriorated, as if he has raised his head disorientedly in a sudden movement, looking up as though being observed from above. His hands are cramped, elongated and anatomically reversed—an allusion to the paralysis of his feet and hands and his inability to control them.

Instead of one of his works on the wall, we see a mullioned window providing a view out over richly coloured mountains: "I'm utterly listless and a bundle of nerves. [...] From my bed I see a few mountains, and sometimes I try painting them, but nothing much comes of it, so I dream on in a semi-coma, exhausted but unable to sleep, and unable to move."[31] And—in the same year, 1917: "I sometimes give up any hope of recovery. It is terrible when you want to work and cannot."[32] The view from the window takes the place of the picture that can't be painted at the moment because of his physical limitations—it represents the picture he longs for. Thus a direct relationship is created between suffering and painting: art is created out of suffering, but it also leaves the painter emaciated and exhausted, a sacrifice to his art. Both themes have here been combined. "If one could only wholly transform the suffering into creativeness," Kirchner wrote in May 1918, "one would have amazing new possibilities; I want to try it as best I can."[33] According to Lucius Grisebach, this picture, produced in October and November 1918, stands "precisely on the threshold between the tense period of existential wartime anxiety and the new reassurance of his life in Davos".[34] It is still marked by personal disruptions, yet the setting promises reassurance and normalcy, now no longer in the metropolis or in the war—Kirchner had fled from both—but in the mountains he had turned to for healing.

According to his letters, in Switzerland he no longer felt the war as a threat, but his health issues persisted: "The eternal struggle with hands and legs often mightily tests my patience,"[35] and in addition he "frequently suffered depressions owing to his physical condition".[36] Otherwise, regardless of all his internal and external problems, there is much talk of business. Kirchner was still able to present one-man shows in 1916 at the

Kunsthandlung Ludwig Schames in Frankfurt am Main, in 1917 at the Kunstverein Jena and in 1918 at the Kunsthaus Zürich. In December 1918, once the war had ended, he was nevertheless relieved that "the external pressure of the war was over", and he could sense a "new beginning in the world".[37]

Though it can be seen that in the years 1915/16 both Kirchner and Beckmann made a new beginning in their art, one has to wonder whether it was the war that played a guiding or even initiating role in this. It was Paul Klee who asked this question as early as 1917, having recently developed a colourful and poetic new pictorial world: "Would my work have soared so quickly under normal circumstances as it did in the years 1916/17?" He answered himself: "A passionate need for transfiguration doubtless has to do with the major change in the way we live"[38] — i.e. to his way of thinking the concentration and wealth of invention at this time were essentially triggered by the different experience of reality, namely the effect of the war and its impact on his powers of imagination (Klee, too, was spared service at the front). Christine Hopfengart has written that what Klee created was the "product of an equally contradictory and powerful perception of war".[39]

The same can be said of Ernst Ludwig Kirchner. Regardless of all his difficulties, it was precisely during the First World War that he managed to realise his great ambition: to express the internal and external disruption in art, and "to create out of the confusion a picture of the time" — in the crisis, in spite of the crisis.

1 Franz Marc to Albert Bloch, letter from 22 November 1914, in *Albert Bloch: Ein amerikanischer Blauer Reiter,* exh. cat. Städtische Galerie im Lenbachhaus (Munich, 1997), p. 166.

2 Franz Marc to Bernhard Koehler, letter from August 1914, Nuremberg, Germanisches Nationalmuseum, Deutsches Kunstarchiv, Franz Marc Estate (copy); see Brigitte Roßbeck, *Franz Marc: Die Träume und das Leben; Biographie* (Munich, 2015), p. 242.

3 Paul Klee to "E. S.", letter from 30 September 1914, in *Der frühe Klee,* exh. cat. Staatliche Kunsthalle Baden-Baden (Baden-Baden, 1964), unpaginated.

4 Ernst Ludwig Kirchner to Eugen Diederichs, letter from 1 November 1914, in Hans Delfs (ed.), *Ernst Ludwig Kirchner: Der gesamte Briefwechsel,* vol. 1, *Briefe von 1901 bis 1923* (Zurich, 2010), p. 96.

5 Ernst Ludwig Kirchner to Gustav Schiefler, letter from 27 January 1915, in Wolfgang Henze et al. (eds.), *Ernst Ludwig Kirchner/Gustav Schiefler: Briefwechsel 1910–1935/1938* (Stuttgart/Zurich, 1991), p. 71, no. 47.

6 Ernst Ludwig Kirchner to Karl Ernst Osthaus, letter from 25 July 1915, in Delfs, *Briefwechsel* (see n. 4), p. 106.

7 Ernst Ludwig Kirchner an Karl Ernst Osthaus, letter from 25 October 1915, in Delfs, *Briefwechsel* (see n. 4), pp. 115–116.

8 Ernst Ludwig Kirchner an Karl Ernst Osthaus, letter from 7 December 1915, in Delfs, *Briefwechsel* (see n. 4), p. 117.

9 Ernst Ludwig Kirchner to Gustav Schiefler, letter from 9 December 1915, in Henze et al., *Kirchner/Schiefler* (see n. 5), p. 72 (no. 49).

10 Oskar Schlemmer to Otto Meyer, letter from 5 January 1915, in Tut Schlemmer (ed.), *Oskar Schlemmer: Briefe und Tagebücher* (Stuttgart, 1977), p. 17.

11 Ernst Ludwig Kirchner to Gustav Schiefler, letter from 17 August 1916, in Henze et al., *Kirchner/Schiefler* (see n. 5), pp. 79–80, no. 60.

12 Franz Marc to Bernhard Koehler, letter from 9 January 1916, in *Franz Marc,* exh. cat. Städtische Galerie im Lenbachhaus (Munich, 1963), unpaginated.

13 Ernst Ludwig Kirchner to Gustav Schiefler, letter from 19 October 1916, in Henze et al., *Kirchner/Schiefler* (see n. 5), pp. 82–83, no. 64.

14 Ernst Ludwig Kirchner to Gustav Schiefler, letter from 12 November 1916, in Henze et al., *Kirchner/Schiefler* (see n. 5), pp. 83–84, no. 65.

15 Ernst Ludwig Kirchner to Gustav Schiefler, letter from March 1917, in Henze et al., *Kirchner/Schiefler* (see n. 5), p. 87, no. 70.

16 Ernst Ludwig Kirchner to Carl Hagemann, letter from 14 October 1917, in Hans Delfs, Mario-Andreas von Lüttichau and Roland Scotti (eds.), *Kirchner, Schmidt-Rottluff, Nolde, Nay ...: Briefe an den Sammler und Mäzen Carl Hagemann, 1906–1940* (Ostfildern-Ruit, 2004), p. 88.

17 Otto Dix in conversation with Hans Kinkel 1961, in Diether Schmidt, *Otto Dix im Selbstbildnis* (East Berlin, 1978, p. 234.

18 *Otto Dix spricht über Kunst, Religion, Krieg,* recording, St. Gallen 1963; also *Otto Dix: Ich folge lieber meinem Dämon: Originaltonaufnahmen,* ed. Robert Eikmeyer and Thomas Knoefel (Nuremberg, 2009).

19 Max Beckmann in conversation with Reinhard Piper, 1919; for the citation in German, see *Max Beckmann: Retrospektive,* ed. Carla Schulz-Hoffmann and Judith Weiss, exh. cat. Haus der Kunst (Munich, 1984), p. 200.

20 Lucius Grisebach, *Ernst Ludwig Kirchner 1880–1938* (Cologne, 1995), p. 129.

21 Ernst Ludwig Kirchner to Gustav Schiefler, letter from 15 December 1915, in Henze et al., *Kirchner/Schiefler* (see n. 5), p. 73, no. 50.

22 Ibid.

23 Ernst Ludwig Kirchner to Gustav Schiefler, letter from 12 November 1916, in Henze et al., *Kirchner/Schiefler* (see n. 5), pp. 83–84, no. 65.

24 Ernst Ludwig Kirchner to Gustav Schiefler, letter probably from March 1917, in Henze et al., *Kirchner/Schiefler* (see n. 5), p. 86, no. 69.

25 Ernst Ludwig Kirchner to Carl Hagemann, letter from 3 December 1915, in Delfs et al., *Kirchner, Schmidt-Rottluff, Nolde, Nay* (see n. 16), p. 45; Ernst Ludwig Kirchner to Gustav Schiefler, letter from 9 December 1915, in Henze et al., *Kirchner/Schiefler* (see n. 5), p. 72, no. 49.

26 Günther Gercken, "Bilder zu Chamissos Peter Schlemihl", in *E. L. Kirchner: Zeichnungen und Druckgraphik 1905–1936,* exh. cat. Kunstverein in Hamburg, Hamburg (Hamburg, 1978), p. 108.

27 Ernst Ludwig Kirchner to Gustav Schiefler, letter from 28 July 1919, in Henze et al., *Kirchner/Schiefler* (see n. 5), pp. 136–137.

28 Gercken, "Bilder" (see n. 26).

29 Kirchner to Schiefler, letter from 28 July 1919 (see n. 27).

30 The painting belongs to the Bayerische Staatsgemäldesammlungen, Munich, Pinakothek der Moderne. Large portions of the picture were later painted over. See Carla Schulz-Hoffmann, "Inszenierte Wirklichkeit: Ernst Ludwig Kirchners Selbstbildnis als Kranker", *arsprototo: Das Magazin der Kulturstiftung der Länder* 1 (2005), pp. 34–36. See also the x-ray photo in *Farbenmensch Kirchner,* ed. Oliver Kase and Heide Skowranek, exh. cat. Pinakothek der Moderne, Munich (Berlin, 2014), p. 122.

31 Ernst Ludwig Kirchner to Gustav Schiefler, letter from 14 July 1917, in Henze et al., *Kirchner/Schiefler* (see n. 5), p. 92, no. 76.

32 Ernst Ludwig Kirchner to Gustav Schiefler, letter from 16 November 1917, in Henze et al., *Kirchner/Schiefler* (see n. 5), p. 94, no. 79.

33 Ernst Ludwig Kirchner to Carl Hagemann, letter from 25 May 1918, in Delfs et al., *Kirchner, Schmidt-Rottluff, Nolde, Nay* (see n. 16), p. 103.

34 Grisebach, *Kirchner* (see n. 20), p. 150.

35 Ernst Ludwig Kirchner to Eberhard Grisebach, letter from 14 May 1918, in Delfs, *Briefwechsel* (see n. 4), p. 286.

36 Ernst Ludwig Kirchner to Eberhard Grisebach, letter from 18 May 1918, in Delfs, *Briefwechsel* (see n. 4), p. 287.

37 Ernst Ludwig Kirchner to Helene Spengler, letter from circa December 1918, in Delfs, *Briefwechsel* (see n. 4), p. 307.

38 Paul Klee, "Tagebuch IV, Gersthofen, 9 September 1917 (1082)", in Paul-Klee-Stiftung (ed.) *Paul Klee: Tagebücher 1898–1918* (Stuttgart/Teufen, 1988), p. 444.

39 Christine Hopfengart, "Creative Enrichment: Paul Klee in the First World War", in *1914: The Avant-Gardes at War,* exh. cat. Bundeskunsthalle, Bonn (Cologne, 2013), p. 281.

Ernst Ludwig Kirchner's Sketches and Woodcuts Based on the Apocalypse

It is unsurprising that during his stay at a sanatorium in Kreuzlingen in 1917/18 Ernst Ludwig Kirchner thought to illustrate the Apocalypse of Saint John[1] with a series of prints, for at the time he felt that his own end was near. In conceiving this plan, he surely had in mind the woodcuts based on the Apocalypse by Albrecht Dürer, whom he greatly revered.[2] Competing with that precursor must have represented a particular challenge for him — and that is precisely what may have stimulated him to set against the historical version a contemporary rendering of the same material.

In his "Preface to the Revelation of Saint John" from 1530, Martin Luther, who did not greatly admire the Apocalypse, if only because of its prophetic pretensions and cryptic threats, wrote, "Many have indeed tried to make something of it but have, to this day, failed to produce anything certain; some have concocted a great many inapt things born of their own imaginations."[3] Today, thanks to historical-critical studies we have a more rational idea of this text, supposedly written around the year AD 90, during the reign of the Roman emperor Domitian. The text is a well-written epistle to seven Christian congregations in Asia Minor, in which they are admonished to endure the horrors of the struggle with Satan and the incipient persecution of Christians in anticipation of Christ's return and the establishment of the Kingdom of God, symbolised as the "New Jerusalem". The Apocalypse is a call to arms against evil and the world's depravity at the time, against the Romans and against false prophets. At the same time, it expresses hope in the revelation of the true world and, with the salvation of the just, provides comfort and courage to the persecuted and oppressed. The expectation of the end of time and beginning of a new era with Christ's return can be understood in the light of the eschatological thinking of Early Christianity. The critical interpretation of that time did not, however, concern itself with the magnificent visionary images in which John attempted to make believable the unbelievable aspects of his prophecies. In their mythical and archetypal nature they transcend time and express the fears and hopes of mankind. As images from our collective human memory, they can be summoned up and reinterpreted at any time. Again and again catastrophic contemporary events have been perceived as the fulfilment of John's prophecies. For example, the colophon to Max Beckmann's illustrated *Apocalypse* begins with the following sentence: "This printing was produced in the fourth year of the Second World War, when visions of the apocalyptic seer became frightening reality."[4] In today's usage the term "apocalypse" generally means simply destruction, chaos and ruin, without any association with the expectation of salvation, as in Ludwig Meidner's *Apocalyptic Landscapes* from 1912/13, which correspond more with the visions of Jakob van Hoddis and Georg Heym than with the message proclaimed by Saint John. This modern, demythologised view accords with Kirchner's stance as well; he did not devote an illustration to Apocalypse's prospect of the imminent start of a new era with the renewal of heaven and earth — "Behold, I make all things new" (Apoc. 21:5). Kirchner and Beckmann interpreted the apocalyptic visions from an enlightened viewpoint, illustrating them with their own imagery coloured by their personal experience of internal or external distress.

Kirchner apparently lacked more suitable drawing materials, for he executed his designs for his *Apocalypse* in pencil or pen and ink over pencil on an unusual material, the cardboard from cigarette packets, limited in format to roughly 6 × 8 cm. The drawings are quick sketches, yet despite their apparent swiftness and small size the assurance of these compositions is astonishing. With the addition of watercolour the tiny depictions become more legible, reflecting the biblical text in many details. This textual precision indicates how carefully Kirchner had read the Apocalypse. He later pasted the twelve compositions into an album that came into the possession of the Davos physician Dr Frédéric Bauer, an important collector of his works. In the Nuremberg catalogue of the Dr F. Bauer Collection the *Album with 12 Designs for an Apocalypse* is listed under "Omnibus Volumes no. 260".[5] When that collection was sold by the Stuttgart Kunstkabinett, the album must have been acquired by Wilhelm F. Arntz, as it found its way with his archive into the Getty Research Institute in Los Angeles in 1985.[6]

At the front of the album Kirchner placed a handwritten title page that reads as follows: "These designs for the Apocalypse are from the year 1917 E L Kirchner." Kirchner's entry is striking on account of the date, 1917, and the fact that he refers to his watercoloured sketches as designs. This early date was questioned by Wolfram Gabler, who was the first to discuss the series in detail and who illustrated it in the original copy of his dissertation. He instead put forward 1918 as the year the series had been produced.[7] But the cigarette packets he used as humble drawing material and the swiftness of the sketches would suggest the beginning of his stay at the Bellevue sanatorium in Kreuzlingen, to which Kirchner was admitted on 15 September 1917. This assumption is also supported by the fact that Hans Mardersteig, at that time working for the Kurt Wolff publishing house, visited the artist in Kreuzlingen in November 1917[8] and in a note, probably for Kurt Wolff, on Kirchner's letter from 9 January 1918 mentions the *Apocalypse* as a graphic portfolio project: "And was he not thinking of the Apocalypse? I would be in favour of it—and then the splendid self-portrait I wrote about as an introductory sheet."[9] Accordingly, Mardersteig, who had probably seen the 1917 woodcut *Head of the Invalid—Self-Portrait as an Invalid* p. 65 during his visit, must have known already in 1917 that Kirchner had planned a self-portrait as the first print in the series p. 79. One can thus assume that the miniature watercoloured sketches were made in preparation for a woodcut sequence.

A short time later, still in Kreuzlingen, Kirchner read in the Old Testament and on 6 January 1918 wrote in a letter to Irene Eucken, "It is like a lovely, powerful fairy tale."[10] During his reading he must have come across the story of Absalom (2 Sam. 13–19), onto which he could project his own personal fate.[11] Apparently he was more concerned with the depiction of his own experience in the guise of a historical text, as we see from the three major cycles *Schlemihl, Triumph of Love* and *Absalom,*[12] than in illustrating the Apocalypse. To fulfil the contract for a portfolio with ten lithographs concluded with the Kurt Wolff publishing house on 23 April 1917,[13] he now offered an "Absalom series in woodcuts".[14] However, the contract with Kurt Wolff was cancelled in 1919.[15] Kirchner carved the *Absalom* series on the Stafelalp in the summer of 1918 but did not print it as an edition, only in a few separate prints.[16]

Around the end of 1918 or the beginning of 1919—i.e. after he had produced the two woodcut cycles *Triumph of Love* and *Absalom*—he translated two of the *Apocalypse* compositions into woodcuts figs. 3, 8.[17] As we learn from a letter to Marie-Luise Binswanger-Schlegel, Kirchner had not yet abandoned his plan for a woodcut portfolio on the Apocalypse in February 1919: "When I have finally finished the cuts for the Apocalypse, I will send you the portfolio."[18] Yet later he appears to have lost interest in continuing the work, possibly because as his health improved, his creative powers and vitality had returned and impressions from nature and alpine life suppressed his apocalyptic mood and shifted the depiction of his immediate experiences into the foreground.

Even though only two woodcuts for the *Apocalypse* were realised, as examples they tell us a great deal about the whole project. From them, one can see that even in the small sketches Kirchner established the possibility of transforming them into woodcuts. The pictorial idea is captured in the shorthand of the sketch. The great similarity between the woodcut and the sketch is astonishing, not only in composition but also in the attention to all the details. Inspired by his reading of the Apocalypse, Kirchner had obviously already envisioned the final form of the illustrations, so that the sketches were no mere experiments but records of internalised images. The two woodcuts are moreover indicative of the development of Kirchner's woodcut technique in the early Swiss years. In Kreuzlingen, in 1917/18, he had clearly refined his woodcut style. The two *Apocalypse* woodcuts are highly detailed and densely composed, and have left the Brücke style far behind. For that reason it is understandable that by this time Kirchner objected to still being described as an Expressionist.

One assumes that Kirchner himself collected the twelve *Apocalypse* watercolours into an album in the same way that he assembled selected sheets from his sketchbooks in albums so as to provide an overview of his draughtsmanship. Well-known examples are the album in the Kupferstichkabinett of the Staatliche Museen zu Berlin, published by Anita Beloubek-Hammer,[19] and the sketchbook in the Museum Folkwang that Paul Vogt published in book form.[20] Kirchner's handwriting provides a clue to the date of his creation of the *Apocalypse* album. Because of a partial paralysis in his hands, in Kreuzlingen he was unable to write clearly. In a letter to Helene Spengler from 21 October 1917 Erna Kirchner wrote of a complete paralysis of his hands and feet that worried her greatly.[21] As late as December 1918 Kirchner was dictating all his letters.[22] The perfectly legible but still shaky handwriting of the album's inscription suggests that it dates from sometime around 1920/21. It is highly unlikely that Kirchner created it specifically for Dr Bauer, its later owner, for it was at precisely this time (late 1920) that he first became acquainted with him. His correspondence with Dr Bauer began in June 1923 and is written in a much more fluid hand. Presumably Kirchner still had the album in 1936, when he dealt with designs from the Apocalypse for the painting of the church in Frauenkirch. The etching *From the Apocalypse* (1936) fig.6, which is similar in motif and composition to the tenth sketch p.88 also belongs in this context. Since the album is never mentioned in the correspondence between Kirchner and Dr Bauer, it is perfectly conceivable that the collector only acquired it from Erna Kirchner after the artist's death.

It is worth noting that the designs in the album are not arranged in the sequence of the text of the Apocalypse. Kirchner isolated the watercolours as single compositions without consideration for a narrative context. Either he no longer recalled the sequence of the text, years after creating the sketches, or, more probably, he considered them not so much illustrations as individual pictorial inventions and pasted them into the album in accordance with pictorial considerations. From the beginning he apparently did not intend to reproduce the narrative sequence but simply selected for his project the most effective motifs. Even so, as in the *Schlemihl* woodcuts, there was no thought of inserting the *Apocalypse* woodcuts into the text, and for the planned unbound portfolio the order of the individual woodcuts would have been arbitrary. Nevertheless, in the album it is possible to identify three pairs of pictures that are associated either thematically or pictorially: sketches 2 and 3 ("The Glory of God"), 6 and 7 ("The Seven Angels") and 9 and 10 ("The Woman of the Apocalypse"). The watercolours in the album are untitled and not related to the respective textual passages. Here they are identified with descriptive titles. Their numbering follows the sequence in the album.

Because of its wealth of graphic textual images, the Apocalypse of Saint John has always inspired artists to render them in pictures. The most famous are the fifteen full-page woodcuts by Albrecht Dürer published in 1498 under the title *The Secret Revelation of John.* In its first edition the Dürer series aroused great interest, for it presented a new, epoch-making woodcut style and demonstrated the artist's stupendous mastery. In Kirchner's sketches Waltraud Neuerburg sees certain echoes of Albrecht Dürer and Lucas Cranach the Elder but maintains that the cycle was produced independently based on his own reading of the text.[23] What were these echoes? It is difficult to find similarities in either the conception of the text or the picture compositions. But the considerable agreement with the Dürer woodcuts in the choice of motifs is striking. It can hardly be coincidental that seven of the watercolours illustrate the same passages, especially since this number is even larger if one takes into account the fact that Kirchner twice splits the complex "figures" of a Dürer woodcut into two sketches. The similarity could perhaps be explained by the fact that Dürer, who likewise based his work on precursors—especially the Cologne Bible from the period around 1478—selected for his work passages that could not be bypassed in new versions of images owing to their considerable significance.

Yet the Apocalypse is so rich in its pictorial descriptions that more illustrations—and different ones—would have been possible, as is shown by Max Beckmann's *Apocalypse*, produced under the most difficult conditions during his exile in Holland in 1941/42. It is illustrated with twenty-seven chalk lithographs, ten of them vignettes,[24] and even there such familiar motifs as *The Four Horsemen of the Apocalypse* and *The Great Whore Babylon* are included.[25]

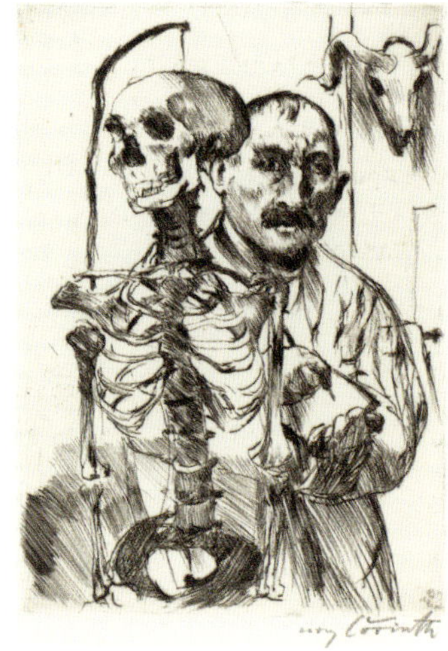

Fig. 1 Lovis Corinth
The Artist and Death II, 1916
Drypoint in black on wove paper, image: 12.1 × 9 cm, sheet: 25.5 × 15.9 cm

National Gallery of Art, Washington, gift of the Marcy Family in memory of Sigbert H. Marcy

Self-Portrait with Death

The first of the album's sketches is a watercolour, *Self-Portrait with Death,* and one has to ask oneself how it relates to the subsequent illustrations. There are two different but obvious explanations for beginning in this way. In their writings the prophets John and Ezekiel and Daniel before him profess to being the authors and recipients of visions. "I John, your brother and your partner in tribulation, and in the kingdom, and patience in Christ Jesus, was in the island, which is called Patmos, for the word of God, and for the testimony of Jesus" (Apoc. 1:9). Kirchner likewise introduces himself as the artist of the watercolours that follow, while his self-portrait marked by illness indicates his existential plight at the time the subsequent sketches were made. With the initial *Self-Portrait* Kirchner virtually assumes the role of John: he himself is the visionary of the sketched images. In this way he describes the visions directly, without revealing that it was actually John who received them and that it was only from his report that the artist obtained his own ideas for the illustrations. As a second explanation, one could argue that he was inspired by Dürer, who, as a prologue to his *Apocalypse* woodcuts, placed a portrait of John the Evangelist, long erroneously considered the author of the Apocalypse. This woodcut, *The Martyrdom of John the Evangelist,* shows John, seated in a vat of boiling oil, suffering martyrdom.[26] Kirchner could have felt a similar sense of being beset during the time he worked on the *Apocalypse.* As he wrote, Kirchner felt he was in a state between life and death. The appearances of paralysis, erroneously diagnosed as syringomyelia (degenerative spinal chord disorder), left no hope of recovery. Instead, it was expected that it would progressively worsen. In concept the watercolour self-portrait is very similar to the woodcut *Head of the Invalid—Self-Portrait as an Invalid* p. 65, to which Mardersteig doubtless refers in his notation on Kirchner's letter. The face with its sunken cheeks and demonstrative presentation of lamed hands call attention to his suffering, both in the woodcut and in the sketch. In its bearing it is not an expression of steadfastness and confidence as in Dürer's portrait of the martyred John, but rather of hopelessness and helplessness. The death's head and skeleton in the left half of the picture symbolise Kirchner's sense of approaching death. Death has placed a hand on his shoulder as though taking possession of him. At this same time Kirchner pictured an identical motif in the woodcut *Self-Portrait with Dancing Death* p. 245. With these works Kirchner takes up a familiar figural motif from art history, "the Artist and Death", for which there are many examples in modern printmaking as well, such as Edvard Munch's lithograph *Dance of Death* from 1915[27] or the drypoint *The Artist and Death II* by Lovis Corinth fig. 1.[28]

Cat. 135

**Self-Portrait with Death
1st sheet of an album with
12 sketches for
the Apocalypse, 1917
Pencil, ink and watercolour on
cigarette-packet paper**

The Getty Research Institute,
Los Angeles

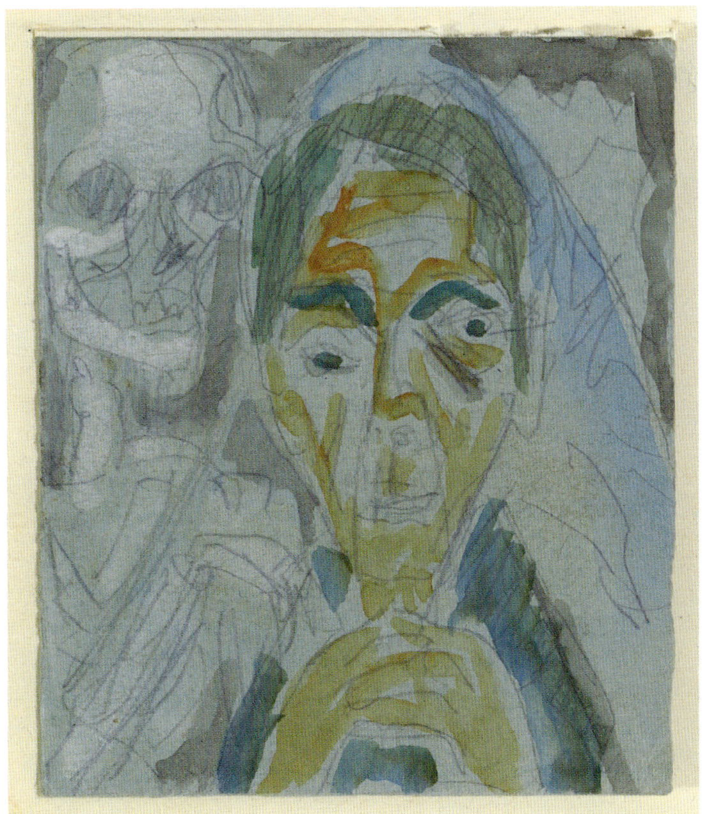

Cat. 135

The Twenty-Four Elders before the Throne
2nd sheet of an album with 12 sketches for the Apocalypse, 1917
Pencil, ink and watercolour on cigarette-packet paper

The Getty Research Institute, Los Angeles

Cat. 135

God Hands the Book with the Seven Seals to the Lamb
3rd sheet of an album with 12 sketches for the Apocalypse, 1917
Pencil, ink and watercolour on cigarette-packet paper

The Getty Research Institute, Los Angeles

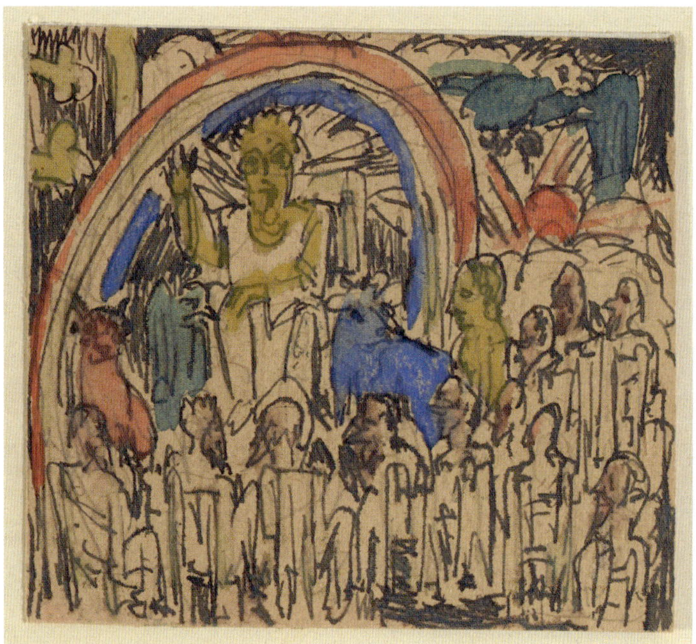

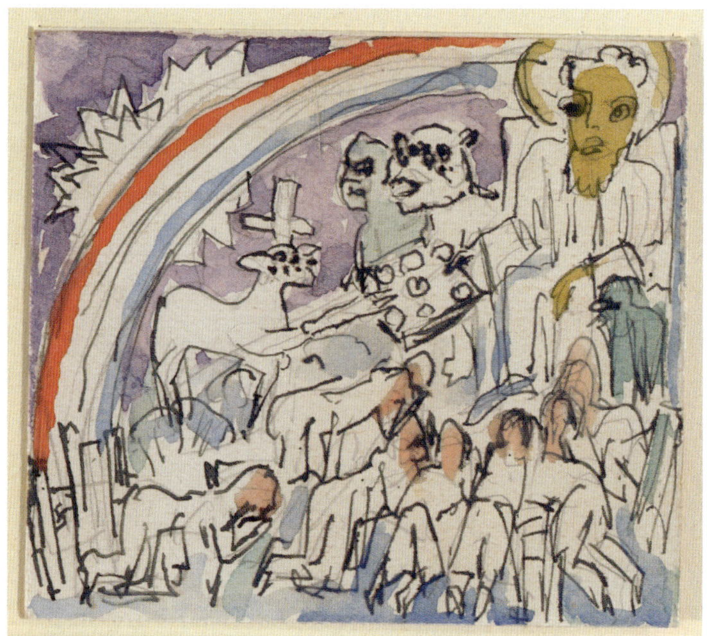

Before the Throne of God (Apoc. 4: 2–8)

In the biblical text, after a door to heaven had been opened, John saw God in his majesty, seated on a throne and surrounded by the twenty-four elders and the four apocalyptic creatures: a lion, an ox, an eagle and one with the face of a man, which in later Christian tradition would become the symbols of the four Evangelists. Kirchner did not include John in the composition, as in the Dürer woodcut, and did not arrange the elders in a circle around God.[29] God is enthroned in monumental size in the centre of the watercolour, his right hand ominously raised. Grouped around the throne are the four living creatures: the eagle and lion on his right, and on his left the ox and the creature with a human face. As in the text, God and his four creatures are overarched and framed by an enormous rainbow. The lower third of the picture is filled by the group of seated elders, though without the crowns mentioned in the Bible. Kirchner also omitted the "sea of glass, like to crystal" between them and God's throne as well as the flashes of lightning and the seven flaming torches.

The Lamb Receives the Book with the Seven Seals (Apoc. 5: 1–8)

In a large-format diagonal composition Kirchner depicted the scene in which God, sitting elevated in the upper-right corner, extends with his outstretched right arm the book with seven seals to the seven-eyed Lamb, identified as Christ by the large cross on its head. For only the Lamb is worthy of opening the book with the seven seals in which the historical plan for coming events is inscribed. On the left, next to God's throne, one sees the lion and the ox, and on the right in front of the throne perches the eagle. The elders in the foreground are shown at the moment in which, with the presentation of the book, they fall to their knees and pray to God. A large rainbow spans the left half of the picture and sets the group of figures on this side apart.

In a dense composition Dürer combined the two visions — the adoration by the twenty-four elders and the presentation of the book — in the woodcut *Saint John Kneeling before Christ and the Twenty-Four Elders.*[30] In it, the twenty-four elders form a circle around God's throne. The Lamb, faithfully depicted with seven horns and seven eyes, is receiving the book from the hand of God. The prophet John kneels in the centre of the picture, above him the heavenly vision and beneath him the earthly world. With this depiction of two worlds Dürer expanded the single visionary image, thereby conforming to the world view on which the entire Apocalypse is based.

By contrast, Max Beckmann reduced the magnificent scene of the handing over of the book to a signet-like depiction of the book with the seven seals and the seven-eyed and seven-horned Lamb, which has a noose around its neck in reference to the biblical text "as it were slain". As in other pictures based on the Apocalypse, Beckmann added a burning candle as a personal symbol of the flame of life.

The Man with the Two-Edged Sword — Vision of the Seven Candlesticks (Apoc. 1: 10–16)

Kirchner's fourth watercolour should actually follow the self-portrait, for it depicts — as in Dürer's woodcut *Vision of the Seven Candlesticks* fig. 2 — the opening text of the Apocalypse. "Dürer's 'figural' sequence on the Apocalypse of Saint John begins with a powerful drum beat and the monumental vision of the Son of Man enthroned in the midst of seven candlesticks."[31] But Kirchner's composition diverges considerably in concept and composition from Dürer's woodcut. The two share essential elements of the vision: the seven candlesticks, standing for the seven churches in Asia Minor addressed in John's epistle and the seven stars in the right hand of Christ, which symbolise the angels of those congregations. The sword is not fiery, as it was said to be in the earlier title of the matching Kirchner woodcut fig. 3, but sharp and two-edged, emerging from Christ's mouth. It stands for the Word of Christ that cleaves, in that at the Last Judgement Christ will separate the blessed from the damned. Whereas Dürer's Christ is seated on a two-arched throne, in Kirchner's version he stands in a long robe amid the seven candlesticks, belted around the chest, as stated in the text, with a golden girdle. In his right hand he holds the bundle of seven stars like a bouquet, and his left is raised as though in proclamation, for he says, "I am the First and the Last" (Apoc. 1: 17).[32] Dürer includes the figure of John in the vision, who kneels in the foreground between the candlesticks, that is to say between the congregations in which he is known as a wandering preacher, thereby making it clear that this is his vision, one with which he legitimises his demand in his epistle to the churches. For the voice commanded him, "Write therefore the things which thou hast seen, and which are, and which must be done hereafter" (Apoc. 1: 19). Kirchner, however, depicts the vision directly, without the intermediary of the prophet, so that on the one hand the distance from the vision is removed and, on the other, its meaning, the call to John to proclaim the event of the Apocalypse, is lost.

The richness and expressiveness that Kirchner is able to extract from the design is documented by the woodcut *The Man with the Two-Edged Sword: Vision of the Seven Candlesticks* (1918/19), which Kirchner printed both in black and white and in colour fig. 3. The colour woodcut, printed in its final state from four or five blocks, develops a colour splendour that causes the burning candlesticks and the stars to glow in yellow against a blue-black background. Christ stands in the foreground in full figure, wearing a red-blue garment reaching down to his feet. In contrast to the watercolour in the sketch, in the woodcut the various colours blend to form a cohesive picture plane.

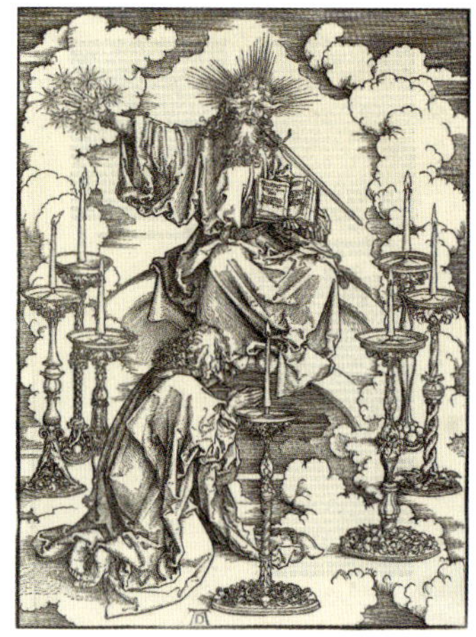

Fig. 2 Albrecht Dürer
The Vision of the Seven Candlesticks, 1498
Woodcut on laid paper, image: 39.5 × 28.5 cm, sheet: 46.5 × 31.5 cm

National Gallery of Art, Washington, Patrons' Permanent Fund and Print Purchase Fund (Horace Gallatin and Lessing J. Rosenwald)

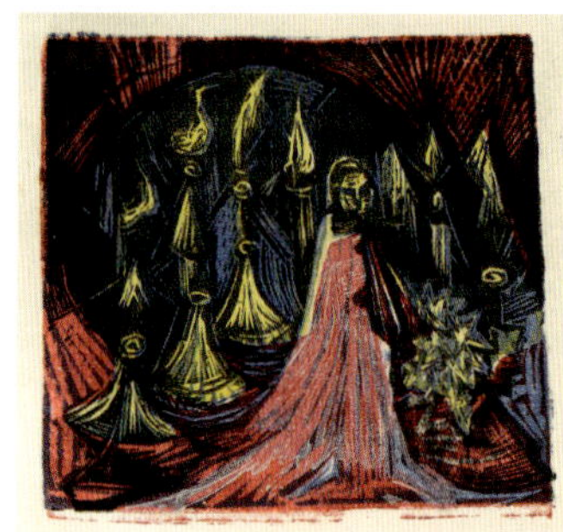

Fig. 3 Ernst Ludwig Kirchner
The Man with the Two-Edged Sword — Vision of the Seven Candlesticks, 1918/19
Colour woodcut on heavy vellum, image: 12.8 × 13.5 cm, sheet: 22.5 × 21 cm
(Gercken 953.3)

Collection E.W.K., Bern/Davos

Cat. 135

Saint John's Vision of the Seven Candlesticks
4th sheet of an album with 12 sketches for the Apocalypse, 1917
Pencil, ink and watercolour on cigarette-packet paper

The Getty Research Institute, Los Angeles

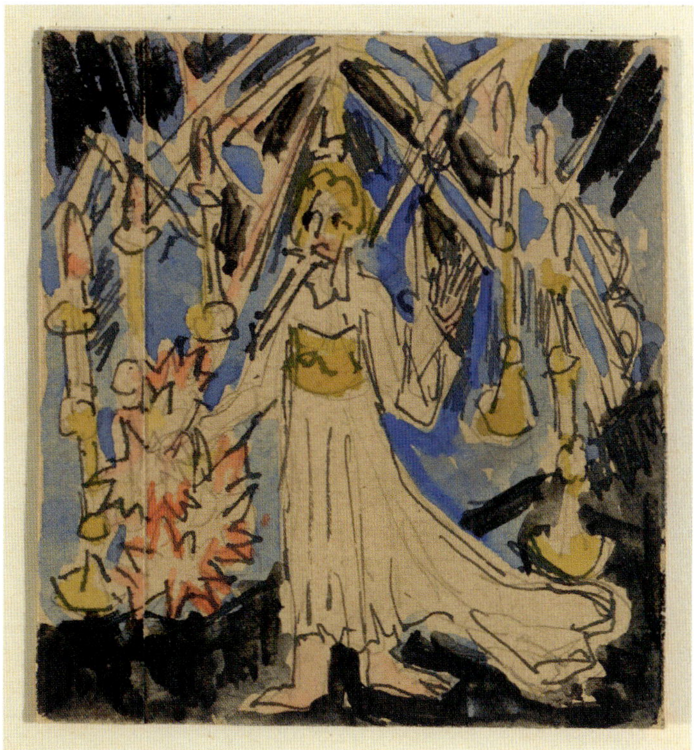

Cat. 135

Saint John Devouring the Book
5th sheet of an album with 12 sketches for the Apocalypse, 1917
Pencil, ink and watercolour on cigarette-packet paper

The Getty Research Institute, Los Angeles

Cat. 135

The Sounding of the Seven Angels
6th sheet of an album with 12 sketches for the Apocalypse, 1917
Pencil, ink and watercolour on cigarette-packet paper

The Getty Research Institute, Los Angeles

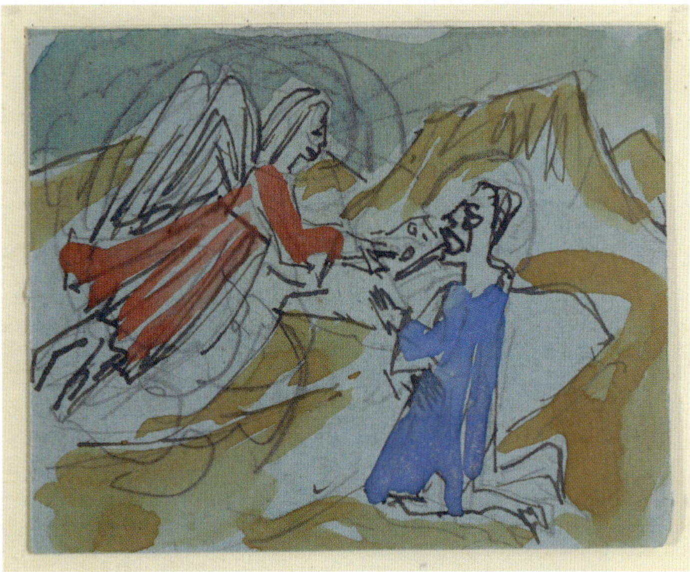

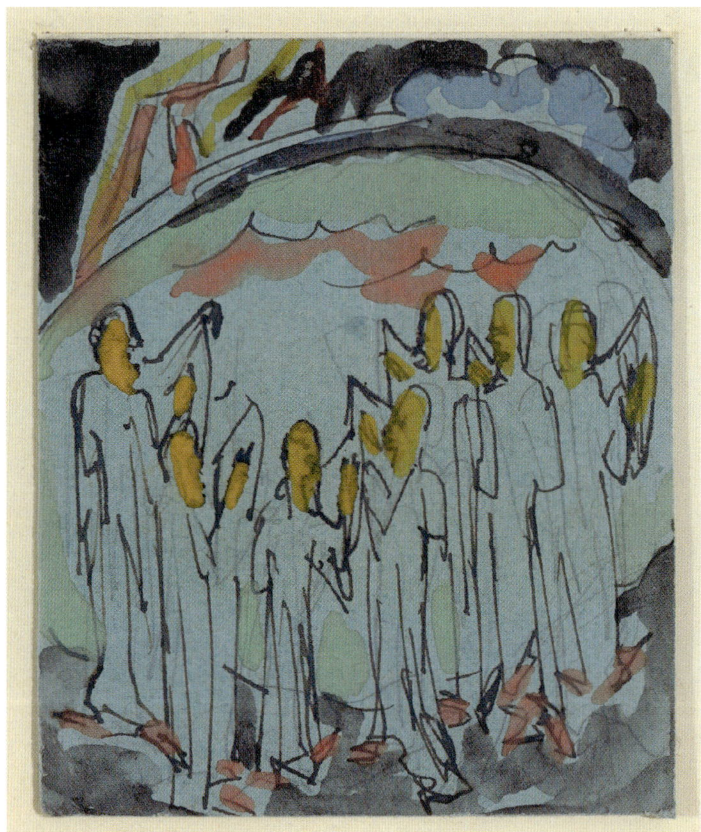

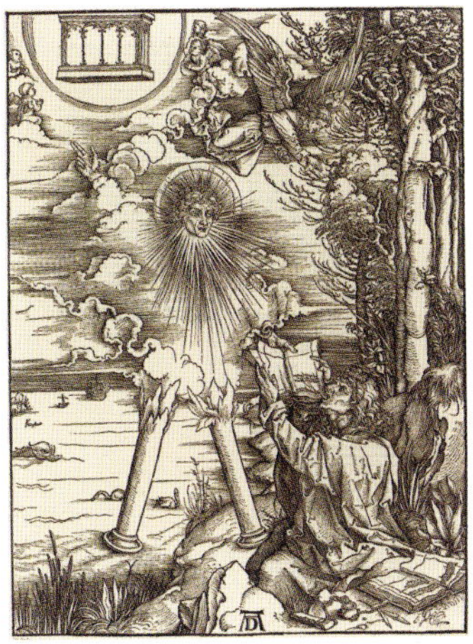

Fig. 4 Albrecht Dürer
Saint John Devouring the Book, 1498
Woodcut on laid paper, image: 39.3 × 28.5 cm, sheet: 45.9 × 31.2 cm

National Gallery of Art, Washington, Patrons' Permanent Fund and Print Purchase Fund (Horace Gallatin and Lessing J. Rosenwald)

John Is Given the Little Book (Apoc. 10:1–10)

Both Kirchner and Dürer illustrate the impressive vision, interesting in terms of depth psychology, in which the angel hands the book to John and says, "Take the book, and eat it up" (Apoc. 10:9). Their pictures depict the decisive scene in the Apocalypse in which John is required to swallow the small book and thus internalise the visions. John, who previously described the visions as though he had observed them from without, is told to acknowledge them with the symbolic ingestion of the book as his own, so as to be able to proclaim them convincingly.[33] In Dürer's woodcut *Saint John Devouring the Book* (1498) fig. 4 John is kneeling on a seashore, receiving the book from the powerful angel with outstretched arms and beginning to eat it.[34] The book in which he meant to write down his visions lies next to him on the ground. Of the angel in the clouds we see only the head, crowned by a rainbow, the two hands, one of them extending the small book, and legs in the form of fiery columns. "Never before had the visionary nature of the angel's appearance been depicted so convincingly."[35] In that the angel spans heaven and earth, he symbolises the link between this world and the hereafter. Kirchner opposed Dürer's imposing scenic design with a simple picture in which John kneels in a mountain landscape and receives the book from the hovering angel. He limits his depiction to the moment in which John opens his mouth in order to swallow the book, without addressing the symbolic meaning of the angelic vision. Thus Kirchner's design lacks the imposing presence of the powerful angel. It was this angel who "swore by him that liveth for ever and ever" that "time shall be no longer" (Apoc. 10:6), which inspired Beckmann to produce an impressive full-page illustration in which two angels support a clock whose hour hand points to twelve fig. 5. Although this suggests that time has run out, the angel does not proclaim the cessation of time but rather its suspension in the eternal now.

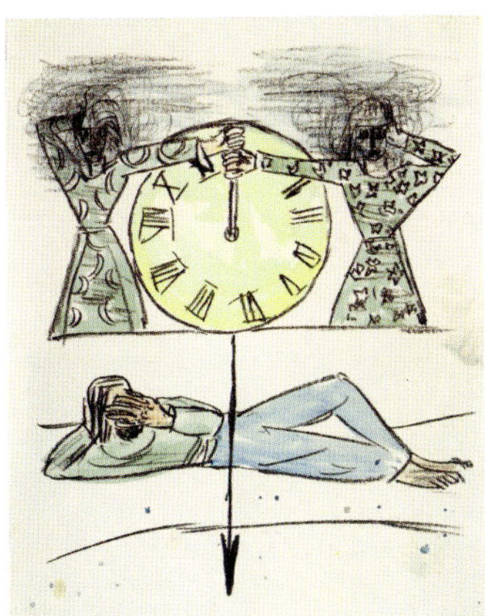

Fig. 5 Max Beckmann
Apocalypse: That Henceforth There Shall Be No More Time, 11–14 April 1942
Chalk lithograph, hand-coloured on paper, image: 31.1 × 25.4 cm, sheet: 34.7 × 26.7 cm

Staatsgalerie Stuttgart

The Seven Trumpeting Angels (Apoc. 8:2–8)

On the opening of the seventh seal, seven angels standing before God are given seven trumpets. With a blast on the trumpet each of them will unleash a new disaster on mankind and on the earth. Kirchner secularises the vision by bringing the angels that form a ring around God in the Dürer woodcut down to earth. Wearing long robes, they stand as a group on a seashore in a shallow semicircle—a compositional form that Kirchner had also used for the painting *Five Women on the Street* (1913) p. 22: fig. 2 and the woodcut *Five Cocottes on the Street* (1913/14) p. 168. With the sounding of the second angel's trumpet "as it were a great mountain, burning with fire, was cast into the sea, and the third part of the sea became blood" (Apoc. 8:8). In his sketch Kirchner adopted the two graphic images of this catastrophe, the sea turning to blood and the mountain spitting fire, which could have referred to the eruption of Vesuvius in AD 79.

In his woodcut *The Opening of the Seventh Seal and the Eagle Crying "Woe"* Dürer pictured both heaven and earth. While in heaven God the Father distributes the trumpets to the angels, on earth in the bottom third of the picture we see the horrors and devastation that follow the separate trumpet blasts from chapters 8 and 9 of the Apocalypse.[36] There is the fire-spitting mountain, which is being sunk in the sea by a pair of hands, the fire that burns a third of the land, and the star that opens the "bottomless pit" (Apoc. 9:2), out of which will rise locusts in human form. Kirchner devoted a separate sketch to this motif, which is not included in Dürer's omnibus woodcut.

The Angels with the Vials of Wrath (Apoc. 16:1–17)

Dürer did not illustrate the seven angels with the vials of wrath, having skipped over chapters 15 and 16 of the Apocalypse. For compositional reasons he limited God's punishments to the first half of his illustration cycle. In Kirchner's watercolour three angels pour perdition onto mankind out of large vials and set the earth on fire. In the foreground of the sketch, set on a seashore, are fleeing figures doubled over in agony and dying, and at the right edge there is a burning tree. When Kirchner was planning the painting of the church in Frauenkirch with pictures from the Apocalypse in 1936, he returned to the theme in the late etching *From the Apocalypse* (1936) fig.6. He then gave it a contemporary twist by associating with the symbolic angels the real airplanes first deployed in battle in the First World War. The vision of mankind's destruction from the air had become reality. In the etching the flying angels have mutated into hybrids, half angel, half airplane. As it happens, Kirchner was already anxious about a new war at the time and wrote to Carl Hagemann, "I chose scenes from the Apocalypse, which is well suited to our time. The angels that pour out vials containing plagues, are they not the planes with gas bombs?"[37]

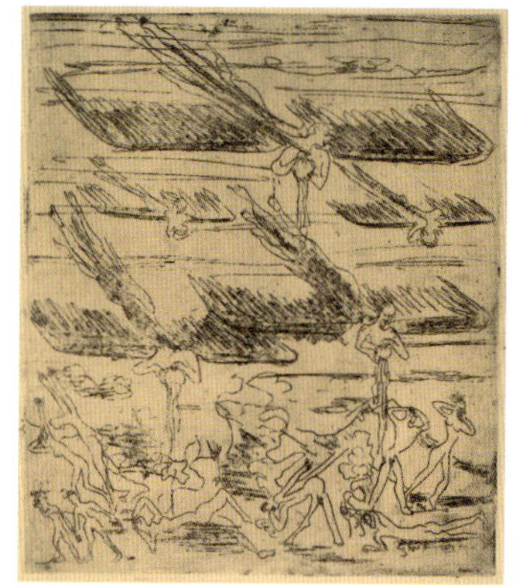

Fig.6 Ernst Ludwig Kirchner
From the Apocalypse, 1936
Line etching and drypoint,
image: 30 × 25 cm,
sheet: 52.2 × 35 cm
(Gercken 1775, Dube R. 650)

National Gallery of Art, Washington, Gift of Ruth Cole Kainen

The Horsemen of the Apocalypse (Apoc. 6:2–8)

No picture of the horsemen of the Apocalypse would become so much a part of our collective visual memory as Dürer's charging riders: three symbolically racing through the air armed with a bow, a sword and scales, and Death on an emaciated nag haunting the earth.[38] That striking image goes beyond the text, ignoring the fact that in the Apocalypse the horsemen do not appear together but individually, at the opening of each of the first four seals. The staggered arrangement of the riders as they charge forward gives the woodcut a stunning sense of drama that has lost none of its impact to this day. By combining the four horsemen of the Apocalypse into a single picture, Kirchner also follows the pictorial tradition that preceded Dürer, not the biblical text. But in contrast to Dürer's depiction, his riders do not suggest the terror of divine punishment. They are quite ordinary, earthly horsemen, reminiscent of Kirchner's pictures of riders from his months in the military in Halle in 1915 p.216. Whereas he appears to have been little interested in the dynamism achieved by Dürer—the group appears to be forming up before setting out—the various colours given to the horses in the Bible were important. The group is led by the rider on the white horse turned to the left and holding a bow in his hand. The centre of the picture is occupied by the second rider on a red horse, whose large sword presages war. Seen from behind and above, the rider with the scales in his hand sits astride a black mount, and at the right edge Death in the form of a skeleton rides a brown steed. In Kirchner's small sketch he also works with different points of view, thereby lending the picture an exciting movement and spaciousness. In contrast to Dürer's woodcut, which is divided into two spheres—the airy sphere with the first three riders and the earthly one with mankind, to which the horsemen are bringing death and destruction—there is no such division in Kirchner's composition. His horsemen come from the secular world. Beckmann invented an interesting variant for the depiction of the horsemen of the Apocalypse, one appropriate to his situation at the time during the Second World War. He had them rage outside the window of his room fig.7. He projected the Apocalypse onto the murderous war he was forced to watch from his exile in Amsterdam.

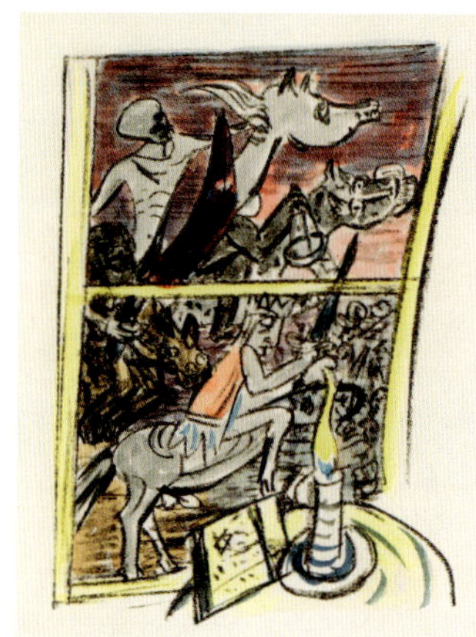

Fig.7 Max Beckmann
Apocalypse: The Four Horsemen of the Apocalypse, 11–14 April 1942
Chalk lithograph, hand-coloured on paper,
image: 24.4 × 16.8 cm,
sheet: 29.5 × 27.1 cm

Staatsgalerie Stuttgart

Cat. 135

The Angels Pouring Out the Vials Filled with God's Wrath
7th sheet of an album with 12 sketches for the Apocalypse, 1917
Pencil, ink and watercolour on cigarette-packet paper

The Getty Research Institute, Los Angeles

Cat. 135

The Four Horsemen of the Apocalypse
8th sheet of an album with 12 sketches for the Apocalypse, 1917
Pencil, ink and watercolour on cigarette-packet paper

The Getty Research Institute, Los Angeles

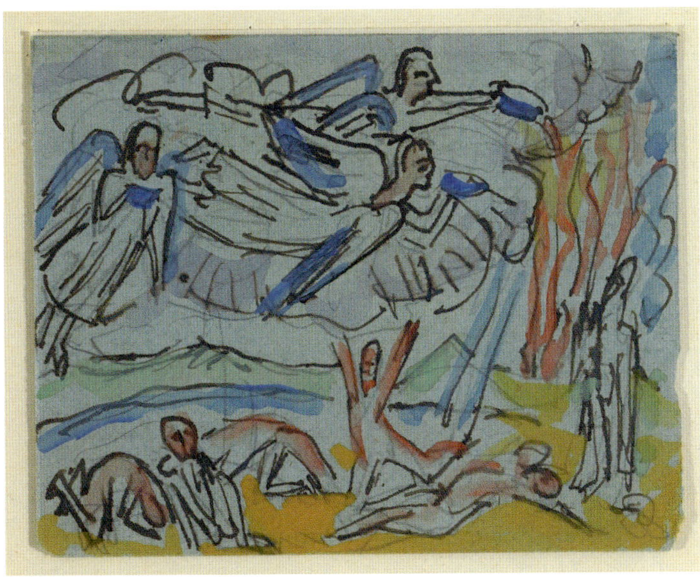

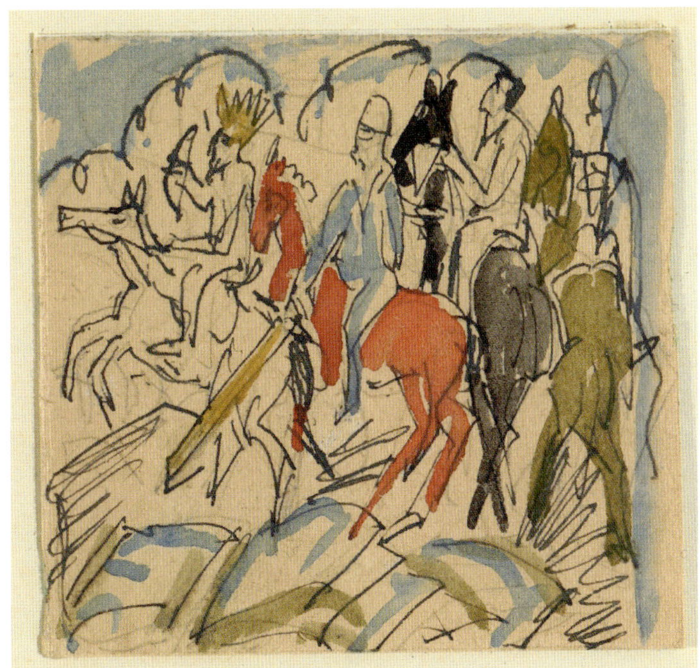

Cat. 135

The Woman Clothed with the Sun and the Dragon
9th sheet of an album with 12 sketches for the Apocalypse, 1917
Pencil, ink and watercolour on cigarette-packet paper

The Getty Research Institute, Los Angeles

Cat. 135

The Woman Clothed with the Sun Flees from the Dragon
10th sheet of an album with 12 sketches for the Apocalypse, 1917
Pencil, ink and watercolour on cigarette-packet paper

The Getty Research Institute, Los Angeles

Cat. 135

The Torment of Humankind by the Locusts
11th sheet of an album with 12 sketches for the Apocalypse, 1917
Pencil, ink and watercolour on cigarette-packet paper

The Getty Research Institute, Los Angeles

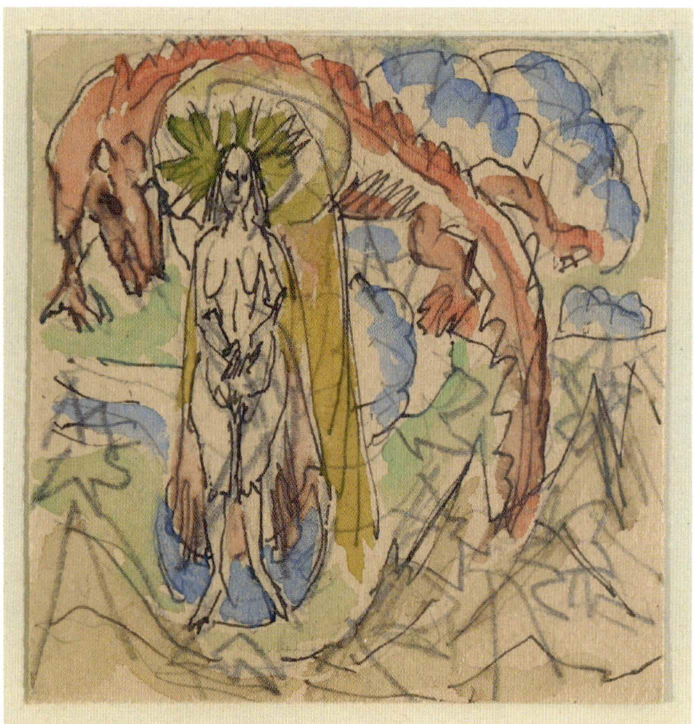

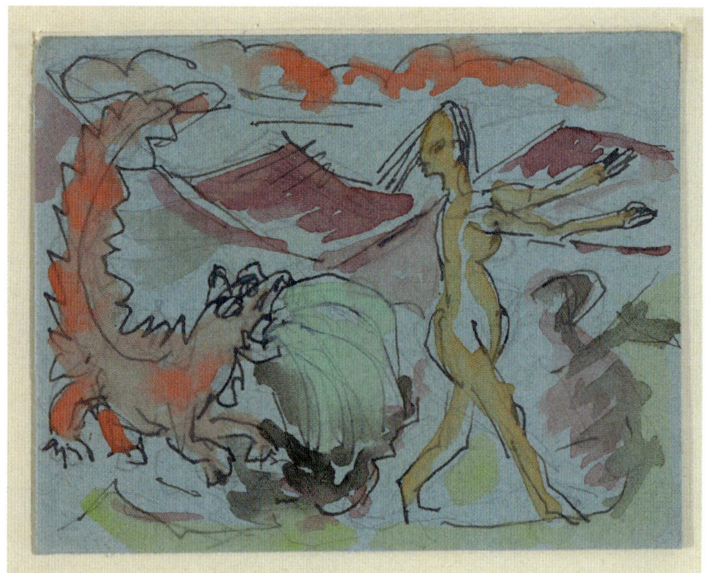

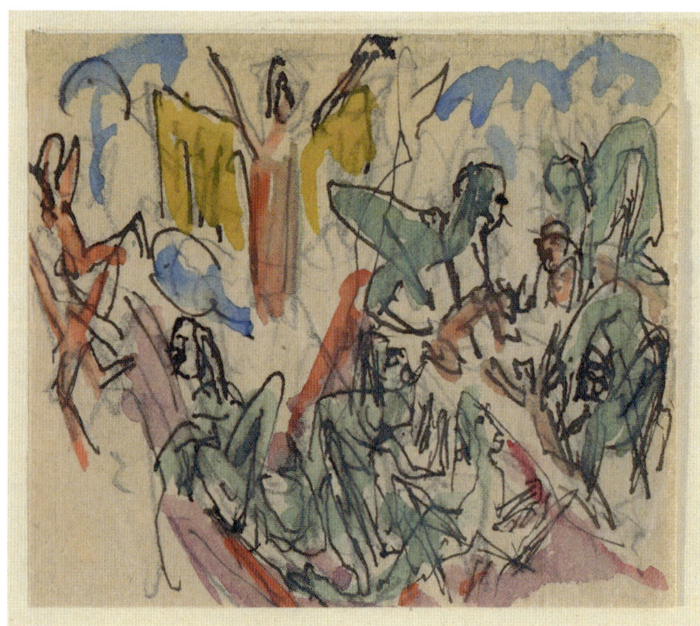

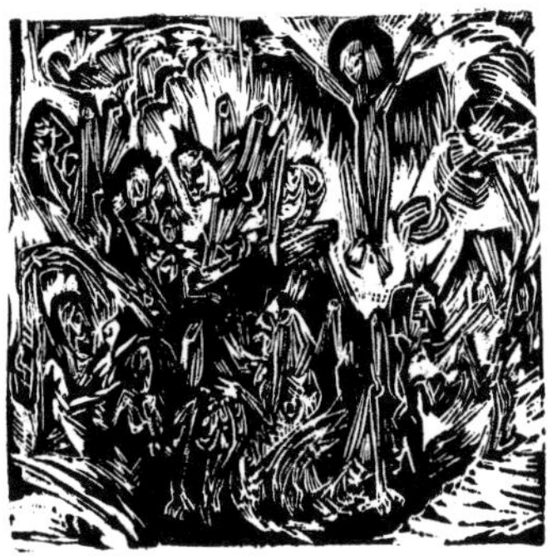

Fig. 8 Ernst Ludwig Kirchner
The Locusts Tormenting Mankind, 1918/19
Woodcut on card-weight vellum, image: 11.8 × 12 cm, sheet: 17.2 × 16.5 cm
(Gercken 954)

Collection E.W.K., Bern/Davos

The Woman and the Dragon (Apoc. 12: 1–5)

One could consider this vision as the turning point in the Apocalypse, for after God's punishments the woman and her childbirth indicate the prospect of the world's renewal. Dürer combines three events in his woodcut *The Woman of the Apocalypse and the Seven-Headed Dragon:* the woman robed with the sun and with the moon beneath her feet, the seven-headed dragon menacing her, and her child being borne up to God.[39] From this complex sequence of events Kirchner takes only two episodes, devoting a watercolour to each of them. His ninth drawing pictures the beautiful woman as a figure standing in front of a tree in a landscape, her feet resting on the blue crescent moon. She is not splendidly gowned as a Madonna surrounded by rays and the crescent moon, as in Dürer, but nude—possibly because the text reads: "a woman clothed with the sun" (Apoc. 12:1)—and she holds her hands protectively in front of her body, for she is about to give birth to the divine child. The red dragon who hopes to devour the expected son curls its long tail around the woman like a lindworm, but without seeming to be menacing. In the powerful vision of the biblical text it sweeps a third of the stars from heaven with its tail, an attempt to deprive mankind of the starry sky as a sign of eternity.

The Flight from the Dragon (Apoc. 12: 13–16)

The vision in the Apocalypse in which the woman has fled on eagle's wings into the desert pursued by the dragon, who hopes to drown her by spewing a flood of water out of its mouth, seems paradoxical. Paradoxical that it should be water that the woman is to be killed with in the desert, where one can die of thirst for the lack of it. But this flood of water is to be seen as a deliberate contrast to the stream of living water that flows from the throne of God in the book's last two chapters. The water the dragon spews forth is deadly, and poisons the world. In his illustration Kirchner stays quite close to the text: despite the eagle's wings that were lent her, the fleeing woman is taking long strides, which have a dance-like quality. Her arms, extended toward the right edge of the picture, indicate the direction of her flight. Since a refuge is promised her, she looks back in triumph as the red dragon spews a river of green water. But the merciful earth opens up and swallows the river to save her.

The Locusts Tormenting Mankind (Apoc. 9: 3–11)

The fifth trumpet blast announces the vision of locusts, as large as horses and with human faces and wafting women's hair, rising up out of the bottomless pit. They are commanded to torture mankind for five months with their scorpion-like stingers, but not to kill. John imagines a terrifying scene of torture in which the people would rather die than endure the pain any longer. Even in his watercolour's small format Kirchner creates a consummate composition with a pyramid of locusts and human figures. In the background, at the top, the king of the locusts, Abaddon, watches over the torture with his arms outspread as though in a gesture of blessing. In the matching woodcut, *The Locusts Tormenting Mankind* (1918/19) fig. 8, Kirchner reproduced the composition of the sketch with its mountain of locusts in the foreground in intricate detail. Thanks to the detail and precision of the woodcut it is easier to understand what is only suggested in the small sketch. The original title, *The Man-Eating Phantoms, Half Knights, Half Women, Rising out of the Earth,* and his description reveal that Gustav Schiefler failed to see the direct reference to the text in the Bible. The plague of locusts must have been firmly anchored in human memory since archaic times, or John could not have evoked it in his vision.

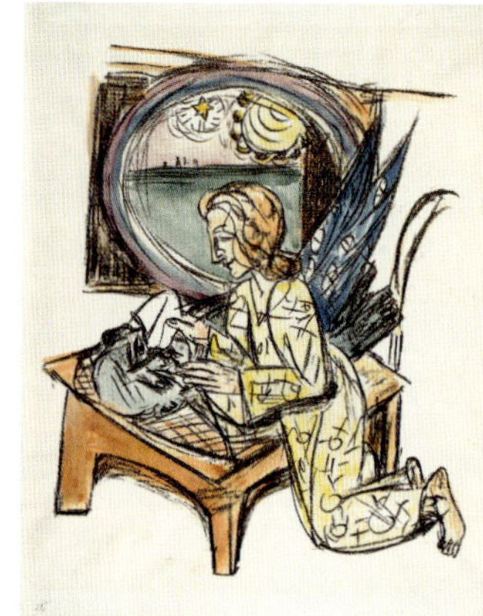

Fig. 9 Max Beckmann
Apocalypse: God Will Wipe Away All Tears, 11–14 April 1942
Chalk lithograph, hand-coloured on paper,
image: 33.2 × 26.3 cm,
sheet: 38.7 × 29.8 cm

Staatsgalerie Stuttgart

The Great Whore Babylon (Apoc. 17:3–6)

The vision of the whore Babylon is a fantastic image that tells in coded form of the depravity of Rome. Dürer pictured *The Whore of Babylon* as a beautiful woman dressed in Venetian garments — following the text "clothed round about with purple and scarlet, and gilt with gold, and precious stones and pearls" — seated on a monstrous beast.[40] With the woman's splendour, the opposite of that of the woman of the Apocalypse, John denounces the extravagance and repugnant wealth of Rome. The monster's seven heads, each with its own specific features, are meant to stand for the seven hills of Rome, and the ten horns for the sequence of ten Roman emperors up to that time. The seductive woman held "a golden cup in her hand, full of the abomination and filthiness of her fornication". John mourns the Romans' persecution of Christians when he writes, "And I saw the woman drunk with the blood of the saints, and with the blood of the martyrs of Jesus." Skipping over chapters, Dürer accommodates in the complex structure of his woodcut the fall of Babylon (chapter 18) and the arrival of the armies of Christ (chapter 19). Kirchner concentrates exclusively on the whore riding on the back of the scarlet-coloured beast. The barren landscape is perhaps meant to recall that with this vision John saw himself translated in spirit to a desert. Illustrating the vision's symbolic meaning appears to have been of little interest to Kirchner; instead, he exploits the scene's erotic potential. In distinct contrast to Dürer's elegantly clad woman, his nearly nude whore is not seated on a symbolic dragon but riding an equine mount alone through a desolate hilly landscape. The sketch emphasises the greatly enlarged goblet she flaunts. On its upper rim Kirchner suggests the fornication, literally following the Bible passage, that takes place inside it. His profane depiction includes no sense of the menace of the seven-headed beast and the balefulness of its lovely rider.

With this twelfth sheet, an illustration of *The Great Whore Babylon,* Kirchner's sequence comes to an end. If one arranges the sketches in the textual sequence — unlike that of the album — one notes that ten sketches apply to the first half of the Apocalypse and that *The Angels Pouring Out the Vials Filled with God's Wrath* p. 87 and *The Whore of Babylon* are all that were drawn from the second part. Kirchner ignored the following chapter in the Apocalypse with the fall of Babylon, the victorious army of Christ and the beginning of the thousand-year kingdom — for which in Dürer there is also only a summary woodcut — for understandable reasons, presumably owing to a greater distance from this part of the prophecy. With the surviving sketches for twelve woodcuts he apparently saw the cycle complete, although we cannot be certain that there were not designs he rejected. As the opening sketch *Self-Portrait with Death* prefigured, the hopeful last part of the Apocalypse did not accord with the sense of despair and his own mortality that coloured his stay in the Kreuzlingen sanatorium. In that desperate situation he was incapable of illustrating the moving passage "And God shall wipe away all tears from their eyes" (Apoc. 21:4), as Max Beckmann did, picturing himself as the one who is comforted; in a ship's cabin an angel — in female form — is wiping away his tears with a cloth fig. 9.[41]

Comparing the Dürer and Kirchner illustrations sharpens our appreciation of the two artists' specific approaches to the text. Their depictions differ not only in style and technique but also as a result of fundamentally different ways of thinking. Dürer worked out of the world of faith, staying close to the biblical text in many details and translating it with an exuberant imagination into his woodcuts. Since these are interleaved with the text, they necessarily follow its narrative progress. The entire work is a retelling of the Apocalypse in such memorable images that when re-reading the text, one cannot help but recall Dürer's visualisation of it. Both his single woodcuts and the sequence as a whole have a narrative structure. Dürer utilises the simultaneity of the picture instead of the successive order of the text by combining successive events from different chapters in a single sheet.

This complex, compressed form was impossible in Kirchner's tiny sketches. In two cases he separated scenes that Dürer had illustrated in a single woodcut into two sketches: motifs from the Dürer woodcut *St John Kneeling before Christ and the Twenty-Four Elders* become sketches 2 and 3 in the album and from *The Woman of the Apocalypse and the*

Cat. 135

The Whore of Babylon
12th sheet of an album with
12 sketches for
the Apocalypse, 1917
Pencil, ink and watercolour on
cigarette-packet paper

The Getty Research Institute,
Los Angeles

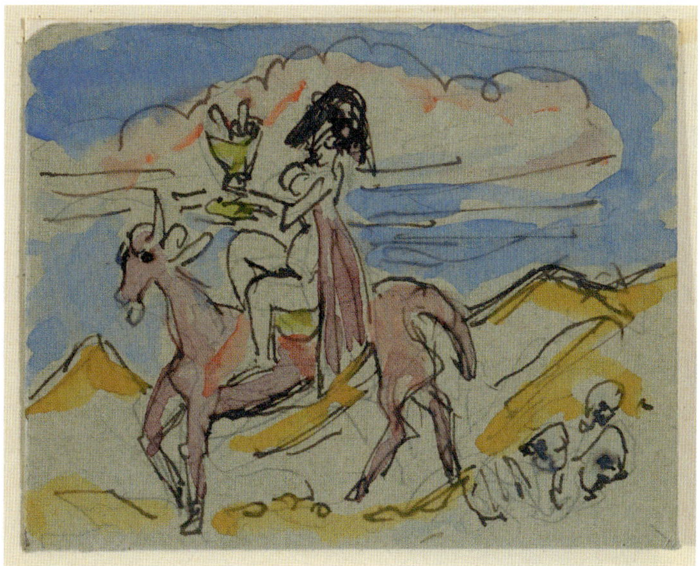

Seven-Headed Dragon, sketches 9 and 10. Neither as single compositions nor in their arbitrary sequence in the album are his sketches narrative in nature. Since he was uninterested in the overarching idea of the prophecy of imminent salvation from this vale of tears through the establishment of the kingdom of God, his separate designs also fail to fit together as components in the overall composition of a cycle as in Dürer.

Whereas the dense graphic structure of the Dürer woodcuts precludes any colouring, in Kirchner's designs, which are painterly in concept, colour is essential. They do not have the look of coloured sketches but rather watercolours over sketched outlines. In this they clearly differ from Beckmann's *Apocalypse* lithographs, which were subsequently hand-coloured and have retained the nature of drawings. Just how effectively Kirchner utilised colour is seen in his only colour woodcut for the *Apocalypse.* The colour is not simply added but a necessary component of the composition. Presumably Kirchner would also have carved colour blocks for the black-and-white woodcut *The Locusts Tormenting Mankind* if he had not abandoned the project.

As in his three major woodcut cycles *Schlemihl, Triumph of Love* and *Absalom,* here too Kirchner is not a mere illustrator interpreting a text with pictures. Instead, he used the text to inspire his own pictorial visions. It was not so much that he served the text but rather that the text triggered his pictorial imagination. The symbolic ingestion of a text — not an original idea of John's, for Ezekiel had already been forced to eat God's letter (Ezek. 3:1–3) — one could apply to the artist, who first had to internalise the text in order to arrive at his own idea for a picture. The pictures Kirchner derived from the Apocalypse are largely secularised, in that he brings the scenes down to earth and fails to identify them as visions of John's. In this way he was able to enjoy a greater freedom vis-à-vis the text, allowing him to realise his artistic intentions. The illustrations are demystifying and matter-of-fact, especially the depictions of female figures and the four horsemen of the Apocalypse. However, he is careful not to subvert the text's historical depth by making references to contemporary war-related events. His imagery takes the form of shorthand notes, yet to consider them only provisional would be to misconceive them. In their idiosyncratic composition, independent of all precursors, they are already fully realised, as we see from the reworking of the designs into the two *Apocalypse* woodcuts. Kirchner valued swift, almost unconscious drawing as the expression of his true feeling. The *Apocalypse* series is not only testimony to Kirchner's own desperate situation, it is a pictorial interpretation of the ancient text in the spirit of our own time.

1 The Apocalypse (Greek apokálypsis = revelation) is the last book of the New Testament.

2 Ernst Ludwig Kirchner to Gustav Schiefler, letter from 22 April 1924: "Yesterday I received Lippmann's major work on Dürer drawings [Friedrich Lippmann (ed.), *Zeichnungen von Albrecht Dürer in Nachbildungen,* 5 of 7 vols. (Berlin, 1883–1929)]. It is a joy to see these drawings that move one as being so related for all their remoteness. How much closer one stands to the entire artistic sensibility of a Dürer than to the best Frenchman or Munch or anyone else. Dürer is inexhaustible, he is frequently so 'modern' in his line that one is simply dumbstruck." In Wolfgang Henze et al. (eds.), *Ernst Ludwig Kirchner/Gustav Schiefler: Briefwechsel 1910–1935/1938* (Stuttgart/Zurich, 1990), p. 290. See also Marcus Andrew Hurttig, "Albrecht Dürer, eine literarische Fiktion als Vorbild für Ernst Ludwig Kirchner", in *Kirchner,* exh. cat. Hamburger Kunsthalle (Bremen, 2010), pp. 58–66.

3 *Luthers Vorreden zur Bibel,* ed. Heinrich Bornkamm (Frankfurt am Main, 1983), p. 220; for Luther's judgement on the text of the Apocalypse, see his preface from 1522.

4 *Apokalypse,* with 27 chalk lithographs by Max Beckmann (Frankfurt am Main, 1943), p. 79; see Corinna Höper, *Max Beckmann: Apokalypse,* exh. cat. Staatsgalerie Stuttgart, Graphische Sammlung (Munich, 2008).

5 *Ernst Ludwig Kirchner: Gemälde und Graphik der Sammlung Dr. F. Bauer,* Davos, exh. cat. Haus der Kunst, Munich (Nuremberg, 1952).

6 Thomas W. Gaehtgens and Anja Foerschner, "Ernst Ludwig Kirchner's Drawings of the Apocalypse", *Getty Research Journal* 6 (2014), pp. 83–102.

7 Wolfram Gabler, *Ernst Ludwig Kirchner als Illustrator* (Ph.D. diss., Berlin, 1988), p. 90.

8 Eberhard W. Kornfeld, *Ernst Ludwig Kirchner: Nachzeichnung seines Lebens* (Bern, 1979), p. 106.

9 Hans Delfs (ed.), *Ernst Ludwig Kirchner: Der gesamte Briefwechsel,* vol. 1, *Briefe von 1901 bis 1923* (Zurich, 2010), p. 231.

10 Ibid., p. 226.

11 See Günther Gercken, *Ernst Ludwig Kirchner: Holzschnittzyklen; Peter Schlemihl, Triumph der Liebe, Absalom* (Stuttgart/Zurich, 1980), pp. 57–59.

12 Ibid., pp. 7–11.

13 Delfs, *Briefwechsel* (see n. 9), pp. 181–182.

14 Ibid., pp. 230–231.

15 Hans Mardersteig to Kurt Wolff, letter from 20 January 1922: "The portfolio contract was cancelled with your approval three years ago." And he goes on to write that "K. was so ill at that time that his own doctor was convinced that he could not be cured, and even predicted that he would die soon. (Syringomyelia!)". In Bernhard Zeller and Ellen Otten (eds.), *Kurt Wolff: Briefwechsel eines Verlegers; 1911–1963* (Frankfurt am Main, 1966), p. 385.

16 For details, see Gercken 945–952.

17 On 26 December 1918 Kirchner wrote to Nele van de Velde that he had carved a "composition on Revelation". Ernst Ludwig Kirchner, *Briefe an Nele und Henry van de Velde* (Munich, 1961), p. 12.

18 Delfs, *Briefwechsel* (see n. 9), p. 343.

19 Anita Beloubek-Hammer, *Ernst Ludwig Kirchner: Erstes Sehen; Das Werk im Berliner Kupferstichkabinett* (Munich, 2004).

20 Paul Vogt, *Ernst Ludwig Kirchner: Skizzenbuch aus der Graphischen Sammlung des Museum Folkwang* (Freren, 1983).

21 Erna Kirchner to Helene Spengler, letter from 21 October 1917, in Lothar Grisebach (ed.), *Maler des Expressionismus im Briefwechsel mit Eberhard Grisebach* (Hamburg, 1962), p. 73.

22 Kornfeld, *Nachzeichnung* (see n. 8), p. 118.

23 Waltraud Neuerburg, *Der graphische Zyklus im deutschen Expressionismus und seine Typen 1905–1925* (Ph.D. diss., Bonn, 1976), p. 101.

24 James Hofmaier, *Max Beckmann: Catalogue Raisonné of His Prints,* 2 vols. (Bern, 1990), pp. 33–356.

25 Max Beckmann could not have known Kirchner's *Apocalypse,* and apparently his interpreters were also unaware of it, so that Stephan von Wiese could claim that Beckmann's *Apocalypse* was unique in the art of Modernism. Stephan von Wiese, "Max Beckmanns Apokalypse, 1941–1942, zwischen Aktualität und Tradition", in Christian Lenz (ed.), *Max Beckmann: Vorträge 1996–1998,* Hefte des Max-Beckmann-Archivs 3 (Munich, 2000), pp. 63–78.

26 Rainer Schoch, Matthias Mende and Anna Scherbaum (eds.), *Albrecht Dürer: Das druckgraphische Werk,* vol. 2 (Munich, 2002), p. 112.

27 Gerd Woll, *Edvard Munch: Werkverzeichnis der Graphik* (Munich, 2001), p. 509.

28 Karl Schwarz, *Das graphische Werk von Lovis Corinth* (San Francisco, 1985), p. 239.

29 Schoch et al., *Dürer: Das druckgraphische Werk* (see n. 26), p. 114.

30 Ibid.

31 Peter Krüger, "Die Apokalypse", in Schoch et al., *Dürer: Das druckgraphische Werk* (see n. 26), p. 72; see also p. 113.

32 Apoc. 1: 8 reads similarly: "I am Alpha and Omega, the beginning and the end, saith the Lord God, who is, and who was, and who is to come."

33 Eugen Drewermann, *Tiefenpsychologie und Exegese 2: Die Wahrheit der Werke und der Worte Wunder, Vision, Weissagung, Apokalypse, Geschichte, Gleichnis* (Munich, 1993), p. 558.

34 Schoch et al., *Dürer: Das druckgraphische Werk* (see n. 26), p. 120.

35 Krüger, "Apokalypse" (see n. 31), p. 90.

36 Schoch et al., *Dürer: Das druckgraphische Werk* (see n. 26), p. 118.

37 Ernst Ludwig Kirchner to Carl Hagemann, letter from 26 March 1936, in Hans Delfs, Mario-Andreas von Lüttichau and Roland Scotti (eds.), *Kirchner, Schmidt-Rottluff, Nolde, Nay …: Briefe an den Sammler und Mäzen Carl Hagemann,* 1906–1940 (Ostfildern-Ruit, 2004), p. 541.

38 Schoch et al., *Dürer: Das druckgraphische Werk* (see n. 26), p. 115.

39 Ibid., p. 121.

40 Ibid., p. 125.

41 Hofmaier, *Beckmann* (see n. 24), p. 354.

Vibrant Metropolis / Idyllic Nature
Kirchner — The Berlin Years

Catalogue

Beginnings in Dresden

1 At twenty-one Kirchner moved from Chemnitz to Dresden, where he studied architecture from 1901 to 1905. A few weeks before graduation, on 7 June 1905, he founded—together with his fellow students Fritz Bleyl, Erich Heckel and Karl Schmidt-Rottluff—the artists' association Brücke. The notion of the unity of art and life, of man and nature played an important role both in their works and in their everyday lives. Their newly created lifestyle and the works they each produced as part of their collaboration are expressions of this. The artists got together regularly to draw from a model. They felt a bond with everyone "who directly and honestly depicts what drives him to create", as they proclaimed in the Brücke programme. They set out to capture the most natural possible aspects and movements, unposed, in a few strokes. To that end they initiated the "quarter-of-an-hour nude", in which their models, generally nude, would assume the same unforced pose for a maximum of fifteen minutes. For this they did not engage professional models but preferred using women friends, lovers or young girls from the neighbourhood. With their anti-academic art and way of life they wanted to emancipate themselves from classical depictions of nudes as well as from social constraints—what they saw as the outmoded conservative values of the empire. Most of the scenes they captured on canvas or paper are set in studios. These modest settings were both work spaces and living quarters, somewhere where they might realise their liberated lifestyle.

One of Brücke's most important models between 1909 and 1911 was the young girl Lina Franziska Fehrmann, called Fränzi. In *Nude behind a Curtain (Fränzi)* p.104, she gazes innocently and at the same time curiously from behind a curtain that Kirchner had painted in a primitive style with erotic scenes. Beyond the curtain we see part of his studio, artfully filled with his own pictures and furniture and fabrics he had made himself. Fränzi, shifted to the left of centre, fills the entire height of the canvas. Standing frontally, her head tilted to the side, she gazes at the viewer. With a blend of childlike innocence and awakening sexuality the young model radiates a subliminal eroticism. Her eyes are emphasised, her face is stylised and draws to a point, and each brush stroke is strongly placed. The angularity of Fränzi's slender body recalls African sculptures, a testament to Kirchner's engagement with non-European cultures at that time. He has reduced his palette to a strong red, yellow-ochre and green, with black shadows and occasional accents in blue that he also used for contours. The entire composition is flat, without depth. Naturalness and spontaneity were meant to be captured on canvas or paper with this kind of unaffected "posing" in the studio.

Studies of bodies, especially the female nude, were made not only in the studios of the Brücke artists but also in nature, not far from Dresden at the Moritzburg Ponds. In secluded spots there they produced a great number of bathing scenes. Many works from this time picture nudes as part of nature and appear as if they were composed and executed in only a few sittings. This "disciplined spontaneity" is readily seen in the summery bathing scene *Four Bathers* p.100 in which four nude women are pictured near the shore. Each is captured in a different natural movement as though in a snapshot. Their faces are merely suggested, and the drawing of their bodies is limited to only the most essential lines. A few lines emphasise the contours of the breasts, their sex, the positions of their arms, and the landscape in the background on the other side of the pond. The rest is sparingly executed with swift, long brush strokes or done so fleetingly that unpainted spots dot the canvas. It is easy to imagine that Kirchner created the composition in only a few minutes. The gaps and the way the tree is cut off by the top edge heighten the impression of the motif having been discovered and executed intuitively. Yet on second glance the spontaneous bathing scene suggests that Kirchner very deliberately distributed his nude figures in different poses in a variety of spatial planes so as to achieve depth despite the flat style of painting.

Kirchner's early work does not yet reveal a clearly defined style; he was still searching for an artistic signature of his own. Only in early 1909 did the so-called Brücke style make its appearance. What this is, becomes particularly clear if one compares pictures from this time with the earlier painting *Fehmarn Houses* p. 101. Kirchner had first visited the Baltic Sea island of Fehmarn in 1908, accompanied by the siblings Emy and Hans Frisch, friends from his school years in Chemnitz. Later, when he was living in Berlin, Fehmarn would become his preferred summer destination. The painting *Fehmarn Houses* clearly betrays the influence of Vincent van Gogh, whose works he had seen in May of that year in Dresden's Kunstsalon Richter. Kirchner captured the farmhouses in thick layers of glowing, unmixed pigments applied with his palette knife or straight out of the tube. The gestural, pastose application of pigment and the resulting contrasts in the texture of the picture are more dominant than the lines and colours. In the Brücke style, however, created in the group's collective development, the application of pigment is thinner and flatter—occasionally one can even see the canvas—and loosely drawn chromatic outlines surround patches of colour. The lines function as colour accents, and not only as boundaries between forms. Radiant, highly contrasting planes of colour and a loose, fluid style of painting are comparable to the style of the Fauves. With just such watercolour-like looseness Kirchner captured an everyday situation in his painting *Streetcar in Dresden* p. 99: an electric streetcar follows an S-bend along a street lined with trees and populated with only a few passers-by and a bicyclist. The motifs are outlined in a dark blue applied with a fluid, rhythmic stroke. The remaining colours are so sparing that, especially in the foreground, large sections of the canvas remain untouched. It was with great virtuosity that he incorporated these empty spots in the overall composition.

The subject of the lively street scene appears for the first time in his lithograph *Street Life in Dresden* p. 98. Here—probably borrowing from Edvard Munch's street scenes—Kirchner schematically depicts figures on Königstrasse in a uniformly applied ink and with numerous scratches and scrapings in the dark surface. There is a painting of the same scene, reversed and with slight deviations in the clothing and the design of the background. Kirchner would only take up the theme of the lively big-city street scene in Berlin in 1913.

In addition to city views and the depictions of nudes both in the studio and in nature, he also pictured motifs from Dresden's nightlife. Dance locales—the music hall, the theatre, the circus—were favourite places that gave him a chance to study more complex sequences of movement and people in refreshingly unforced poses and to capture them in art. In *Two Dancing Girls* p. 102 two women dressed in a radiant yellow dance on a light-brown stage. In the background there is the suggestion of an outdoor scene with green trees and blue water. This is in fact a theatre backdrop. Kirchner closely cropped the scene and pictures the two dancers slightly from below, from the perspective of the audience. The few, strong colours and the flat application of pigment emphasise the movement motif. Kirchner creates rhythm and dynamism with the swinging skirts with their irregularly painted black hems that permit a glimpse of the women's white bloomers, and by depicting the dancers in an unstable pose that they could assume only for a brief moment.

Cat. 103

Street Life in Dresden, 1908
Lithograph on chamois blotting paper

Kassel, Museumslandschaft Hessen Kassel, Graphische Sammlung

Cat. 3

Streetcar in Dresden, 1909
Oil on canvas

Staatsgalerie Stuttgart, on loan from a private collection

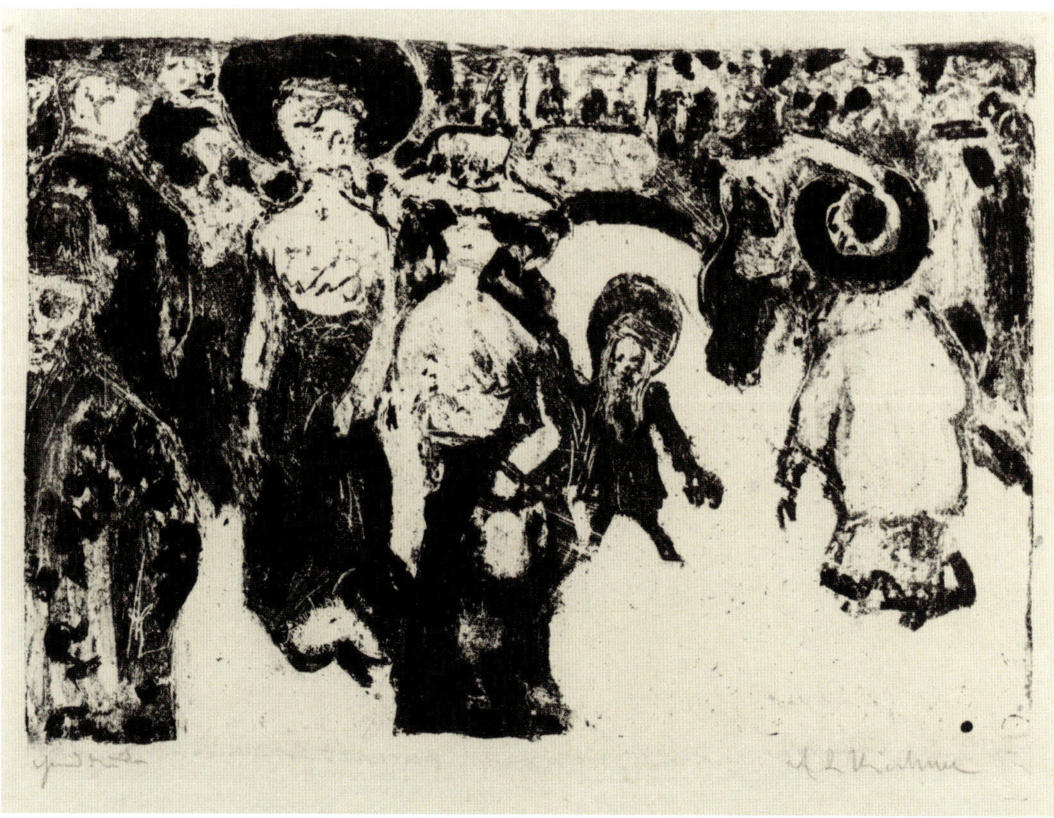

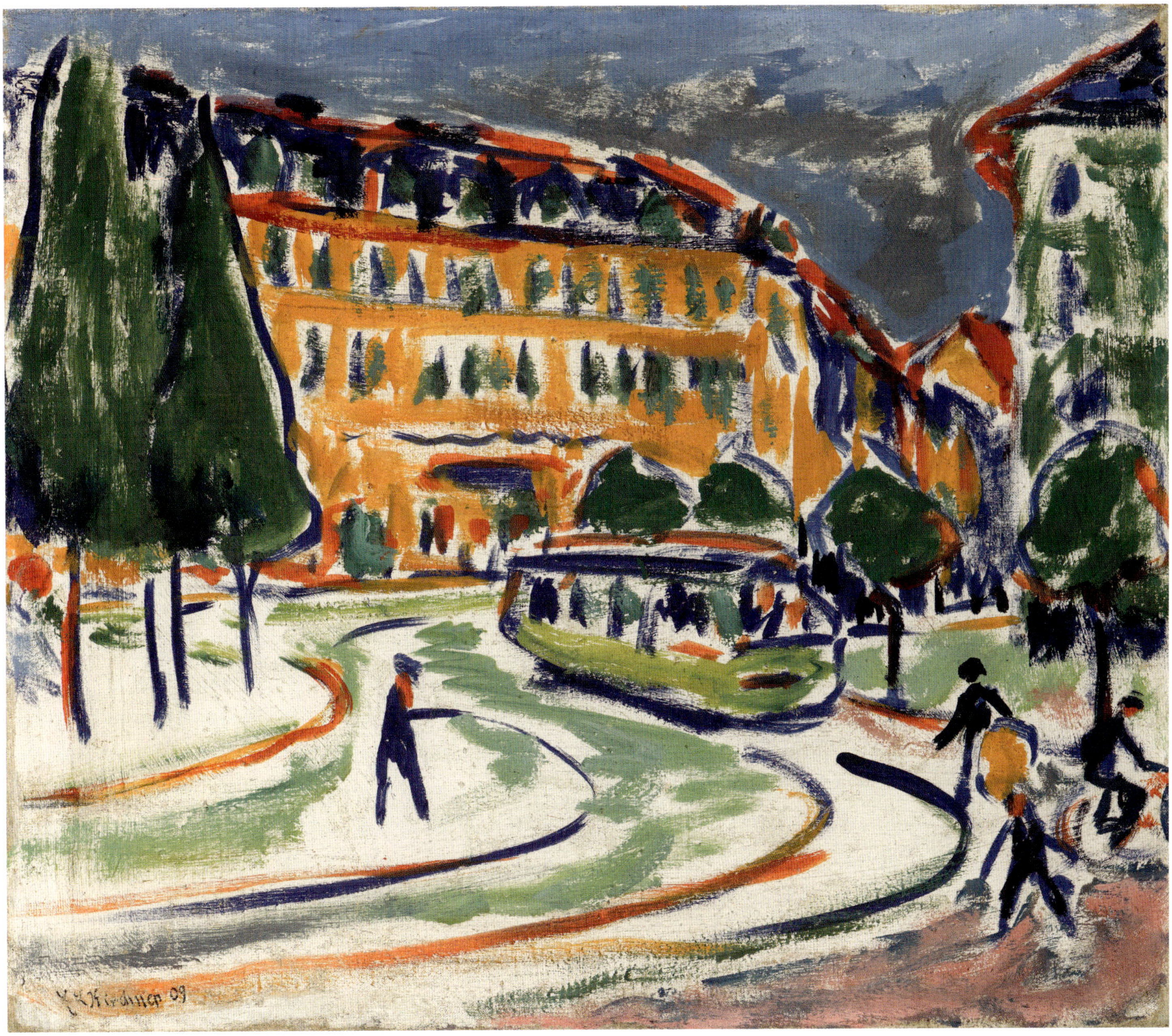

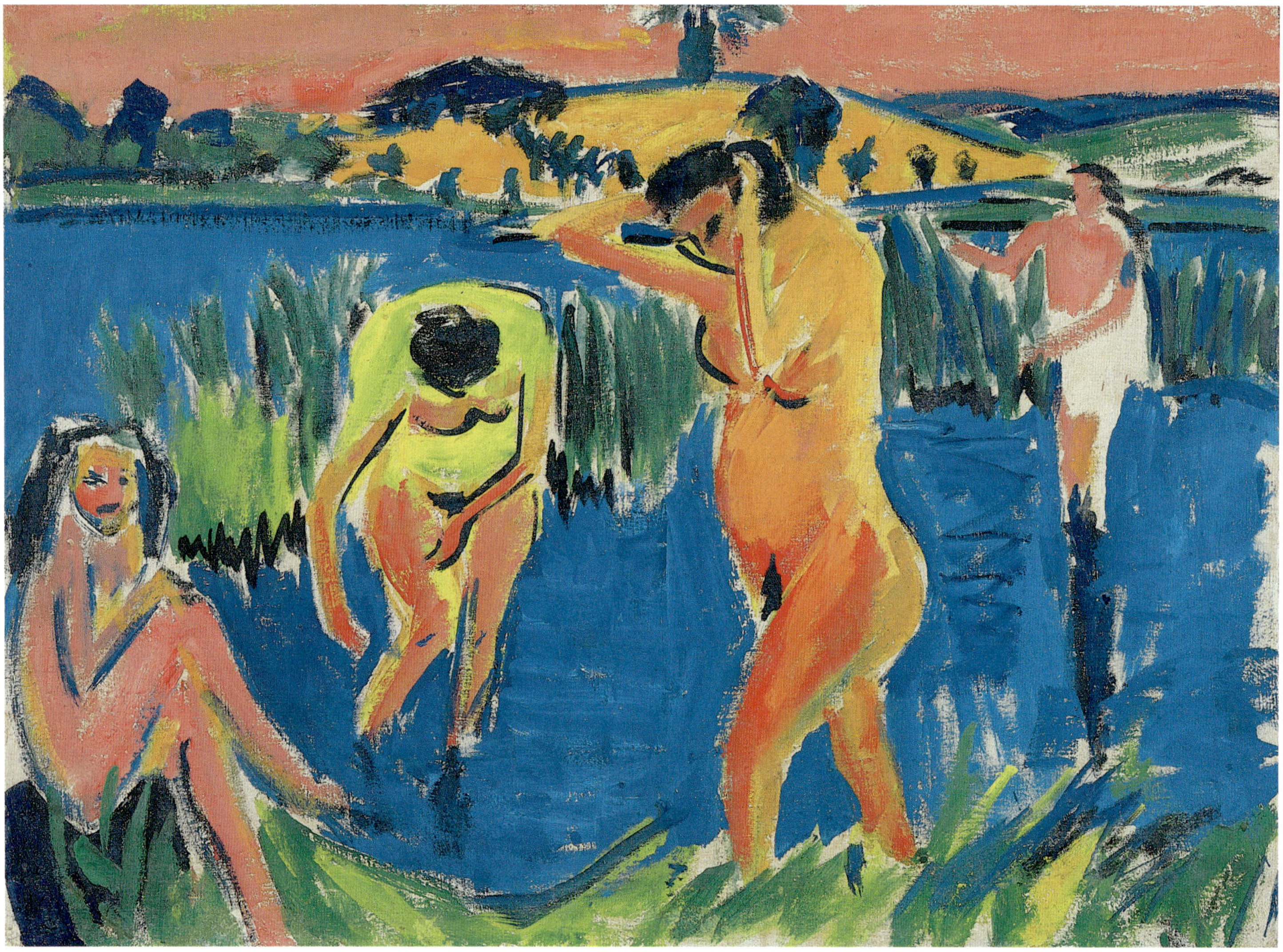

Cat. 2

Four Bathers, 1909
Oil on canvas

Von der Heydt-Museum Wuppertal

Cat. 1

Fehmarn Houses, 1908
Oil on canvas

Städel Museum, Frankfurt am Main, on permanent loan from a private collection

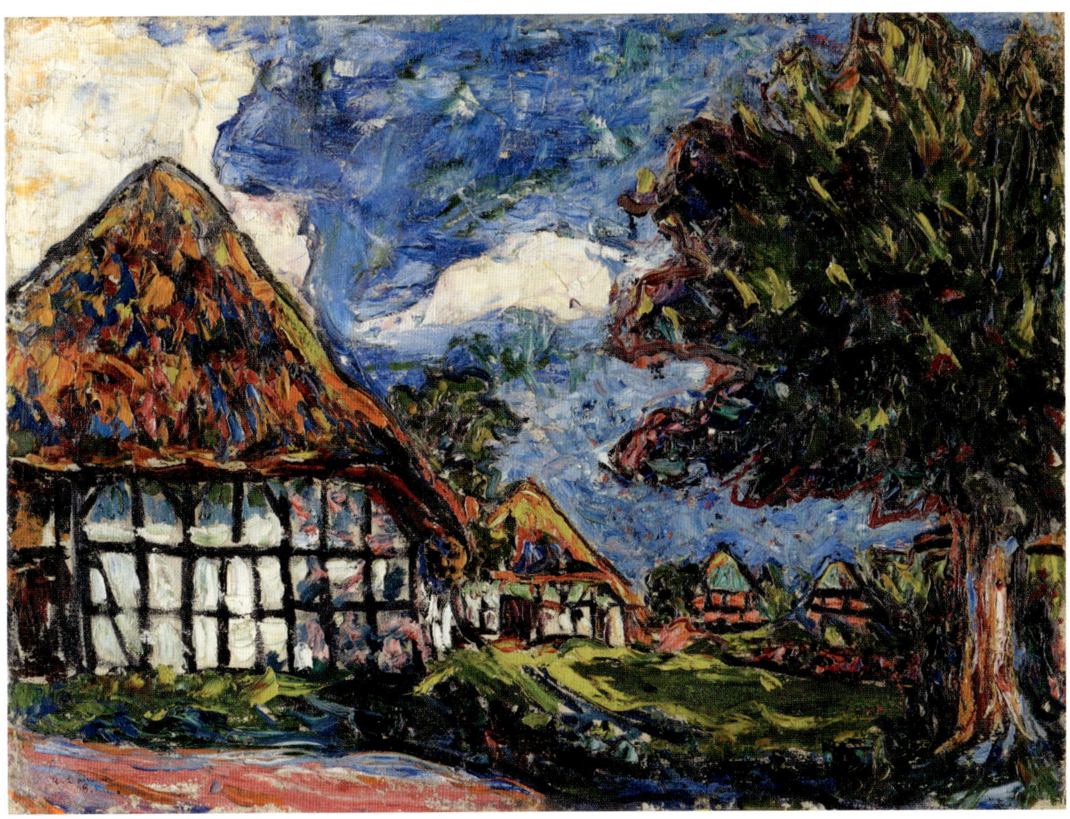

Cat. 9

Two Dancing Girls, 1910/11
Oil on canvas

Franz Marc Museum, Kochel am See, on permanent loan from a private collection

Cat. 7

Artist – Marcella, 1910
Oil on canvas

Brücke-Museum, Berlin

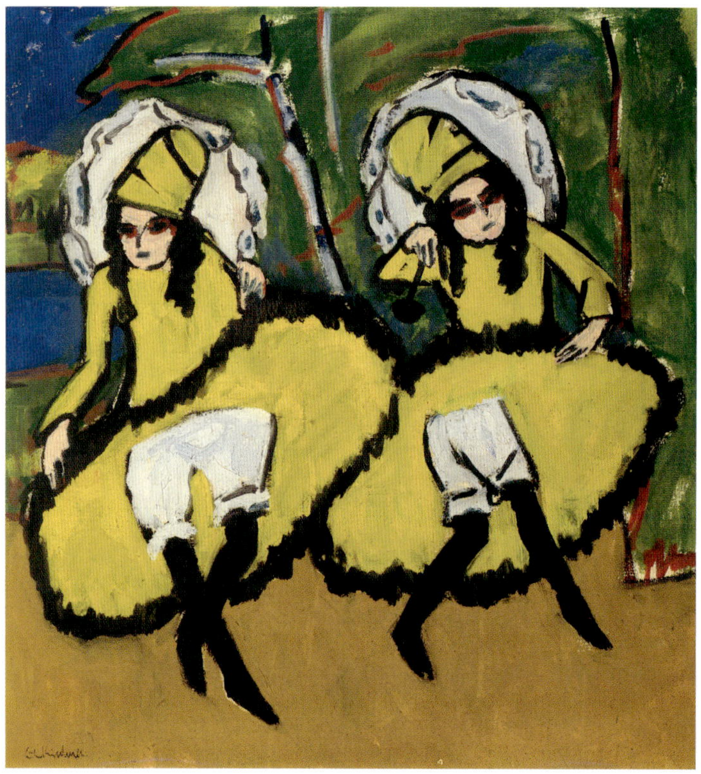

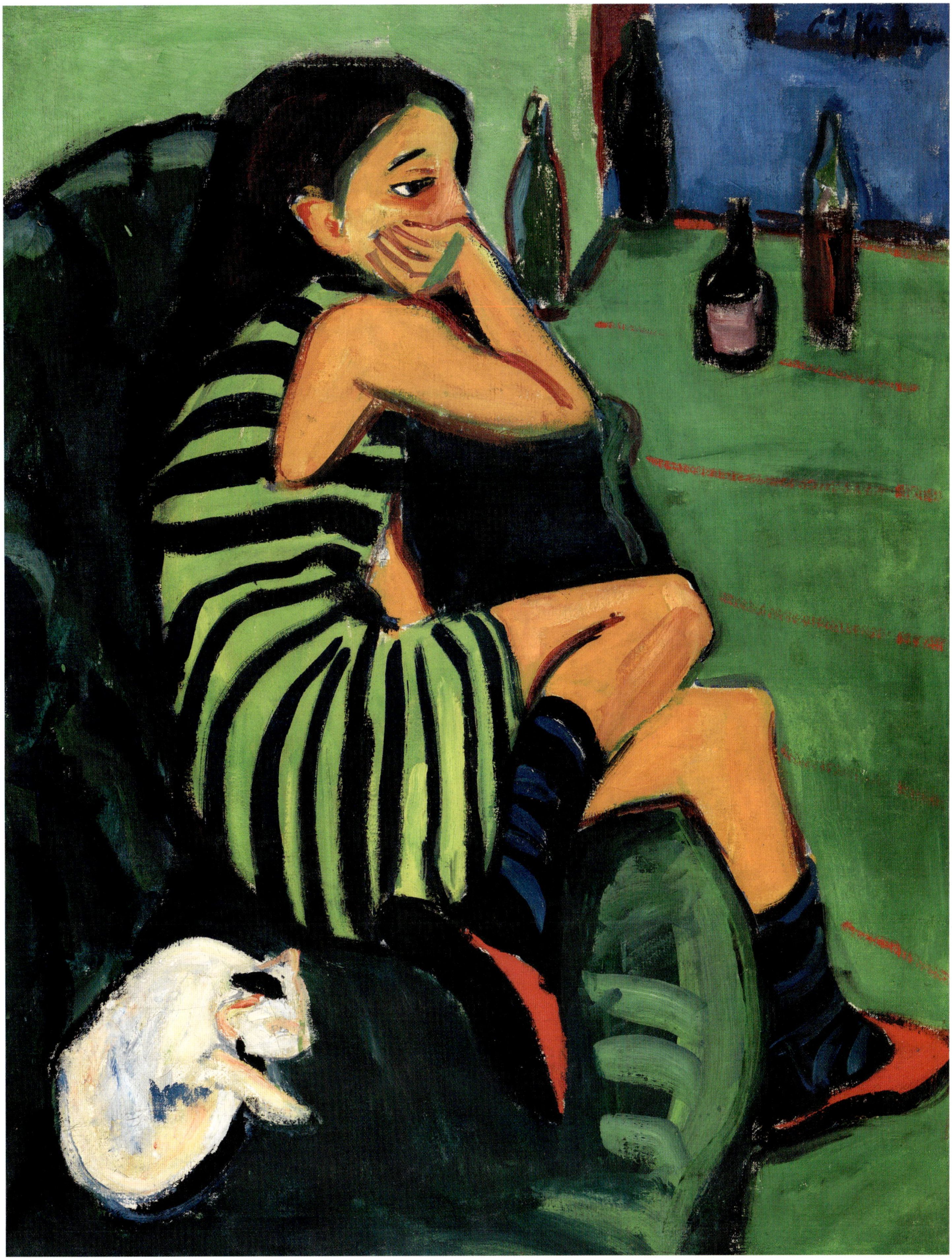

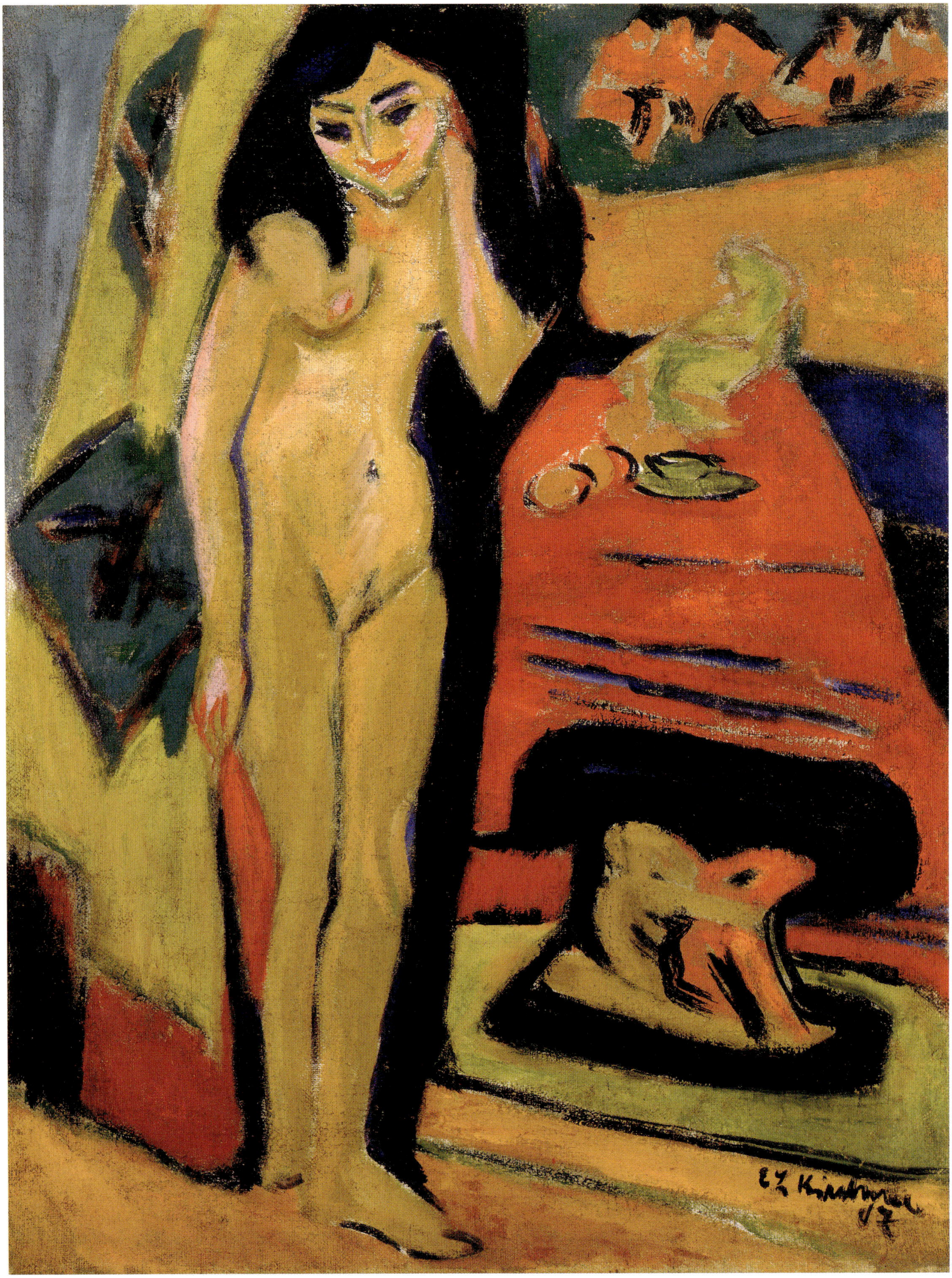

Cat. 8

Nude behind a Curtain (Fränzi), 1910/1926
Oil on canvas

Collection Stedelijk Museum, Amsterdam

Cat. 6

Girl with Cat, Fränzi, 1910
Oil on canvas

Merzbacher Kunststiftung

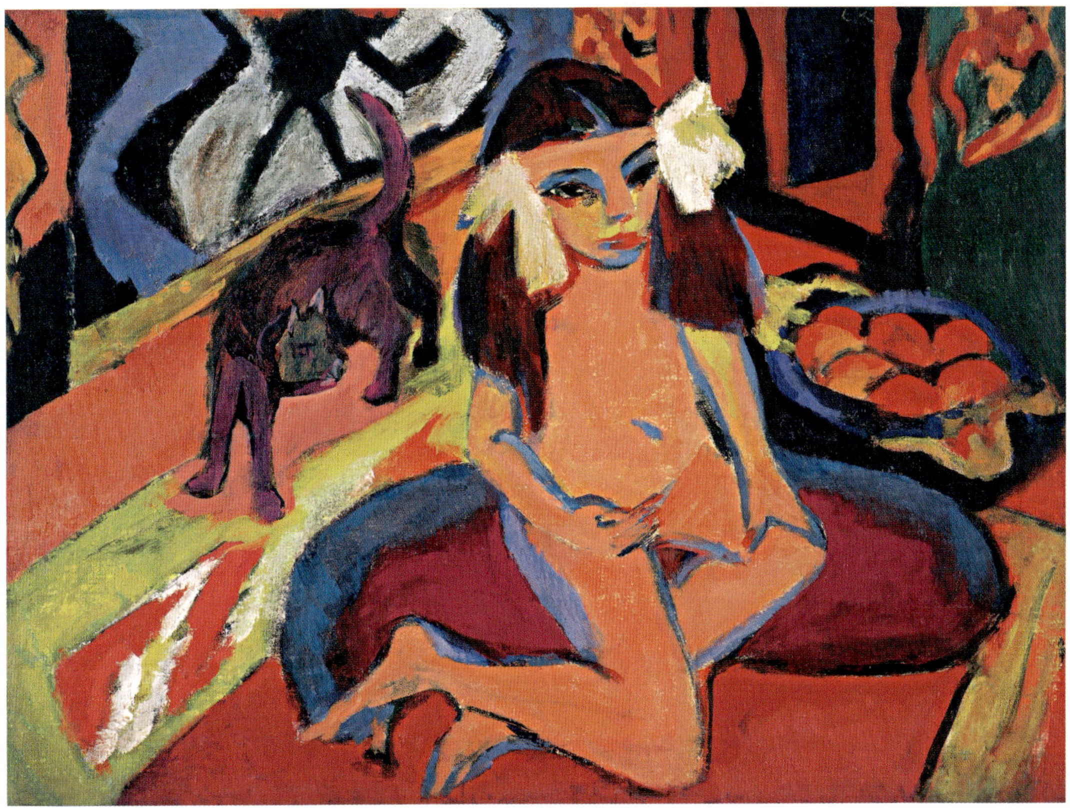

Cat. 4

Reclining Nude in Front of a Mirror, 1909/10
Oil on canvas

Brücke-Museum, Berlin

Cat. 5

Fränzi and Marcella, 1910
Oil on painting pad

E. W. K. Collection, Bern/Davos

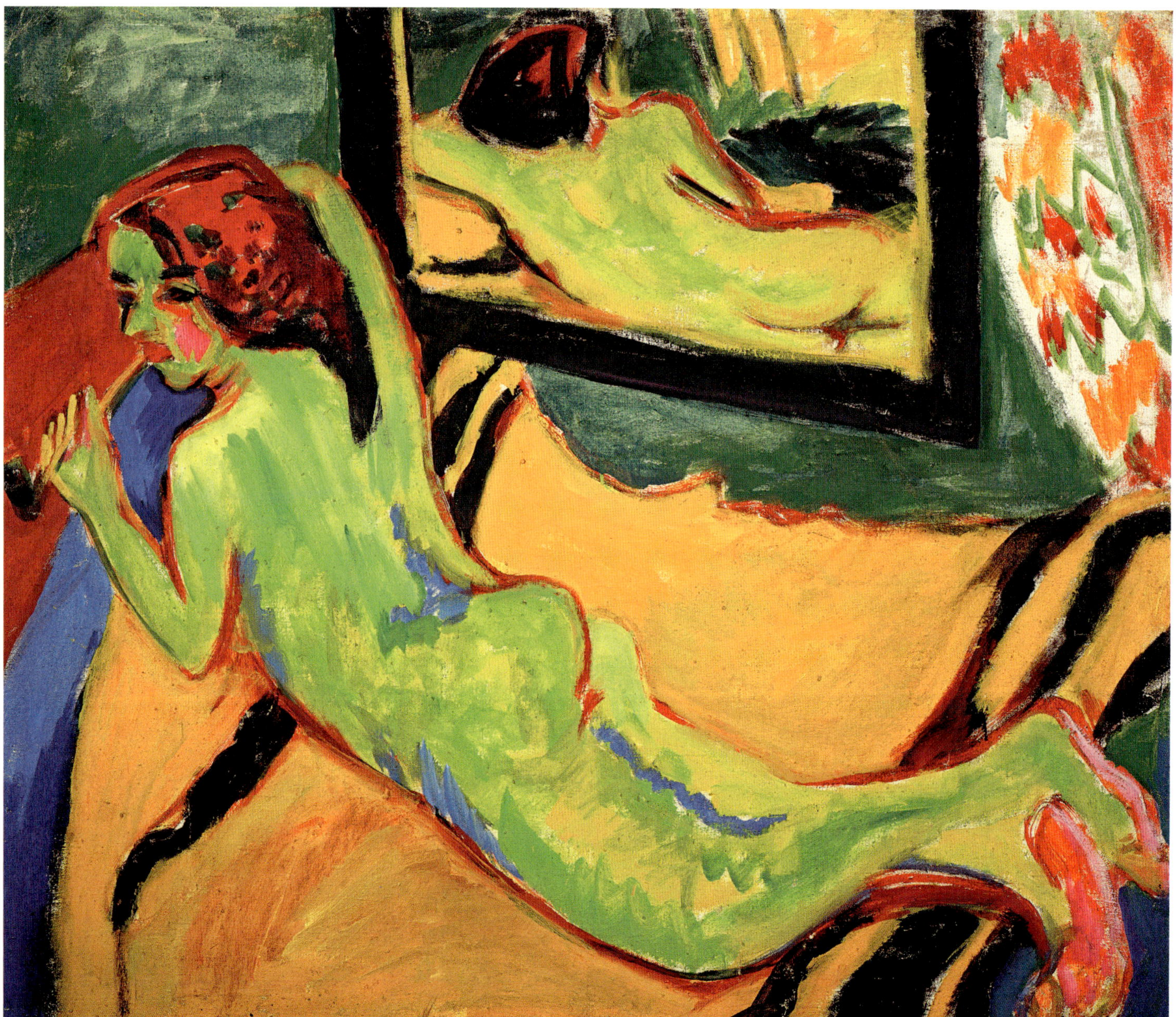

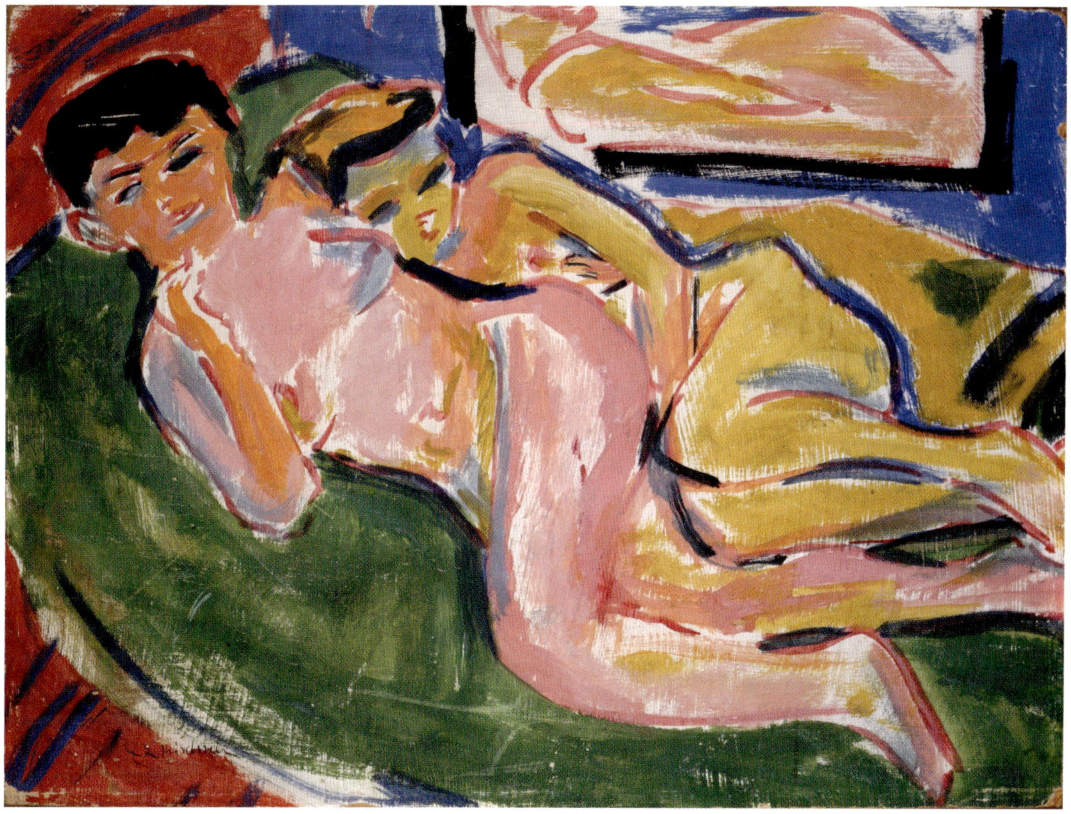

From Dresden to Berlin (1911–1912)

2

In the fall of 1911 Kirchner moved from Dresden to Berlin. The metropolis had only recently become one of Germany's leading art centres, and he hoped to be better able to establish himself as an artist in Berlin. Kirchner's expectations of the city were not fulfilled, however, and he was at first disappointed. The art school he founded with Max Pechstein shortly after his arrival in Berlin—the MUIM Institut (Moderner Unterricht in Malerei/Modern Instruction in Painting), which was housed in the same building as their studios and from which they hoped for additional income—had to be closed after a year as it did not attract enough pupils. Kirchner's extremely productive Berlin years are characterised by dynamic impressions of the big city, its amusements and vices, as well as by his stays during the summer months on the Baltic Sea island of Fehmarn. However, it was not merely the move to Berlin that was responsible for the change in style that appears in 1911 but rather Kirchner's engagement with non-European art, especially India's Ajanta frescoes, which he had discovered in the library of the Dresden museums in John Griffiths's book *The Paintings in the Buddhist Cave-Temples of Ajantá, Khandesh, India* (London, 1896/97). The figures in the wall paintings of the Buddhist cave temples are characterised by softly rounded forms that contrasted with Kirchner's flat and angular style at the time. He subsequently attempted to adapt this quality for his figures by means of outlining and unobtrusive hatching. A new aesthetic thus enters Kirchner's work and gradually replaces the use of radiant planes of colour evident in his paintings of the previous years.

Kirchner would develop his newly acquired style still further in the first works he produced in Berlin. In *Two Female Nudes in Vertical Format* p.111 the contours as well as the figures' protruding buttocks recall the well-formed bodies of the Ajanta frescoes, although here the zigzag hatching along the contours is even more dominant. The work introduces Kirchner's "flatter" style typical of his later Berlin works. His use of new models, namely the two sisters Gerda and Erna Schilling—pictured in this painting—whom Kirchner had met shortly after his arrival in Berlin, also stimulated his abandonment of "soft Saxon bodies" and androgynous, childlike models in favour of "beautiful, architecturally structured bodies" (Kirchner, 1925/26). In the painting, Erna, standing and bending over, is sponging her sister Gerda, who is seated on a rug and turned towards the viewer. Their pink and beige tones stand out against the green background, in which one can make out the fabrics Kirchner had designed himself.

A short time later Erna Schilling became Kirchner's new girlfriend and he spent the summer of 1912 together with her on Fehmarn. The couple chose a secluded spot for their stay, living in the house of the lighthouse keeper Lüthmann at Staberhuk on the island's south-eastern tip. Kirchner not only used the island as an escape but made it his own personal Arcadia. How important his visits to the island were in the summer months of 1912, 1913 and 1914 is obvious from the large number of works in various techniques with Fehmarn motifs. The island's characteristic landscape and the search for a unity of man and nature—which he had begun at the Moritzburg Ponds—inspired the artist to paint a large number of bathing scenes and depictions of nudes.

Taking up his new concept of the figure, he applied the outline painting style, hatching and a more muted palette to the Fehmarn pictures. In *Bather between Rocks* p.119 Erna is seated nude between the large boulders that were a distinctive feature of the beach below the lighthouse. The forms of her body, especially her thighs, are repeated in the rocks. Hatching in a dark grey was used to suggest volumes in the painting as a whole. Kirchner chose a tight cropping for the scene: Erna's head is close to the top edge and the lighthouse in the background is cut off by it. This serves to draw the depiction closer to the viewer.

Moreover, a sparing use of colour underscores the nature of the island's raw and craggy landscape. The only colour accent is Erna's red sun hat. This same head covering appears in many Fehmarn pictures, for example *Two Nudes by a Tree, Fehmarn* p. 118 or *Erna near the Sea, Fehmarn* p. 146. In *Bather between Rocks* the colour and shape of the hat are taken up again on the head of a man at the far-left edge and in the roof of the building next to the lighthouse. Kirchner also photographed his girlfriend in a similar scene, but from somewhat farther off and shifted away from centre p. 114.

Kirchner recorded everyday experiences as well as specific stretches of the island landscape. The artist was fascinated by its raw and rich variety. He considered the vegetation on Fehmarn exotic, and gave certain paintings corresponding titles, like *Mexico Bay, Fehmarn* p. 122. The laburnum tree in the lighthouse keeper's garden was probably one of the plants that gave him that impression. In the painting *Laburnum Tree* p. 120 it is seen in full bloom in the centre of the scene. Kirchner used the glowing yellow blossoms that hung from the tree as accents in the painting's colour harmony, contrasting them with the cooler green of the lush vegetation and the blue of the sea in the background, which he also used as the colour of the shadows.

In addition to depictions of figures and landscapes, there is a third group of pictures from Fehmarn featuring the island's buildings pp. 162, 163. One recurring motif is the Staberhuk lighthouse, from whose elevation there was a good view of the bathing beach below. *The Lighthouse of Fehmarn* p. 121 is a good example of how Kirchner was inspired by actual motifs and translated them into his own pictorial imagery. He pictured the lighthouse and its adjacent buildings in a bird's-eye view. The individual structures are treated three-dimensionally and are still clearly separated from each other and from the background, in contrast to *Laburnum Tree* p. 120, where the background appears to blend in with the foliage of the tree in the foreground. Kirchner creates compositional excitement with his colouring and his idiosyncratic treatment of space: he depicts the two houses from different perspectives from an elevated standpoint but shows the lighthouse frontally, while the entire composition is held together by the unrealistic curving horizon line that runs parallel to the bend of the shore.

Back in Berlin, in the second half of 1912 he began painting a series of cityscapes in addition to nudes in his studio pp. 126, 127. In them he chose both architectural motifs and everyday metropolitan subjects that he had previously captured in his sketchbooks on his frequent wanderings through the city. *Nollendorfplatz* p. 112 and *Street at Schöneberg City Park* p. 125 both picture an intersection—one seen at a diagonal and one frontally. In *Nollendorfplatz* the streets are teeming with people and two streetcars appear to crash into each other, but in *Street at Schöneberg City Park* there are only isolated, fashionably dressed strollers on streets devoid of traffic. It is only in the background that a locomotive can be seen passing across a bridge. In both paintings Kirchner magisterially combines views from above and below: he shows the buildings, streets, sidewalks and people from different points of view and plays with different perspectives, so that the building in the centre in *Nollendorfplatz* and the two clusters of buildings in *Street at Schöneberg City Park* thrust forward as though distended. In addition to the alienating perspectives, in both pictures Kirchner concentrates on only few colours: yellow-blue and black or respectively grey-blue-green.

Cat. 11

Unicycle Rider, 1911
Oil on canvas

Merzbacher Kunststiftung

Cat. 12

Two Female Nudes in Vertical Format, 1911/12
Oil on canvas

Kunstmuseum Bern,
Gift of Hilde Thannhauser, Bern,
from the Justin Thannhauser Collection

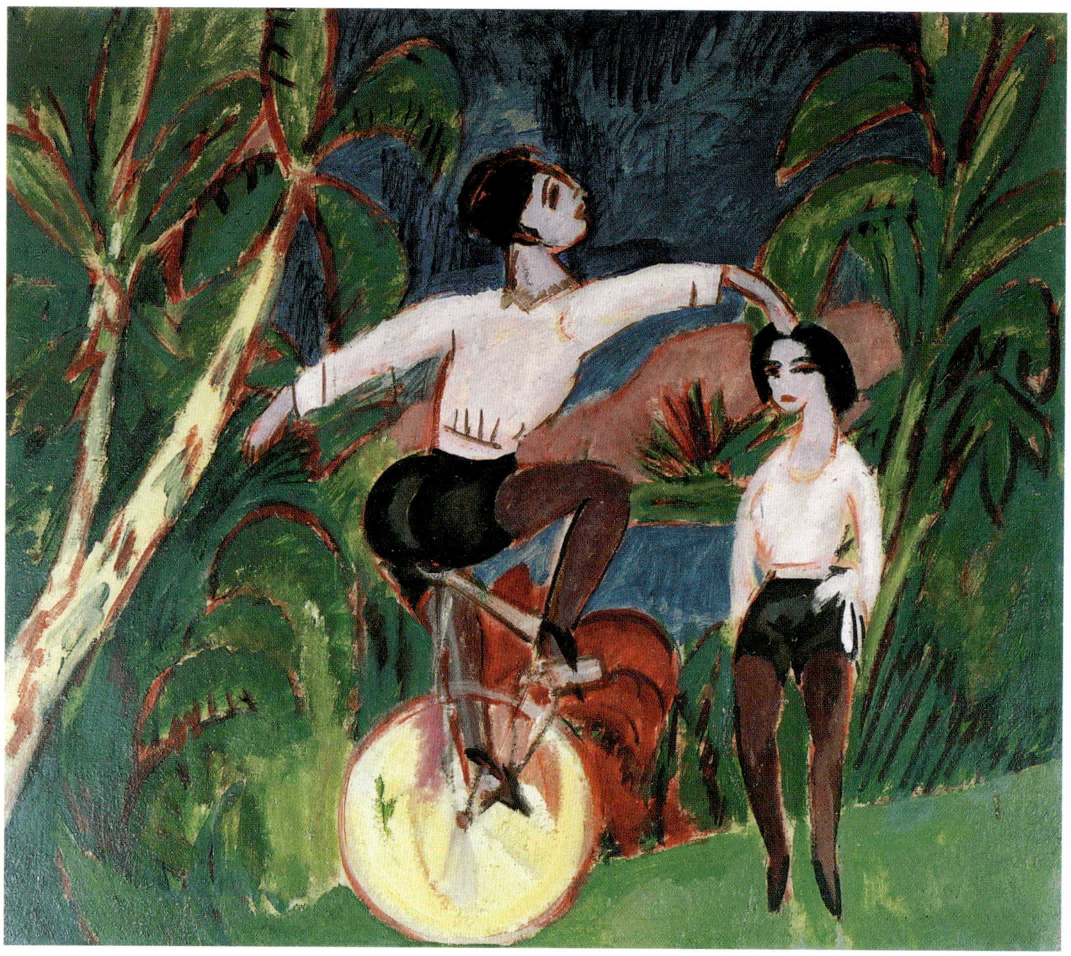

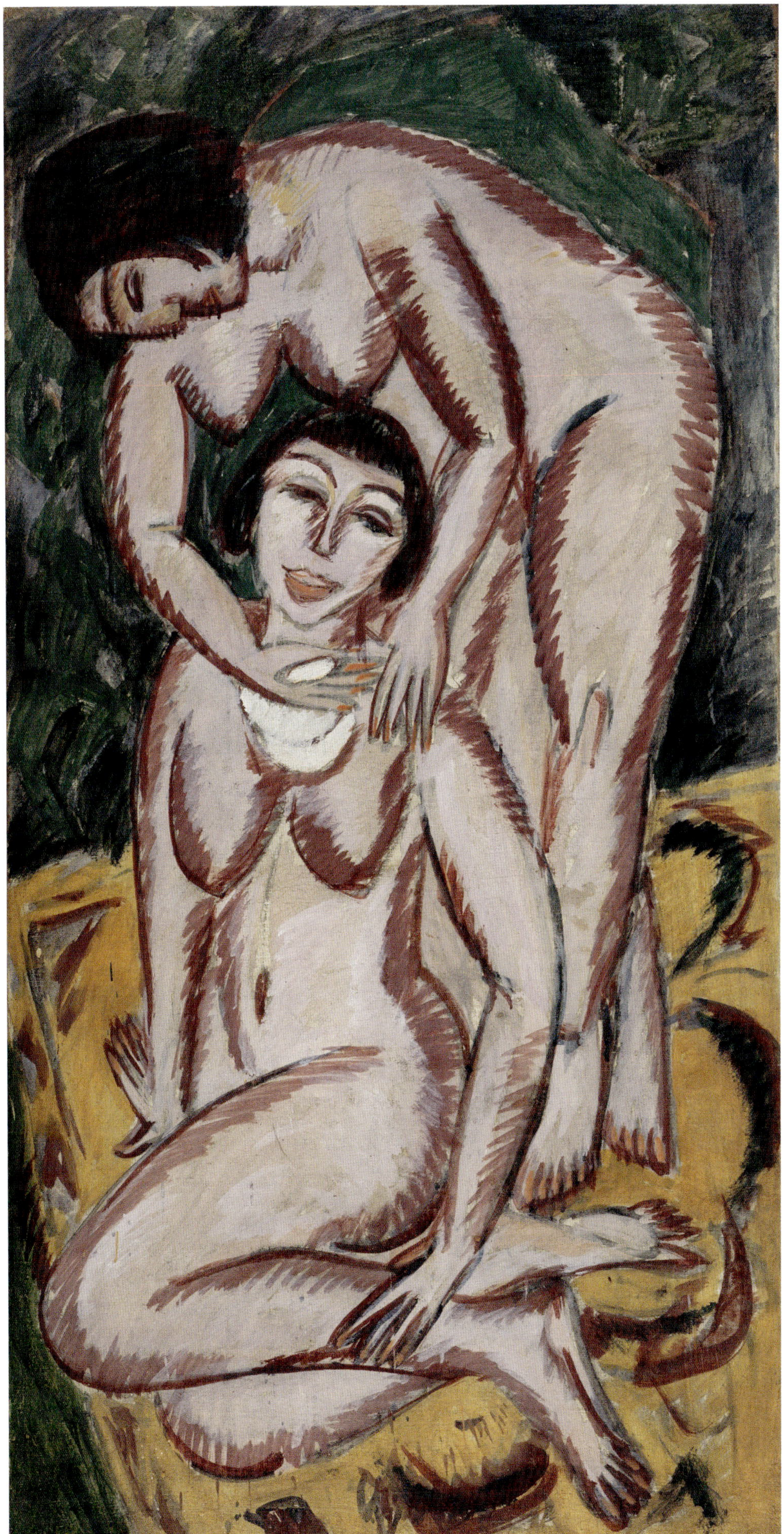

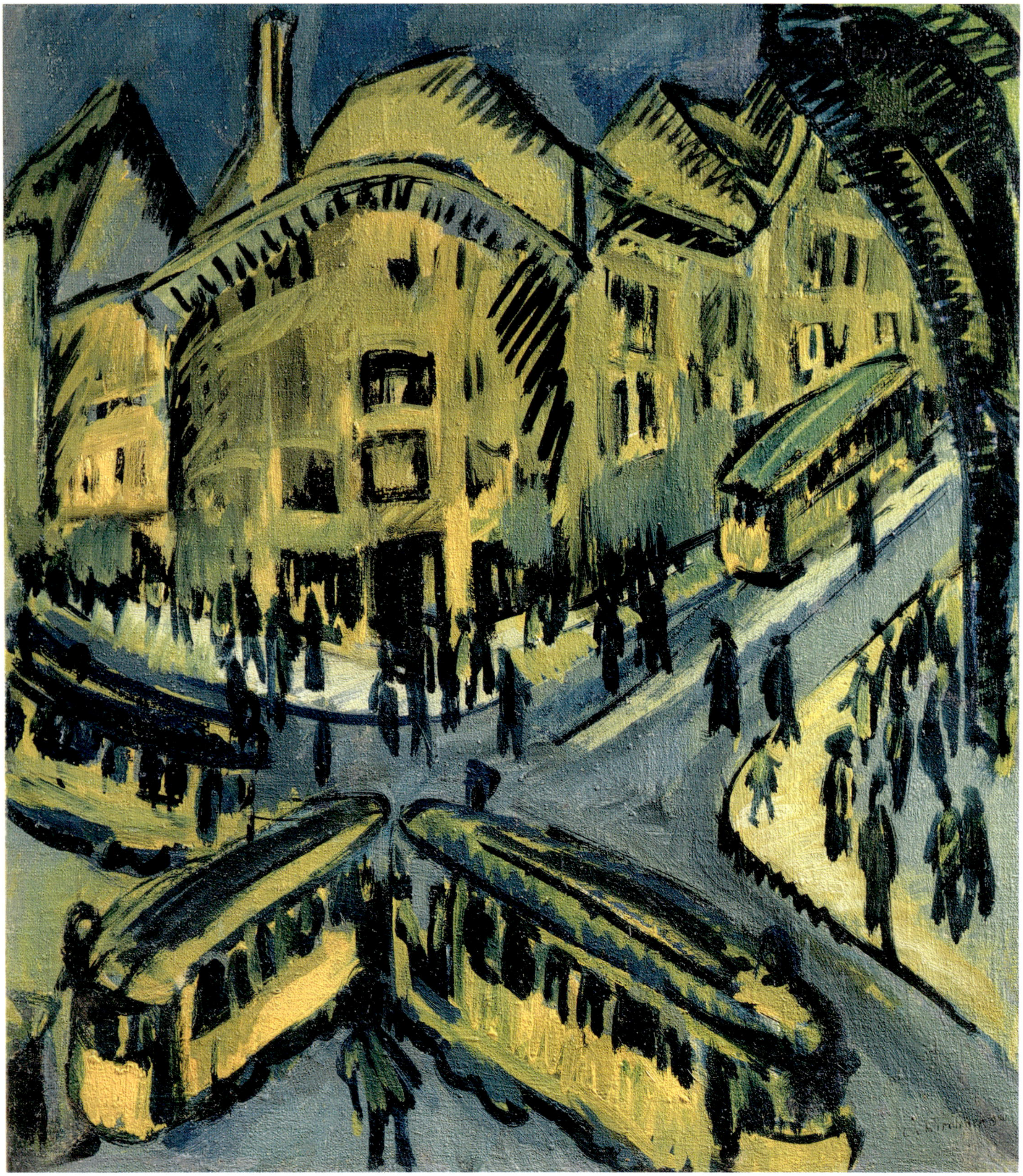

Cat. 19

Nollendorfplatz, 1912
Oil on canvas

Stadtmuseum Berlin Foundation

Cat. 10

City Tower, 1911
Oil on canvas

Kunstsammlungen Chemnitz – Museum Gunzenhauser, property of the Gunzenhauser Foundation

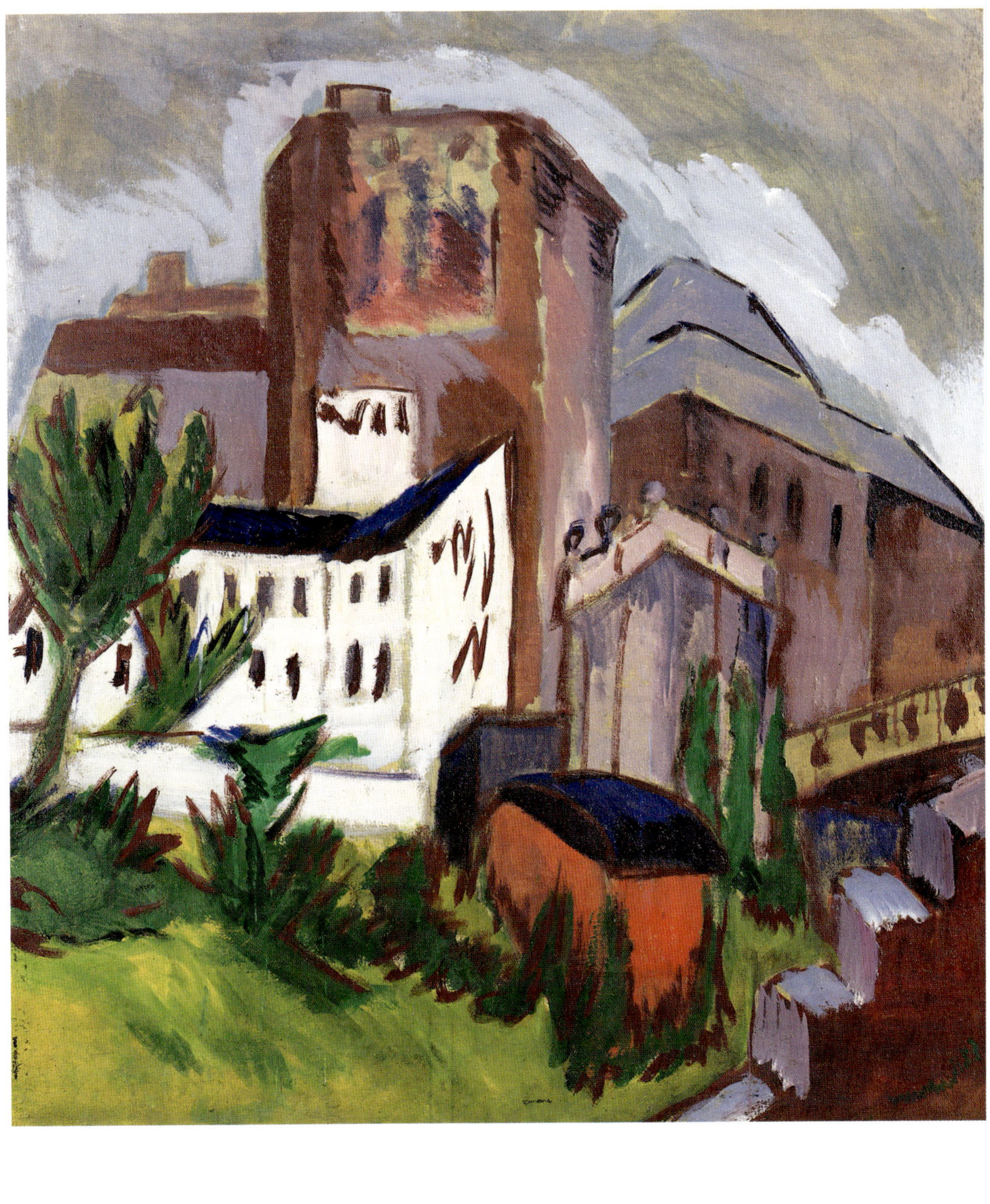

Cat. 139

Erna Schilling on the rocks on the coast, Fehmarn, 1913 Contact print (modern print)

Kirchner Museum Davos, Gift of the Ernst Ludwig Kirchner Estate 1992

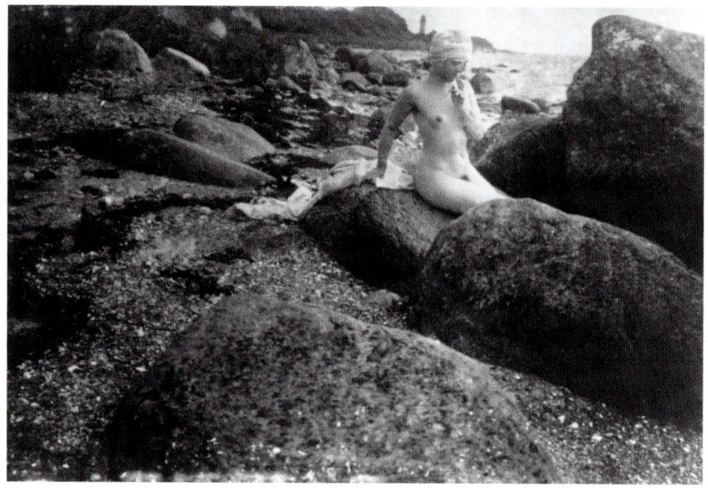

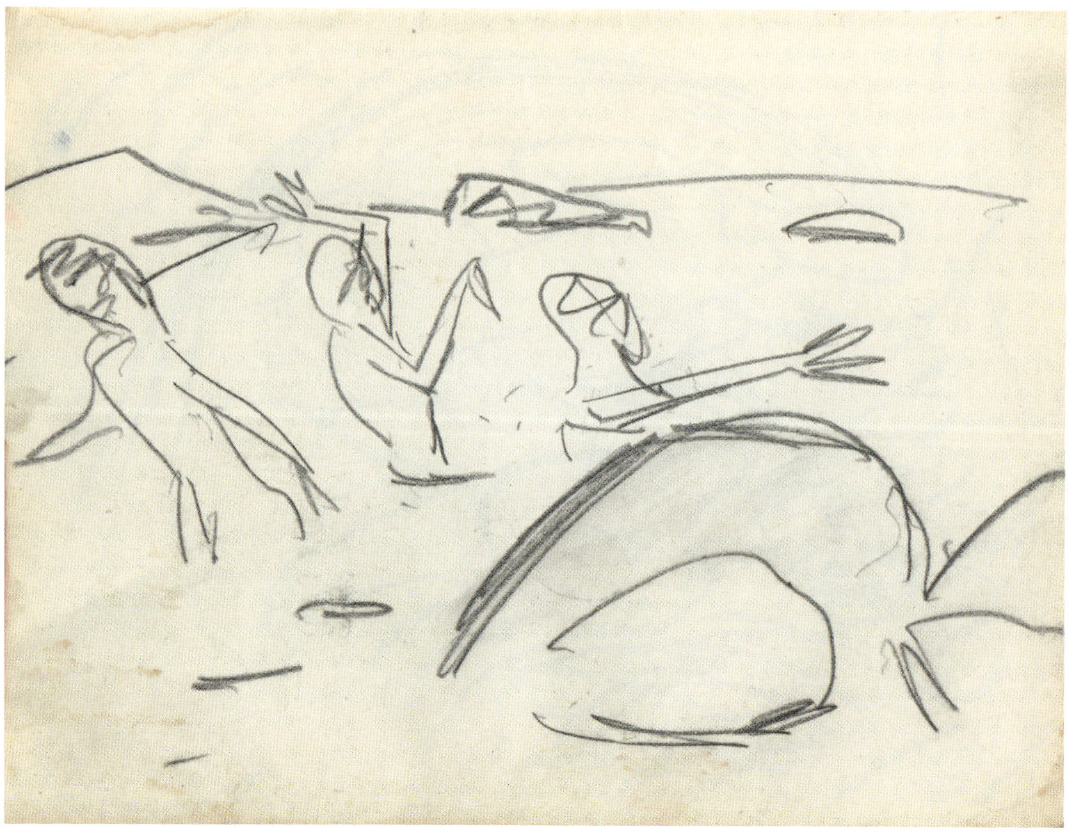

Cat. 132

Page (Fol. 15) in Sketchbook 26, 1912
Oilcloth booklet with 3 metal clasps

Kirchner Museum Davos, Gift of the Ernst Ludwig Kirchner Estate 1990

Cat. 76

Two Women and Sculpture on the Beach, c.1912
Pencil on paper

Kunstmuseum Winterthur, Gift of Balthasar and Nanni Reinhard-Schinz, 1999

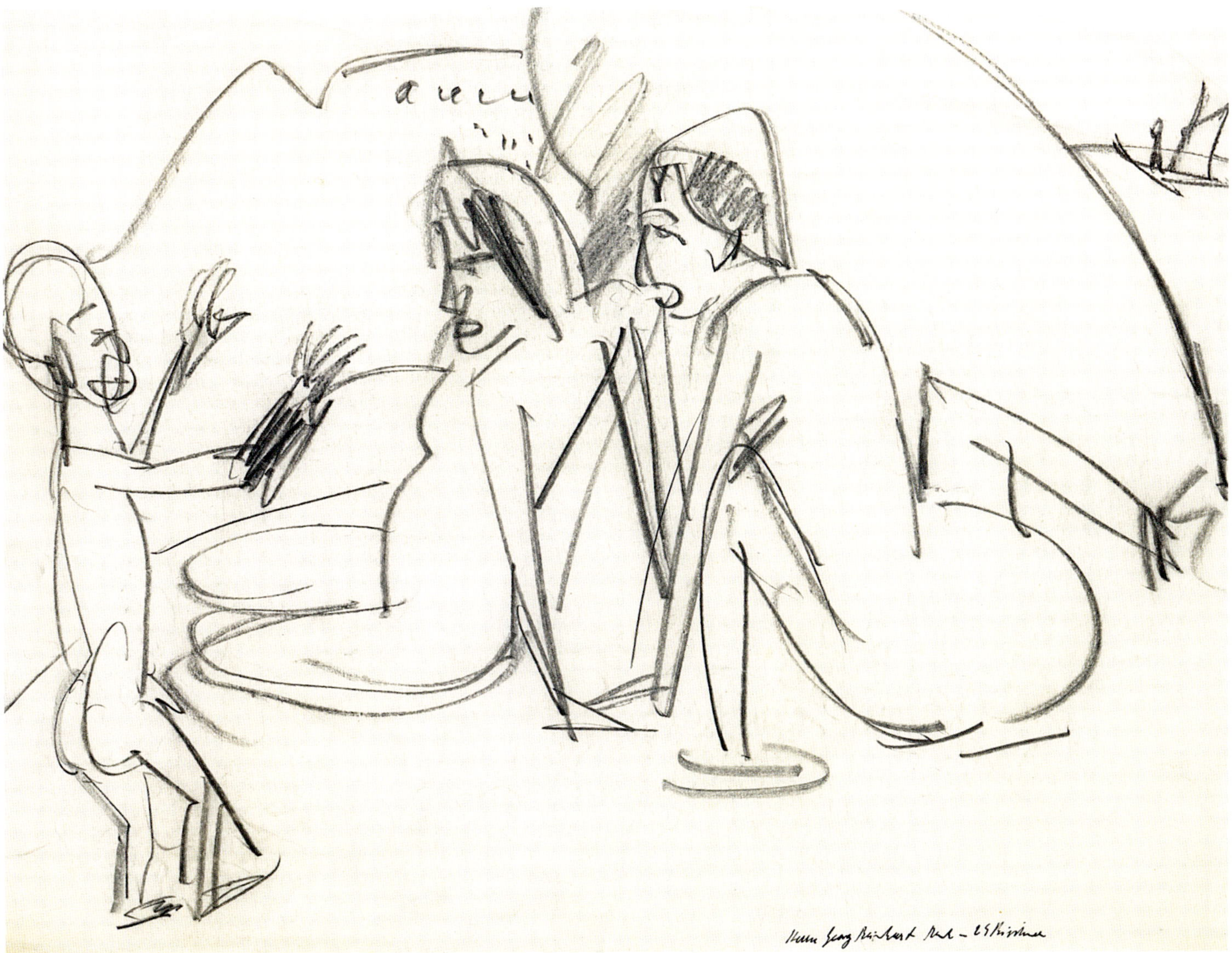

Cat. 75

Seated Bather, 1912
Blue crayon and watercolour on paper

Kunstmuseum Basel, Kupferstichkabinett

Cat. 104

Women Bathing between White Rocks, Fehmarn, 1912
Colour woodcut on vellum

Brücke-Museum, Berlin

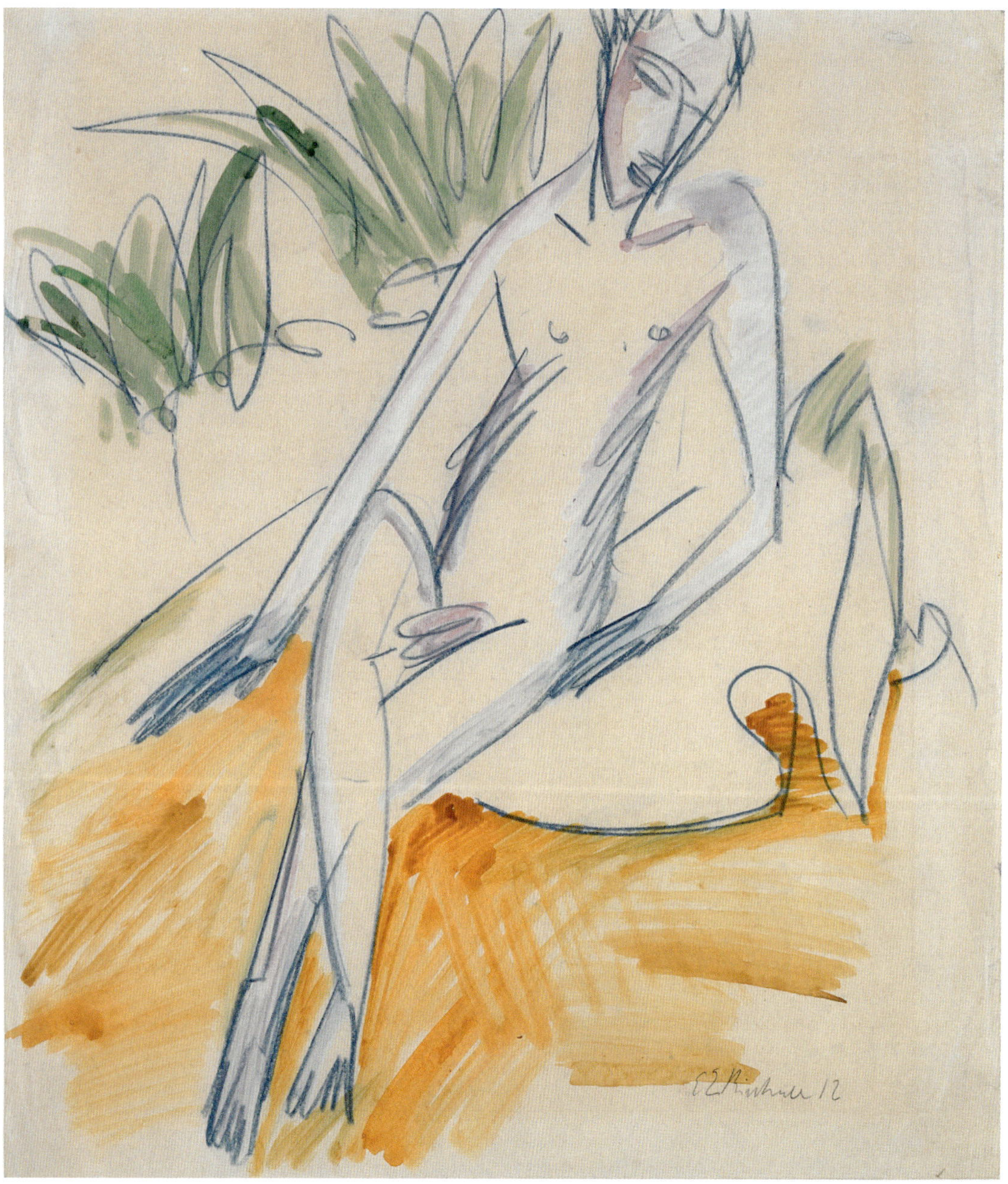

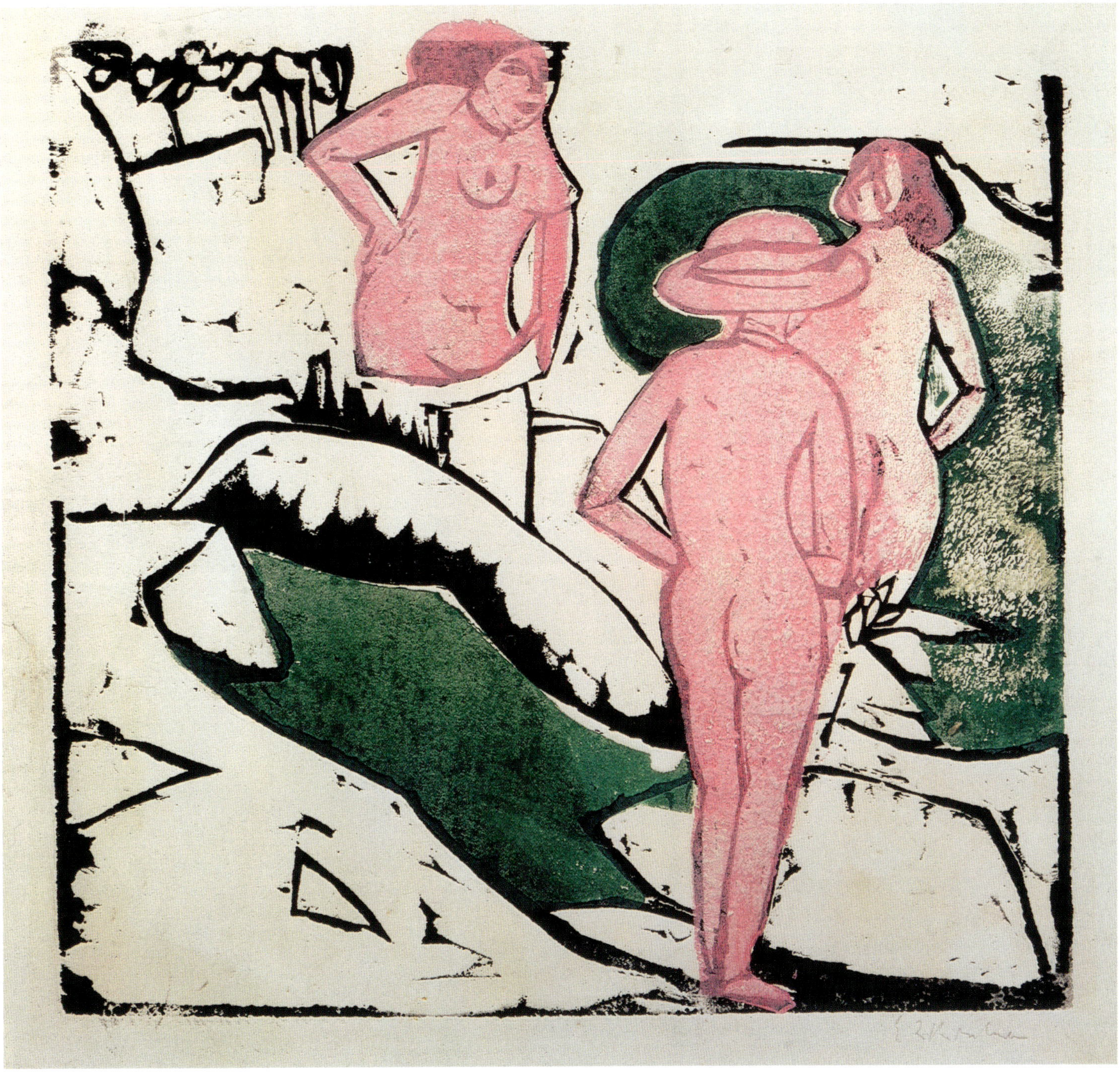

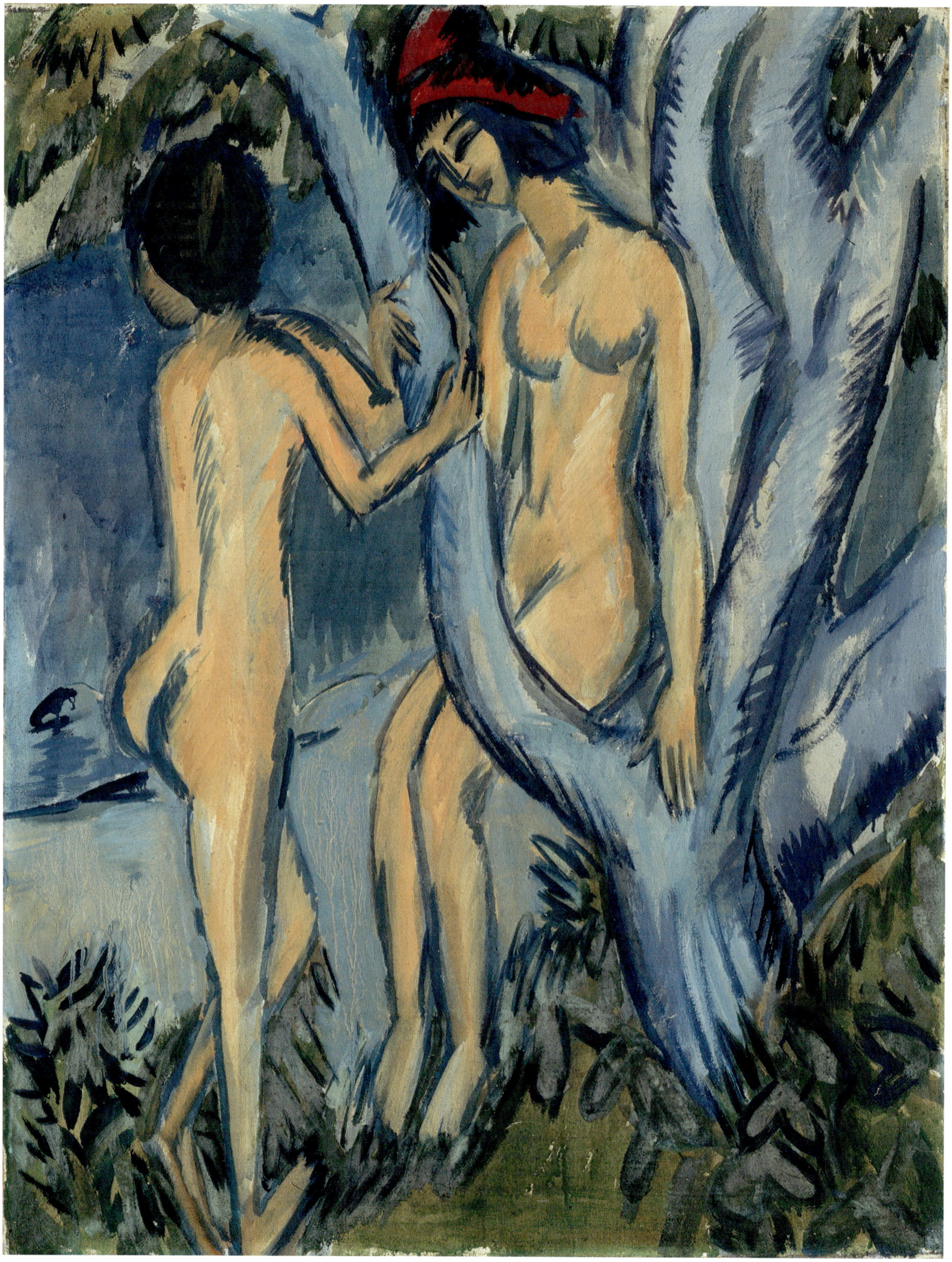

Cat. 20

Two Nudes by a Tree, Fehmarn, 1912/13
Oil on canvas

Private collection

Cat. 17

Bather between Rocks, 1912
Oil on canvas

Städel Museum, Frankfurt am Main, on permanent loan from a private collection

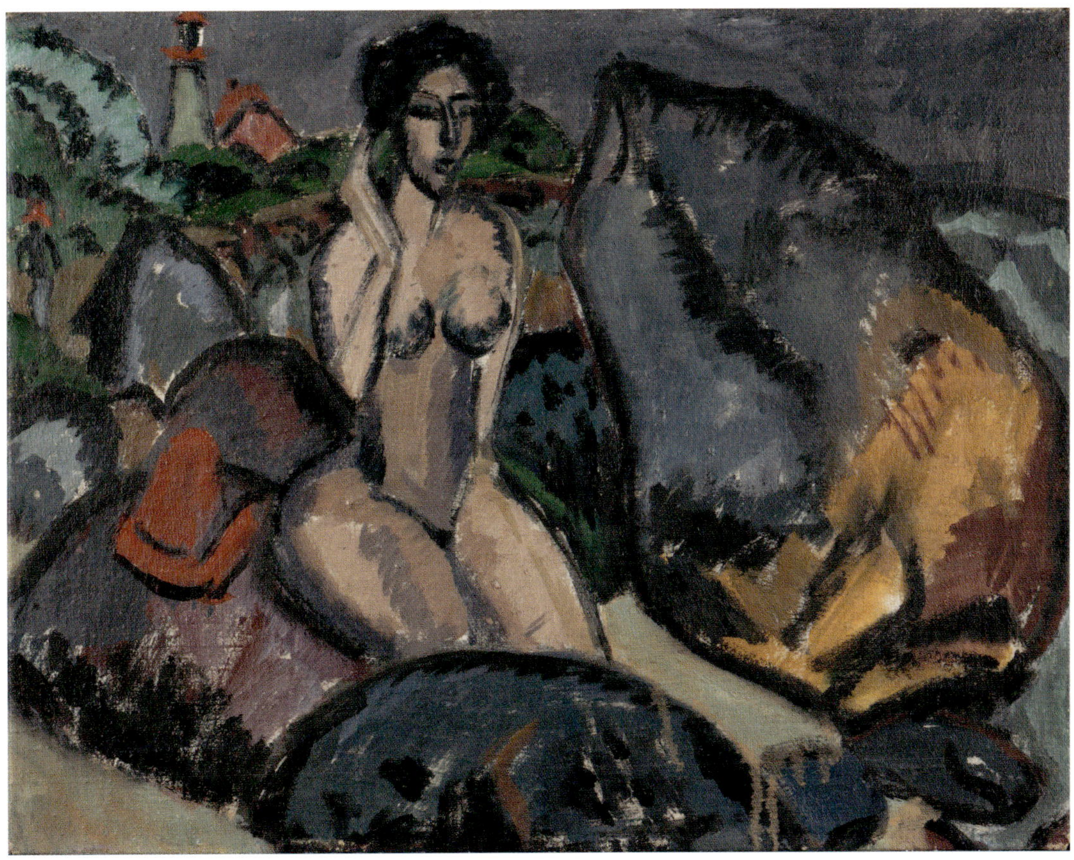

Cat. 21

Laburnum Tree, 1912/13
Oil on canvas

Colby College Museum of Art,
Gift of Gertrud A. Mellon

Cat. 16

The Lighthouse of Fehmarn, 1912
Oil on canvas

Carnegie Museum of Art,
Pittsburgh: Patrons Art Fund

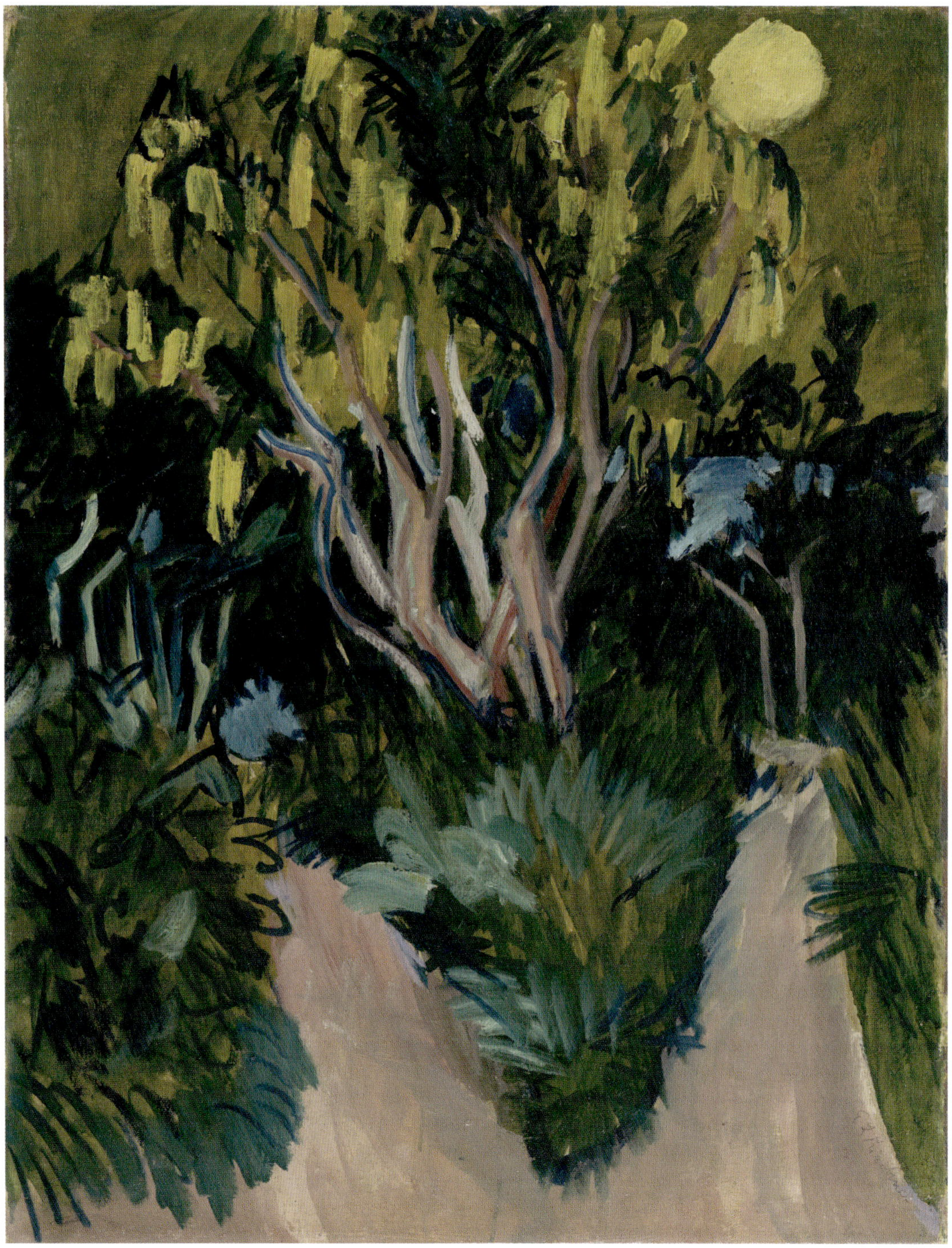

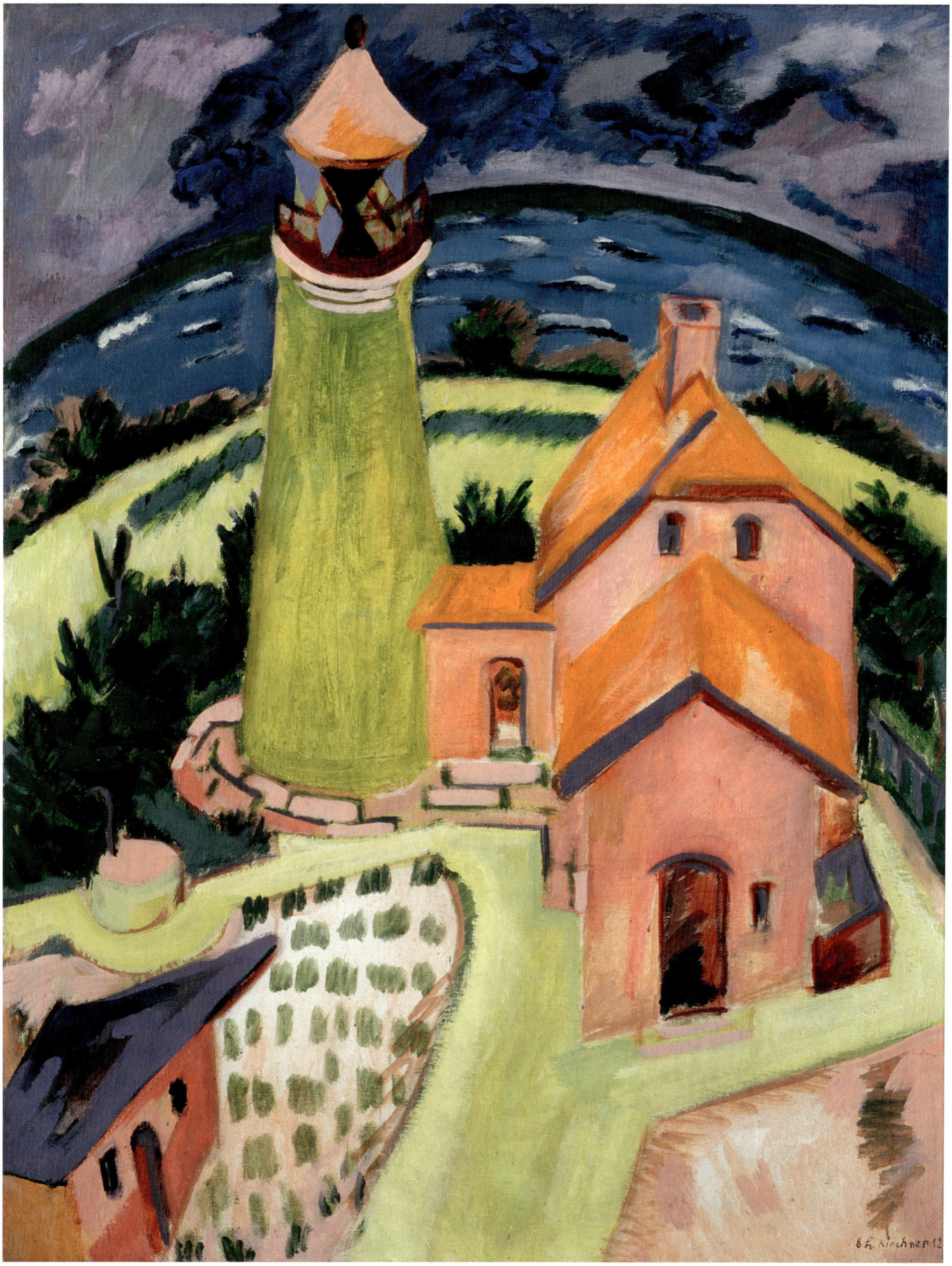

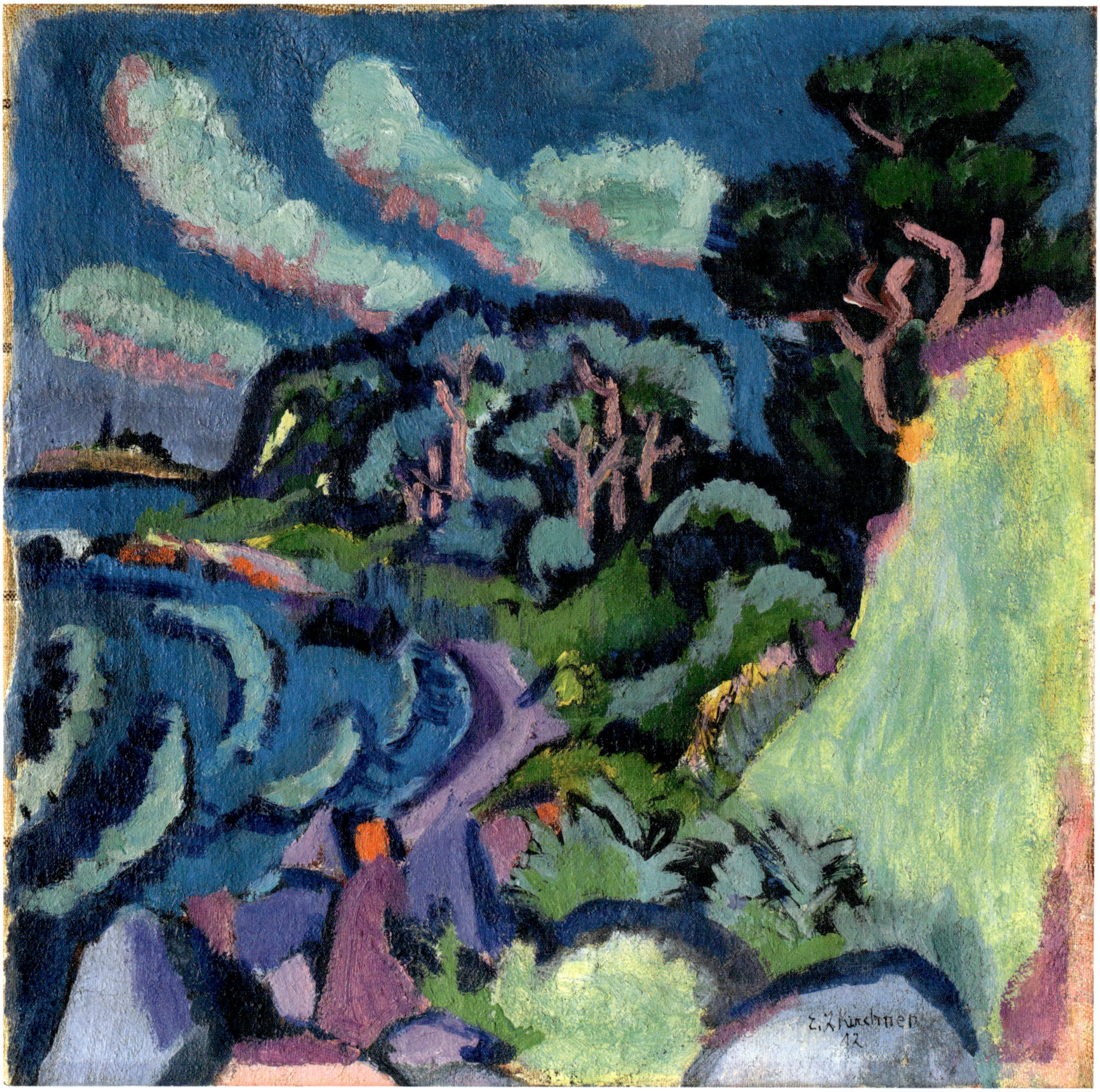
E.L.Kirchner
12

Cat. 14

Mexico Bay, Fehmarn, 1912
Oil on canvas

Private collection, Germany

Cat. 15

Trees above Sandy Path, 1912
Oil on canvas

Kunstmuseum Liechtenstein,
Vaduz/Gift of Gerda Techow, Vaduz

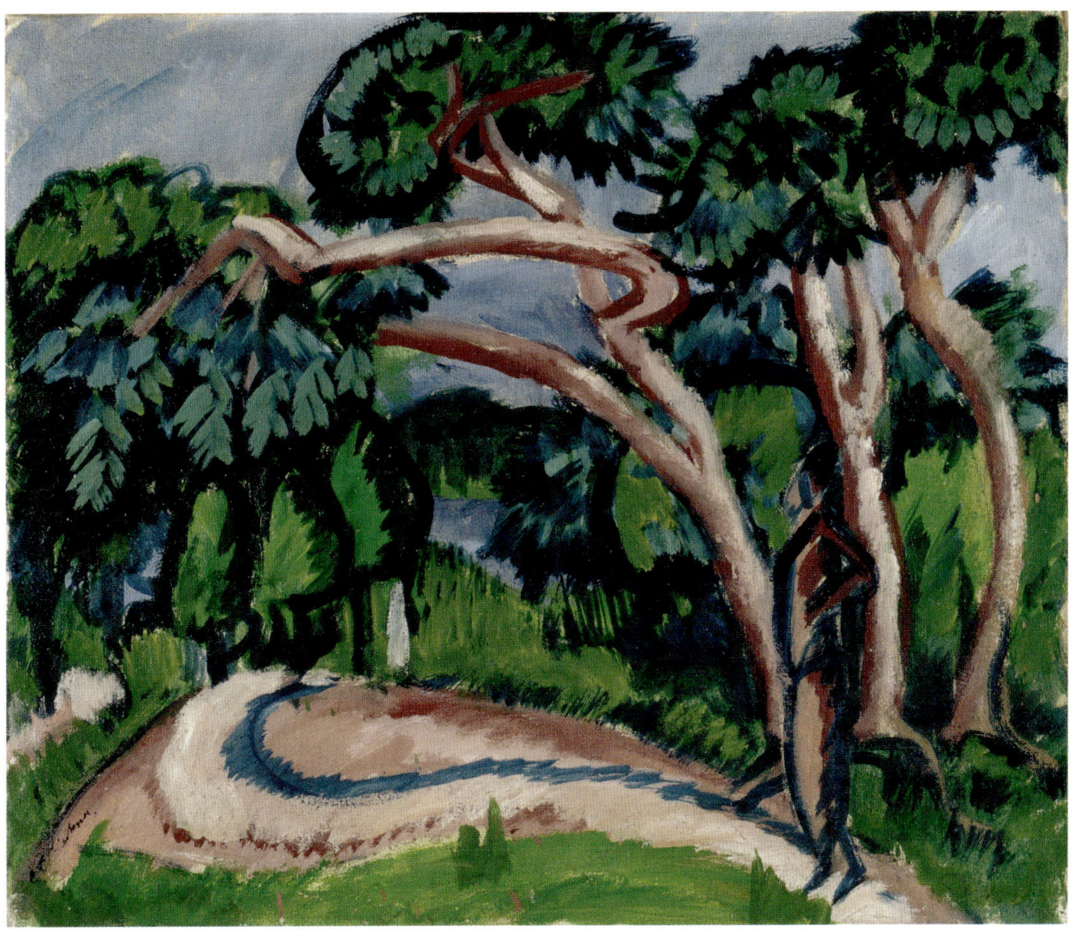

Cat. 23

Elisabethufer, 1912/13
Oil on canvas

Bayerische Staatsgemälde-sammlungen, Munich, Pinakothek der Moderne

Cat. 24

Street at Schöneberg City Park, 1912/13
Oil on canvas

Milwaukee Art Museum, Gift of Mrs Harry Lynde Bradley

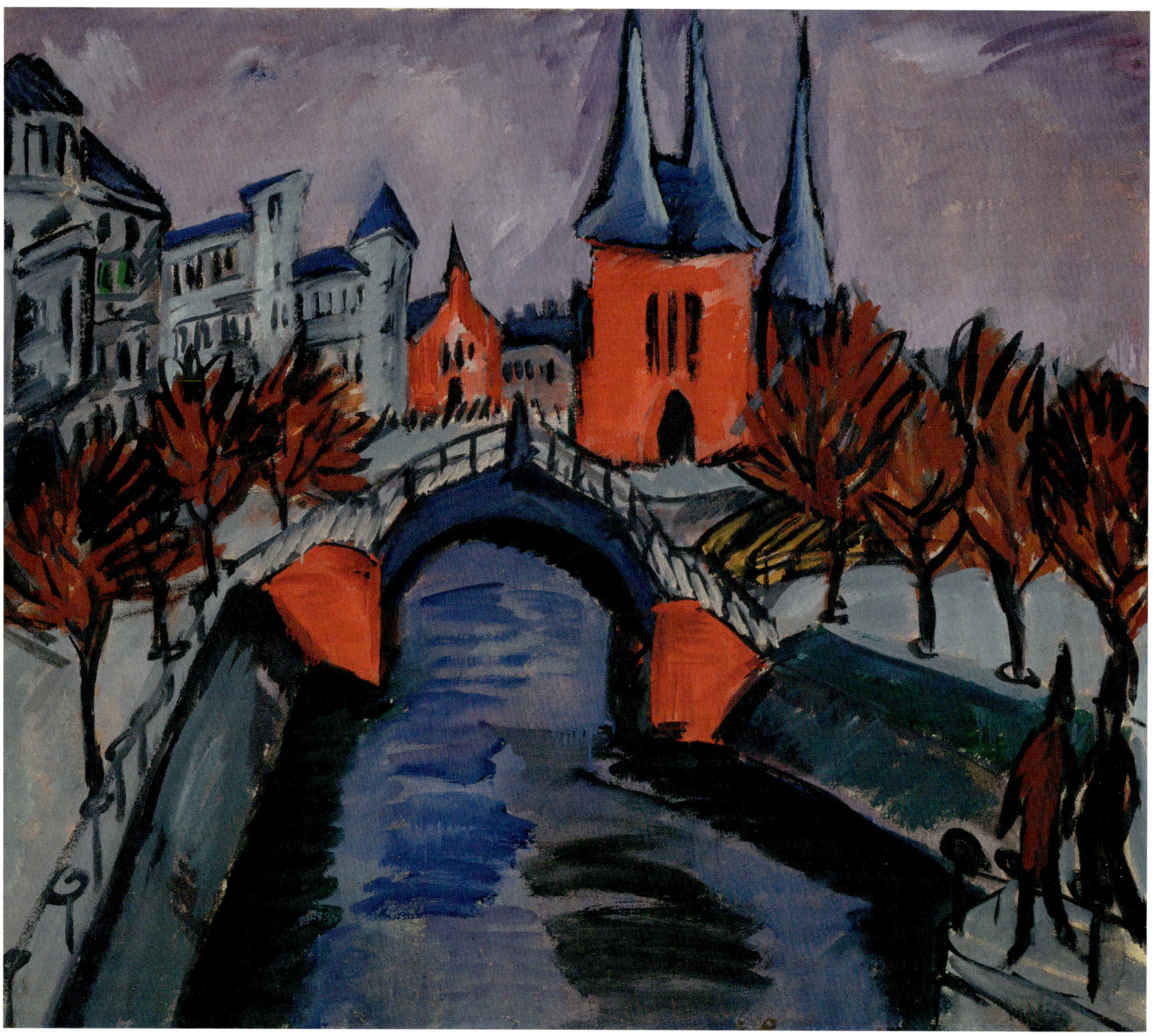

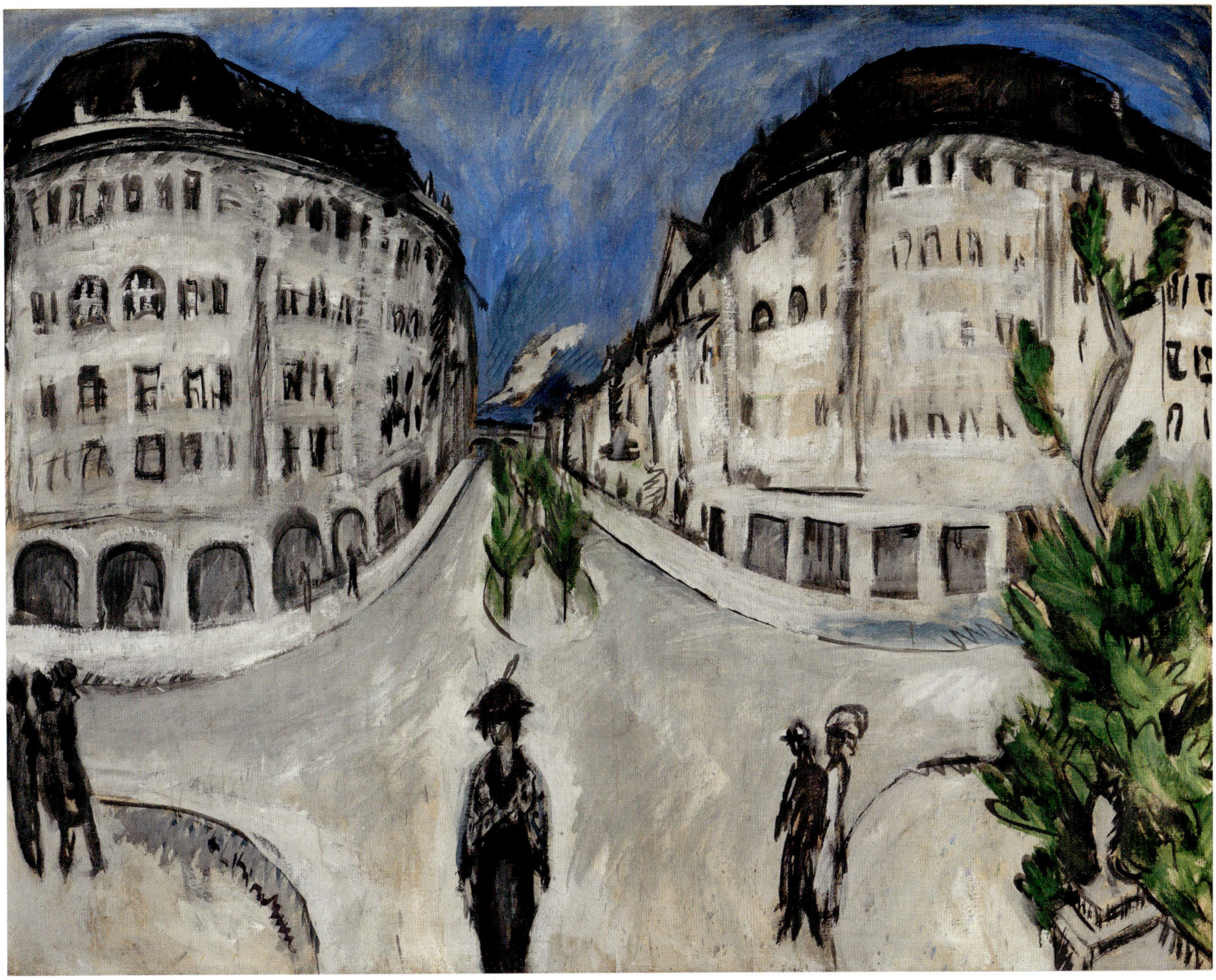

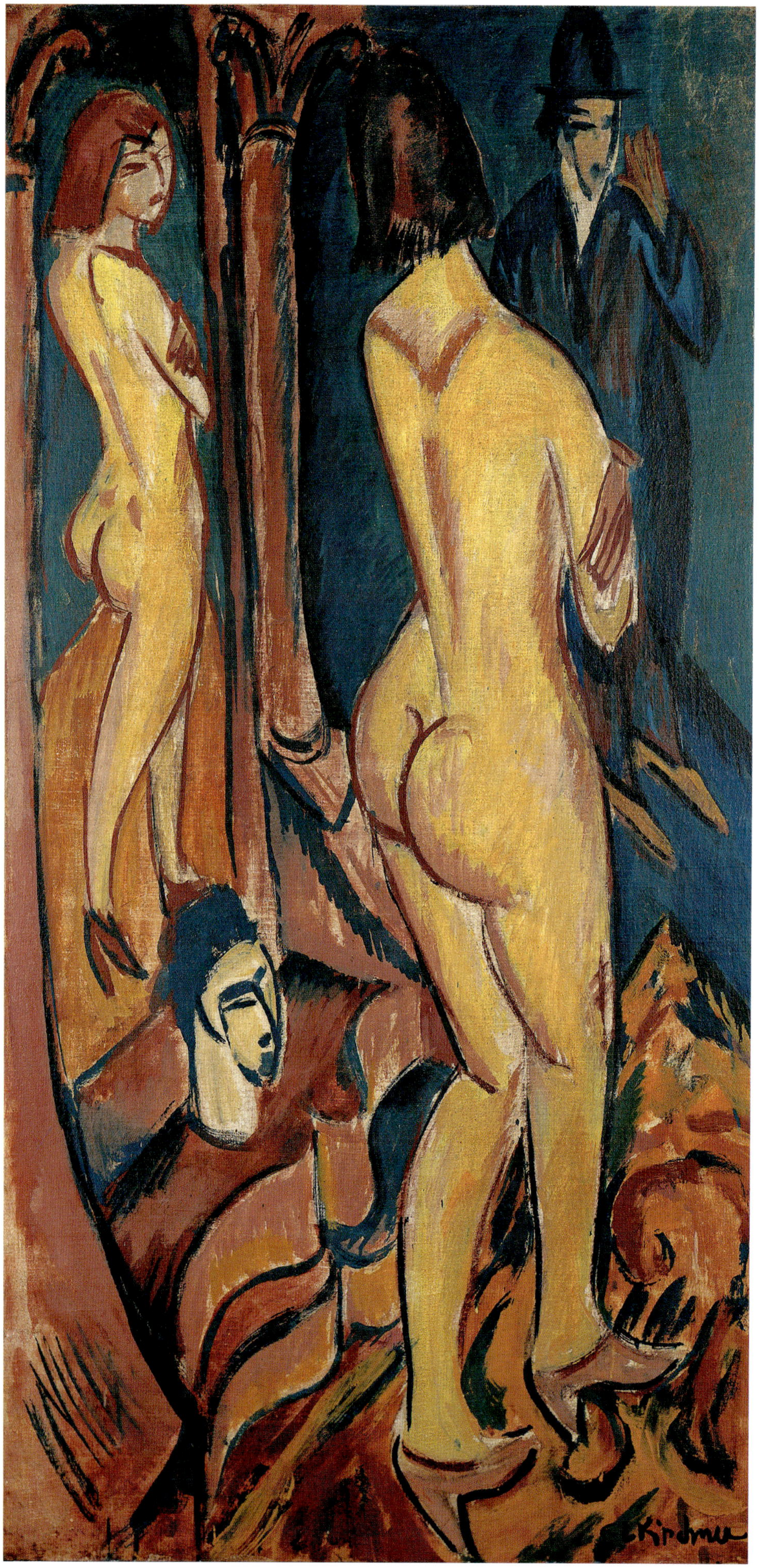

Cat. 13

Nude from the Back with Mirror and Man, 1912
Oil on canvas

Brücke-Museum, Berlin

Cat. 18

Nudes in the Studio, 1912
Oil on canvas

Leopold Museum, Vienna

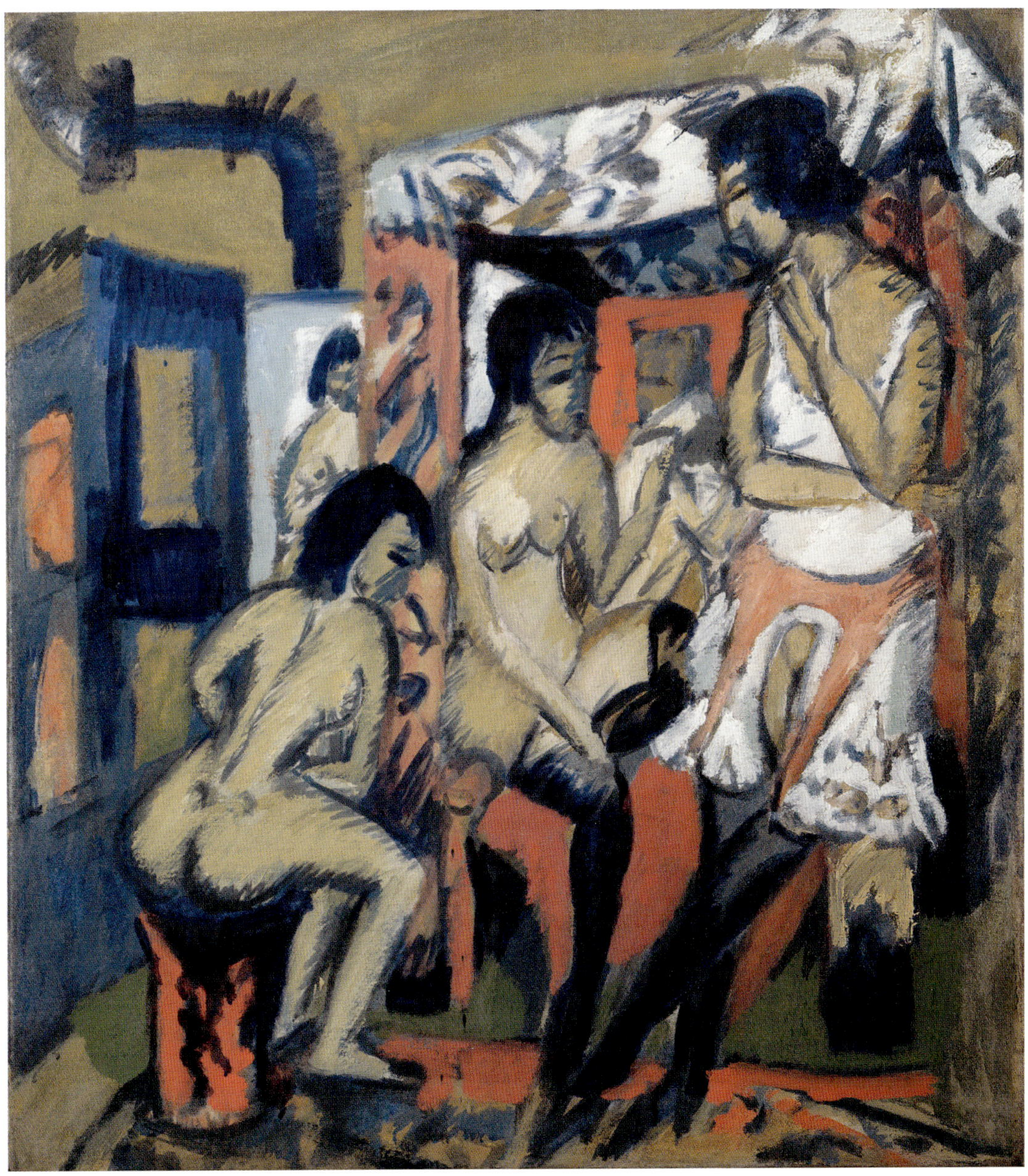

Between Big-City Dynamism and Island Idylls (1913)

3

Within half a century Berlin had grown into a modern metropolis with two million inhabitants, and in the years before the First World War it was one of Germany's most exciting cities for artists. As before in Dresden, Kirchner set up his Berlin studio as a place to live and work in, with fabrics and furniture he had made himself as expressions of his unconventional lifestyle. In *Erich Heckel and Otto Mueller Playing Chess* p. 133 his two Brücke colleagues are seated across from each other in Kirchner's studio. In contrast to the two fully clothed men, behind them a nude woman is lying on a divan with her arms crossed behind her head. This could be Erna Schilling, who had been Kirchner's partner since 1912. The picture's dynamism comes from his choice of a view from above and from formal elements: Kirchner no longer used crude hatching only along the contours, as at the beginning of his Berlin period, but across entire planes. The brush strokes are fragmented, the forms angular, and the lines collide. At the same time Kirchner distorts perspectives and proportions to the extent that the figures threaten to fall away from the chessboard, and the lamp on the table, though standing farther back in the picture, appears as large as Mueller's torso in the foreground. The painting is one of the last documents showing his Brücke colleagues in his studio. In Berlin the group's cohesiveness was lost and owing to irreconcilable differences of opinion Brücke was finally officially dissolved in May 1913.

Despite this breakup and his existential difficulties, Kirchner was fascinated by the metropolis and would continue to explore it artistically for the next two years. A new world was opening up to him through literature as well. He got in with the avant-garde literary circle around Herwarth Walden's gallery and journal *Der Sturm.* Through it he got to know the psychiatrist and writer Alfred Döblin, and made contact with the writers of Der Neue Club among them Simon Guttmann. His friendship with them is documented in a series of sketched, painted and photographed portraits pp. 142, 143. Like Kirchner, in their works the two writers dealt with issues relating to the metropolis, modern life, and prostitution. In a few brief years Kirchner would produce city views, streetscapes with strolling cocottes, and bordello, café, music hall and circus scenes in various techniques. Kirchner's fascination with these places of amusement and their questionable habitués is fully expressed in the painting *Circus* p. 139. In a red-walled manège that is cut off on the right a female acrobat hanging upside down on a galloping grey horse is performing a daredevil trick. Kirchner captures the scene in the manège and the anonymous crowd of spectators dressed in black in the left of the picture from the elevated vantage point of an upper tier, while at the same time presenting a frontal view of the figure in the foreground, who is seen from the back, and of the three characters dressed in red in the upper right. The horse and the acrobatic artiste take up both perspectives, and thus seem overly large and distorted. Kirchner emphasises them not only in his composition but also in his choice of colours: around the pinkish artiste, seemingly nude, he places light-green accents in the horse's hide that heighten the colour contrast and together with the dark contours and distinct hatching along the body make the two stand out even further. As a result, the depiction seems more dynamic than Georg Seurat's Pointillist painting *The Circus* from 1881 (Musée d'Orsay, Paris), which Kirchner may well have known.

For his cityscapes Kirchner occasionally chose unspectacular locations that exercised a certain charm for him. *Elisabethufer* p. 124 shows the two-tower Melanchthon Church on Planufer, which was destroyed in the war—and behind it the Garnison Church, restored in 1909 after a fire—depicted in bright red. The rust-brown foliage on the trees along the bank and the dark grey-violet overcast sky indicate that it is autumn. The picture is dominated by the bright red of the church, which is repeated in the abutments of the bridge that crossed the Luisenstadt Canal, which has since been filled in. Despite the pair of strollers in the bottom-right corner, the cityscape seems totally deserted.

Kirchner spent the summer of 1913 with Erna again on Fehmarn. Although it was relatively accessible by train and ferry, the Baltic Sea island was by no means a tourist destination at the time. In addition to its peacefulness, it was above all its varied landscape, promising endless motifs, that made Fehmarn so captivating for him. There he developed his painting style even further. Instead of using outlines and shading to model his forms as he had continued to do the previous year, hatching now covers the entire picture surface, adding excitement to a wild, pristine nature as in *Fehmarn Windmill* p.162 and *Bay on the Fehmarn Coast* p.152. Behind the lighthouse at Staberhuk, where Kirchner and Erna were staying, the land falls off steeply to a broad beach. The curving line of the shore with its large granite boulders that he pictured from various angles with or without bathers made this section of the coast one of his favourite motifs during his Fehmarn visits. In *Bay on the Fehmarn Coast* he captures its expanse from the edge of the slope in bird's-eye perspective in the ochre, blue and green colours that Kirchner found so characteristic of the island. The coast is depicted as a sharp, dynamic curve that is taken up in the upper-right edge by the horizon line. In the picture *Erna with Japanese Umbrella (Japanese Girl)* p.148 the bay with its steep slope and rocks on the beach serves as background. Erna, fashionably dressed, is seated in the dunes, turned away from the sea, with a Japanese umbrella. Between 1909 and 1913 Japanese umbrellas turn up in a number of Kirchner's paintings. In this same year, for example, he also painted *Couple under Japanese Umbrella* p.144, the location of which becomes clear only after a second look. In it Kirchner plays with the confusion between exterior and interior space. Only by comparing the work to photographs of his studio from the same time p.44 does it become apparent that the seemingly outdoor scene with lush vegetation is, in fact, set in his studio at Durlacher Strasse 14 and features his painted wall hangings in the background. It is unclear whether the couple in the closely cropped picture represents Otto Mueller and his wife Maschka or Kirchner himself with Erna Schilling. The entire painting is flat in concept. Tension is created by the greatly abstracted forms and the hatching that holds the composition together, while at the same time making it all the more difficult for the viewer to distinguish between foreground and background.

Another double portrait that definitely depicts the artist and his partner is *Tower Room, Fehmarn (Self-Portrait with Erna)* p.151. It shows the two in a bright red in a room painted blue that the couple had moved into for the summer months in the gable of the lighthouse keeper's house. Kirchner, dressed and seated, smoking his pipe, and Erna, standing naked, face each other and are apparently conversing. In the painting the room's back wall, depicted parallel to the canvas, is interrupted by two windows, through which we can see vegetation and the sea with a sailing boat. Yet the objects in the room are painted from different points of view.

Next to the rocks on the beach Kirchner built a grass shack into which he could retreat with Erna and gaze out at the sea. This hut is the motif of the watercolour drawing *Fehmarn Coast with Yellow Nude* p.156. In addition to the live nude, he also incorporated a wood sculpture that is not immediately recognisable as such in the drawing. The sculpture in question is a piece called *Figure Looking Back* p.154, which he carved on Fehmarn that same summer out of driftwood. The original shape of the beam from which he carved the female figure is still recognisable. She is plump at the bottom and slender at the top and caught in considerable torsion, so that the viewer can appreciate the figure from multiple angles. On Fehmarn Kirchner sought to lead an uncontrived life in nature. The grass hut on the beach and his many works created there reflect that yearning.

In addition to Erna, the children of the lighthouse keeper and friends who visited him served Kirchner as models for his work. The painting *Three Bathers* p.160 stands out from the other works produced on Fehmarn — if only for its almost life-size format — and seems to have been painted less spontaneously. It was also not painted until after his return to his Berlin studio. Based on the drawing *Three Bathers in the Surf* p.161, in which the figure at the back still appears to be a man, the painting pictures three standing female bathers, a bird flying by in the upper right and a rounded rock behind the figures. Unlike in the drawing, the rock in the painting is covered with root-like excrescences that are probably seaweed. The view includes neither the beach nor the horizon. The women stand in the water like sculptures; as though rooted, they defy the waves, whose sequential breaking on the beach is ornamentally stylised and encircles the trio of bathers. The figures are stacked vertically, one behind the other, just as Kirchner would later picture cocottes in the street.

In addition to scenes with bathers, on Fehmarn Kirchner painted a number of pictures with nudes in the woods, cavorting between trees. Whereas *Two Nudes by a Tree, Fehmarn* p.118, with its detailed depiction of the figures, rounder forms and graduated colours as well as more restrained brush strokes, recalls works from the previous year, the figures and forest landscape in *Nudes Next to the Shore Woods* p.158 are only sketchily captured. They are greatly elongated, harmonise with the tree trunks and are virtually absorbed into nature. This impression is supported by the energetic, fanning brush strokes that lead to uncertainties in the picture space, since foreground and background are meshed. At the same time, this swift painting style suggests a high degree of immediacy and spontaneity. The use of colour is also simplified, reduced, as in *Three Bathers,* to only a few tones: orange, green and ochre.

Back in Berlin Kirchner began painting a series of street scenes. As compared to the cityscapes with only incidental figures, in the group of works produced between late 1913 and early 1915, which includes some seven to eleven paintings, numerous pastels, drawings and graphics, people become the focus in the dynamic metropolis. In *Street, Berlin* p.169 two extravagantly dressed women are pictured in the centre of the painting strolling along a pinkish sidewalk. To their right a man has deliberately turned away and bent down to study a blue-lit display window, presumably observing the women's reflection in the mirroring windowpane. Stacked behind are a number of other male passers-by. In the upper left one can see an automobile and, beneath an arcade on the opposite side of the street, other men. In these street scenes Kirchner combines artistic depictions of the night-time activities of the metropolis with the subject of prostitution, which could be practised only discreetly on the street. Cocottes, as prostitutes were called at the time, were among the tolerated attractions of Berlin nightlife. In order to stand out, they adorned themselves with large feather hats and pointed collars that emphasised their cleavage, yet they had to be careful not to attract the attention of the moral police by their behaviour. Kirchner captured in paint one such discreet contact between cocottes and their johns by means of a quick glance or the placement of a hand on a crotch. The tension-laden scene is captured by the structure of the composition and dynamic compositional devices: the extreme perspective foreshortening and the arrangement of the visual elements along the two diagonals of the picture draw the viewer into the painting, focusing attention on the elongated female figures moving outwards from the centre. Kirchner develops the individual forms out of dense hatching fringing out to the edges. Vibrant brush strokes across the entire painting underscore the pointed shapes along the diagonals.

The two women in *Street, Berlin* recall in composition and dress the painting *Two Women with Washbasin; The Sisters* p.145, which pictures Erna and Gerda Schilling elegantly dressed in the artist's studio. They are seated next to a washbasin that stands in the space like some foreign object and in which Erna is washing her hands. When Kirchner met them, the two were working as dancers in a dance hall. This perhaps explains their heavily made-up faces and the dresses with the bright white collars typically seen in Kirchner's Berlin street scenes. Yet the angular, feathery forms, which would be so characteristic of the street scenes, are here still balanced by the graceful curves evident in the figures and the red armchair in the background next to them.

With the motif of cocottes on the streets and his now characteristic vibrant painting style, Kirchner found an artistic equivalent for the flood of attractions and movement in the modern metropolis before the First World War.

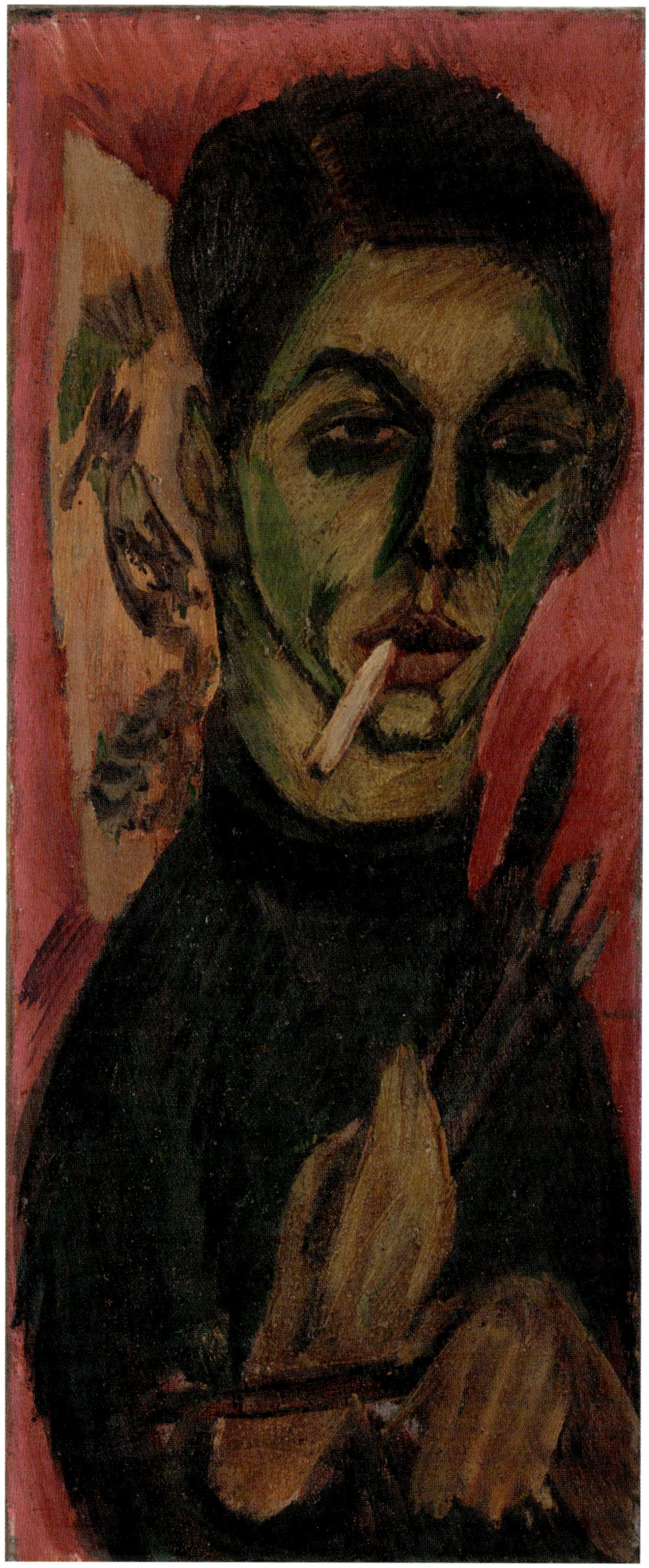

Cat. 27

Self-Portrait, 1913
Oil on canvas

Private collection

Cat. 29

Erich Heckel and Otto Mueller Playing Chess, 1913
Oil on canvas

Brücke-Museum, Berlin

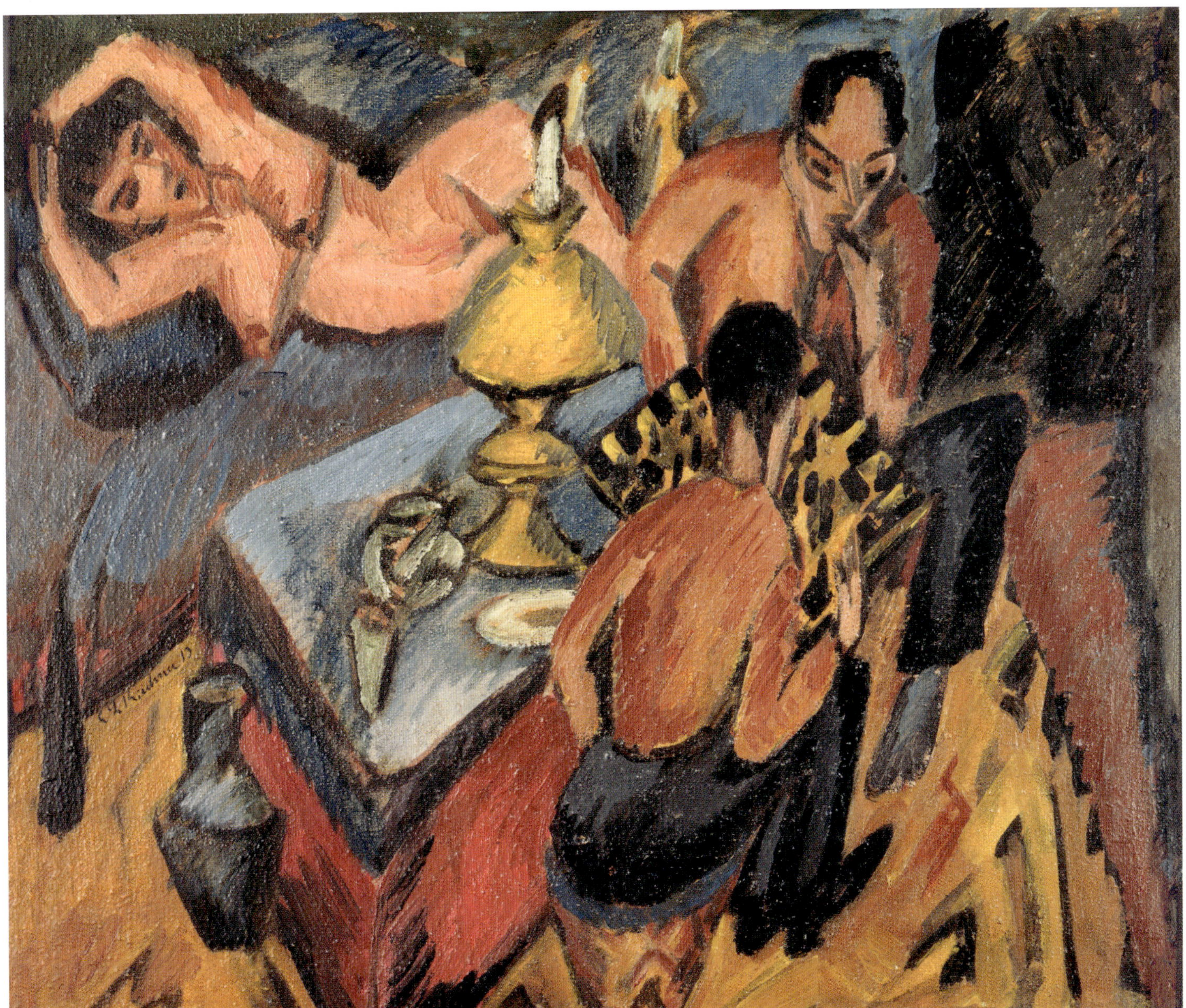

Cat. 28

Artist Sketching with Two Women/Artists, 1913
Oil on canvas

Collection Stedelijk Museum, Amsterdam

Cat. 30

Yellow Engelufer, Berlin, 1913
Oil on canvas

Kunsthalle Mannheim

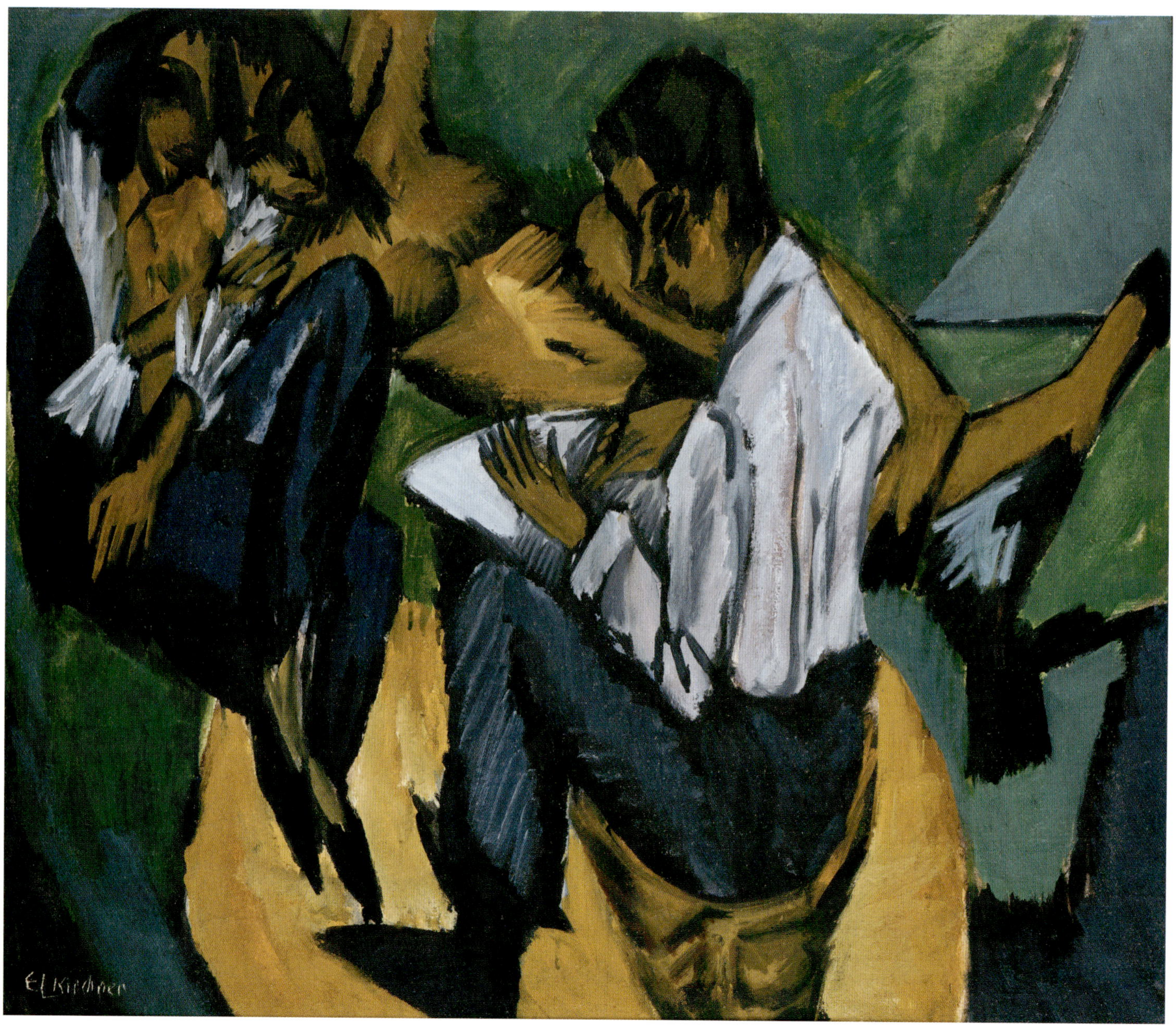

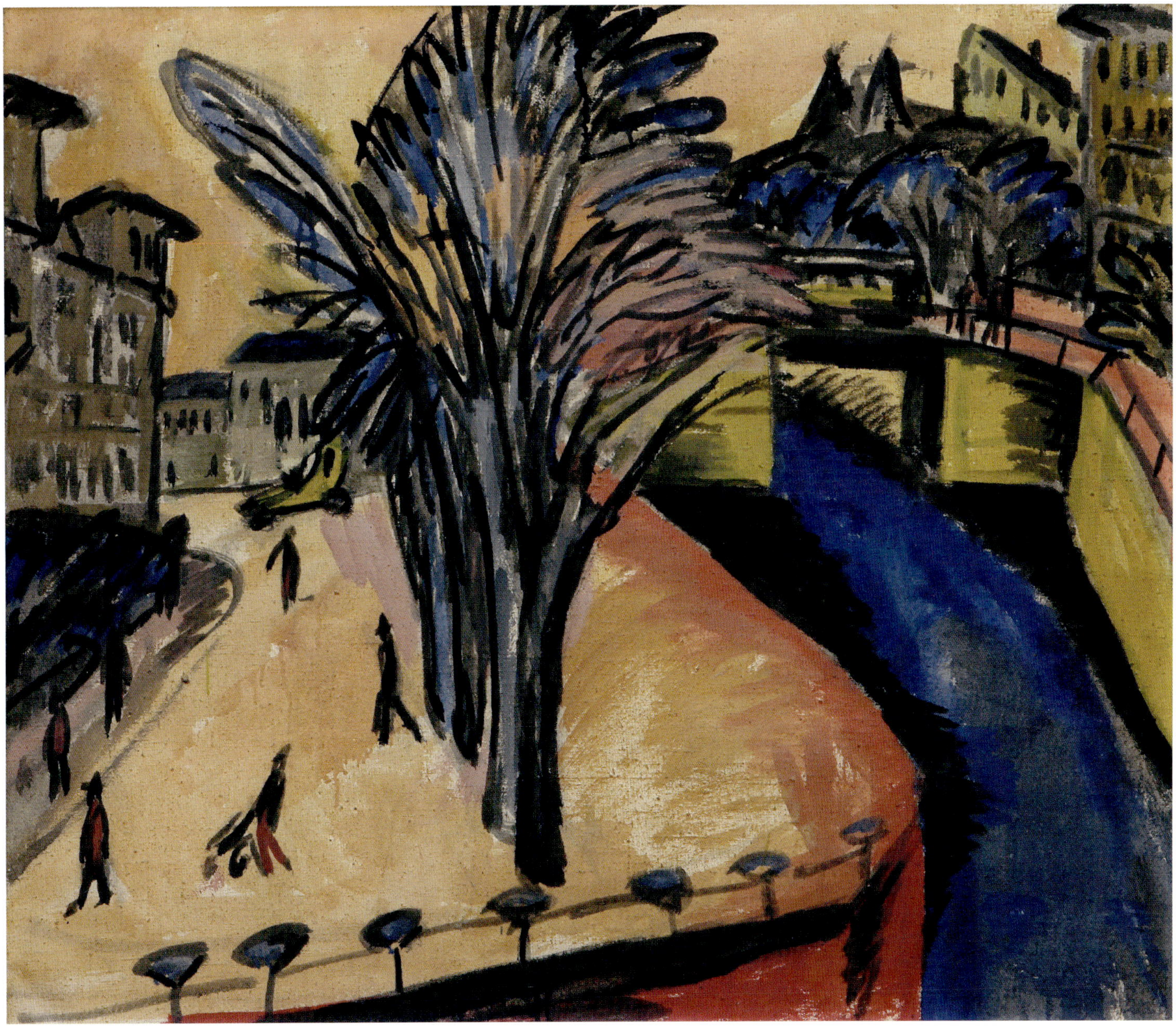

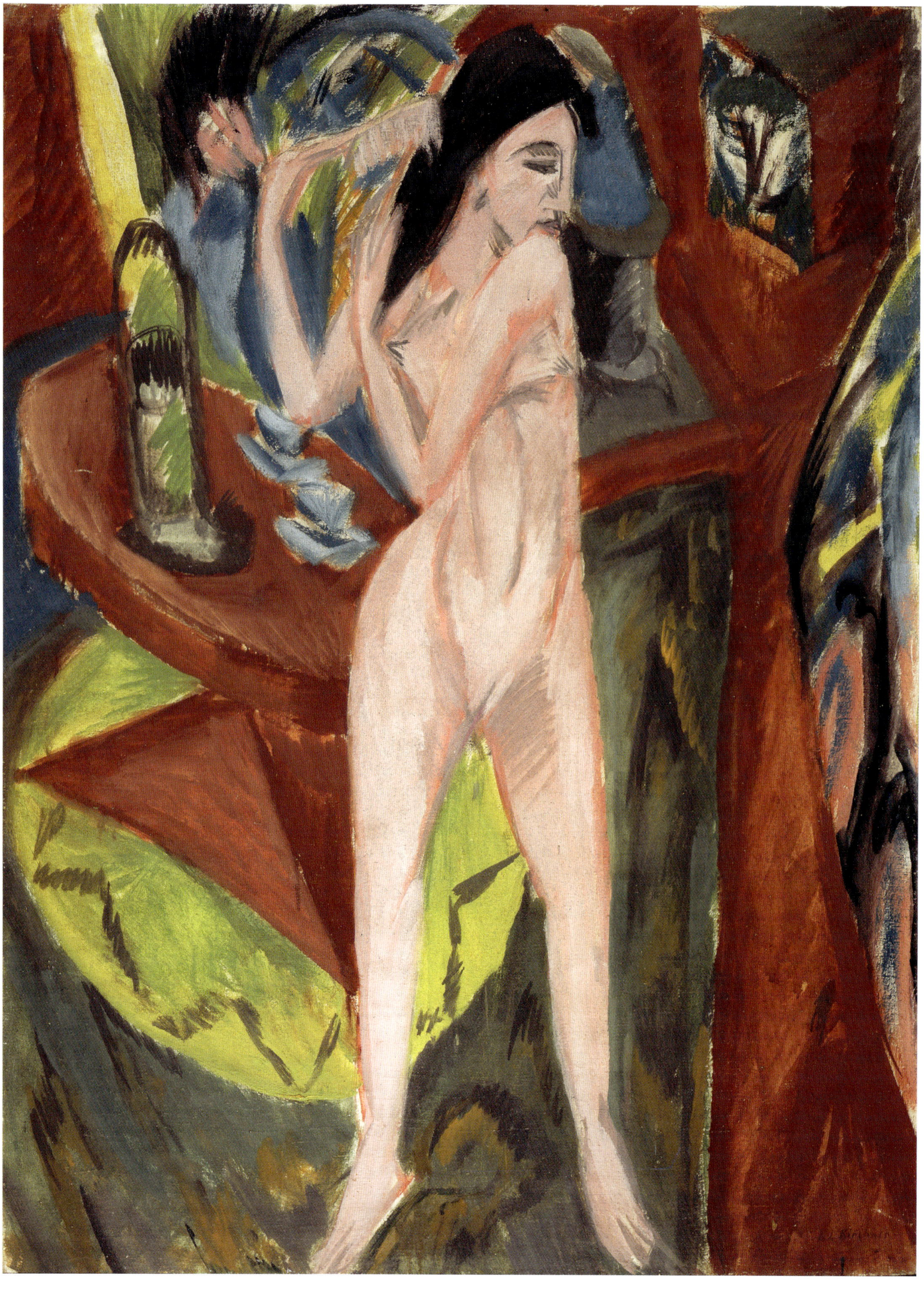

Cat. 43

Female Nude Combing Her Hair, 1913
Oil on canvas

Brücke-Museum, Berlin

Cat. 22

Bridge by the City Gate, Chemnitz, 1912/13
Oil on canvas

Museum Frieder Burda, Baden-Baden

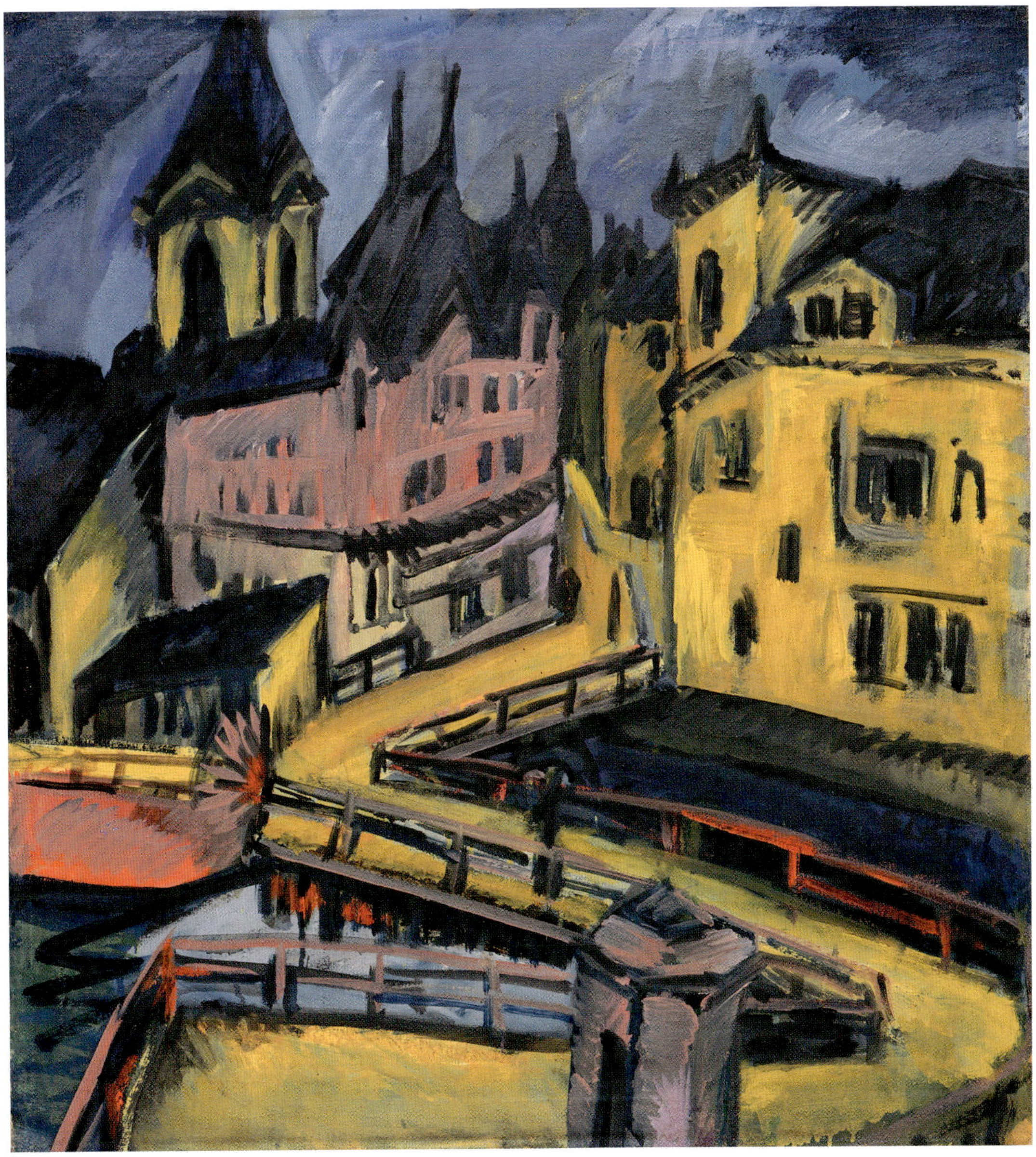

Cat. 105

Cartwheeling Acrobatic Dancers, 1913
Colour woodcut on blotting paper

Werner Coninx Foundation, Zurich

Cat. 25

Circus, 1913
Oil on canvas

Bayerische Staatsgemälde-sammlungen, Munich, Pinakothek der Moderne

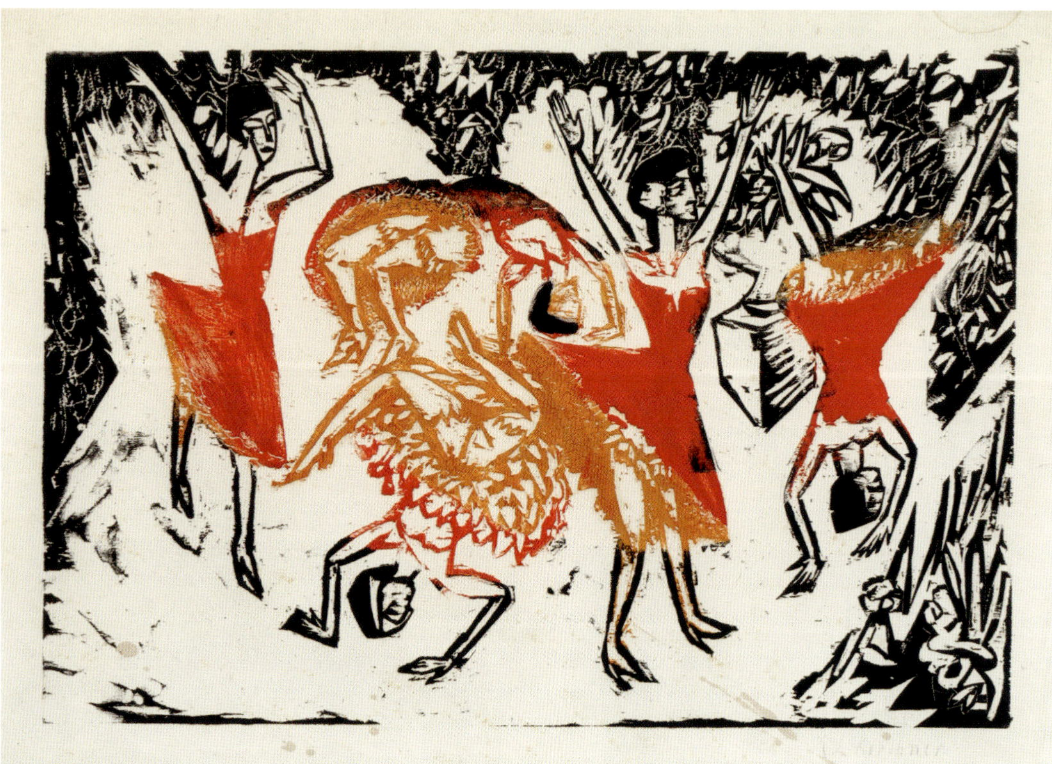

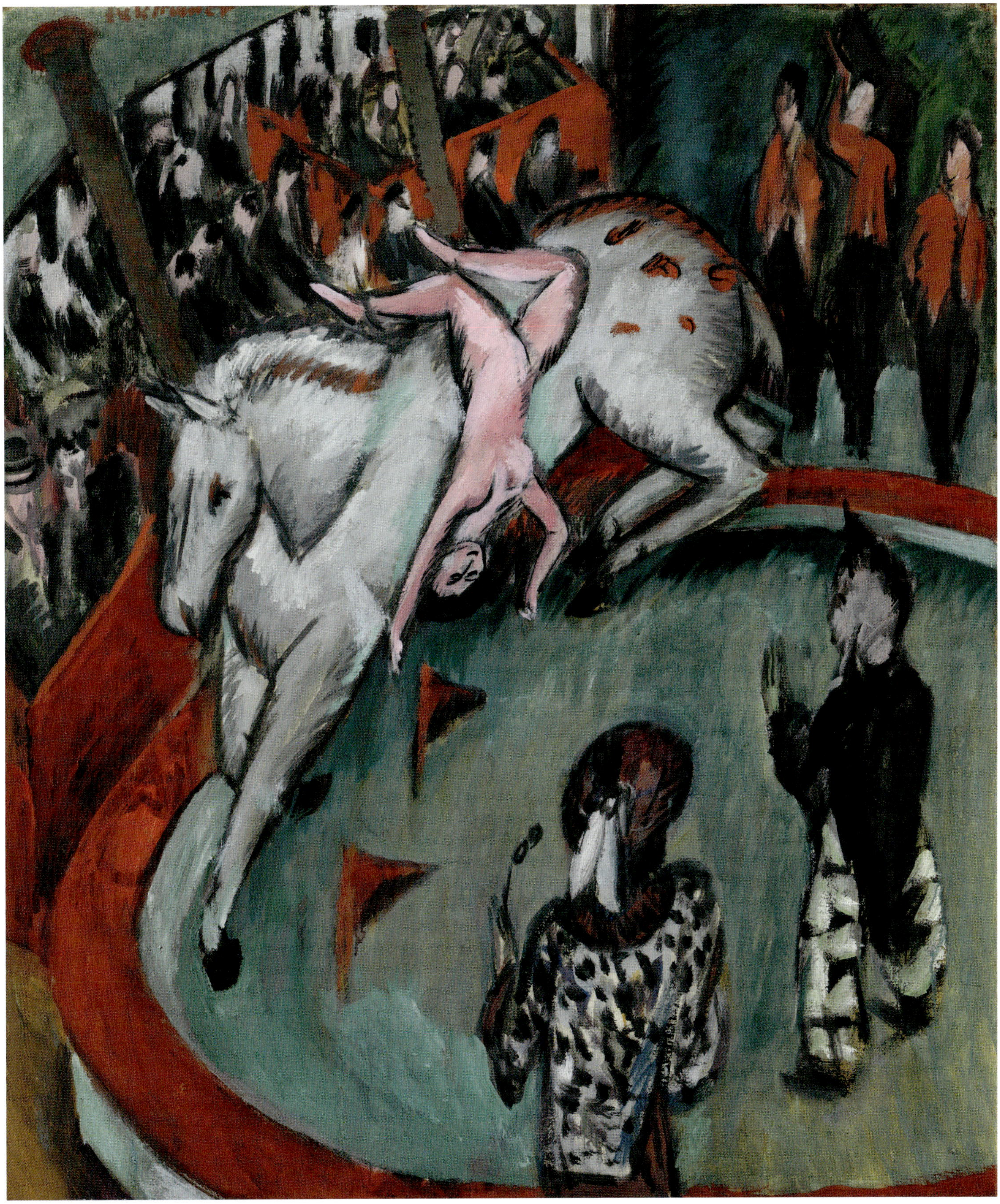

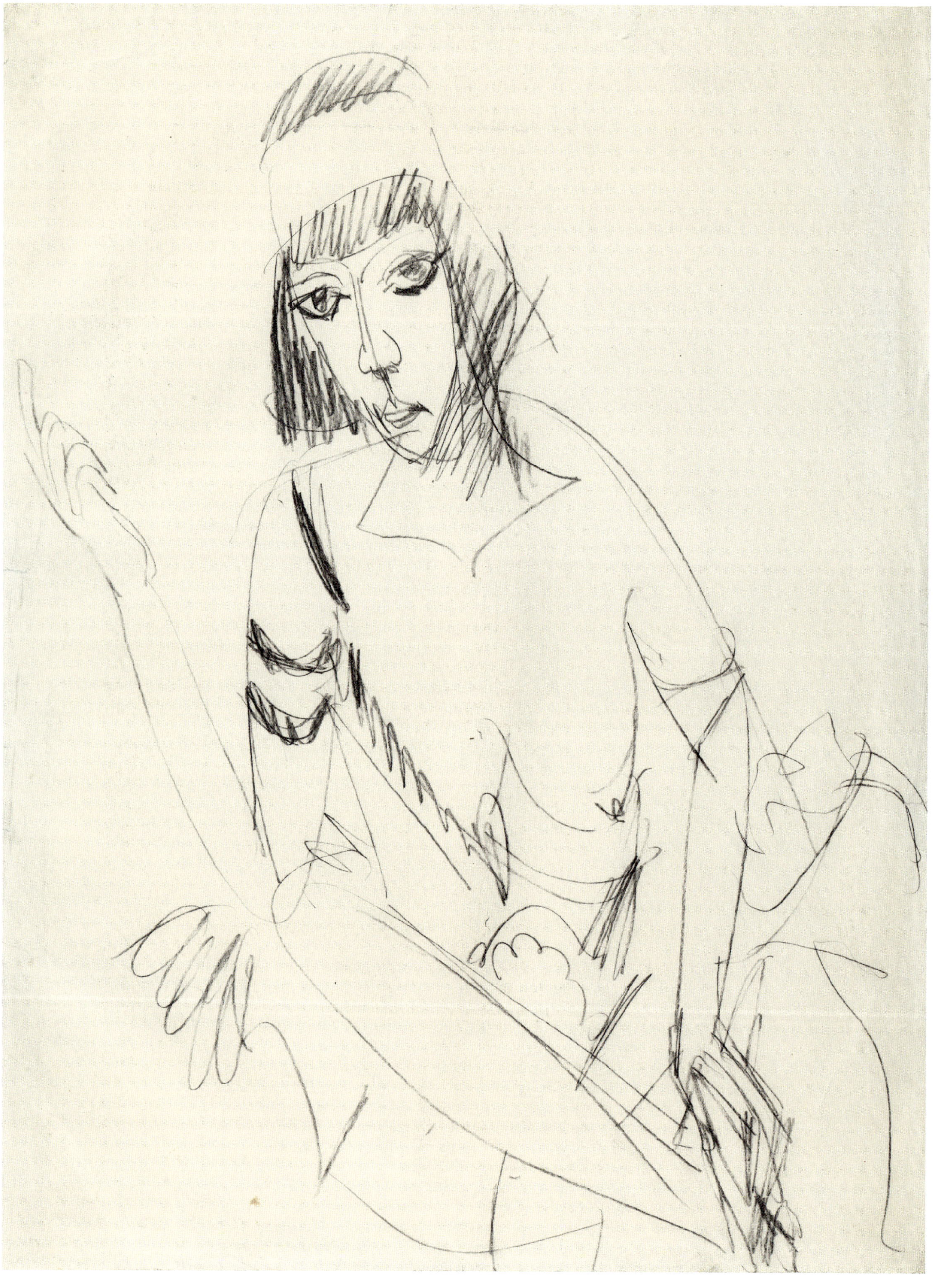

Cat. 78

Seated Dancer (Erna), 1913
Pencil on paper

Brücke-Museum, Berlin

Cat. 77

Bordello, 1913
Pen, brush and ink on paper

Brücke-Museum, Berlin, Karl and Emy Schmidt-Rottluff Foundation

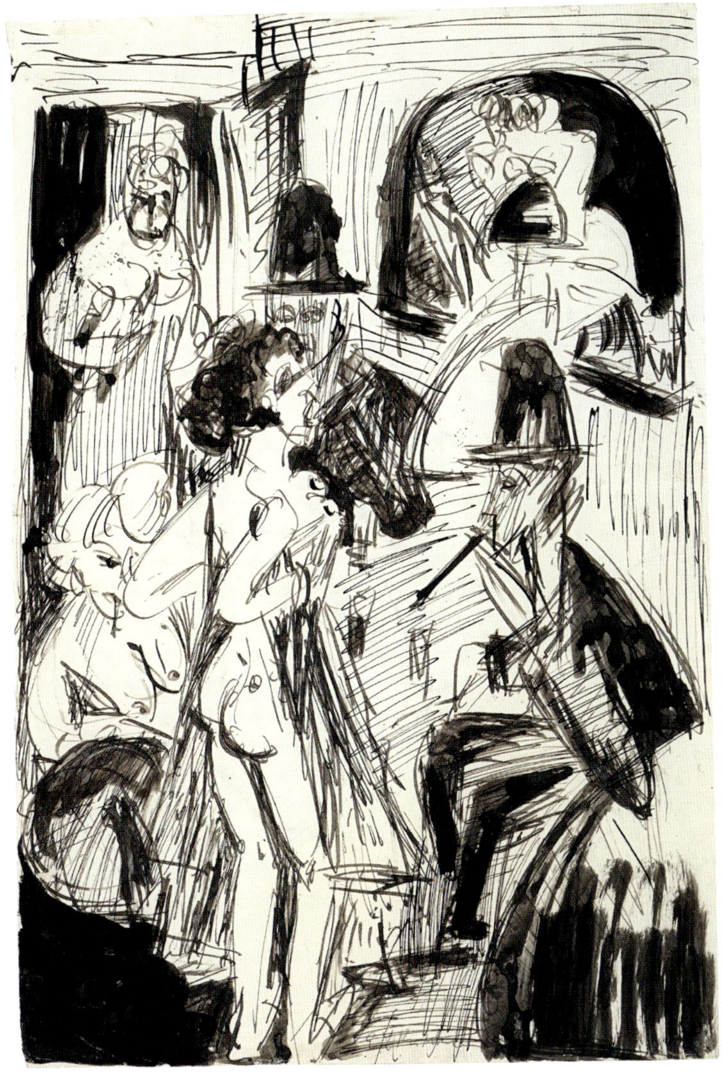

Cat. 79

Portrait of Alfred Döblin, 1913
Pencil on paper

Brücke-Museum, Berlin

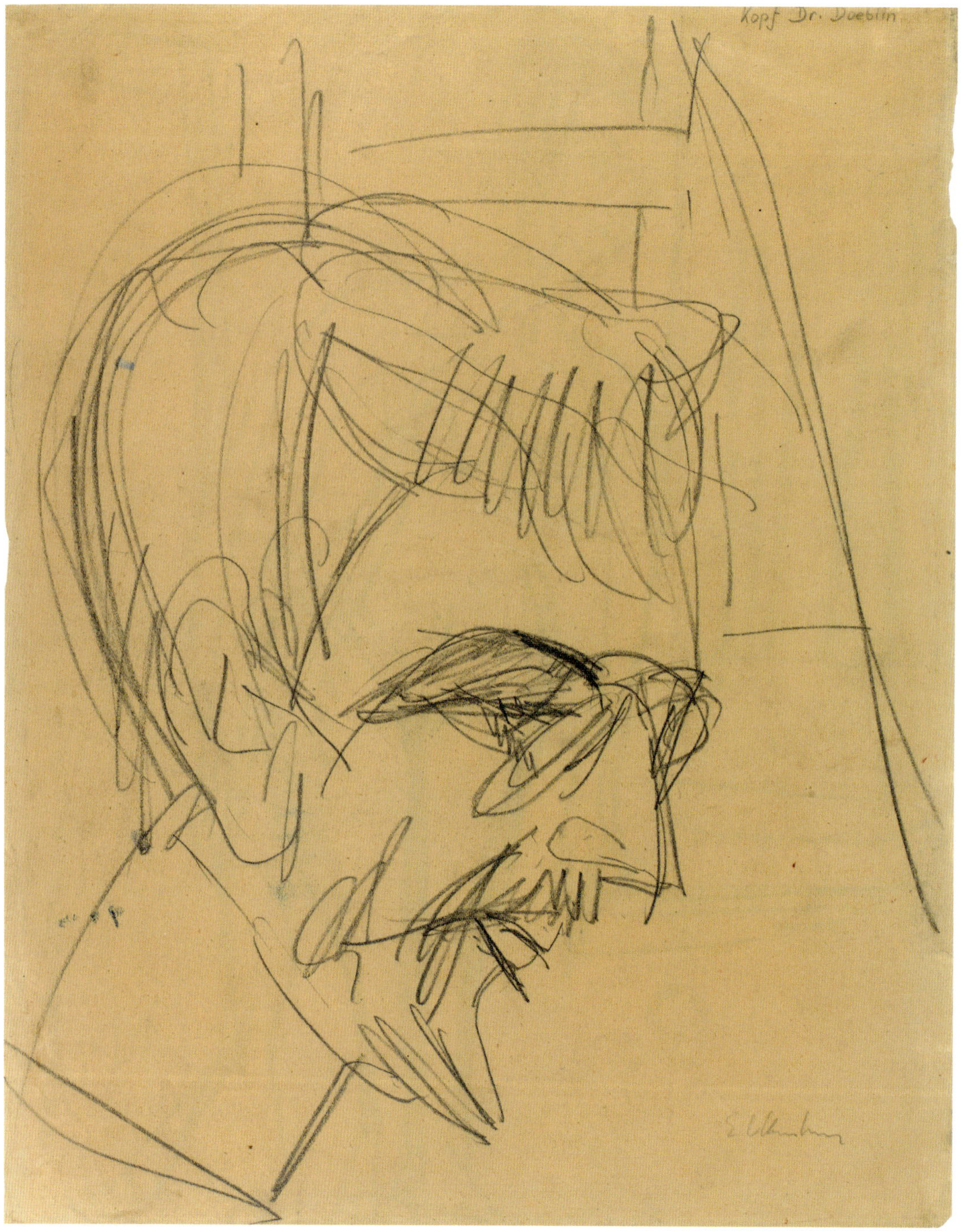

Cat. 136

Alfred Döblin in Kirchner's live-in studio, 1912/13
Gelatine silver (modern print)

Kirchner Archive, Wichtrach/Bern, Kirchner Museum Davos

Cat. 74

Young Poet (Simon Guttmann), 1911
Pencil on paper

Brücke-Museum, Berlin

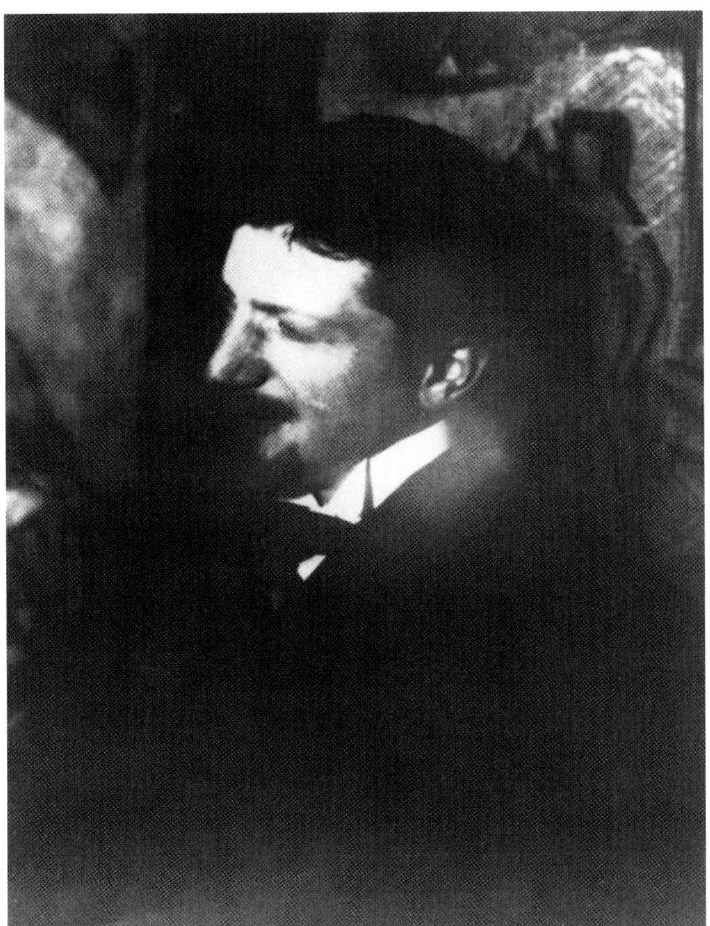

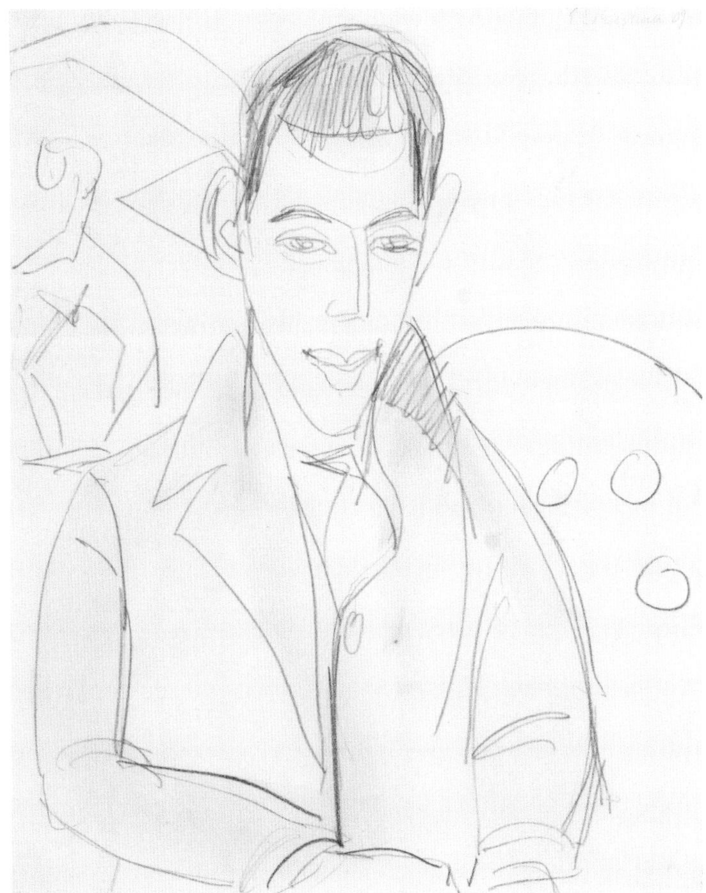

Cat. 35

Couple under Japanese Umbrella, 1913
Oil on canvas

Hilti Art Foundation, Schaan, Liechtenstein

Cat. 26

Two Women with Washbasin; The Sisters, 1913
Oil on canvas

Städel Museum, Frankfurt am Main, property of the Städelscher Museums-Verein e. V.

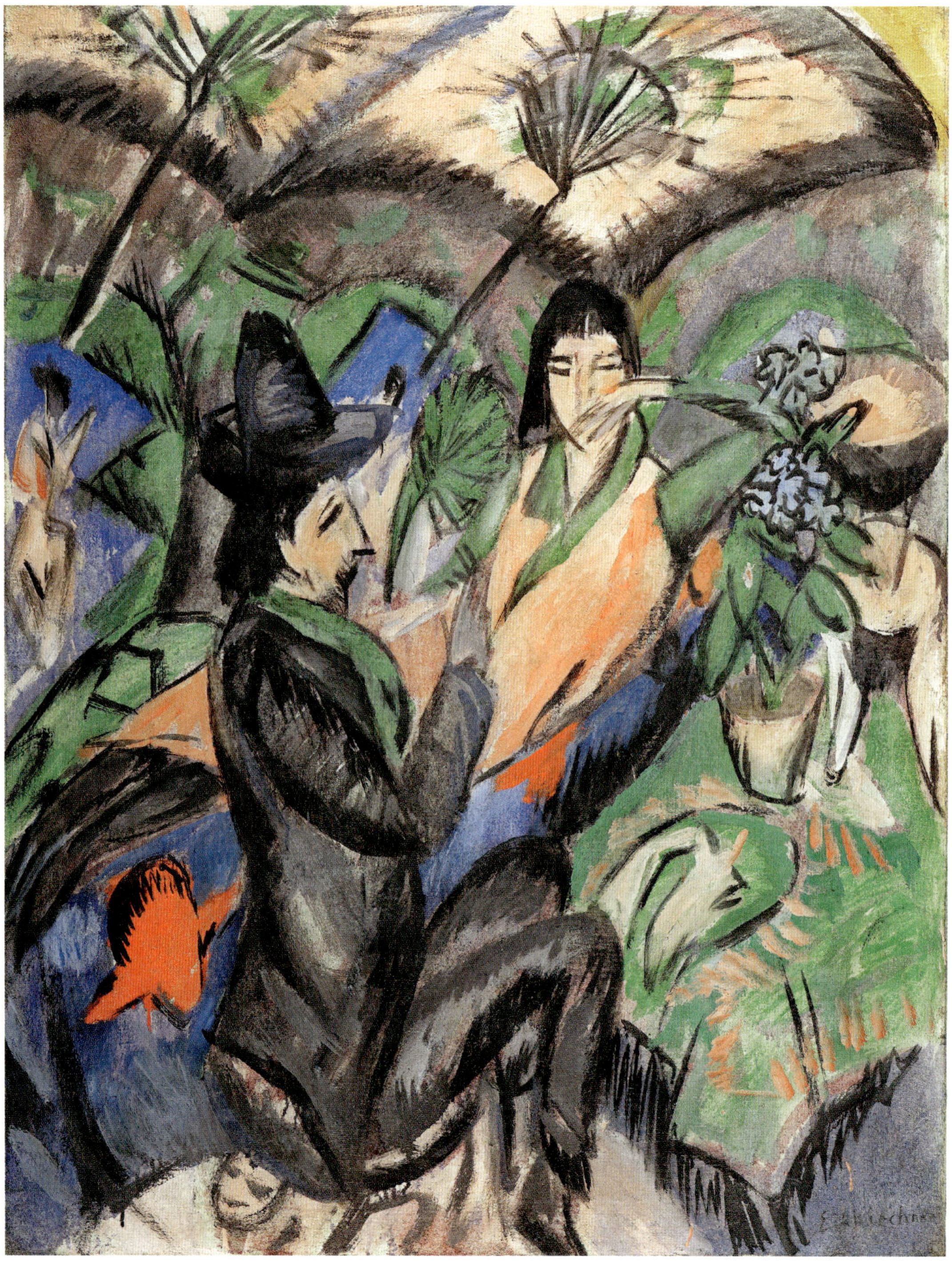

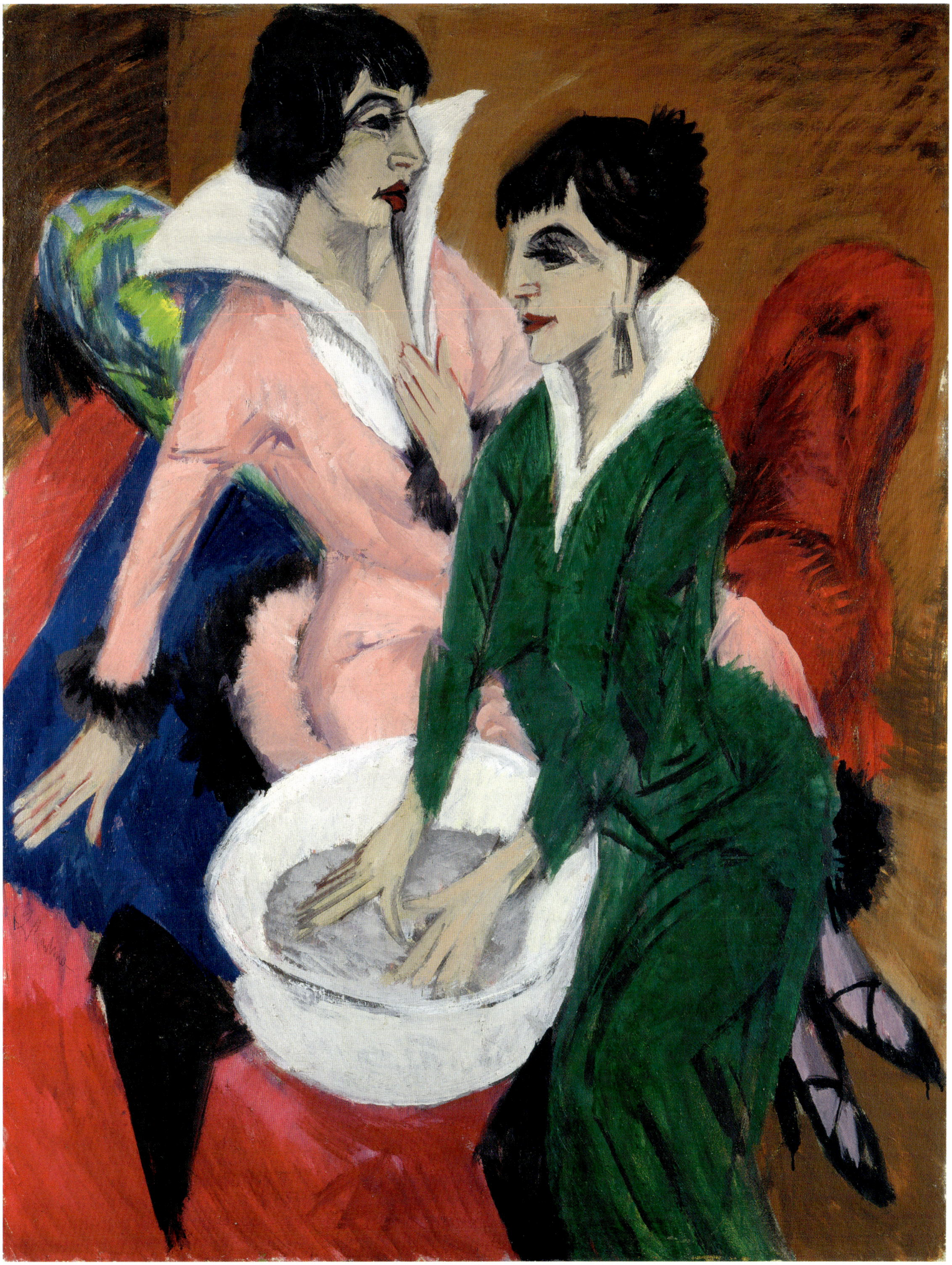

Cat. 33

Erna near the Sea, Fehmarn, 1913
Oil on canvas

Merzbacher Kunststiftung

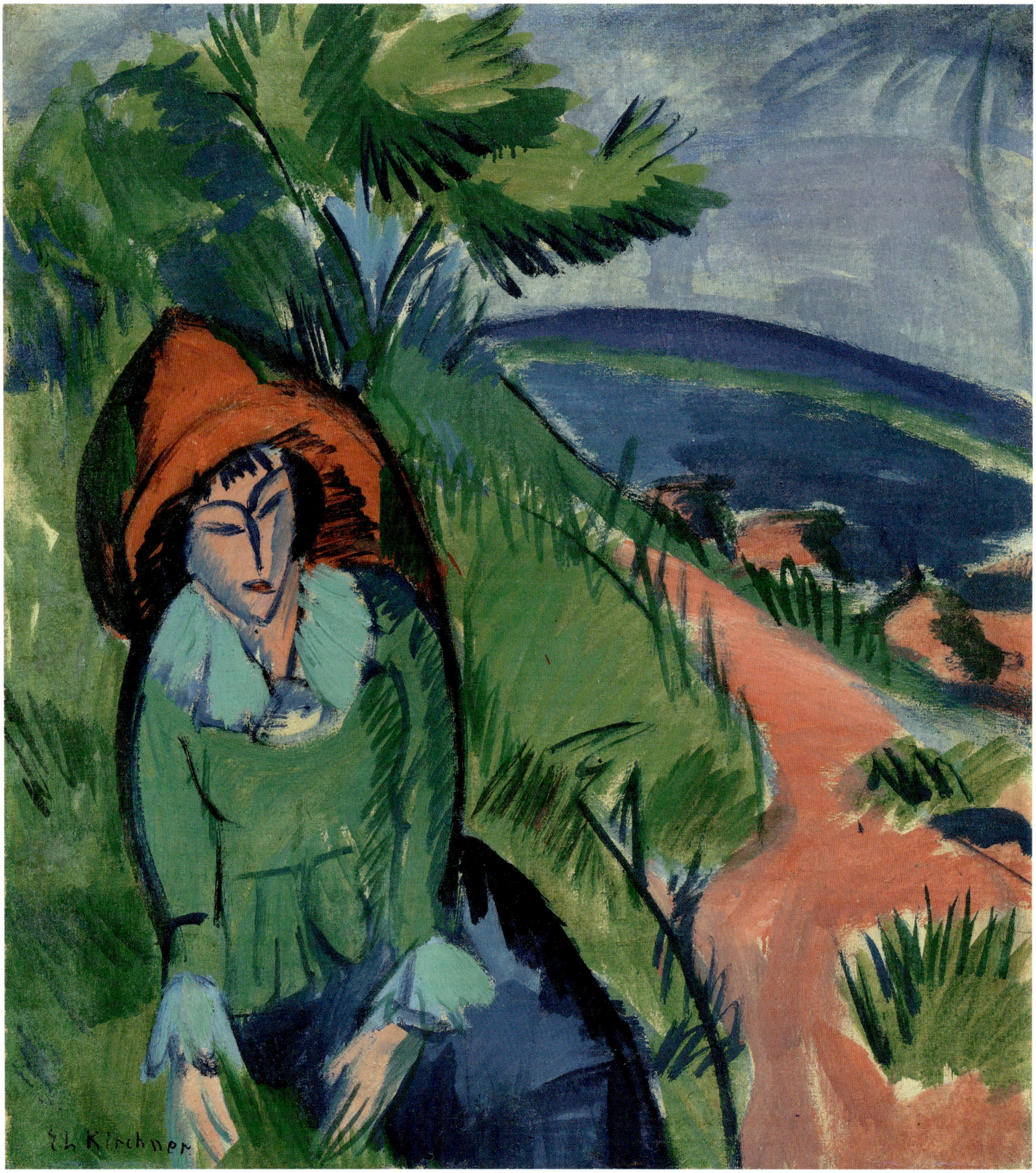

Cat. 82

Woman in the Hammock, 1913
Black crayon on paper

Brücke-Museum, Berlin

Cat. 83

Dancing Female Nude
on the Beach, Fehmarn, 1913
Carpenter pencil
on thick paper

Kirchner Museum Davos,
Gift of the Ernst Ludwig
Kirchner Estate 1994

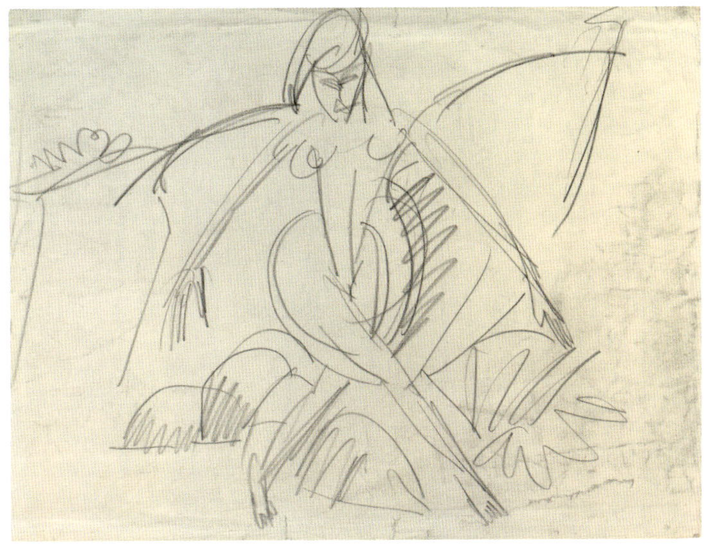

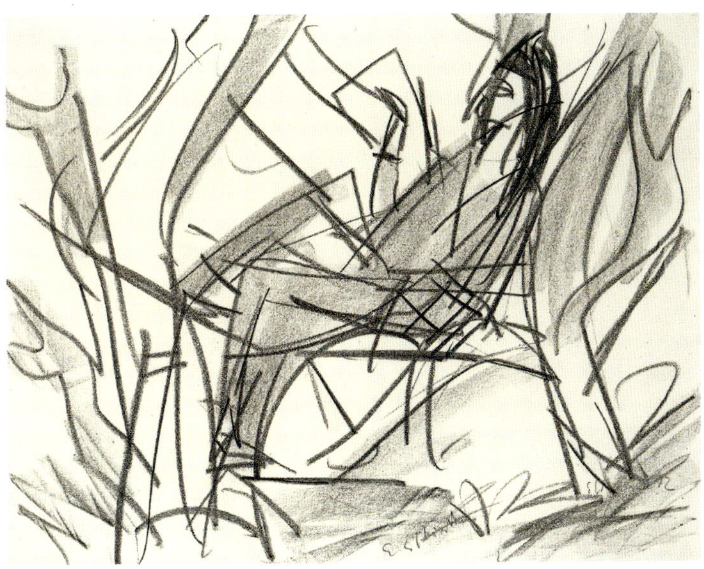

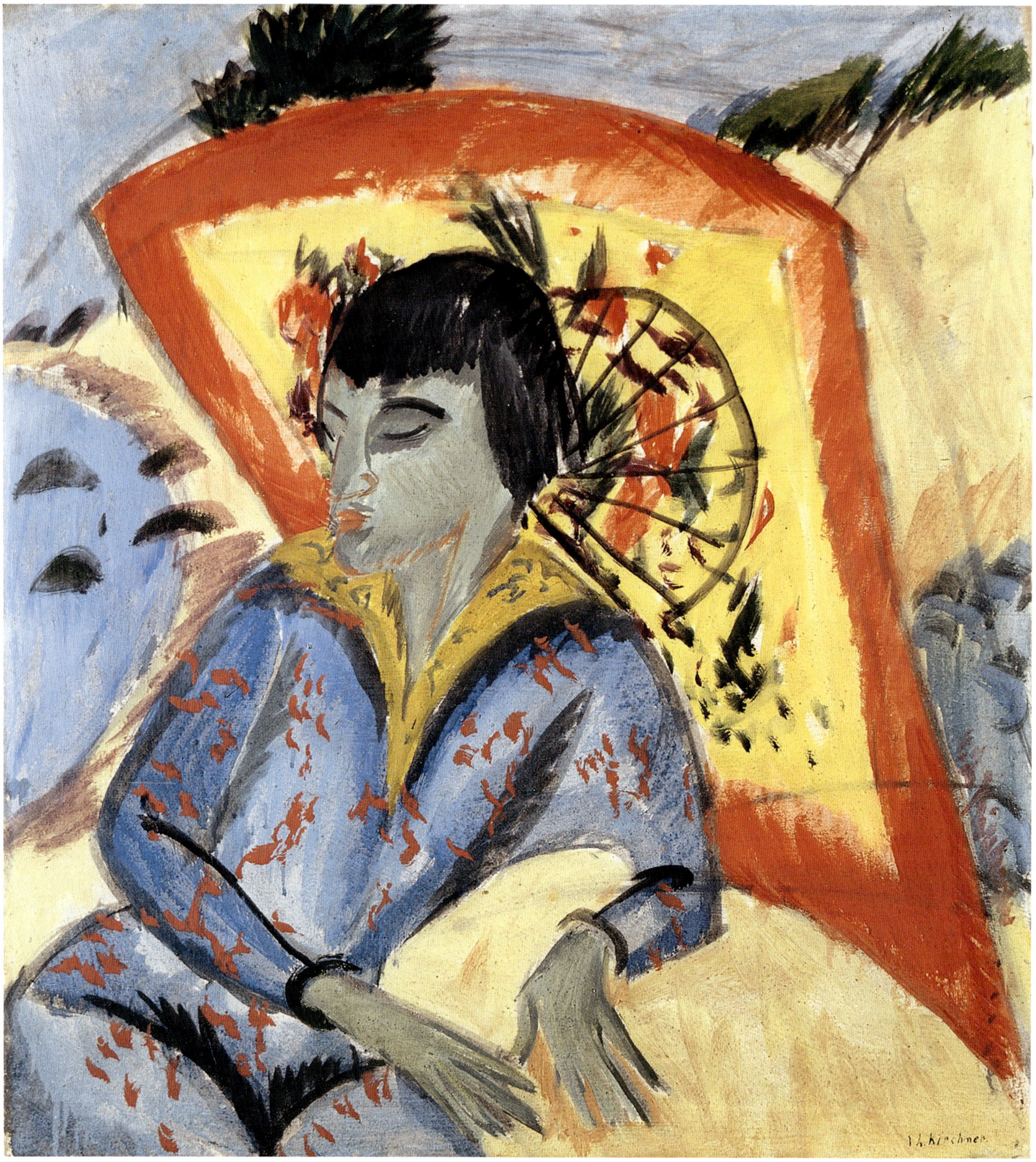
E.L.Kirchner

Cat. 34

Erna with Japanese Umbrella (Japanese Girl), 1913
Oil on canvas

Aargauer Kunsthaus Aarau/ Bequest of Dr Othmar and Valerie Häuptli

Cat. 42

Red Tree on the Shore, 1913
Oil on canvas

Private collection

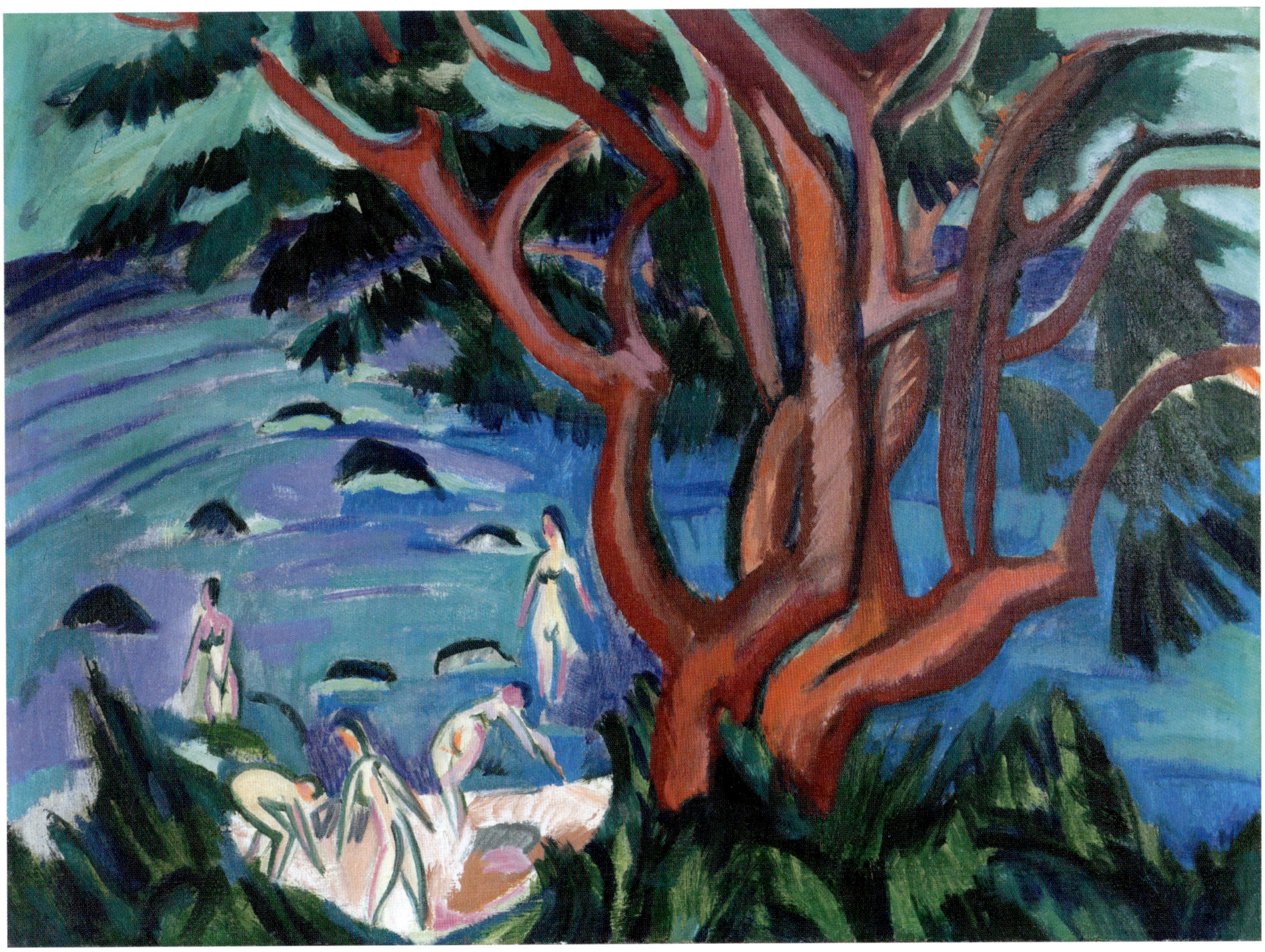

Cat. 37

Fehmarn Coast with Lighthouse, 1913
Oil on canvas

Hermann Gerlinger Collection, in the Kunstmuseum Moritzburg Halle (Saale)

Cat. 32

Tower Room (Self-Portrait with Erna), 1913
Oil on canvas

Columbus Museum of Art, Ohio, Gift of Howard D. and Babette L. Sirak, the Donors to the Campaign for Enduring Excellence, and the Derby Fund

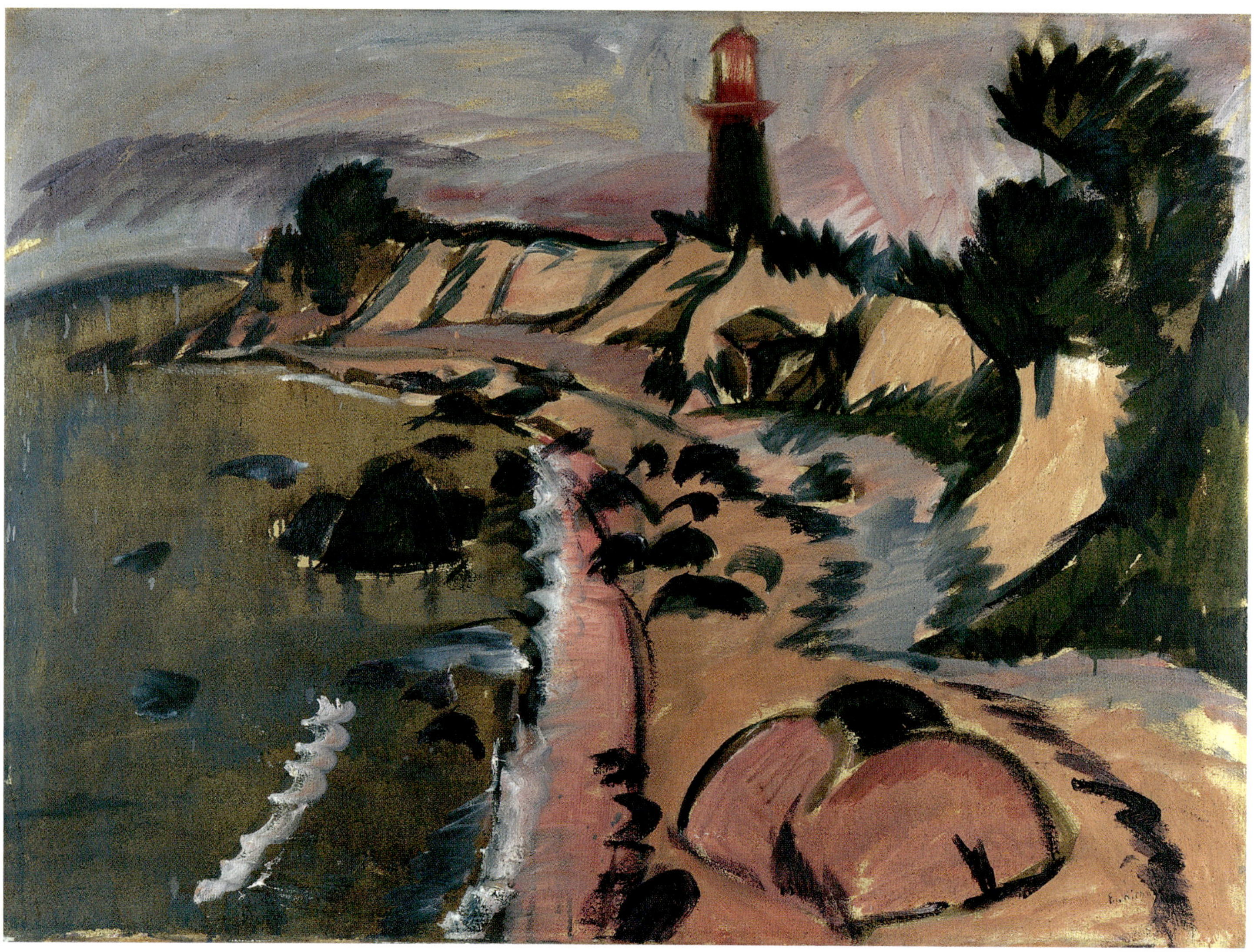

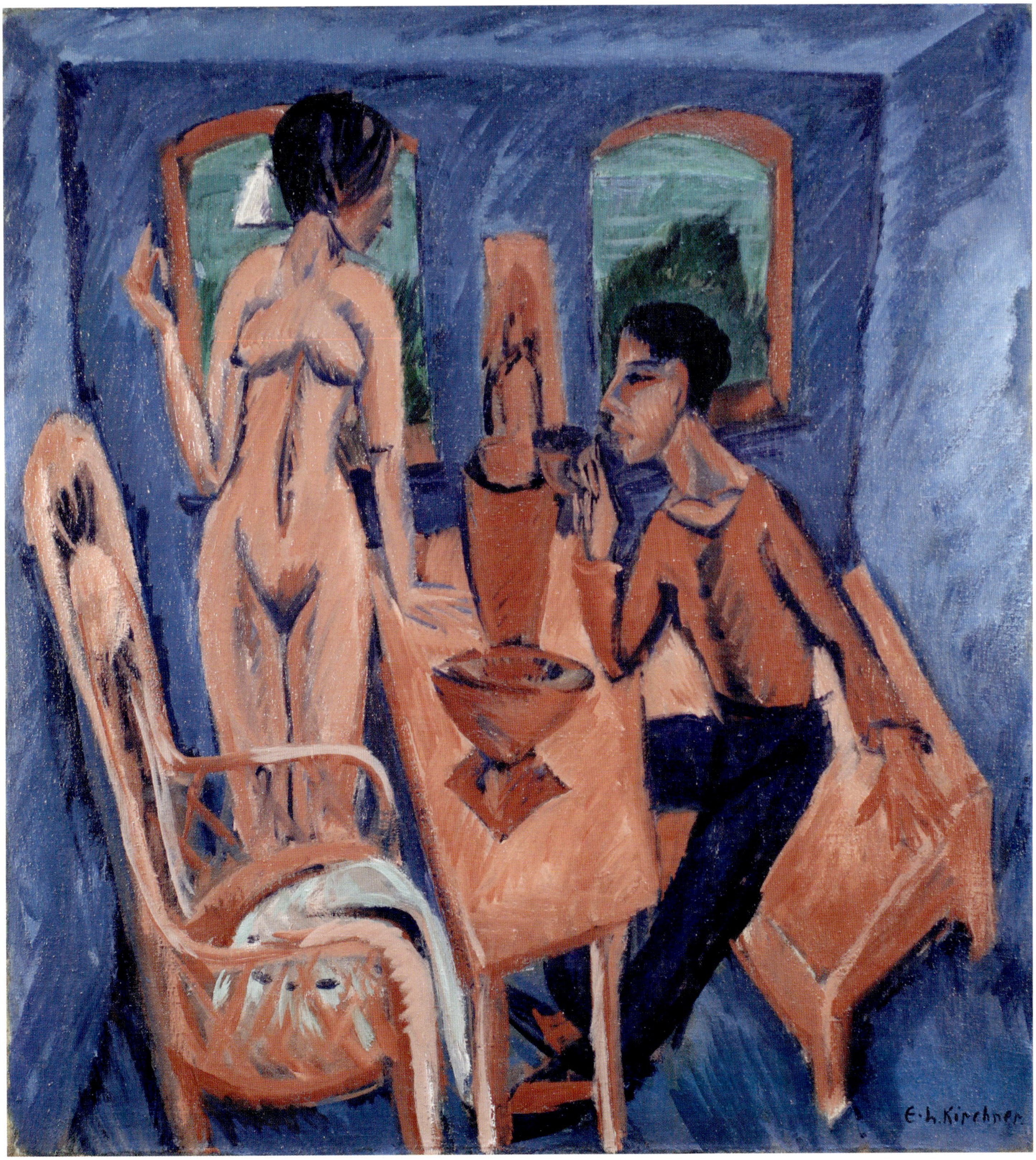
E.L.Kirchner

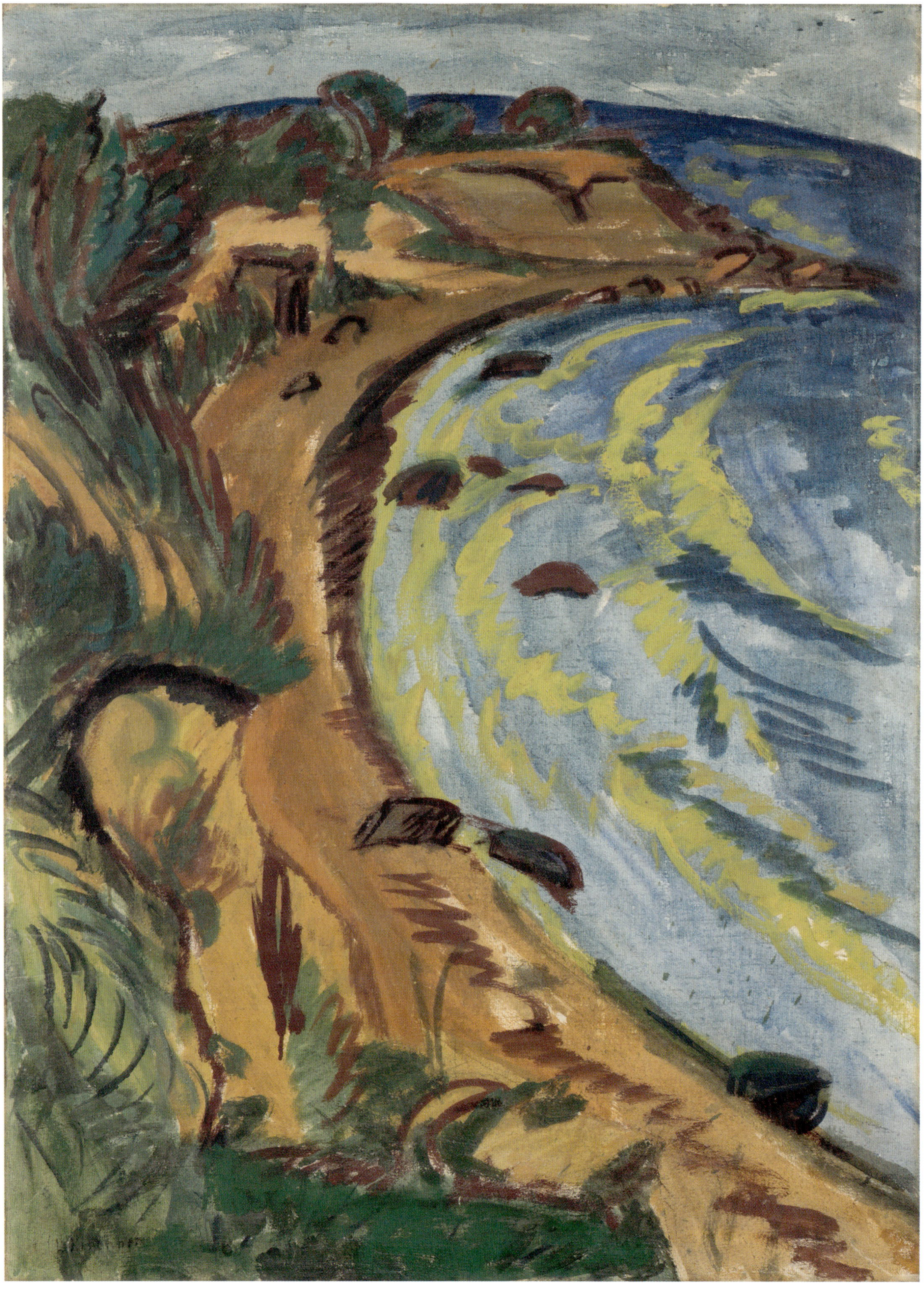

Cat. 38

Bay on the Fehmarn Coast, 1913
Oil on canvas

Städel Museum, Frankfurt am Main, on permanent loan from a private collection

Cat. 138

Bay on the east coast of the Baltic Sea island of Fehmarn, 1913
Glass negative

Kirchner Museum Davos, Gift of the Ernst Ludwig Kirchner Estate 1992

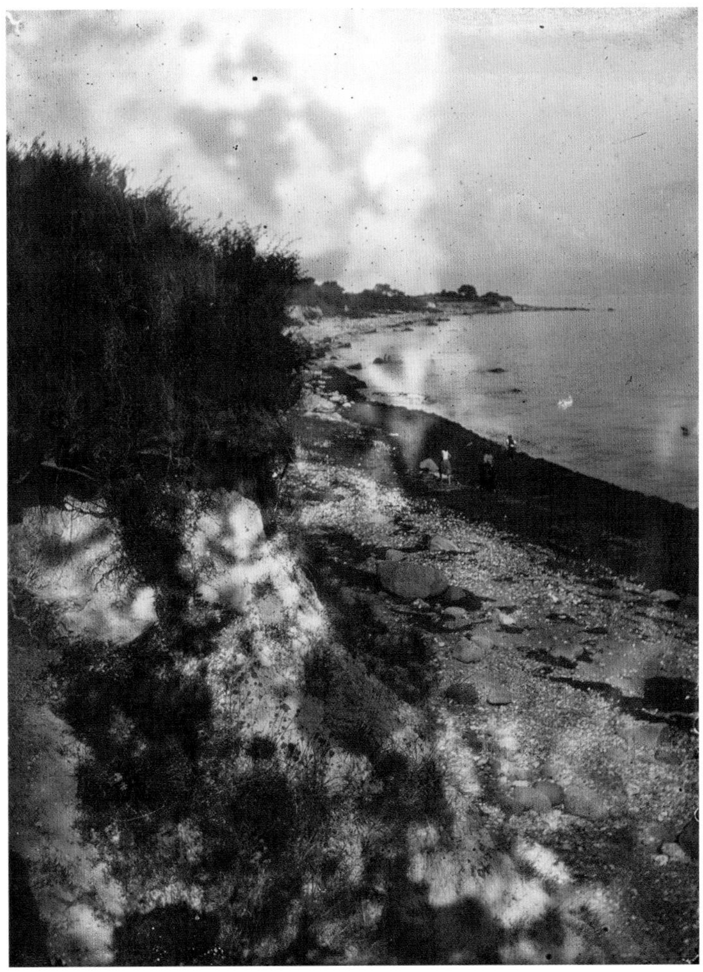

Cat. 106

Trees and Shrubs Next to the Beach, Fehmarn, 1913
Colour woodcut on blotting paper, mounted on cardboard

Brücke-Museum, Berlin, Karl and Emy Schmidt-Rottluff Foundation

Cat. 148

Figure Looking Back, 1913
Wood (oak, from a single trunk), stained dark

Museum Kunstpalast, Düsseldorf

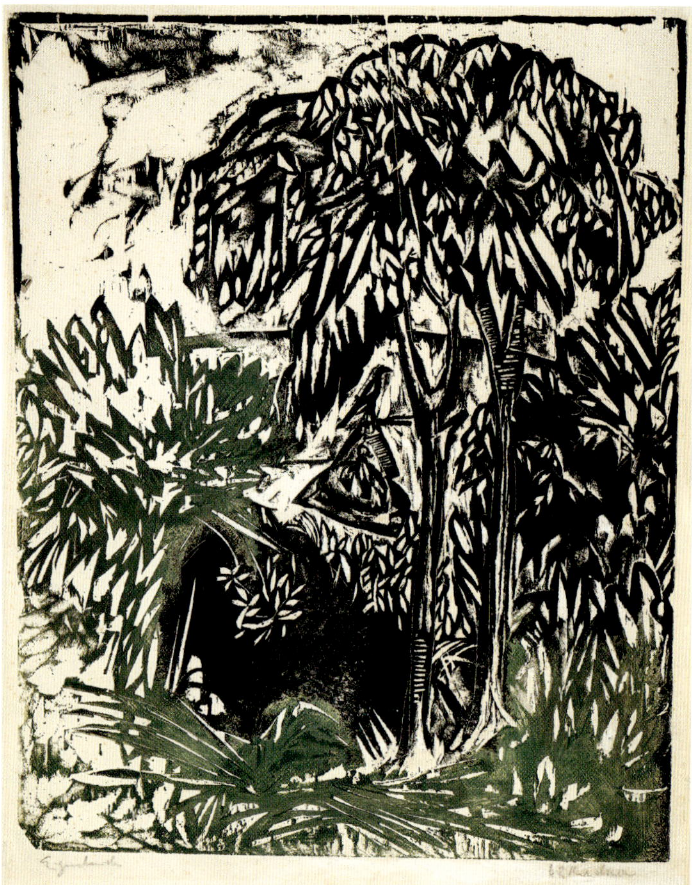

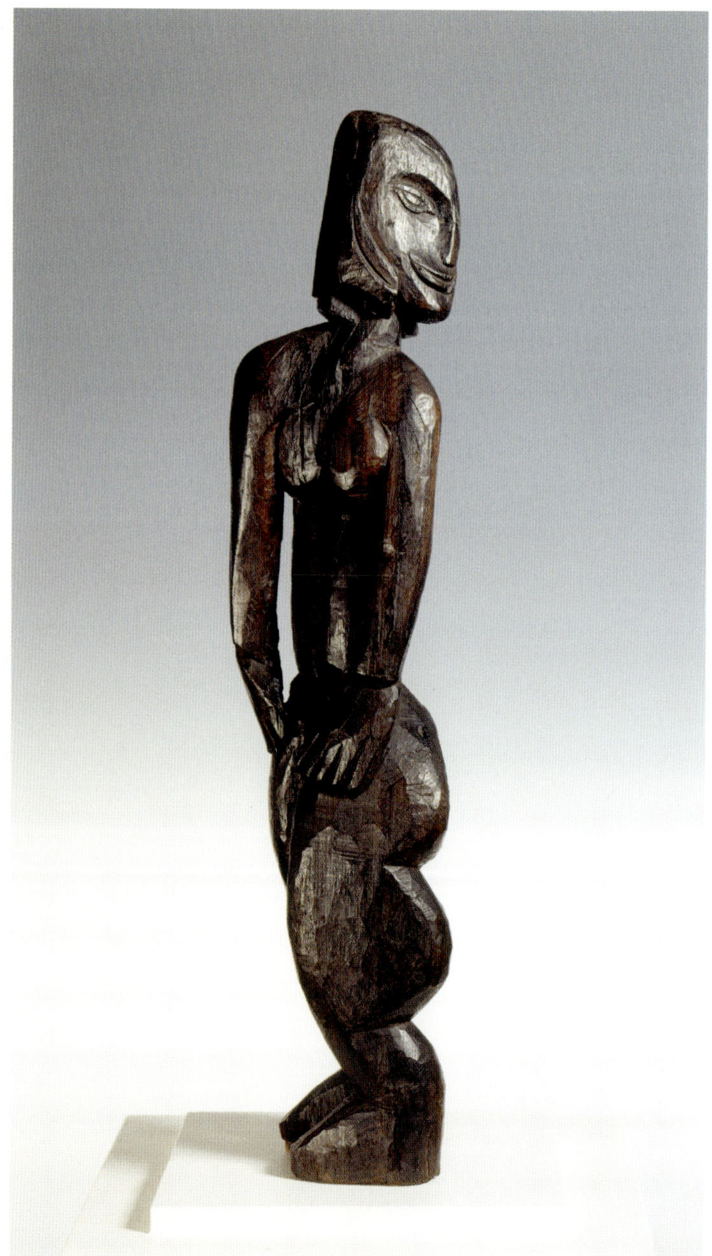

Cat. 109

Three Bathers Next to Rocks, Fehmarn, 1913
Colour lithograph on smooth cardboard

Kunstmuseum Basel, Kupferstichkabinett

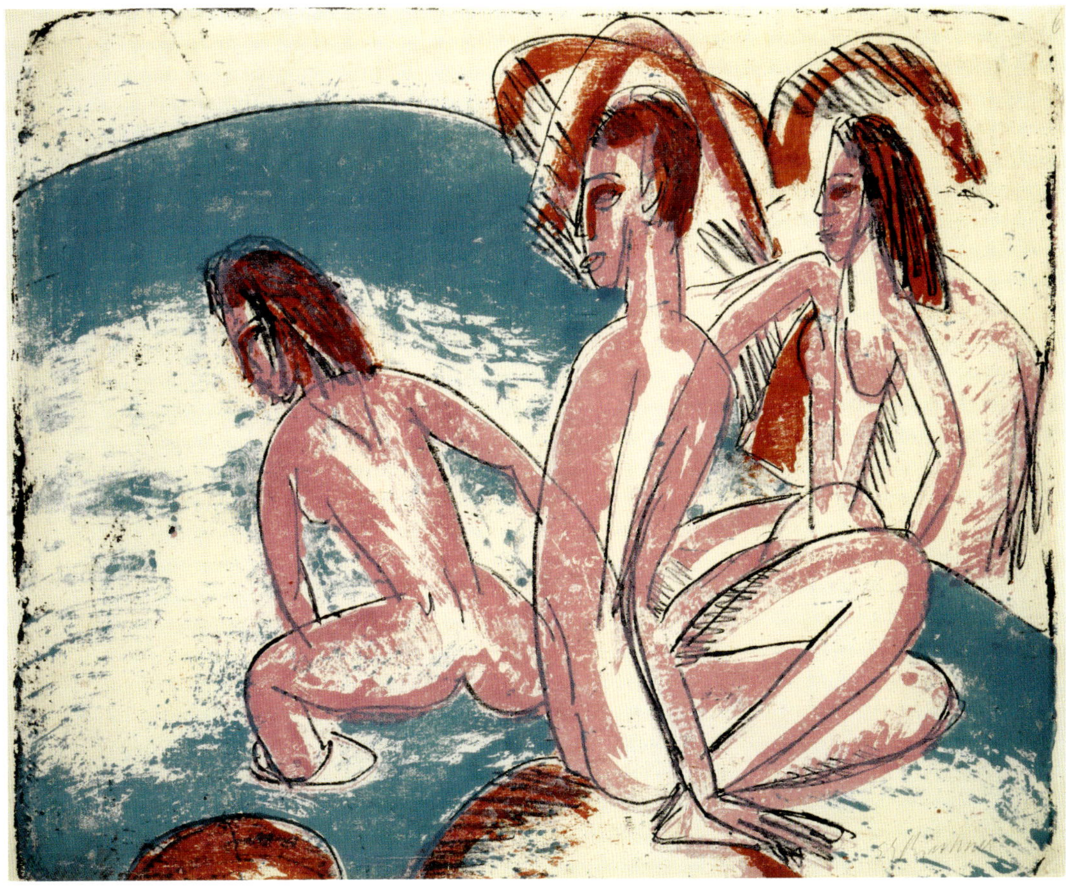

Cat. 81

Fehmarn Coast with Yellow Nude, 1913
Watercolour over pencil on paper

Kirchner Museum Davos, on loan from the Rosemarie Ketterer Foundation

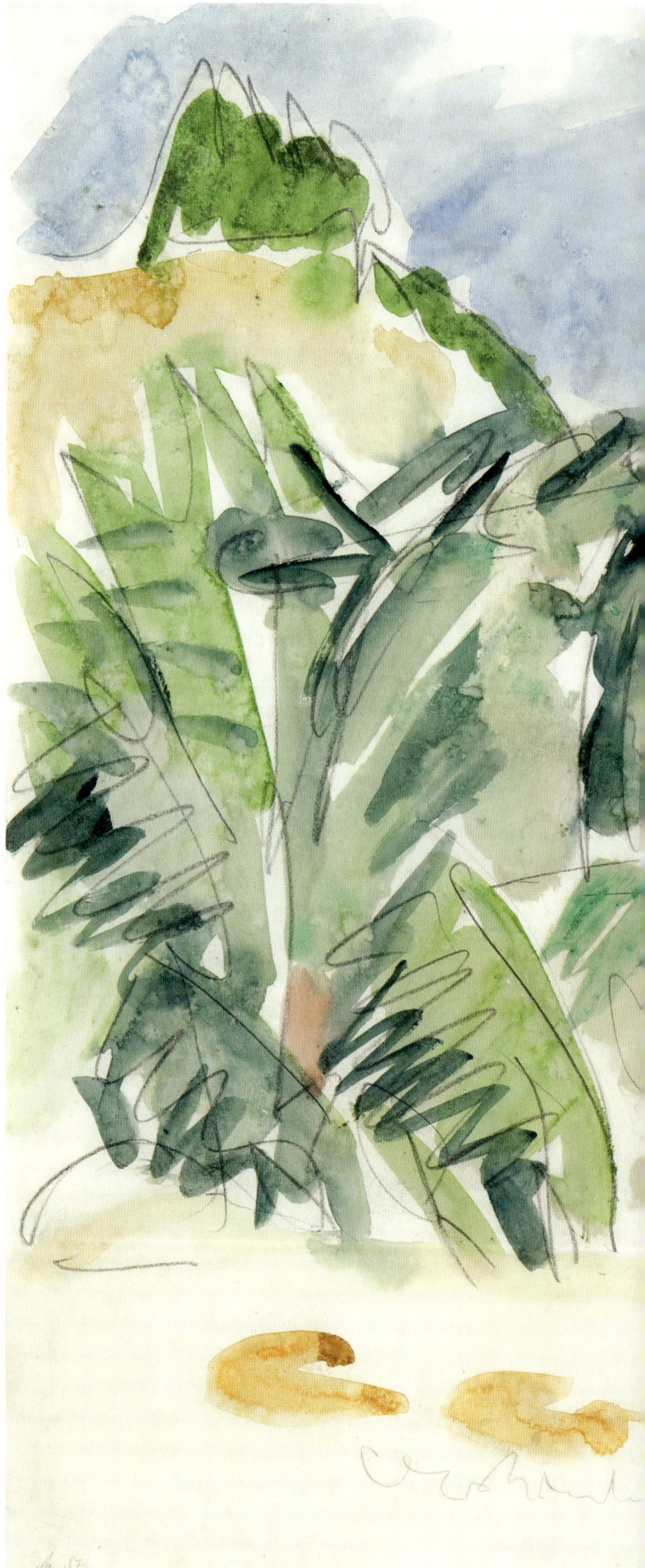

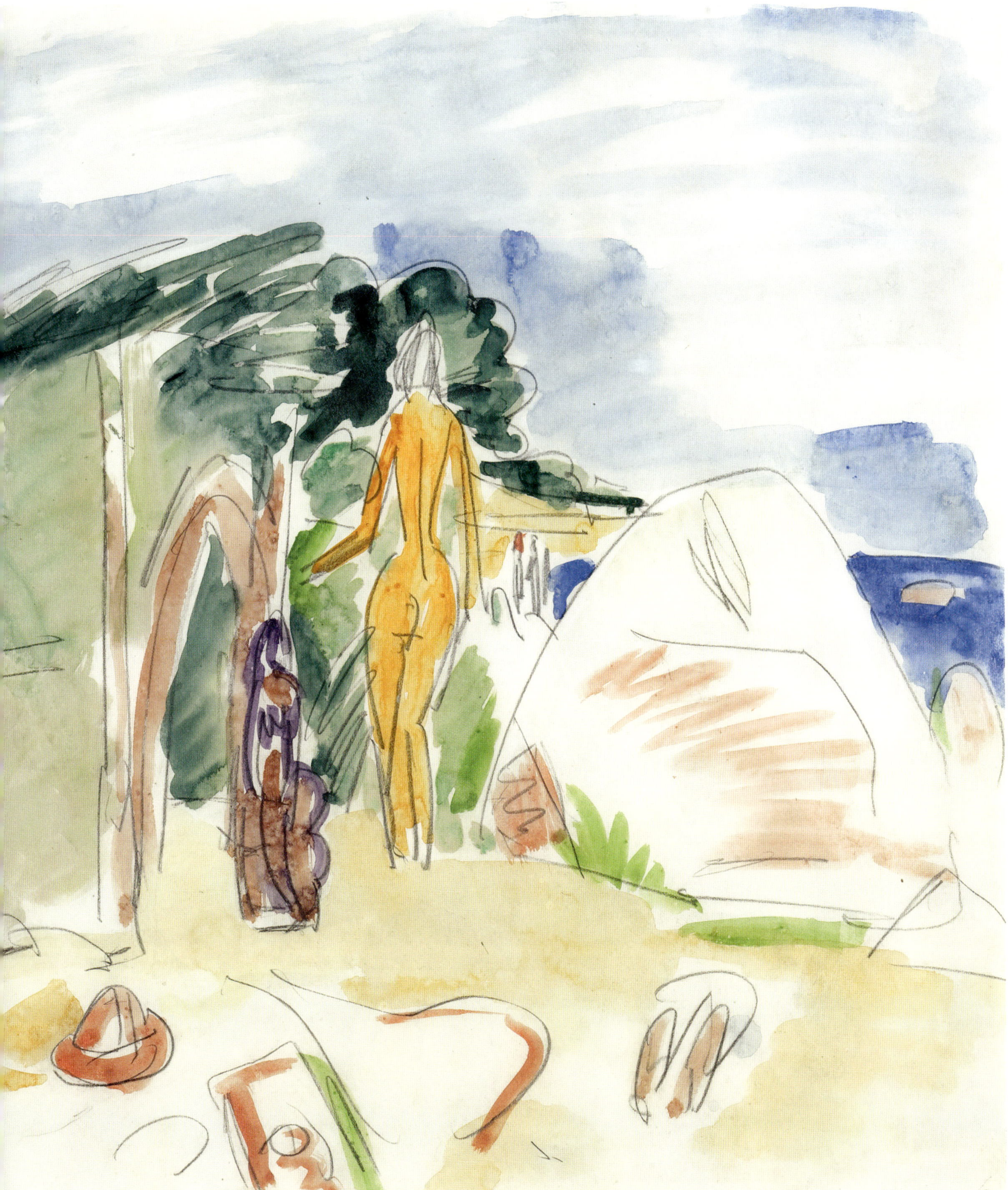

Cat. 40

Nudes Next to the Shore Woods, 1913
Oil on canvas

Kunstmuseum Moritzburg Halle (Saale)

Cat. 39

Girls, Fehmarn, 1913
Oil on canvas

Lehmbruck Museum, Duisburg

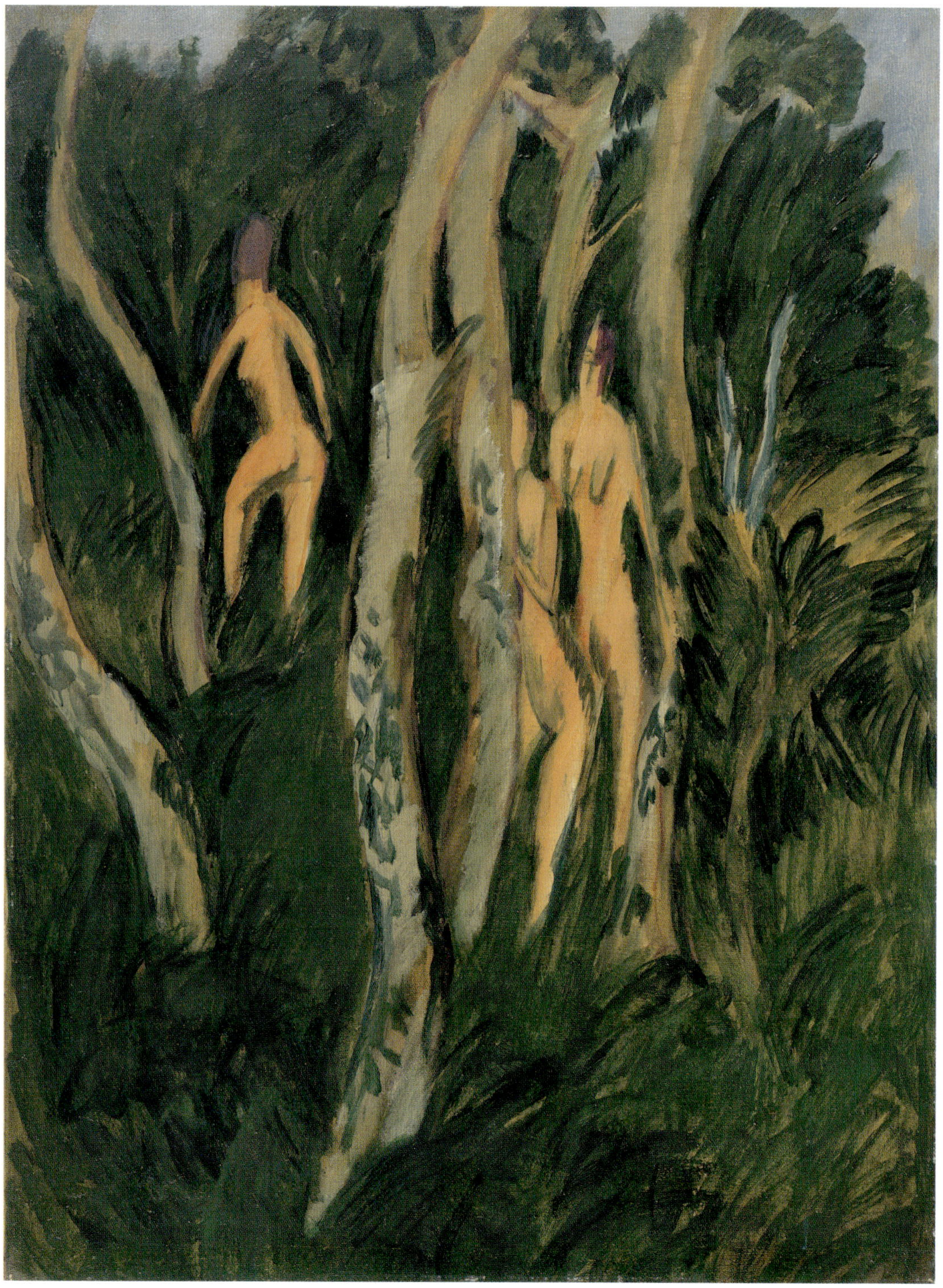

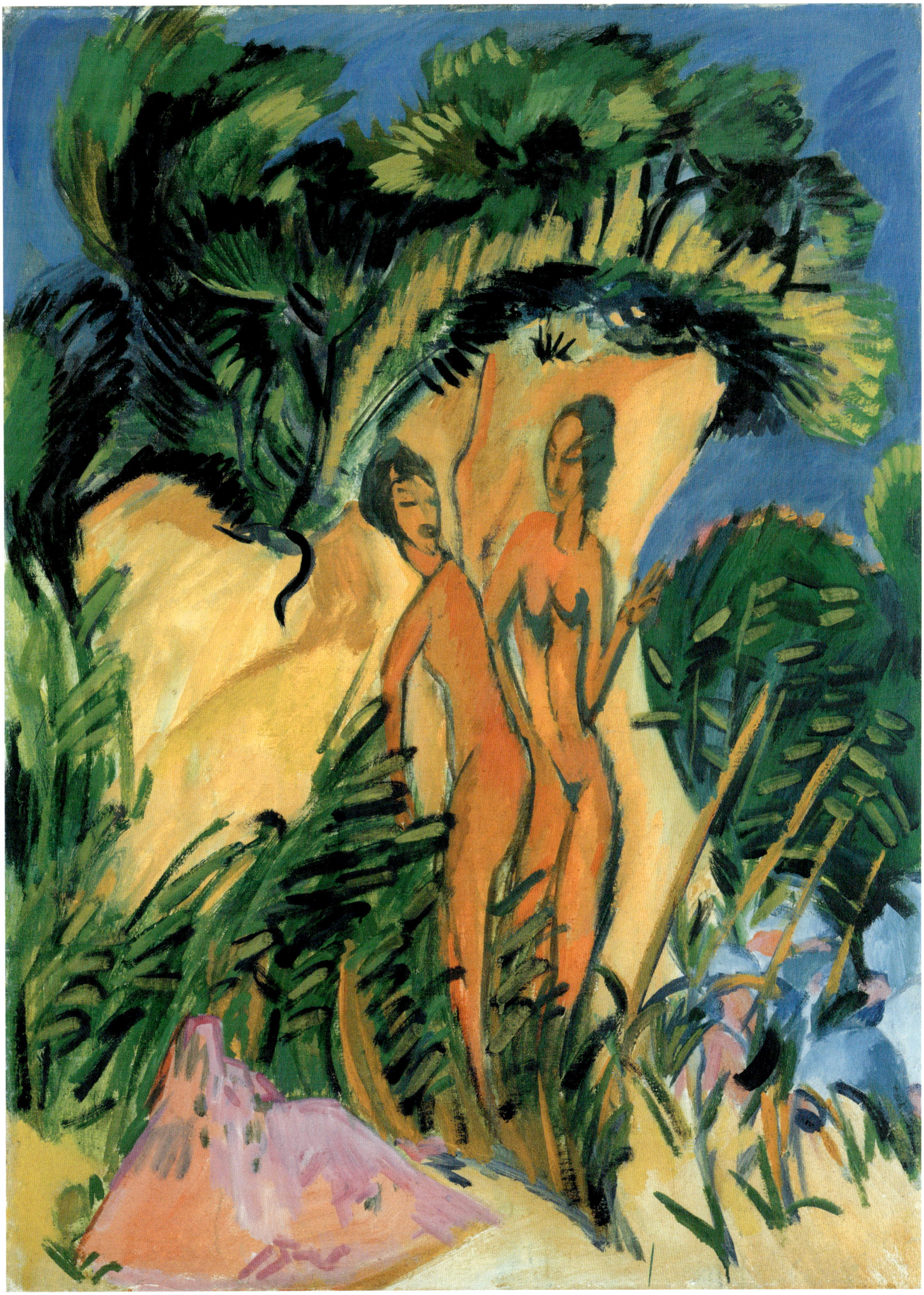

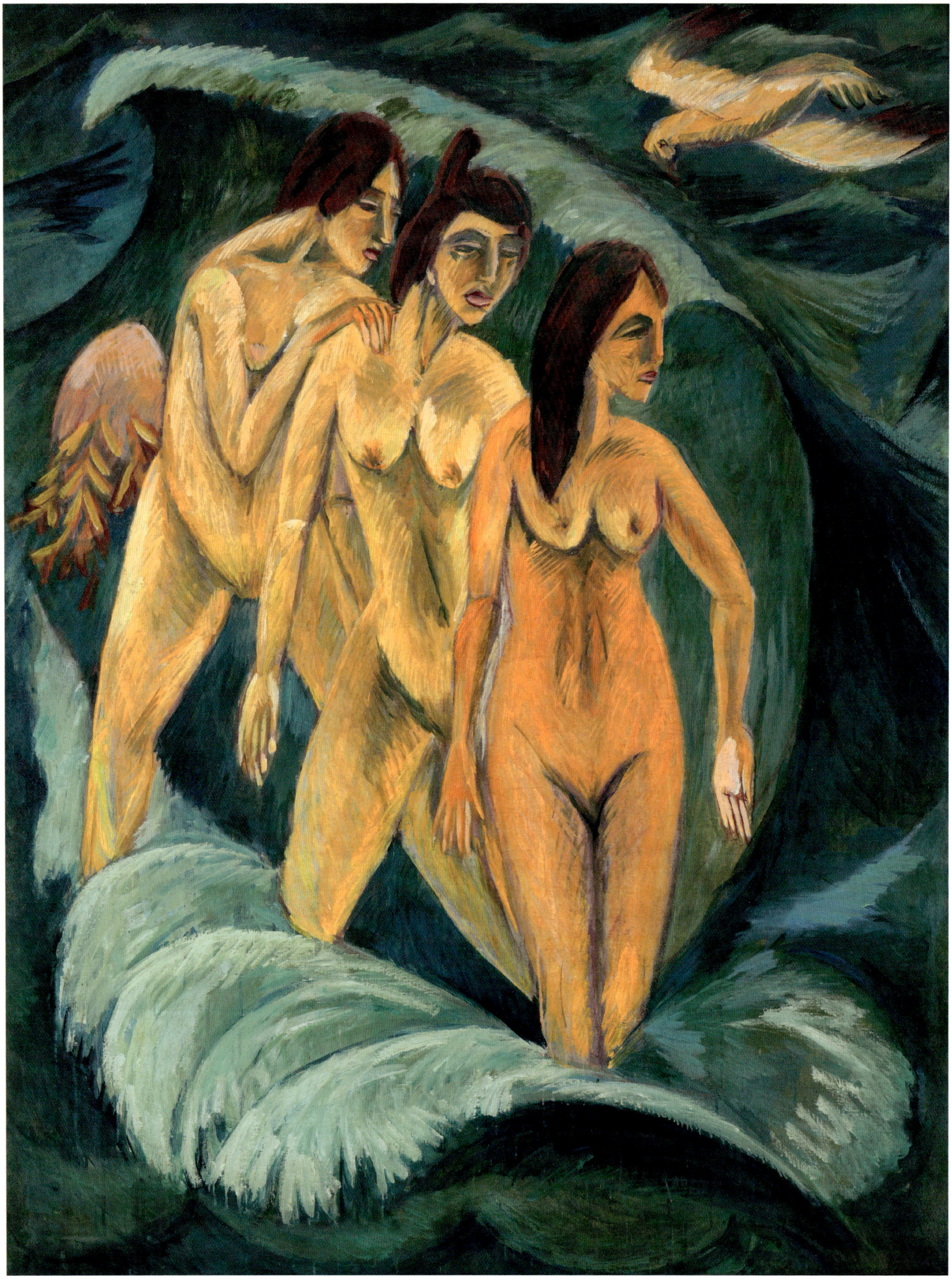

Cat. 41

Three Bathers, 1913
Oil on canvas

Collection: Art Gallery of New South Wales, Sydney – Art Gallery of New South Wales Foundation Purchase 1984

Cat. 84

Three Bathers in the Surf, 1913
Charcoal on paper

E.W.K. Collection, Bern/Davos

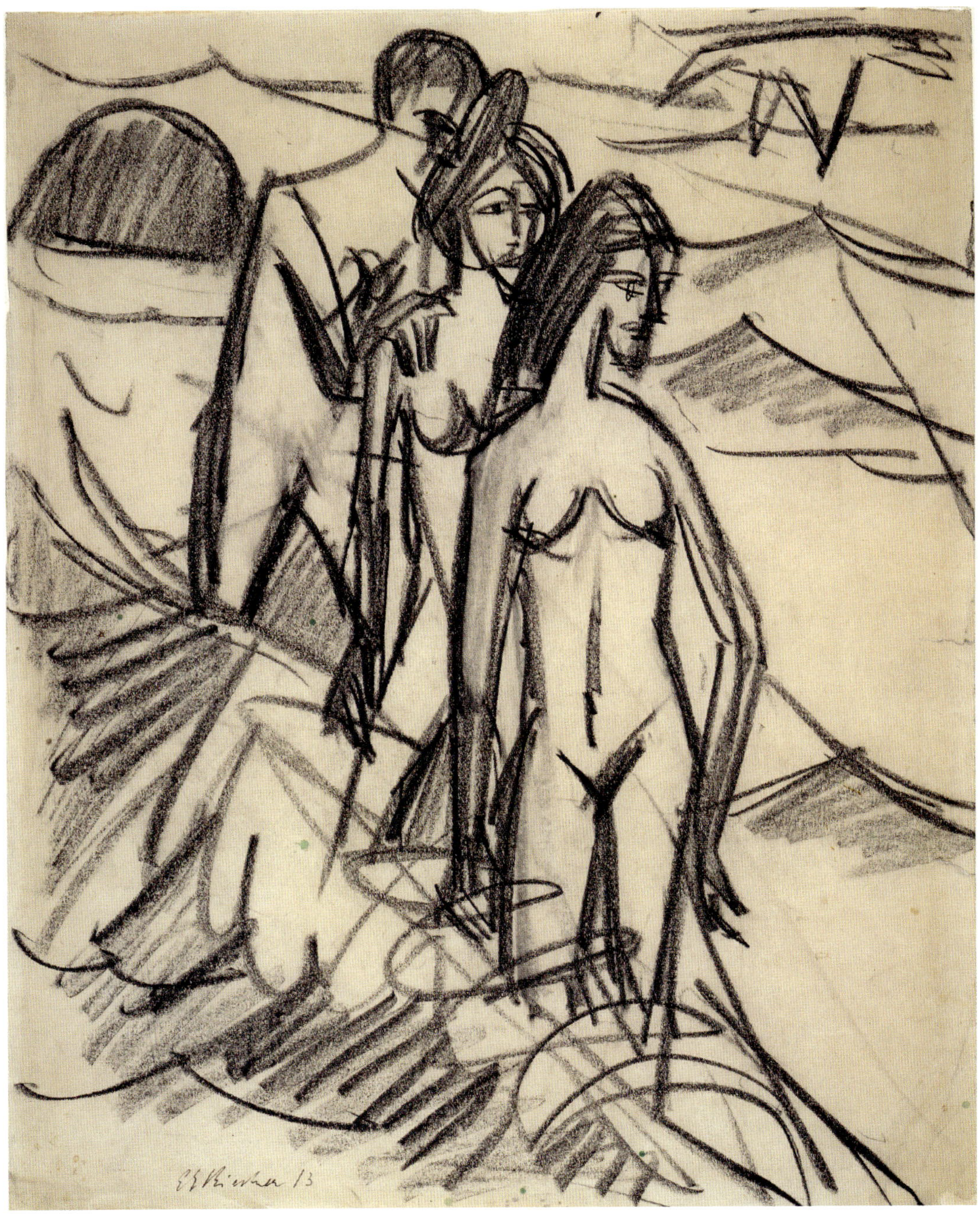

Cat. 31

Fehmarn Windmill, 1913
Oil on canvas

Von der Heydt-Museum
Wuppertal

Cat. 36

Staberhof Country Seat, Fehmarn I, 1913
Oil on canvas

Hamburger Kunsthalle

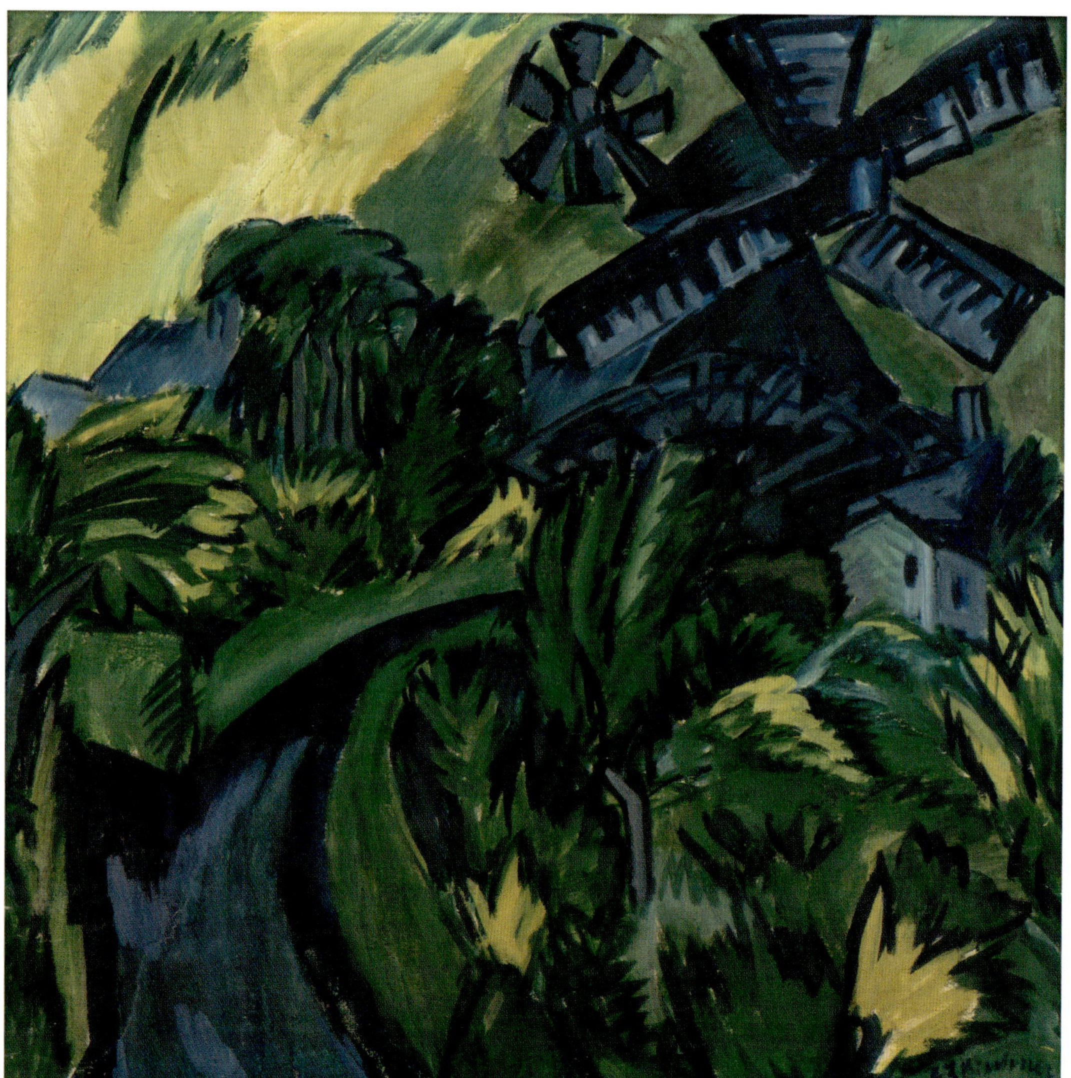

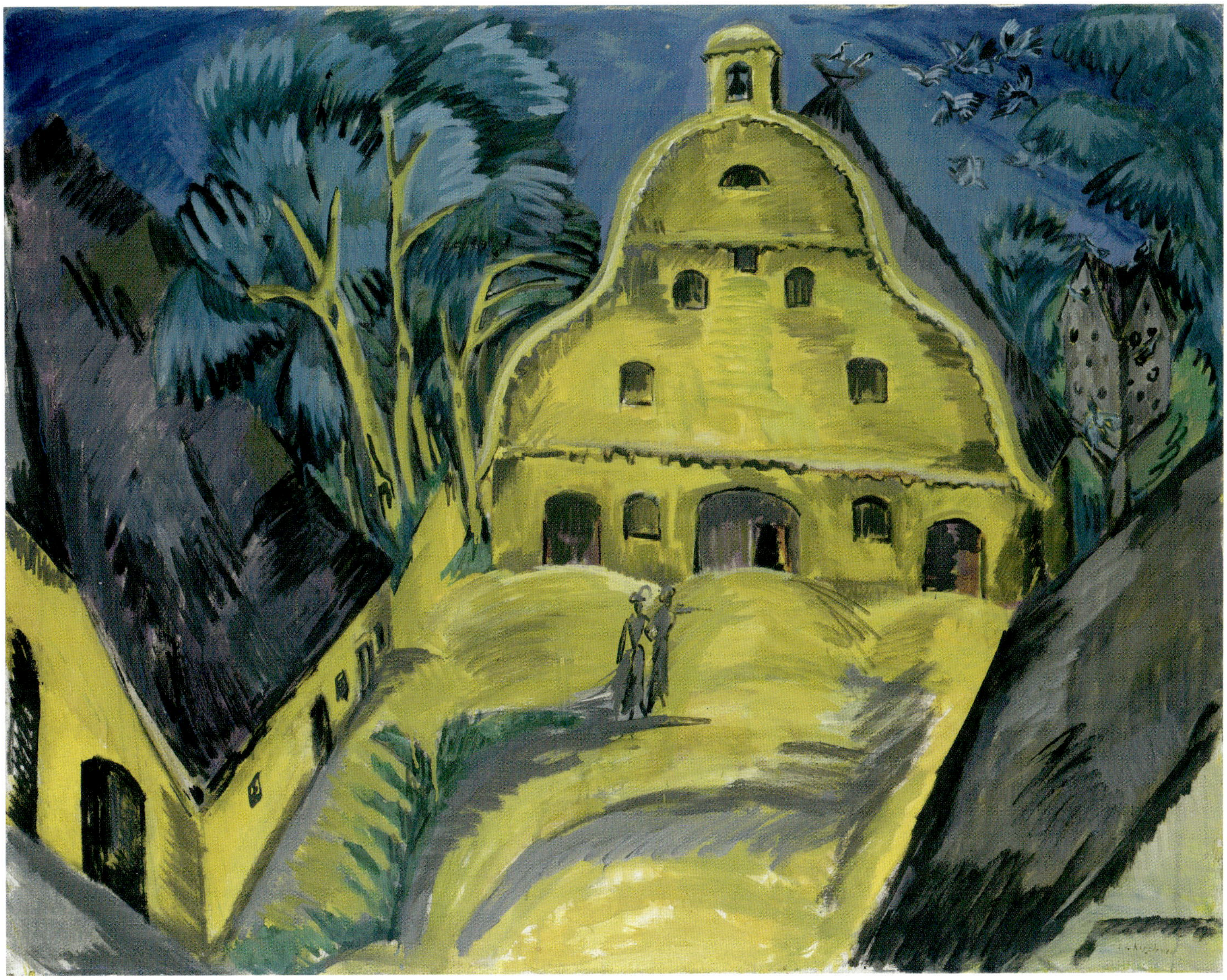

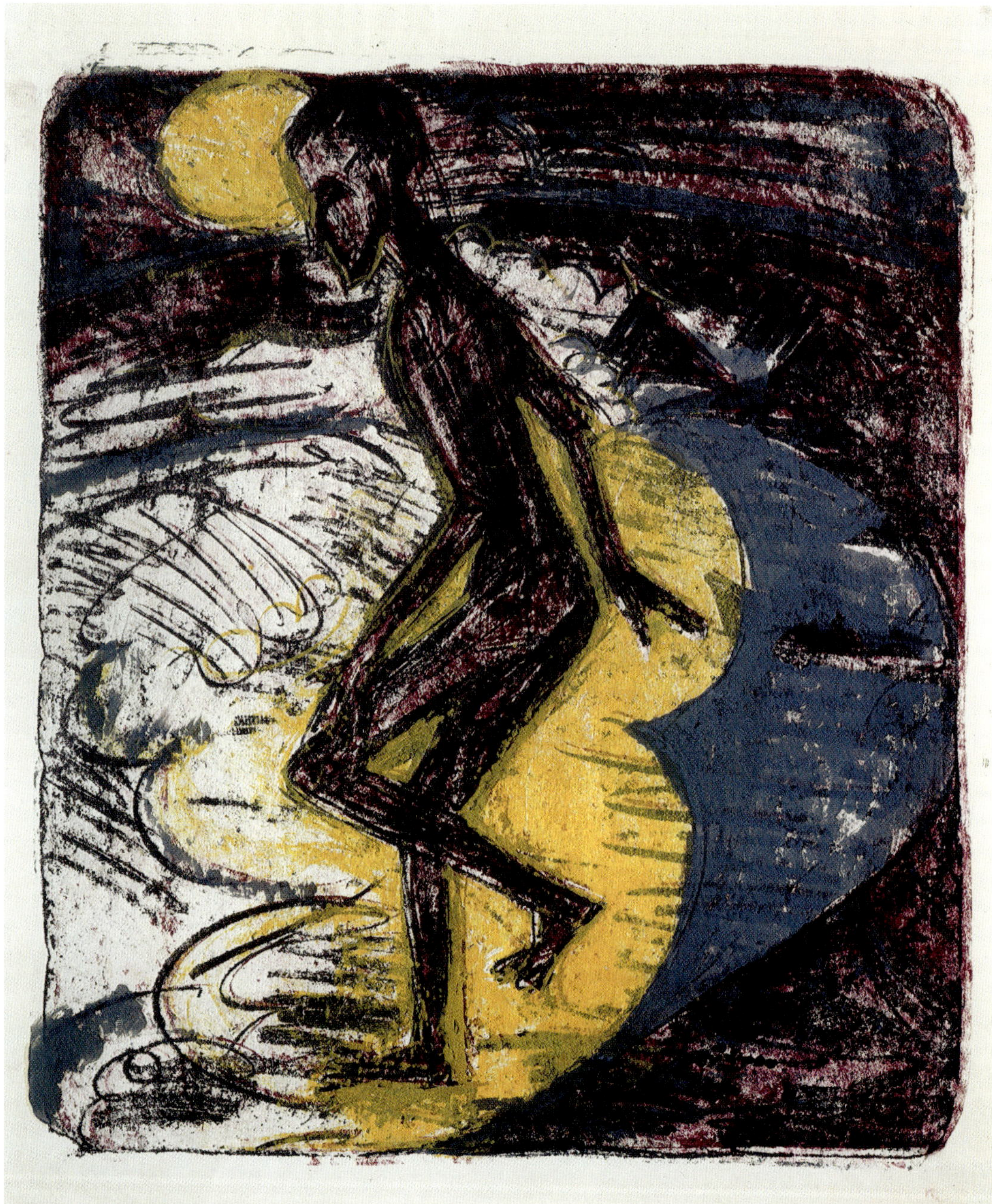

Cat. 108

Man Entering the Sea (Hans Gewecke), 1913
Colour lithograph on smooth cardboard

Private collection, Courtesy W. Wittrock, Berlin

Cat. 107

Three Bathers in the Surf, 1913
Colour woodcut on blotting paper

Werner Coninx Foundation, Zurich

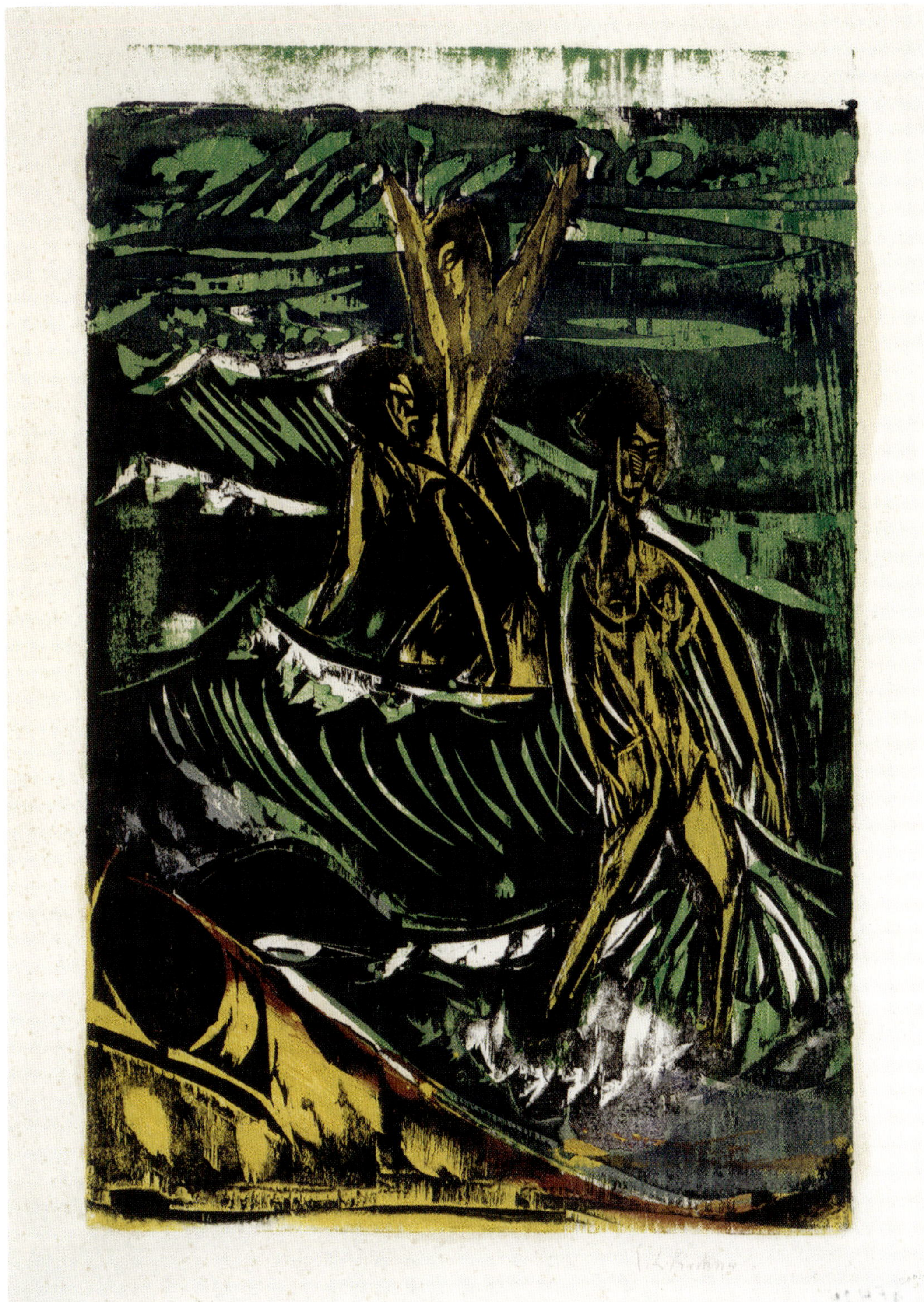

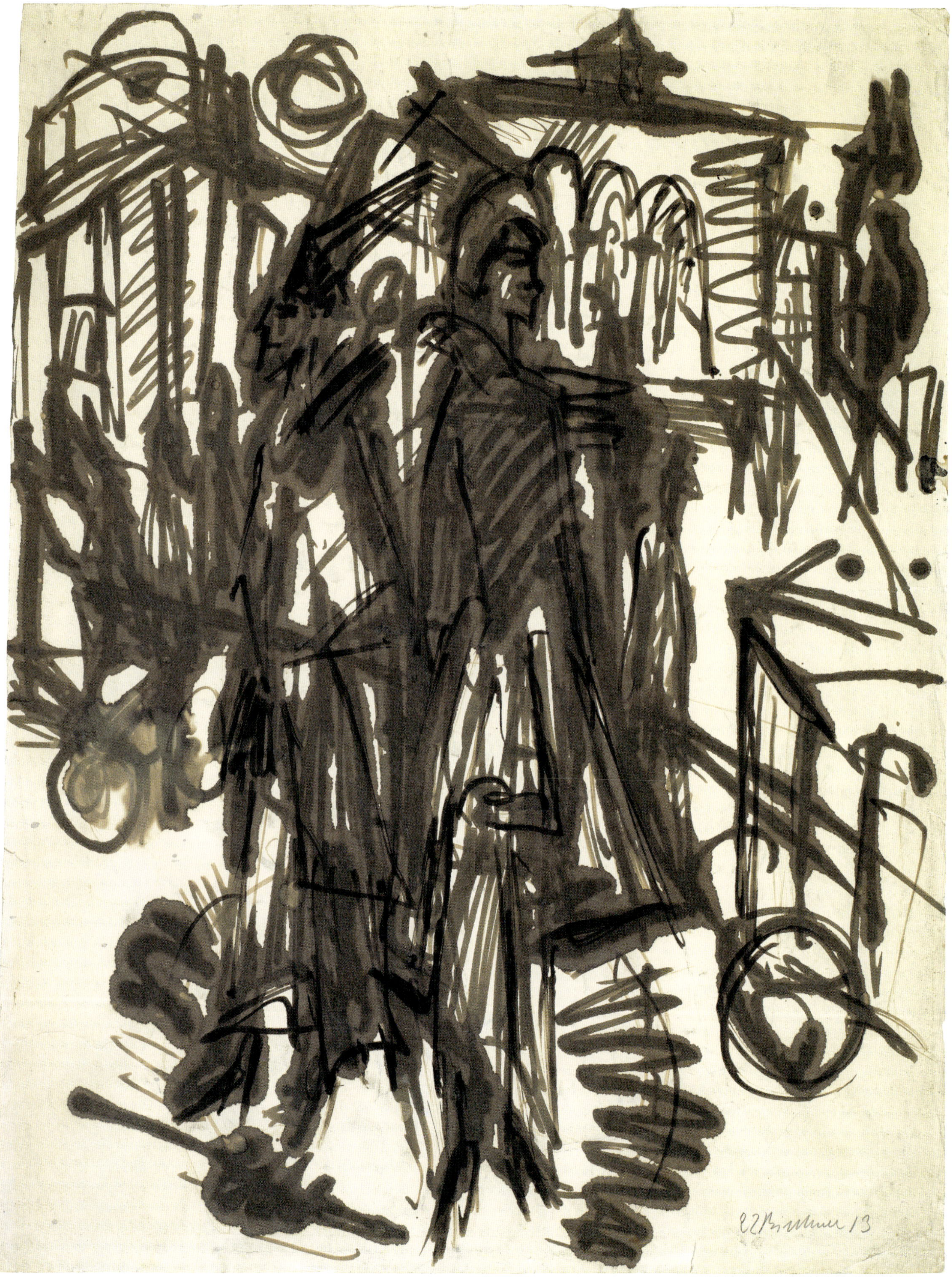
ELKirchner 13

Cat. 80

Potsdamer Platz, 1913
Reed pen and black ink, brush and dark-brown ink on paper

E. W. K. Collection, Bern/Davos

Cat. 88

Street Scene in Berlin, 1913/14
Pencil on paper

E. W. K. Collection, Bern/Davos

Cat. 89

Street Scene in Berlin, 1913/14
Pencil on paper

E. W. K. Collection, Bern/Davos

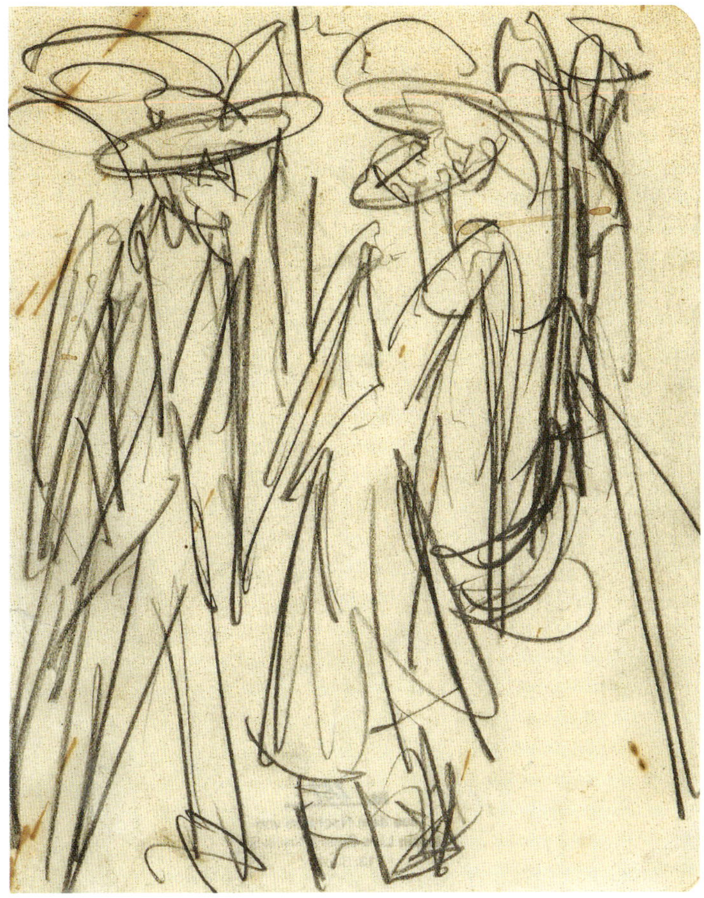

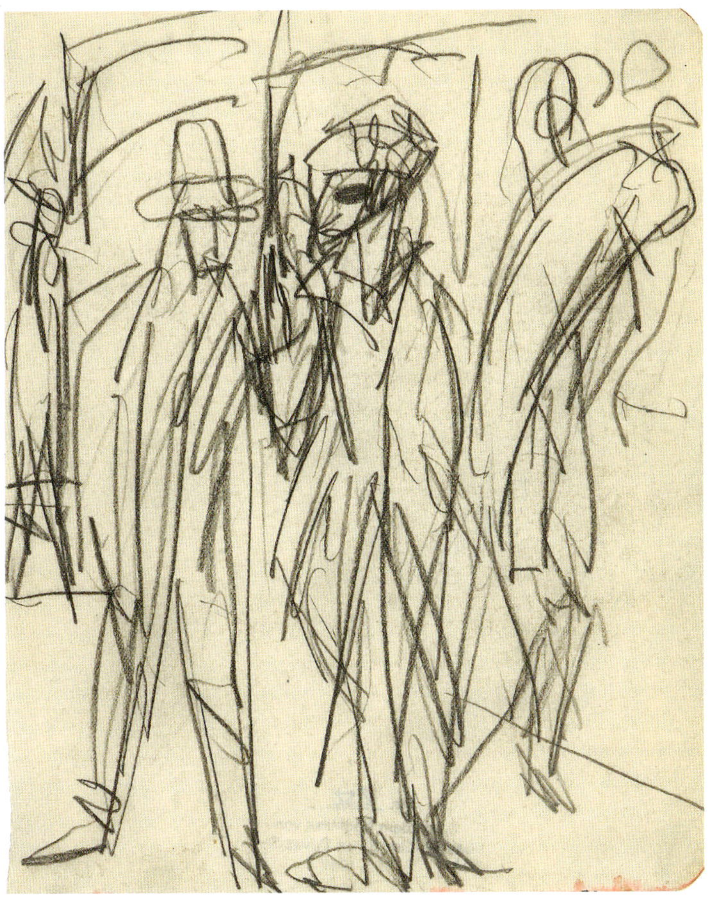

Cat. 110

Five Cocottes on the Street, 1913/14
Woodcut on vellum card

Städel Museum, Graphische Sammlung, Frankfurt am Main

Cat. 44

Street, Berlin, 1913
Oil on canvas

The Museum of Modern Art, New York, purchase, 1939

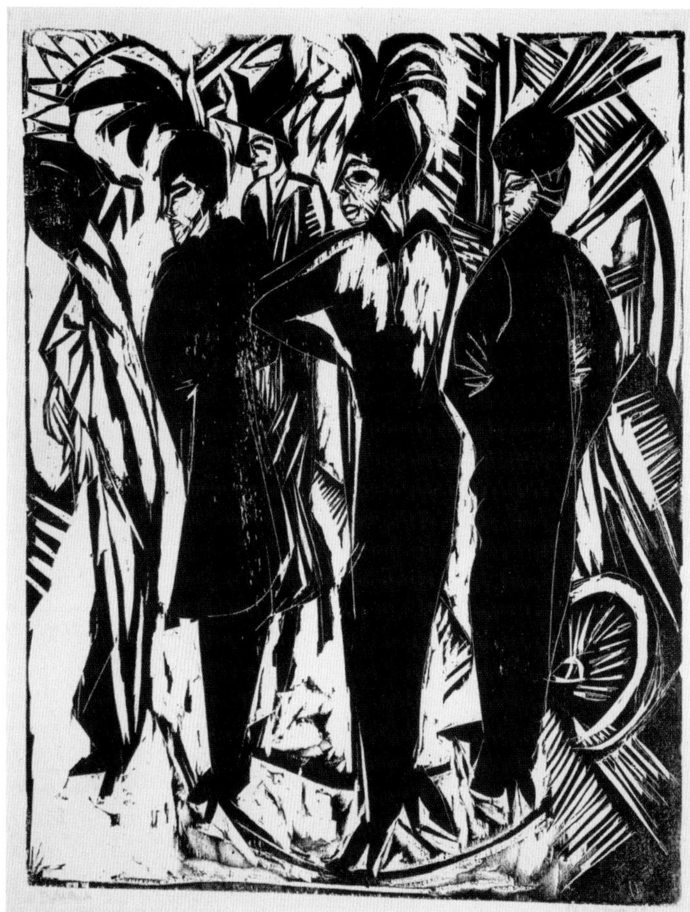

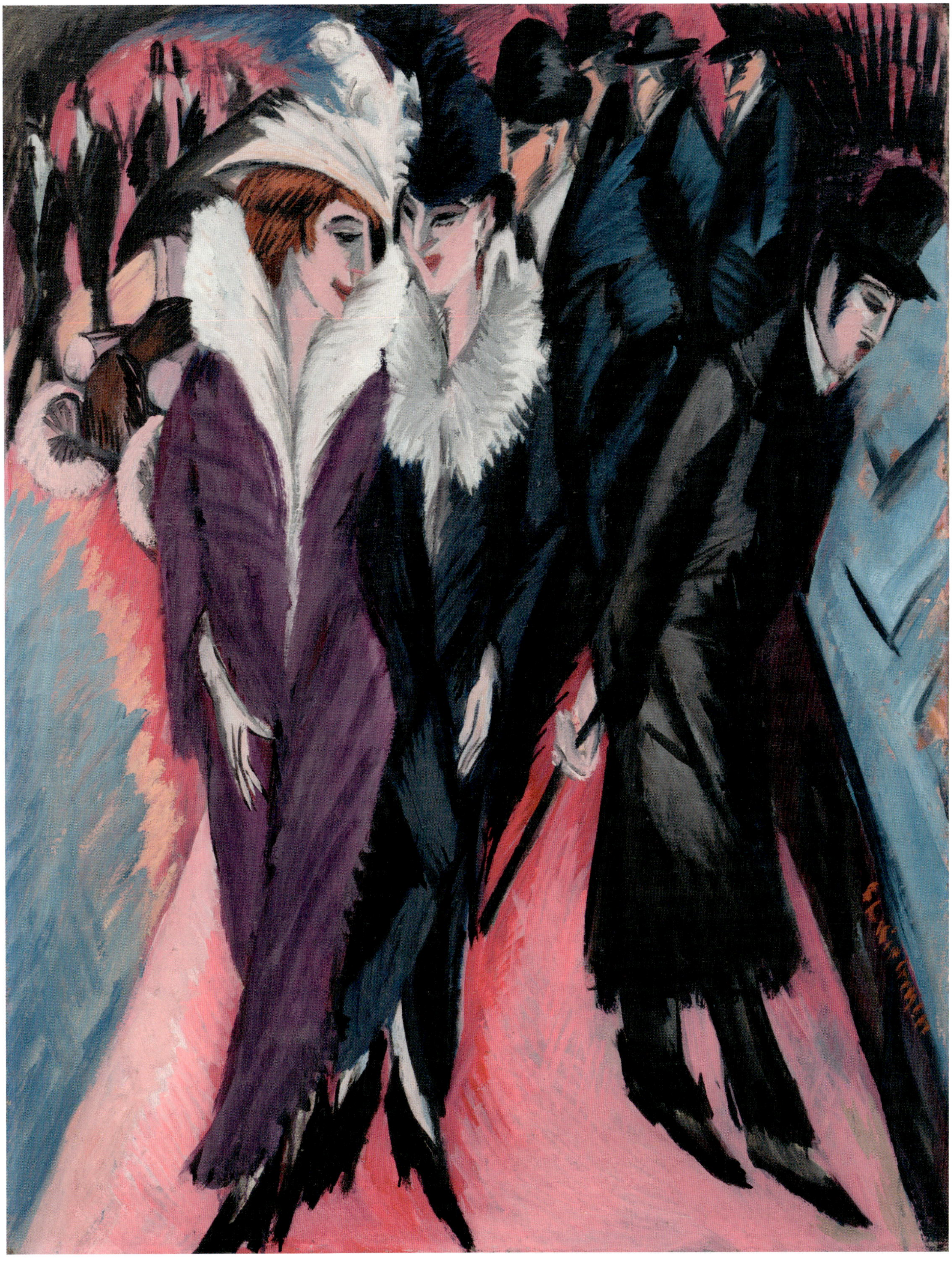

In the Maelstrom of the Metropolis and Farewell to Arcadia (1914)

4

Kirchner continued to work on the street scenes in 1914. He took a sketchbook along wherever he went, capturing everything around him in quick pictorial shorthand: intuitively and swiftly he registered his surroundings on paper, then later reworked these snapshots pp.167,188 in his studio in other techniques. *Friedrichstrasse, Berlin* p.191 is the first painting from the series of street scenes whose title identifies a specific location. Nevertheless, it is impossible to locate the scene precisely, since the background is only suggested. Three women—one slightly behind and the one in front with an inviting gaze and hand on hip—are approaching the viewer. In Berlin at that time Friedrichstrasse was one of the places where cocottes could be encountered. So these women, elegantly dressed in blue, wearing hats with long feathers and heavily made up, are prostitutes in search of tricks in the white-green artificial night-time light. The thin, elongated figures, as is often the case in this series, fill almost the entire height of the picture. Behind them, stacked diagonally from the centre of the picture to the upper-right corner is a row of men without individual features in dark coats and hats. On the right one can see part of a passing vehicle that has frightened a dog on the street. On the left edge an almost unrecognisable man looks out from behind the street lamp. The sequence of strollers could also be interpreted as an optical multiplication, the simultaneous registry of a single person in motion. Kirchner might have been inspired in this by Futurism, for example, which he knew from publications and from exhibitions at Herwarth Walden's. Movement, speed and rhythm were featured in the works of the Futurists. But unlike the Italian Futurists, who created movement in the static picture through the mechanisation and fragmentation of individual forms, Kirchner gave his street scene a pulsing activity and vitality by depicting movement in different directions, with strong, feathery hatching, fragmented outlines, pointed shapes and a dense network of lines that he himself referred to as "lines of force" (*Kraftlinien*).

In his attempt to capture the dynamism of the metropolis, Kirchner also turned to motifs from the demi-monde, from dance, the circus and music hall. Eroticism and the depiction of movement were important aspects, as, for example, in the painting *Dancing Couple* p.187. The two figures fill the entire pictorial space. While the man appears almost motionless, he spins his partner around so violently that she is upside down, with one leg extended vertically, giving the viewer a glimpse of her undergarments. Kirchner heightens the erotically charged scene with his colouring: the brightest spot in the picture is the dancer's bright-pink flounced bloomers, from which the brush strokes fan out like rays, growing darker toward the hem of her skirt, and thus focus the viewer's gaze. The trapezoidal shape in the background could be one of the hand-painted fabrics with which Kirchner furnished the mansard niches of his second Berlin studio at Körnerstrasse 45. The dancers are in all probability Kirchner and Gerda Schilling, Erna's sister.

In October 1913 Kirchner had moved from Berlin-Wilmersdorf into a larger studio apartment in Berlin-Friedenau. From one of the windows of his new studio he could look out at the urban landscape. The view of the tracks, the railway bridge, the passing trains and streetcars and the backs of the apartment blocks across the way inspired numerous pictures pp.173–175. The train was still a relatively new mode of modern mass transit, providing rapid and comfortable transportation. At the same time, it was changing the cityscape in those years: routes were being upgraded and bridges and signal boxes constructed. In *Railway Overpass* p.175 one can see a stretch of the Wannseebahn, which passed directly in front of Kirchner's front door on its way from Berlin-Mitte to Potsdam. The dominant element in the picture is the way the bridge, on which a streetcar is travelling, crosses the train tracks at an angle. Smoke issuing from the locomotive and wafting towards the back indicates that the train is in motion. The rest of the painting is done in swift hatching and the people on the bridge are merely suggested with short vertical strokes. Whereas Kirchner reproduced the actual colours in *Railway Overpass*, in the painting *Streetcar and Train* p.173 he captured the same motif in brighter, unnatural tones. At the same time the brushwork is less agitated.

In addition to the fascinating motifs it offered him, the city was filled with the tense atmosphere that accompanied the outbreak of the First World War. In Kirchner's oeuvre there are again and again self-portraits that attest to the fact that the artist observed and depicted himself in various roles. Yet it is striking that after the outbreak of war his artistic self-examination greatly increases and in part documents the fears that plagued him when faced with impending conscription. In his *Self-Portrait* from 1914 p.206 Kirchner pictures himself as a painter, behind a canvas but without painting utensils. His head is framed by two canvases placed diagonally—one seen from the back on an easel in the foreground on the right and another hanging crooked in the background on the left. He gazes directly at the viewer, his eyes and mouth emphasised with dark brush strokes. For his portrait he has selected muted tertiary colours and a reduced palette of brown, ochre and violet tones that reflect his depressed spirits at the time.

When war was declared between Austria-Hungary and Serbia on 28 July 1914, Kirchner and Erna were on Fehmarn. On 1 August the island was declared a strategically important military zone and they were suddenly required to leave. Accordingly, in that brief time on Fehmarn Kirchner produced comparatively few works, and many of these were probably completed in Berlin. *Curving Bay (Laburnum Tree)* p.201 shows how the stylistic change in Kirchner's imagery also made itself felt in the Fehmarn works. As in the street scenes, nature is captured with dense parallel brush strokes and interrupted outlines. But instead of the pointed shapes, here rounded ones predominate, as bands of clouds in the sky, waves in the sea, blossoms on the laburnum tree or as the horizon line and wreath of rays from the setting sun. Seen from a bird's-eye perspective, a laburnum tree occupies the entire right half of the picture, while on the left side three bathers—or is it only a single one captured in motion?—cavort on the beach. The colour triad red–blue–yellow dominates the painting, with the vegetation in the foreground picked out in green.

Cat. 51

Streetcar and Train, 1914 (recto)/ Dune Landscape, 1912 (verso) Oil on canvas

Die Lübecker Museen, Museum Behnhaus Drägerhaus

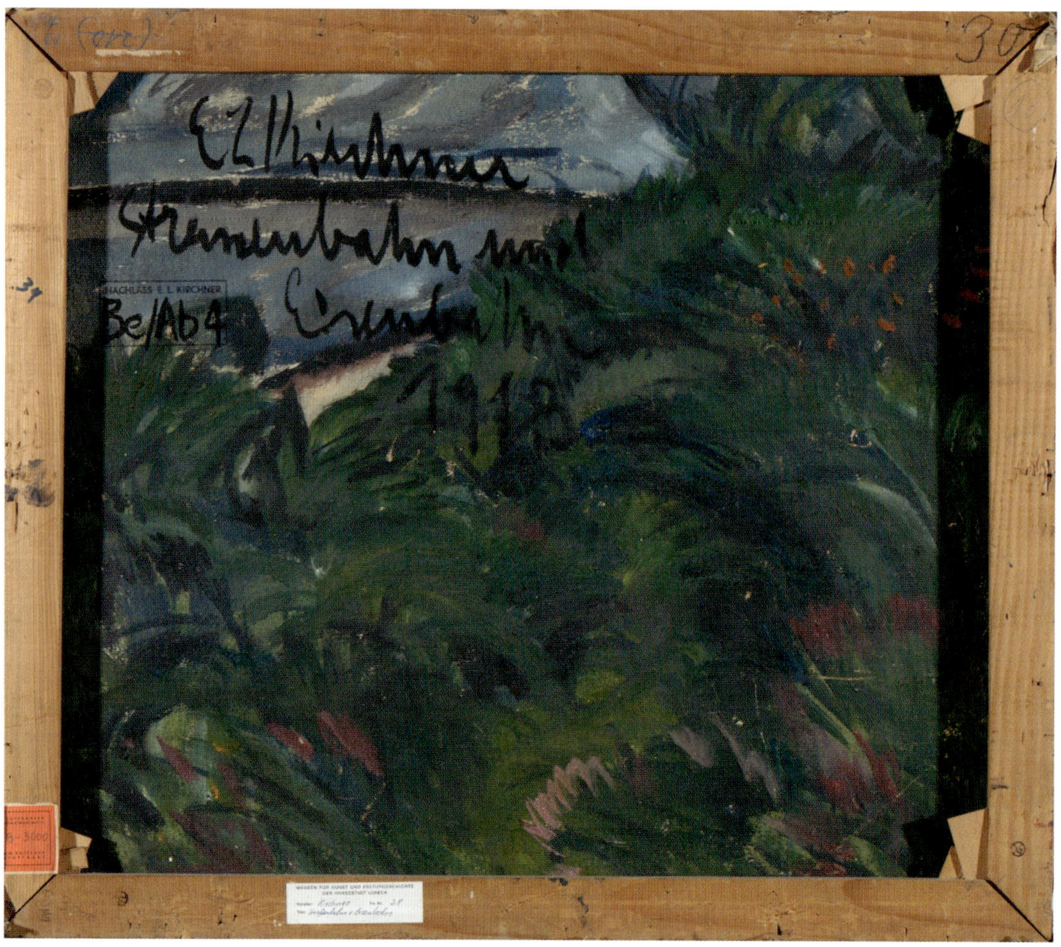

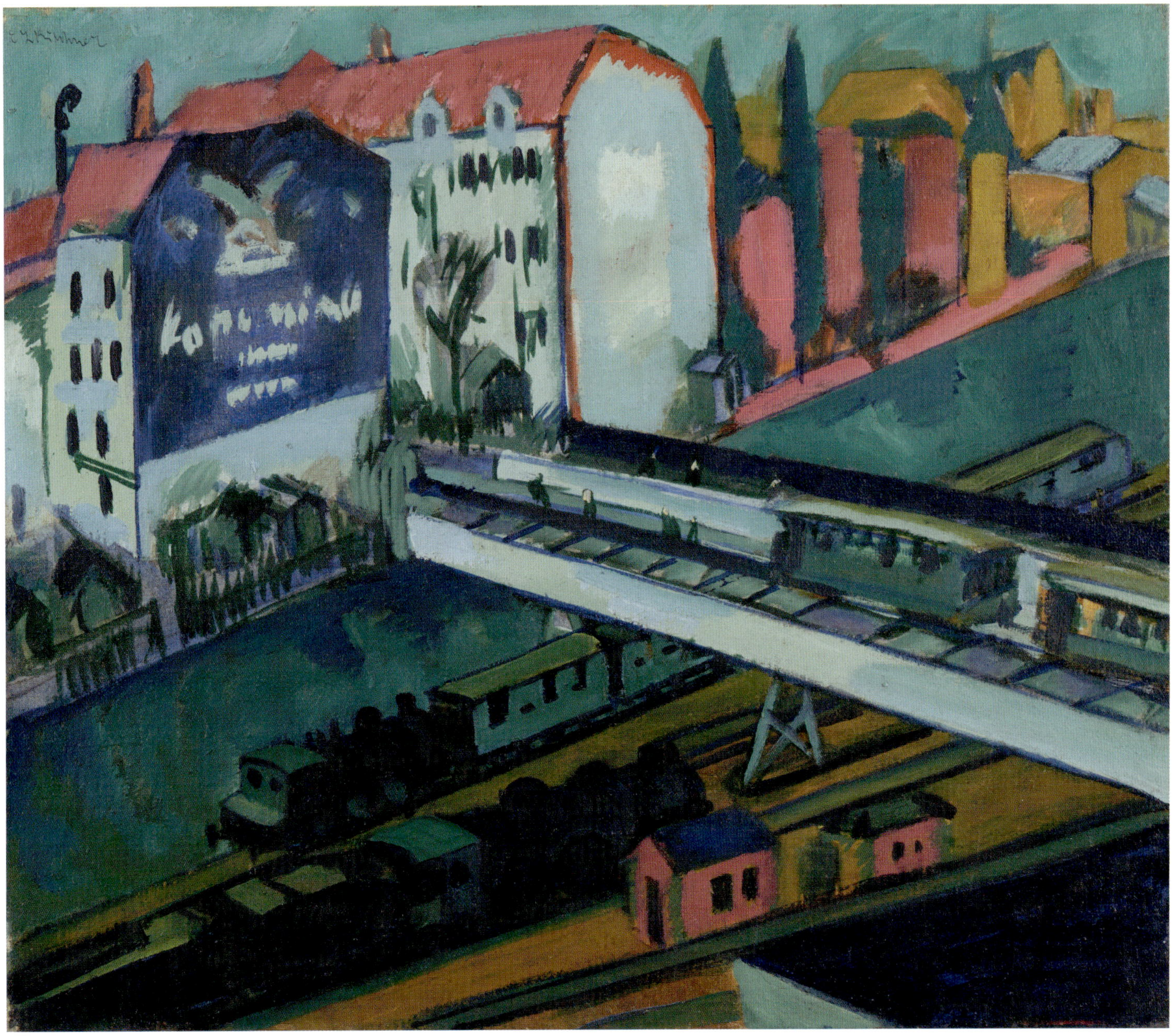

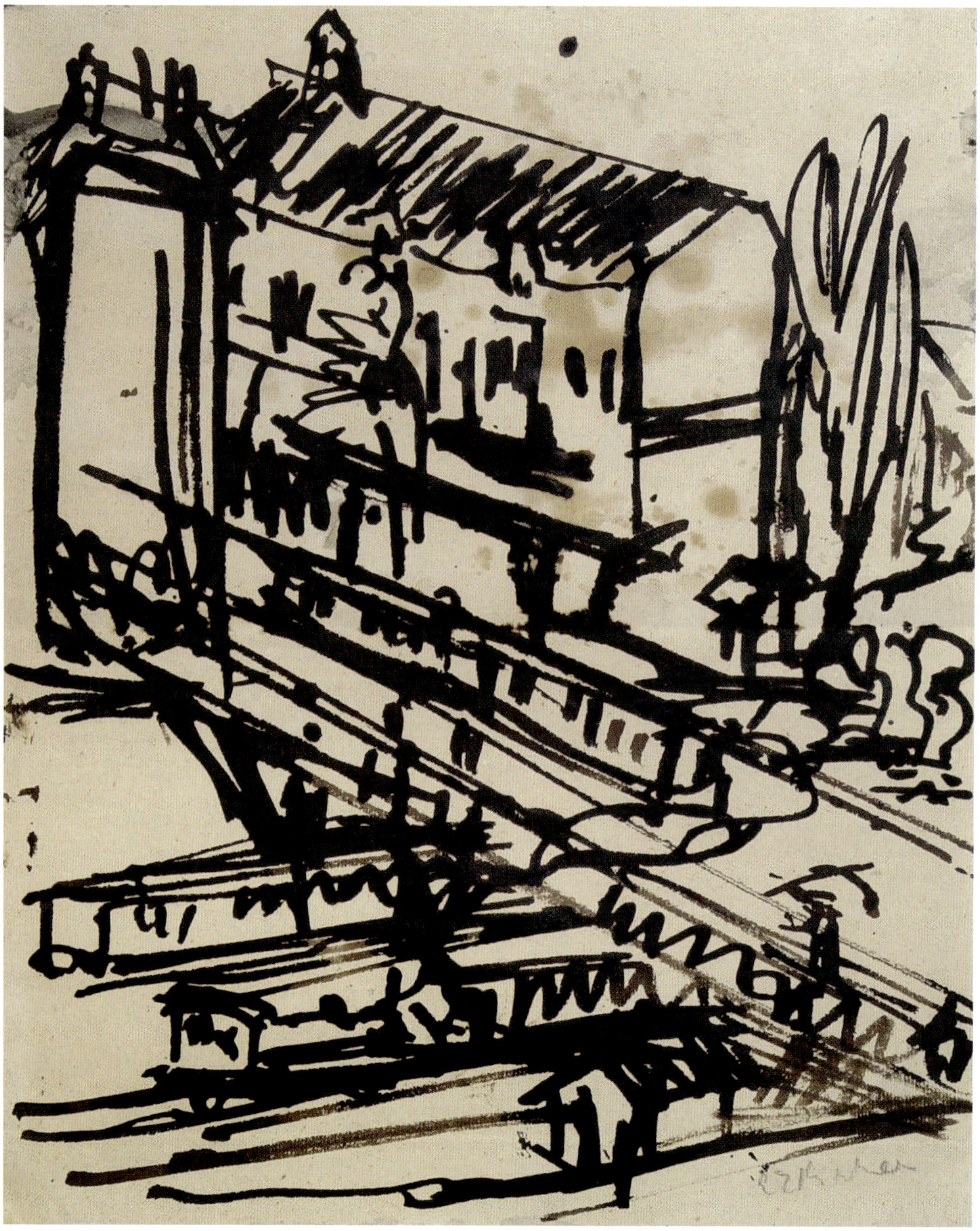

Cat. 92

The Railway Overpass, 1914
Brush and ink on paper

Stadtmuseum Berlin Foundation

Cat. 50

Railway Overpass, 1914
Oil on canvas

Museum Ludwig, Cologne

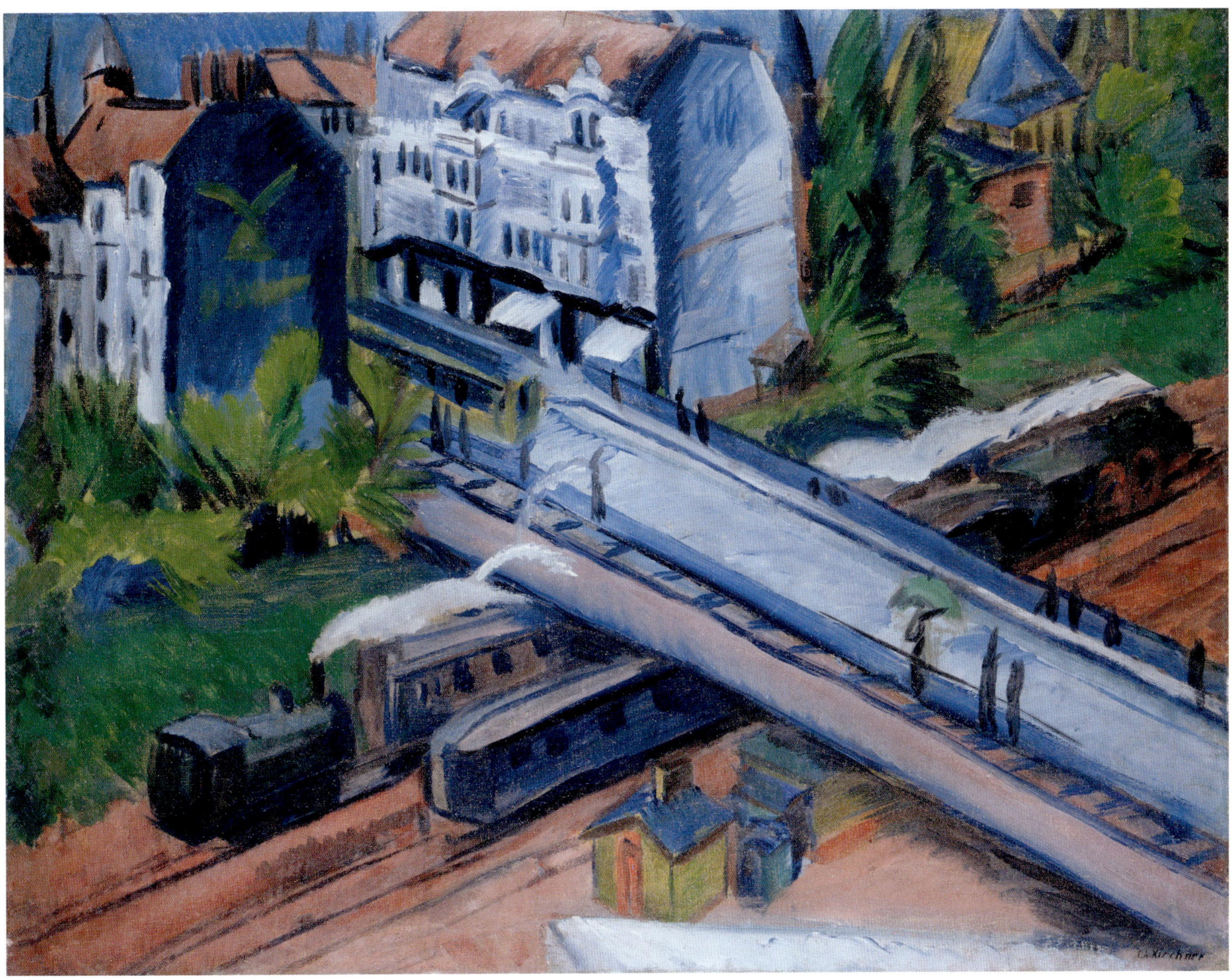

Cat. 52

Gas Tanks and Suburban Railway, 1914/1920
Oil on canvas

Staatliche Kunsthalle Karlsruhe

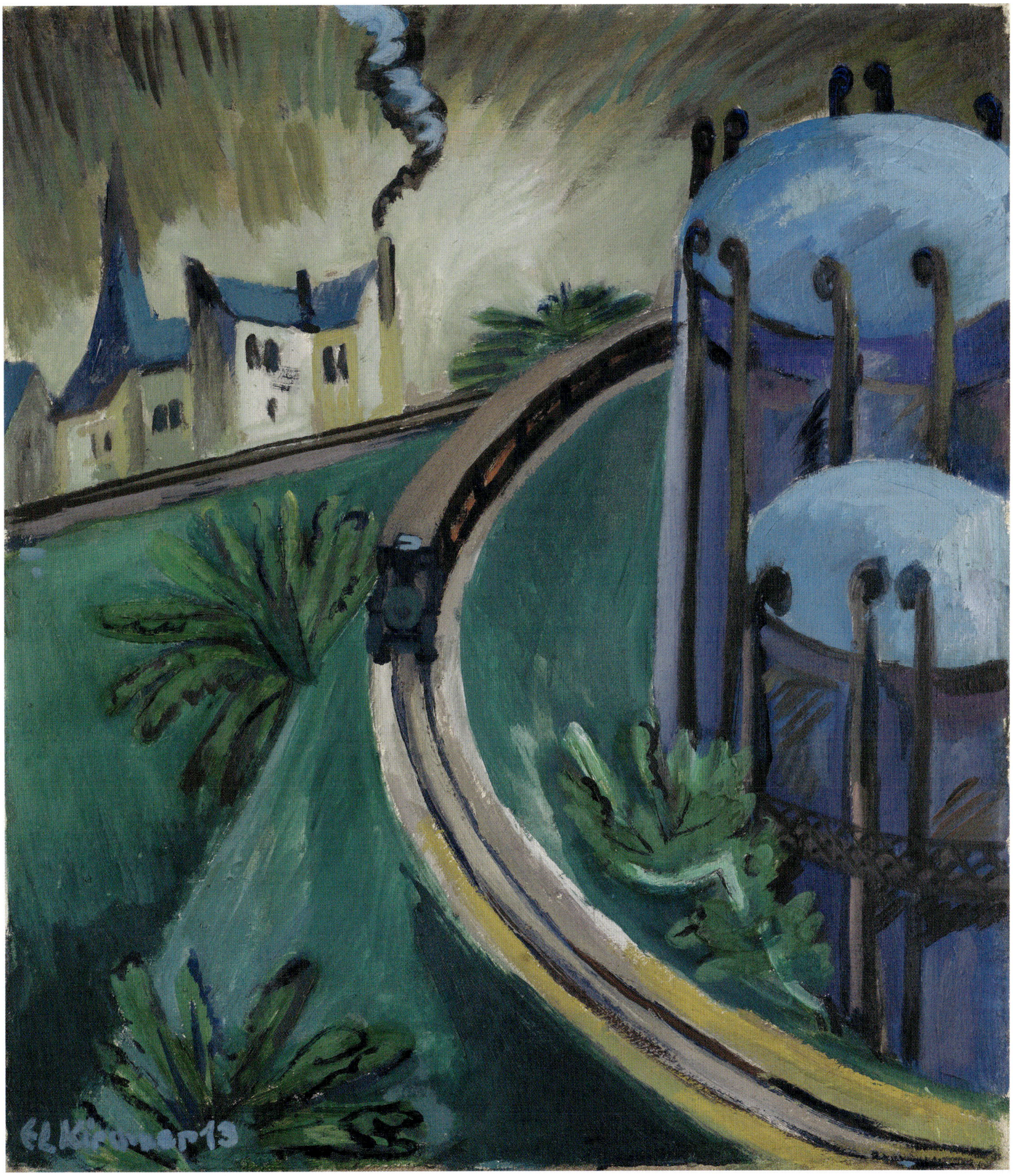

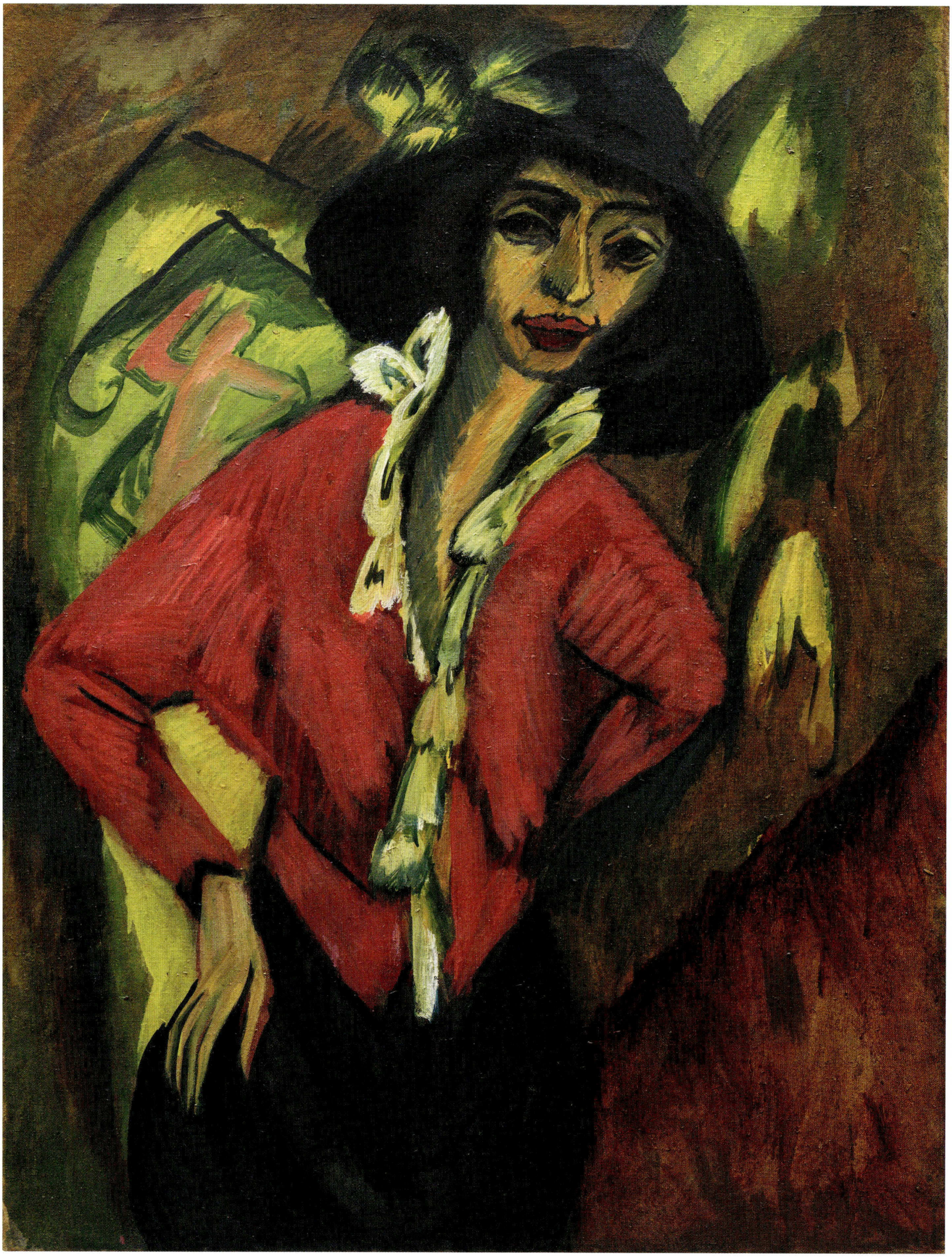

Cat. 49

Gerda, Half-Length Portrait, 1914
Oil on canvas

Solomon R. Guggenheim Museum, New York, partial gift, Mr and Mrs Mortimer M. Denker, 1978

Cat. 59

Portrait of Oskar Schlemmer, 1914
Oil on canvas

Hessisches Landesmuseum Darmstadt

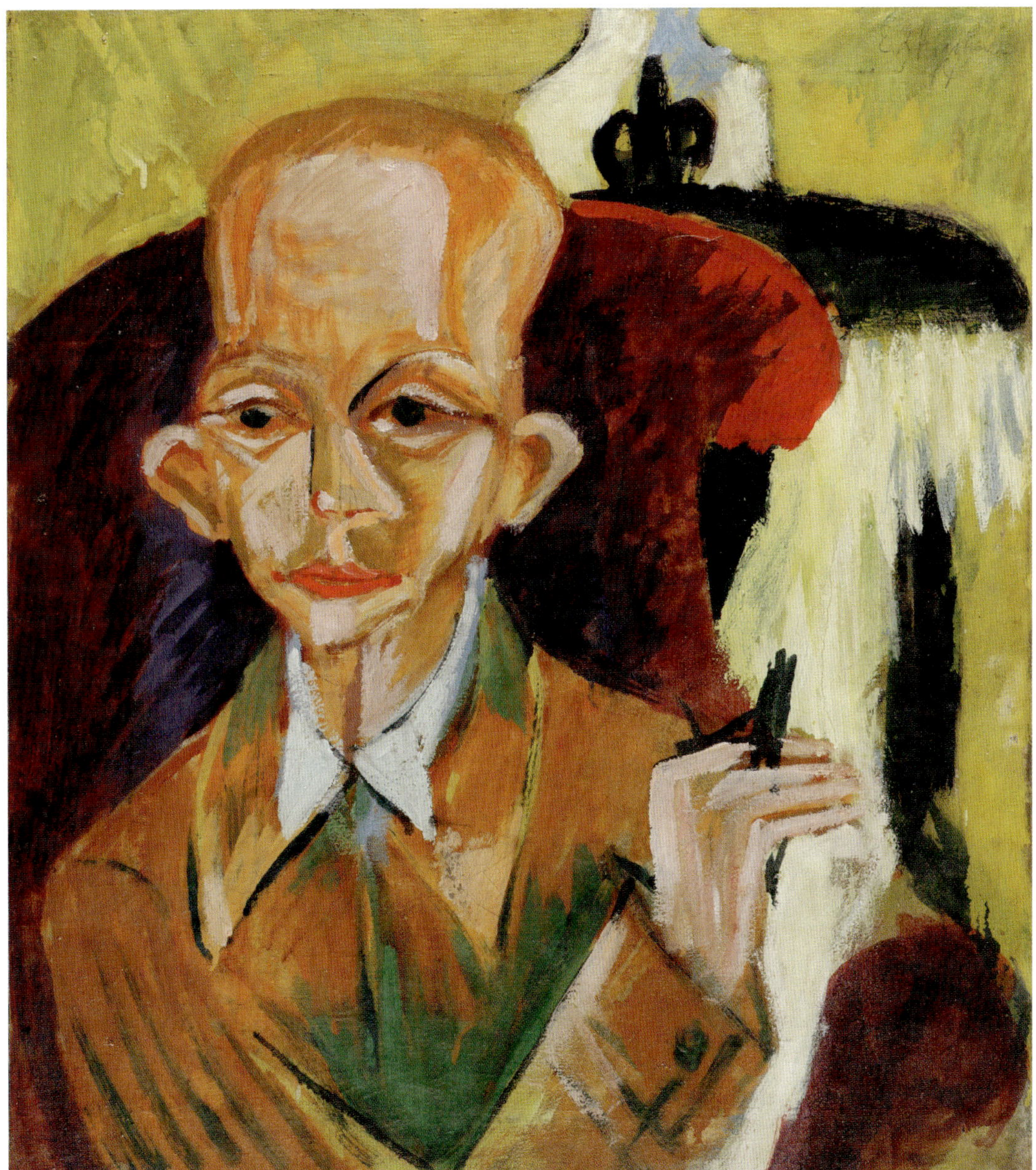

Cat. 144

Botho Graef in Kirchner's live-in studio, Berlin-Friedenau, 1914/15
Glass negative

Kirchner Museum Davos, Gift of the Ernst Ludwig Kirchner Estate 1992

Cat. 140

Erna Schilling in Kirchner's live-in studio, 1913/14
Gelatine silver (vintage print)

E. W. K. Collection, Bern/Davos, Courtesy Kirchner Museum Davos

Cat. 91

Portrait of Botho Graef, 1914
Charcoal on paper

Brücke-Museum, Berlin

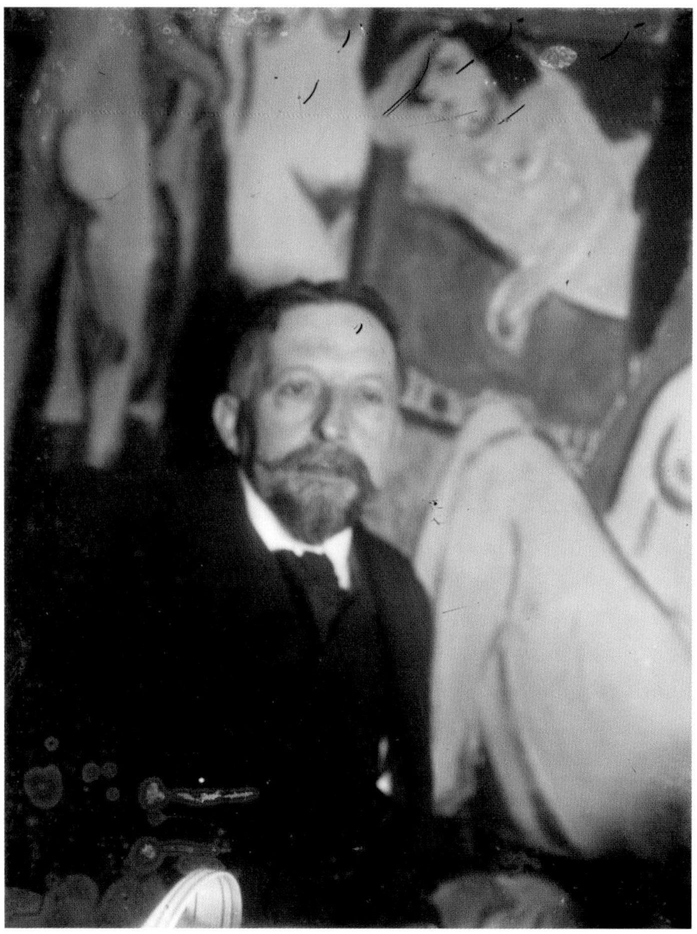

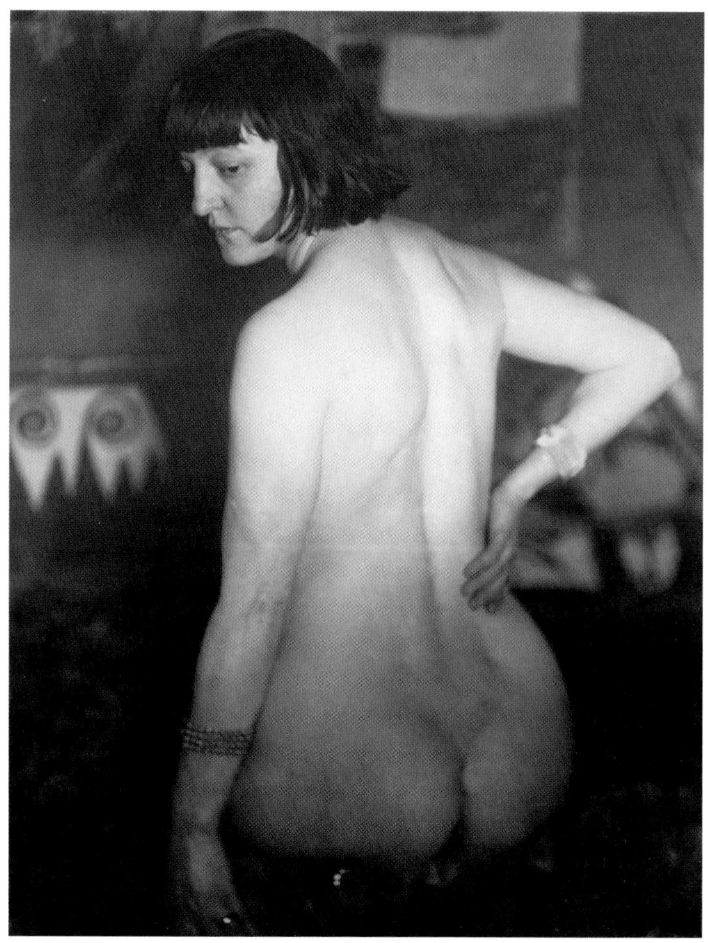

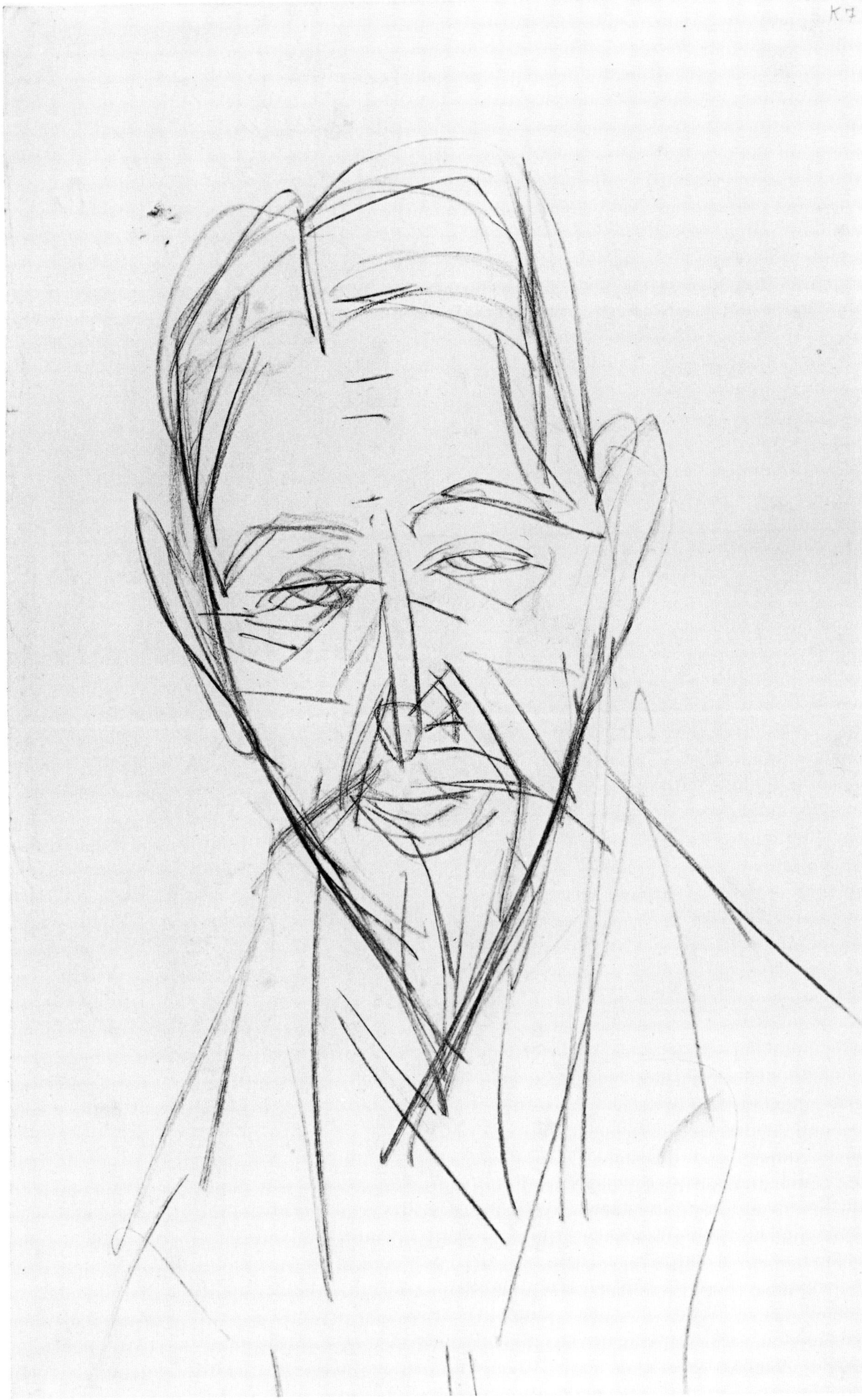

Cat. 96

Two Figures in a Room, 1914
Coloured crayon over charcoal on paper

Brücke-Museum, Berlin

Cat. 90

Standing Nude in Front of the Tent, c.1913/14
Coloured crayon on handmade paper

Museum Kunstpalast, Düsseldorf

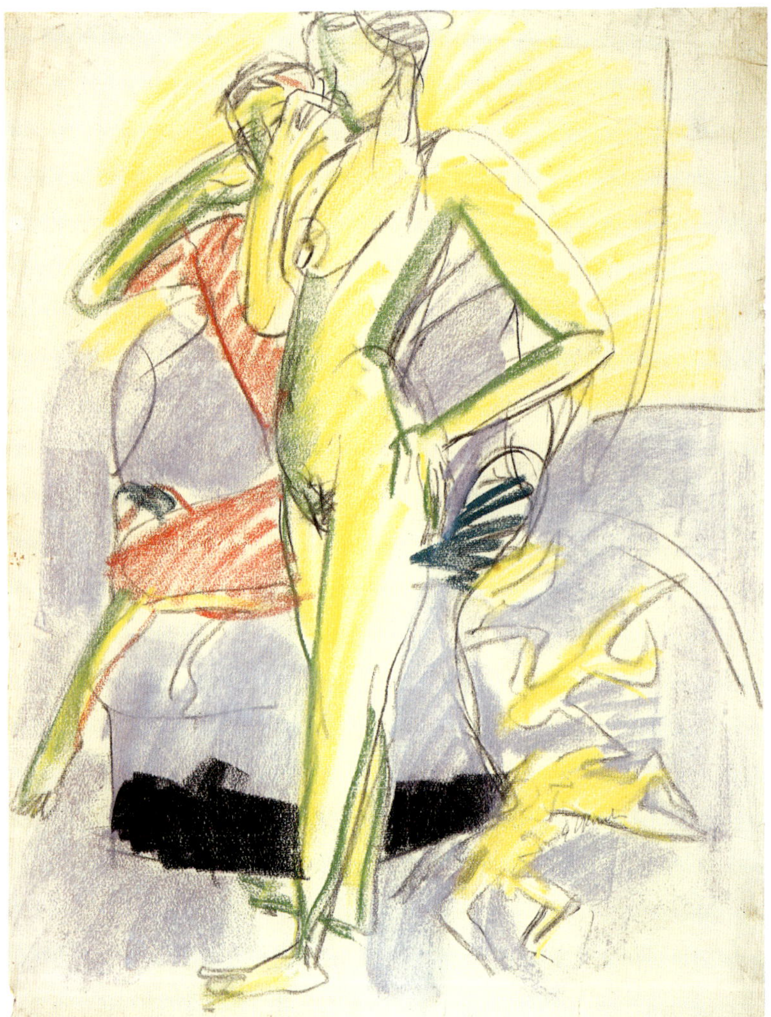

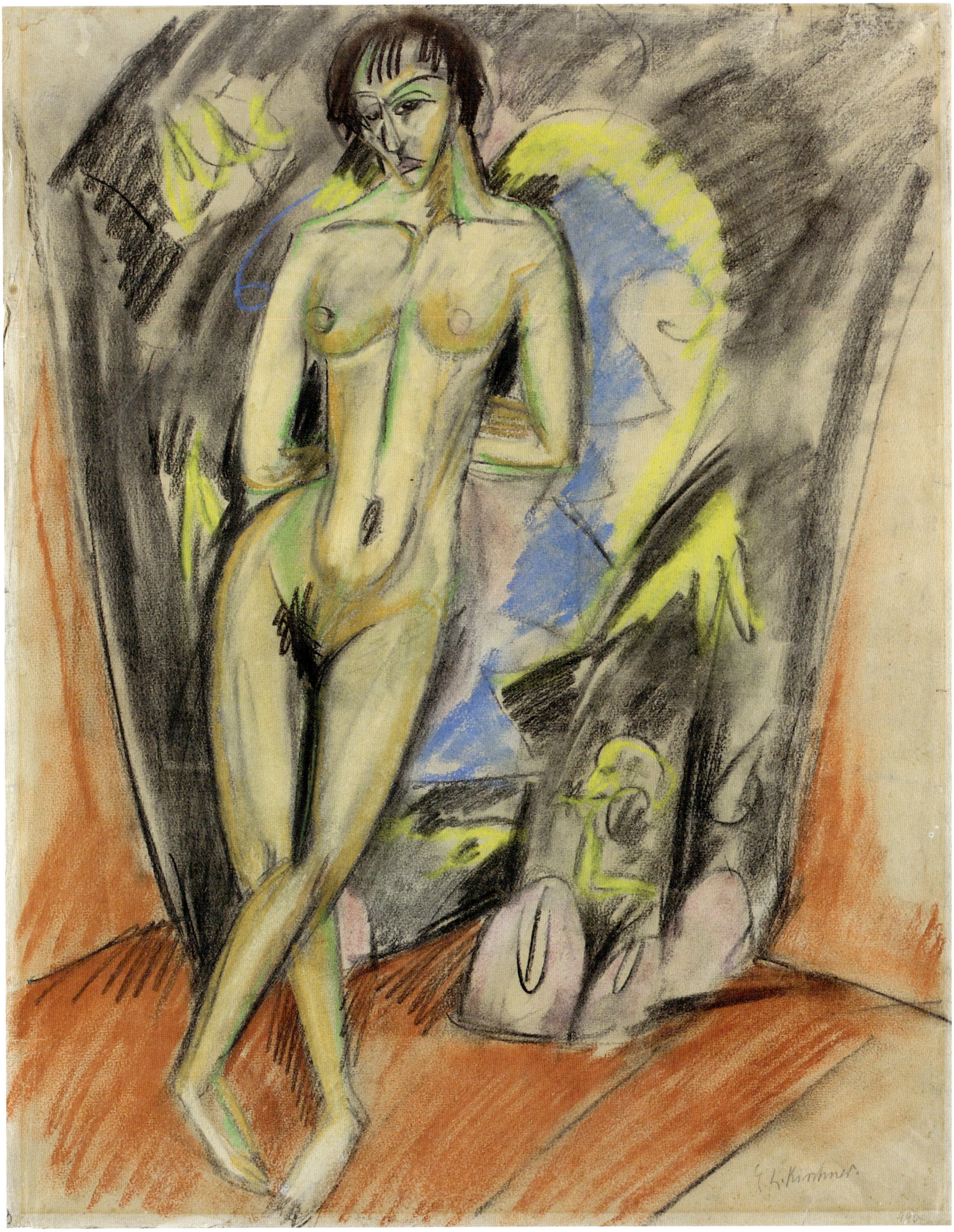
E. L. Kirchner

Cat. 116

Dancing Nudes, 1914
Lithograph on yellow paper

Estate of Erich Heckel,
Hemmenhofen (DE)

Cat. 113

Music Restaurant, 1914
Lithograph on yellow paper

Brücke-Museum,
Berlin

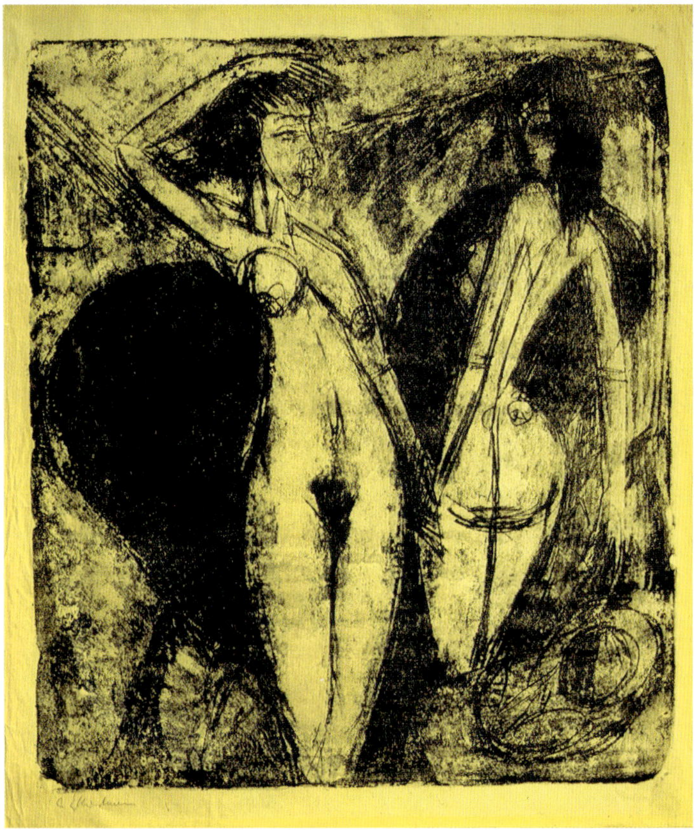

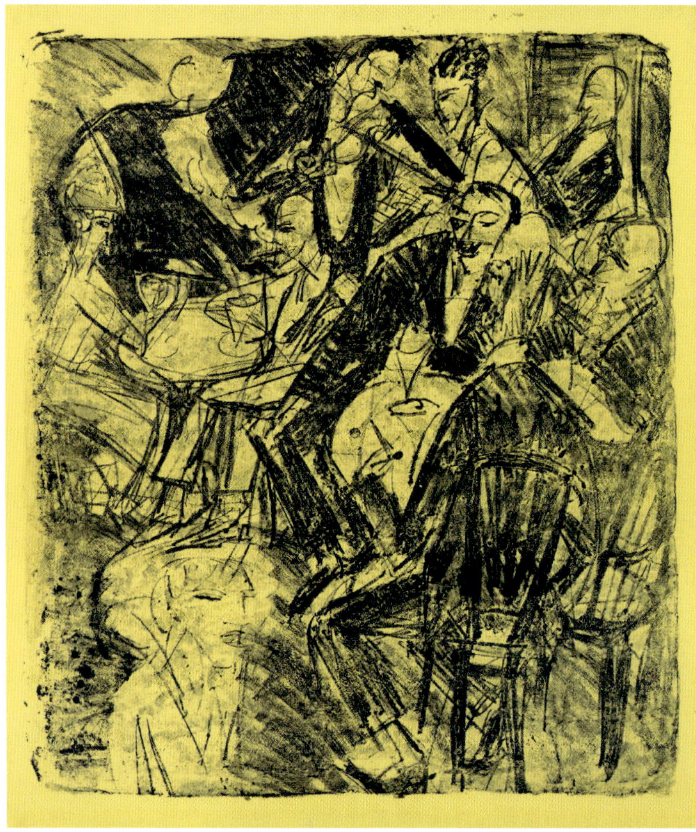

Cat. 114

Cocottes on Kurfürstendamm, 1914
Lithograph on yellow paper

Olbricht Collection

Cat. 115

Leipziger Strasse, Intersection, 1914
Lithograph on yellow paper

Brücke-Museum, Berlin, Karl and Emy Schmidt-Rottluff Foundation

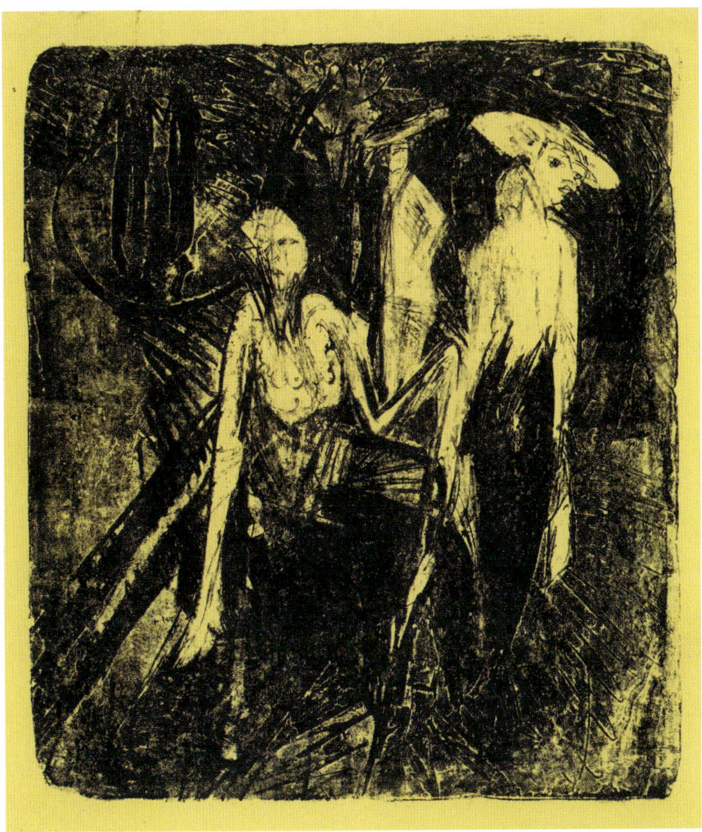

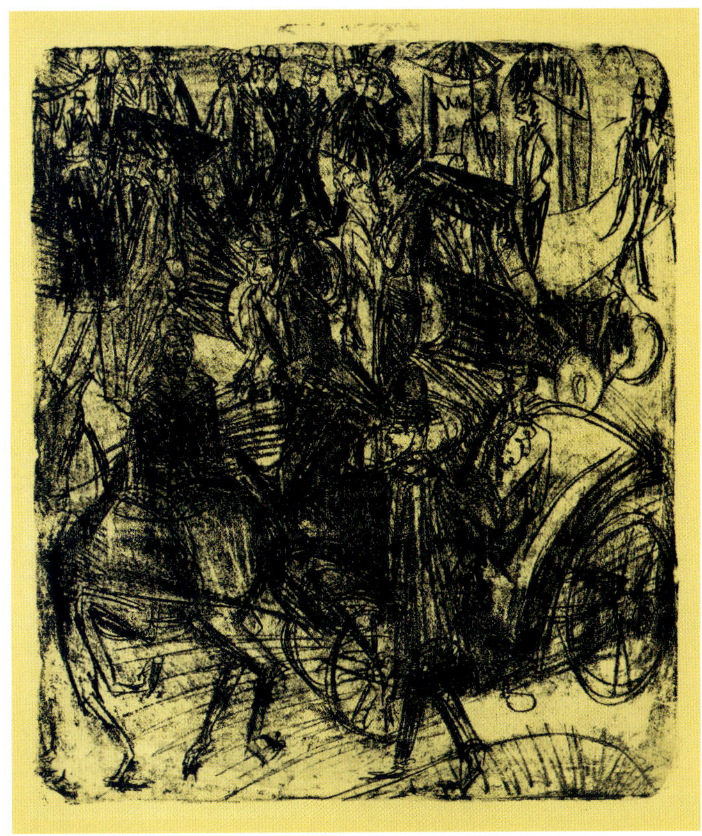

Cat. 48

In the Café Garden, 1914
Oil on canvas

Brücke-Museum, Berlin

Cat. 53

Dancing Couple, 1914
Oil on canvas

Museum Folkwang, Essen

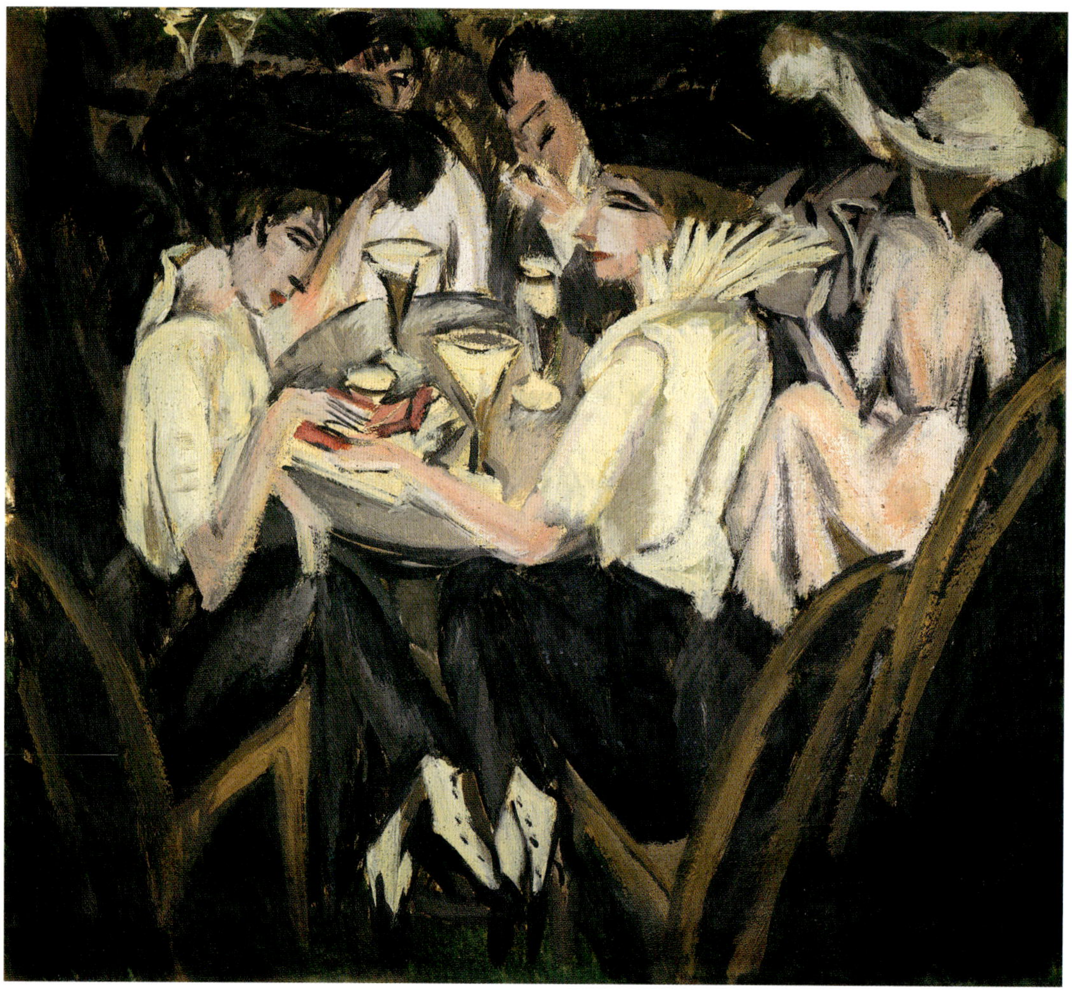

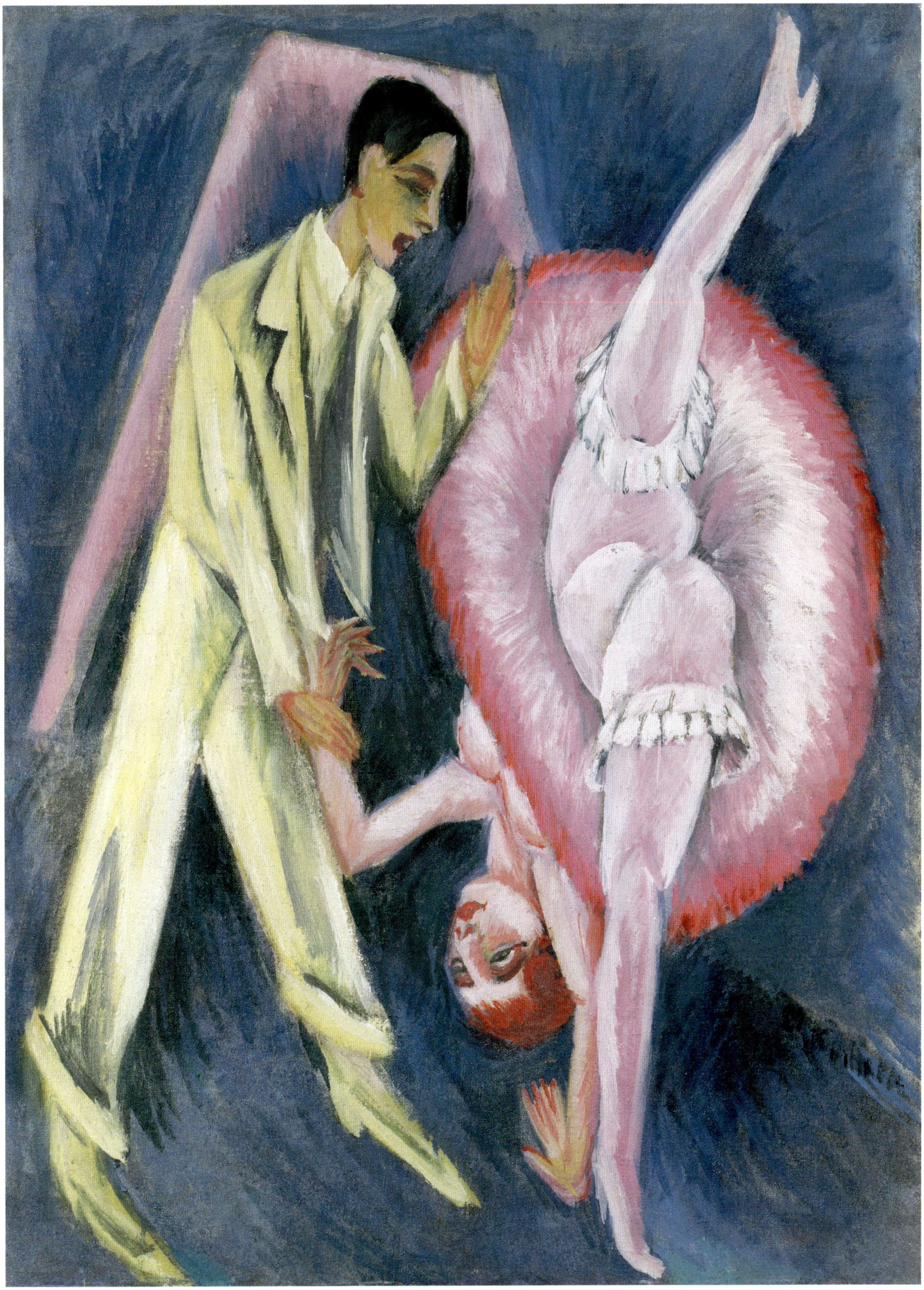

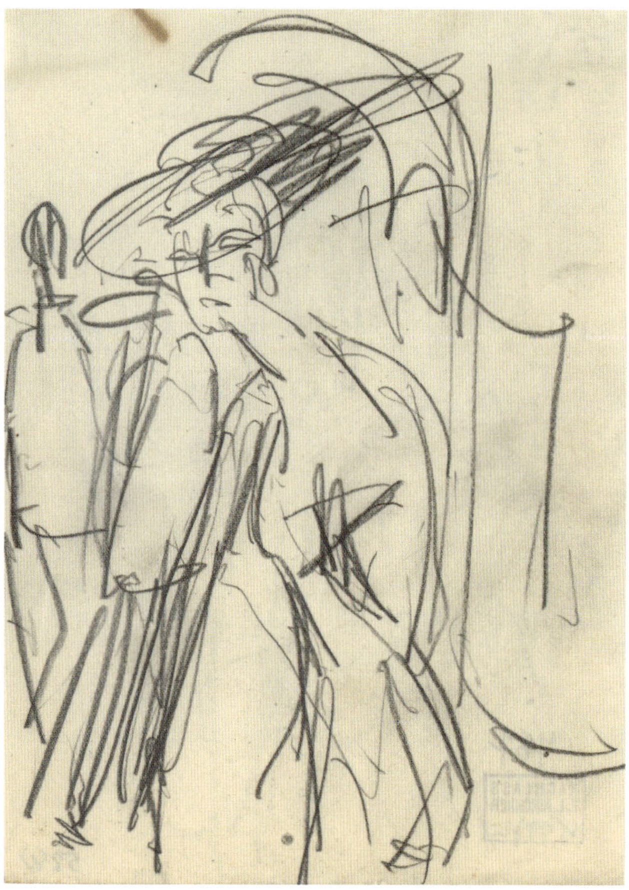

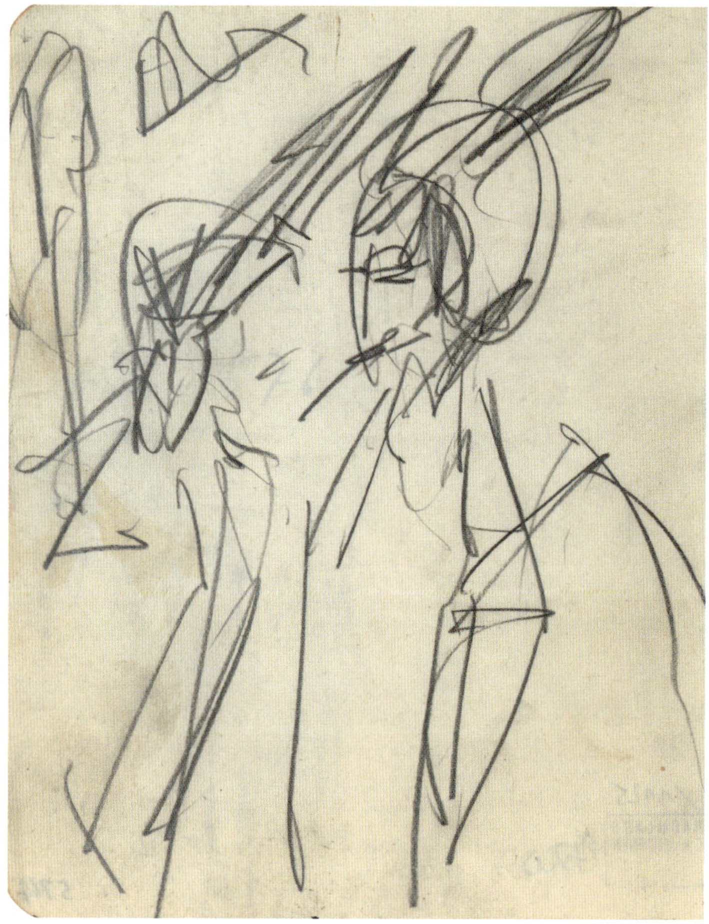

Cat. 94

Woman with Hat (Street Scene), 1914
Carpenter pencil on light chamois paper with foxing

Kirchner Museum Davos, Gift of the Ernst Ludwig Kirchner Estate 1994

Cat. 95

Two Women with Hats (Street Scene), 1914
Carpenter pencil on paper with foxing

Kirchner Museum Davos, Gift of the Ernst Ludwig Kirchner Estate 1994

Cat. 85

Women on the Street, 1913/14
Pastel and mixed media on paper

Leopold-Hoesch-Museum & Papiermuseum Düren

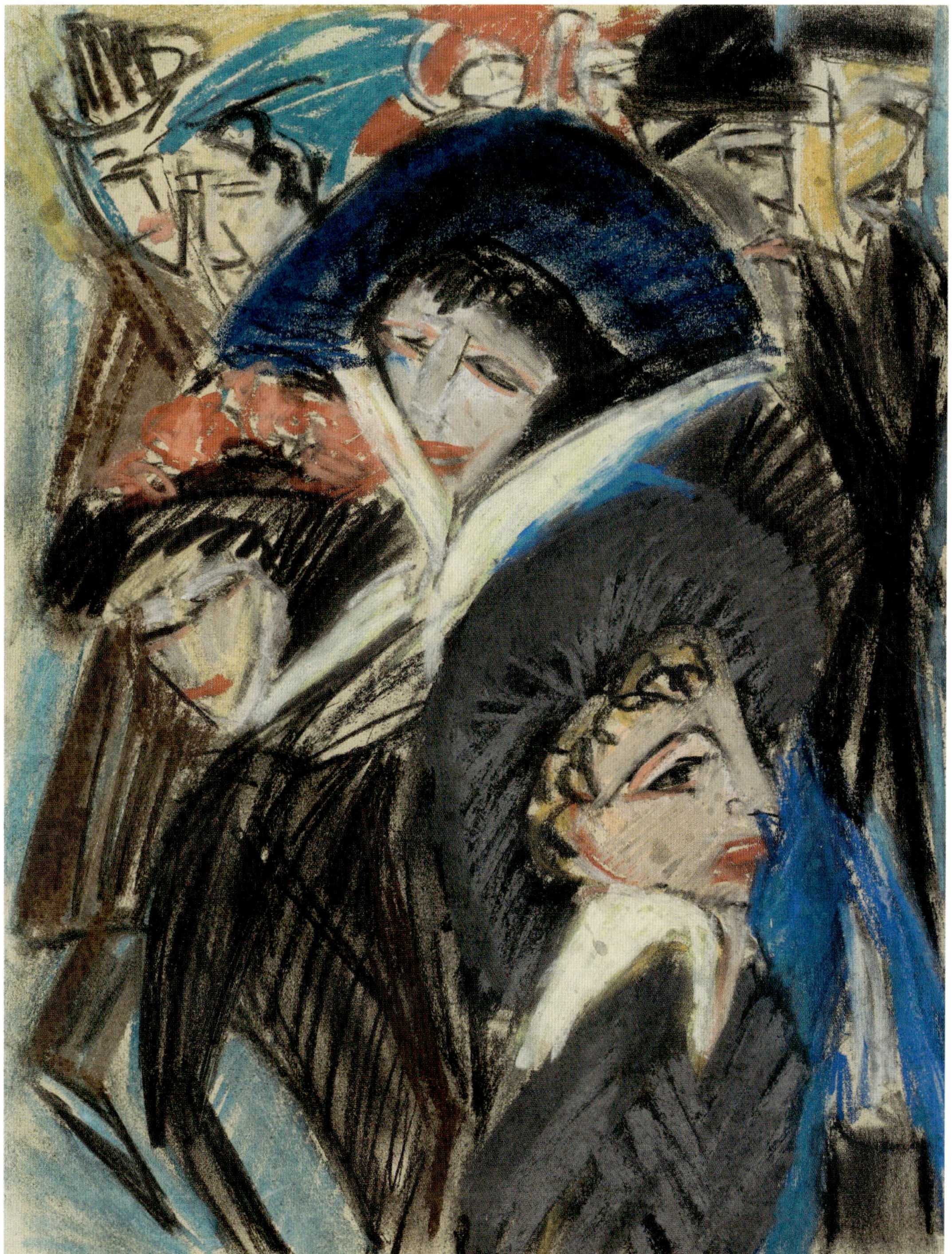

Cat. 86

Cocottes on the Street, 1913/14
Pastel on paper

Kirchner Museum Davos, on loan from the Rosemarie Ketterer Foundation

Cat. 46

Friedrichstrasse, Berlin, 1914
Oil on canvas

Staatsgalerie Stuttgart

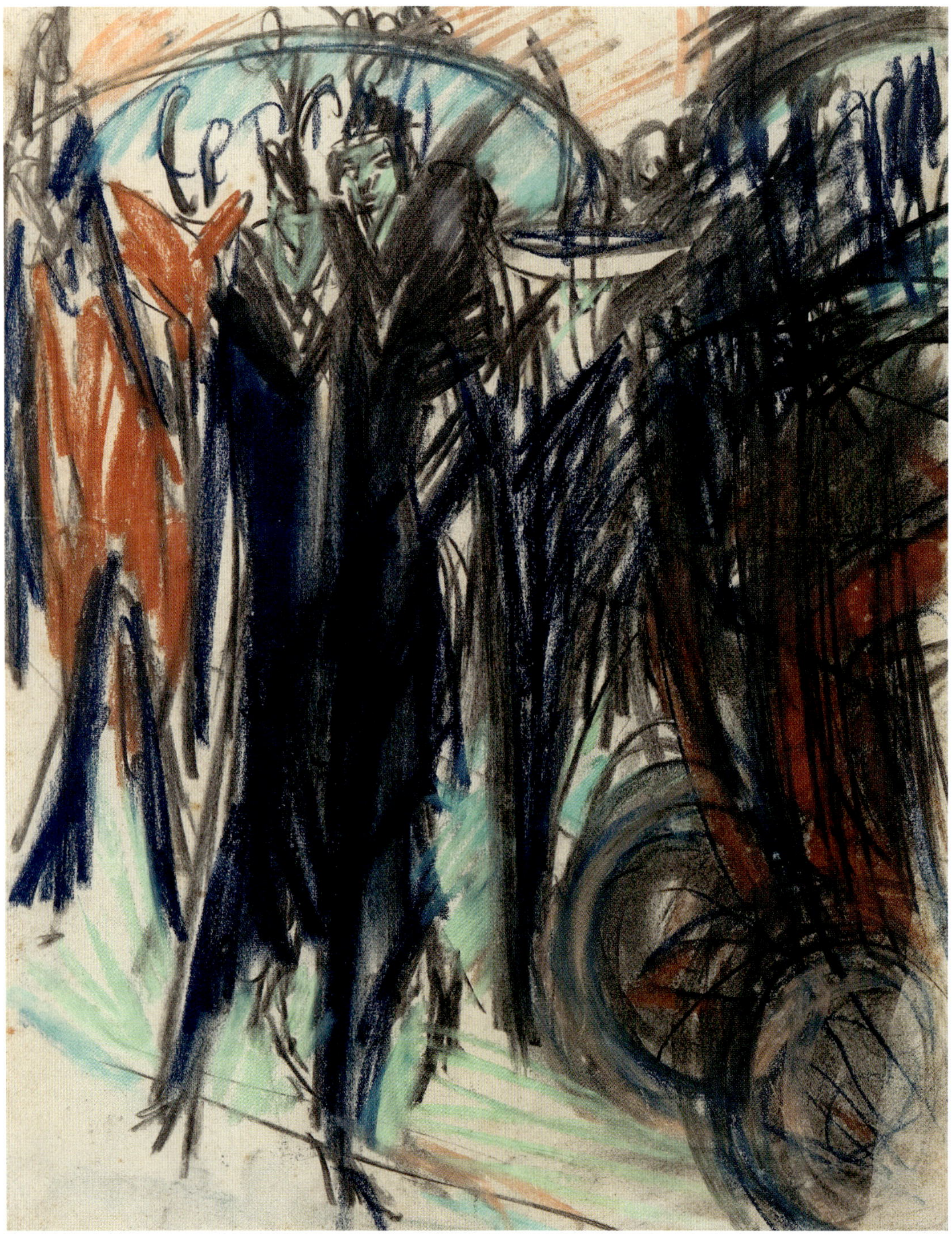

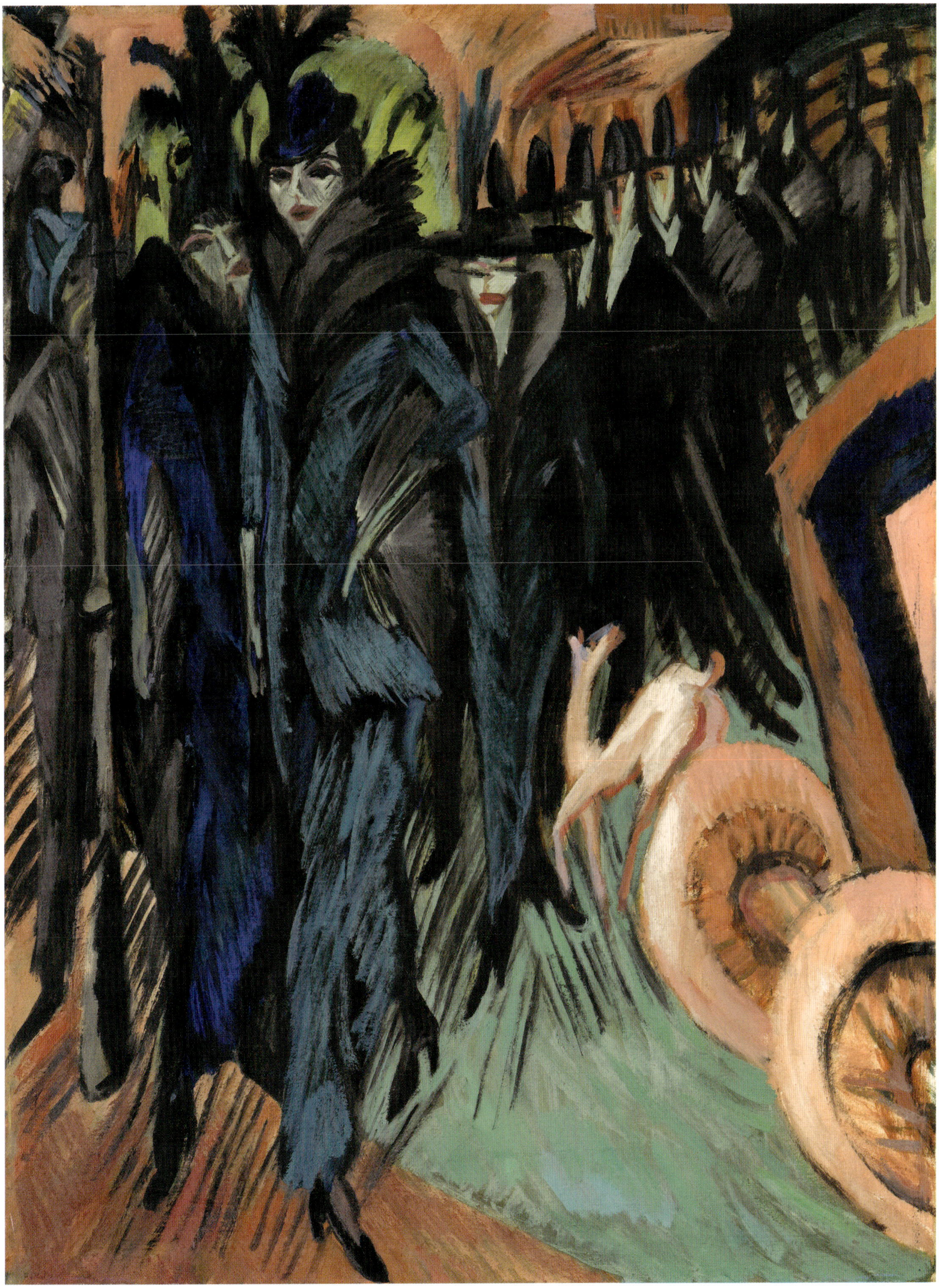

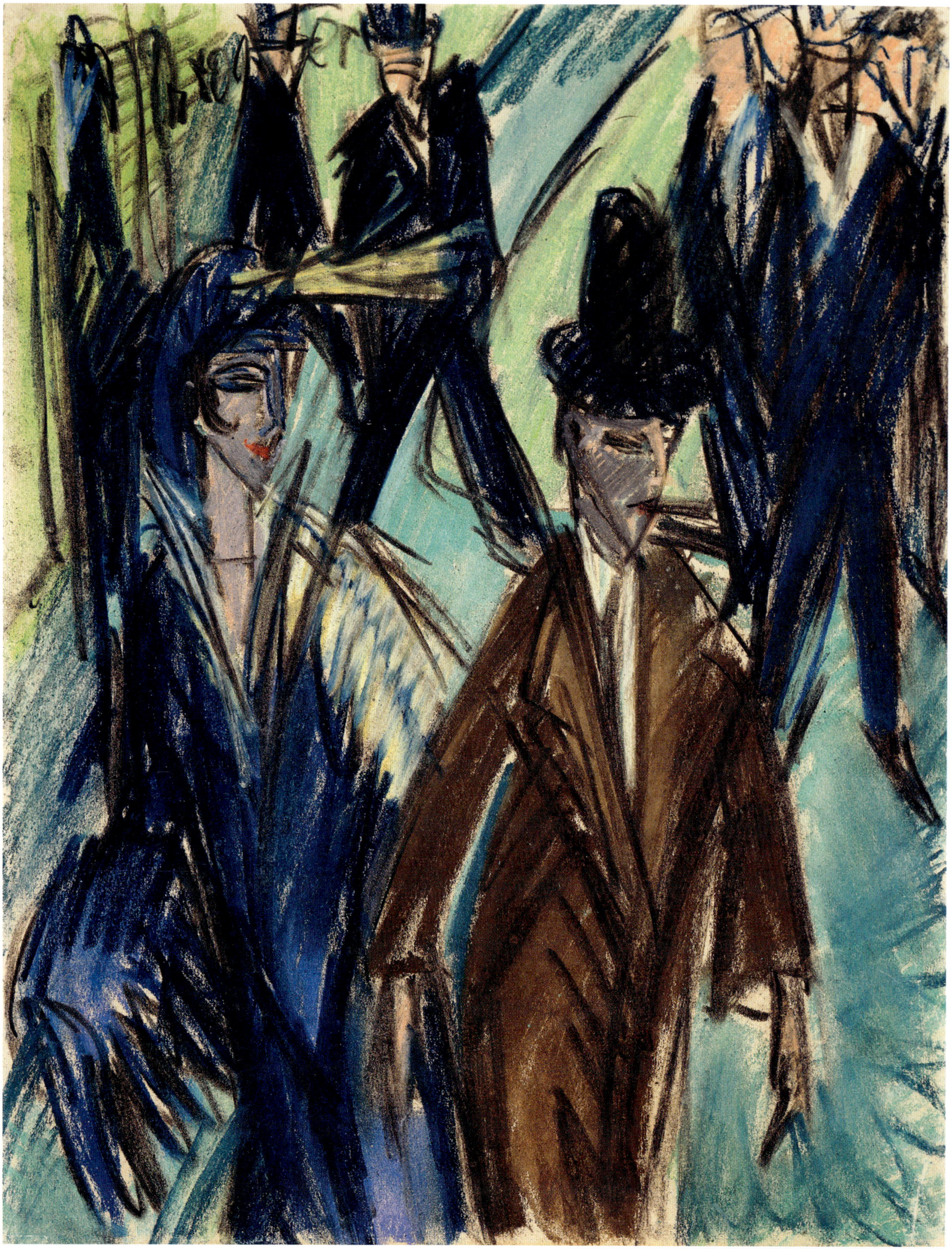

Cat. 87

Street Scene, 1913/14
Pastel on paper

Brücke-Museum, Berlin

Cat. 93

Street Scene, 1914
Pastel on paper

E. W. K. Collection, Bern/Davos

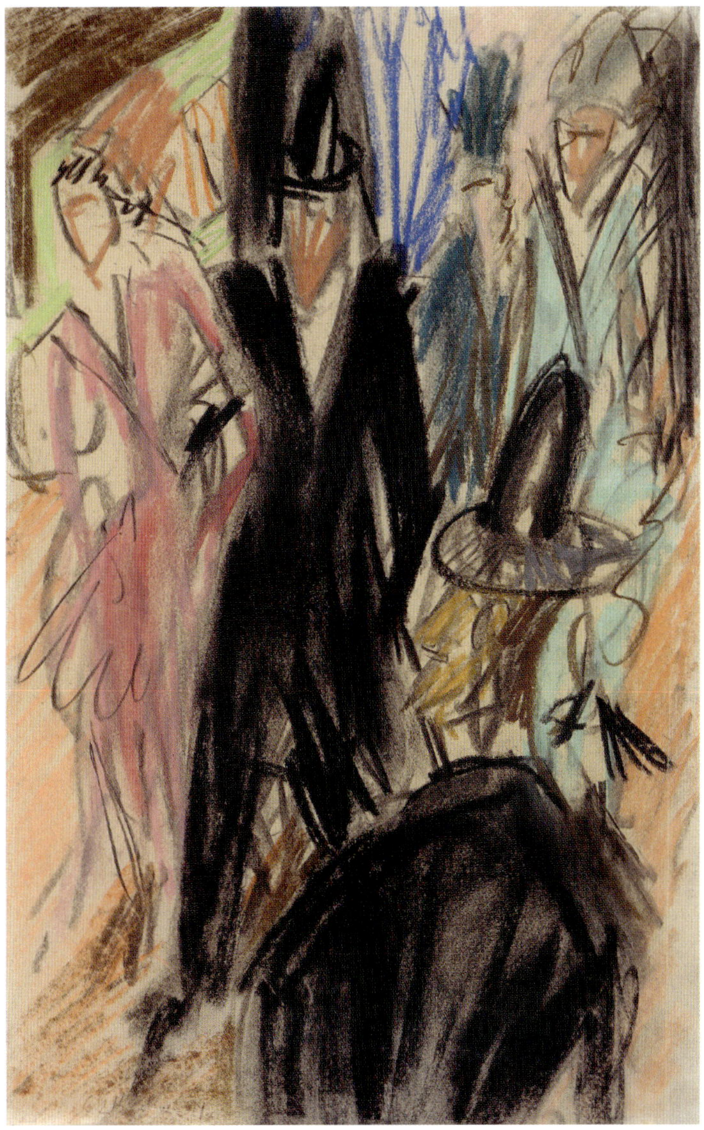

Cat. 112

Cocotte Offering Herself, 1914
Line and surface-tone etching on zinc, on soft vellum

Brücke-Museum, Berlin

Cat. 111

Women on Potsdamer Platz, Berlin, 1914
Woodcut on blotting paper

Museum Folkwang, Essen

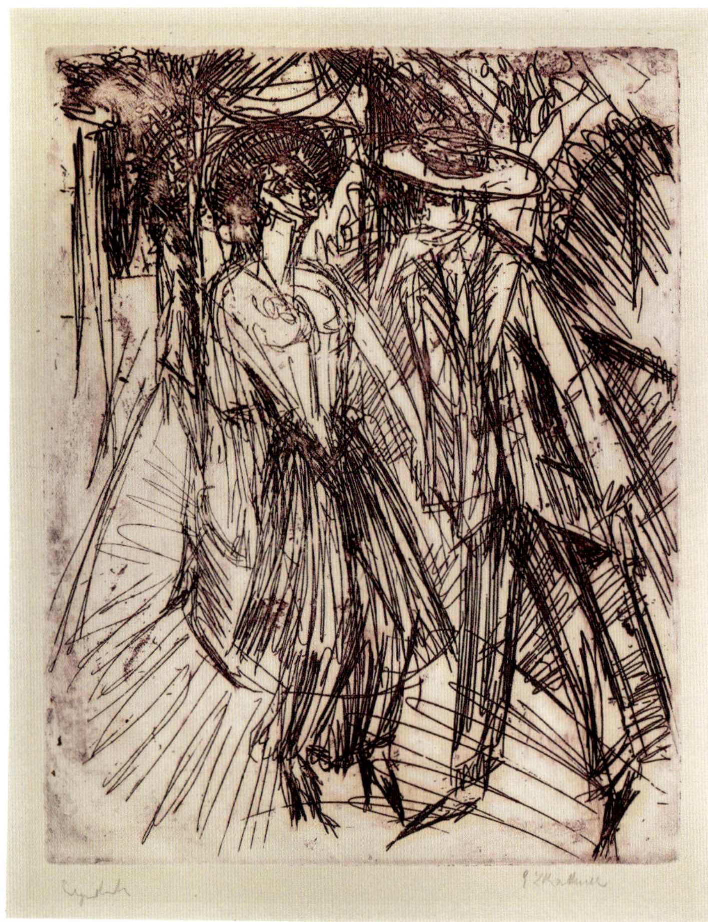

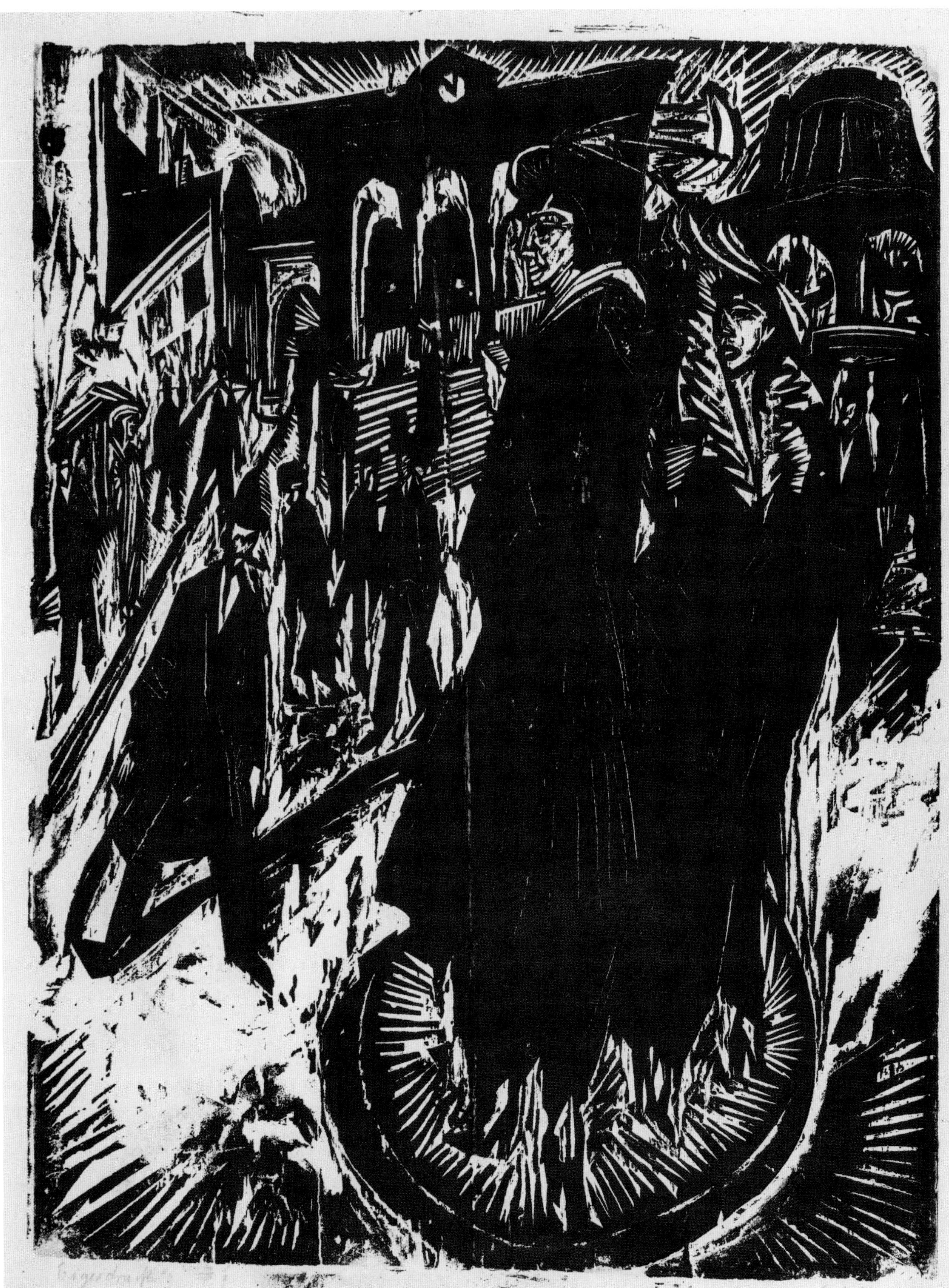

Cat. 47

Two Women on the Street, 1914 (recto)/ Two Bathers in Surf, 1912 (verso) Oil on canvas

Kunstsammlung Nordrhein-Westfalen, Düsseldorf

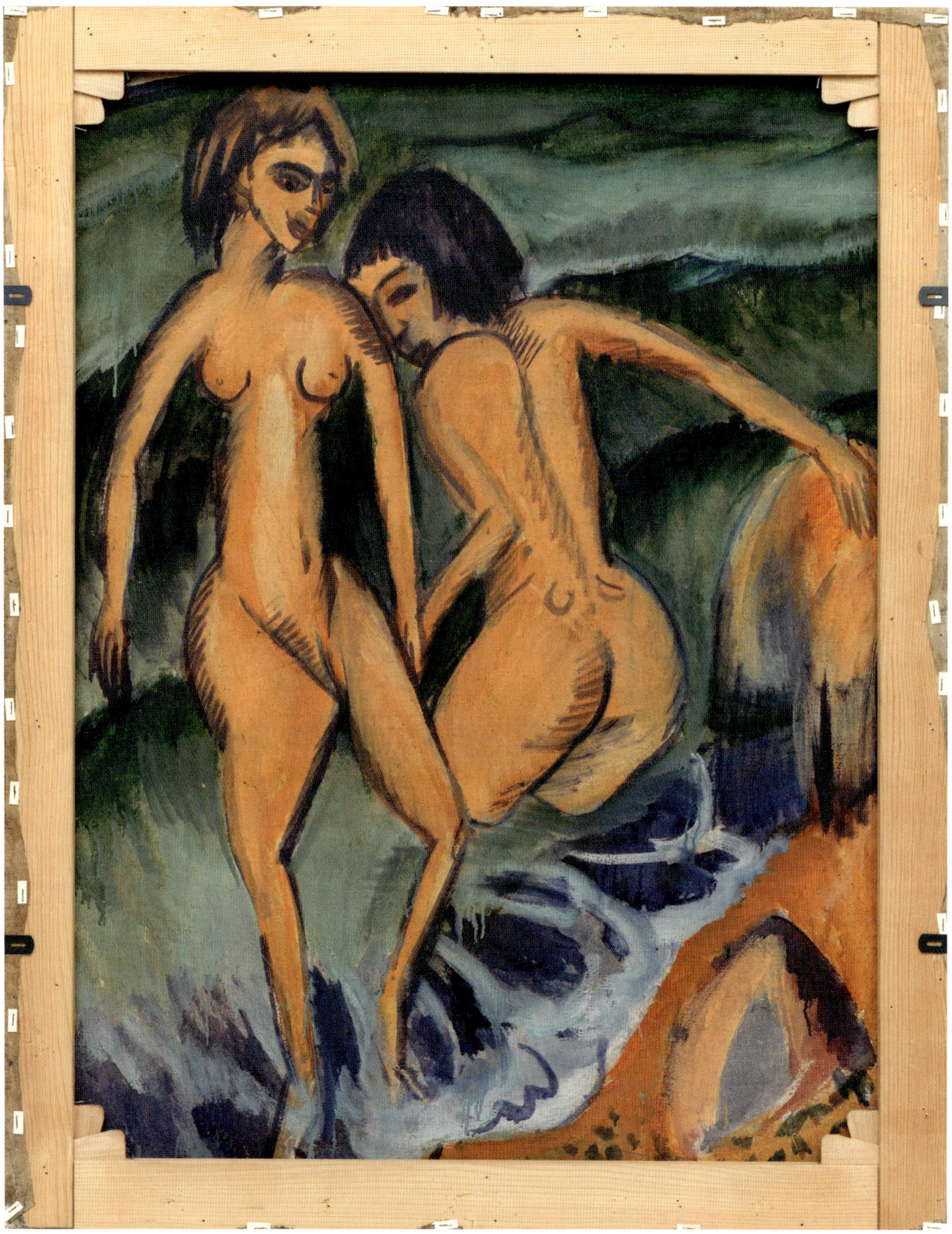

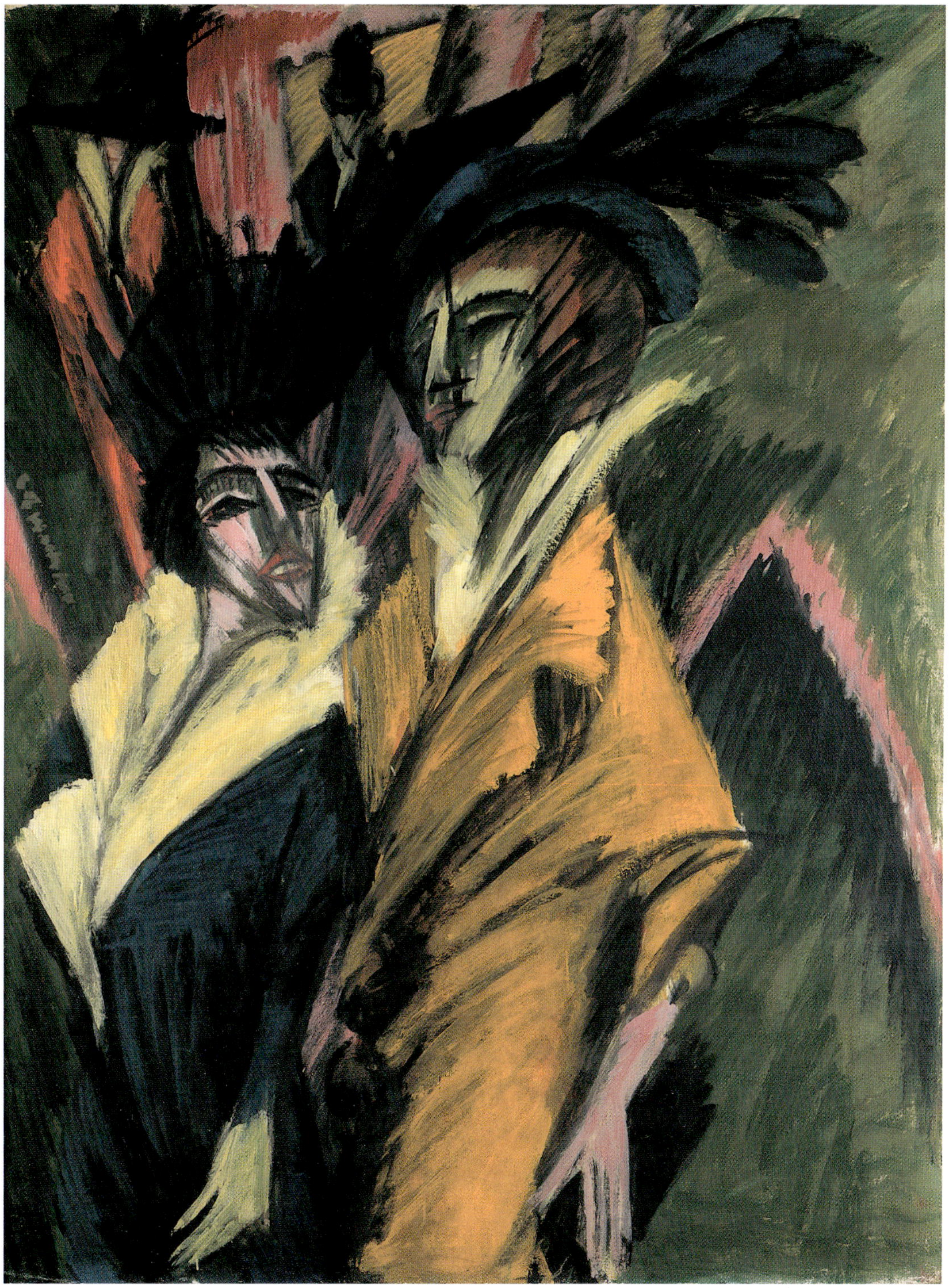

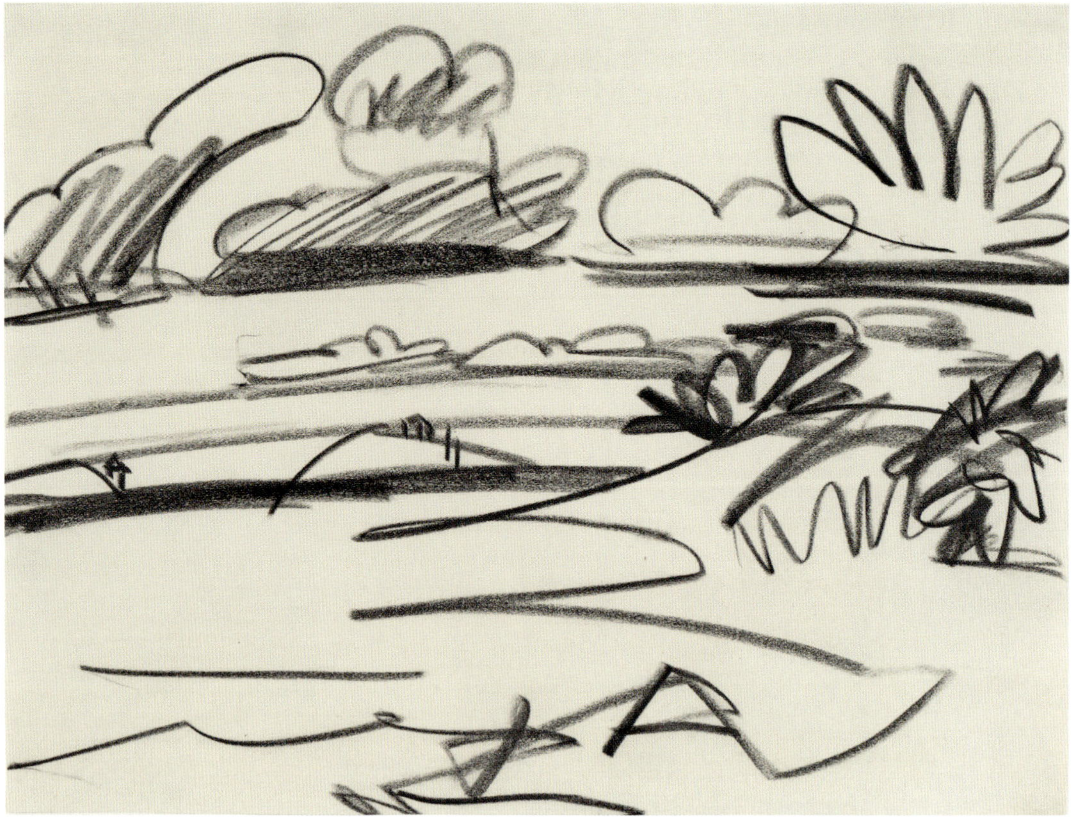

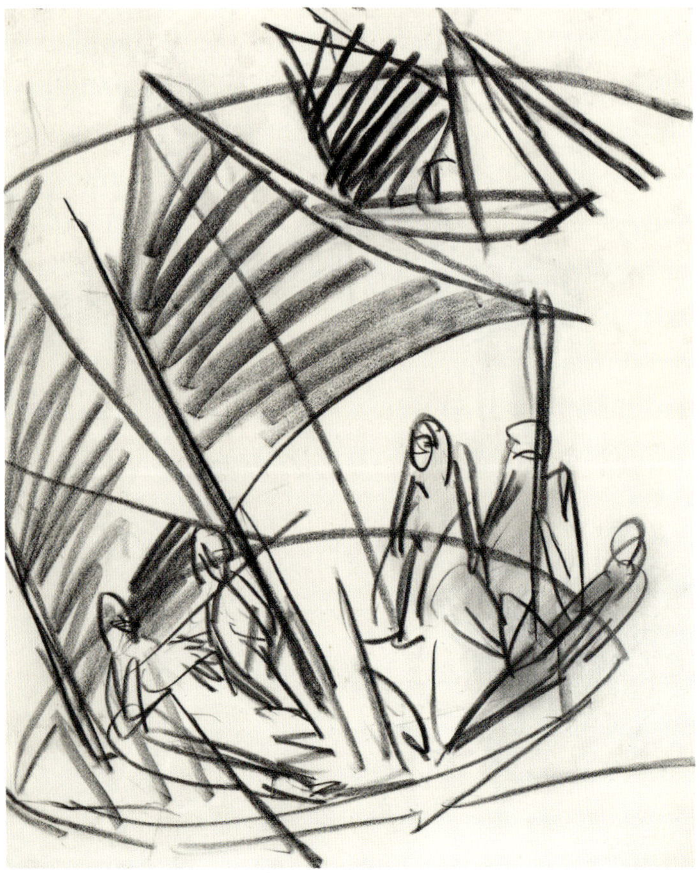

Cat. 97

Sailing Boats off Fehmarn, 1914
Black crayon on paper

Brücke-Museum, Berlin

Cat. 98

Expansive Fehmarn Coast, c.1914
Charcoal on slightly satinised chamois paper

Kirchner Museum Davos, Gift of the Ernst Ludwig Kirchner Estate 1990

Cat. 117

Sailing Boats off Fehmarn, 1914
Woodcut on light-grey blotting paper

Brücke-Museum, Berlin

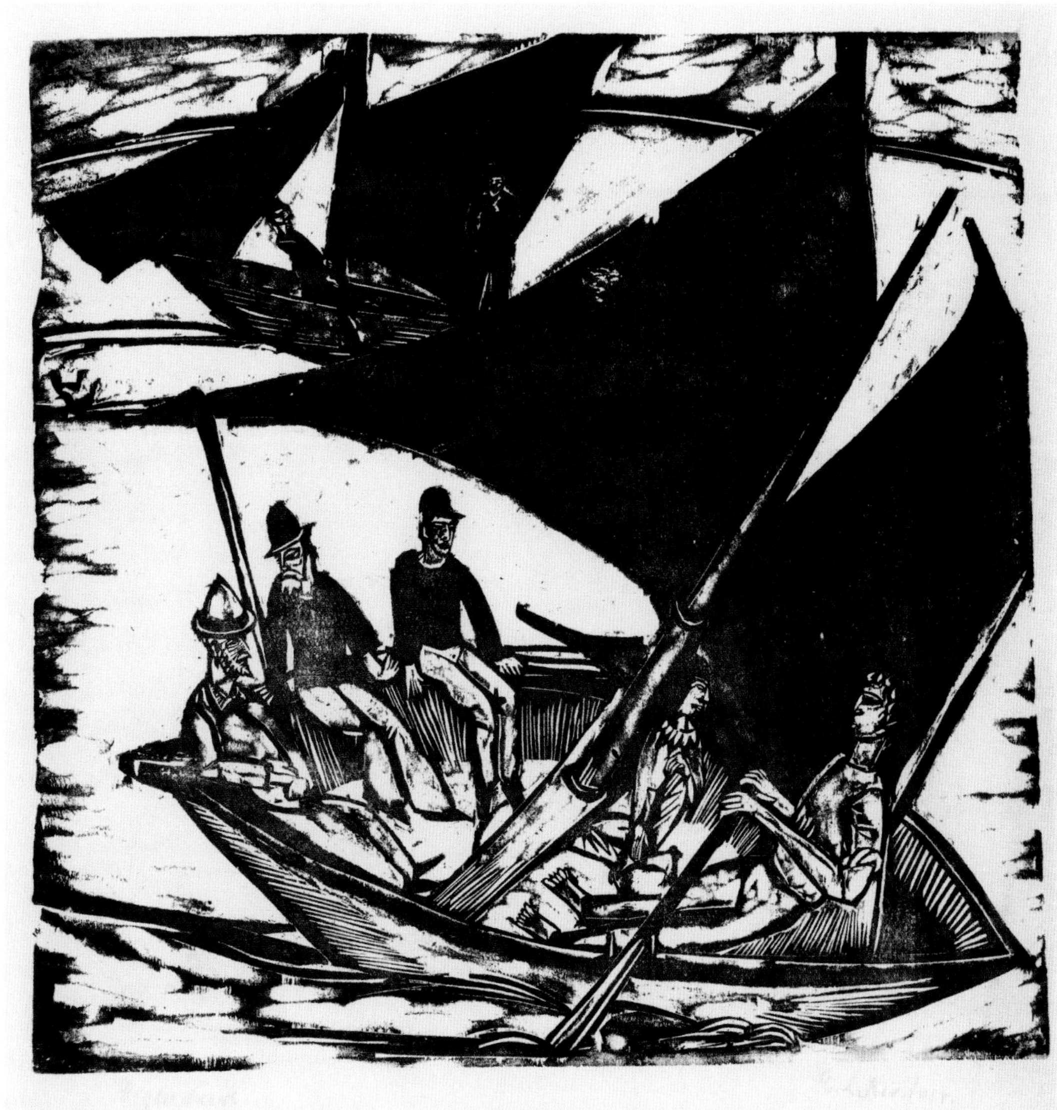

Cat.55

Bathers by the Sea, 1914
Oil on canvas

Private collection

Cat.56

Curving Bay
(Laburnum Tree), c.1914
Oil on canvas

Museo Thyssen-Bornemisza, Madrid

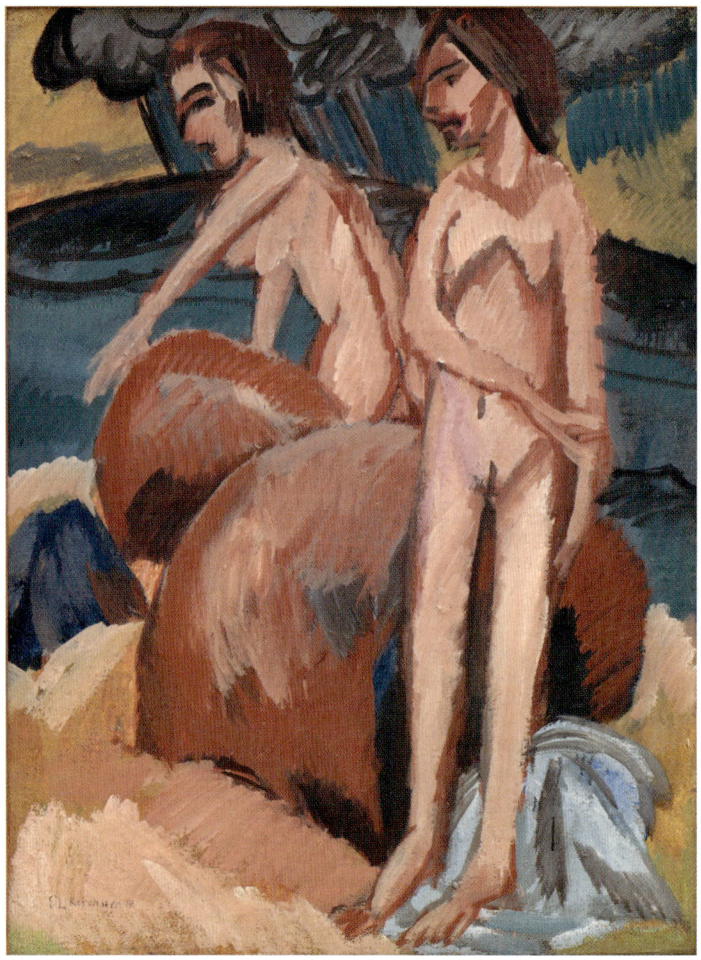

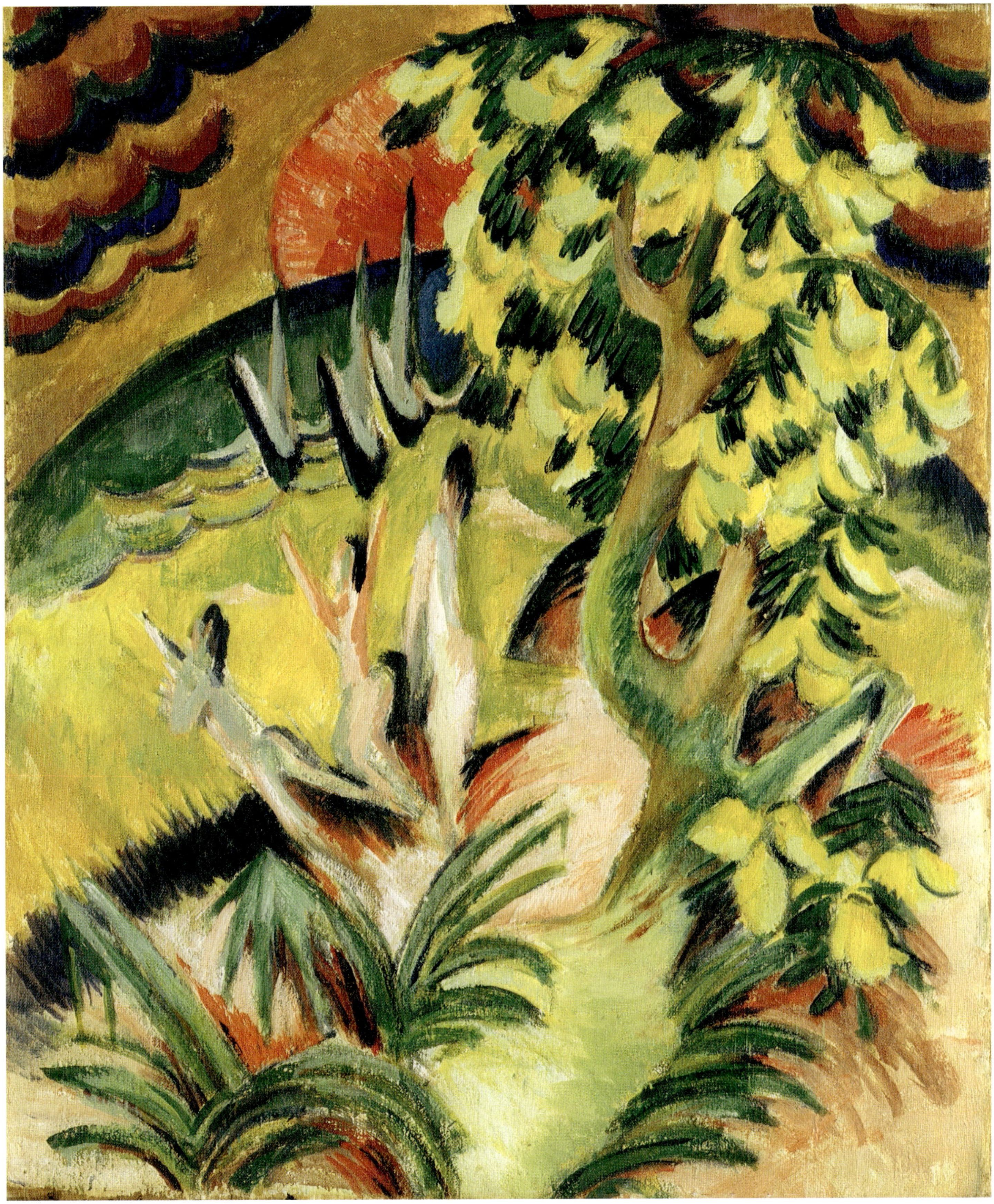

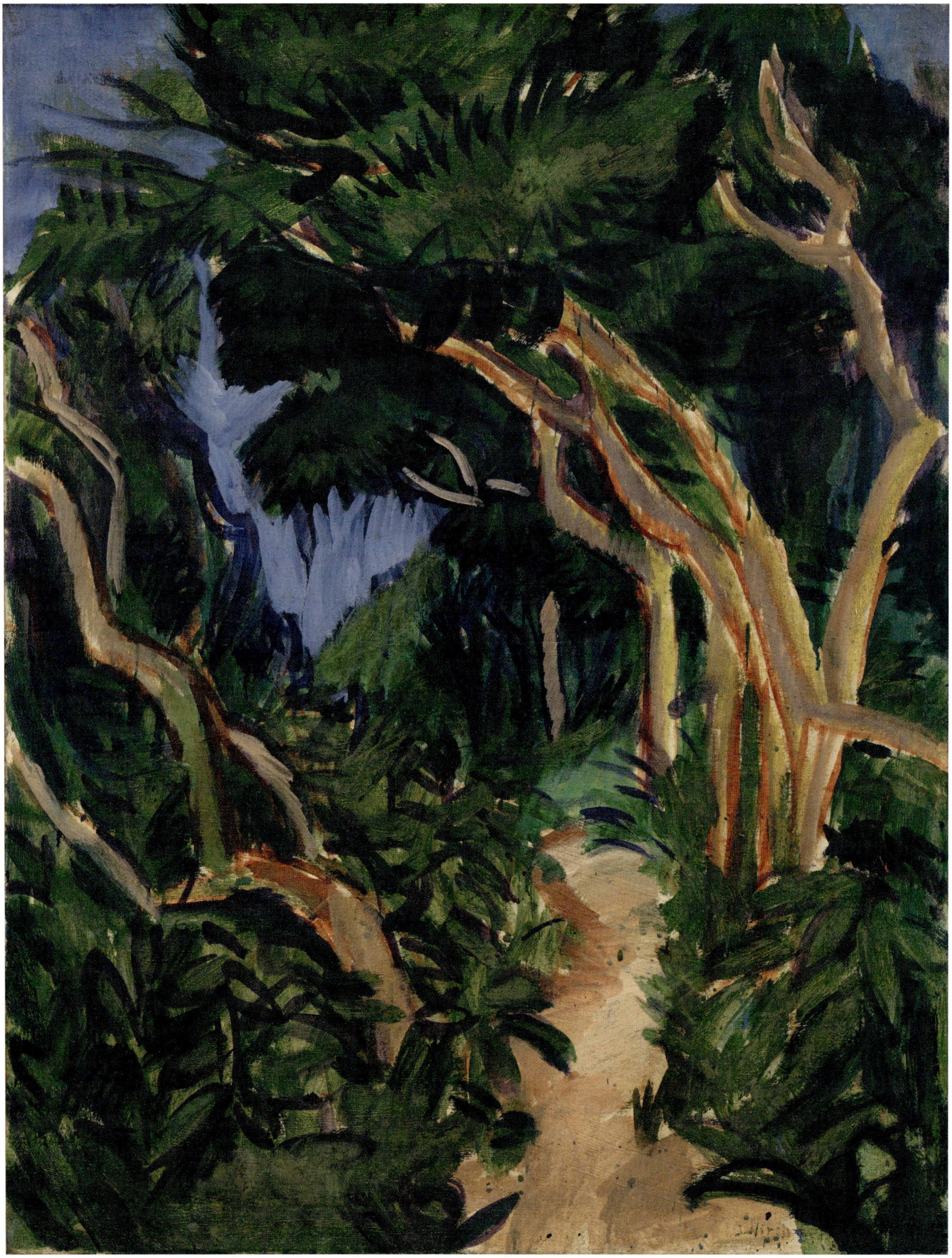

Cat. 54

Forest Path between Young Trees on the Fehmarn Coast, 1914
Oil on canvas

Private collection

Cat. 45

Nude Youth and Girl on the Beach, 1913 (recto)
Oil on canvas

Albertina, Vienna —
Batliner Collection

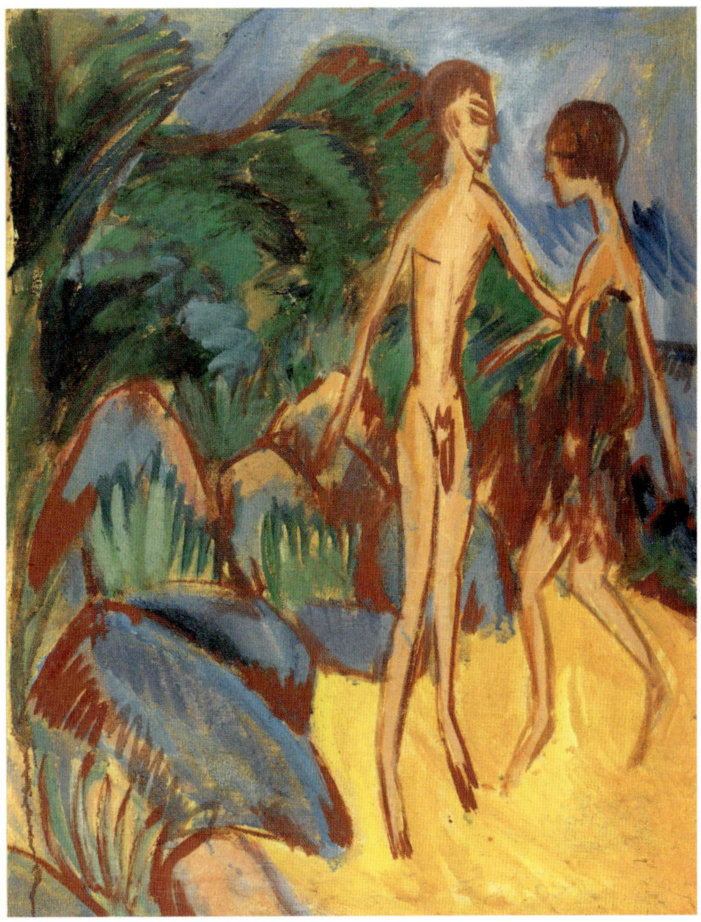

Cat. 57

Two Yellow Nudes with Bouquet of Flowers, 1914
Wax-oil emulsion on canvas

Bündner Kunstmuseum Chur, purchase

Cat. 45

Two Female Nudes in a Room, 1914 (verso)
Oil on canvas

Albertina, Vienna — Batliner Collection

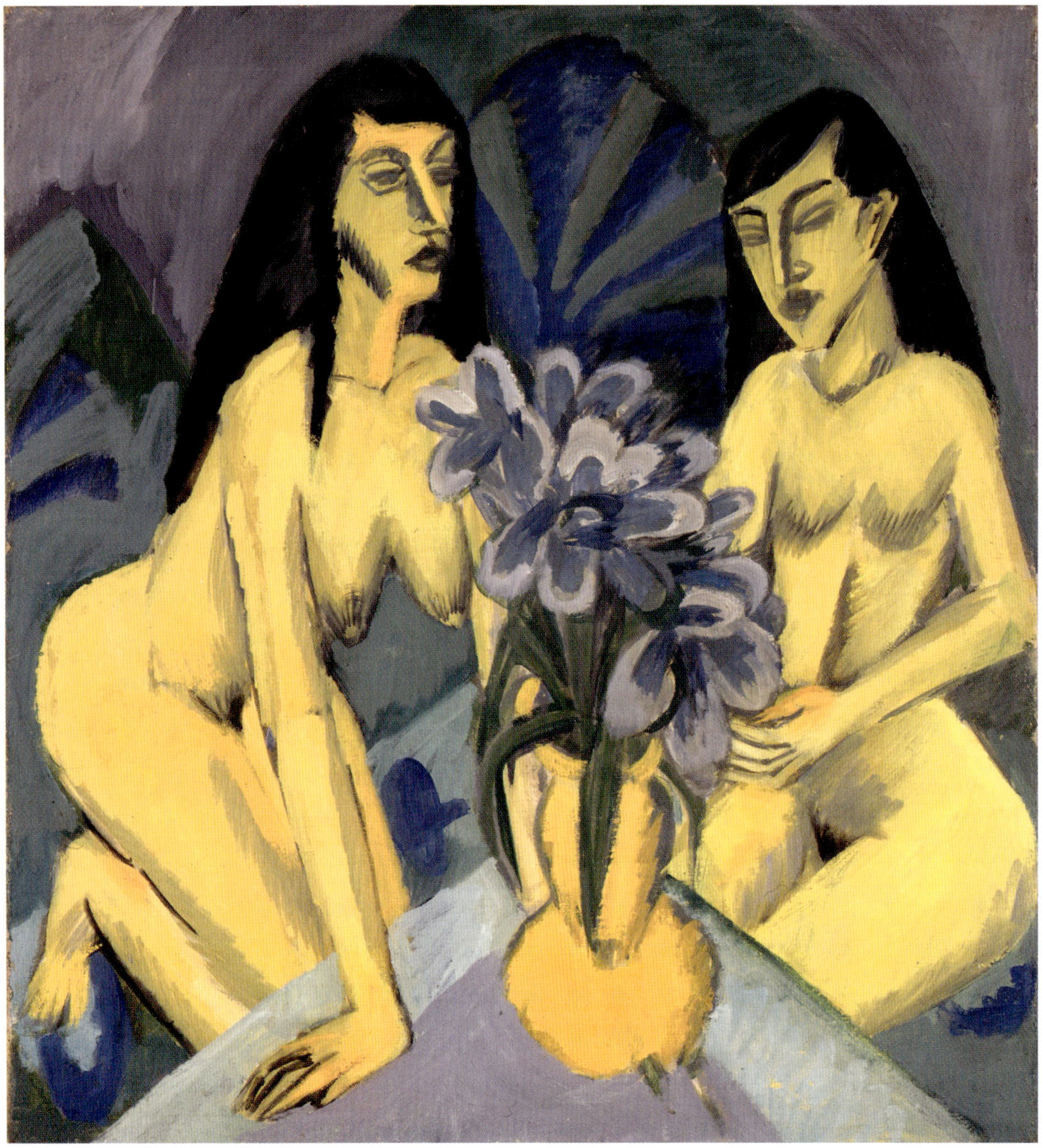

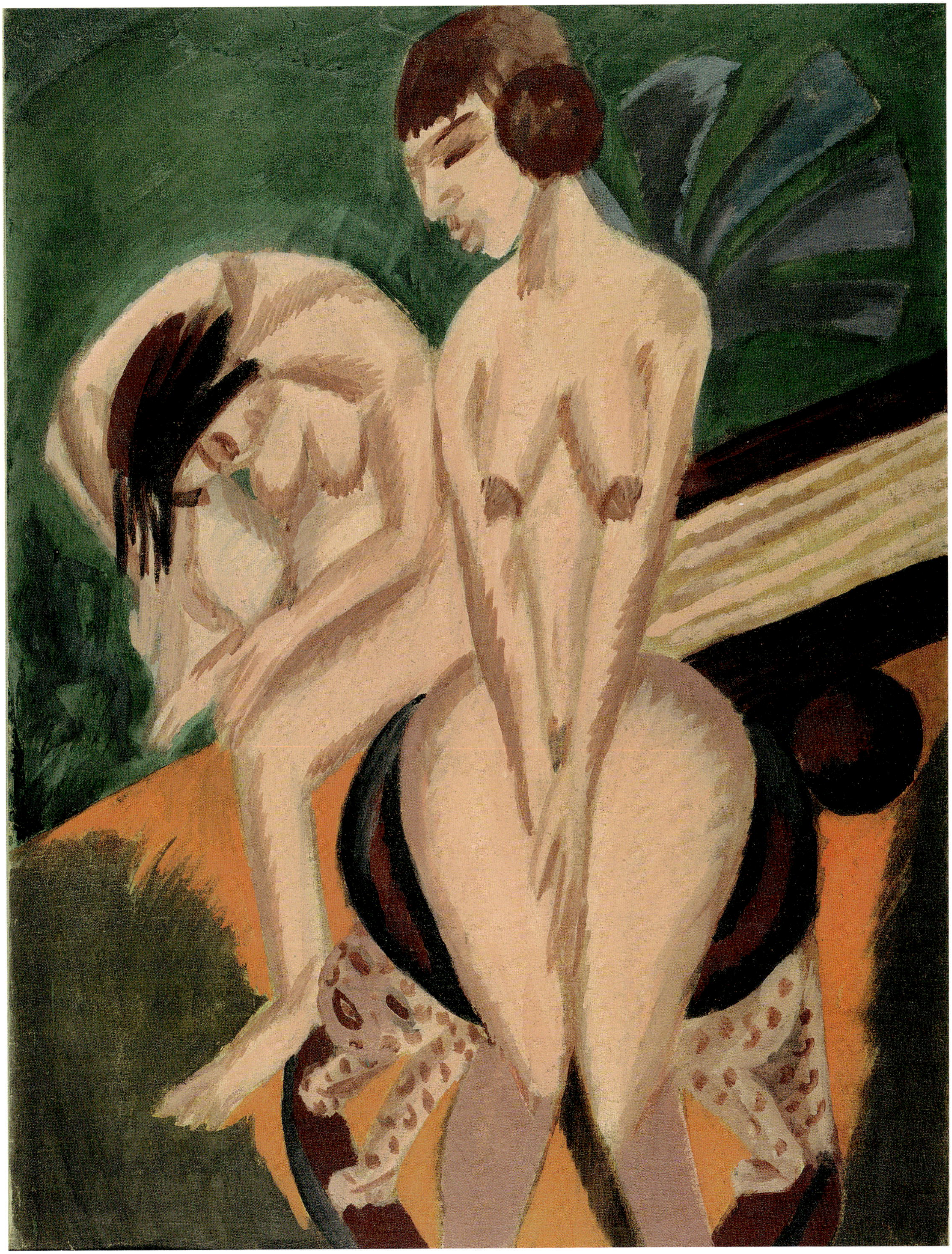

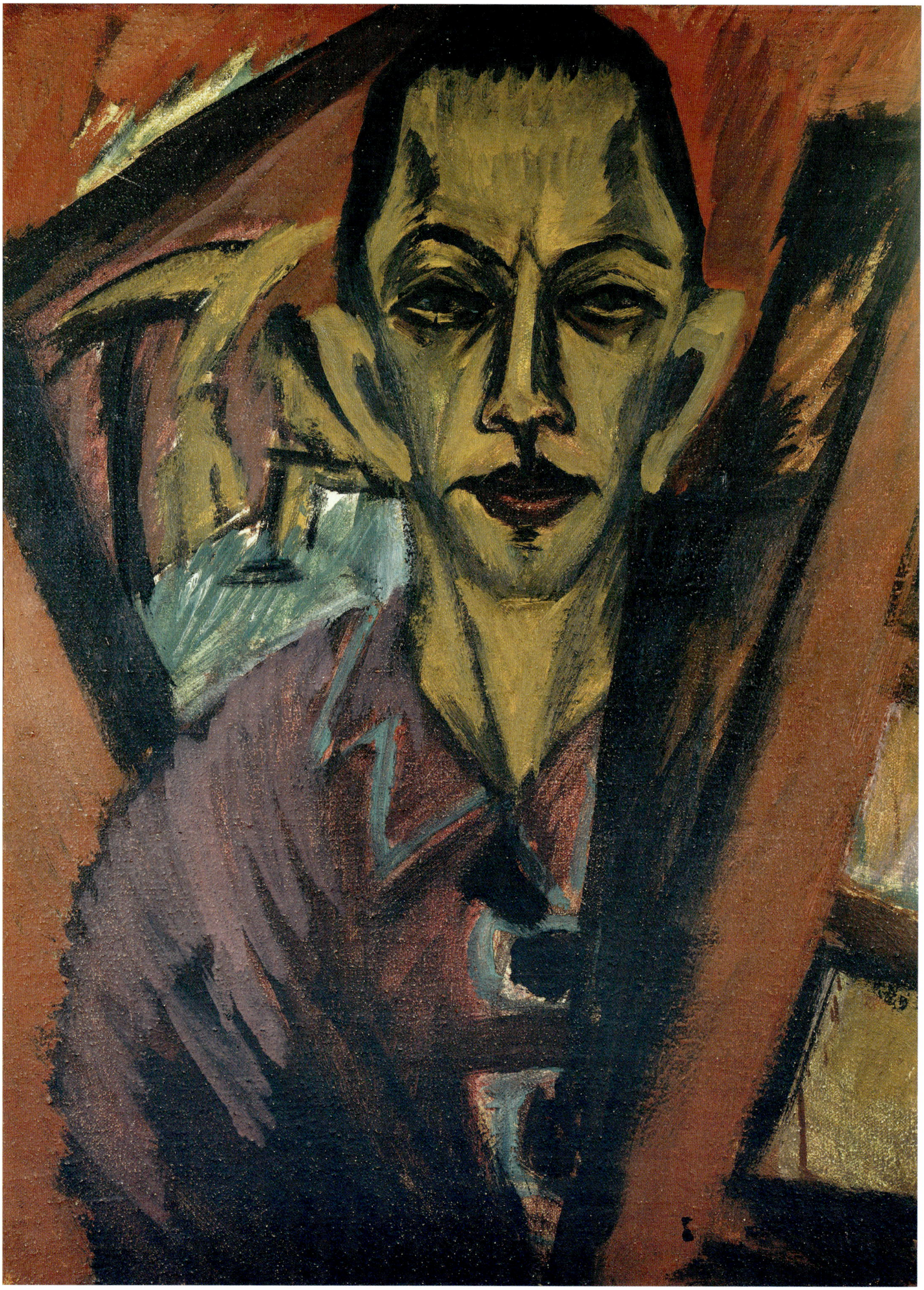

Cat. 60

Self-Portrait, 1914
Oil on canvas

Brücke-Museum, Berlin

Cat. 58

Portrait of Hugo, 1914
Oil on canvas

Ernst Ludwig Kirchner Estate, Courtesy Galerie Henze & Ketterer, Wichtrach/Bern

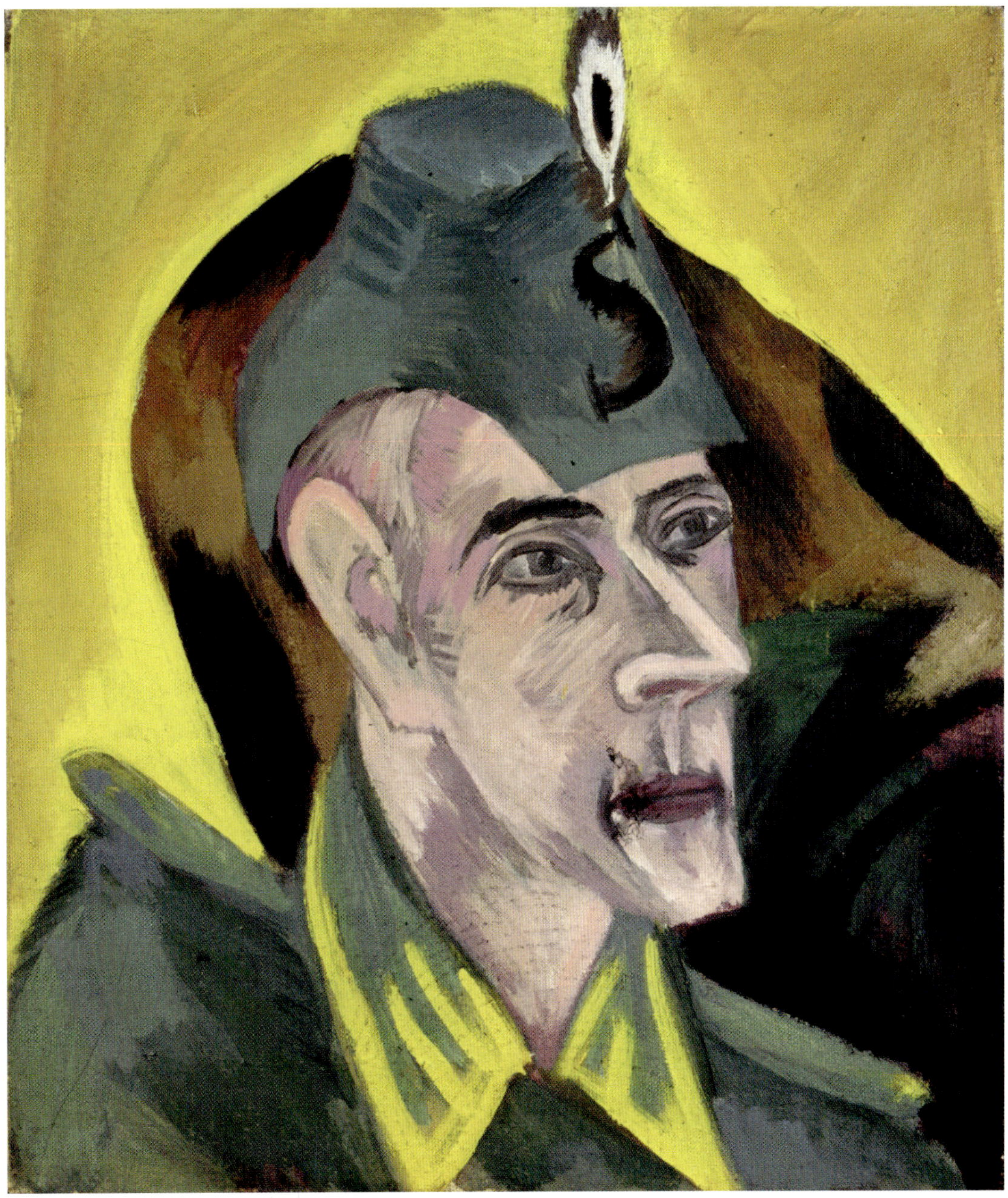

War and Crisis (1915–1917)

5

The outbreak of the First World War marked a turning point in Kirchner's life. His last works in Berlin were produced in a state of physical and mental collapse. He had always been temperamental, but the war and his experience of military service intensified his existential angst and led to excessive consumption of alcohol and drugs.

Before Kirchner joined up in the summer of 1915, he once more took up the cocottes theme. In the last of his series of Berlin street scenes, *Women on the Street* p.213, two cocottes are seen on Friedrichstrasse in a garish yellow light. The women are looking directly at the viewer, while a john right next to them on the right lowers his gaze in their direction. Other men, buildings and arcades are suggested in the background. The sharp-pointed forms Kirchner used in many of his paintings and prints of street motifs dominate this composition as well: everything seems to be staggered wedge-shaped towards the centre and tapering down to the bottom edge. In this way, the green-clad woman in front becomes the scene's protagonist. Compared to earlier street scenes, the brushwork has become less agitated in this painting, so that the image seems less hectic. Also dating from this same period is the tension-filled picture *Brandenburg Gate, Berlin* p.212. It shows the symbol of Prussia's striving for power, a structure built in the neoclassical style, depicted in bright yellow and seen from a worm's-eye view. Three red-black automobiles shoot out of the gate's shadows; given the prevailing atmosphere of war at the time the work was painted, one automatically assumes that these are armoured cars. Pariser Platz, just in front of it, is pictured from above, however, which makes the architectural monument even more imposing and causes the few people suggested at the bottom left to seem lost. Some have even lost their heads, for Kirchner painted the picture at such great speed that in suggesting a street with a light-blue colour, he actually painted over some of them. The vigorous brush strokes and pigment applied in all directions as well as the distorted perspective heighten the scene's dynamism.

It was in this ominous climate that Kirchner voluntarily enlisted in the spring of 1915, hoping to be able to choose which branch of the service he would enter. On 1 July he was drafted to the Mansfelder Field Artillery in Halle (Saale). Although he was temporarily released after only three months in very bad health, his soldier's training supplied him with new motifs drawn from military life. During his convalescent leave in Berlin he painted *Hussars on Horseback; The Riders* p.216. In its composition it is reminiscent of the paintings of the Berlin cocottes being observed by possible johns, only here it is two soldiers in uniform trotting past a group of civilians. Kirchner sketched the people with a few strokes; they are only anonymous observers of an everyday wartime scene. In the centre the uniformed riders are making their way through a yellow declivity into the depth of the picture and towards an unrealistic background resembling a violet cloud. Another work that captures Kirchner's artistic reaction to impressions from his military training period is the lithograph *Artillerists' Bath—Bathing Soldiers* p.217. The print shows a group of nude soldiers in the shower, overseen by a man in uniform—a metaphor for the loss of individuality in wartime. During his leave he also took an unconventional *Self-Portrait as a Soldier* p.66, which pictures the artist in uniform with sabre and spiked helmet in his Berlin-Friedenau live-in studio. The contrast between his life as an artist freed from Wilhelmine notions of morality and his experience of military drill as a soldier could not have been greater and is impressively documented in this photograph.

In the following months the artist turned to alcohol and drugs in excess and thus in part helped to make himself unfit for service. To avoid being called up again after his two-month period of leave, he declared his readiness to check into a sanatorium. But he kept postponing his departure for Königstein so as to be able to complete the woodcut cycle on Adelbert von Chamisso's 1814 novella *Peter Schlemihl's Wondrous Story.* The six colour woodcuts with title page pp.220–225 do not so much illustrate the novella as they do Kirchner's frame of mind around 1915.

In December 1915, at the recommendation of his friend Botho Graef, whom he had got to know in February 1914 at his first major one-man exhibition at the Kunstverein in Jena, Kirchner finally sought a cure at Dr Oskar Kohnstamm's sanatorium in Königstein im Taunus. His moves were also frequently associated with changes in subject matter: whereas his military training in Halle had inspired several motifs from the life of soldiers, his stays in Königstein and the hilly Taunus landscape heightened his interest in motifs from nature, some executed on-site, some in his Berlin studio, where he could work far away from a therapeutic regimen and undisturbed by other patients. Characteristic of the works produced at this time are his use of glowing colours, disparities in the proportions and constantly changing perspectives within a single composition. *Königstein with Red Church* p.228 depicts figures that are overly large in relation to the buildings and seen frontally at eye level with the viewer, while the village street is shown from a bird's-eye perspective. The observer's gaze is drawn towards the village church standing at the vanishing point, above which an ominous storm cloud and two black ravens hover. In his clothing the man in the foreground is reminiscent of the johns in the Berlin street scenes; only the cocottes are missing. Kirchner also chose different points of view in *Village with Blue Paths* p.227: he painted the village in frontal view, but the blue paths, which look more like rivers, from high above. In the foreground one can see two figures doing field work. These two paintings are characterised by the harmony of the primary colours red–blue–yellow, which is further heightened in *Village with Blue Paths* by the absence of white and the complementary contrast of red and green.

Driven by inner turmoil, in the first half of the year 1916 Kirchner interrupted his course of treatment on several occasions, each time after less than a month; he restlessly travelled between Berlin, Jena and Königstein and beginning in 1917 he also went for treatment in Davos and Kreuzlingen. In this peripatetic period he also dealt with his fear of the war and the precarious state of his health in a number of self-portraits pp.236,237. In "a night when I had half lost consciousness", he produced the etching *Self-Portrait, Drawing* p.233, picturing himself drawing with an etching needle in his right hand, which is placed at the bottom edge of the picture. With fine lines he tried to capture his own physiognomy but the crude drawing only hints at his portrait: his sunken face remains schematic, without fixed contours, and the black eyes are emphasised without betraying any expression. This self-portrait, with its nervous lines is an impressive testimony to his terrible state of mind in these months, which would only improve years later in Davos after he had conquered his addiction to the medications he was taking.

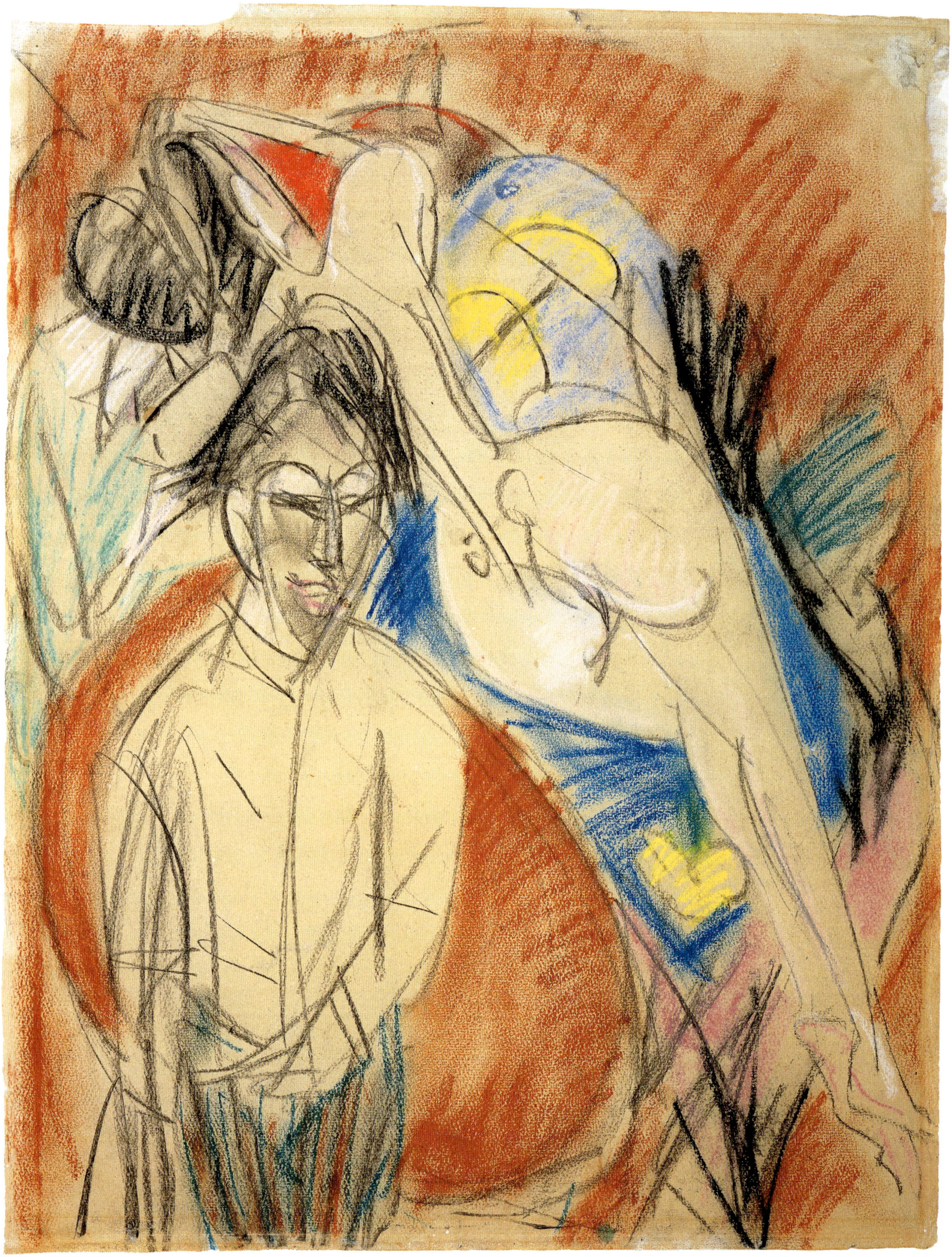

Cat. 99

Painter and Nude Woman (Self-Portrait with Model), 1915
Pastel on paper

Brücke-Museum, Berlin

Cat. 100

Self-Portrait, 1915
Pencil on paper

Private collection

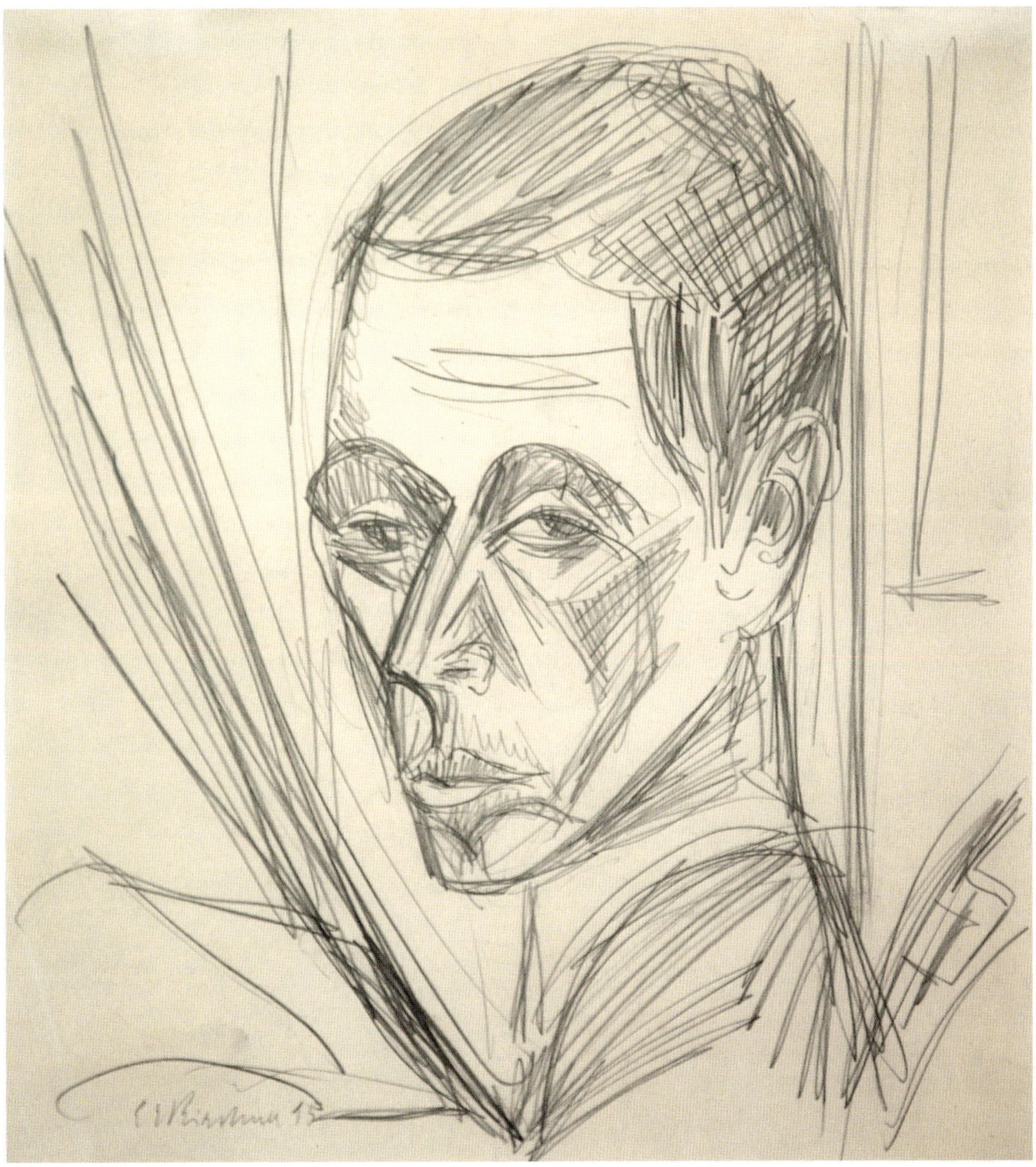

Cat. 63

Brandenburg Gate, Berlin, 1915
Oil on canvas,
on art panel and wood

Würth Collection

Cat. 61

Women on the Street, 1915
Oil on canvas

Von der Heydt-Museum
Wuppertal

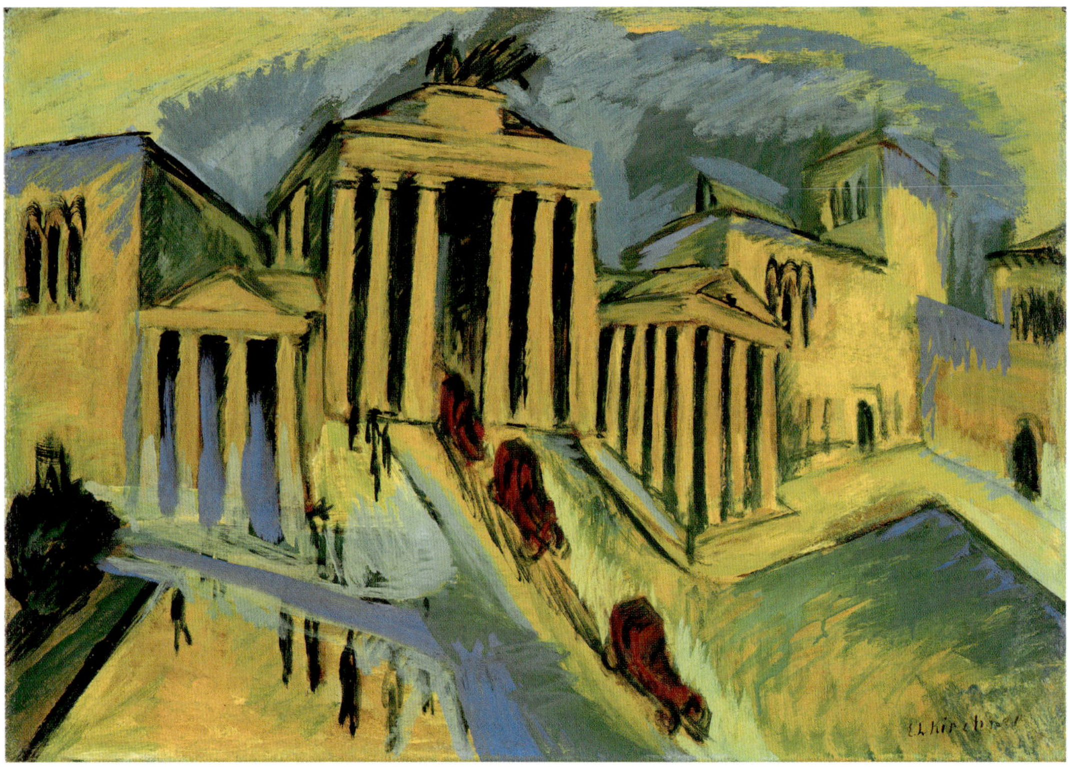

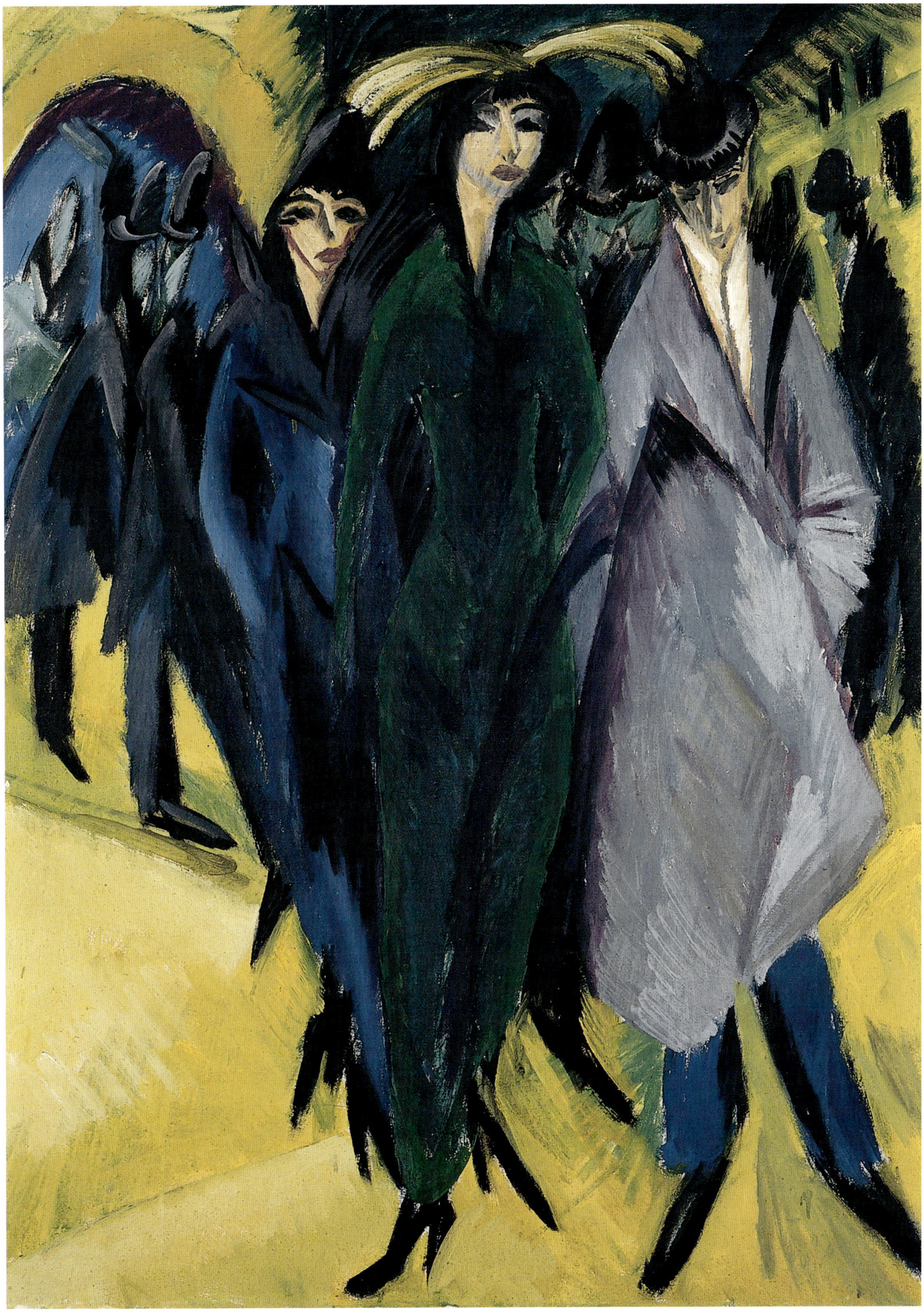

Cat. 120

Cocotte on the Street, 1915
Woodcut on yellow paper, print from drawing block in black

Städel Museum, Graphische Sammlung, Frankfurt am Main

Cat. 121

Cocotte on the Street, 1915
Woodcut on thin Japan paper, print from colour block in black

Städel Museum, Graphische Sammlung, Frankfurt am Main

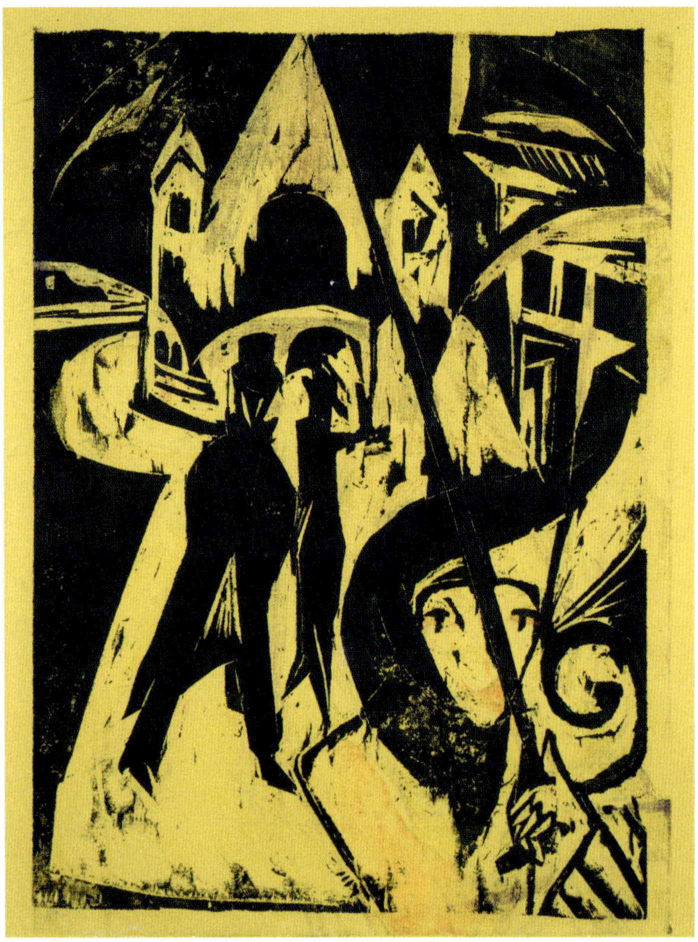

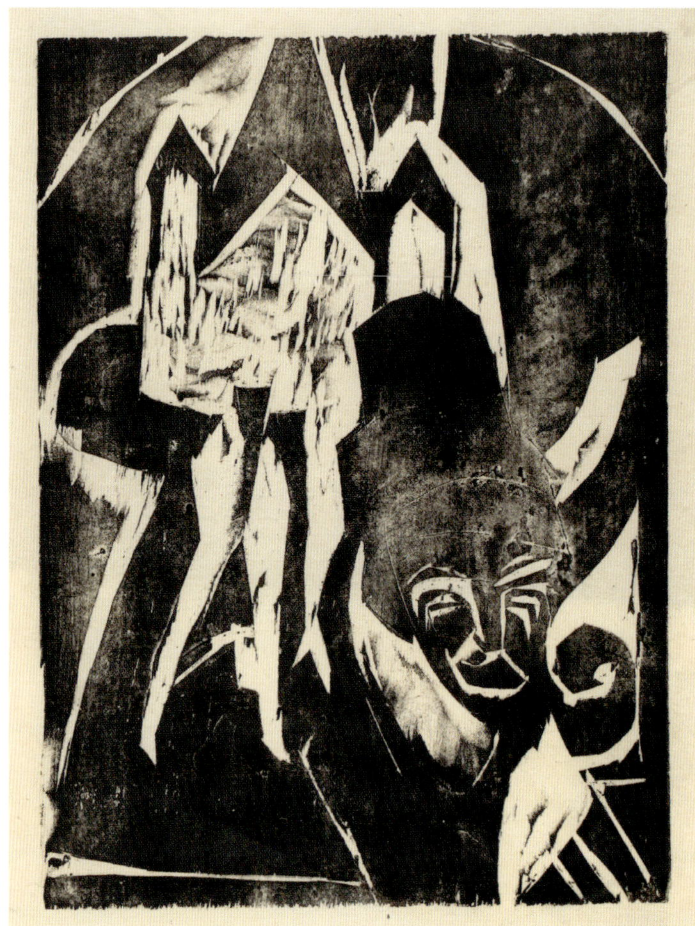

Cat. 122

Cocotte on the Street, 1915
Colour woodcut on blotting paper, print from 2 blocks in black, red, yellow, blue and green

Städel Museum, Graphische Sammlung, Frankfurt am Main

Cat. 123

Cocotte on the Street, 1915
Colour woodcut on stiff vellum, print from 2 blocks in violet, red, yellow, blue and green

Private collection, Courtesy W. Wittrock, Berlin

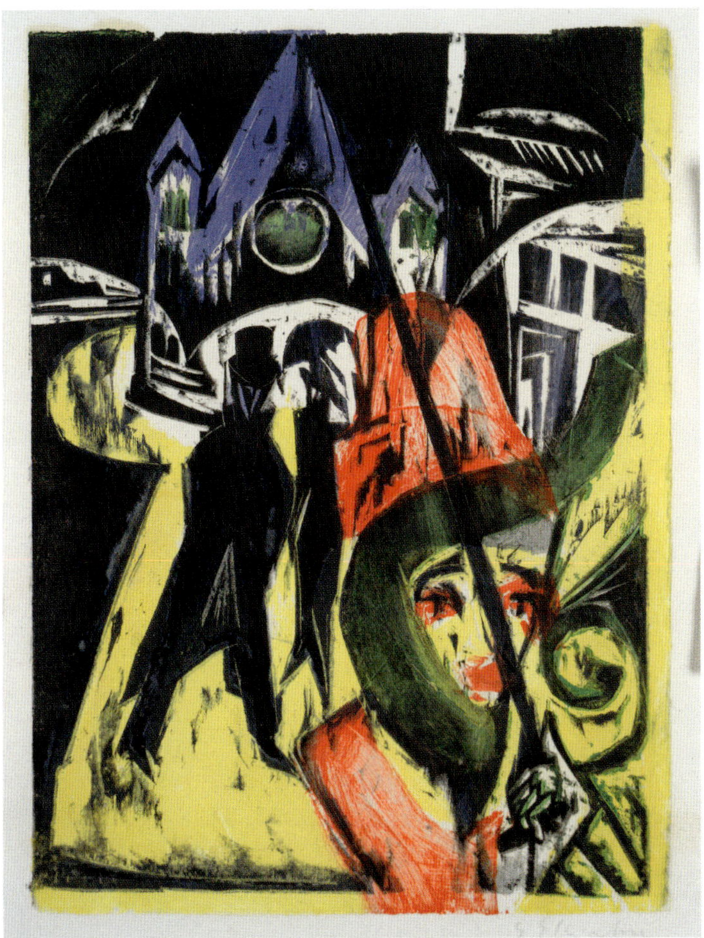

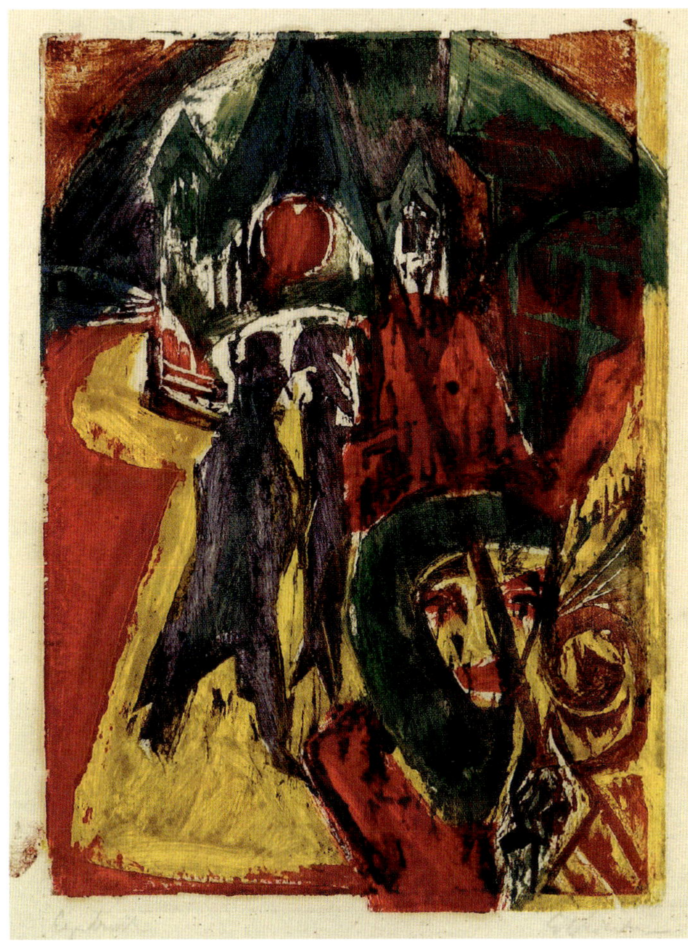

Cat. 62

Hussars on Horseback; The Riders, 1915
Oil on canvas

Private collection

Cat. 118

Artillerists' Bath — Bathing Soldiers, 1915
Lithograph on yellow paper

E. W. K. Collection, Bern/Davos

Cat. 119

Mounted Patrol in the Evening, 1915
Lithograph on yellow paper

Werner Coninx Foundation, Zurich

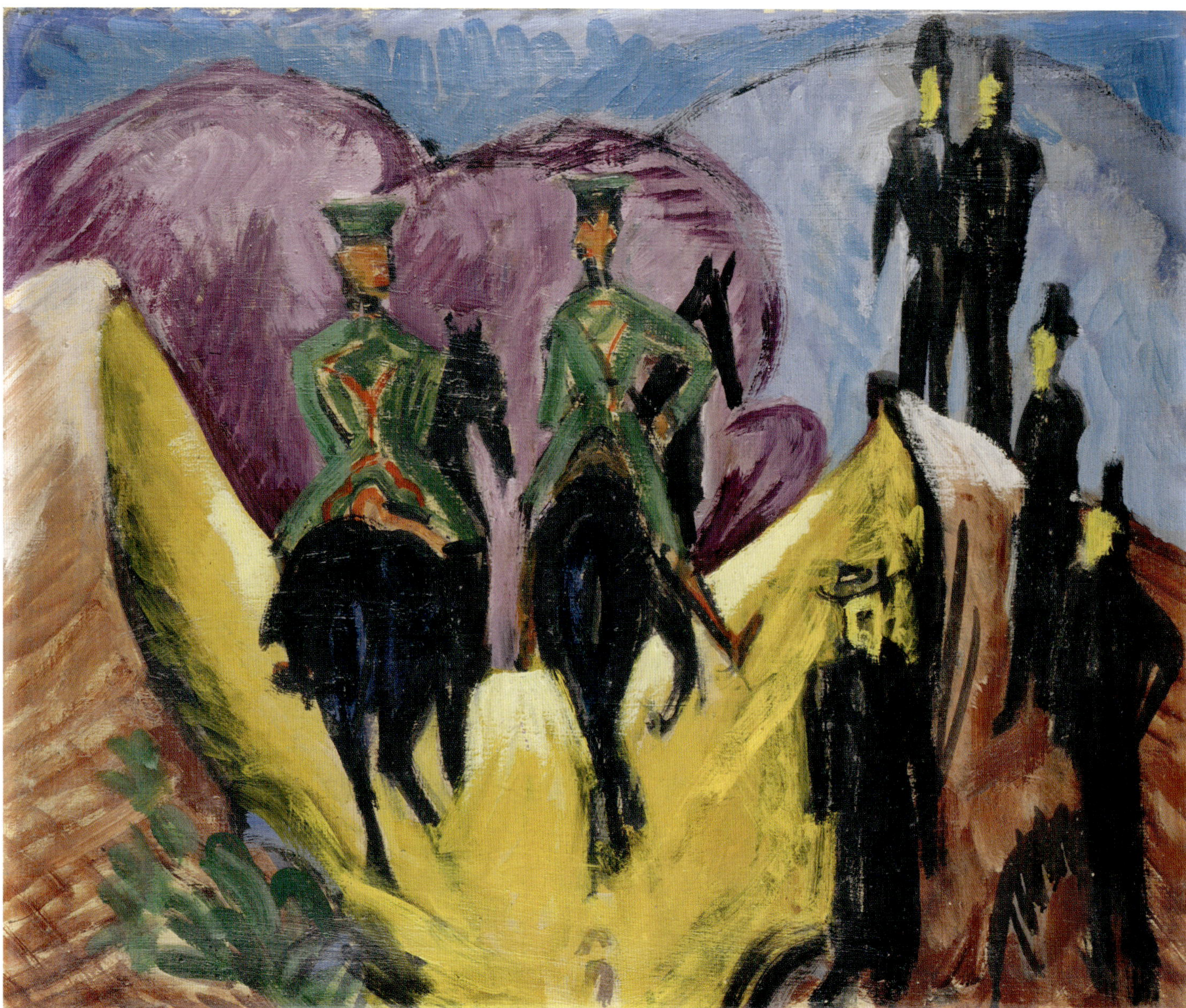

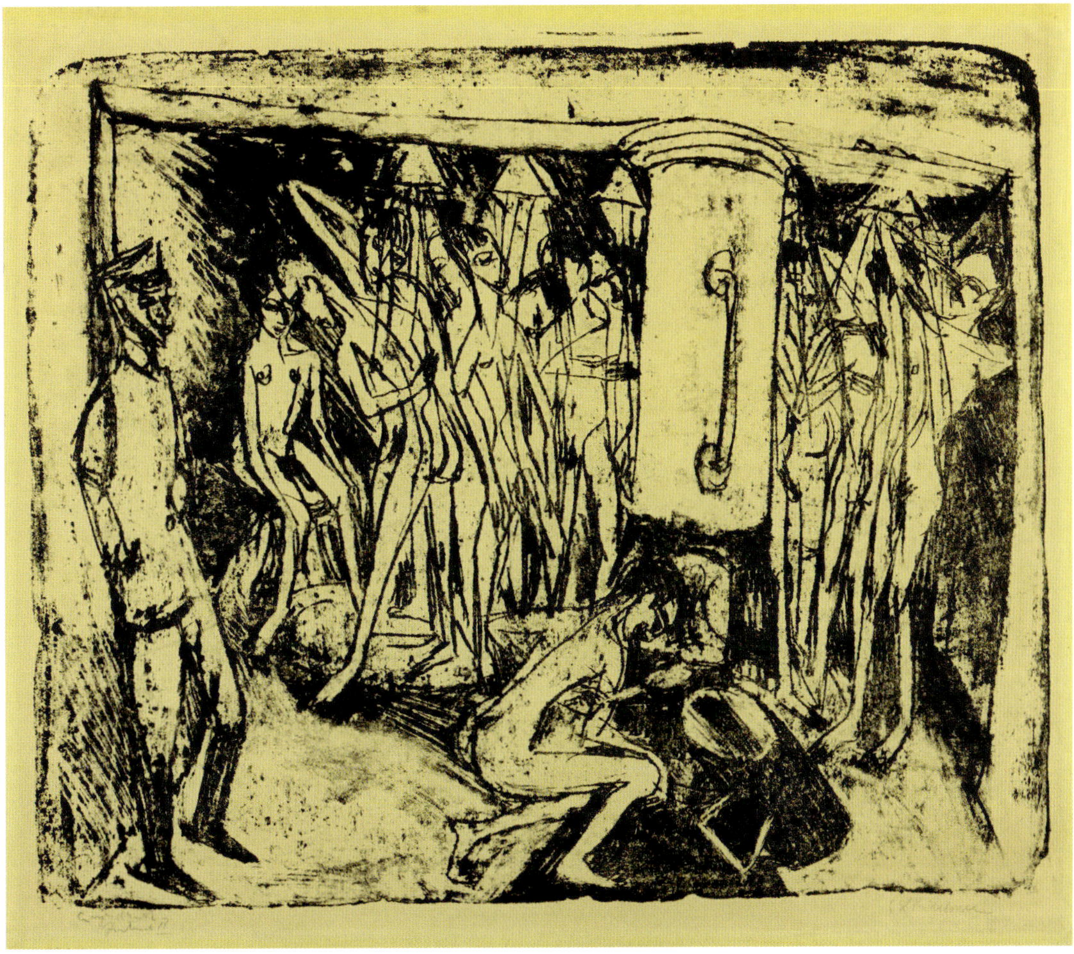

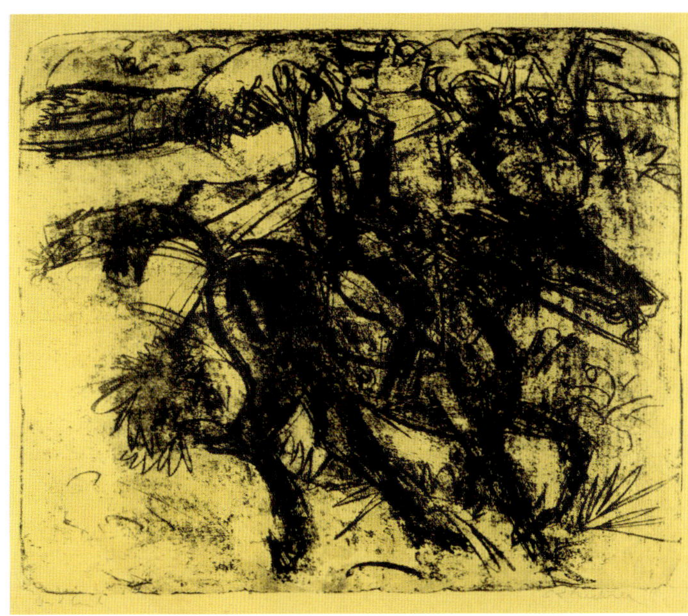

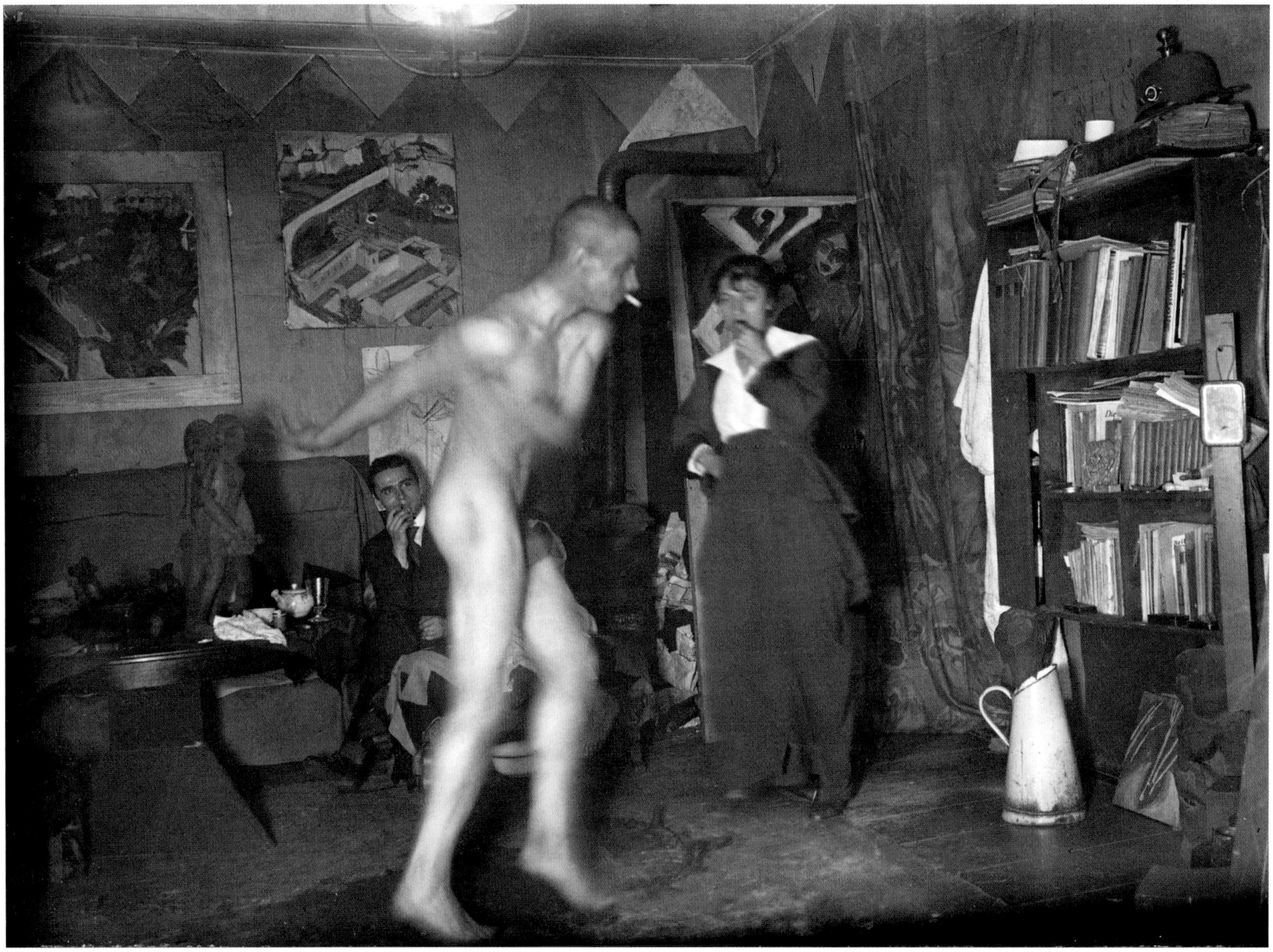

Cat. 146

Werner Gothein, unknown young woman obscured next to him (Gerda Schilling?), Ernst Ludwig Kirchner (?) and Erna Schilling in Kirchner's live-in studio, Berlin-Friedenau, 1915
Glass negative

E.W.K. Collection, Bern/Davos, Courtesy Kirchner Museum Davos

Cat. 101

Dance between the Women, 1915/16
Pen and ink on paper

E.W.K. Collection, Bern/Davos

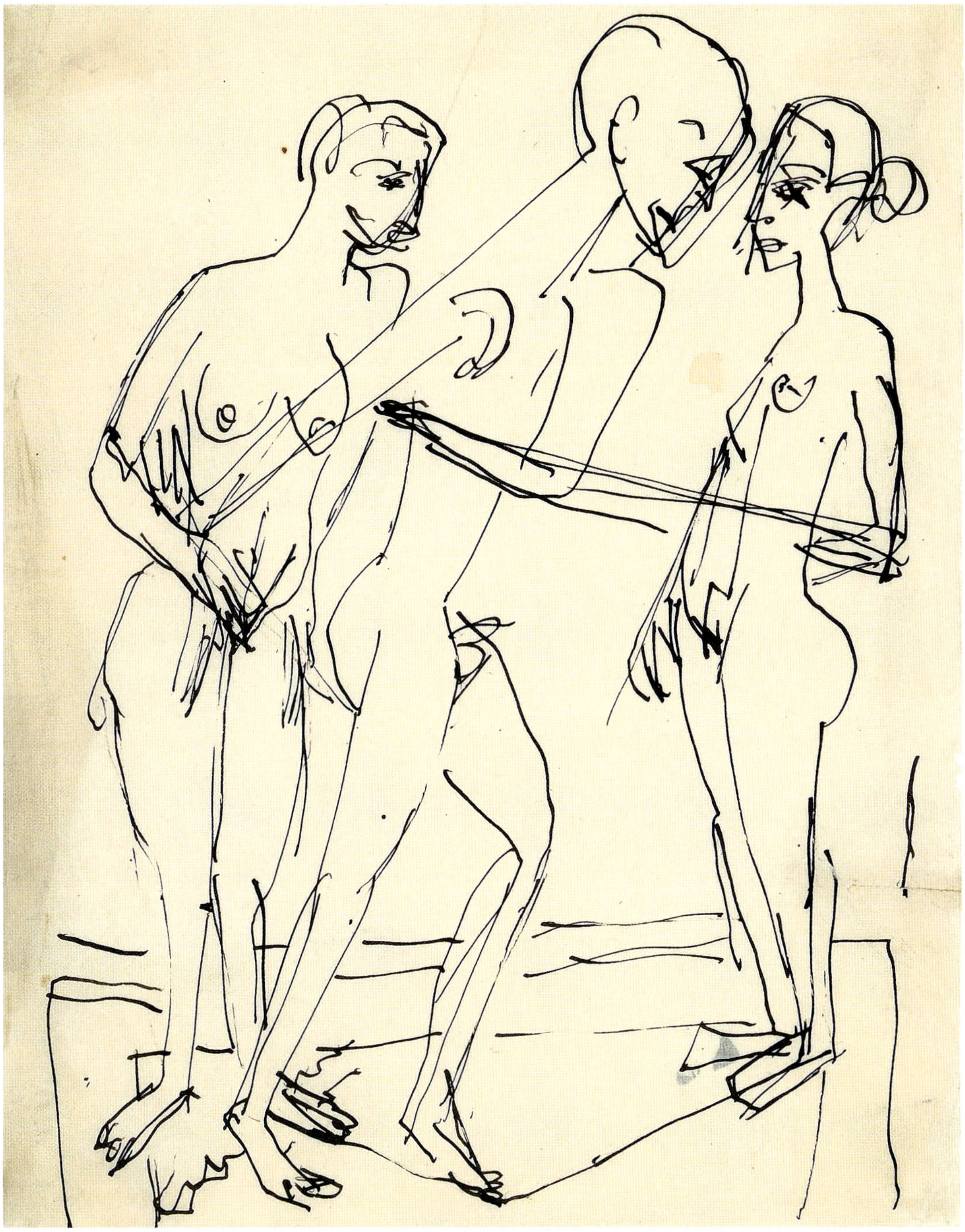

Cat. 124 a

Schlemihl cycle, cover illustration with title "Adelbert von Chamisso/Schlemihl", 1915
Lithograph on violet paper, pasted onto yellow cover paper

Brücke-Museum, Berlin, Karl and Emy Schmidt-Rottluff Foundation

Cat. 124 b

Schlemihl cycle, title page for "Peter Schlemihl's Wondrous Story", 1915
Colour woodcut on blotting paper

Brücke-Museum, Berlin, Karl and Emy Schmidt-Rottluff Foundation

Cat. 124 c

Schlemihl cycle, sheet 1: The Sale of the Shadow, 1915
Colour woodcut on blotting paper

Brücke-Museum, Berlin, Karl and Emy Schmidt-Rottluff Foundation

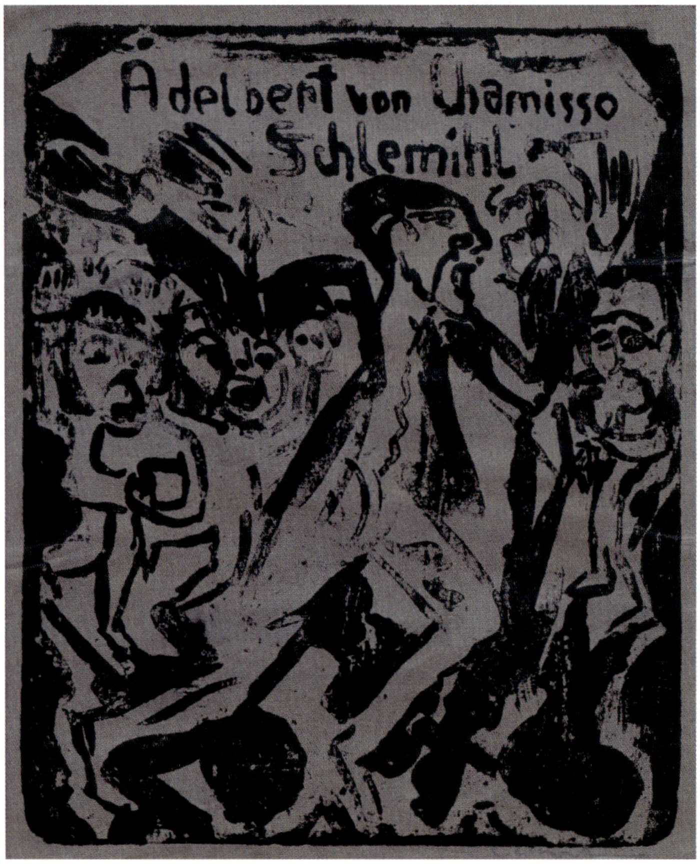

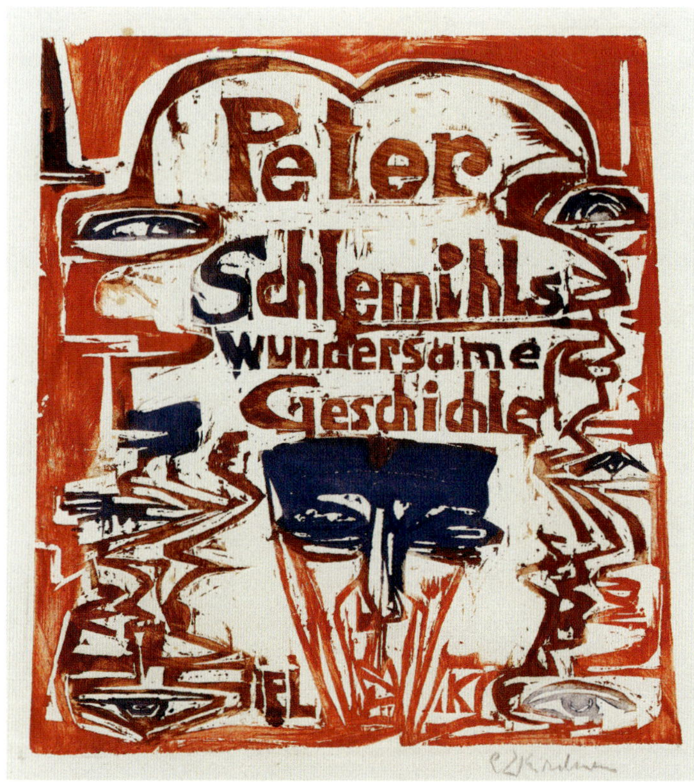

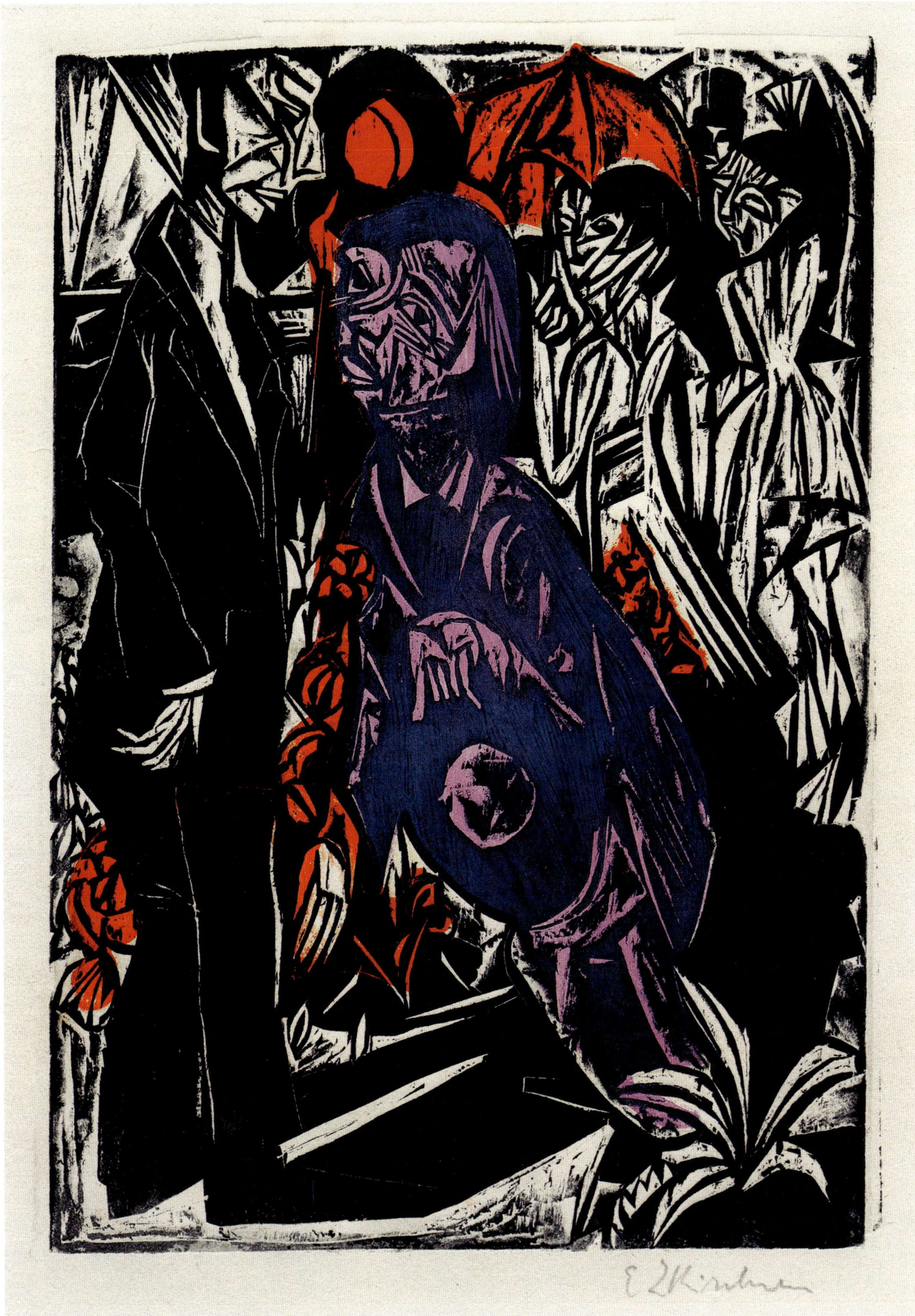

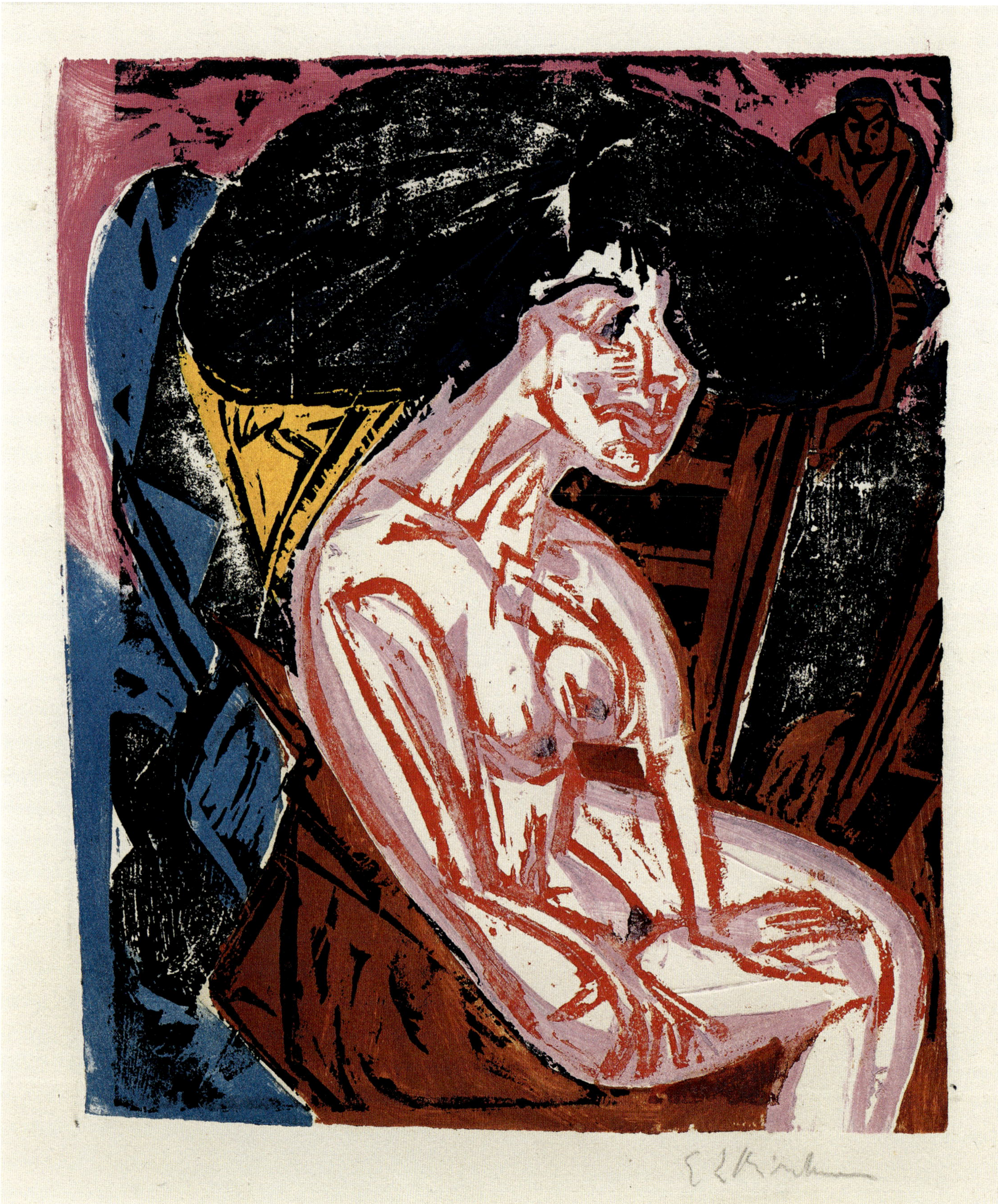

Cat. 124 d

Schlemihl cycle, sheet 2:
The Beloved, 1915
Colour woodcut on blotting paper

Brücke-Museum, Berlin, Karl and Emy Schmidt-Rottluff Foundation

Cat. 124 e

Schlemihl cycle, sheet 3:
Struggles — Pangs of Love, 1915
Colour woodcut on blotting paper

Brücke-Museum, Berlin, Karl and Emy Schmidt-Rottluff Foundation

Cat. 124 f

Schlemihl cycle, sheet 4:
Schlemihl in the Solitude of His Room, 1915
Colour woodcut on blotting paper

Brücke-Museum, Berlin, Karl and Emy Schmidt-Rottluff Foundation

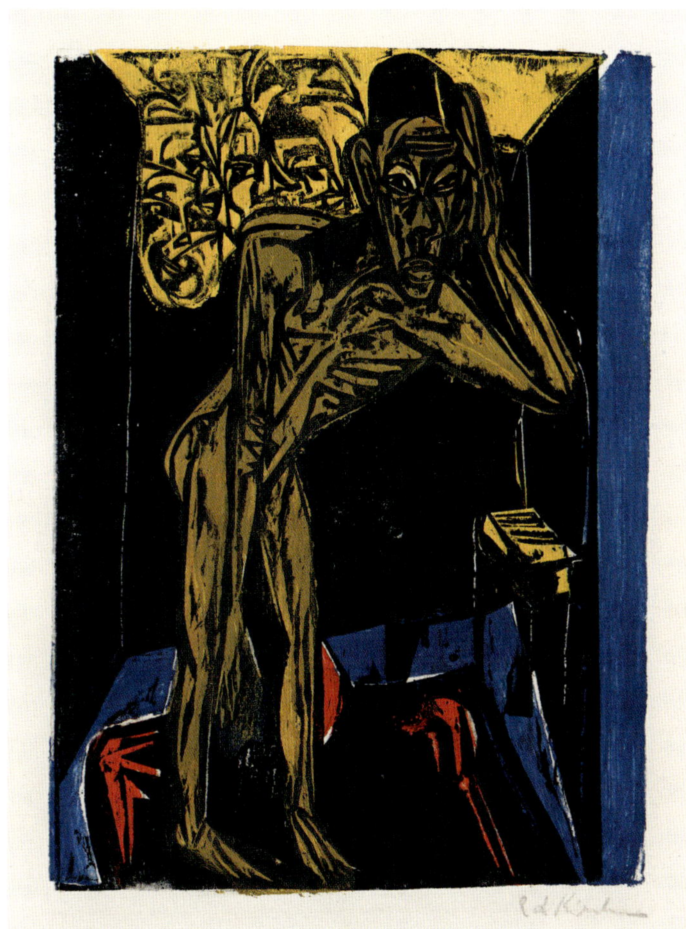

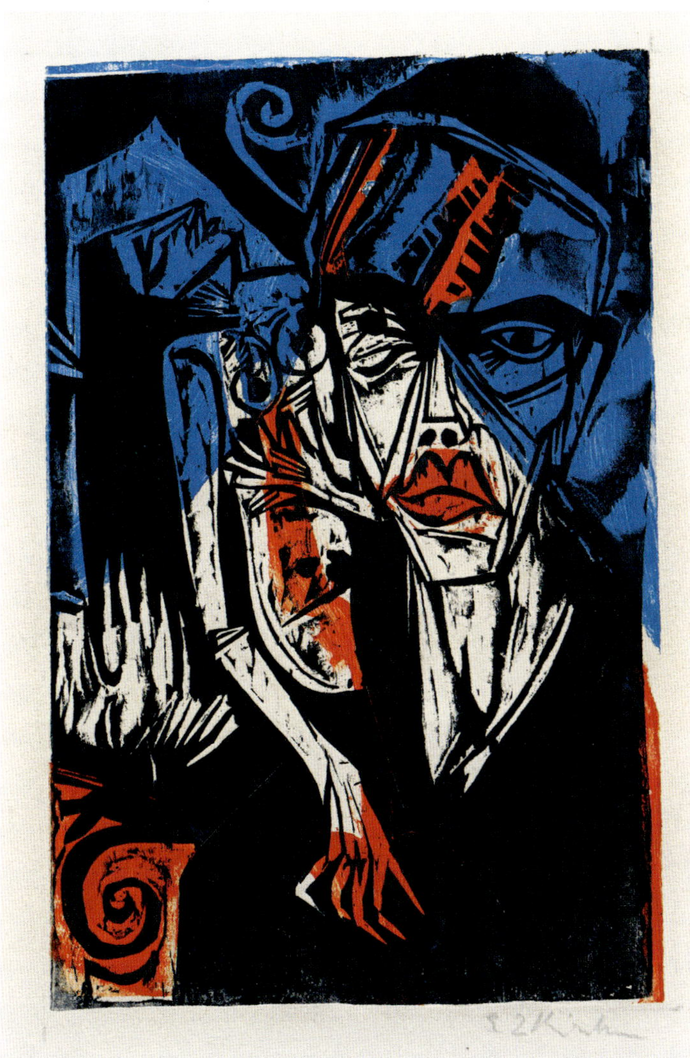

Cat. 124 g

Schlemihl cycle, sheet 5: Schlemihl Encounters the Little Grey Man on the Country Road, 1915
Colour woodcut on blotting paper

Brücke-Museum, Berlin, Karl and Emy Schmidt-Rottluff Foundation

Cat. 124 h

Schlemihl cycle, sheet 6: Schlemihl's Encounter with the Shadow, 1915
Colour woodcut on blotting paper

Brücke-Museum, Berlin, Karl and Emy Schmidt-Rottluff Foundation

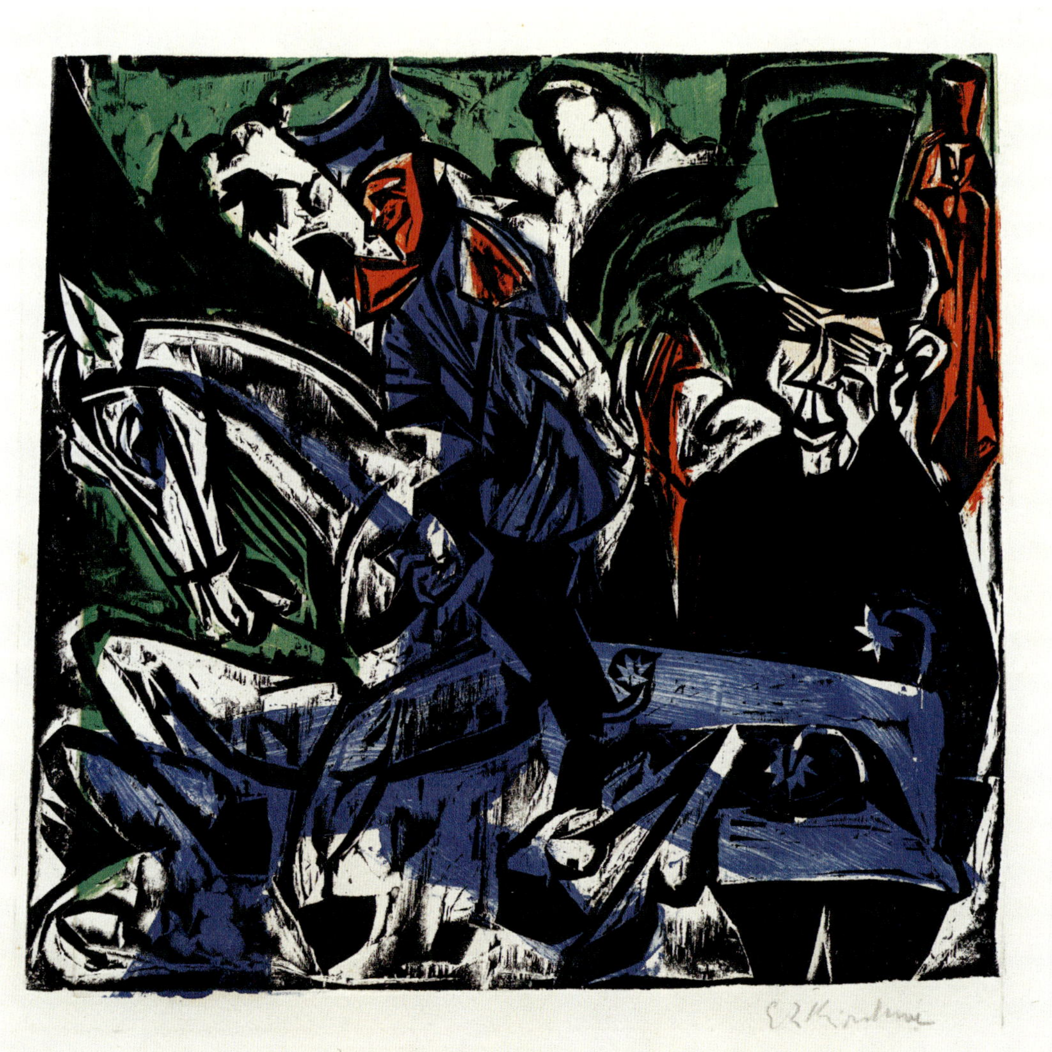

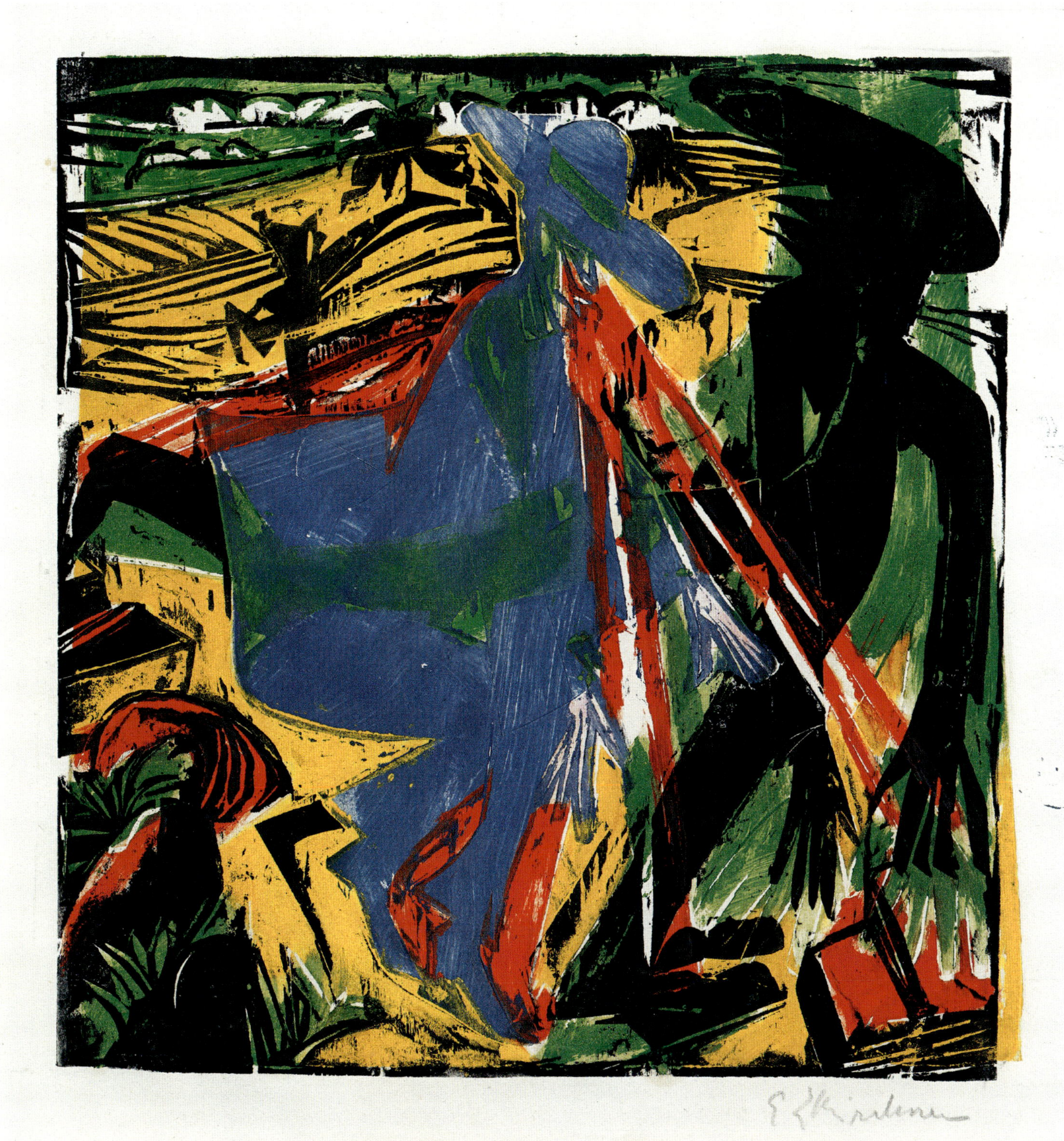

Cat. 65

Village with Blue Paths, 1916/1920
Oil on canvas

Museum Ostwall im Dortmunder U, Dortmund

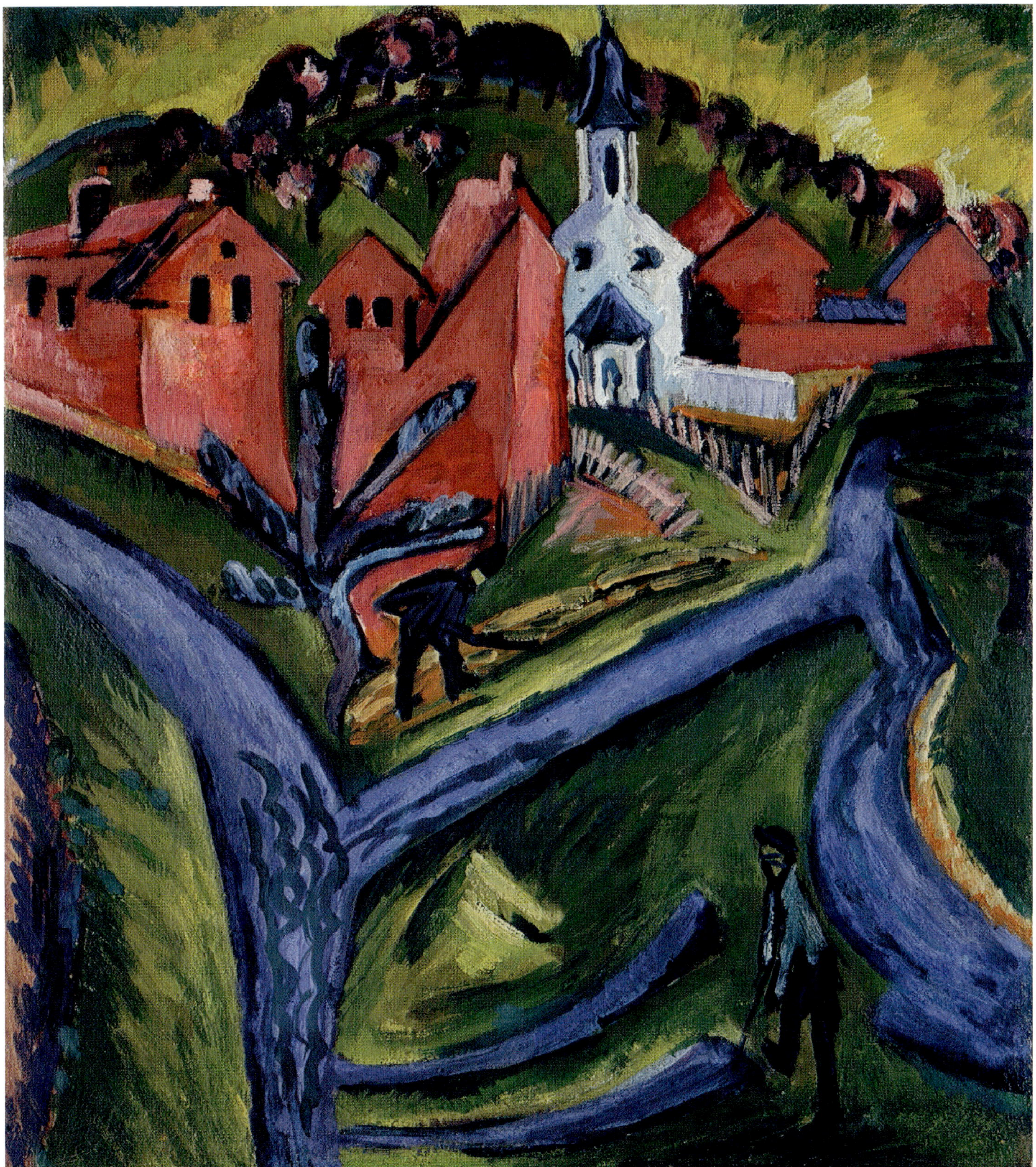

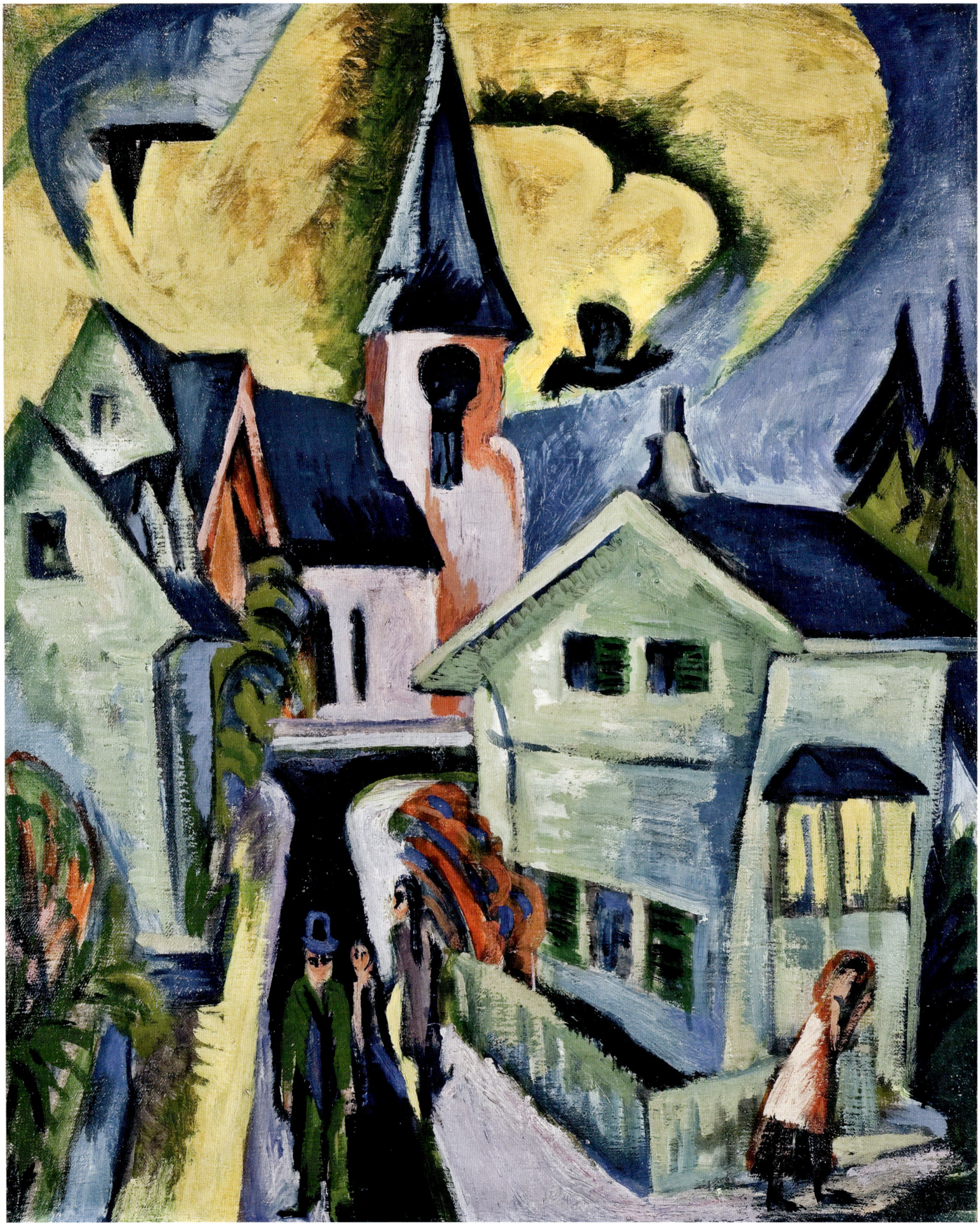

Cat. 66

Königstein with Red Church, 1916
Oil on canvas

Private collection

Cat. 67

The Patient's Bath, 1916
Oil on board

Private collection

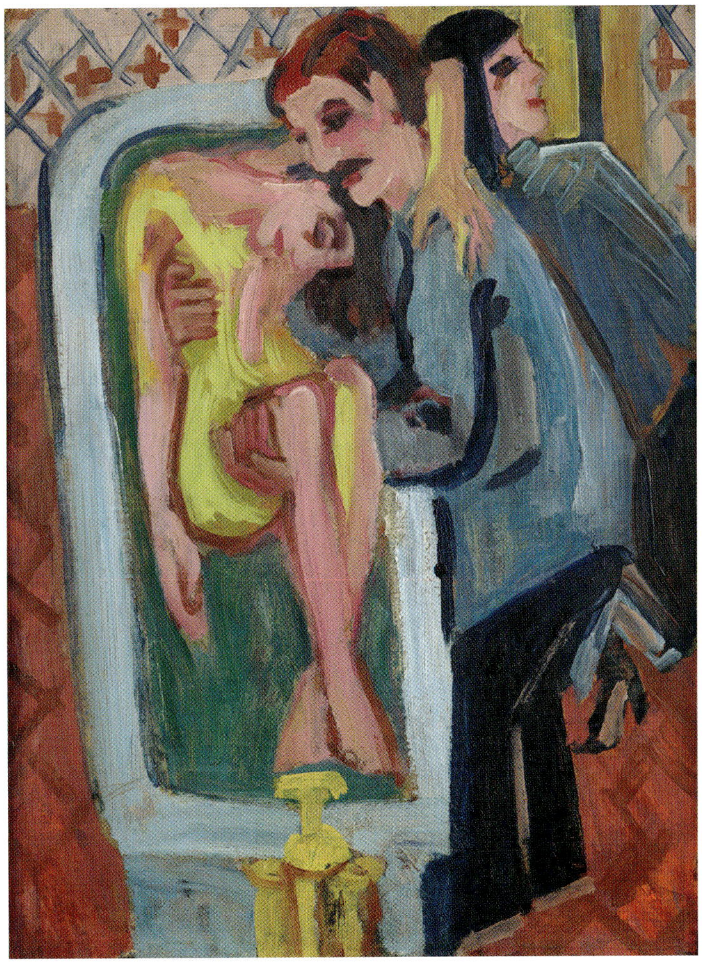

Cat. 64

Graef's Garden in Jena, 1916
Oil on canvas

Kunstsammlungen Chemnitz,
on permanent loan from the
Claus Hüppe Collection

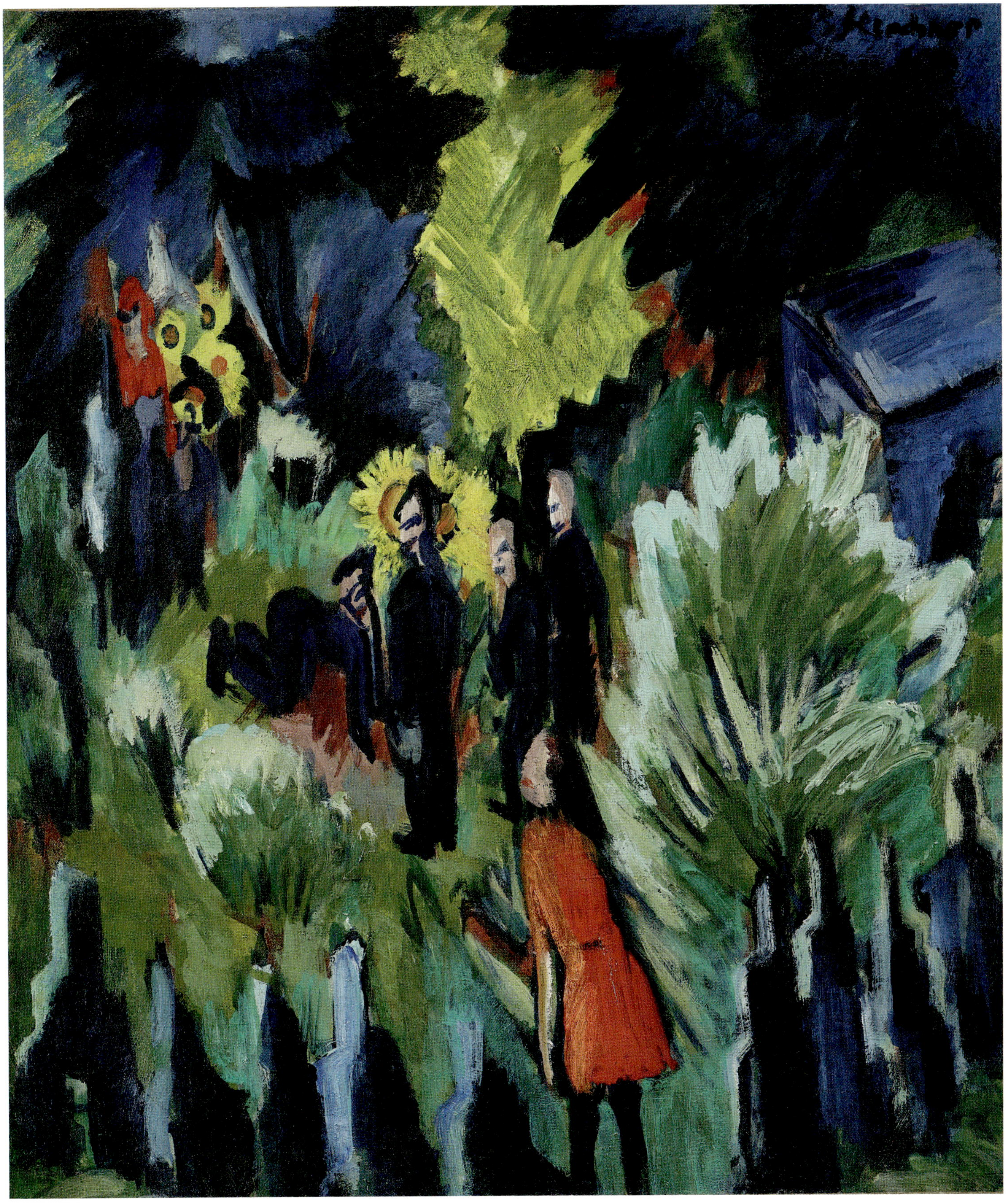

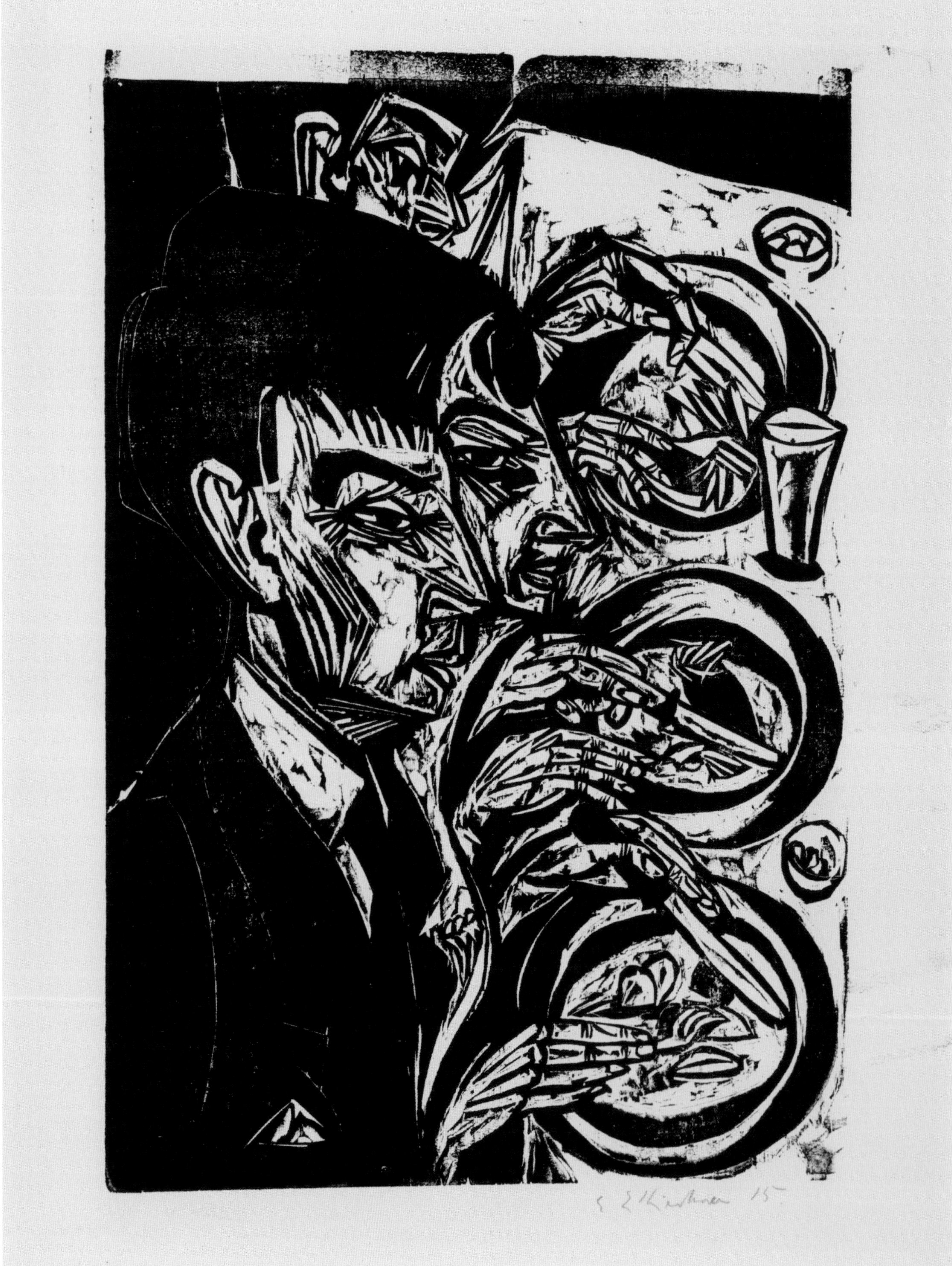

Cat. 126

Nervous Persons at Table (Kohnstamm Sanatorium), 1916
Woodcut on cardboard

Kassel, Museumslandschaft Hessen Kassel, Graphische Sammlung, Städtischer Kunstbesitz

Cat. 125

Self-Portrait, Drawing, 1916
Line and surface-tone etching on zinc, on copperplate printing paper

Brücke-Museum, Berlin

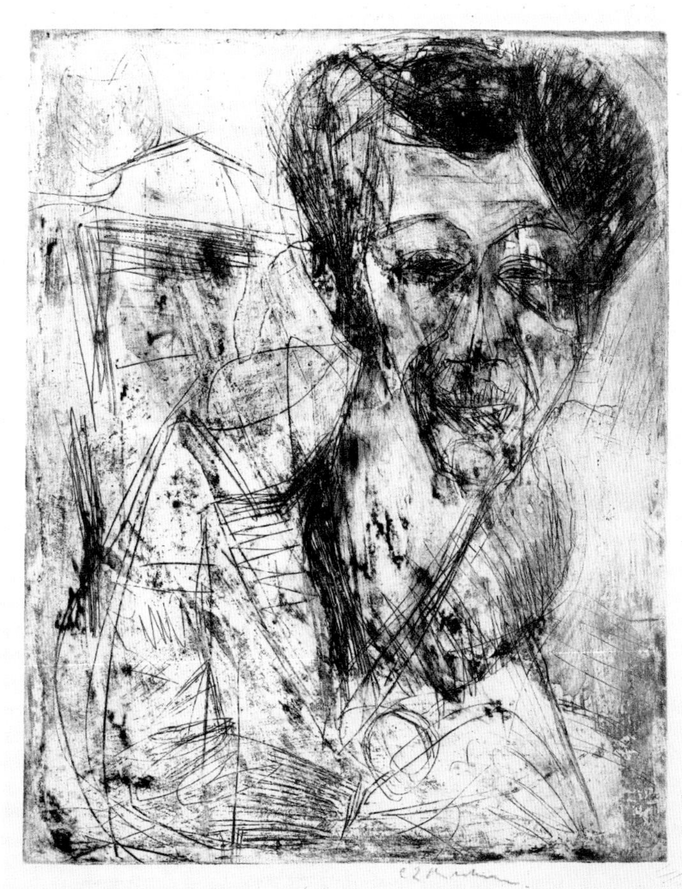

Cat. 128

Head of Henry van de Velde, dark, 1917
Woodcut on blotting paper

Kunsthaus Zürich,
Grafische Sammlung,
Gift of the artist

Cat. 129

Head of Eberhard Grisebach (en face), 1917
Woodcut on blotting paper

Private collection

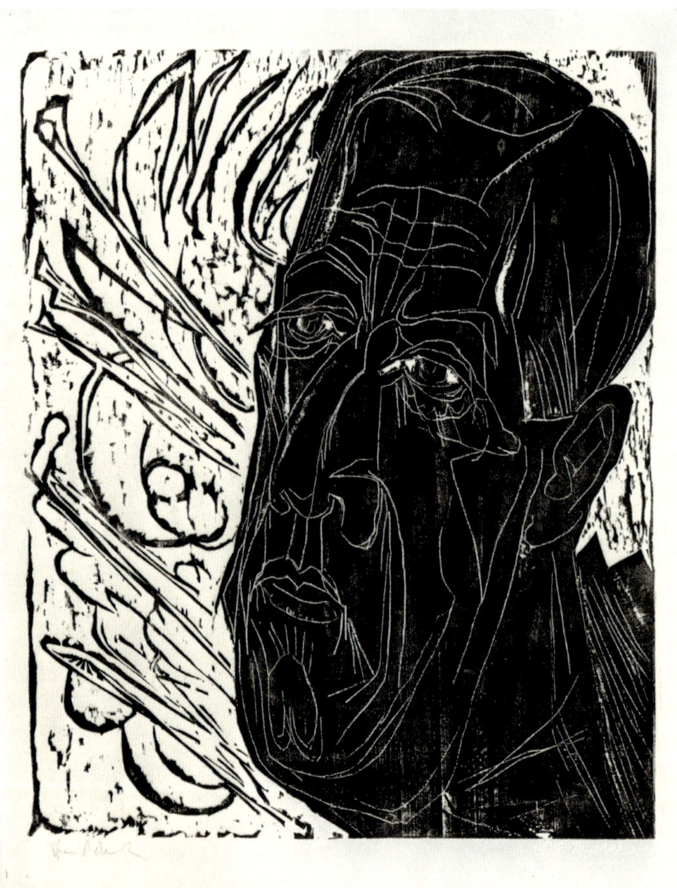

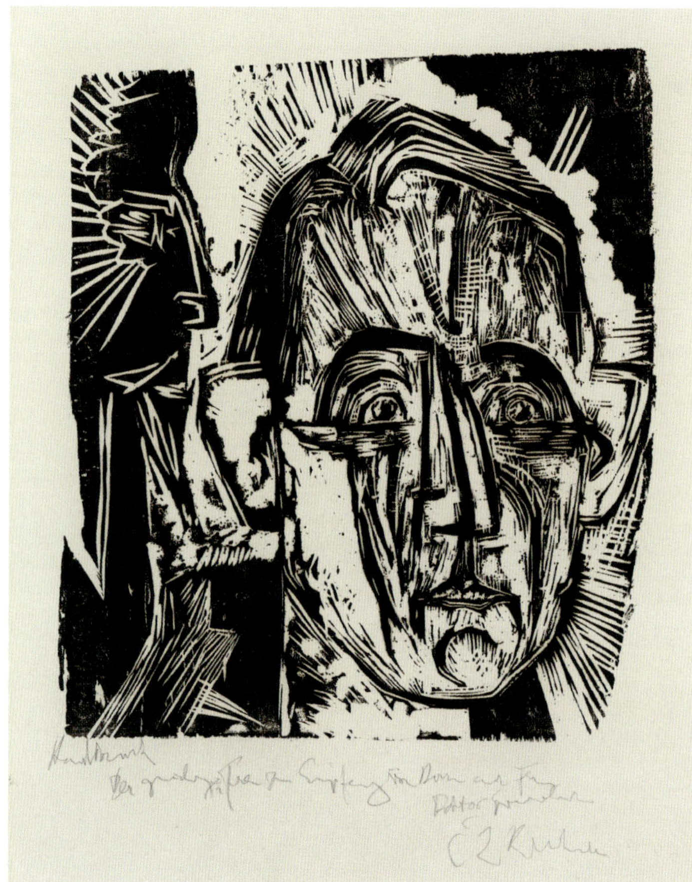

Cat. 69

Head of Erna, 1917
Oil on canvas

Kirchner Museum Davos,
Gift of the Baumgart-Möller
Foundation 2000

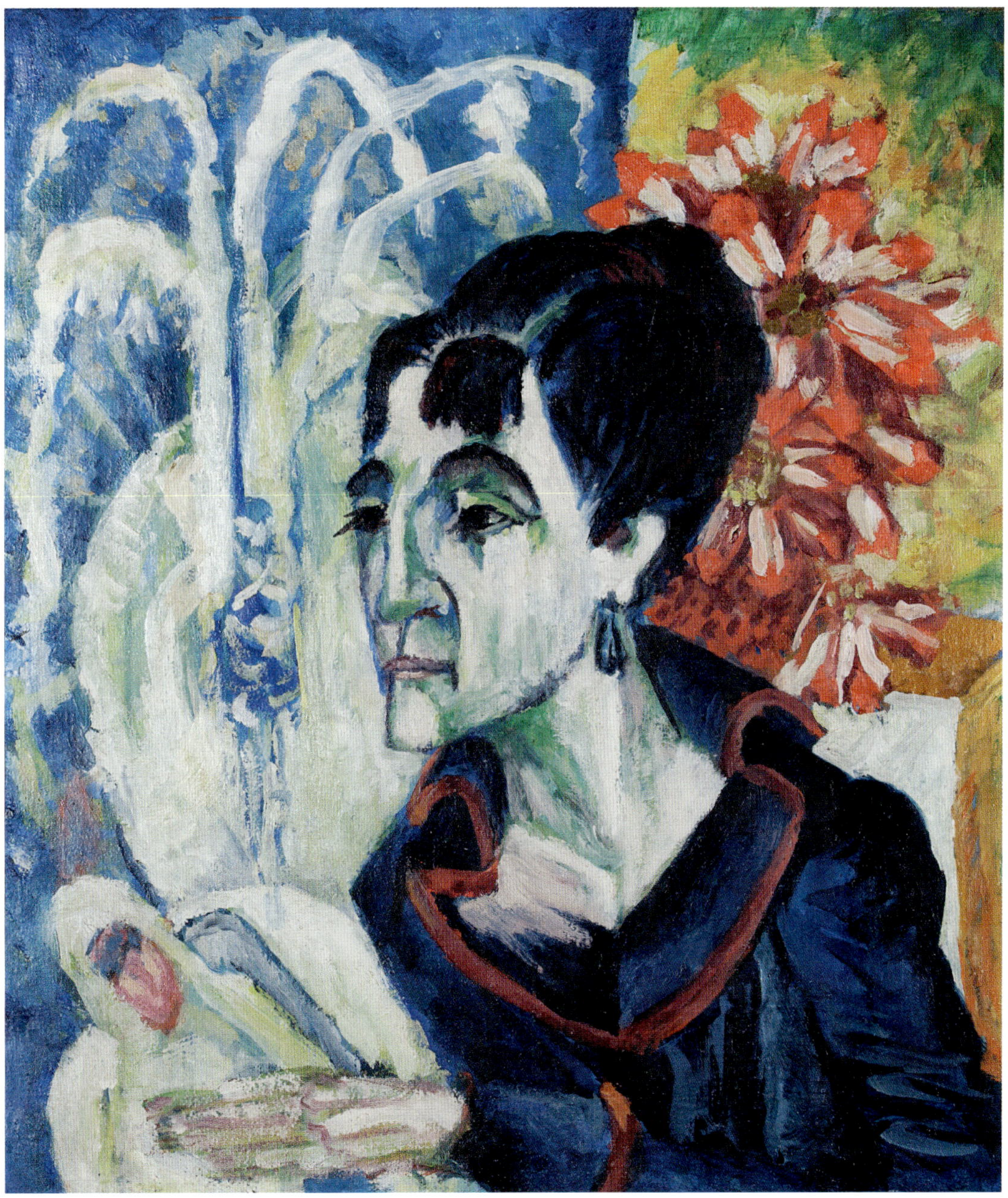

Cat. 134

Double page (Fol. 5–6) in Sketchbook 54, 1917–1918
Oilcloth booklet

Kirchner Museum Davos, Gift of the Ernst Ludwig Kirchner Estate 1990

Cat. 102

Self-Portrait in Morphine Rush, 1917
Reed pen and ink on gessoed paper

Brücke-Museum, Berlin

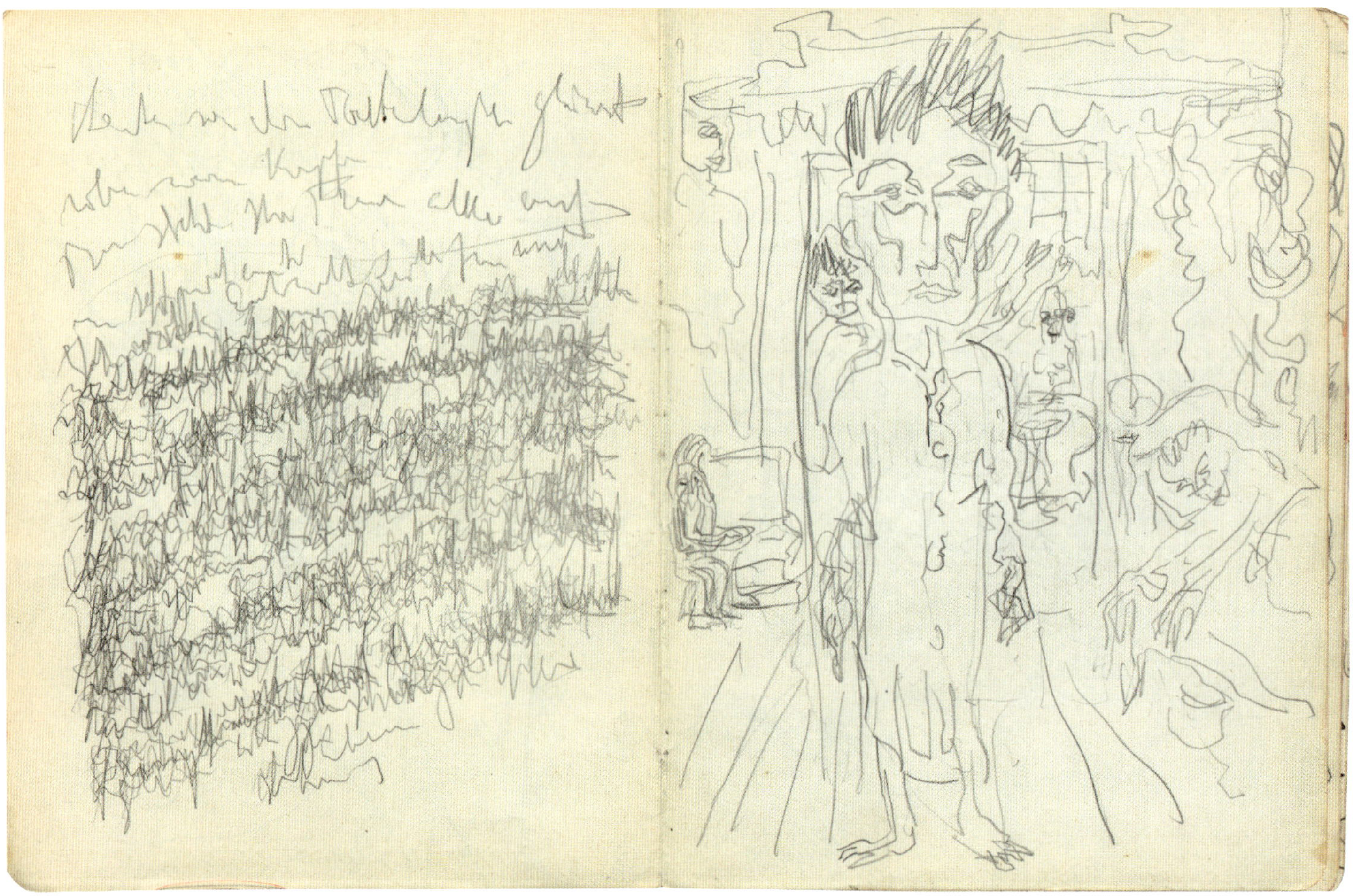

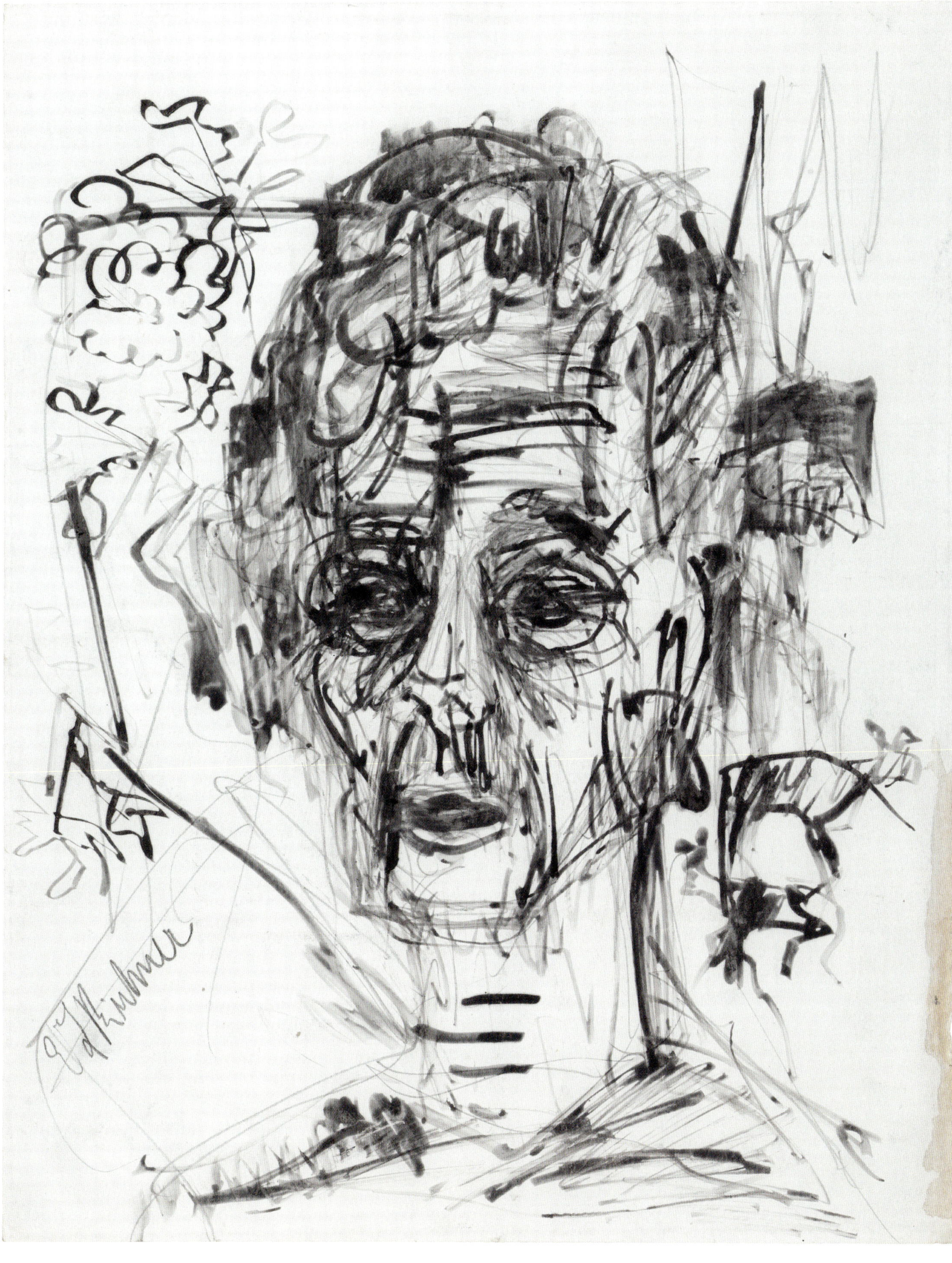

From Berlin to Davos

6

After Kirchner's condition had worsened despite his release from military service and repeated stays in sanatoriums in Königstein and Berlin, he first went to Davos in January 1917 to be treated by Dr Lucius Spengler. This first stay was brief. After only two weeks Kirchner departed in haste because he found it too cold. In early May 1917 he returned and spent the summer in the care of a nurse in the Rüesch hut on the Stafelalp above Davos Frauenkirch. His heavy misuse of medications had weakened him physically. Kirchner suffered paralysis and a lack of feeling in his hands and feet, which made any kind of artistic work more difficult. In September 1917, at the urging of Henry van de Velde, he transferred to Kreuzlingen, where he stayed for almost a year in order to receive treatment from Dr Ludwig Binswanger at the Bellevue Sanatorium.

At first the move to Switzerland, where Kirchner would spend the rest of his life, did not occasion a change in style. Some of his early Swiss works feature the same fan-like application of pigment and similar changes of perspective as in the paintings produced in Berlin. The shift to a flatter, more ornamental style with less agitated brushwork would only appear after 1921, as he began to recover both physically and mentally.

In Switzerland he took up subject matter he had not dealt with before. Though at first he mainly produced portraits of the people taking care of him as well as a number of self-portraits, his picture motifs soon register his new immediate surroundings: mountain landscapes, their inhabitants and animals in their everyday lives. One of the first of the paintings inspired by his new surroundings is *Rhaetian Railway in Snow* p.240. It was probably on such a train that he himself had first travelled through snow and cold weather to Davos. The painting pictures a locomotive with a blue roof and red railway carriage heading up the mountain in front of a steep slope. The smoke issuing from its smokestack shows it to be moving and immediately blends with the clouds and the snow. The painting achieves its dynamism from the curve the train makes from left to right. Beside the locomotive an overlarge figure stands isolated in the snow, probably the conductor, who is not watching the train but staring out of the picture. In the background one sees a row of trees that are still green, despite the deep snow. The rest of the picture is painted only sketchily, almost non-objectively, the background delineated with undefined spots of colour. The pigments are greatly thinned and applied with various types of brush strokes, not completely opaque. The fanning out of forms and the agitated brushwork recall the Berlin street scenes. This piece was then painted in his Berlin studio, where in December 1917 Karl Ernst Osthaus chose it for the Museum Folkwang he had founded, and with other paintings made the first museum purchase of Kirchner's work.

Between 1917 and 1919 Kirchner painted a series of Alpine landscapes depicting his own dwelling and its views of the landscape p.241–243. The painting *Stafelalp in Snow* p.243 is one such view from the mountain looking out over the surrounding houses. In the distance one can see the characteristic shape of the Tinzenhorn. In the foreground on the right a male figure is wading through the snow with a horse. Both are captured as mere silhouettes. The picture space is organised from different points of view rather than from one fixed spot. This is obvious from the shadows on the roofs of the houses, which are cast in different directions. The painting is also striking for its unusual colouring: the snow appears pink in the foreground and a bright yellow in the middle distance. Kirchner used the same green for the firs and for the sky, in which there are a few pinkish-orange clouds.

Inspired by moonlit nights in the mountains, which deeply impressed him, Kirchner created paintings, woodcuts and drawings of landscapes with a rising or setting moon. *Moonrise on the Stafelalp* p.241. pictures three houses in red-blue as seen from the artist's own hut. They seem to have been shifted close to the distant mountains, which are depicted in the same green as the meadow in the foreground. Two figures are lying in the meadow, and at the right edge stand three figures dressed in blue: they are elongated and greatly simplified, and their clothing recalls that of the pedestrians in the Berlin street scenes. The moon, which here looks more like the sun, is rising behind stylised mountain peaks and, with its halo of alternating orange and pink, seems huge against the sky.

Although Kirchner's condition was considered hopeless at the time, it is astonishing how much he accomplished during his stays in Davos and Kreuzlingen, despite poor coordination and bouts of paralysis. Among the most impressive works from this time is a series of woodcut portraits of visitors, patients and himself, including *Head of the Invalid—Self-Portrait as an Invalid* p.65. It is a depressing composition. In a constricted picture space the artist unsparingly depicts himself with a narrow, elongated head, sunken cheeks, deep creases in his forehead and slanting eyes that gaze in different directions. Most impressive are the hands with splayed fingers that he holds twisted in front of his chest—symbolising his limited mobility. Because of the paralysis, in these years Kirchner mainly carved his wood blocks in short, strong gouges with the goat's foot, a carving tool with a V-shaped blade. The restless rhythm and the changing direction of the lines deform his face and convey to the viewer a sense of the artist's suffering. At times Kirchner gave up hope of ever recovering and even wrote his will. Thoughts of death also directly inspired another woodcut. In *Self-Portrait with Dancing Death* p.245 the artist's body is atrophied and his head, seen in profile, is overly large. The back of his head, or rather his brain, is occupied by Death, depicted as a dancing skeleton; his legs replace the body in this emblematic view of himself. Death has taken over the artist's mind.

After a year's treatment in Kreuzlingen his condition improved to the point that he was again able to spend the summer on the Stafelalp. The painting *Alpine Kitchen* p.247 provides an impression of Kirchner's simple existence. In it he shows the interior of the hut—with its spare, rustic furnishings—in which he lived from July to mid-September 1918. On the left of the space is a cooking stove and in the foreground on the right a person is sitting, bent over a table. It is unclear whether this is the artist drawing or Erna busy writing or embroidering. The vanishing lines on the ceiling, the floor and the wall cupboard on the right lead the viewer's gaze towards the open door with its view of the mountains in the background.

Cat. 68

Rhaetian Railway in Snow, 1917
Oil on canvas

Deutsche Bank Collection

Cat. 71

Moonrise on the Stafelalp, 1917
Oil on canvas

Kirchner Museum Davos, on loan from the Rosemarie Ketterer Foundation

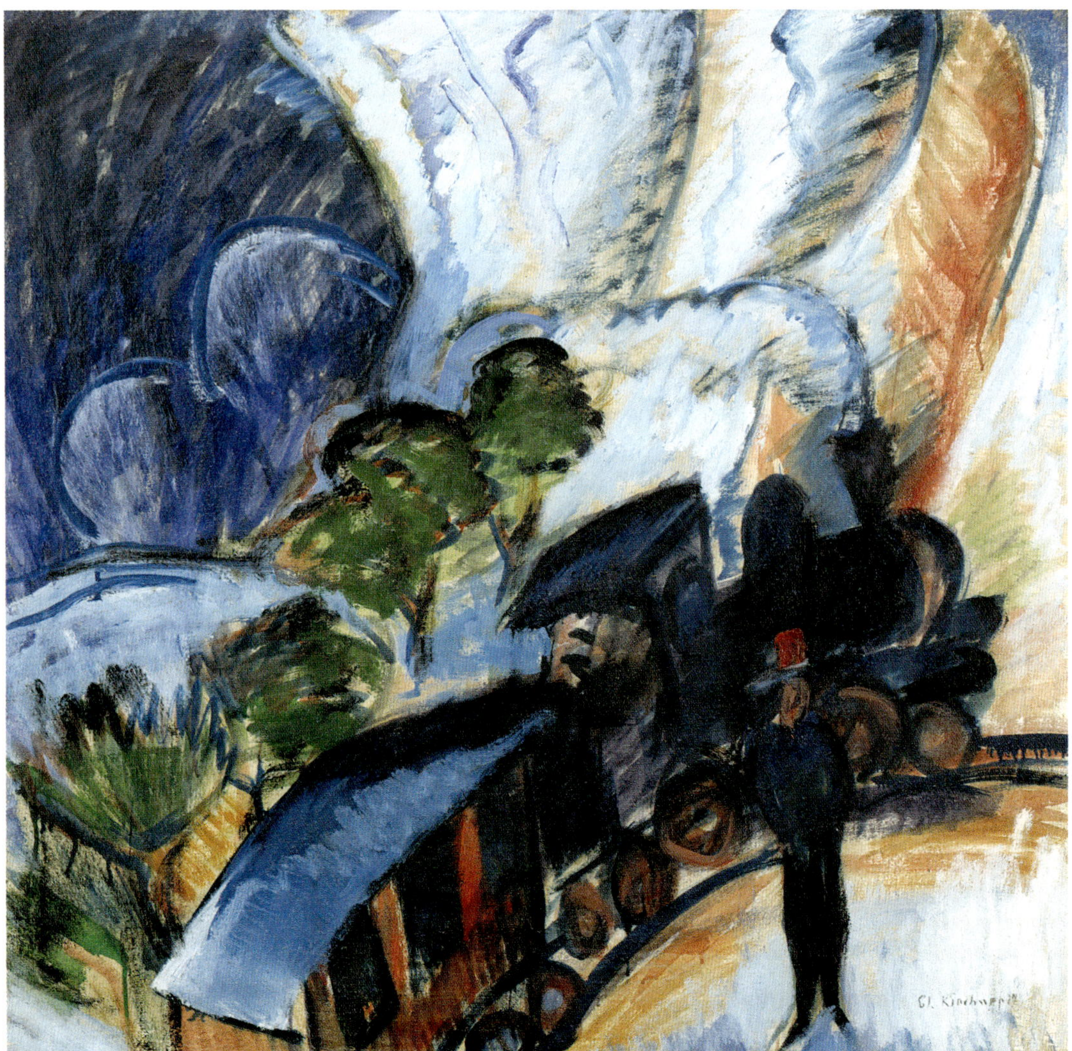

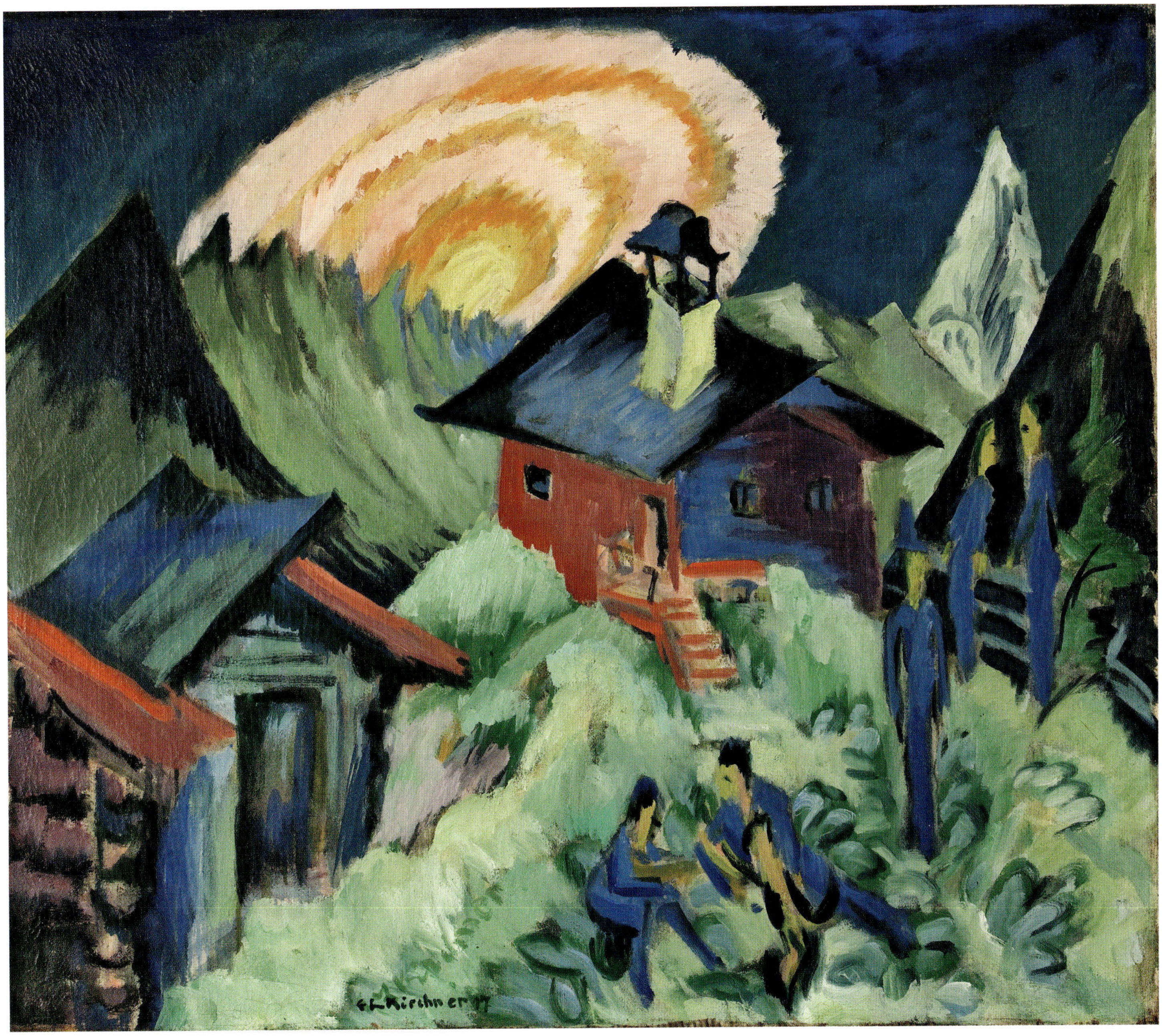
E L Kirchner 17

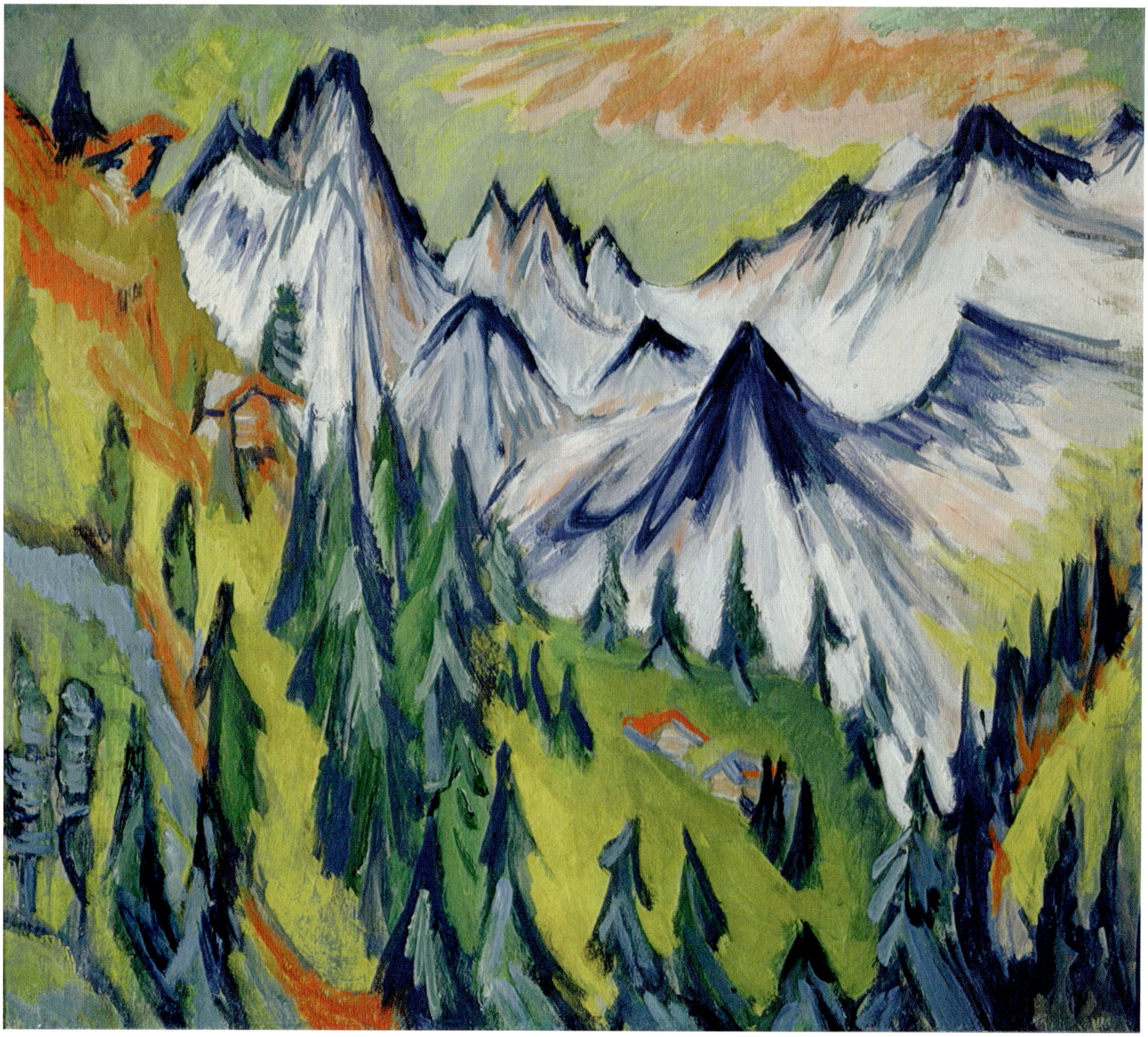

Cat. 72

Mountain Peaks, 1918
Oil on canvas

Private collection

Cat. 70

Stafelalp in Snow, 1917
Oil on cloth

E. W. K. Collection, Bern/Davos

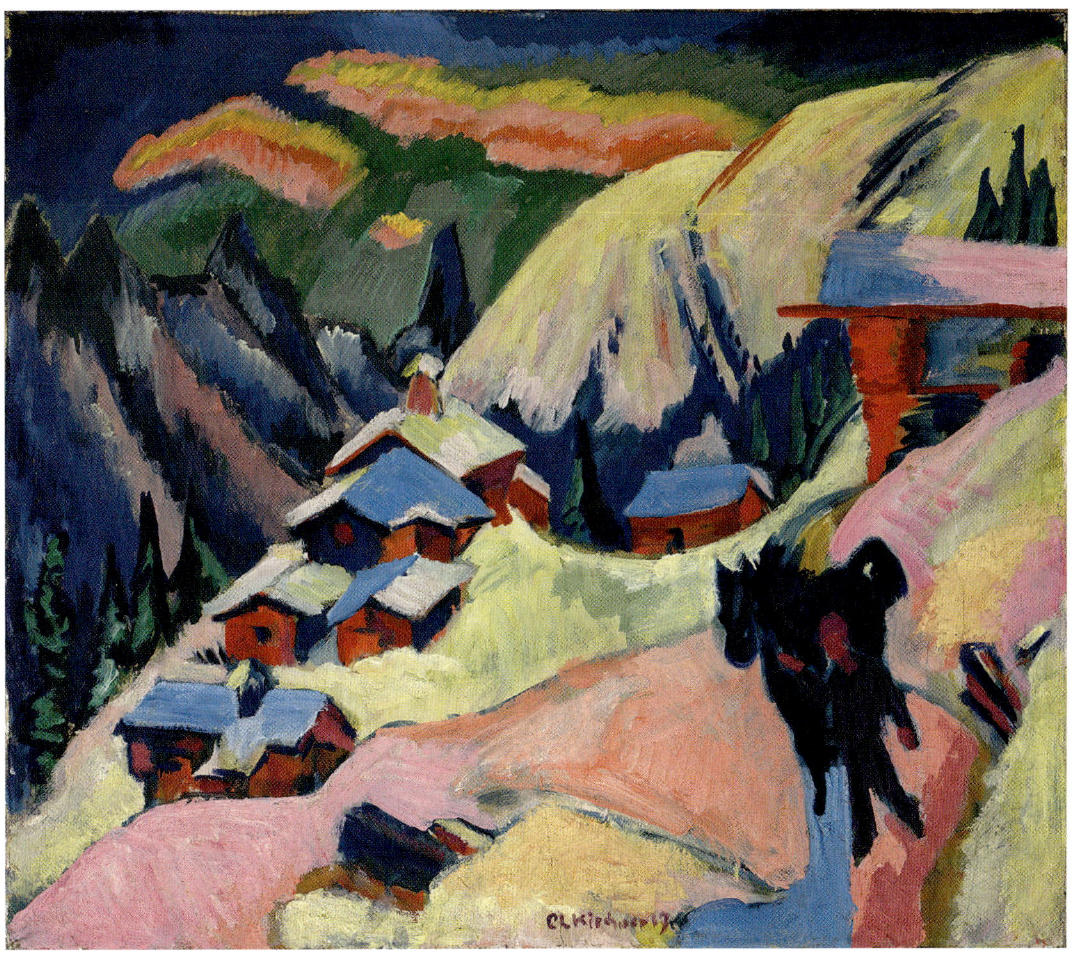

Cat. 127

Three Paths, Stafelalp, 1917
Woodcut on grey blotting paper

Kunsthaus Zürich,
Grafische Sammlung

Cat. 131

Self-Portrait with Dancing Death, 1918
Woodcut on paper

Museum Folkwang, Essen

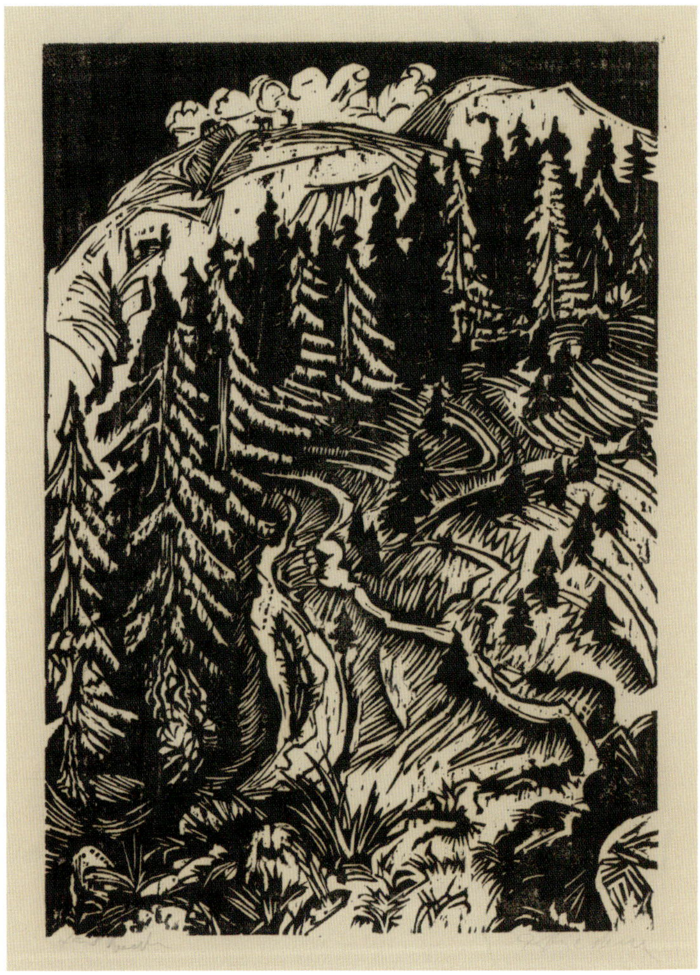

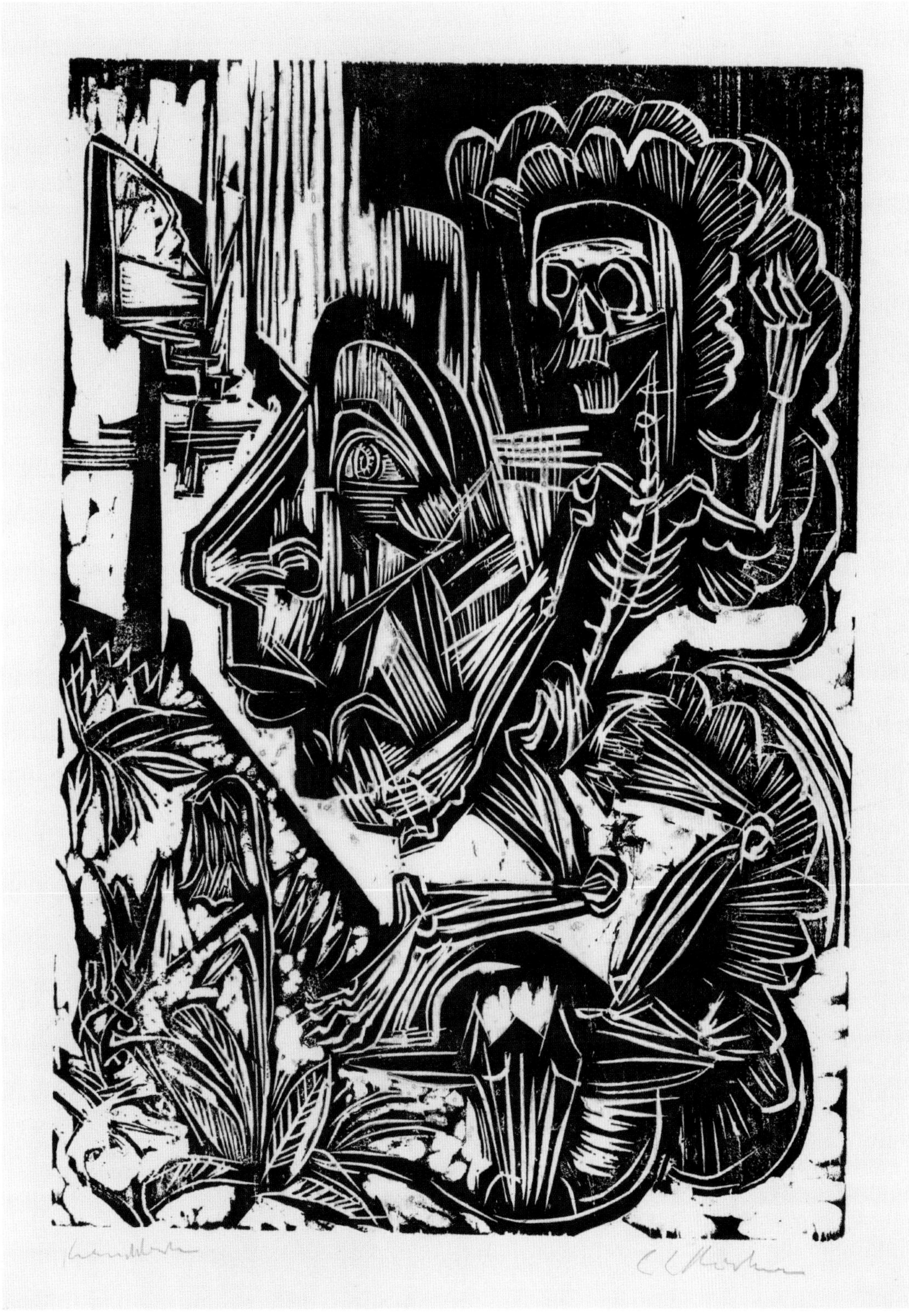

Cat. 73

Alpine Kitchen, 1918
Oil on canvas

Museo Thyssen-Bornemisza, Madrid

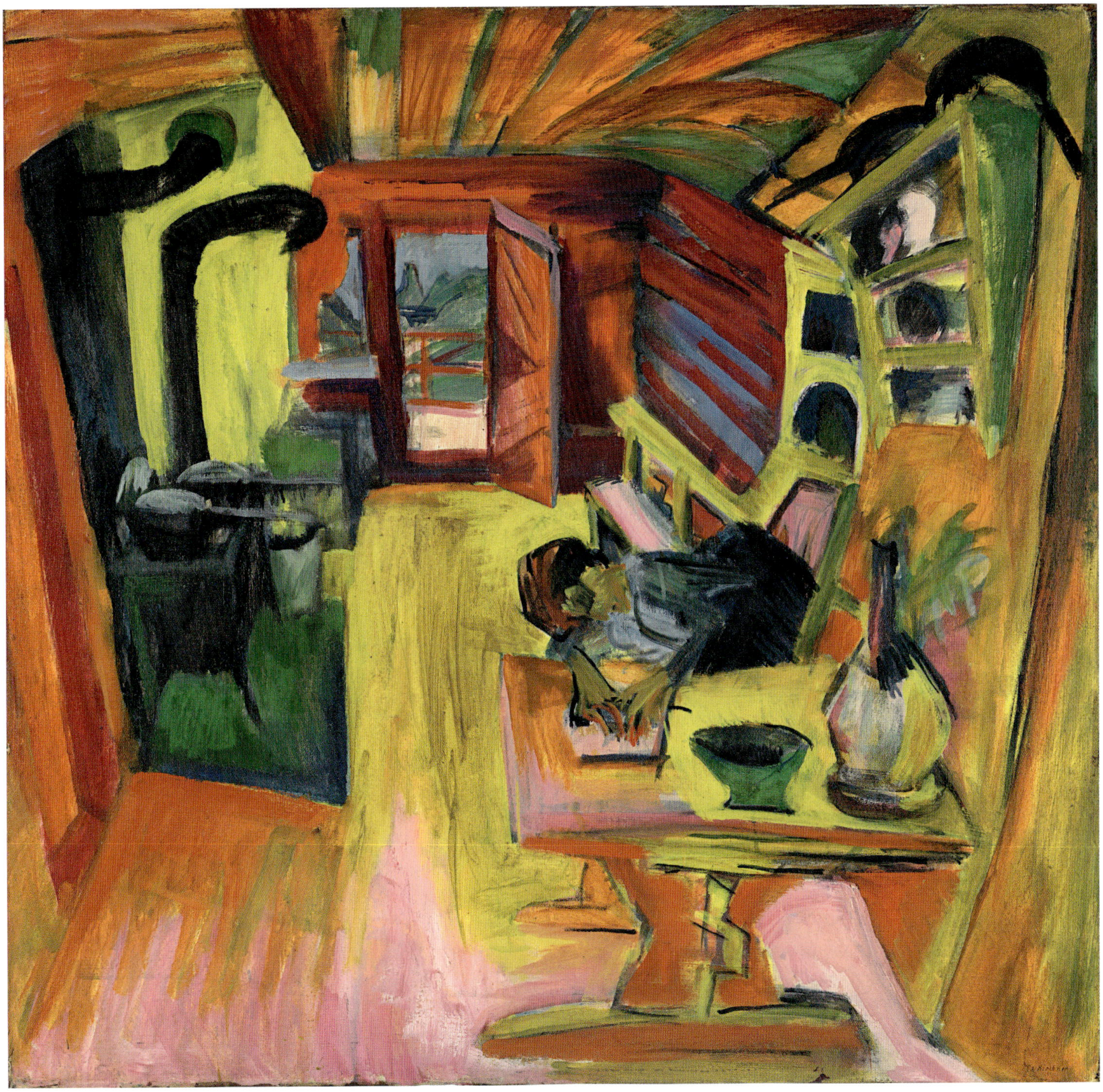

Vibrant Metropolis / Idyllic Nature
Kirchner—The Berlin Years

Appendix

Biography Ernst Ludwig Kirchner (1880–1938)

This biography draws in large part on the extensive chronologies by Hans Bolliger in his *Ernst Ludwig Kirchner: Zeichnungen und Pastelle,* ed. Roman Norbert Ketterer, with the collaboration of Wolfgang Henze (Stuttgart, 1979); by Roland Scotti in *Ernst Ludwig Kirchner,* ed. Magdalena M. Moeller and Roland Scotti, exh. cat. Kunstforum Wien and Kunsthalle der Hypo-Kulturstifung (Munich, 1998); by Birgit Gudat in *Ernst Ludwig Kirchner: Mountain Life: The Early Years in Davos 1917–1926,* exh. cat. Kunstmuseum Basel (Ostfildern-Ruit, 2003); by Hyun Ae Lee, *"Aber ich stelle doch nochmals einen neuen Kirchner auf": Ernst Ludwig Kirchners Davoser Spätwerk* (Ph.D. diss., 2007/08; Münster, 2008); by Lucius Grisebach in *Ernst Ludwig Kirchner,* exh. cat. Museum der Moderne Salzburg (Clogne, 2009); and in Hans Delfs (ed.), *Ernst Ludwig Kirchner: Der gesamte Briefwechsel,* 4 vols. (Zurich, 2010).

1880–1900

Kirchner is born in Aschaffenburg as the oldest of three brothers on 6 May 1880. His father Ernst (1847–1921) is a civil engineer, builder and inventor in the field of papermaking; his mother Maria Elise née Franke (1852–1928) comes from a merchant family. In 1886 the family move to Frankfurt am Main, then in 1887 to Perlen, near Lucerne. In 1890 they move again to Chemnitz, where Kirchner's father assumes a director's post at the C. G. Haubold papermaking machine factory. Two years later he becomes a lecturer at the state technical school, where he teaches papermaking, amongst other things, until 1914.

1901–1902/03

In 1901, after finishing high school, Kirchner follows his father's wishes and begins studying architecture at Dresden's Königlich Sächsische Technische Hochschule (Royal Saxon Technical College). But he really aspires to become a painter. He produces his first independent paintings in 1902/03.

1903

After earning an intermediate diploma in April, he transfers to the Königlich Bayerische Technische Hochschule (Royal Bavarian Technical College) in Munich for the winter semester 1903/4. In Munich he takes courses in composition and life drawing under professors Wilhelm von Debschitz (1871–1948) and Hermann Obrist (1862–1927), as well as the professional course in graphic arts taught by Hugo Steiner-Prag at the private Versuchs- und Lehranstalt für Angewandte und Freie Kunst (Research and Teaching Institute for Fine and Applied Arts). In October he takes a study trip to Nuremberg, where he marvels at Albrecht Dürer's original printing blocks in the Germanisches Nationalmuseum. The 8th exhibition of the Munich artists' group Phalanx is presented from November to December; there he sees prints from Julius Meier-Graefe's *Germinal* portfolio, including works by Gauguin, Van Gogh and Vallotton.

1904

The 10th Phalanx exhibition in Munich, including works by Signac, van Rysselberghe, Vuillard and Vallotton, runs from the end of March to the beginning of May. Kirchner returns to Dresden and resumes his architecture studies in the summer semester. Together with his fellow student Fritz Bleyl (1880–1966) he goes on his first outings to the landscape of ponds around the baroque Moritzburg Chateau near Dresden. He becomes acquainted with Erich Heckel (1883–1970) and produces his first woodcuts.

1905

On 7 June, together with his fellow students Erich Heckel, Fritz Bleyl and Karl Schmidt-Rottluff (1884–1976), he founds the artists' association Brücke. They initiate the practice of "quarter-of-an-hour nudes", drawings from nude models either in his studio or in nature. On 1 July he completes his study as a graduate engineer. In November the first Brücke exhibition is held in the art shop P. H. Beyer and Son in Leipzig, with works on paper. By the time the group disbands in 1913 it will have presented seventy Brücke exhibitions and participated collectively in thirty more. In November the Galerie Arnold in Dresden exhibits fifty paintings by Van Gogh.

1906

Brücke formulates its programme, published as both a typographic notice and a Kirchner woodcut. In February the Sächsischer Kunstverein (Saxon Art Society) in Dresden presents a show with works by Edvard Munch. On 24 September the first show of Brücke paintings opens in Karl-Max Seifert's lamp factory in Dresden-Löbtau. Brücke opens up to passive members (collectors and friends), who are to receive an annual portfolio of prints. The Swiss painter Cuno Amiet (1868–1961), Emil Nolde (1867–1956) and Max Pechstein (1881–1955) become active members. Kirchner produces his first etchings and lithographs as well as his first sculptures, mostly small-format works in stone. In all probability he begins visiting Dresden's Völkerkundemuseum (ethnology museum): Hans Frisch (1875–1941), a friend from his youth in Chemnitz, has worked there since 1905. Doris Grosse (called Dodo; 1884–after 1936), a modiste from Dresden, becomes Kirchner's model and girlfriend (until 1911).

1907

Kirchner carves the first Brücke members' list in wood. Starting at the end of June the *I. Gemälde-Kollektion* (1st Painting Collection) is presented as Brücke's first show at the Museum Folkwang in Hagen. During the summer Kirchner works with Max Pechstein in Goppeln, near Dresden. In September Brücke presents its first exhibition in Dresden's Kunstsalon Emil Richter. In the early autumn Kirchner takes over Erich Heckel's studio (a former butcher's shop) at Berliner Strasse 60. Kirchner uses it as a live-in studio, and begins to make his own furniture and textiles for it.

1908

In January he presents a joint show with Karl Schmidt-Rottluff in the Kunstsalon August Dörbrandt in Braunschweig, and in May he visits the *Van Gogh* exhibition at the Kunstsalon Richter, with seventy-five paintings and twenty graphics. He enjoys his first stay on the Baltic Sea island of Fehmarn, accompanied by Hans Frisch and his sister Emy (1884–1975), who will later marry Karl Schmidt-Rottluff. Kirchner learns photography from her. In September the Kunstsalon Richter in Dresden runs parallel shows, one with works by the Fauves, the other a Brücke show. Around the end of the year Kees van Dongen (1877–1968), from the circle of the Paris Fauves, becomes a Brücke member.

1909

In January, together with Max Pechstein and Karl Schmidt-Rottluff, he visits the Matisse show in Paul Cassirer's gallery in Berlin. He arranges his first longer stays at the Moritzburg Ponds near Dresden (in the summer with Erich Heckel and Pechstein; in October, alone). The young girl Fränzi (actually Lina Franziska) Fehrmann becomes Brücke's most important model. As of 1 November Kirchner's address is Berliner Strasse 80, where he again sets up a live-in studio with furniture and textiles he has designed himself. In November he visits the extensive Cézanne exhibition at the Galerie Paul Cassirer in Berlin. While in Berlin, he visits Pechstein, who has moved to the metropolis in August 1908. He carves his first sculptures in wood.

1910

In March he works with Erich Heckel at Max Pechstein's in Berlin. He visits the 20th Exhibition of the Berlin Secession with works by Henri Matisse. Kirchner, along with the other Brücke artists, joins the Neue Secession (New Secession) in Berlin; at that time Pechstein is serving as president of the new artists' association. In May, in Berlin, Kirchner meets the painter Otto Mueller (1874–1930), who becomes a member of Brücke. He spends the summer at the Mortizburg Ponds together with Heckel, Pechstein and their models. In September the most important Brücke exhibition to date opens at the Galerie Arnold in Dresden; their first catalogue appears with twenty woodcut illustrations. At the same time Galerie Arnold presents a show with works by Paul Gauguin, for which Kirchner designs the poster. In October, in Hamburg, he visits the regional court director and art collector Gustav Schiefler (1857–1935) and Karl Schmidt-Rottluff's friend the art historian Rosa Schapire (1874–1954). In November he enters into correspondence with Karl Ernst Osthaus (1874–1921), the founder of the Museum Folkwang in Hagen. In December he becomes a member of the Deutscher Künstlerbund (German Artists' League).

Cat. 141

Self-portrait in the live-in studio in Berlin-Friedenau, 1913/1915
Glass negative

Kirchner Museum Davos,
Gift of the Ernst Ludwig
Kirchner Estate 2001

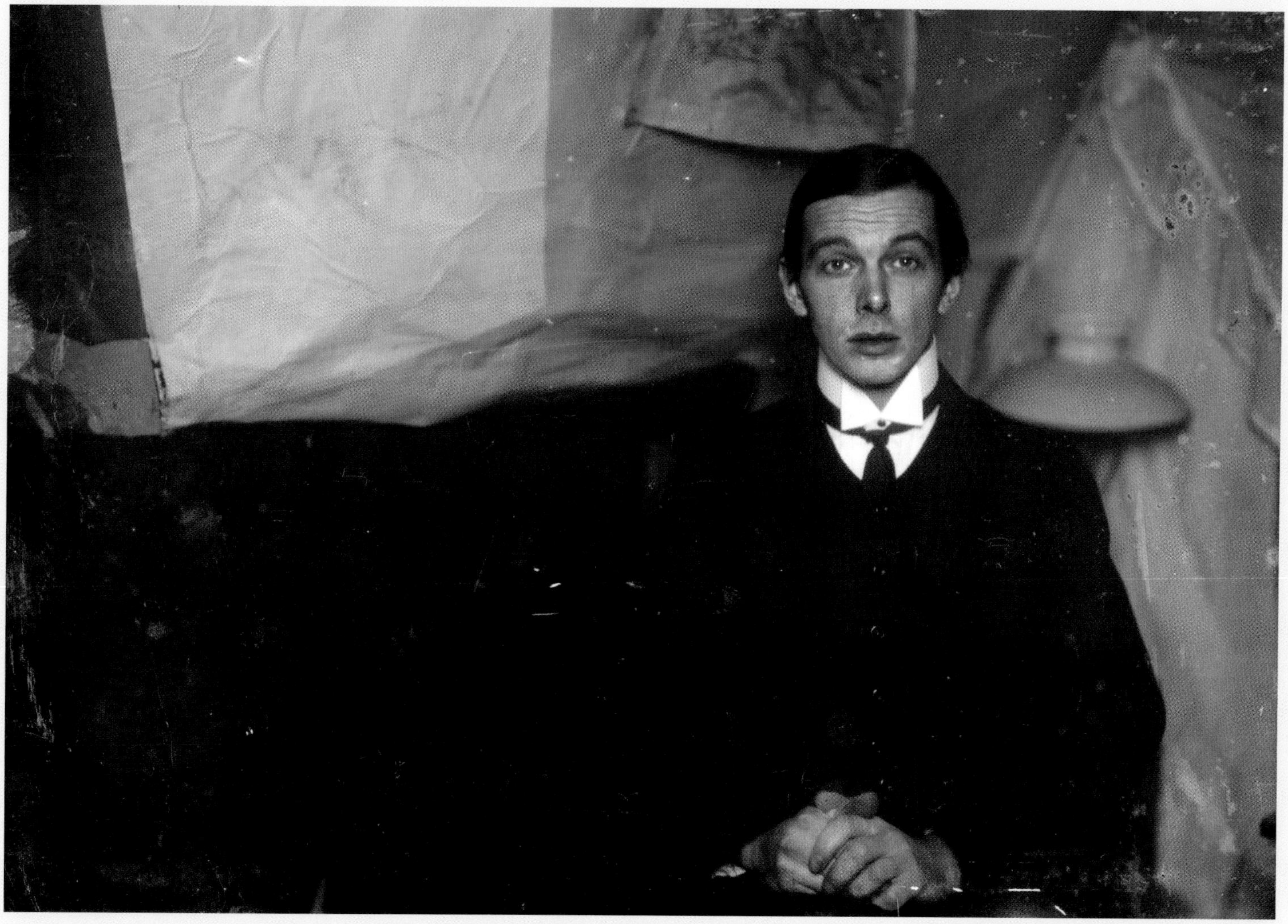

The Berlin Years 1911–1917

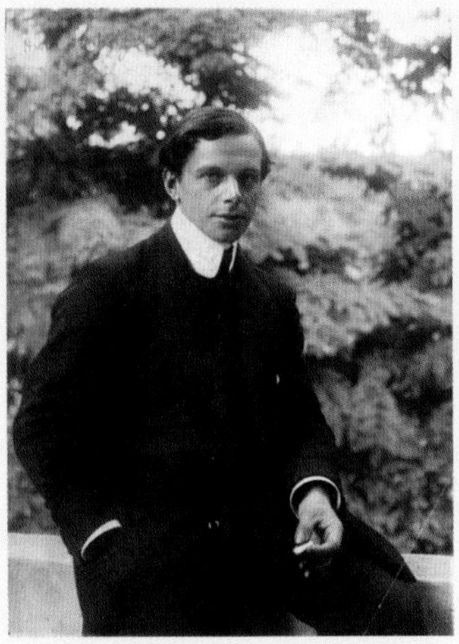

Aura Hertwig-Brendel
Ernst Ludwig Kirchner, 1913/14
Pigment print on barite paper (original: vintage print), dimensions unknown

E.W.K. Collection, Bern/Davos, Courtesy Kirchner Museum, Davos

1911

In January he is in Berlin, where he frequently gets together with Otto Mueller and Max Pechstein. In February and March the large travelling Brücke exhibition *I. Kollektion 1911* (1st Collection 1911) is mounted at the Kunstverein Jena; it is reviewed positively by the archaeologist and art historian Botho Graef (1857–1917), who, as of 1914, will become a kind of father figure for Kirchner. He stays for the last time at the Moritzburg Ponds together with Erich Heckel. He considers moving to Paris, but instead, at more or less the same time, moves with Karl Schmidt-Rottluff and Heckel to Berlin in October. He rents a studio at Durlacher Strasse 14, where Pechstein has been living since 1908. There the two found the MUIM Institute (Moderner Unterricht in Malerei/Modern Instruction in Painting); its only pupils are Hans Gewecke (1886–?) and Werner Gothein (1890–1968). He gets to know the poet Simon Guttmann (1891–1990), the man who actually "discovered" Georg Heym (1887–1912) and the co-founder of Der Neue Club and the Neopathetisches Cabaret. Among the club's regulars are Kurt Hiller (1885–1972), Erwin Loewenson (1888–1963) and Jacob van Hoddis (1887–1942), who have presented public lectures and recitation evenings there since June 1910. Between April 1911 and March 1912 the journal *Der Sturm,* published by Herwarth Walden (1878–1941), reproduces ten of Kirchner's woodcuts and one of his drawings. It is presumed that Kirchner meets the sisters Gerda (1893–1923) and Erna Schilling (1884–1945) before the year is out.

1912

Intensive exchanges between the artists' groups Der Blaue Reiter and Brücke. In February Kirchner participates in the *Der Blaue Reiter* exhibition at the Galerie Hans Goltz in Munich. In April a large Brücke exhibition is mounted in Berlin's Galerie Fritz Gurlitt, and from August to September the same show is presented in the Galerie Commeter in Hamburg. From mid-April to the end of May Herwarth Walden shows works by the Italian Futurists in his Sturm gallery. On 15 May Max Pechstein, having taken part in the exhibition of the Berlin Secession, is expelled from Brücke. The group is invited to the Sonderbund's International Art Exhibition in Cologne (25 May–30 September); within the framework of this exhibition Kirchner and Erich Heckel paint a chapel there. In Cologne Kirchner meets Edvard Munch (1863–1944). From there he visits the Museum Folkwang in Hagen to see about possible exhibitions there. In June/July he first considers moving to the Rhineland, where he hopes to find easier living conditions, but ends up staying in Berlin. He enjoys a second summer stay (from the end of July at the latest to at least mid-August) on the island of Fehmarn, this time with Erna Schilling, who is now his girlfriend, along with Heckel and his friend the dancer Sidi Riha (1891–1982). He makes the acquaintance of the writer and practising psychiatrist Alfred Döblin (1878–1957). In December the MUIM Institute is shut down for want of sufficient enrolment.

1913

Thanks to the Munich gallerist Hans Goltz (1873–1927), a painting of Kirchner's (Gordon 211) is included in the Armory Show in New York from February to March; the show then moves to Chicago and Boston. Kirchner composes the *Chronik KG Brücke* at the behest of the group's members, but owing to differences of opinion about this text, Brücke formally disbands on 27 May. Kirchner publishes a very few copies of the *Chronik* privately. He spends his third summer on Fehmarn with Erna Schilling (from mid-July at the latest to at least the end of September); there he is visited by Hans Gewecke, Werner Gothein, and Otto Mueller and his wife Maschka. In October he has his first one-man show at the Museum Folkwang in Hagen. In late October he moves to a larger studio apartment at Körnerstrasse 45 in Berlin-Friedenau and again he and Erna fix it up with their own handmade furnishings. In November he has a solo exhibition at the Galerie Gurlitt in Berlin. Kirchner illustrates Alfred Döblin's novella *Das Stiftsfräulein und der Tod* (The Canoness and Death), which will be published in Berlin in 1914. At the end of the year he works on illustrations for Döblin's one-act *Comtesse Mizzi* (Countess Mizzi).

1914

From February to March he has an important one-man show at the Kunstverein Jena at the invitation of its director, the philosopher Eberhard Grisebach (1880–1945). Through him Kirchner is introduced into the intellectual circle in Jena that had formed around the archaeologist Botho Graef and his lover Hugo Biallowons (1879–1916), the writer Karl Theodor Bluth (1892–1964) and the philosopher Rudolf Eucken (1846–1926) and his wife, the artist Irene Eucken (1863–1941), all of whom become important friends and patrons of his art. For the Cologne tobacco merchant Josef Feinhals, Kirchner designs a booth at the Werkbund exhibition in Cologne with wall textiles. In Cologne he becomes acquainted with Oskar Schlemmer (1888–1943). With Erna he spends a last summer on Fehmarn from the beginning of July to the outbreak of the war, when the island is declared an important strategic zone. He suffers increasingly from attacks of nervous anxiety and consumes large amounts of absinthe.

1915

In the spring Kirchner volunteers for the military, hoping to be able to choose which branch he would serve in. In July he is detailed to the mounted Mansfelder Field Artillery Regiment No. 75 in Halle (Saale). But he cannot stand the pressure of the training and suffers a mental and physical collapse; in August, thanks to the intervention of the regimental riding instructor and former passive member of Brücke Hans Fehr (1874–1961), he is placed on leave until 29 October. Kirchner spends this time in Berlin. Through the agency of Karl Ernst Osthaus he designs three wooden models for an "Iron Smithy", which is to be set up in Hagen as an emblem of the war; his project is rejected by the committee. Osthaus nevertheless purchases the three sculptural models for the Museum Folkwang—the first museum acquisition of Kirchner's sculpture. At the beginning of November he is declared unfit for service until he recovers. After 15 December he travels to the sanatorium of Dr Oskar Kohnstamm (1871–1917) in Königstein im Taunus, where he stays until roughly 23 January 1916. The chemist Carl Hagemann (1867–1940) in Frankfurt am Main becomes one of Kirchner's most important collectors. Despite his precarious condition, he begins making large-format paintings and carves woodcuts for the *Schlemihl* cycle pp. 220–225.

1916

At the beginning of the year, again thanks to a recommendation from Karl Ernst Osthaus, he works on the design for a relief in a house built by J. L. M. Lauweriks (1864–1932) in Hagen. Additional stays at the Kohnstamm Sanatorium (23 March–18 April and 20 June–15 July); between them alternating stays in Berlin, Halle and Jena. On 9 July his friend Hugo Biallowons is killed near Verdun. In Königstein he paints wall paintings with motifs of bathers in the sanatorium's well tower (destroyed after 1933). There is no improvement in his health. The sanatorium's director, Oskar Kohnstamm, diagnoses dependency on Veronal, a sleeping pill, in combination with alcoholism and an incipient morphine addiction. In Königstein he makes the acquaintance of the conductor Otto Klemperer (1885–1973) and the writer Carl Sternheim (1878–1942). During this time Kirchner is generously supported by private collectors like Carl Hagemann and Rosi (1869–1926) and Ludwig Fischer (1860–1922), by museum directors like Karl Ernst Osthaus, Ernst Gosebruch (1872–1953) and Eberhard Grisebach and by his circle of friends in Jena. In October the Frankfurt art dealer Ludwig Schames (1852–1922), to whom Kirchner has been introduced through Botho Graef, mounts a first show of his work. In December he stays for a time in Dr Edel's sanatorium in Berlin-Charlottenburg. At the latest by the end of the year Erna Schilling is signing her letters with the name Kirchner, although they are unmarried.

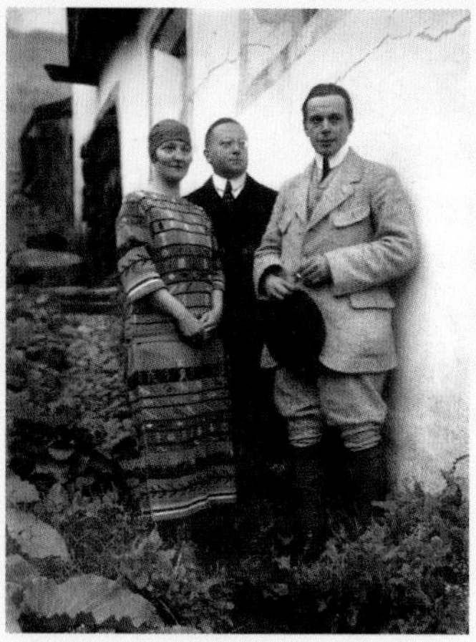

Ernst Ludwig Kirchner
Erna Schilling, Walter Kirchner and Ernst Ludwig Kirchner in front of the house "In den Lärchen", 1923
Glass negative, 24 × 18 cm

Kirchner Museum Davos, Gift of the Ernst Ludwig Kirchner Estate 2001

1917

He is released from Dr Edel's sanatorium at the intervention of his father. His first stay in Davos, from 19 January to 4 February, is arranged by Eberhard Grisebach. There he makes the acquaintance of the Spengler family of physicians; the daughter Lotte Spengler is Grisebach's wife. Because of the unusually severe cold Kirchner hastens back to Berlin. On his return trip he visits the collection and an exhibit with Swiss and German artists at the Kunsthaus Zürich. In March he has another solo exhibition at the Kunstverein Jena. On 9 April Kirchner's friend and mentor Botho Graef dies of a heart attack. In the spring Kirchner is contacted by Henry van de Velde (1863–1957), who had seen his work at the Kunstverein Jena in 1916; van de Velde tells him of his plan to establish a school in Uttwil, on Lake Constance, and Kirchner is prepared to be involved in it. On 8 May he begins a second stay in Davos, where he is treated by Dr Lucius Spengler (1858–1923) with the assistance of his wife Helene Spengler (1870–1943); he is placed on a regimen of withdrawal from his morphine and Veronal addiction that will continue until 1921. In late June he meets Henry van de Velde in person in Davos. For the summer he moves with a nurse into the Rüesch hut on the Stafelalp, where van de Velde visits him in late August. At van de Velde's urging on 15 September Kirchner transfers to the Bellevue Sanatorium in Kreuzlingen, run by the important psychiatrist Dr Ludwig Binswanger (1881–1966). There he becomes acquainted with the Winterthur collector Georg Reinhart (1877–1955) and the writer Leonhard Frank (1882–1961). In September Kirchner is visited by Edwin Redslob (1884–1973), who will later become German National Art Commissioner. At the beginning of his stay in Kreuzlingen Kirchner produces the drawings for a planned woodcut series on the Apocalypse pp. 79–91. Erna Kirchner has been staying in Berlin for the time being, tending to business and personal contacts; she arrives in Kreuzlingen for a month at the beginning of October. Suffering from paralysis in his limbs and impaired consciousness, the artist mainly produces graphics and drawings. In December Gustav Schiefler, on the suggestion of Graef and Grisebach, shares with Kirchner his plan of publishing a catalogue raisonné of his graphic works. Late in the year Eberhard Grisebach writes a monograph on Kirchner, which — with the exception of a single chapter — will not be published until 2014.

Cat. 147

Ernst Ludwig Kirchner,
Davos Frauenkirch, c.1919
Glass negative

Kirchner Museum Davos,
Gift of the Ernst Ludwig
Kirchner Estate 1992

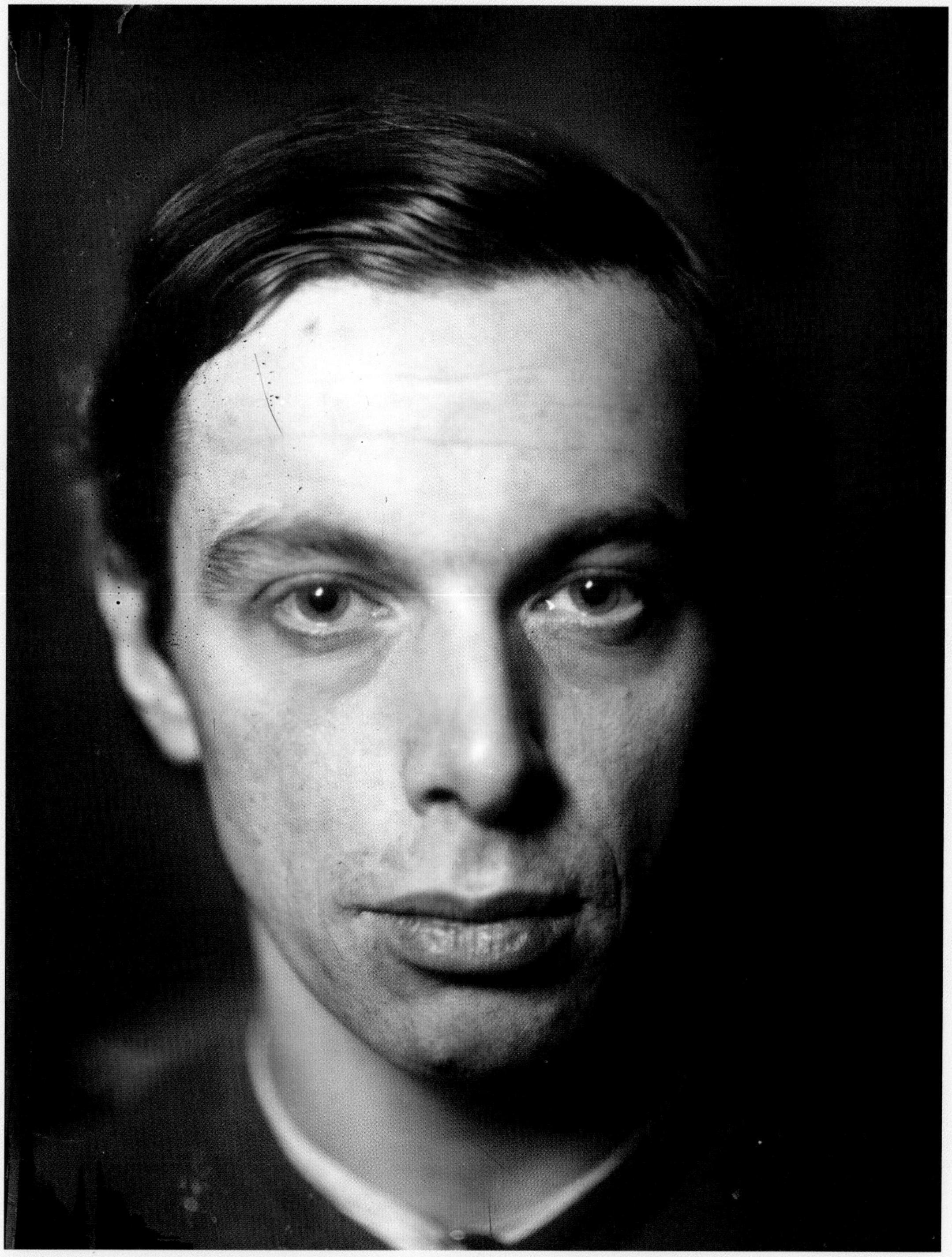

1918

In January Karl Ernst Osthaus acquires four paintings, three of which find their way into the collection of the Museum Folkwang (Gordon 218, 416, 476); this is the first museum purchase of Kirchner's paintings. In the same month Kirchner is visited in Kreuzlingen by Hans Mardersteig (1892–1977), from the Kurt Wolff Verlag, the leading publisher of Expressionism. During his sanatorium stay Kirchner sorts and arranges his entire graphic work — sent from Berlin in February — for Gustav Schiefler. He also works with Henry van de Velde on a monograph about his art that never materialises. In Kreuzlingen he begins a friendship with Nele van de Velde (1897–1965), van de Velde's daughter. From March to April he takes part in an exhibition at the Kunsthaus Zürich, from which the Zürcher Kunstgesellschaft (Zurich Art Society) purchases a print p. 234 to add to one donated to it by the artist p. 244. In May, acting in cooperation with the Kunstverein Jena, Kirchner establishes the Botho-Graef-Stiftung (Botho-Graef Foundation), in memory of his friend, a gift of more than 250 graphic works and drawings. On 14 July, accompanied by Erna and a nurse, he again moves up to the Stafelalp. There he is visited by Eberhard Grisebach and van de Velde. At the beginning of September Kirchner is granted permission to settle in Davos, and on 20 September moves into a house "In den Lärchen", a cluster of farm houses in Davos Frauenkirch; he furnishes his domicile with textiles he has designed himself and his own hand-carved vessels, later supplemented by sculptural furniture. In the autumn of 1918 he writes the "Glaubensbekenntnis eines Malers" (A Painter's Profession of Faith), which will be published in 1919 in *Die literarische Gesellschaft* and *Das Kunstblatt*. His health continues to be precarious.

1919

In January he receives a first shipment of his possessions from Berlin — in addition to artworks, these include his printing press and a few rugs; later this year stones and zinc plates for lithographs will come as well. Now he can again work in all the graphic techniques. From February to March there is an exhibition at the Galerie Ludwig Schames in Frankfurt am Main. He produces embroidery designs for Erna and Lene Spengler. Erna is once again given a temporary resident permit for Switzerland (as in 1920 and 1921) and arrives in Davos Frauenkirch in early April. In June the Nationalgalerie Berlin plans to purchase three Kirchner paintings; but during negotiations Kirchner quarrels with its director, Ludwig Justi (1876–1957), so that ultimately only one of them (Gordon 387) is acquired. Kirchner begins keeping a diary on 5 July. He again spends the summer on the Stafelalp. He begins to partially "restore" and even overpaint his early pictures and to predate some of his works in order to ensure that they will be seen as pioneering artistic achievements. In addition to his painting and drawing he again takes up furniture-making and carving relief doors and wood sculptures. With a large camera he begins taking photographs of people and landscapes as well as his own works. He continues to be in contact with German collectors and gallerists.

1920

In January and February there is a show of Kirchner's graphic works at the Kunstsalon Schames in Frankfurt am Main; its catalogue includes Karl Theodor Bluth's poem "Hymnus", which is dedicated to the artist, as well as the chapter on his graphics from Eberhard Grisebach's unpublished monograph. Kirchner publishes the first of a total of six texts about his own works under the pseudonym Louis de Marsalle in the journal *Genius;* in it he introduces the term "hieroglyph". By posing as a French art critic, Kirchner is able to discuss his artistic development "objectively". In his diary he makes extensive notes about his own role in the history of modern art. He comes into contact for the first time with other artists living in Davos, the German Philipp Bauknecht (1884–1933) and the Dutch painter Jan Wiegers (1893–1959), who becomes his friend and first pupil.

He produces a stage set for the amateur theatre in Davos. In the summer he stays briefly on the Stafelalp. In October and November he paints alongside Nele van de Velde. Late in the year he becomes acquainted with the Davos sanatorium physician Dr Frédéric Bauer (1883–1957), who in the following years will become one of Kirchner's most important collectors and patrons. In addition to his artistic work, Kirchner devotes himself intensively to readings in art history and art criticism and assembles an extensive library.

1921

Early in the year Kirchner temporarily conquers his morphine addiction. In February there is an exhibition in Berlin's Kronprinzenpalais with fifty of his works. During a stay in Zurich in early May, Kirchner meets the dancer Nina Hard (née Engelhardt; 1899 or 1900–1971), who visits him during the summer and serves as his model for a number of pictures. Kirchner also gets to know the writer Jakob Bosshart (1862–1924), who lives in Davos Clavadel, and through him the weaver Lise Gujer (1883–1967), who in the following years will create numerous tapestries based on Kirchner's designs.

1922

In January Ludwig Schames presents Kirchner's "Swiss Work" in his Frankfurt art salon; a few months later the gallerist dies. His nephew Manfred Schames will continue to operate the Kunstsalon until 1934 and handle business contacts with Kirchner. In March the live-in studio in Berlin is vacated and from now on Erna Kirchner stays in Davos full-time. In June Kirchner travels to Zurich, where he visits a Munch exhibition at the Kunsthaus Zürich and on that occasion meets the art historian Curt Glaser (1879–1943). In July Schiefler and his wife visit in Davos. Three of Kirchner's paintings are exhibited at the 23rd Art Biennale in Venice.

1923

After the death of his physician, Dr Lucius Spengler, on 12 February there is a falling out with the Grisebach and Spengler family members over Kirchner's medical records, which can no longer be found. Dr Frédéric Bauer takes over Kirchner's treatment. In June a large one-man show is presented at the Kunsthalle Basel, which has a major influence on Basel's young artists. Kirchner meets the artists Hermann Scherer (1893–1927) and Albert Müller (1897–1926), also the subsequent director of the art museum Georg Schmidt (1896–1965). From mid-June to the end of July Schiefler works with Kirchner on the catalogue raisonné of his graphic work. In August he receives a first visit from Scherer. In October he moves into an old farmhouse on the "Wildboden" in Davos Frauenkirch.

1924

In January he begins to correspond with the Basel painter Albert Müller, who will come to Davos to work with him in April. Will Grohmann (1887–1968), an art critic from Dresden, visits the artist for the first time in April, to prepare a monograph on Kirchner's drawings. In June and July there is a large solo exhibition with works from his entire career at the Kunstmuseum Winterthur, which is not altogether appreciated by the public. Kirchner resists being labelled an "Expressionist". In July a collection of Georg Heym's poems, designed and illustrated by Kirchner, is published under the title *Umbra Vitae*. His relationship with Hans Mardersteig intensifies.

1925

Kirchner writes an essay in his diary titled "Das Werk", in which he sketches his artistic development. During the Prussian Academy's spring exhibition in Berlin, Kirchner is awarded the "Prize of the Republic" for his painting *Junkerboden*, 1919 (Gordon 569). In the spring Ernst Gosebruch, director of the Museum Folkwang in Essen, visits Kirchner in Davos and discusses with him the possibility of his designing wall paintings for the ballroom of the museum then under construction; this commission will be solidified in 1927 and become a "life's work" that will occupy him until 1934. In June and July Kirchner and Albert Müller work closely together.

In September he travels with Müller to the International Art Exhibition at the Kunsthaus Zürich; Kirchner is impressed only by Picasso. In October Kirchner agrees with his patron Dr Frédéric Bauer to build up an extensive collection of his own work for him. On 18 December Kirchner takes his first trip back to Germany, with initial stops in Zurich and Basel. In Zurich he meets with Wilhelm Wartmann (1882–1970), director of the Kunsthaus Zürich, who wishes to put together a major exhibition for him with some 50 paintings and 100 graphic works; the show, planned for 1926, is ultimately abandoned because of scheduling problems.

1926

Until 11 March Kirchner continues his travels to Frankfurt, Chemnitz, Dresden and Berlin, where he visits friends, gallerists and family members. He is being considered for a professorship in Dresden. There he meets the dancers Mary Wigman (1886–1973) and Gret Palucca (1902–1993). He reconnects with Karl Schmidt-Rottluff — first in Chemnitz then in Berlin — who wants to found a new artists' association; Kirchner declines. On 5 March he is given a reception by the National Art Commissioner Edwin Redslob and makes the acquaintance of Chancellor Hans Luther. In Berlin he also visits Max Liebermann (1847–1935). In February and March he has a solo exhibition at the Kölnischer Kunstverein in Cologne. For the summer International Art Exhibition in Dresden he puts together a selection of "young Swiss art"; along with works by the Basel group Rot/Blau he also inserts some of his own. The Basel painter Paul Camenisch (1893–1970) works with Kirchner the entire summer. In November and December there are one-man shows in Berlin (Galerie Paul Cassirer), Dresden and Davos. Will Grohmann's *Das Werk Ernst Ludwig Kirchners,* the text of which Kirchner has considerably reworked, appears in Munich. The first volume of Gustav Schiefler's *Das druckgraphische Werk von Ernst Ludwig Kirchner* is published in Berlin; the second volume will follow in 1931.

1927

In May and June there are solo exhibitions in Wiesbaden and Dresden, and in June and July a major one-man show of his graphic works at the Galerie Aktuaryus in Zurich. In his diary Kirchner sketches out two programmatic essays on colour problems in painting and academic training. He makes the acquaintance of the German couple Hansgeorg (1899–1982) and Elfriede (died 1937) Knoblauch, with whom he will maintain a regular correspondence from 1927 to 1938. In late June Gret Palucca arrives in Davos for a dance performance. With Georg Schmidt and the artist and organ restorer Julius Hembus (1903–1983), with whom he had become acquainted in 1925, Kirchner enjoys an outing to St Moritz-Maloja, where they look up Alberto Giacometti (1901–1966) and admire his sculptures. The Basel painter Hans-Rudolf Schiess (1904–1978) stays with Kirchner for several weeks. In September Kirchner begins making preparations for the memorial exhibition for Albert Müller, which is presented in Basel in October and November.

1928

Kirchner mainly works on the wall-painting designs for the Museum Folkwang ballroom, a commission that has now been confirmed. Oskar Schlemmer is entrusted with the painting for the museum's fountain room. In February Kirchner organises the memorial exhibition for Hermann Scherer in Basel. Kirchner's painting *Sleigh Ride* (Schlittenfahrt; Gordon 713) is exhibited in the German Pavilion at the 16th Art Biennale in Venice. In the summer he shows five works at the exhibition of the Neue Secession (New Secession) in Munich. The Nationalgalerie Berlin purchases the painting *An Artists' Group (The Brücke Painters)* (Eine Künstlergemeinschaft [Die Maler der Brücke], 1926/27; Gordon 855). In October he is visited by the Berlin art dealer Ferdinand Möller (1882–1956). Kirchner expresses a desire to build a studio. On 23 December, the day of his mother's death, he makes a last entry in the diary begun in 1919, which has a number of major gaps.

1929

In February he contacts the Galerie Jeanne Bucher in Paris with a view to organising an exhibition, which is never realised. Erna Kirchner travels to Germany in the spring; from now on she will frequently stay in Berlin, mainly for health reasons. In April Kirchner begins to correspond with the German painter and Bauhaus pupil Fritz Winter (1905–1976), who will visit him in the coming four summers. In the last half of June he travels to Germany, with stops in Essen and Berlin, visiting Ernst Gosebruch and Ferdinand Möller. He plans to rent a studio in Berlin in which to produce the cartoons for Essen but the plan does not come to fruition. Late in the year he resumes correspondence with Emil Nolde. The *Kunstblatt* publishes the essay by Gustav Schiefler commissioned by Kirchner in 1927, "E.L. Kirchners Entwürfe für Wandgestaltung in einem Festsaal des Folkwang-Museums: Wandmalerei und Miniatur im Werk E.L. Kirchners".

1930

In January there is a solo exhibition of his graphic work in Wiesbaden. In the same month Gret Palucca presents several evenings of dance in Davos and visits Kirchner in the Wildboden house. Hans Arp (1886–1966) visits in March; Curt Glaser, in September. Kirchner becomes acquainted with the director of the Davos Treatment and Tourism Association Walter Kern (1898–1966), who will feature him in various future publications.

1931

In March and April he has four paintings in the exhibition *German Paintings and Sculpture* at New York's Museum of Modern Art, as well as four paintings in the show *L'Art vivant en Europe* in Brussels (April–May). The MoMA catalogue names museum collections in thirteen cities as owners of Kirchner's works (Berlin, Chemnitz, Dresden, Elberfeld, Essen, Frankfurt am Main, Halle, Hamburg, Jena, Mannheim, Stuttgart, Wiesbaden and Vienna). In mid-June Kirchner visits his art dealer, Manfred Schames, and Carl Hagemann in Frankfurt, then proceeds to Berlin. He is named a member of the Prussian Academy of Arts. He makes initial contact with Max Huggler (1903–1994), the director of the Kunsthalle Bern.

1932

Owing to political developments, the state of the art market, so crucial for Kirchner, becomes increasingly uncertain. In March he is visited by Alfred Döblin, who is in the middle of a lecture tour through Germany and Switzerland. Kirchner once again becomes addicted to medication and in July presses Dr Frédéric Bauer to prescribe drugs containing morphine. In late October he visits the major Picasso exhibition at the Kunsthaus Zürich with Max Huggler.

1933

There is an important retrospective at the Kunsthalle Bern in March and April; the catalogue for the show includes his last essay under the pseudonym Louis de Marsalle, whom Kirchner now declares dead. After the National Socialist takeover Kirchner follows German cultural policies with grave concern; in May he is pressed to withdraw his membership of the Prussian Academy. In June Ernst Gosebruch is forced to resign as director of the Museum Folkwang, shattering any hope Kirchner had of realising the wall paintings. At the end of the year he meets the French Surrealist René Crevel (1900–1935) in Davos.

1934

In March he receives a visit from Oskar Schlemmer in Davos. In May there is a show of his woodcuts in the Galerie Commeter in Hamburg. In late May Kirchner meets Paul Klee (1879–1940) in Bern. At an exhibition of modern German art at the Kunsthaus Zürich in late June Kirchner resumes contact with Wilhelm Wartmann and asks about the possibility of a one-man show. In late June or early July Kirchner visits Carl Hagemann in Frankfurt am Main, who returns the visit in Davos in September.

1935

In March he travels to Bern to see the Paul Klee exhibition at the Kunsthalle. In May and June Kirchner's watercolours and drawings are on view in the Kunstmuseum Basel's Kupferstichkabinett. He becomes acquainted with Christian Anton Laely (1913–1992), his last "pupil". Until the following year Kirchner will occupy himself with the plan to paint the church in Frauenkirch, in part with scenes from the Apocalypse. He publishes his text "Anfänge und Ziele" (Beginnings and Aims) in the Dutch journal *Kroniek van hedendaagsche Kunst en Kultur.*

1936

In late March Wilhelm Wartmann, director of the Kunsthaus Zürich, asks Kirchner about a July solo exhibition that has been planned since 1934 with roughly 100 paintings and as many works on paper but, owing to disagreements about the hanging and the catalogue, the exhibition fails to materialise. In the summer Kirchner carves a five-figure relief for the portal of the new schoolhouse in Davos Frauenkirch, which is dedicated on 18 October. During a visit to Davos in September the director of the Detroit Institute of Arts, Wilhelm R. Valentiner (1880–1958) offers the artist a first one-man show in the United States. In October he is visited by the art dealer Curt Valentin (1902–1954), who will emigrate to America in the following year. In late October Kirchner learns that the Deutscher Künstlerbund (German Artists' League) has been disbanded. In Germany political actions against modern art intensify. Kirchner's health again seriously deteriorates; for pain he takes a drug containing morphine.

1937

In January there is an exhibition at the Detroit Institute of Arts. In February Kirchner is in contact with Alfred Barr (1902–1981), the director of New York's Museum of Modern Art, about the possibility of his taking over the show. In late July and early August modern art is confiscated from German museums as being "degenerate" and presented in an exhibition that travels through various German cities until 1941. Some 770 works by Kirchner (including 54 paintings) are removed from museums and later either sold abroad or destroyed. In late July Kirchner is expelled from the Prussian Academy. At the end of the year there are further solo shows at the Buchholz Gallery in New York, run by Curt Valentin, and at the Kunsthalle Basel. His text "Ein paar Worte zur Arbeit" appears in the journal *Kroniek van hedendaagsche Kunst en Kultur.* At the end of the year he considers applying for Swiss citizenship.

1938

His health deteriorates further. Germany's annexation of Austria on 13 March sends Kirchner into a panic, as he fears that the Germans could march across the Austrian border into Grisons. He destroys some of his printing blocks and some sculptures of his that surround his house. On his 58th birthday on 6 May there is not a single word of congratulation from Germany. In a letter from 9 May Kirchner asks Wilhelm Wartmann about the planned exhibition of modern German art in London, and at the same time about the possibility of a show at the Kunsthaus Zürich. On 10 May he applies to the Davos authorities for a marriage licence with Erna but on 12 June he withdraws this request. On 15 June he ends his life with a pistol not far from his house. On 18 June he is buried in the Davos Waldfriedhof, very near his last residence. Erna, who can now officially use the name Kirchner, continues to live in the Wildboden house until her death on 4 October 1945. In July five Kirchner works are on view as part of the exhibition *Twentieth Century German Art* in London, presented as a riposte to the *Degenerate Art* show in Munich.

Select Bibliography

Catalogues Raisonnés

Gordon

Donald E. Gordon, *Ernst Ludwig Kirchner* (Cambridge, MA, 1968).

Dube

Annemarie and Wolf-Dieter Dube, *E. L. Kirchner: Das graphische Werk*, 2 vols. (Munich, 1967; 2nd enlarged edn., 1980).

Presler

Gerd Presler, *Ernst Ludwig Kirchner: Die Skizzenbücher; "Ekstase des ersten Sehens"; Monographie und Werkverzeichnis* (Karlsruhe/Davos, 1996).

Henze

Wolfgang Henze, *Die Plastik Ernst Ludwig Kirchners: Monographie mit Werkverzeichnis* (Wichtrach/Bern, 2002).

Scotti

Roland Scotti, *Ernst Ludwig Kirchner: The Photographic Work* (Göttingen 2006).

Gercken

Günther Gercken in collaboration with Annemarie Gercken, *Ernst Ludwig Kirchner: Kritisches Werkverzeichnis der Druckgraphik*, vol. 1 (1904–1908), vol. 2 (1909–1911), vol. 3 (1912–1916), vol. 4 (1917–1919) (Bern, 2013–2015); further volumes in preparation.

Correspondence and the Artist's Own Key Writings

Ernst Ludwig Kirchner, "Bemerkungen über Leben und Arbeit", *Das Werk* 17, no. 1 (1930), pp. 2–12.

Louis de Marsalle [Ernst Ludwig Kirchner], "[untitled]" in *Ernst Ludwig Kirchner*, ed. Max Huggler, exh. cat. Kunsthalle Bern (Bern, 1933), pp. 14–16.

Ernst Ludwig Kirchner, *Briefe an Nele und Henry van de Velde*, with an afterword by Mary van Deventer (Munich, 1961).

Eberhard Grisebach, *Maler des Expressionismus im Briefwechsel mit Eberhard Grisebach* (Hamburg, 1962); new edn., *"Ich bin den friedlichen Bürgern zu modern": Aus Eberhard Grisebachs Briefwechsel mit seinen Malerfreunden*, ed. Kirchner Museum Davos, compiled by Lothar Grisebach; reworked and with new commentary by Lucius Grisebach (Zurich, 2010).

Lothar Grisebach, *E. L. Kirchners Davoser Tagebuch: Eine Darstellung des Malers und eine Sammlung seiner Schriften* (Cologne, 1968; new edn., rev. by Lucius Grisebach, Stuttgart, 1997) [with Kirchner's writings under the pseudonym Louis de Marsalle].

Ernst Ludwig Kirchner und das Folkwang-Museum Hagen: Briefe von, an und über Kirchner, compiled and with commentary by Herta Hesse-Frielinghaus (Münster, 1974).

Eberhard W. Kornfeld, *Ernst Ludwig Kirchner: Nachzeichnung seines Lebens; Katalog der Sammlung von Werken Ernst Ludwig Kirchners im Kirchner-Haus Davos*, exh. cat. Kunstmuseum Basel (Bern, 1979).

Annemarie Dube-Heynig, *Ernst Ludwig Kirchner: Postkarten und Briefe an Erich Heckel im Altonaer Museum in Hamburg*, ed. Roman Norbert Ketterer, with the collaboration of Wolfgang Henze (Cologne, 1984).

Wolfgang Henze in collaboration with Annemarie Dube-Heynig and Magdalena Kraemer-Noble (eds.), *Ernst Ludwig Kirchner/Gustav Schiefler: Briefwechsel, 1910–1935/1938* (Stuttgart/Zurich, 1990).

Bettina Heil and Andrea Sinzel, *Briefe an Karl Ernst Osthaus* (Kulturstiftung der Länder, Patrimonia 189; Hagen, 2000).

Harry Joelson (ed.), *Das ungewohnte Neue: Briefwechsel Ernst Ludwig Kirchner und Georg Reinhart*, with a foreword by Dieter Schwarz (Winterthur, 2002).

Hans Delfs, Mario-Andreas von Lüttichau and Roland Scotti (eds.), *Kirchner, Schmidt-Rottluff, Nolde, Nay...: Briefe an den Sammler und Mäzen Carl Hagemann, 1906–1940* (Ostfildern-Ruit, 2004).

Hans Delfs (ed.), *Ernst Ludwig Kirchner: Der gesamte Briefwechsel*, 4 vols. (Zurich, 2010).

Beat Stutzer, "Der Briefwechsel mit Ernst Ludwig Kirchner (1880–1938)", in *"Sie lieber Herr Im Obersteg sind unser Schweizer für alles": Briefwechsel mit Cuno Amiet, Robert Genin, Alexej von Jawlensky, Alexander und Clotilde Sacharoff, Marc Chagall, Ernst Ludwig Kirchner und Wassily Kandinsky in der Sammlung Im Obersteg*, published in conjunction with the exhibition *Künstlerfreundschaften: Karl Im Obersteg im Dialog mit Amiet, Chagall, Jawlensky*, Kunstmuseum Basel (Basel, 2011), pp. 205–216.

Most Important Monographic Publications from the Last Twenty Years

Ernst Ludwig Kirchner: Gemälde, Aquarelle, Zeichnungen und Druckgraphik; Eine Ausstellung zum 60. Todestag, ed. Magdalena M. Moeller and Roland Scotti, exh. cat. Kunstforum Wien and Kunsthalle der Hypo-Kulturstiftung München (Munich, 1998).

Ernst Ludwig Kirchner, ed. Rudy Chiappini, exh. cat. Museo d'Arte Moderna della Città di Lugano, Villa Malpensata, Lugano (Geneva, 2000).

Ernst Ludwig Kirchner, ed. Magdalena M. Moeller and Roland Scotti, exh. cat. Fondazione Antonio Mazzotta, Milan (Milan, 2002).

Ernst Ludwig Kirchner: The Dresden and Berlin Years, ed. Jill Lloyd and Magdalena M. Moeller, exh. cat. National Gallery of Art, Washington, DC, and Royal Academy of Arts, London (London, 2003).

Ernst Ludwig Kirchner: Mountain Life; The Early Years in Davos, 1917–1926, exh. cat. Kunstmuseum Basel (Ostfildern-Ruit, 2003).

Magdalena M. Moeller, *Von Dresden nach Davos: Ernst Ludwig Kirchner, Zeichnungen; Die Sammlung des Brücke-Museums Berlin* (Munich, 2003).

Ernst Ludwig Kirchner: Erstes Sehen; Das Werk im Berliner Kupferstichkabinett, exh. cat. Kupferstichkabinett, Staatliche Museen zu Berlin, Kulturforum Potsdamer Platz, Berlin, and elsewhere (Munich, 2004).

Brücke und Berlin: 100 Jahre Expressionismus, ed. Anita Beloubek-Hammer, Magdalena M. Moeller and Dieter Scholz, exh. cat. Neue Nationalgalerie, Kulturforum Potsdamer Platz, Berlin (Berlin, 2005).

Brücke: Die Geburt des deutschen Expressionismus, ed. Magdalena M. Moeller and Javier Arnaldo, exh. cat. Brücke-Museum Berlin in der Berlinischen Galerie and elsewhere (Munich, 2005).

Ernst Ludwig Kirchner in Berlin, ed. Magdalena M. Moeller, exh. cat. Brücke-Museum, Berlin (Berlin, 2008).

Lucius Grisebach, *Ernst Ludwig Kirchner,* exh. cat. Museum der Moderne Salzburg (Cologne, 2009).

Ernst Ludwig Kirchner: Retrospective, ed. Felix Krämer, exh. cat. Städel Museum, Frankfurt am Main (Ostfildern-Ruit, 2010).

Kirchner, exh. cat. Hamburger Kunsthalle (Bremen, 2011).

"No One Else Has These Colors": Kirchner's Painting, ed. Karin Schick and Heide Skowranek, exh. cat. Kirchner Museum Davos (Ostfildern-Ruit, 2011).

Farbenmensch Kirchner, ed. Oliver Kase and Heide Skowranek, exh. cat. Pinakothek der Moderne, Munich (Berlin, 2014).

Eberhard Grisebach, *Ernst Ludwig Kirchner,* ed. Lucius Grisebach (Bern, 2014) [previously unpublished typescript from 1917].

Ernst Ludwig Kirchner: Das expressionistische Experiment, ed. Magdalena M. Moeller, exh. cat. Brücke-Museum, Berlin and Bucerius Kunst Forum, Hamburg (Munich, 2014).

Der doppelte Kirchner: Die zwei Seiten der Leinwand, ed. Inge Herold, Ulrike Lorenz and Thorsten Sadowsky, exh. cat. Kunsthalle Mannheim and Kirchner Museum Davos (Cologne, 2015).

Ernst Ludwig Kirchner: Hieroglyphen, ed. Joachim Jäger, exh. cat. Hamburger Bahnhof, Berlin (Berlin, 2016).

On the Metropolis

Ewald Rathke, *Ernst Ludwig Kirchner: Straßenbilder* (Stuttgart, 1969).

Lucius Grisebach, *Ernst Ludwig Kirchner: Großstadtbilder* (Munich/ Zurich, 1979).

Rosalyn Deutsche, "Alienation in Berlin. Kirchner's Street Scenes", *Art in America* 71, no. 1 (1983), pp. 64–72.

Ich und die Stadt: Mensch und Großstadt in der deutschen Kunst des 20. Jahrhunderts, ed. Eberhard Roters and Bernhard Schulz, exh. cat. Berlinische Galerie, Martin-Gropius-Bau 1987 (Berlin, 1987).

Dominik Bartmann, "Das Großstadtbild Berlins in der Weltsicht der Expressionisten", in *Stadtbilder: Berlin in der Malerei vom 17. Jahrhundert bis zur Gegenwart,* exh. cat. Berlin Museum (Berlin, 1987), pp. 243–294.

Charles W. Haxthausen, "Images of Berlin in the Art of the Secession and Expressionism", in *Art in Berlin 1815–1989,* ed. Kelly Morris and Amanda Woods, exh. cat. High Museum of Art, Atlanta (Atlanta, 1989), pp. 61–82.

Charles W. Haxthausen, "'A New Beauty': Ernst Ludwig Kirchner's Images of Berlin", in Charles W. Haxthausen and Heidrun Suhr, *Berlin: Culture and Metropolis* (Minneapolis/ Oxford, 1990), pp. 58–94.

Magdalena M., Moeller, *Ernst Ludwig Kirchner: Die Straßenszenen 1913–1915* (Munich, 1993).

Martina Padberg, *Großstadtbild und Großstadtmetaphorik in der deutschen Malerei: Vorstufen und Entfaltung 1870–1918* (Ph.D. diss., 1995, Bonner Studien zur Kunstgeschichte 10; Münster, 1995).

Katharina Sykora, *Weiblichkeit, Großstadt, Moderne: Ernst Ludwig Kirchners Berliner Straßenszenen 1913–1915* (Berlin, 1996).

Rita E. Täuber, *Der häßliche Eros: Darstellungen zur Prostitution in der Malerei und Grafik 1855–1930* (Berlin, 1997).

Wolfgang Henze, "Maler der Großstadt — Maler der Bergwelt", in *Ernst Ludwig Kirchner,* ed. Rudy Chiappini, exh. cat. Museo d'Arte Moderna della Città di Lugano, Villa Malpensata, Lugano (Geneva, 2000), pp. 111–141.

Sherwin Simmons, "Ernst Kirchner's Streetwalkers: Art, Luxury, and Immorality in Berlin, 1913–16", *The Art Bulletin,* 82 (2000), pp. 117–148.

Der Potsdamer Platz: Ernst Ludwig Kirchner und der Untergang Preußens, ed. Katharina Henkel and Roland März, exh. cat. Neue Nationalgalerie, Staatliche Museen zu Berlin (Berlin, 2001).

Ernst Ludwig Kirchner: Großstadt, Eros und Natur; Aus den verborgenen Sammlungen der Region, ed. Barbara Alms, exh. cat. Städtische Galerie Delmenhorst (Bremen, 2005).

Magdalena M. Moeller, "Kirchner in Berlin: Die 'Straßenszenen' als Höhepunkt expressionistischer Kunst", in *Brücke: Die Geburt des deutschen Expressionismus,* ed. Magdalena M. Moeller and Javier Arnaldo, exh. cat. Brücke-Museum Berlin in der Berlinischen Galerie and elsewhere (Munich, 2005), p. 79–86.

Javier Arnaldo, "Großstadt Berlin", in *Brücke: Die Geburt des deutschen Expressionismus,* ed. Magdalena M. Moeller and Javier Arnaldo, exh. cat. Brücke-Museum Berlin in der Berlinischen Galerie and elsewhere (Munich, 2005), pp. 349–353.

Pamela Kort, *Ernst Ludwig Kirchner: Berlin Street Scene* (New York, 2007).

Kirchner and the Berlin Street, ed. Deborah Wye, exh. cat. The Museum of Modern Art, New York (New York, 2008).

Expressionismus: Auftakt zur Moderne in der Großstadt, ed. Katharina Heise and Antje Tietken, exh. cat. Horst-Janssen-Museum, Oldenburg (Bremen, 2008).

Olaf Peters, "Die Straße als transitorischer Ort in der Großstadtmalerei des deutschen Expressionismus und der Neuen Sachlichkeit", in *Großstadt: Motor der Künste in der Moderne,* ed. Burcu Dogramaci (Berlin, 2010), pp. 173–187.

Eleanor Moseman, "At the Intersection: Kirchner, Kubišta, and 'Modern Morality', 1911–14", *Art Bulletin,* 93 (2011), pp. 79–100.

Charles W. Haxthausen, "Framing Movement: Kirchner in Berlin", in Joseph Masheck (ed.), *Mostly Modern: Essays in Art and Architecture* (Stockbridge, MA, 2014), p. 104–117.

On Fehmarn

Andreas Hüneke, "'Es ist unglaublich, wie stark man die Farben hier findet': Die Sommeraufenthalte der 'Brücke'-Maler bis 1914", in *Künstler der Brücke in Moritzburg,* ed. Volkmar Billig, exh. cat. Museum Schloss Moritzburg (Dresden, 1995), pp. 25–34.

Wolfgang Büche, "Ernst Ludwig Kirchner auf Fehmarn", in Kulturstiftung der Länder and Staatliche Galerie Moritzburg, Halle (eds.), *Ernst Ludwig Kirchner: Akte im Strandwald* (Kulturstiftung der Länder, Patrimonia 112; Bonn, 1996), pp. 21–33.

Ernst Ludwig Kirchner auf Fehmarn, ed. Hermann Gerlinger and Heinz Spielmann, exh. cat. Schleswig-Holsteinisches Landesmuseum, Schloß Gottorf, Schleswig (Brücke-Almanach 5; Schleswig, 1997).

Wolfgang Henze, "Die Badeszene in der Natur oder die Realisierung eines arkadischen Traumes: Ernst Ludwig Kirchner auf Fehmarn 1912–1914", in *Ernst Ludwig Kirchner: Gemälde, Aquarelle, Zeichnungen und Druckgraphik; Eine Ausstellung zum 60. Todestag,* ed. Magdalena M. Moeller and Roland Scotti, exh. cat. Kunstforum Wien and Kunsthalle der Hypo-Kulturstiftung München (Munich, 1998), pp. 35–48.

Die Badenden: Mensch und Natur im deutschen Expressionismus, ed. Jutta Hülswig-Johnen and Thomas Kellein, exh. cat. Kunsthalle Bielefeld (Bielefeld, 2000).

Ulrich Pfarr, "Zwischen Ekstase und Alltag: Zur Rezeption der Lebensreform in der künstlerischen Praxis der Brücke", in *Die Lebensreform: Entwürfe zur Neugestaltung von Leben und Kunst um 1900,* exh. cat. Mathildenhöhe, Darmstadt (Darmstadt, 2001), vol. 1, pp. 251–256.

Andreas Hüneke, "Nahe und ferne Paradiese: Erotik und Exotik — Die Einheit von Mensch und Natur", in *Brücke und Berlin: 100 Jahre Expressionismus,* ed. Anita Beloubek-Hammer, Magdalena M. Moeller and Dieter Scholz, exh. cat. Neue Nationalgalerie, Kulturforum Potsdamer Platz, Berlin (Berlin, 2005), pp. 100–101.

Janina Dahlmanns, "Akte in der Landschaft", in *Brücke: Die Geburt des deutschen Expressionismus,* ed. Magdalena M. Moeller and Javier Arnaldo, exh. cat. Brücke-Museum Berlin in der Berlinischen Galerie and elsewhere (Munich, 2005), pp. 297–300.

Jutta Hülsewig-Johnen, "Der freie Mensch in freier Natürlichkeit: Ernst Ludwig Kirchner in Moritzburg und Fehmarn", in *Ernst Ludwig Kirchner: Großstadt, Eros und Natur; Aus den verborgenen Sammlungen der Region,* ed. Barbara Alms, exh. cat. Städtische Galerie Delmenhorst (Bremen, 2005), pp. 124–133.

Steffen Krautzig, *Ernst Ludwig Kirchner auf Fehmarn* (Stationen, ed. Roland Krischke, vol. 22; Heidelberg, 2016).

On the Berlin Studios

Erika Billetter, "Ernst Ludwig Kirchner: Kunst als Lebensentwurf", in *Ernst Ludwig Kirchner 1880–1938*, exh. cat. Nationalgalerie Berlin and elsewhere (Berlin, 1979), pp. 16–25.

Die Pracht der Farben: Ernst Ludwig Kirchner; Textile Werke nach seinen Entwürfen; Bildteppiche von Lise Gujer und Bildstickereien, exh. cat. Kirchner Museum Davos (Davos, 1999).

Mario-Andreas von Lüttichau, "Das Atelier als selbstgeschaffene Welt", in *Die Brücke in Dresden 1905–1911*, ed. Birgit Dalbajewa and Ulrich Bischoff, exh. cat. Galerie Neue Meister, Staatliche Kunstsammlungen Dresden (Cologne, 2001), pp. 283–288.

Beat Stutzer, "Auf den Spuren eines Leoparden: Ein Hocker aus Kamerun als Anregung und Bildmotiv für Ernst Ludwig Kirchner", in Christine E. Stauffer (ed.), *Festschrift für Eberhard W. Kornfeld zum 80. Geburtstag* (Bern, 2003), pp. 233–244.

Roland März, "Berliner Ateliers der Brücke: Orte der Begegnung", in *Brücke und Berlin: 100 Jahre Expressionismus*, ed. Anita Beloubek-Hammer, Magdalena M. Moeller and Dieter Scholz, exh. cat. Neue Nationalgalerie, Kulturforum Potsdamer Platz, Berlin (Berlin, 2005), pp. 307–313.

Hanna Strzoda, *Die Ateliers Ernst Ludwig Kirchners: Eine Studie zur Rezeption "primitiver" europäischer und außereuropäischer Kulturen* (Ph.D. diss., 2004; Petersberg, 2006).

Leonie Beiersdorf, "'... dass Leben und Arbeit eines sind': Gelebte Utopie bei Ernst Ludwig Kirchner und Rosa Schapire", in *Gesamtkunstwerk Expressionismus: Kunst, Film, Literatur, Theater, Tanz und Architektur 1905 bis 1925*, ed. Ralf Beil and Claudia Dillmann, exh. cat. Mathildenhöhe Darmstadt (Ostfildern-Ruit, 2010), pp. 70–77.

Hanna Strzoda, "Expressionistische Gegenwelten: Die Ateliers von Ernst Ludwig Kirchner, Gabriele Münter und Wassily Kandinsky", in *Mythos Atelier: Von Spitzweg bis Picasso, von Giacometti bis Nauman*, ed. Ina Conzen, exh. cat. Staatsgalerie Stuttgart (Munich, 2012), pp. 105–113.

On Wartime and Crisis

Ernst Ludwig Kirchner: Von Jena nach Davos; Eine Ausstellung zum 90. Gründungsjubiläum des Jenaer Kunstvereins, exh. cat. Stadtmuseum Göhre in Jena (Leipzig, 1993).

Philip Larson, "Loser on Leave: Ernst Ludwig Kirchner's Woodcuts for 'Peter Schlemihls wundersame Geschichte'", *On Paper: The Journal on Prints, Drawings, and Photography* 1, no. 5 (1997), pp. 12–16.

Günther Gercken, "Die Krisenjahre 1914–1918 im Spiegel der Graphik", in *Ernst Ludwig Kirchner: Gemälde, Aquarelle, Zeichnungen und Druckgraphik; Eine Ausstellung zum 60. Todestag*, ed. Magdalena M. Moeller and Roland Scotti, exh. cat. Kunstforum Wien and Kunsthalle der Hypo-Kulturstiftung München (Munich, 1998), pp. 49–60.

Ernst Ludwig Kirchner: "Kirchner in Königstein"; Aquarelle, Zeichnungen, Druckgrafik, Fotografien, exh. cat. Galerie Jahrhunderthalle Hoechst (Frankfurt am Main, 1999).

Titia Hoffmeister, "1915–1917: Die Jahre der Krise", in *Ernst Ludwig Kirchner*, ed. Rudy Chiappini, exh. cat. Museo d'Arte Moderna della Città di Lugano, Villa Malpensata, Lugano (Geneva, 2000), pp. 91–109.

Peter Springer, *Hand and Head: Ernst Ludwig Kirchner's Self-Portrait as Soldier* (Berkeley, CA, 2002).

Michael F. Zimmermann, "Art and Crisis: Kirchner Paints Kirchner", in *Ernst Ludwig Kirchner: Mountain Life; The Early Years in Davos 1917–1926*, exh. cat. Kunstmuseum Basel (Ostfildern-Ruit, 2003), pp. 59–70.

Roland Scotti, "War, Art and Crisis: Ernst Ludwig Kirchner 1914–1918" in *Ernst Ludwig Kirchner: The Dresden and Berlin Years*, ed. Jill Lloyd and Magdalena M. Moeller, exh. cat. National Gallery of Art, Washington, DC, and Royal Academy of Arts, London (London, 2003), pp. 27–31.

Sherwin Simmons, "Split-Identity in Ernst Ludwig Kirchner's Woodcut Cycle 'Peter Schlemihls wundersame Geschichte'", *Zeitschrift für Kunstgeschichte* 70 (2007), pp. 409–432.

Bettina Gockel, *Die Pathologisierung des Künstlers: Künstlerlegenden der Moderne* (Berlin, 2010).

Javier Arnaldo, "War and Breakdown", in *Ernst Ludwig Kirchner: Retrospective*, ed. Felix Krämer, exh. cat. Städel Museum, Frankfurt am Main (Ostfildern-Ruit, 2010), pp. 151–155.

1914: The Avant-Gardes at War, exh. cat. Kunst- und Ausstellungshalle der Bundesrepublik Deutschland, Bonn (Cologne, 2013).

Aya Soika, "Ernst Ludwig Kirchner", in ead., *Weltenbruch: Die Künstler der Brücke im Ersten Weltkrieg; 1914–1918*, ed. Magdalena M. Moeller, exh. cat. Brücke-Museum, Berlin (Munich, 2014), pp. 59–80.

Magdalena M. Moeller and Günther Gercken, *Ernst Ludwig Kirchner: Peter Schlemihl's Wondrous Story*, exh. cat. Brücke-Museum, Berlin (Munich, 2014).

Thomas W. Gaehtgens and Anja Foerschner, "Ernst Ludwig Kirchner's Drawings of the Apocalypse", *Getty Research Journal* 6 (2014), pp. 83–102.

Thomas W. Gaethgens, "Ernst Ludwig Kirchner: An Inner War", in *Nothing but the Clouds Unchanged: Artists in World War I*, ed. Gordon Hughes and Philipp Blom, publication in conjunction with the exhibition *World War I: War of Images, Images of War*, The Getty Research Institute, Los Angeles, and the Mildred Lane Kemper Art Museum at Washington University, St. Louis (Los Angeles, 2014), pp. 118–127.

Günther Gercken, "E. L. Kirchners graphische Werke aus der Zeit seines Sanatoriumsaufenthaltes in Kreuzlingen 1917/18", in *Ernst Ludwig Kirchner: Das expressionistische Experiment*, ed. Magdalena M. Moeller, exh. cat. Brücke-Museum, Berlin (Munich, 2014), pp. 35–47.

Exhibition Checklist

Paintings

Cat. 1 p. 101
Fehmarn Houses / Fehmarn-Häuser, 1908
Oil on canvas, 75 × 99.5 cm
Gordon 37
Städel Museum, Frankfurt am Main, on permanent loan from a private collection

Cat. 2 p. 100
Four Bathers / Vier Badende, 1909
Oil on canvas, 75 × 100.5 cm
Gordon 95
Von der Heydt-Museum Wuppertal

Cat. 3 p. 99
Streetcar in Dresden / Strassenbahn in Dresden, 1909
Oil on canvas, 70 × 78.5 cm
Gordon 99
Staatsgalerie Stuttgart, on loan from a private collection

Cat. 4 p. 106
Reclining Nude in Front of a Mirror / Liegender Akt vor Spiegel, 1909/10
Oil on canvas, 83.5 × 95.5 cm
Gordon 56
Brücke-Museum, Berlin

Cat. 5 p. 107
Fränzi and Marcella / Fränzi und Marcella, 1910
Oil on painting pad, 50 × 65.5 cm
Not in Gordon
E.W.K. Collection, Bern/Davos

Cat. 6 p. 105
Girl with Cat, Fränzi / Mädchen mit Katze, Fränzi, 1910
Oil on canvas, 88.5 × 119 cm
Gordon 124
Merzbacher Kunststiftung

Cat. 7 p. 103
Artist — Marcella / Artistin — Marcella, 1910
Oil on canvas, 101 × 76 cm
Gordon 125
Brücke-Museum, Berlin

Cat. 8 p. 104
Nude behind a Curtain (Fränzi) / Nacktes Mädchen hinter Vorhang (Fränzi), 1910/1926
Oil on canvas, 120.5 × 90 cm
Gordon 154
Collection Stedelijk Museum, Amsterdam

Cat. 9 p. 102
Two Dancing Girls / Zwei Tänzerinnen, 1910/11
Oil on canvas, 65 × 59.5 cm
Gordon 192
Franz Marc Museum, Kochel am See, on permanent loan from a private collection

Cat. 10 p. 113
City Tower / Der Stadtturm, 1911
Oil on canvas, 96.5 × 84 cm
Gordon 210
Kunstsammlungen Chemnitz — Museum Gunzenhauser, Inv. no. GUN_M-0177, property of the Gunzenhauser Foundation

Cat. 11 p. 110
Unicycle Rider / Einradfahrer, 1911
Oil on canvas, 80 × 90 cm
Gordon 221
Merzbacher Kunststiftung

Cat. 12 p. 111
Two Female Nudes in Vertical Format / Zwei weibliche Akte in Hochformat, 1911/12
Oil on canvas, 150.5 × 75.5 cm
Gordon 224
Kunstmuseum Bern, Gift of Hilde Thannhauser, Bern, from the Justin Thannhauser Collection

Cat. 13 p. 126
Nude from the Back with Mirror and Man / Rückenakt mit Spiegel und Mann, 1912
Oil on canvas, 150 × 75.5 cm
Gordon 225
Brücke-Museum, Berlin

Cat. 14 p. 122
Mexico Bay, Fehmarn / Mexikobucht auf Fehmarn, 1912
Oil on canvas, 50.5 × 50.5 cm
Gordon 243
Private collection, Germany

Cat. 15 p. 123
Trees above Sandy Path / Bäume über Sandweg, 1912
Oil on canvas, 70 × 80 cm
Gordon 248
Kunstmuseum Liechtenstein, Vaduz / Gift of Gerda Techow, Vaduz

Cat. 16 p. 121
The Lighthouse of Fehmarn / Leuchtturm Staberhuk, Fehmarn, 1912
Oil on canvas, 119.5 × 91 cm
Gordon 252
Carnegie Museum of Art, Pittsburgh: Patrons Art Fund, 55.56

Cat. 17 p. 119
Bather between Rocks / Badende zwischen Steinen, 1912
Oil on canvas, 45.5 × 60.5 cm
Gordon 256
Städel Museum, Frankfurt am Main, on permanent loan from a private collection

Cat. 18 p. 127
Nudes in the Studio / Akte im Atelier, 1912
Oil on canvas, 80.5 × 70.5 cm
Gordon 286
Leopold Museum, Vienna

Cat. 19 p. 112
Nollendorfplatz, 1912
Oil on canvas, 69 × 60 cm
Gordon 291
Stadtmuseum Berlin Foundation

Cat. 20 p. 118
Two Nudes by a Tree, Fehmarn / Zwei Akte an einem Baum, Fehmarn, 1912/13
Oil on canvas, 100 × 75 cm
Gordon 261
Private collection

Cat. 21 p. 120
Laburnum Tree / Goldregenbaum, 1912/13
Oil on canvas, 101.5 × 76 cm
Gordon 332
Colby College Museum of Art, Gift of Gertrud A. Mellon, 1961.007

Cat. 22 p. 137
Bridge by the City Gate, Chemnitz / Pfortensteg Chemnitz, 1912/13
Oil on canvas, 89 × 80 cm
Gordon 168
Museum Frieder Burda, Baden-Baden

Cat. 23 p. 124
Elisabethufer, 1912/13
Oil on canvas, 83.5 × 94 cm
Gordon 275
Bayerische Staatsgemälde-sammlungen, Munich, Pinakothek der Moderne

Cat. 24 p. 125
Street at Schöneberg City Park / Strasse am Stadtpark Schöneberg, 1912/13
Oil on canvas, 121 × 151 cm
Gordon 292
Milwaukee Art Museum, Gift of Mrs Harry Lynde Bradley M1964.55

Cat. 25 p. 139
Circus / Zirkus, 1913
Oil on canvas, 120 × 100 cm
Gordon 288
Bayerische Staatsgemälde-sammlungen, Munich, Pinakothek der Moderne

Cat. 26 p. 145
Two Women with Washbasin; The Sisters / Zwei Frauen mit Waschbecken; Die Schwestern, 1913
Oil on canvas, 121 × 90.5 cm
Gordon 295
Städel Museum, Frankfurt am Main, property of the Städelscher Museums-Verein e.V.

Cat. 27 p. 132
Self-Portrait/
Selbstbildnis, 1913
Oil on canvas, 68 × 28 cm
Gordon 297
Private collection

Cat. 28 p. 134
Artist Sketching with Two Women/Artists/
Skizzierender Künstler mit zwei Frauen/Künstlergruppe, 1913
Oil on canvas, 70 × 80 cm
Gordon 301
Collection Stedelijk Museum, Amsterdam

Cat. 29 p. 133
Erich Heckel and Otto Mueller Playing Chess/
Erich Heckel und Otto Mueller beim Schach, 1913
Oil on canvas, 35.5 × 40.5 cm
Gordon 302
Brücke-Museum, Berlin

Cat. 30 p. 135
Yellow Engelufer, Berlin/
Gelbes Engelufer, Berlin, 1913
Oil on canvas, 71.5 × 80.5 cm
Gordon 306
Kunsthalle Mannheim

Cat. 31 p. 162
Fehmarn Windmill/
Windmühle auf Fehmarn, 1913
Oil on canvas, 95.5 × 95.5 cm
Gordon 310
Von der Heydt-Museum Wuppertal

Cat. 32 p. 151
Tower Room (Self-Portrait with Erna)/
Turmzimmer (Selbstbildnis mit Erna), 1913
Oil on canvas, 91 × 81 cm
Gordon 312
Columbus Museum of Art, Ohio, Gift of Howard D. and Babette L. Sirak,the Donors to the Campaign for Enduring Excellence, and the Derby Fund

Cat. 33 p. 146
Erna near the Sea, Fehmarn/
Erna am Meer, Fehmarn, 1913
Oil on canvas, 79 × 69 cm
Gordon 316
Merzbacher Kunststiftung

Cat. 34 p. 148
Erna with Japanese Umbrella (Japanese Girl)/
Erna mit Japanschirm (Japanerin), 1913
Oil on canvas, 80 × 70.5 cm
Gordon 317
Aargauer Kunsthaus Aarau/Bequest of Dr Othmar and Valerie Häuptli

Cat. 35 p. 144
Couple under Japanese Umbrella/
Paar unter Japanschirm, 1913
Oil on canvas, 100 × 75 cm
Gordon 318
Hilti Art Foundation, Schaan, Liechtenstein

Cat. 36 p. 163
Staberhof Country Seat, Fehmarn I/
Gut Staberhof, Fehmarn I, 1913
Oil on canvas, 121 × 151 cm
Gordon 322
Hamburger Kunsthalle

Cat. 37 p. 150
Fehmarn Coast with Lighthouse/
Fehmarnküste mit Leuchtturm, 1913
Oil on canvas, 90.5 × 120.5 cm
Gordon 325
Hermann Gerlinger Collection in the Kunstmuseum Moritzburg Halle (Saale)

Cat. 38 p. 152
Bay on the Fehmarn Coast/
Bucht an der Fehmarnküste, 1913
Oil on canvas, 126 × 90 cm
Gordon 336
Städel Museum, Frankfurt am Main, on permanent loan from a private collection

Cat. 39 p. 159
Girls, Fehmarn/
Mädchen auf Fehmarn, 1913
Oil on canvas, 125 × 90.5 cm
Gordon 348
Lehmbruck Museum, Duisburg

Cat. 40 p. 158
Nudes Next to the Shore Woods/
Akte im Strandwald, 1913
Oil on canvas, 124 × 90 cm
Gordon 354
Kunstmuseum Moritzburg Halle (Saale)

Cat. 41 p. 160
Three Bathers/
Drei Badende, 1913
Oil on canvas, 197.5 × 147.5 cm
Gordon 356
Collection: Art Gallery of New South Wales, Sydney — Art Gallery of New South Wales Foundation Purchase 1984

Cat. 42 p. 149
Red Tree on the Shore/
Roter Baum am Strand, 1913
Oil on canvas, 76 × 100 cm
Gordon 359
Private collection

Cat. 43 p. 136
Female Nude Combing Her Hair/
Sich kämmender Akt, 1913
Oil on canvas, 125 × 90 cm
Gordon 361
Brücke-Museum, Berlin

Cat. 44 p. 169
Street, Berlin/
Die Strasse, 1913
Oil on canvas, 120.5 × 91 cm
Gordon 364
The Museum of Modern Art, New York, purchase, 1939

Cat. 45 pp. 203/205
Two Female Nudes in a Room/
Zwei Akte im Raum, 1914 (verso)/
Nude Youth and Girl on the Beach/
Nackter Jüngling und Mädchen am Strand, 1913 (recto)
Oil on canvas, 104 × 76 cm
Gordon 351
Albertina, Vienna — Batliner Collection

Cat. 46 p. 191
Friedrichstrasse, Berlin, 1914
Oil on canvas, 125 × 91 cm
Gordon 367
Staatsgalerie Stuttgart

Cat. 47 pp. 196/197
Two Women on the Street/
Zwei Frauen auf der Strasse, 1914 (recto)/
Two Bathers in Surf/
Zwei Badende in Wellen, 1912 (verso)
Oil on canvas, 120.5 × 91 cm
Gordon 369
Kunstsammlung Nordrhein-Westfalen, Düsseldorf

Cat. 48 p. 186
In the Café Garden/
Im Cafégarten, 1914
Oil on canvas, 70.5 × 76 cm
Gordon 374
Brücke-Museum, Berlin

Cat. 49 p. 178
Gerda, Half-Length Portrait/
Frauenkopf, Gerda, 1914
Oil on canvas, 99 × 75.5 cm
Gordon 375
Solomon R. Guggenheim Museum, New York, partial gift of Mr and Mrs Mortimer M. Denker, 1978

Cat. 50 p. 175
Railway Overpass/
Eisenbahnüberführung, 1914
Oil on canvas, 79 × 99.5 cm
Gordon 378
Museum Ludwig, Cologne

Cat. 51 pp. 172/173
Streetcar and Train/
Strassenbahn und Eisenbahn, 1914 (recto)/
Dune Landscape/
Dünenlandschaft, 1912 (verso)
Oil on canvas, 71 × 81 cm
Gordon 379
Die Lübecker Museen, Museum Behnhaus Drägerhaus

Cat. 52 p. 177
Gas Tanks and Suburban Railway/
Gaskessel und Vorortbahn, 1914/1920
Oil on canvas, 70.5 × 60.5 cm
Gordon 385
Staatliche Kunsthalle Karlsruhe

Cat. 53 p. 187
Dancing Couple/
Tanzpaar, 1914
Oil on canvas, 91 × 65 cm
Gordon 389
Museum Folkwang, Essen

Cat. 54 p. 202
Forest Path between Young Trees on the Fehmarn Coast/
Waldweg zwischen jungen Bäumen an der Küste von Fehmarn, 1914
Oil on canvas, 120 × 90.5 cm
Not in Gordon
Private collection

Cat. 55 p. 200
Bathers by the Sea/
Badende am Meer, 1914
Oil on canvas, 95.5 × 71 cm
Gordon 399
Private collection

Cat. 56 p. 201
Curving Bay (Laburnum Tree)/
Runde Bucht (Goldregenbaum), c. 1914
Oil on canvas, 146 × 123 cm
Gordon 479
Museo Thyssen-Bornemisza, Madrid

Cat. 57 p. 204
Two Yellow Nudes with Bouquet of Flowers/
Zwei gelbe Akte mit Blumenstrauss, 1914
Wax-oil emulsion on canvas, 80 × 71 cm
Gordon 409
Bündner Kunstmuseum Chur, purchase

Cat. 58 p. 207
Portrait of Hugo/
Porträt Hugo, 1914
Oil on canvas, 60 × 50 cm
Gordon 415
Ernst Ludwig Kirchner Estate, Courtesy Galerie Henze & Ketterer, Wichtrach/Bern

Cat. 59 **p. 179**
Portrait of Oskar Schlemmer/
Porträt Oskar Schlemmer, 1914
Oil on canvas, 70 × 60 cm
Gordon 416
Hessisches Landesmuseum Darmstadt

Cat. 60 **p. 206**
Self-Portrait/
Selbstbildnis, 1914
Oil on canvas, 65 × 47 cm
Gordon 421
Brücke-Museum, Berlin

Cat. 61 **p. 213**
Women on the Street/
Frauen auf der Strasse, 1915
Oil on canvas, 126 × 90 cm
Gordon 427
Von der Heydt-Museum Wuppertal

Cat. 62 **p. 216**
Hussars on Horseback; The Riders/
Husarenritt; Die Reiter, 1915
Oil on canvas, 60.5 × 71 cm
Gordon 432
Private collection

Cat. 63 **p. 212**
Brandenburg Gate, Berlin/
Brandenburger Tor, Berlin, 1915
Oil on canvas, on art panel and wood, 50.5 × 70.5 cm
Gordon 437
Würth Collection

Cat. 64 **p. 231**
Graef's Garden in Jena/
Garten Graef in Jena, 1916
Oil on canvas, 65 × 54.5 cm
Gordon 446
Kunstsammlungen Chemnitz, on permanent loan from the Claus Hüppe Collection

Cat. 65 **p. 227**
Village with Blue Paths/
Dorf mit blauen Wegen, 1916/1920
Oil on canvas, 80 × 70 cm
Gordon 462
Museum Ostwall im Dortmunder U, Dortmund

Cat. 66 **p. 228**
Königstein with Red Church/
Königstein mit roter Kirche, 1916
Oil on canvas, 80.5 × 64 cm
Gordon 467
Private collection

Cat. 67 **p. 229**
The Patient's Bath/
Bad des Kranken, 1916
Oil on board, 53 × 39 cm
Gordon 488
Private collection

Cat. 68 **p. 240**
Rhaetian Railway in Snow/
Rhätische Bahn im Schnee, 1917
Oil on canvas, 94 × 94 cm
Gordon 476
Deutsche Bank Collection

Cat. 69 **p. 235**
Head of Erna/
Kopf Erna, 1917
Oil on canvas, 70.5 × 60.5 cm
Gordon 500
Kirchner Museum Davos, Gift of the Baumgart-Möller Foundation 2000

Cat. 70 **p. 243**
Stafelalp in Snow/
Stafelalp im Schnee, 1917
Oil on cloth, 80 × 90 cm
Gordon 555
E. W. K. Collection, Bern/Davos

Cat. 71 **p. 241**
Moonrise on the Stafelalp/
Mondaufgang auf der Stafelalp, 1917
Oil on canvas, 80 × 90 cm
Gordon 561
Kirchner Museum Davos, on loan from the Rosemarie Ketterer Foundation

Cat. 72 **p. 242**
Mountain Peaks/
Berggipfel, 1918
Oil on canvas, 79.5 × 90 cm
Gordon 512
Private collection

Cat. 73 **p. 247**
Alpine Kitchen/
Alpküche, 1918
Oil on canvas, 121.5 × 121.5 cm
Gordon 518
Museo Thyssen-Bornemisza, Madrid

Drawings and Pastels

Cat. 74 **p. 143**
Young Poet (Simon Guttmann)/
Junger Dichter (Simon Guttmann), 1911
Pencil on paper, 34.4 × 27 cm
Brücke-Museum, Berlin

Cat. 75 **S. 116**
Seated Bather/
Sitzender Badender, 1912
Blue crayon and watercolour on paper, 46 × 39.1 cm
Kunstmuseum Basel, Kupferstichkabinett

Cat. 76 **p. 115**
Two Women and Sculpture on the Beach/
Zwei Frauen und Skulptur am Strand, c.1912
Pencil on paper, 43.3 × 57 cm
Kunstmuseum Winterthur, Gift of Balthasar and Nanni Reinhard-Schinz, 1999

Cat. 77 **p. 141**
Bordello/
Bordell, 1913
Pen, brush and ink on paper, 49.8 × 33 cm
Brücke-Museum, Berlin, Karl and Emy Schmidt-Rottluff Foundation

Cat. 78 **p. 140**
Seated Dancer (Erna)/
Sitzende Tänzerin (Erna), 1913
Pencil on paper, 52.8 × 39.3 cm
Brücke-Museum, Berlin

Cat. 79 **p. 142**
Portrait of Alfred Döblin/
Porträt Alfred Döblin, 1913
Pencil on paper, 43.5 × 34.5 cm
Brücke-Museum, Berlin

Cat. 80 **p. 166**
Potsdamer Platz, 1913
Reed pen and black ink, brush and dark-brown ink on paper, 53 × 39 cm
E. W. K. Collection, Bern/Davos

Cat. 81 **p. 156**
Fehmarn Coast with Yellow Nude/
Fehmarnküste mit gelbem Akt, 1913
Watercolour over pencil on paper, 45.5 × 59 cm
Kirchner Museum Davos, on loan from the Rosemarie Ketterer Foundation

Cat. 82 **p. 147**
Woman in the Hammock/
Frau in der Hängematte, 1913
Black crayon on paper, 40 × 49 cm
Brücke-Museum, Berlin

Cat. 83 **p. 147**
Dancing Female Nude on the Beach, Fehmarn/
Tanzender weiblicher Akt am Strand, Fehmarn, 1913
Carpenter pencil on thick paper, 40.5 × 47.5 cm
Kirchner Museum Davos, Gift of the Ernst Ludwig Kirchner Estate 1994

Cat. 84 **p. 161**
Three Bathers in the Surf/
Drei Badende in der Welle, 1913
Charcoal on paper, 49.5 × 40 cm
E. W. K. Collection, Bern/Davos

Cat. 85 **p. 189**
Women on the Street/
Frauen auf der Strasse, 1913/14
Pastel and mixed media on paper, 40.3 × 29.4 cm
Leopold-Hoesch-Museum & Papiermuseum Düren

Cat. 86 **p. 190**
Cocottes on the Street/
Kokotten auf der Strasse, 1913/14
Pastel on paper, 40 × 30 cm
Kirchner Museum Davos, on loan from the Rosemarie Ketterer Foundation

Cat. 87 **p. 192**
Street Scene/
Strassenszene, 1913/14
Pastel on paper, 40 × 30 cm
Brücke-Museum, Berlin

Cat. 88 **p. 167**
Street Scene in Berlin/
Strassenszene in Berlin, 1913/14
Pencil on paper, 20.6 × 16.2 cm
E. W. K. Collection, Bern/Davos

Cat. 89 **p. 167**
Street Scene in Berlin/
Strassenszene in Berlin, 1913/14
Pencil on paper, 20.6 × 16 cm
E. W. K. Collection, Bern/Davos

Cat. 90 **p. 183**
Standing Nude in Front of the Tent/
Stehender Akt vor dem Zelt, c.1913/14
Coloured crayon on handmade paper, 67.5 × 51.2 cm
Museum Kunstpalast, Düsseldorf

Cat. 91 **p. 181**
Portrait of Botho Graef/
Bildnis Botho Graef, 1914
Charcoal on paper, 48 × 30 cm
Brücke-Museum, Berlin

Cat. 92 **p. 174**
The Railway Overpass/
Die Eisenbahnüberführung, 1914
Brush and ink on paper, 43 × 34.5 cm
Stadtmuseum Berlin Foundation

Cat. 93 **p. 193**
Street Scene/
Strassenszene, 1914
Pastel on paper, 47.2 × 29.4 cm
E. W. K. Collection, Bern/Davos

Cat. 94 **p. 188**
Woman with Hat (Street Scene)/
Frau mit Hut (Strassenszene), 1914
Carpenter pencil on light chamois paper with foxing, 20.1 × 14.4 cm
Kirchner Museum Davos, Gift of the Ernst Ludwig Kirchner Estate 1994

Cat. 95 **p. 188**
Two Women with Hats (Street Scene)/
Zwei Frauen mit Hüten (Strassenszene), 1914
Carpenter pencil on paper with foxing, 20.5 × 15.3 cm
Kirchner Museum Davos, Gift of the Ernst Ludwig Kirchner Estate 1994

Cat. 96 p. 182
Two Figures in a Room/
Zwei Figuren im Raum, 1914
Coloured crayon over charcoal on paper, 67 × 50 cm
Brücke-Museum, Berlin

Cat. 97 p. 198
Sailing Boats off Fehmarn/
Segelboote bei Fehmarn, 1914
Black crayon on paper, 49 × 39 cm
Brücke-Museum, Berlin

Cat. 98 p. 198
Expansive Fehmarn Coast/
Ausgedehnte Fehmarnküste, c.1914
Charcoal on slightly satinised chamois paper, 36 × 46 cm
Kirchner Museum Davos, Gift of the Ernst Ludwig Kirchner Estate 1990

Cat. 99 p. 210
Painter and Nude Woman (Self-Portrait with Model)/
Maler und nackte Frau (Selbstbildnis mit Modell), 1915
Pastel on paper, 68.5 × 50 cm
Brücke-Museum, Berlin

Cat. 100 p. 211
Self-Portrait/
Selbstbildnis, 1915
Pencil on paper, 37 × 32 cm
Private collection

Cat. 101 p. 219
Dance between the Women/
Der Tanz zwischen den Frauen, 1915/16
Pen and ink on paper, 28.7 × 22.3 cm
E. W. K. Collection, Bern/Davos

Cat. 102 p. 237
Self-Portrait in Morphine Rush/
Selbstbildnis im Morphiumrausch, 1917
Reed pen and ink on gessoed paper, 50 × 38 cm
Brücke-Museum, Berlin

Prints

Cat. 103 p. 98
Street Life in Dresden/
Strassenleben in Dresden, 1908
Lithograph on chamois blotting paper,
image: 27 × 38 cm,
sheet: 43.9 × 54.5 cm
Gercken 210
Kassel, Museumslandschaft Hessen Kassel, Graphische Sammlung

Cat. 104 p. 117
Women Bathing between White Rocks, Fehmarn/
Badende Frauen zwischen weissen Steinen, Fehmarn, 1912
Colour woodcut on vellum,
image: 28.5 × 29 cm,
sheet: 35.4/34.8 × 35.4/34.5 cm
Gercken 577/I
Brücke-Museum, Berlin

Cat. 105 p. 138
Cartwheeling Acrobatic Dancers/
Sich überschlagende akrobatische Tänzerinnen, 1913
Colour woodcut on blotting paper,
image: 34 × 49 cm,
sheet: 41.1 × 56.8 cm
Gercken 593.2
Werner Coninx Foundation, Zurich

Cat. 106 p. 154
Trees and Shrubs Next to the Beach, Fehmarn/
Bäume und Büsche am Strand, Fehmarn, 1913
Colour woodcut on blotting paper, mounted on cardboard,
image: 50.0/5 × 38.5/40.2 cm,
sheet: 57.2/5 × 42.2/0 cm
Gercken 616/II.2
Brücke-Museum, Berlin, Karl and Emy Schmidt-Rottluff Foundation

Cat. 107 p. 165
Three Bathers in the Surf/
Drei Badende in den Wellen, 1913
Colour woodcut on blotting paper,
image: 40.5 × 27.5 cm,
sheet: 47.9 × 34.6 cm
Gercken 622/II.1
Werner Coninx Foundation, Zurich

Cat. 108 p. 164
Man Entering the Sea (Hans Gewecke)/
Ins Meer Schreitender (Hans Gewecke), 1913
Colour lithograph on smooth cardboard,
image: 59.5 × 51 cm,
sheet: 67.3 × 57.4 cm
Gercken 625
Private collection, Courtesy W. Wittrock, Berlin

Cat. 109 p. 155
Three Bathers Next to Rocks, Fehmarn/
Drei Badende an Steinen, Fehmarn, 1913
Colour lithograph on smooth cardboard,
image: 50 × 59 cm,
sheet: 50 × 60.9 cm
Gercken 626/I
Kunstmuseum Basel, Kupferstichkabinett

Cat. 110 p. 168
Five Cocottes on the Street/
Fünf Kokotten auf der Strasse, 1913/14
Woodcut on vellum card,
image: 49 × 37 cm,
sheet: 52.5 × 39.5 cm
Gercken 645/I
Städel Museum, Graphische Sammlung, Frankfurt am Main

Cat. 111 p. 195
Women on Potsdamer Platz, Berlin/
Frauen am Potsdamer Platz, Berlin, 1914
Woodcut on blotting paper,
image: 52.2 × 38.4 cm,
sheet: 58 × 43 cm
Gercken 646/III.1
Museum Folkwang, Essen

Cat. 112 p. 194
Cocotte Offering Herself/
Sich anbietende Kokotte, 1914
Line and surface-tone etching on zinc, on soft vellum,
image: 35 × 27 cm,
sheet: 46.5 × 38.8 cm
Gercken 661/I.2
Brücke-Museum, Berlin

Cat. 113 p. 184
Music Restaurant/
Musikrestaurant, 1914
Lithograph on yellow paper,
image: 59.5 × 50.5 cm,
sheet: 65 × 54.5 cm
Gercken 666/I
Brücke-Museum, Berlin

Cat. 114 p. 185
Cocottes on Kurfürstendamm/
Kokotten am Kurfürstendamm, 1914
Lithograph on yellow paper,
image: 59.3 × 50.5 cm,
sheet: 66.3 × 56.2 cm
Gercken 668/II
Olbricht Collection

Cat. 115 p. 185
Leipziger Strasse, Intersection/
Leipziger Strasse, Kreuzung, 1914
Lithograph on yellow paper,
image: 59 × 50.6 cm,
sheet: 70.5 × 55.9 cm
Gercken 669/III
Brücke-Museum, Berlin, Karl and Emy Schmidt-Rottluff Foundation

Cat. 116 p. 184
Dancing Nudes/
Tanzende Akte, 1914
Lithograph on yellow paper,
image: 59.2 × 50.6 cm,
sheet: 66 × 56 cm
Gercken 680/II
Estate of Erich Heckel, Hemmenhofen (DE)

Cat. 117 p. 199
Sailing Boats off Fehmarn/
Segelboote bei Fehmarn, 1914
Woodcut on light grey blotting paper,
image: 41.9/7 × 39/40.3 cm,
sheet: 56.7 × 42.2/0 cm
Gercken 710/II
Brücke-Museum, Berlin

Cat. 118 p. 217
Artillerists' Bath — Bathing Soldiers/
Artilleristenbad — Badende Soldaten, 1915
Lithograph on yellow paper,
image: 50.5 × 59,0/4 cm,
sheet: 56.8/3 × 62.6/63 cm
Gercken 760/II
E. W. K. Collection, Bern/Davos

Cat. 119 p. 217
Mounted Patrol in the Evening/
Patrouillenritt am Abend, 1915
Lithograph on yellow paper,
image: 50.5 × 59.5 cm,
sheet: 57 × 67 cm
Gercken 762/III
Werner Coninx Foundation, Zurich

Cat. 120 p. 214
Cocotte on the Street/
Kokotte auf der Strasse, 1915
Woodcut on yellow paper, print from drawing block in black,
drawing block: 34.5 × 24.5 cm,
sheet: 40.8 × 27.8 cm
Gercken 771/I.1
Städel Museum, Graphische Sammlung, Frankfurt am Main

Cat. 121 p. 214
Cocotte on the Street/
Kokotte auf der Strasse, 1915
Woodcut on thin Japan paper, print from colour block in black,
colour block: 34.5 × 24 cm,
sheet: 45.5 × 39.8 cm
Gercken 771/I.2
Städel Museum, Graphische Sammlung, Frankfurt am Main

Cat. 122 p. 215
Cocotte on the Street/
Kokotte auf der Strasse, 1915
Colour woodcut on blotting paper, print from 2 blocks in black, red, yellow, blue and green,
colour block: 34.6/8 × 25 cm,
drawing block: 34.5 × 24.7 cm,
sheet: 57 × 42 cm
Gercken 771/II.a
Städel Museum, Graphische Sammlung, Frankfurt am Main

Cat. 123 p. 215
Cocotte on the Street/
Kokotte auf der Strasse, 1915
Colour woodcut on stiff vellum, print from 2 blocks in violet, red, yellow, blue and green,
colour block: 34.6/8 × 25 cm,
drawing block: 33.5 × 24 cm,
sheet: 53.3 × 38.4 cm
Gercken 771/II.c
Private collection, Courtesy W. Wittrock, Berlin

Cat. 124 a p. 220
Schlemihl cycle, cover illustration with title "Adelbert von Chamisso/Schlemihl"/ Schlemihl-Zyklus, Umschlag-zeichnung mit Titel "Adelbert von Chamisso/Schlemihl", 1915
Lithograph on violet paper, pasted onto yellow cover paper, image: 26.7 × 21.5 cm, sheet: 28.4 × 23 cm
Gercken 772
Brücke-Museum, Berlin, Karl and Emy Schmidt-Rottluff Foundation

Cat. 124 b p. 220
Schlemihl cycle, title page for "Peter Schlemihl's Wondrous Story"/ Schlemihl-Zyklus, Titelblatt zu "Peter Schlemihls wundersame Geschichte", 1915
Colour woodcut on blotting paper, image: 29.3 × 26.3 cm, sheet: 57.9 × 41.7 cm
Gercken 773
Brücke-Museum, Berlin, Karl and Emy Schmidt-Rottluff Foundation

Cat. 124 c p. 221
Schlemihl cycle, sheet 1: The Sale of the Shadow/ Schlemihl-Zyklus, Blatt 1: Der Verkauf des Schattens, 1915
Colour woodcut on blotting paper, image: 32.3 × 22 cm, sheet: 57.8 × 41.8 cm
Gercken 774.2
Brücke-Museum, Berlin, Karl and Emy Schmidt-Rottluff Foundation

Cat. 124 d p. 222
Schlemihl cycle, sheet 2: The Beloved/ Schlemihl-Zyklus, Blatt 2: Die Geliebte, 1915
Colour woodcut on blotting paper, image: 28.8 × 23.6 cm, sheet: 57.8 × 41.7 cm
Gercken 775/III.2.a
Brücke-Museum, Berlin, Karl and Emy Schmidt-Rottluff Foundation

Cat. 124 e p. 223
Schlemihl cycle, sheet 3: Struggles — Pangs of Love/ Schlemihl-Zyklus, Blatt 3: Kämpfe — Qualen der Liebe, 1915
Colour woodcut on blotting paper, image: 33.6 × 21.7 cm, sheet: 57 × 41.9 cm
Gercken 776.2
Brücke-Museum, Berlin, Karl and Emy Schmidt-Rottluff Foundation

Cat. 124 f p. 223
Schlemihl cycle, sheet 4: Schlemihl in the Solitude of His Room/ Schlemihl-Zyklus, Blatt 4: Schlemihl in der Einsamkeit des Zimmers, 1915
Colour woodcut on blotting paper, image: 33.3 × 23.8 cm, sheet: 57.9 × 41.7 cm
Gercken 777.2
Brücke-Museum, Berlin, Karl and Emy Schmidt-Rottluff Foundation

Cat. 124 g p. 224
Schlemihl cycle, sheet 5: Schlemihl Encounters the Little Grey Man on the Country Road/ Schlemihl-Zyklus, Blatt 5: Begegnung Schlemihls mit dem grauen Männlein auf der Landstrasse, 1915
Colour woodcut on blotting paper, image: 30.5 × 31 cm, sheet: 57.9 × 41.7 cm
Gercken 778/II.b
Brücke-Museum, Berlin, Karl and Emy Schmidt-Rottluff Foundation

Cat. 124 h p. 225
Schlemihl cycle, sheet 6: Schlemihl's Encounter with the Shadow/ Schlemihl-Zyklus, Blatt 6: Schlemihls Begegnung mit dem Schatten, 1915
Colour woodcut on blotting paper, image: 30.5 × 29.3 cm, sheet: 58 × 41.5 cm
Gercken 779/II.a
Brücke-Museum, Berlin, Karl and Emy Schmidt-Rottluff Foundation

Cat. 125 p. 233
Self-Portrait, Drawing/ Selbstbildnis, zeichnend, 1916
Line and surface-tone etching on zinc, on copperplate printing paper, image: 40.5 × 31 cm, sheet: 56.2 × 36.5 cm
Gercken 780/II
Brücke-Museum, Berlin

Cat. 126 p. 232
Nervous Persons at Table (Kohnstamm Sanatorium)/ Nervöse beim Diner (Sanatorium Kohnstamm), 1916
Woodcut on cardboard, image: 42 × 28 cm, sheet: 56.8 × 39.3 cm
Gercken 807/II
Kassel, Museumslandschaft Hessen Kassel, Graphische Sammlung, Städtischer Kunstbesitz

Cat. 127 p. 244
Three Paths, Stafelalp/ Drei Wege, Stafelalp, 1917
Woodcut on grey blotting paper, image: 50 × 33.7 cm, sheet: 56.6/56 × 41.8/42 cm
Gercken 855
Kunsthaus Zürich, Grafische Sammlung

Cat. 128 p. 234
Head of Henry van de Velde, dark/ Kopf Henry van de Velde, dunkel, 1917
Woodcut on blotting paper, image: 49.5 × 39.5 cm, sheet: 57.5 × 44.5 cm
Gercken 862
Kunsthaus Zürich, Grafische Sammlung, Gift of the artist

Cat. 129 p. 234
Head of Eberhard Grisebach (en face)/ Kopf Eberhard Grisebach (en face), 1917
Woodcut on blotting paper, image: 33/34 × 24/28 cm, sheet: 59 × 40 cm
Gercken 871/I
Private collection

Cat. 130 p. 65
Head of the Invalid — Self-Portrait as an Invalid/ Kopf des Kranken — Selbstportrait als Kranker, 1917
Woodcut on blotting paper, image: 56.9 × 27.3 cm, sheet: 58.8 × 38 cm
Gercken 872/II
Brücke-Museum, Berlin

Cat. 131 p. 245
Self-Portrait with Dancing Death/ Selbstportrait mit tanzendem Tod, 1918
Woodcut on paper, image: 50.3 × 34 cm, sheet: 59 × 46 cm
Gercken 886/I
Museum Folkwang, Essen

Sketchbooks and Albums

Cat. 132 p. 114
Sketchbook 26, 1912
Oilcloth booklet with 3 metal clasps, 21 × 17.3 × 1.1 cm (closed)
Presler Skb. 26
Kirchner Museum Davos, Gift of the Ernst Ludwig Kirchner Estate 1990

Cat. 133 no illus.
Sketchbook 28, 1912–1913
Oilcloth booklet, 20.6 × 17.2 × 0.7 cm (closed)
Presler Skb. 28
Kirchner Museum Davos, Gift of the Ernst Ludwig Kirchner Estate 1990

Cat. 134 p. 236
Sketchbook 54, 1917–1918
Oilcloth booklet, 20 × 15 × 0.6 cm (closed)
Presler Skb. 54
Kirchner Museum Davos, Gift of the Ernst Ludwig Kirchner Estate 1990

Cat. 135 pp. 79–91
Album with 12 sketches for the Apocalypse/ Album mit 12 Skizzen zur Apokalypse, 1917
Pencil, ink and watercolour on cigarette-packet paper, each max. 8 × 10 cm, album 18.1 × 17.5 × 1.8 cm (closed)
The Getty Research Institute, Los Angeles (850463)

Photographs

The exhibited works include contact prints produced by the Kirchner Museum Davos from the original plates/glass negatives

Cat. 136 p. 143
Alfred Döblin in Kirchner's live-in studio, 1912/13
Gelatine silver (modern print), 16.5 × 12 cm
Scotti 319
Kirchner Archive, Wichtrach/Bern, Kirchner Museum Davos

Cat. 137 p. 44
Erna Schilling and Ernst Ludwig Kirchner in the live-in studio in Berlin-Wilmersdorf, c. 1913
Glass negative, 18 × 24 cm
Scotti 18
Kirchner Museum Davos, Gift of the Ernst Ludwig Kirchner Estate 1992

Cat. 138 p. 153
Bay on the east coast of the Baltic Sea island of Fehmarn, 1913
Glass negative, 11.8 × 8.8 cm
Scotti 20
Kirchner Museum Davos, Gift of the Ernst Ludwig Kirchner Estate 1992

Cat. 139 p. 114
Erna Schilling on the rocks on the coast, Fehmarn, 1913
Contact print (modern print), 6 × 9 cm
Scotti 21
Kirchner Museum Davos, Gift of the Ernst Ludwig Kirchner Estate 1992

Cat. 140 p. 180
Erna Schilling in Kirchner's live-in studio, 1913/14
Gelatine silver (vintage print), 16.5 × 11 cm
Scotti 239
E.W.K. Collection, Bern/Davos, Courtesy Kirchner Museum Davos

Cat. 141 p. 251
Self-portrait in the live-in studio in Berlin-Friedenau, 1913/1915
Glass negative, 13 × 18 cm
Scotti 27
Kirchner Museum Davos, Gift of the Ernst Ludwig Kirchner Estate 2001

Cat. 142 p. 59
Mansard niche in Kirchner's live-in studio, Berlin-Friedenau, 1914/15
Glass negative, 24 × 18 cm
Scotti 28
Kirchner Museum Davos, Gift of the Ernst Ludwig Kirchner Estate 2001

Cat. 143 p. 58
Unknown young woman (Gerda Schilling?), Ernst Ludwig Kirchner, Erna Schilling and Hans Gewecke in Kirchner's live-in studio, Berlin-Friedenau, 1914/15
Glass negative, 18 × 24 cm
Scotti 32
Kirchner Museum Davos, Gift of the Ernst Ludwig Kirchner Estate 1992

Cat. 144 p. 180
Botho Graef in Kirchner's live-in studio, Berlin-Friedenau, 1914/15
Glass negative, 24 × 18 cm
Scotti 34
Kirchner Museum Davos, Gift of the Ernst Ludwig Kirchner Estate 1992

Cat. 145 p. 66
Self-portrait as a soldier in the live-in studio in Berlin-Friedenau, 1915
Glass negative, 18 × 13 cm
Scotti 41
Kirchner Museum Davos, Gift of the Ernst Ludwig Kirchner Estate 1992

Cat. 146 p. 218
Werner Gothein, unknown young woman obscured next to him (Gerda Schilling?), Ernst Ludwig Kirchner (?) and Erna Schilling in Kirchner's live-in studio, Berlin-Friedenau, 1915
Glass negative, 13 × 18 cm
Scotti 241
E.W.K. Collection, Bern/Davos, Courtesy Kirchner Museum Davos

Cat. 147 p. 255
Ernst Ludwig Kirchner, Davos Frauenkirch, c.1919
Glass negative, 24 × 18 cm
Scotti 71
Kirchner Museum Davos, Gift of the Ernst Ludwig Kirchner Estate 1992

Sculptures

Cat. 148 p. 154
Figure Looking Back/ Rückschauende, 1913
Wood (oak, from a single trunk), stained dark,
H: c.81 cm, base: 20 × 20 cm
Henze 1913/06
Museum Kunstpalast, Düsseldorf

Cat. 149 p. 60
Anonymous, leopard stool (from the former collection of Ernst Ludwig Kirchner), 19th century
African obeche wood,
H: 35 cm, ø 42 cm
Bündner Kunstmuseum Chur, Gift of Prof. Otto Tschumi, Bern (1954)

Textiles

Ernst Ludwig Kirchner (design) and Erna Schilling (execution)

Cat. 150 p. 61
Supraporte from Kirchner's live-in studio, Berlin-Friedenau, 1914/15
Wool embroidery on linen, 113 cm wide at top, side strips each 235 cm long and 44 cm wide at the bottom
E.W.K. Collection, Bern/Davos

Cat. 151 p. 63
Backrest cover from Kirchner's live-in studio, Berlin-Friedenau, 1914/15
Wool embroidery on linen, 79 × 251cm
E.W.K. Collection, Bern/Davos

Cat. 152 p. 63
Backrest cover from Kirchner's live-in studio, Berlin-Friedenau, 1914/15
Wool embroidery on linen, 79 × 165 cm
E.W.K. Collection, Bern/Davos

Cat. 153 p. 62
Divan throw from Kirchner's live-in studio, Berlin-Friedenau, 1914/15
Wool embroidery on linen, 114 × 160 cm
Private collection

Cat. 154 p. 63
Tablecloth from Kirchner's live-in studio, Berlin-Friedenau, 1914/15
Wool embroidery on linen, 67 × 164 cm
E.W.K. Collection, Bern/Davos

About the Authors

Günther Gercken, **Studied medicine and psychology at the universities of Freiburg and Cologne. Doctorate in medicine in 1956 and medical licence in 1959. Professor of biochemistry at Hamburg University. In 1968 director of the graphics/objects working committee of the documenta council. Long-time president of the Kunstverein in Hamburg, organising and participating in many exhibition projects. Numerous writings on contemporary artists, books about Horst Antes, Georg Baselitz, Ernst Ludwig Kirchner and Gustav Kluge. Author of *Ernst Ludwig Kirchner: Kritisches Werkverzeichnis der Druckgraphik.* In 2016 established the Stiftung Günther und Annemarie Gercken at the Staatliche Kunstsammlungen Dresden with works by contemporary artists.**

Sandra Gianfreda, **Studied history of art and architecture as well as psychology in Bern and Rome, dissertation on the half-figure history painting in the Seicento in 2001. From 1998 to 2002 assistant to the chair of modern art history in Bern, then research fellowship in the 19th Century and Classical Modernism Department of the Kunstmuseum Basel. From 2005 to 2009 curator at the Kunstmuseum Winterthur. From 2009 to early 2015 project manager and curator of special exhibitions at the Museum Folkwang, Essen, and since summer 2015 curator at the Kunsthaus Zürich. Exhibitions and publications on Impressionism, Classical Modernism and post-war American, German and Italian art.**

Charles Werner Haxthausen, **Ph.D. in art history, Columbia University, New York, in 1976; dissertation: "Paul Klee: The Formative Years". From 1975 to 1983 assistant then associate professor of fine arts and curator of the Busch-Reisinger Museum, Harvard University. From 1985 to 1993 associate professor of art history at the University of Minnesota. From 1993 to 2016 professor of art history at Williams College, Williamstown, MA; since 2016 professor emeritus. Author of numerous publications on modern and contemporary art and art criticism. In 2012 curated the exhibition *Sol LeWitt: The Well-Tempered Grid,* Williams College Museum of Art.**

Martina Pfister, **Studied medieval, modern and East Asian art history and political science at the University of Zurich. In 2007 internship at the Peggy Guggenheim Collection in Venice; from 2008 to 2010 position at the Daros Latinamerica Collection, Zurich. Following a period at the Kunstmuseum Winterthur, exhibition organisation at the Kunsthaus Zürich since 2012.**

Karin Schick, **Art history, philosophy and German studies in Tübingen and Boston; dissertation on Paul Cézanne's reception in the United States. After positions at the Hamburger Kunsthalle and the Kunstmuseum Stuttgart from 1998 to 2006, appointed director of the Kirchner Museum Davos. Since December 2012 head of the Modern Art department at the Hamburger Kunsthalle. Publications, exhibitions and lectures on Max Beckmann, Otto Dix, Ernst Ludwig Kirchner, Emil Nolde, Sophie Taeuber-Arp and others.**

Uwe M. Schneede, **Doctorate in art history, 1965. Assistant at the Kunsthalle Düsseldorf 1966–1967, director of the Württembergischer Kunstverein, Stuttgart, and the Kunstverein in Hamburg, 1968–1984; until 1990 professor of modern art history at Ludwig-Maximilians-Universität in Munich, then director of the Hamburger Kunsthalle until 2006. Author of numerous publications on modern art. In 2010 curated the exhibition *Das schönste Museum der Welt* (The Most Beautiful Museum in the World) at the Museum Folkwang in Essen, in 2011 the exhibition *Gerhard Richter: Bilder einer Epoche* (Gerhard Richter: Pictures of an Epoch) at the Bucerius Kunst Forum in Hamburg, and in 2013 the exhibition *1914: Die Avantgarden im Kampf* (1914: The Avant-Gardes at War) at the Bundeskunsthalle in Bonn. Since 2015 director of the German Lost Art Foundation in Magdeburg.**

Photo Credits

Front cover

Ernst Ludwig Kirchner, *Street at Schöneberg City Park* (detail), 1912/13 (Cat. 24); photo: Courtesy Milwaukee Art Museum, photo credit: Larry Sanders

Back cover

Ernst Ludwig Kirchner, *Women Bathing between White Rocks, Fehmarn* (detail), 1912 (Cat. 104); photo: Brücke-Museum, Berlin

Front endpapers

Max Missmann, Unter den Linden at Friedrichstrasse in Berlin, 1909; photo: ullstein bild–Imagno; Ernst Ludwig Kirchner, Bay on the east coast of the Baltic Sea island of Fehmarn, 1913 (Cat. 138); photo: Kirchner Museum Davos/digitised: Stephan Bösch

Back endpapers

Waldemar Titzenthaler, Berlin Leipziger Strasse at Friedrichstrasse, 1904, photo: ullstein bild–Waldemar Titzenthaler; Ernst Ludwig Kirchner, Bathers in the Baltic Sea on Fehmarn, 1913, glass negative, 8.8 × 11.84 cm, Kirchner Museum Davos, Gift of the Ernst Ludwig Kirchner Estate 1992; photo: Kirchner Museum Davos/digitised: Stephan Bösch

Photo: AGNSW: p. 160

Albertina, Vienna: pp. 203, 205

Alinari Archives, Florence: p. 49 (right)

Allen Memorial Art Museum, Oberlin College, Ohio: p. 67 (right)

© Antje Zeis-Loi, Medienzentrum Wuppertal: p. 102

Archive Karin Schick: p. 34

Photo: Archive Museum Gunzenhauser: p. 113

© ARTOTHEK: p. 25

Photo: Bernd Kirtz: p. 159

©Blauel/Gnamm–ARTOTHEK: pp. 41(right), 124

© bpk/Bayerische Staatsgemäldesammlungen: p. 70

© bpk/Bayerische Staatsgemäldesammlungen/Sybille Forster: p. 139

© bpk/Hamburger Kunsthalle/Elke Walford: p. 163

© bpk/Kunstsammlung Nordrhein-Westfalen, Düsseldorf/Achim Kukulies: pp. 196, 197

© bpk/Nationalgalerie, Staatliche Museen zu Berlin/Jörg P. Anders: pp. 21, 39 (left)

© bpk/Staatliche Kunsthalle Karlsruhe/Annette Fischer/Heike Kohler: p. 177

© bpk/Staatsgalerie Stuttgart: pp. 38 (right), 85 (bottom), 86 (bottom), 90, 99, 191

Bridgeman Images: p. 48

Brücke-Museum, Berlin: pp. 27 (right), 38 (left), 65, 103, 106, 117, 126, 133, 136, 140, 141, 142, 143 (right), 147 (top), 154 (left), 181, 182, 184 (right), 185 (right), 186, 192, 194, 198 (bottom), 199, 206, 210, 220–225, 233, 237

© Bündner Kunstmuseum: pp. 60, 204

Photo © 2016 Carnegie Museum of Art, Pittsburgh: p. 121

Colby College Museum of Art: p. 120

Columbus Museum of Art, Ohio: p. 151

Deutsche Bank Collection: p. 240

Photo: Ebersold GmbH: p. 28

Estate of Erich Heckel, Hemmenhofen (DE): p. 184 (left)

E.W.K. Collection, Bern/Davos: pp. 61, 63, 82 (bottom), 89, 107, 161, 166, 167, 193, 217 (top), 219, 243

Photo: Courtesy Galerie Henze & Ketterer, Wichtrach/Bern pp. 37 (left), 207

Photo: Courtesy Galerie Kornfeld, Bern: pp. 27 (left), 36, 185 (left)

The Getty Research Institute, Los Angeles: pp. 79, 80, 83, 84, 87, 88, 91

Groninger Museum, photo: Marten de Leeuw: p. 40 (left)

Hessisches Landesmuseum Darmstadt, photo: Wolfgang Fuhrmannek: p. 179

Hilti Art Foundation, Schaan, Liechtenstein: p. 144

Photo credit: Jörg Müller: p. 148

Kassel, Museumslandschaft Hessen Kassel: pp. 98, 232

Photo: Courtesy Kirchner Museum Davos: p. 252

Kirchner Museum Davos: pp. 50 (left), 114 (bottom), 147 (bottom), 156, 188, 190, 198 (top), 235

Kirchner Museum Davos/digitised: Stephan Bösch: pp. 2–3, 44, 46, 47, 66 (right), 51, 52, 54, 58, 59, 114 (top), 143 (left), 153, 180, 218, 251, 254, 255

Kirchner Museum Davos/photo: Jakob-Jägli: p. 241

Kirchner Museum Davos/photo: Stephan Bösch: p. 236

Photo: Klaus E. Göltz, Halle (Saale): pp. 150, 158

Kunsthalle Mannheim, photo: Cem Yücetas: p. 135

Kunsthaus Zürich: pp. 234 (left), p. 244

Kunstmuseum Basel, Martin P. Bühler: pp. 116, 155

Kunstmuseum Bern: p. 111

Kunstmuseum Liechtenstein/Heinz Freute, Vaduz: p. 123

Photo: Kunstsammlungen Chemnitz/PUNCTUM/Bertram Kober: p. 231

Lenders: pp. 62, 118, 122, 132, 149, 211, 216, 229, 234 (right), 242

Leopold Museum, Vienna: p. 127

Die Lübecker Museen, Museum Behnhaus Drägerhaus: pp. 172, 173

LWL-Mkuk/ARTOTHEK: p. 33

Photo: Medienzentrum, Antje Zeis-Loi/Kunst- und Museumsverein Wuppertal: p. 69

Medienzentrum, Antje Zeis-Loi/Von der Heydt-Museum Wuppertal: pp. 100, 162, 213

Merzbacher Kunststiftung: pp. 105, 110, 146

Courtesy Milwaukee Art Museum, photo credit: Larry Sanders: p. 125

Museo Thyssen-Bornemisza, Madrid: pp. 201, 247

© Museum Folkwang, Essen–ARTOTHEK: pp. 187, 195, 245

Museum Frieder Burda, Baden-Baden: p. 137

Museum Kunstpalast/ARTOTHEK: p. 41 (left)

© Museum Kunstpalast–Horst Kolberg–ARTOTHEK: p. 183

© Museum Kunstpalast–Manos Meisen–ARTOTHEK: p. 154 (right)

© 2016. Digital image, The Museum of Modern Art, New York/SCALA, Florence: p. 169

Museum Ostwall im Dortmunder U, Dortmund: p. 227

Image courtesy of the National Gallery of Art, Washington: pp. 37 (right), 78, 82 (top), 85 (top), 86 (top)

Photo: Peter Hinschläger: p. 189

Photo: Reto Rodolfo Pedrini, Zurich: pp. 200, 202

Photo: © Rheinisches Bildarchiv, rba_d024729: p. 22

Photo: © Rheinisches Bildarchiv, rba_c010738: p. 175

Photo: © Rheinisches Bildarchiv, rba_d022399: p. 228

© Swiss Institute for Art Research (SIK-ISEA), Zurich, Jean-Pierre Kuhn: p. 115

Solomon R. Guggenheim Museum, New York: pp. 67 (left), 178

© Städel Museum–U. Edelmann/ARTOTHEK: pp. 66 (left), 168, 214, 215 (left)

© Städel Museum–ARTOTHEK: pp. 101, 119, 145, 152

Photo: Städtische Sammlungen Freital: p. 68

© Stadtmuseum Berlin Foundation: pp. 26, 112, 174

Stedelijk Museum Amsterdam: pp. 104, 134

© Virginia Museum of Fine Arts, photo: Travis Fullerton: p. 50 (right)

Werner Coninx Foundation, Zurich: pp. 10–11, 138, 165, 217 (bottom)

Wilhelm-Hack-Museum, Ludwigshafen: pp. 39 (right), 40 (right)

Courtesy W. Wittrock, Berlin: pp. 164, 215 (right)

Würth Collection/photo: Volker Naumann, Schönaich: p. 212

VONTOBEL
-STIFTUNG

Schweizerische Eidgenossenschaft
Confédération suisse
Confederazione Svizzera
Confederaziun svizra

Swiss Confederation

Federal Department of Home Affairs FDHA
Federal Office of Culture FOC

ArsRhenia
Stiftung zur überregionalen Förderung
von Kunst und Kultur

**A-Charity
Foundation**

TRUUS UND GERRIT
VAN RIEMSDIJK STIFTUNG

DR. GEORG
UND JOSI
GUGGEN
HEIM STIF
TUNG

Colophon

This book is published in conjunction with the exhibition *Vibrant Metropolis / Idyllic Nature Kirchner — The Berlin Years,* Kunsthaus Zürich, 10 February–7 May 2017.

The exhibition was conceived in cooperation with the Brücke-Museum, Berlin.

EXHIBITION

Concept
Magdalena M. Moeller and Sandra Gianfreda

Curator
Sandra Gianfreda

Co-curator
Magdalena M. Moeller

Project assistant
Martina Pfister

Coordinator
Franziska Lentzsch

Insurance and transport
Gerda Kram

Public relations
Björn Quellenberg and Kristin Steiner

Sponsoring
Monique Spaeti

Conservation and restoration
Hanspeter Marty and Tobias Haupt

Documentation
Cécile Brunner

Technical services
Gabriel Cantieni and team

Exhibition architecture
Ulrich Zickler

Reconstruction of mansard niche
Johann-Christoph Knospe

Typography
Lena Huber

CATALOGUE

Editor
Zürcher Kunstgesellschaft/ Kunsthaus Zürich

Content editing
Sandra Gianfreda and Martina Pfister

Editing
Markus Kersting

Translations
Russell Stockman

Copy-editing and proofreading
Simon Cowper, Tradukas GbR

Graphic design
Lena Huber

Typesetting
Lena Huber and
Etc. pp., Berlin – Ralf Klöden

Production
Katja Durchholz

Lithography
Repromayer Medienproduktion GmbH, Reutlingen

Printing and binding
Printer Trento SRL, Trento
Printed in Italy

Bibliographic information published by the Deutschen Nationalbibliothek: the Deutsche Nationalbibliothek lists this publication in the Deutsche Nationalbibliografie; detailed bibliographic data is available on the Internet at "http://www.dnb.de".

ISBN 978-3-7774-2729-4
(English edition)

ISBN 978-3-7774-2728-7
(German edition)

Hirmer Verlag GmbH
Nymphenburgerstr. 84
80636 Munich
Germany

www.hirmerverlag.de

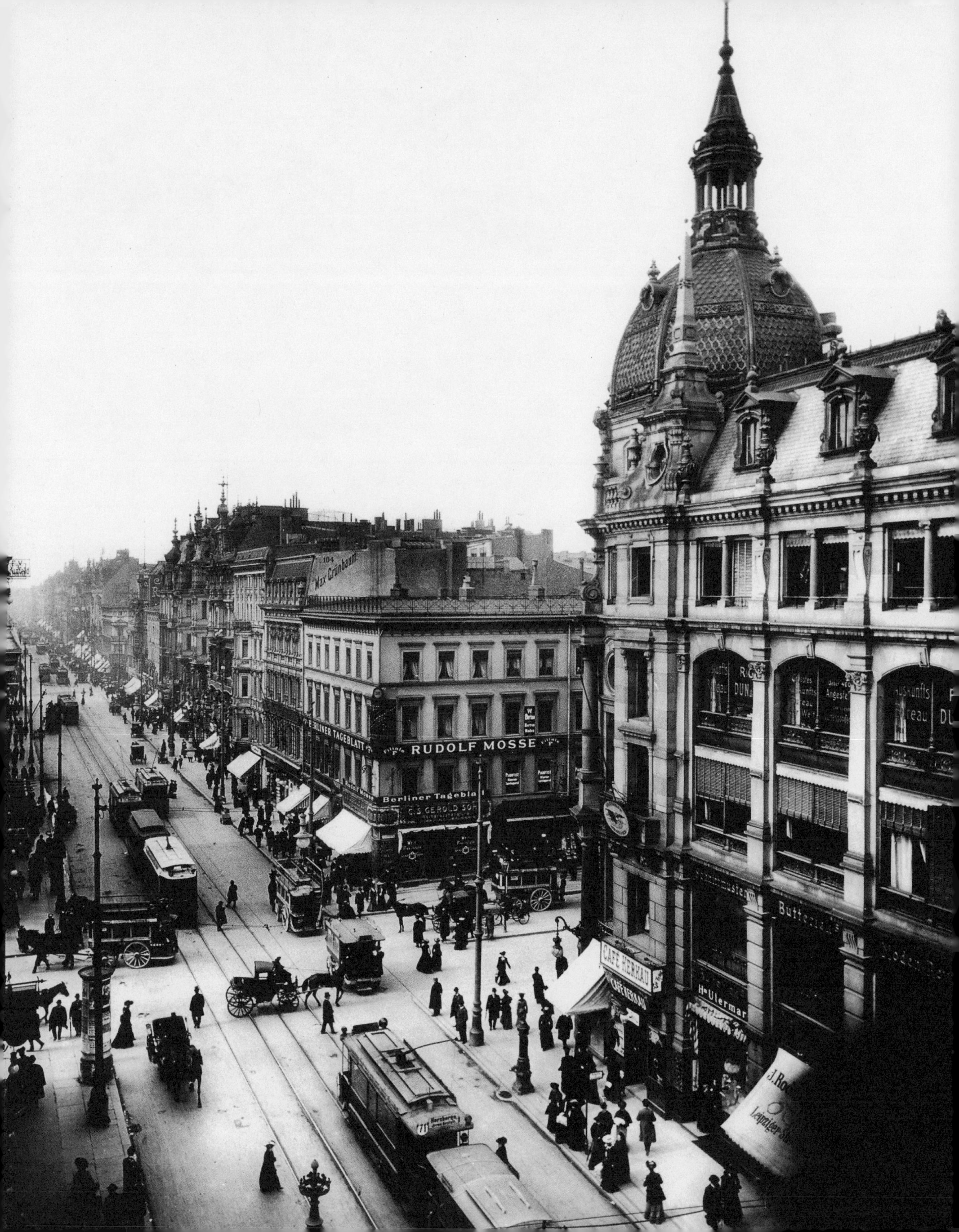
104
Max Grünbaum
BERLINER TAGEBLATT
RUDOLF MOSSE
Berliner Tageblatt
CAFE KERKAU

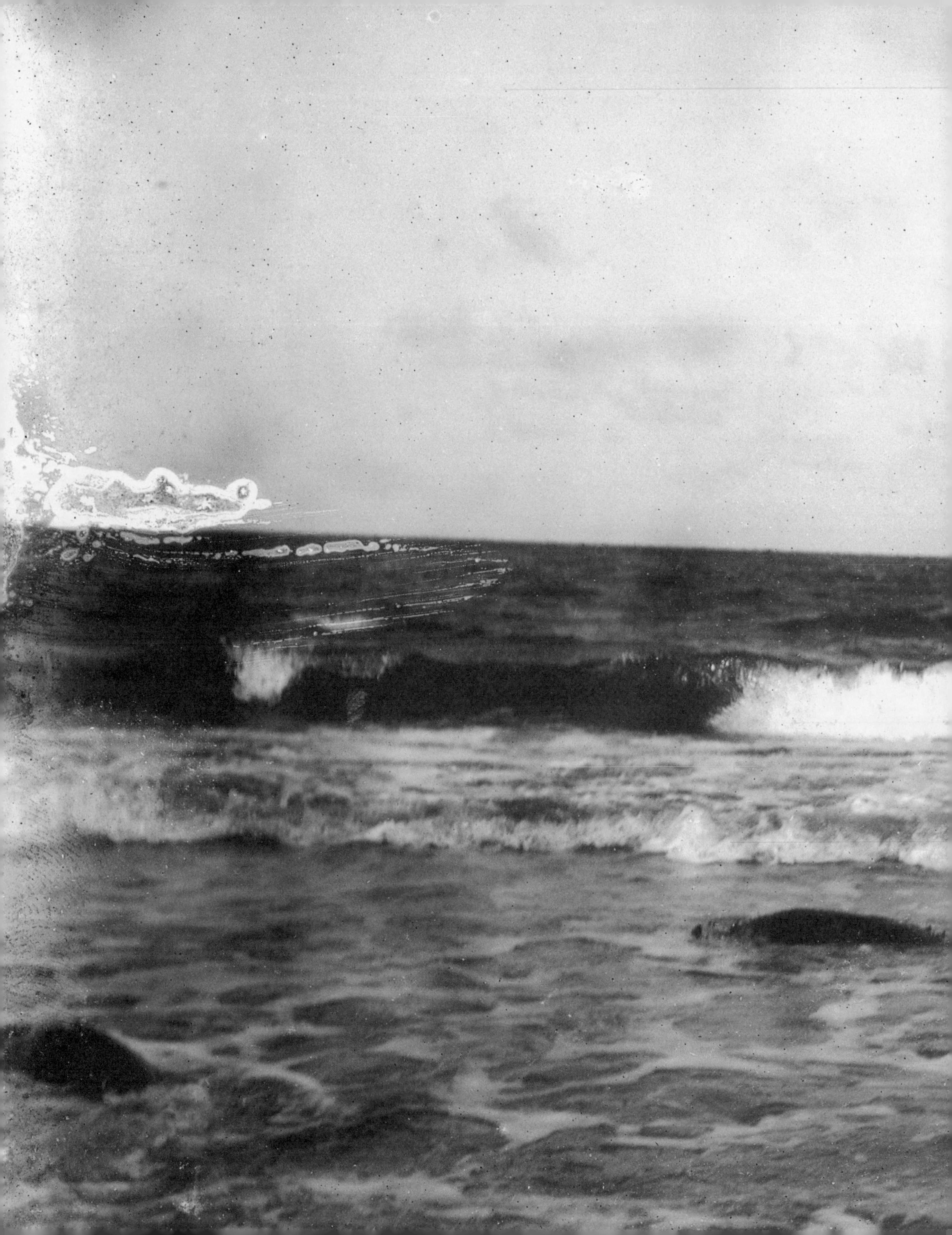